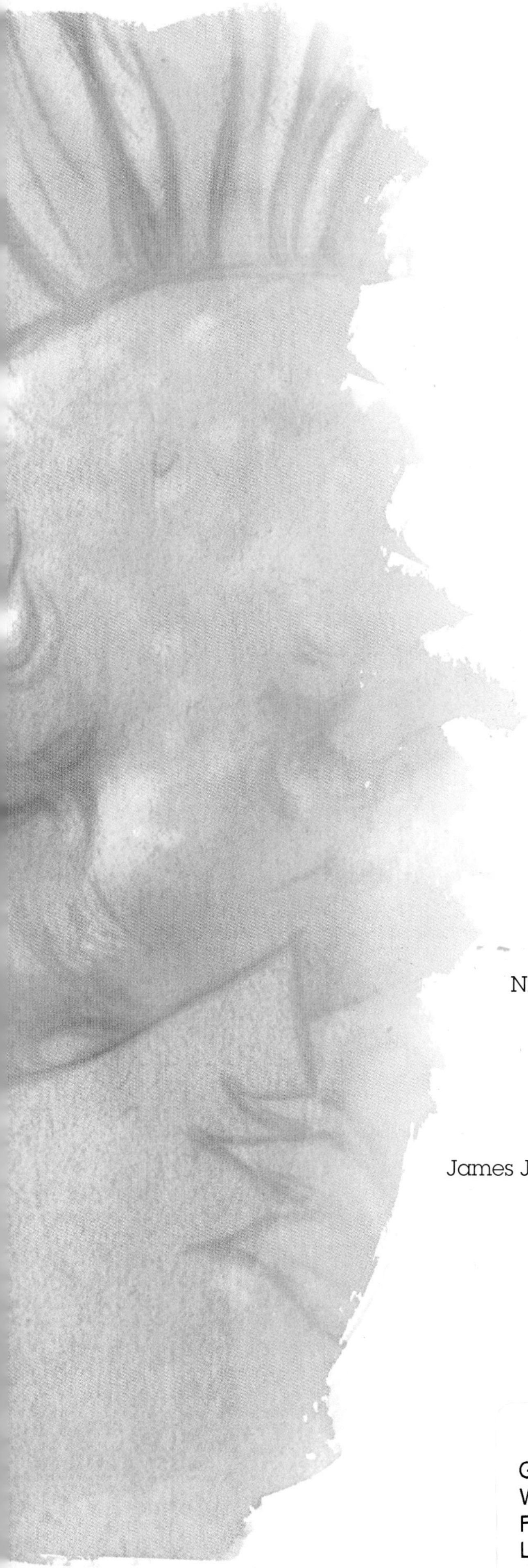

FABLES: THE DELUXE EDITION BOOK NINE

Bill Willingham Writer

Mark Buckingham Steve Leialoha
Niko Henrichon Michael Allred Peter Gross
David Hahn Andrew Pepoy Artists

Lee Loughridge Niko Henrichon
Laura Allred Colorists

Todd Klein Letterer

Daniel Dos Santos Cover Art

James Jean Mark Buckingham Original Series Covers

FABLES created by Bill Willingham

This volume of war and the darkness that follows is dedicated to Mark Buckingham, who makes the stories work, and who's about the brightest and un-warlike person I know.
— Bill Willingham

Dedicated to my father-in-law, Cefe, the kindest and most generous of men. It is also in loving memory of his wife, and Irma's mother, Marisa, a wonderful woman who sadly passed away whilst I was working on the stories contained in this volume. She is always in our thoughts.
— Mark Buckingham

Shelly Bond Editor – Original Series and Executive Editor – Vertigo
Angela Rufino Assistant Editor – Original Series
Scott Nybakken Editor
Robbin Brosterman Design Director – Books
Louis Prandi Publication Design

Hank Kanalz Senior VP – Vertigo and Integrated Publishing

Diane Nelson President
Dan DiDio and Jim Lee Co-Publishers
Geoff Johns Chief Creative Officer
Amit Desai Senior VP – Marketing and Franchise Management
Amy Genkins Senior VP – Business and Legal Affairs
Nairi Gardiner Senior VP – Finance

Jeff Boison VP – Publishing Planning
Mark Chiarello VP – Art Direction and Design
John Cunningham VP – Marketing
Terri Cunningham VP – Editorial Administration
Larry Ganem VP – Talent Relations and Services
Alison Gill Senior VP – Manufacturing and Operations
Jay Kogan VP – Business and Legal Affairs, Publishing
Jack Mahan VP – Business Affairs, Talent
Nick Napolitano VP – Manufacturing Administration
Sue Pohja VP – Book Sales
Fred Ruiz VP – Manufacturing Operations
Courtney Simmons Senior VP – Publicity
Bob Wayne Senior VP – Sales

Logo design by Brainchild Studios/NYC

FABLES: THE DELUXE EDITION BOOK NINE

Published by DC Comics. Copyright © 2014 Bill Willingham and DC Comics. All Rights Reserved.

Originally published in single magazine form as FABLES 70-82. Copyright © 2008, 2009 Bill Willingham and DC Comics.

Library of Congress Cataloging-in-Publication Data

Willingham, Bill, author.
  Fables : the deluxe edition book nine / Bill Willingham, Mark Buckingham.
      pages cm
  ISBN 978-1-4012-5004-1 (hardback)

All Rights Reserved. All characters, their distinctive likenesses and related elements featured in this publication are trademarks of Bill Willingham. VERTIGO is a trademark of DC Comics. The stories, characters and incidents featured in this publication are entirely fictional. DC Comics does not read or accept unsolicited submissions of ideas, stories or artwork.

  1. Fairy tales—Adaptations—Comic books, strips, etc. 2. Legends—Adaptations—Comic books, strips, etc. 3. Graphic novels. I. Buckingham, Mark, illustrator. II. Title. III. Title: Fables. Book nine.
  PN6727.W52F36 2014
  741.5'973—dc23
       2014014690

DC Comics, 1700 Broadway, New York, NY 10019
A Warner Bros. Entertainment Company. Printed in Canada. First Printing.
ISBN: 978-1-4012-5004-1

SUSTAINABLE FORESTRY INITIATIVE
Certified Chain of Custody
Promoting Sustainable Forestry
www.sfiprogram.org
SFI-00507
This label only applies to the text section.

Table of Contents

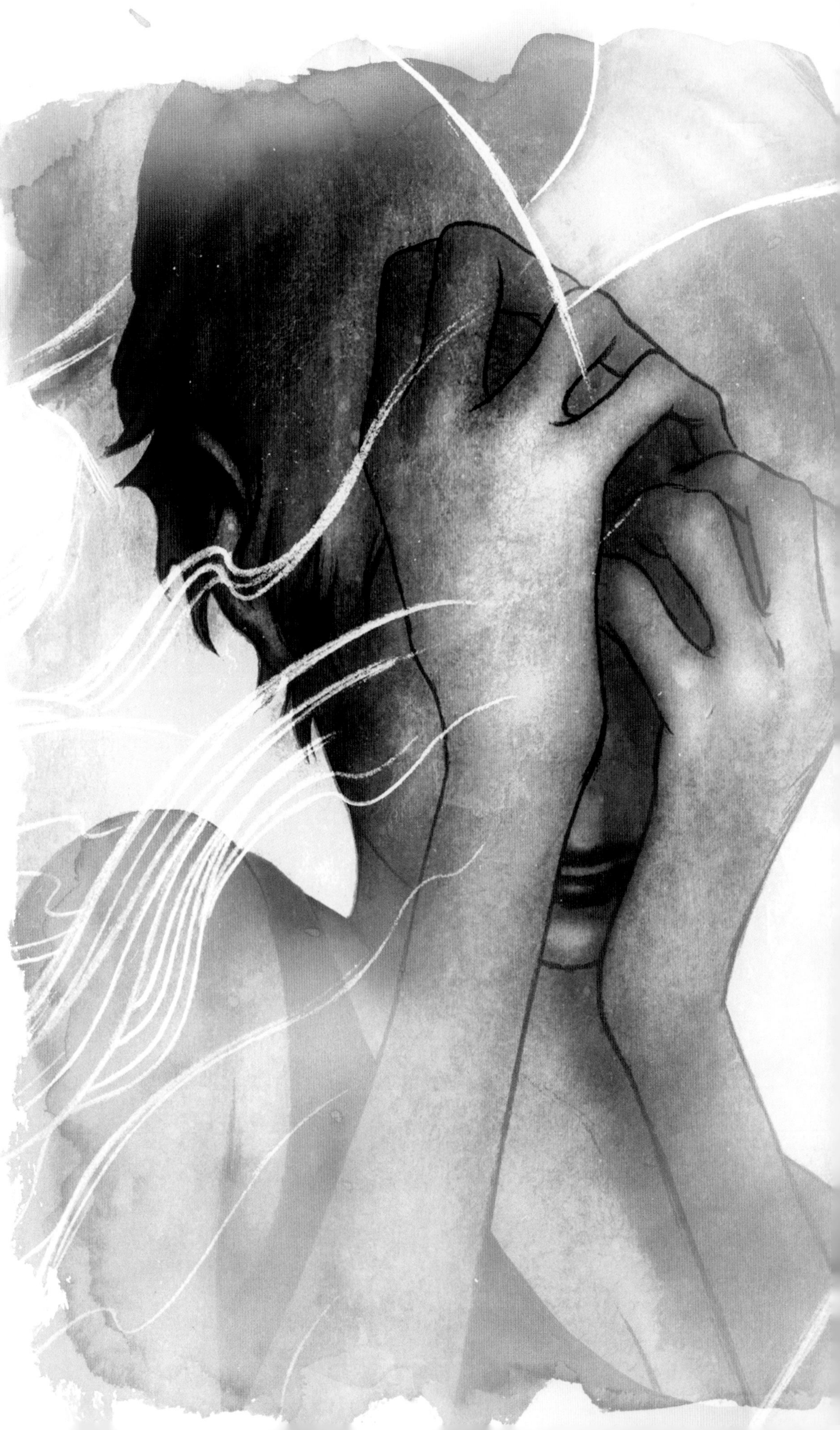

Introduction

I love FABLES.

If someone asks me what I'm reading it's always the first thing out of my mouth. I *love* this book.

Now, I know that "love" doesn't mean much coming from a comic book fan. Comic book fans are easy. Really easy. We're hos. We're junkies. No, scratch that, we're worse. No junkie would show up at his dealer's place every Wednesday at lunchtime just because that's when the new drugs arrive.

All of this is to say that the "love" a comic book fan feels generally doesn't require much to keep it going. You find a book when you're twelve, wrap a blanket around your neck to make a cape, and boom, you're together forever. It's habit. It's nostalgia. It's comfort. You're the middle-aged couple sleeping in the Lucy & Ricky twin beds, each just content to know the other is there every month (crises and reboots notwithstanding.) What are you going to do, *not* pick up the ol' ball and chain when it comes out? C'mon, it's on your pull list! You kind of have to.

But how amazing is it when the book you love reminds you of *why* you love it? When new issues, instead of being mediocre reminders of the great ones you used to read, are so good that they only make you think about what's ahead?

How great is it when you don't just love a book, you're *in* love with it?

If you're a FABLES reader, "War and Pieces" and "The Dark Ages" are the personification of True Love. If the book grabbed you at issue #1, 70 issues later it grips you more tightly than ever. It's like if you're dating someone smart, sexy, and beautiful, and then they pull you from a fiery car crash. You thought you loved them before — but now!

(Warning: there will be spoilers. So if you're some FABLES dilettante who likes to get into a hobby hardcover first, welcome — and please come back to this after you've been initiated.)

***

"War and Pieces" is the story of a war, from beginning to end. (By the way, who does that? Who writes a war? George Lucas tried, but FABLES succeeds. It's like *The Iliad* with talking animals. Wait... were there talking animals in *The Iliad*? That many years, that many gods, somebody must have gotten their anthropomorph on. Wikipedia that and get back to me.) Glorious, methodical, and somehow, between the spells, goblins, and trans-dimensional gateways, realistic — part 007, part History Channel, part *Bridge on the River Kwai* — it is the culmination of the backstory underlying every FABLES issue that came before it. A tale six years (or several centuries, depending on your point of view) in the making, the War Against the Adversary to Reclaim the Homelands is finally unveiled here. The result is everything you could have hoped for, and more. Seriously, your relationship with this book might already be great, but after reading this you're going to have to up you game. I think you'll need to start working out.

One of the story's greatest strengths is the way it incorporates all of the FABLES elements that we've gotten to know fairly deeply (the animal Fables, the 13th Floor, Cinderella) as well as several that are, up to this point, new or just barely familiar (Sleeping Beauty, the Arabian Fables). We see how, and how well, the Fables prepare for war, and we see how it affects everyone from the Farm to the Woodland Building to the tourists. We see tactics both ancient (a well-timed finger prick) and modern (sniper rifles), and combinations of the two (*The Glory of Baghdad* is certainly the best use of "bringing a gun to a swordfight" since *Raiders of the Lost Ark*).

We peer further into the Homelands and the Empire's capital city, and get a glimpse of the Emperor as an active ruler rather than a shadowy, fantastical image. And we see the wartime leadership of Bigby — it's good to finally see why everyone is so afraid of him, though what's most surprising, I think, is how well the lone wolf plays with others.

We also see the quiet heroism of Boy Blue. It's amazing how this character goes from a fifth- or sixth-banana supporting character to a real leading man.

Finally, we see the long-hidden good side of Prince Charming. C'mon, you know Snow would never have married him if he didn't have *some* redeeming qualities.

***

Romantic songs often say "don't ever change," but no one says it with the fervor of comic book fans. We of the "comfortable love" are devoted to our adventure stories, but the emphasis is usually on the "our." We want the same thing over and over. We'll call you boring but we'll lose our minds if you try to do something new.

FABLES don't play that. Comic book people talk a lot about continuity, but really, most comic books are just about *continuing*. The arch-nemesis is never really killed, the hero never really changes (except his costume), because if you write real changes then things have to end. Aside from the corporate problem of eliminating "properties" that may still be moving "units" on the toy shelves, ending things brings up an even tougher creative problem: once you've gotten to the end, what happens next?

FABLES is not afraid of the challenge. FABLES knows that in any good relationship, you grow and change together.

So, immediately after re-dedicating our love with "War and Pieces," FABLES gets freaky on us and brings another man into the relationship with "The Dark Ages."

"The Dark Ages" shows the coming of Mister Dark and the unbinding of Fabletown in ways both figurative and literal. It begins in the Homelands with a couple of characters that I'm not sure I would call "Fables," but my 7th grade

sword & sorcery-reading self is thrilled by their inclusion. At least until they open the box.

Mister Dark is about fear — fear for the reader, fear for the characters, and fear for the worlds. Seeing that fear expressed by the powerful and normally impassive Frau Totenkinder is a nice touch, and sets a particularly menacing tone. This lady cooks children, and she's afraid? It lets you know that you are in new territory and you cannot know what to expect.

"The Dark Ages" does what horror movie producers have been trying to do for decades: give "The Boogeyman" a personality. But while Mister Dark is undoubtedly the most important element of "The Dark Ages," the story isn't really about him.

Many books have killed off beloved characters, some multiple times (*cough* Jean Grey *cough*), but it's usually touted as a "Very Special Issue" — "After this, the world of ____ Will Never Be The Same!" Following which, of course, things are pretty much the same. Maybe the main character comes back with a slightly darker tone, missing a youthful sidekick, or even sporting some new epaulets.

Not here. What's to come is a profound change that affects every soul in Fabletown and resonates through all of the stories to come. FABLES is letting you know that life is not going to be all litters of flying babies, parades, and returns to normalcy. There is no up without down, no good without bad, no battle without sacrifice, and like any relationship worth its salt, this comic book love affair is going to challenge you.

Reading this collection will not only rekindle that love, but also show you how the mystery and excitement that you remember from the beginning mean so much more now that you've gotten to know these characters so intimately. You're no longer just going through the motions — you're bragging to your friends about this book. Heck, you might even go back to buying the monthly issues! You may not wrap blankets around your neck anymore, but hey, that old trenchcoat would make a pretty good Bigby cosplay. With a love like this, and a book like FABLES, anything is possible.

— Phil LaMarr
February 28th, 2014

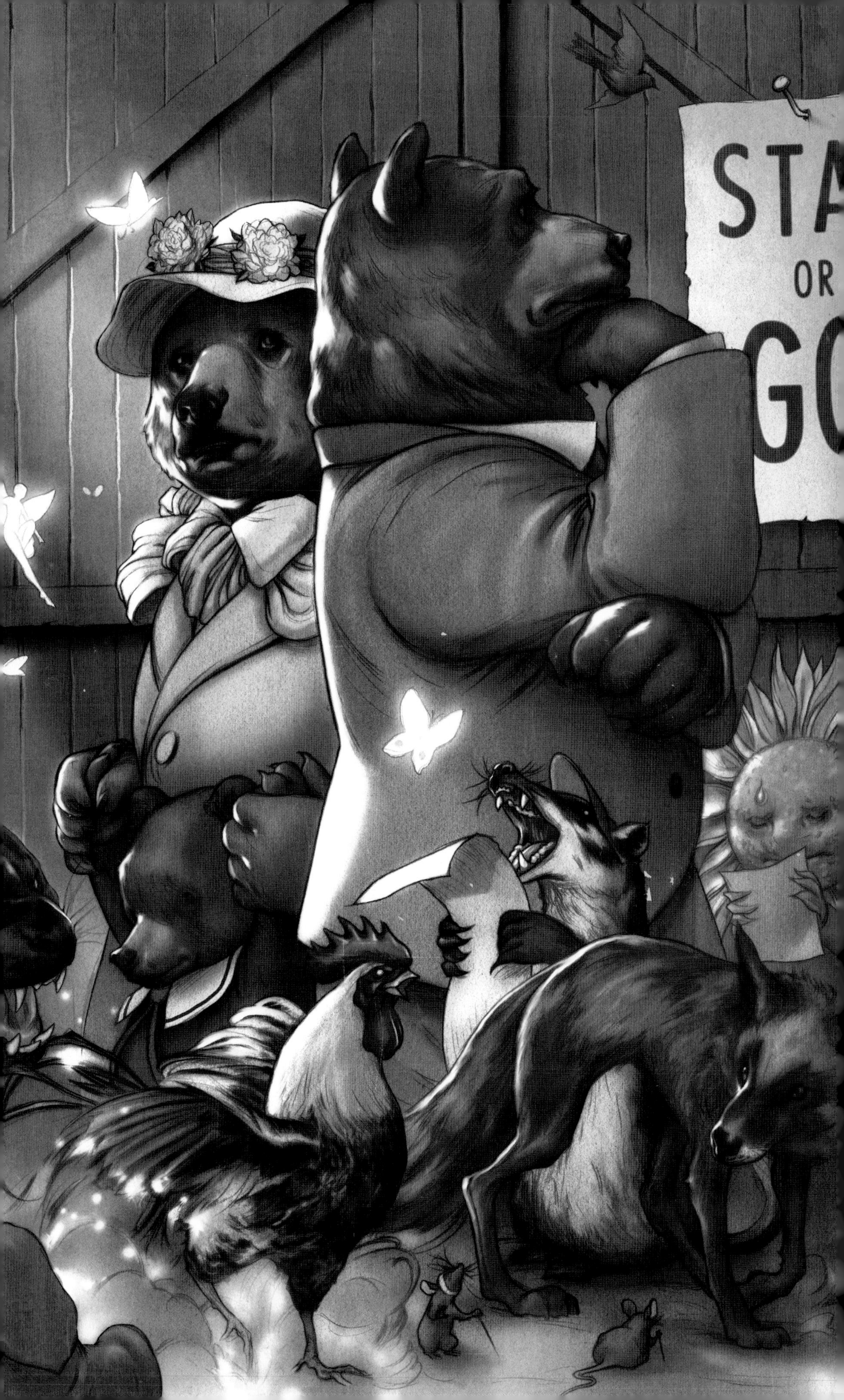
STA
OR
G

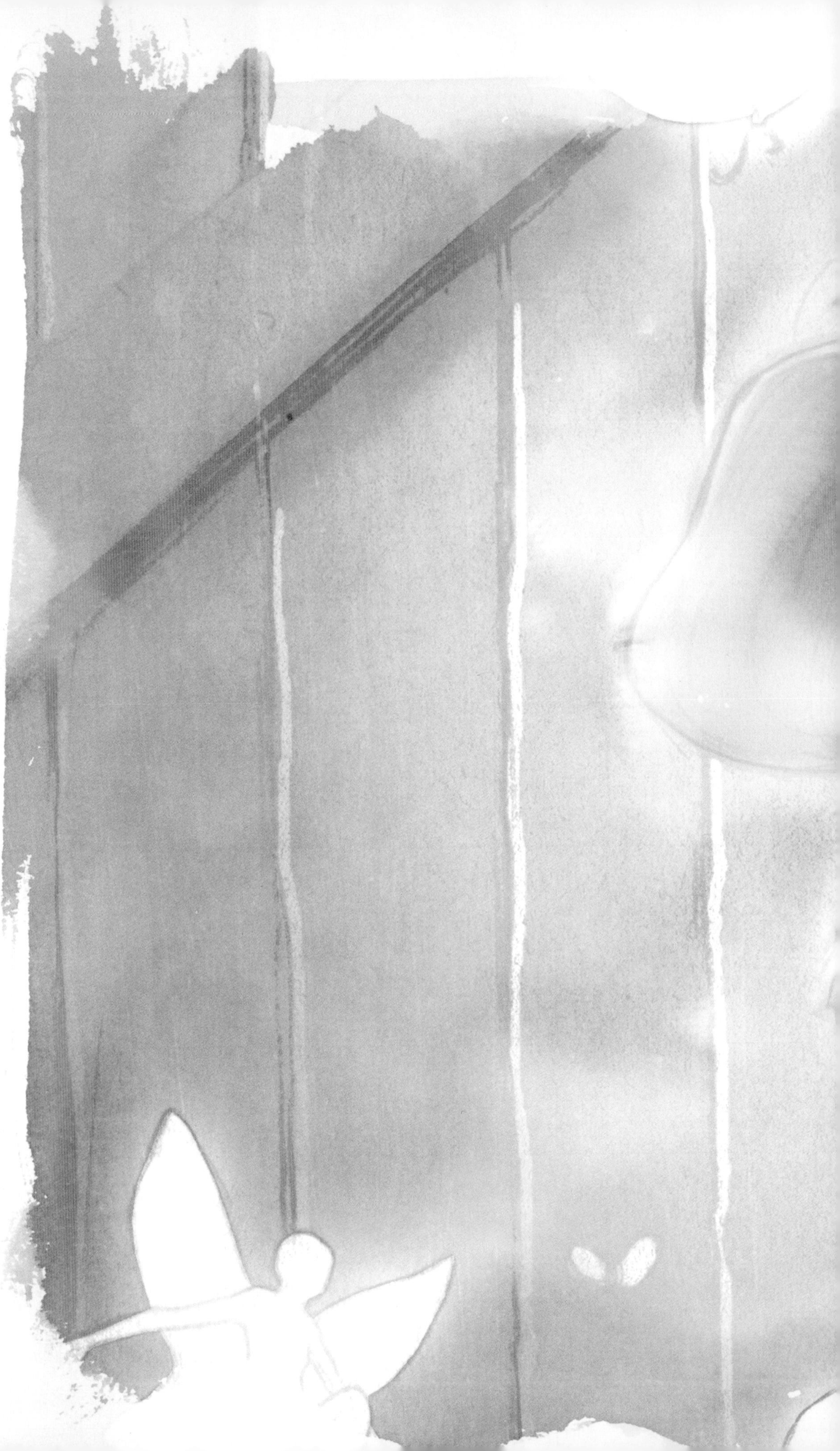

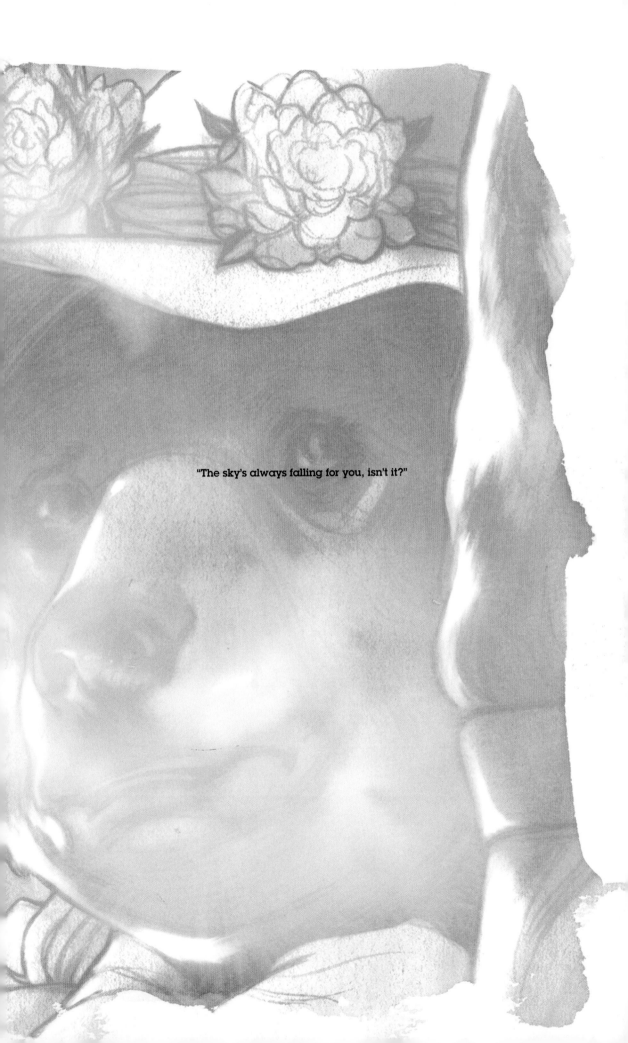

"The sky's always falling for you, isn't it?"

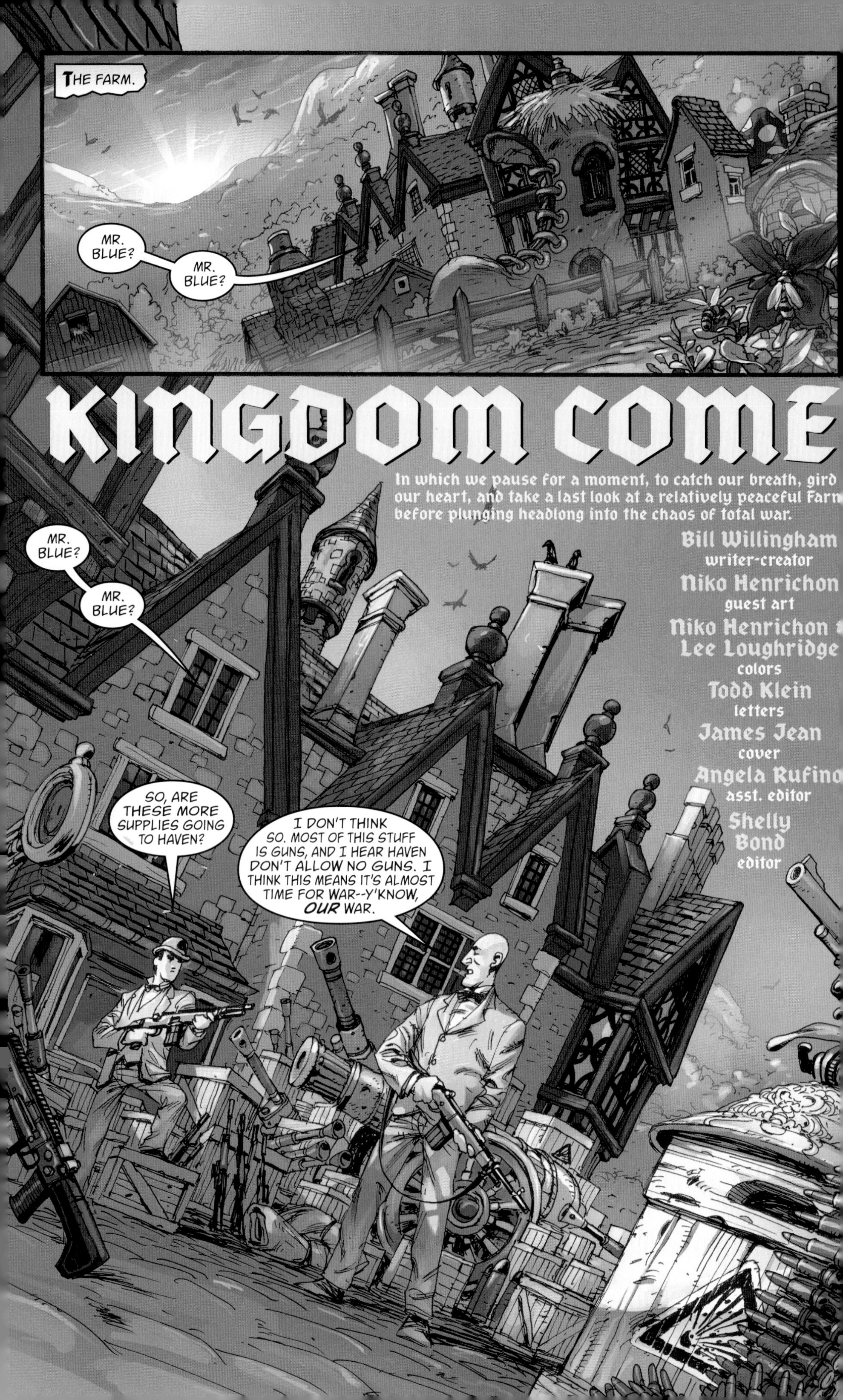

THE FARM.
MR. BLUE?
MR. BLUE?
KINGDOM COME
In which we pause for a moment, to catch our breath, gird our heart, and take a last look at a relatively peaceful Farm before plunging headlong into the chaos of total war.
Bill Willingham writer-creator
Niko Henrichon guest art
Niko Henrichon Lee Loughridge colors
Todd Klein letters
James Jean cover
Angela Rufino asst. editor
Shelly Bond editor
MR. BLUE?
MR. BLUE?
SO, ARE THESE MORE SUPPLIES GOING TO HAVEN?
I DON'T THINK SO. MOST OF THIS STUFF IS GUNS, AND I HEAR HAVEN DON'T ALLOW NO GUNS. I THINK THIS MEANS IT'S ALMOST TIME FOR WAR--Y'KNOW, OUR WAR.

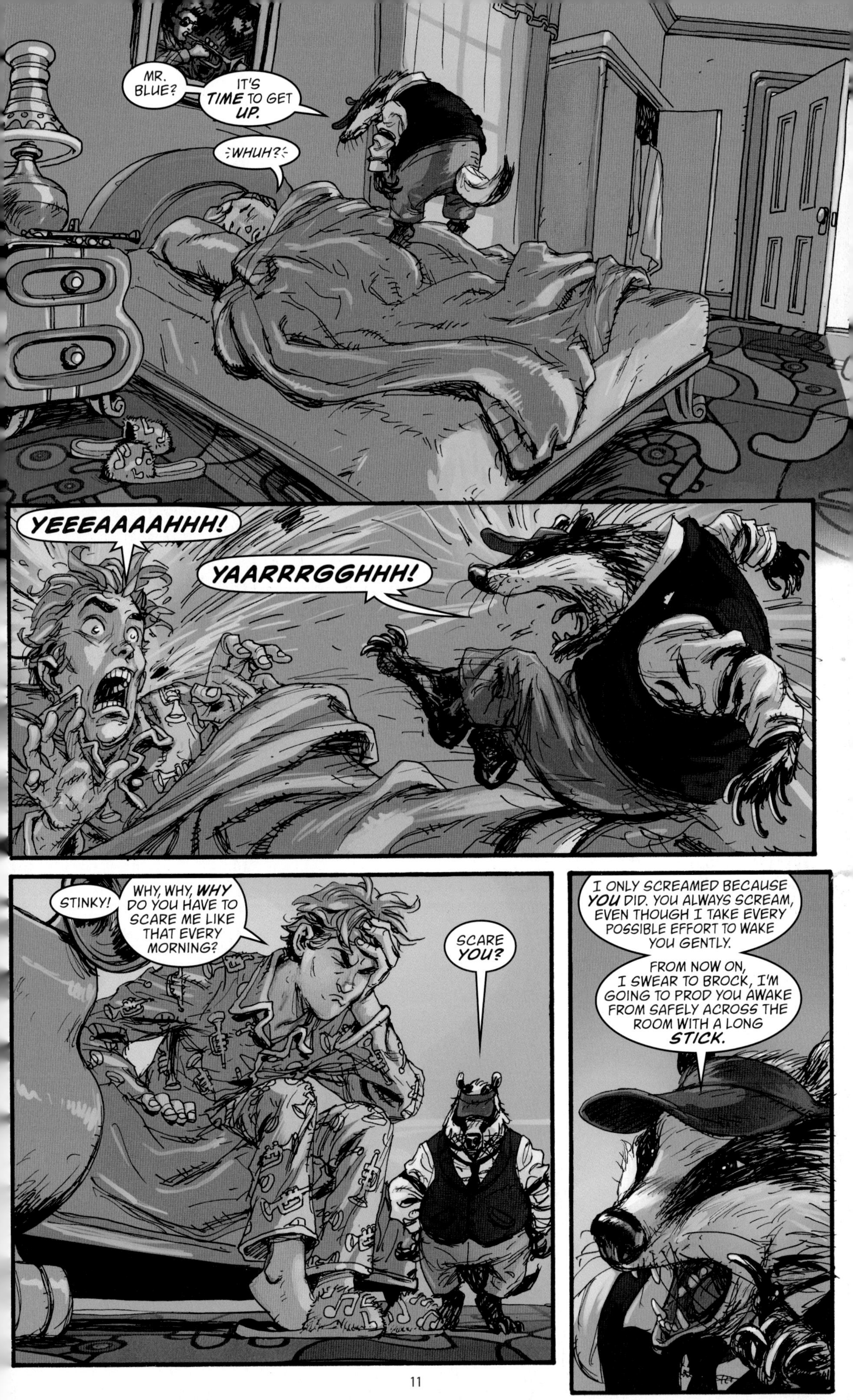
MR. BLUE?
IT'S TIME TO GET UP.
WHUH?
YEEEAAAAHHH!
YAARRRGGHHH!
STINKY!
WHY, WHY, WHY DO YOU HAVE TO SCARE ME LIKE THAT EVERY MORNING?
SCARE YOU?
I ONLY SCREAMED BECAUSE YOU DID. YOU ALWAYS SCREAM, EVEN THOUGH I TAKE EVERY POSSIBLE EFFORT TO WAKE YOU GENTLY.
FROM NOW ON, I SWEAR TO BROCK, I'M GOING TO PROD YOU AWAKE FROM SAFELY ACROSS THE ROOM WITH A LONG STICK.

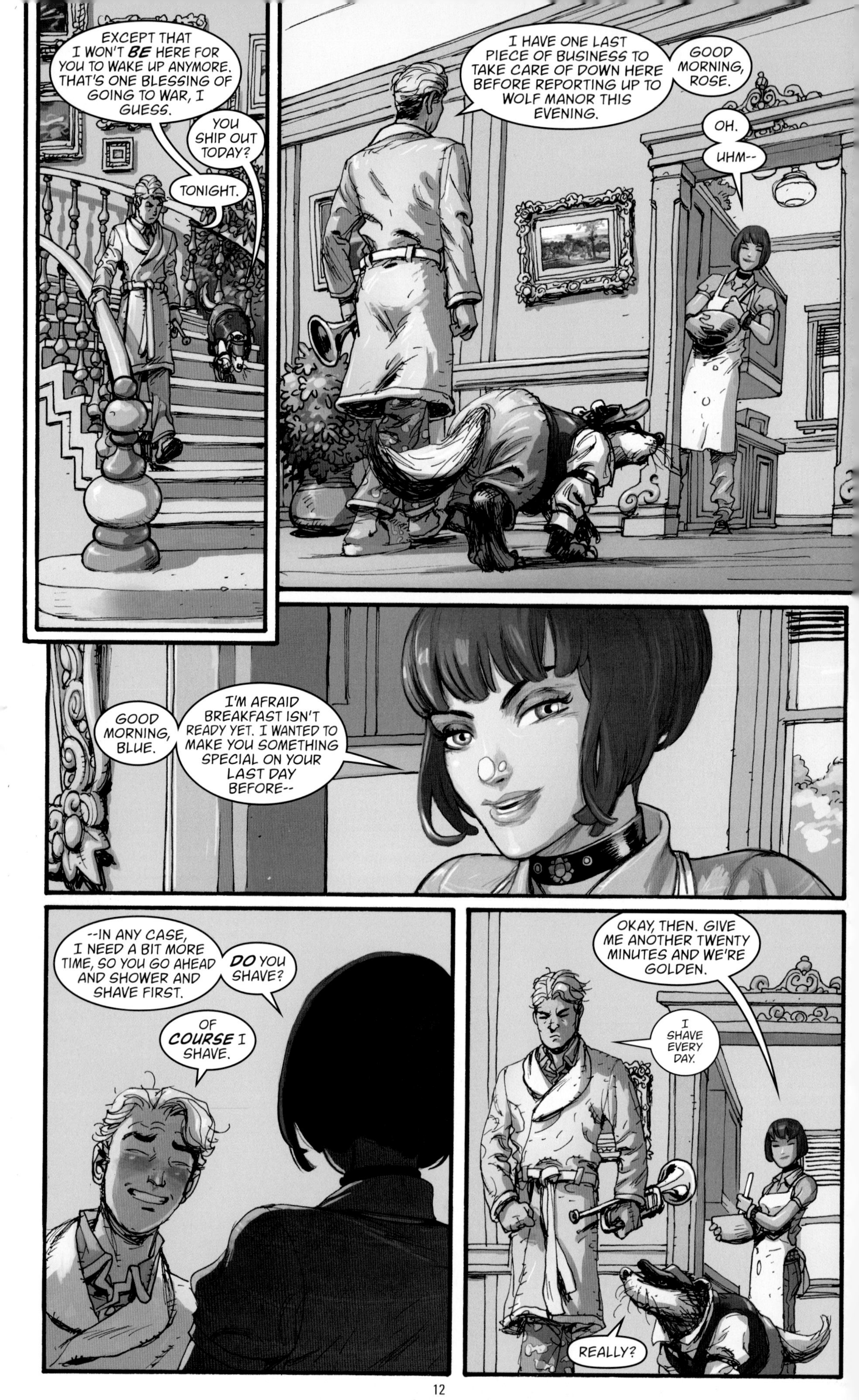
EXCEPT THAT I WON'T **BE** HERE FOR YOU TO WAKE UP ANYMORE. THAT'S ONE BLESSING OF GOING TO WAR, I GUESS.
YOU SHIP OUT TODAY?
TONIGHT.
I HAVE ONE LAST PIECE OF BUSINESS TO TAKE CARE OF DOWN HERE BEFORE REPORTING UP TO WOLF MANOR THIS EVENING.
GOOD MORNING, ROSE.
OH.
UHM--
GOOD MORNING, BLUE.
I'M AFRAID BREAKFAST ISN'T READY YET. I WANTED TO MAKE YOU SOMETHING SPECIAL ON YOUR LAST DAY BEFORE--
--IN ANY CASE, I NEED A BIT MORE TIME, SO YOU GO AHEAD AND SHOWER AND SHAVE FIRST.
DO YOU SHAVE?
OF **COURSE** I SHAVE.
OKAY, THEN. GIVE ME ANOTHER TWENTY MINUTES AND WE'RE GOLDEN.
I SHAVE EVERY DAY.
REALLY?

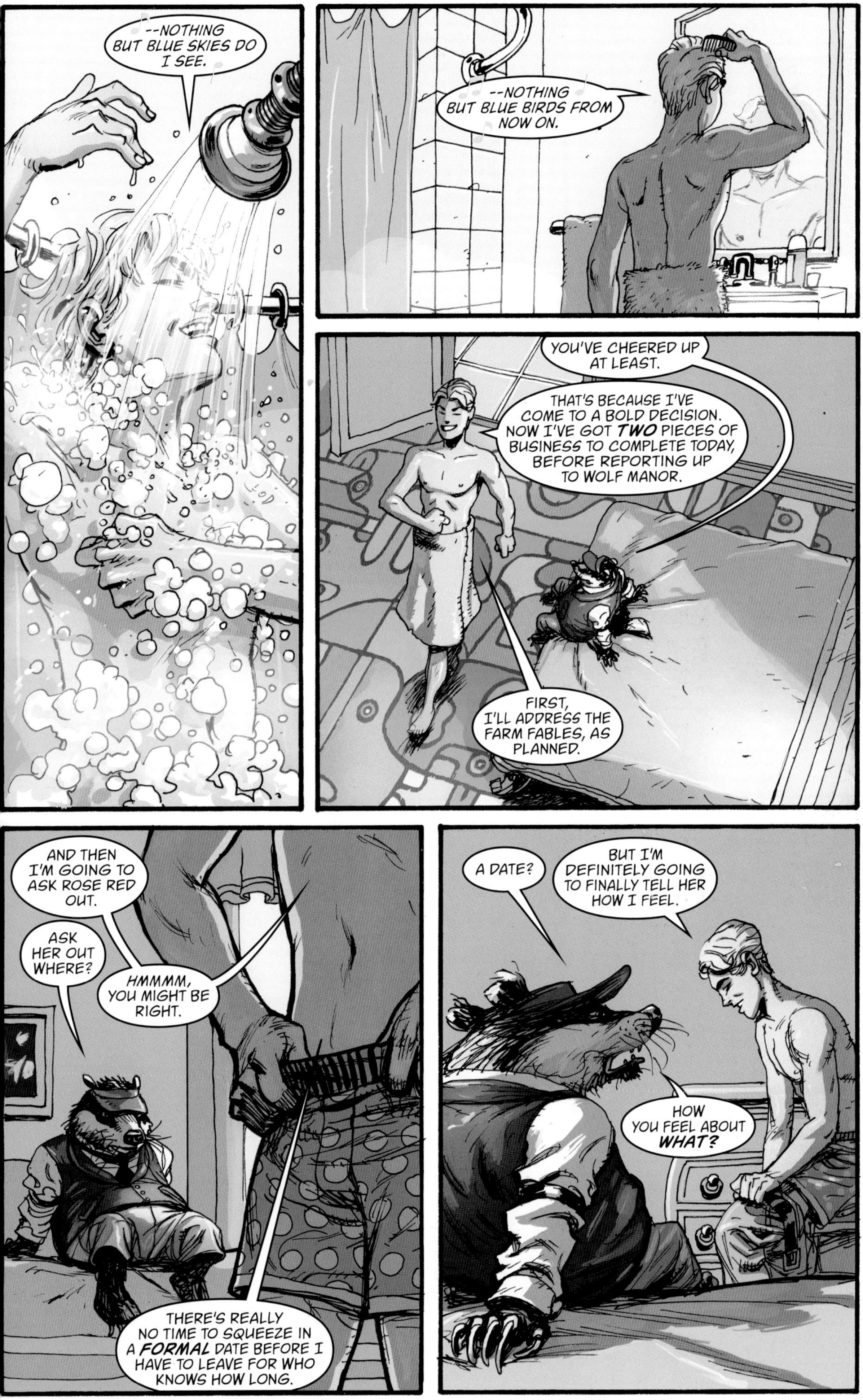
--NOTHING BUT BLUE SKIES DO I SEE.
--NOTHING BUT BLUE BIRDS FROM NOW ON.
YOU'VE CHEERED UP AT LEAST.
THAT'S BECAUSE I'VE COME TO A BOLD DECISION. NOW I'VE GOT **TWO** PIECES OF BUSINESS TO COMPLETE TODAY, BEFORE REPORTING UP TO WOLF MANOR.
FIRST, I'LL ADDRESS THE FARM FABLES, AS PLANNED.
AND THEN I'M GOING TO ASK ROSE RED OUT.
ASK HER OUT WHERE?
HMMMM, YOU MIGHT BE RIGHT.
THERE'S REALLY NO TIME TO SQUEEZE IN A **FORMAL** DATE BEFORE I HAVE TO LEAVE FOR WHO KNOWS HOW LONG.
A DATE?
BUT I'M DEFINITELY GOING TO FINALLY TELL HER HOW I FEEL.
HOW YOU FEEL ABOUT **WHAT?**

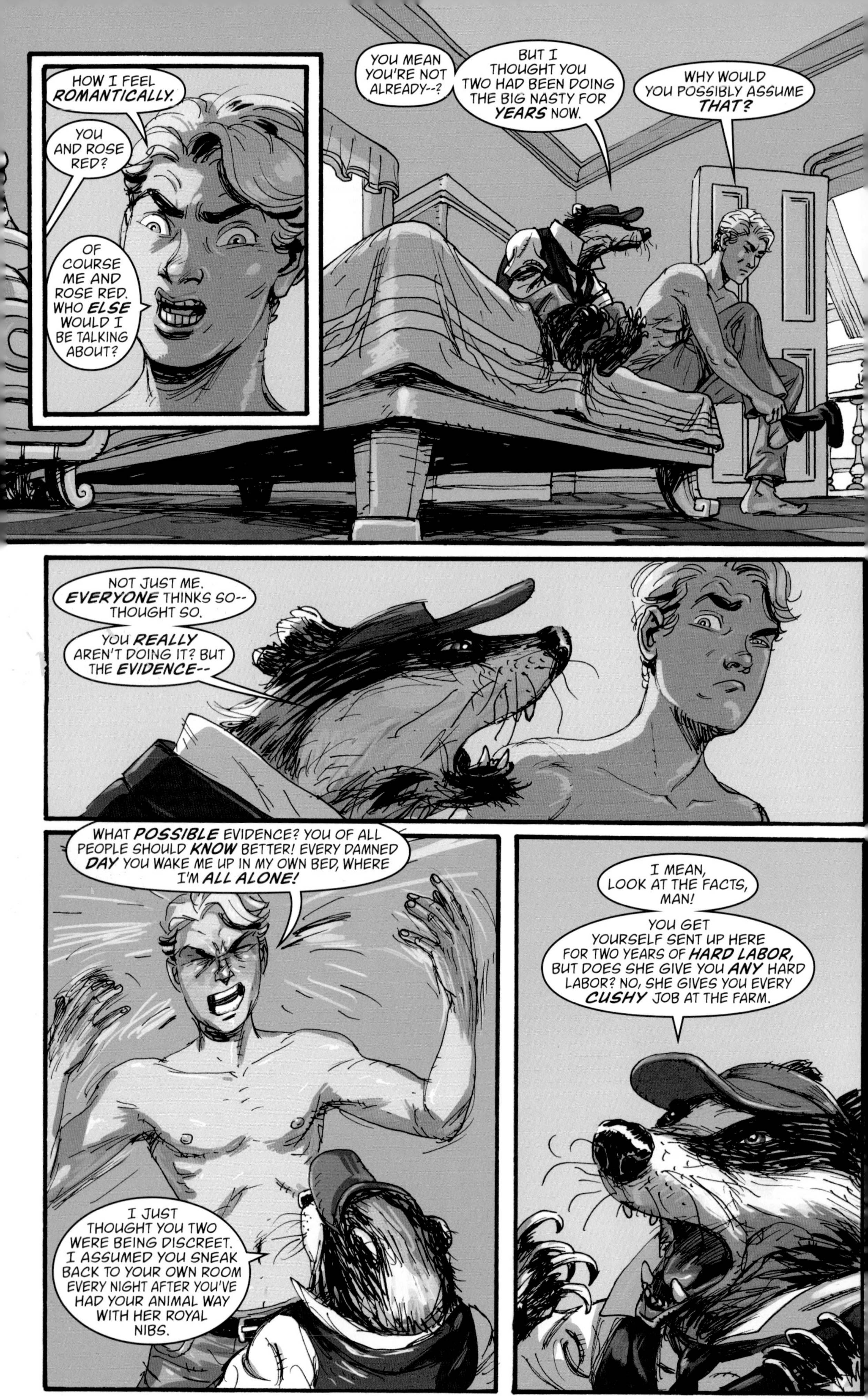
HOW I FEEL ROMANTICALLY.
YOU AND ROSE RED?
OF COURSE ME AND ROSE RED. WHO ELSE WOULD I BE TALKING ABOUT?
YOU MEAN YOU'RE NOT ALREADY--?
BUT I THOUGHT YOU TWO HAD BEEN DOING THE BIG NASTY FOR YEARS NOW.
WHY WOULD YOU POSSIBLY ASSUME THAT?
NOT JUST ME. EVERYONE THINKS SO-- THOUGHT SO.
YOU REALLY AREN'T DOING IT? BUT THE EVIDENCE--
WHAT POSSIBLE EVIDENCE? YOU OF ALL PEOPLE SHOULD KNOW BETTER! EVERY DAMNED DAY YOU WAKE ME UP IN MY OWN BED, WHERE I'M ALL ALONE!
I JUST THOUGHT YOU TWO WERE BEING DISCREET. I ASSUMED YOU SNEAK BACK TO YOUR OWN ROOM EVERY NIGHT AFTER YOU'VE HAD YOUR ANIMAL WAY WITH HER ROYAL NIBS.
I MEAN, LOOK AT THE FACTS, MAN!
YOU GET YOURSELF SENT UP HERE FOR TWO YEARS OF HARD LABOR, BUT DOES SHE GIVE YOU ANY HARD LABOR? NO, SHE GIVES YOU EVERY CUSHY JOB AT THE FARM.

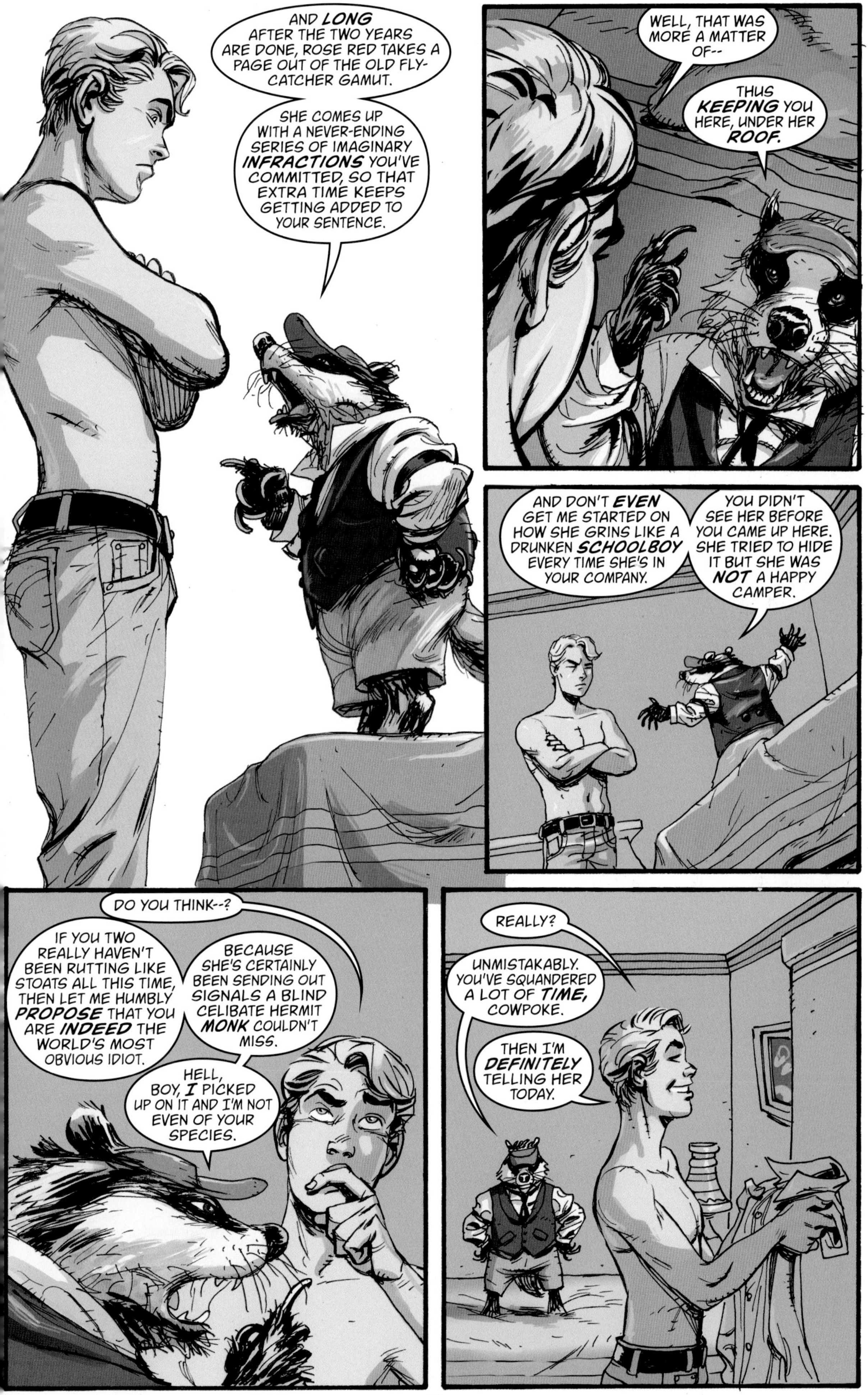

AND LONG AFTER THE TWO YEARS ARE DONE, ROSE RED TAKES A PAGE OUT OF THE OLD FLY-CATCHER GAMUT.
SHE COMES UP WITH A NEVER-ENDING SERIES OF IMAGINARY INFRACTIONS YOU'VE COMMITTED, SO THAT EXTRA TIME KEEPS GETTING ADDED TO YOUR SENTENCE.
WELL, THAT WAS MORE A MATTER OF--
THUS KEEPING YOU HERE, UNDER HER ROOF.
AND DON'T EVEN GET ME STARTED ON HOW SHE GRINS LIKE A DRUNKEN SCHOOLBOY EVERY TIME SHE'S IN YOUR COMPANY.
YOU DIDN'T SEE HER BEFORE YOU CAME UP HERE. SHE TRIED TO HIDE IT BUT SHE WAS NOT A HAPPY CAMPER.
DO YOU THINK--?
IF YOU TWO REALLY HAVEN'T BEEN RUTTING LIKE STOATS ALL THIS TIME, THEN LET ME HUMBLY PROPOSE THAT YOU ARE INDEED THE WORLD'S MOST OBVIOUS IDIOT.
BECAUSE SHE'S CERTAINLY BEEN SENDING OUT SIGNALS A BLIND CELIBATE HERMIT MONK COULDN'T MISS.
HELL, BOY, I PICKED UP ON IT AND I'M NOT EVEN OF YOUR SPECIES.
REALLY?
UNMISTAKABLY. YOU'VE SQUANDERED A LOT OF TIME, COWPOKE.
THEN I'M DEFINITELY TELLING HER TODAY.

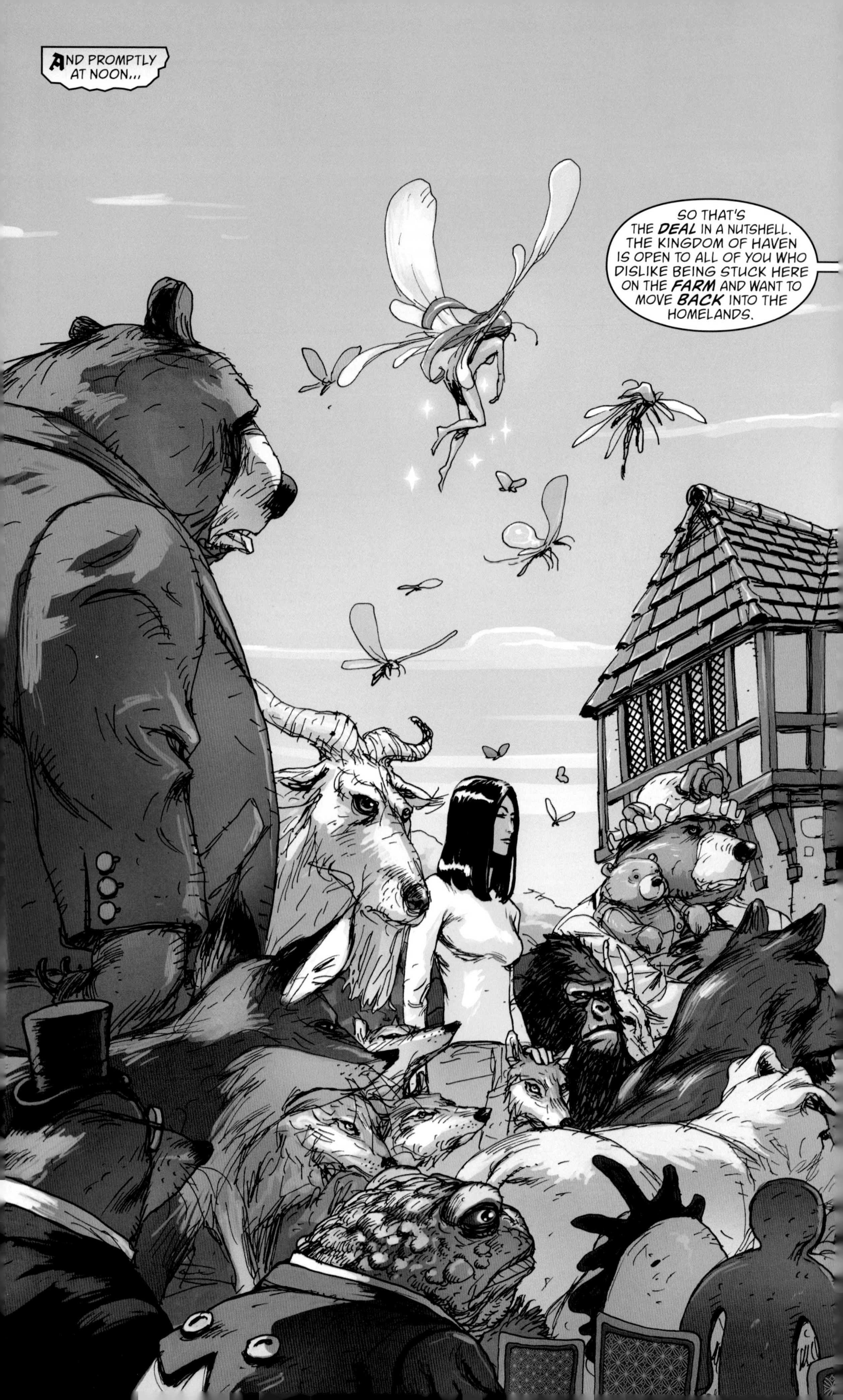
AND PROMPTLY AT NOON...
SO THAT'S THE DEAL IN A NUTSHELL. THE KINGDOM OF HAVEN IS OPEN TO ALL OF YOU WHO DISLIKE BEING STUCK HERE ON THE FARM AND WANT TO MOVE BACK INTO THE HOMELANDS.

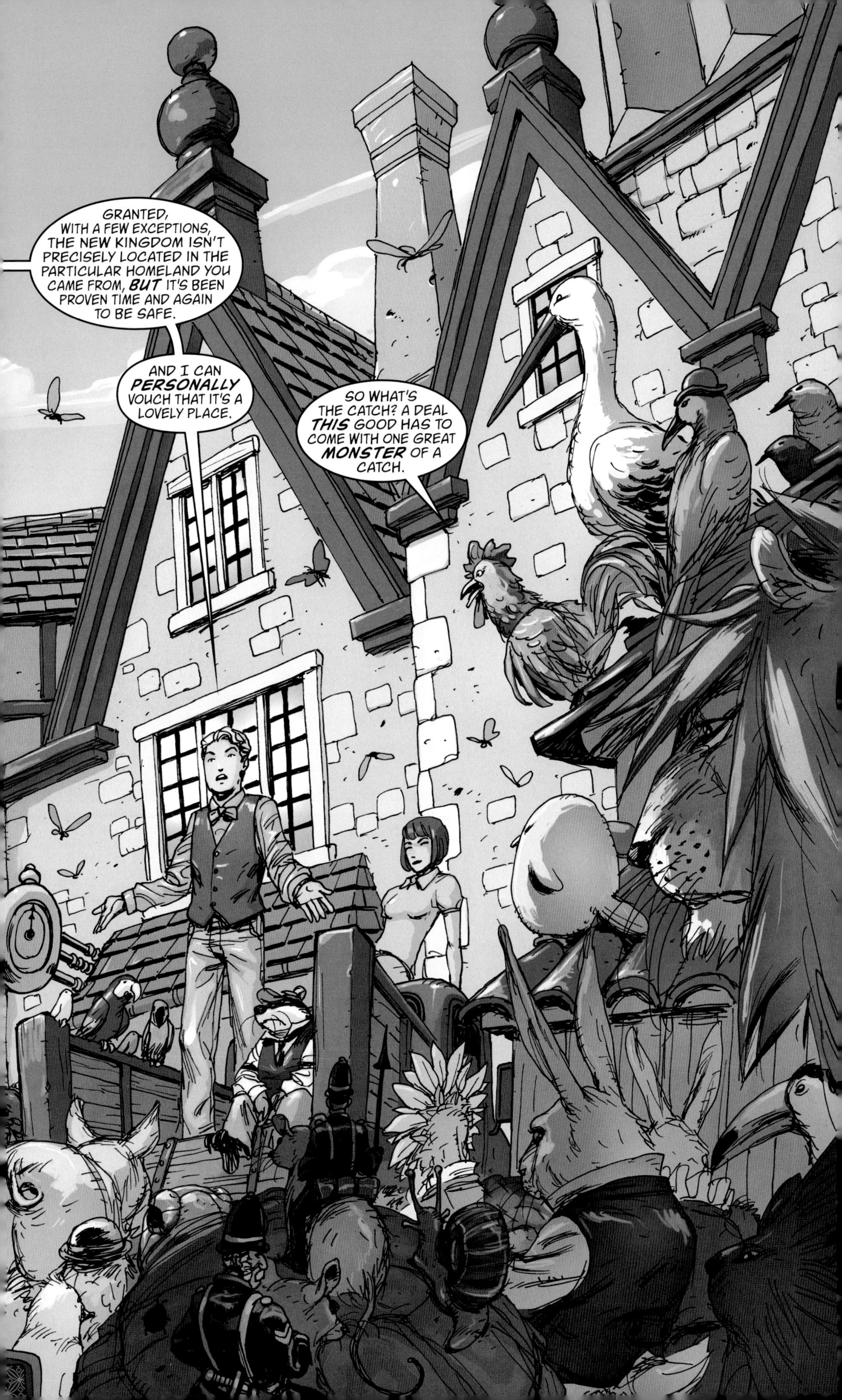
GRANTED, WITH A FEW EXCEPTIONS, THE NEW KINGDOM ISN'T PRECISELY LOCATED IN THE PARTICULAR HOMELAND YOU CAME FROM, BUT IT'S BEEN PROVEN TIME AND AGAIN TO BE SAFE.
AND I CAN PERSONALLY VOUCH THAT IT'S A LOVELY PLACE.
SO WHAT'S THE CATCH? A DEAL THIS GOOD HAS TO COME WITH ONE GREAT MONSTER OF A CATCH.

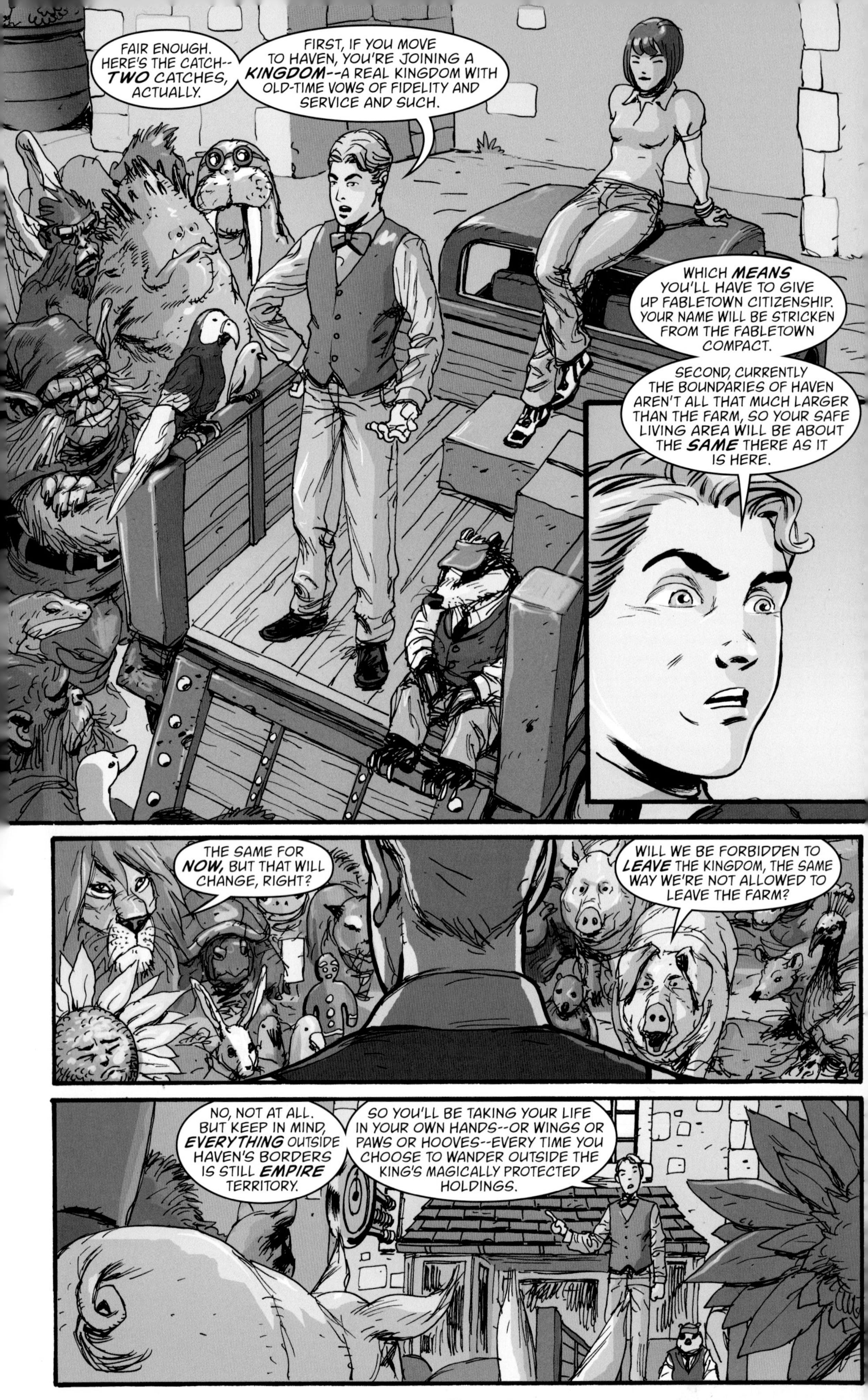
FAIR ENOUGH. HERE'S THE CATCH--TWO CATCHES, ACTUALLY.
FIRST, IF YOU MOVE TO HAVEN, YOU'RE JOINING A KINGDOM--A REAL KINGDOM WITH OLD-TIME VOWS OF FIDELITY AND SERVICE AND SUCH.
WHICH MEANS YOU'LL HAVE TO GIVE UP FABLETOWN CITIZENSHIP. YOUR NAME WILL BE STRICKEN FROM THE FABLETOWN COMPACT.
SECOND, CURRENTLY THE BOUNDARIES OF HAVEN AREN'T ALL THAT MUCH LARGER THAN THE FARM, SO YOUR SAFE LIVING AREA WILL BE ABOUT THE SAME THERE AS IT IS HERE.
THE SAME FOR NOW, BUT THAT WILL CHANGE, RIGHT?
WILL WE BE FORBIDDEN TO LEAVE THE KINGDOM, THE SAME WAY WE'RE NOT ALLOWED TO LEAVE THE FARM?
NO, NOT AT ALL. BUT KEEP IN MIND, EVERYTHING OUTSIDE HAVEN'S BORDERS IS STILL EMPIRE TERRITORY.
SO YOU'LL BE TAKING YOUR LIFE IN YOUR OWN HANDS--OR WINGS OR PAWS OR HOOVES--EVERY TIME YOU CHOOSE TO WANDER OUTSIDE THE KING'S MAGICALLY PROTECTED HOLDINGS.

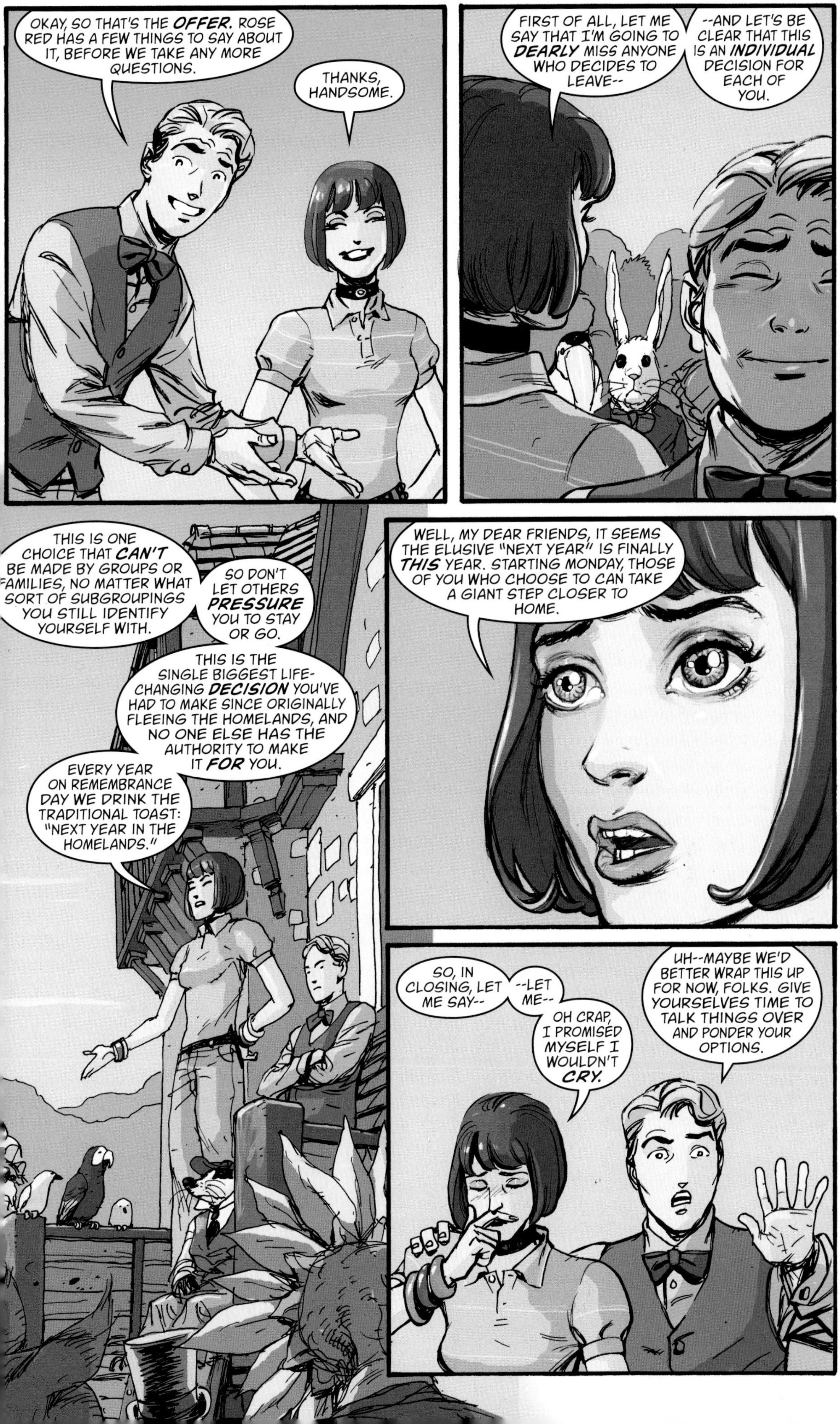
OKAY, SO THAT'S THE OFFER. ROSE RED HAS A FEW THINGS TO SAY ABOUT IT, BEFORE WE TAKE ANY MORE QUESTIONS.
THANKS, HANDSOME.
FIRST OF ALL, LET ME SAY THAT I'M GOING TO DEARLY MISS ANYONE WHO DECIDES TO LEAVE--
--AND LET'S BE CLEAR THAT THIS IS AN INDIVIDUAL DECISION FOR EACH OF YOU.
THIS IS ONE CHOICE THAT CAN'T BE MADE BY GROUPS OR FAMILIES, NO MATTER WHAT SORT OF SUBGROUPINGS YOU STILL IDENTIFY YOURSELF WITH.
SO DON'T LET OTHERS PRESSURE YOU TO STAY OR GO.
THIS IS THE SINGLE BIGGEST LIFE-CHANGING DECISION YOU'VE HAD TO MAKE SINCE ORIGINALLY FLEEING THE HOMELANDS, AND NO ONE ELSE HAS THE AUTHORITY TO MAKE IT FOR YOU.
EVERY YEAR ON REMEMBRANCE DAY WE DRINK THE TRADITIONAL TOAST: "NEXT YEAR IN THE HOMELANDS."
WELL, MY DEAR FRIENDS, IT SEEMS THE ELUSIVE "NEXT YEAR" IS FINALLY THIS YEAR. STARTING MONDAY, THOSE OF YOU WHO CHOOSE TO CAN TAKE A GIANT STEP CLOSER TO HOME.
SO, IN CLOSING, LET ME SAY--
--LET ME--
OH CRAP, I PROMISED MYSELF I WOULDN'T CRY.
UH--MAYBE WE'D BETTER WRAP THIS UP FOR NOW, FOLKS. GIVE YOURSELVES TIME TO TALK THINGS OVER AND PONDER YOUR OPTIONS.

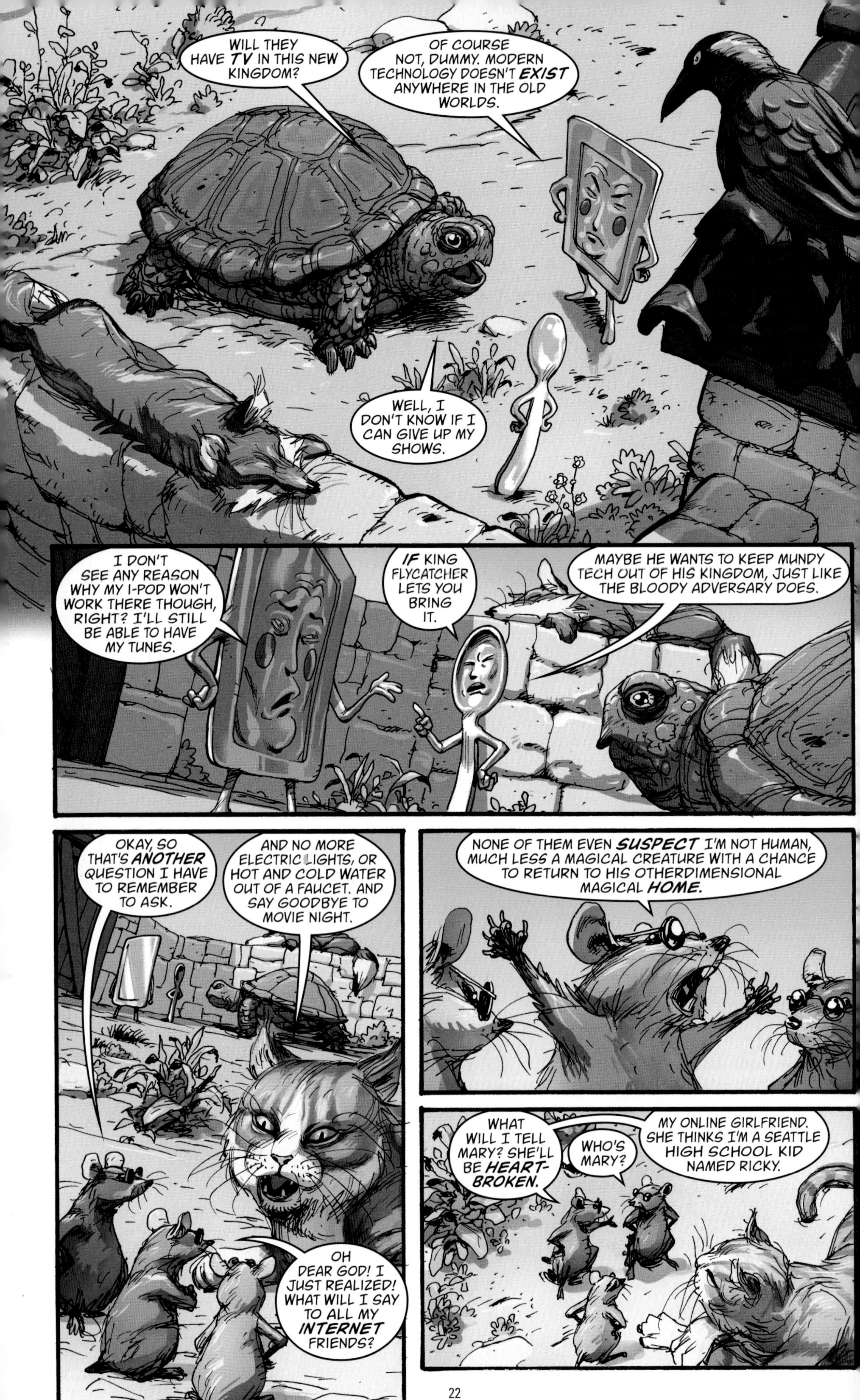
WILL THEY HAVE TV IN THIS NEW KINGDOM?
OF COURSE NOT, DUMMY. MODERN TECHNOLOGY DOESN'T EXIST ANYWHERE IN THE OLD WORLDS.
WELL, I DON'T KNOW IF I CAN GIVE UP MY SHOWS.
I DON'T SEE ANY REASON WHY MY I-POD WON'T WORK THERE THOUGH, RIGHT? I'LL STILL BE ABLE TO HAVE MY TUNES.
IF KING FLYCATCHER LETS YOU BRING IT.
MAYBE HE WANTS TO KEEP MUNDY TECH OUT OF HIS KINGDOM, JUST LIKE THE BLOODY ADVERSARY DOES.
OKAY, SO THAT'S ANOTHER QUESTION I HAVE TO REMEMBER TO ASK.
AND NO MORE ELECTRIC LIGHTS, OR HOT AND COLD WATER OUT OF A FAUCET. AND SAY GOODBYE TO MOVIE NIGHT.
OH DEAR GOD! I JUST REALIZED! WHAT WILL I SAY TO ALL MY INTERNET FRIENDS?
NONE OF THEM EVEN SUSPECT I'M NOT HUMAN, MUCH LESS A MAGICAL CREATURE WITH A CHANCE TO RETURN TO HIS OTHERDIMENSIONAL MAGICAL HOME.
WHAT WILL I TELL MARY? SHE'LL BE HEART-BROKEN.
WHO'S MARY?
MY ONLINE GIRLFRIEND. SHE THINKS I'M A SEATTLE HIGH SCHOOL KID NAMED RICKY.

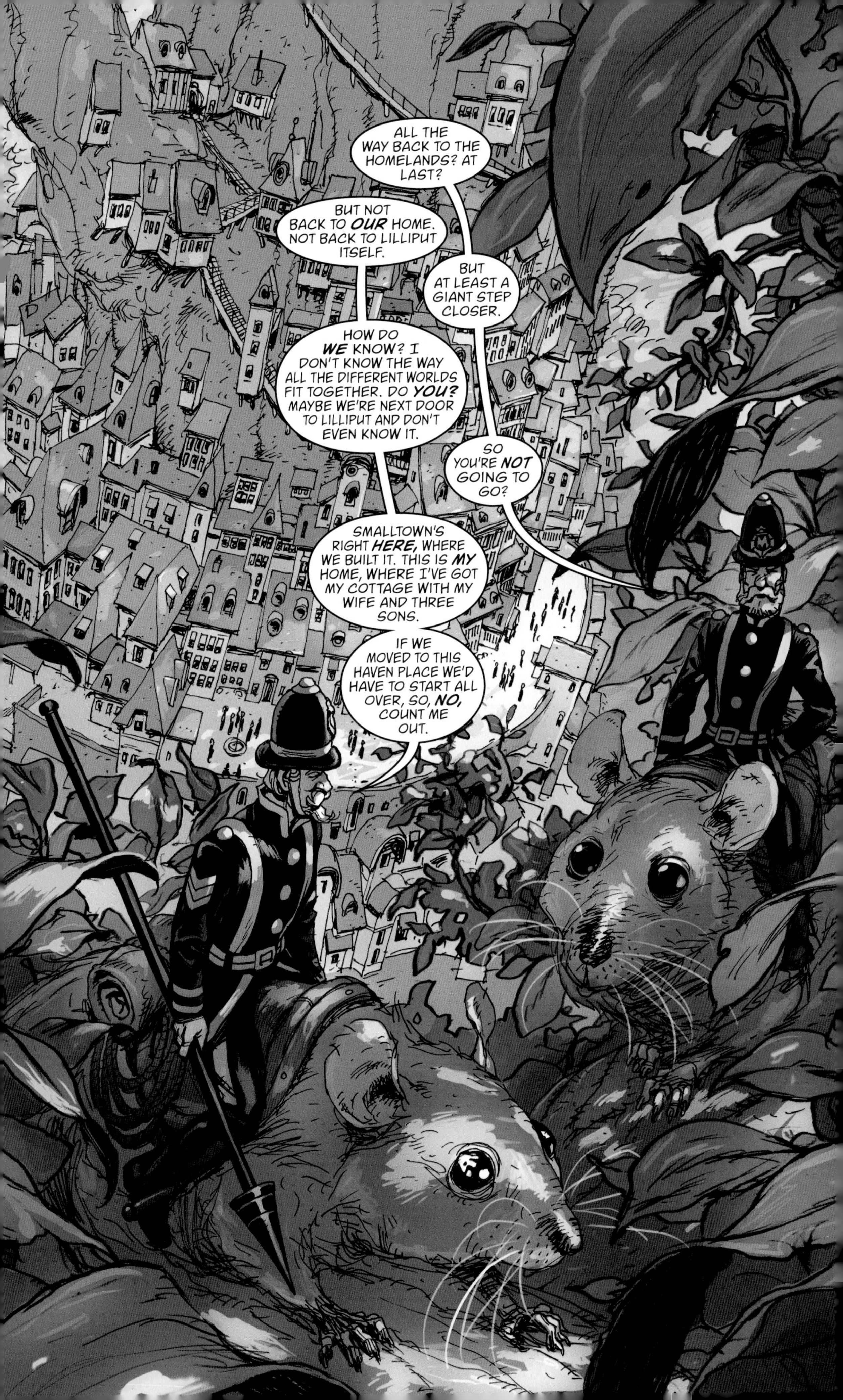
ALL THE WAY BACK TO THE HOMELANDS? AT LAST?
BUT NOT BACK TO **OUR** HOME. NOT BACK TO LILLIPUT ITSELF.
BUT AT LEAST A GIANT STEP CLOSER.
HOW DO **WE** KNOW? I DON'T KNOW THE WAY ALL THE DIFFERENT WORLDS FIT TOGETHER. DO **YOU?** MAYBE WE'RE NEXT DOOR TO LILLIPUT AND DON'T EVEN KNOW IT.
SO YOU'RE **NOT** GOING TO GO?
SMALLTOWN'S RIGHT **HERE,** WHERE WE BUILT IT. THIS IS **MY** HOME, WHERE I'VE GOT MY COTTAGE WITH MY WIFE AND THREE SONS.
IF WE MOVED TO THIS HAVEN PLACE WE'D HAVE TO START ALL OVER, SO, **NO,** COUNT ME OUT.

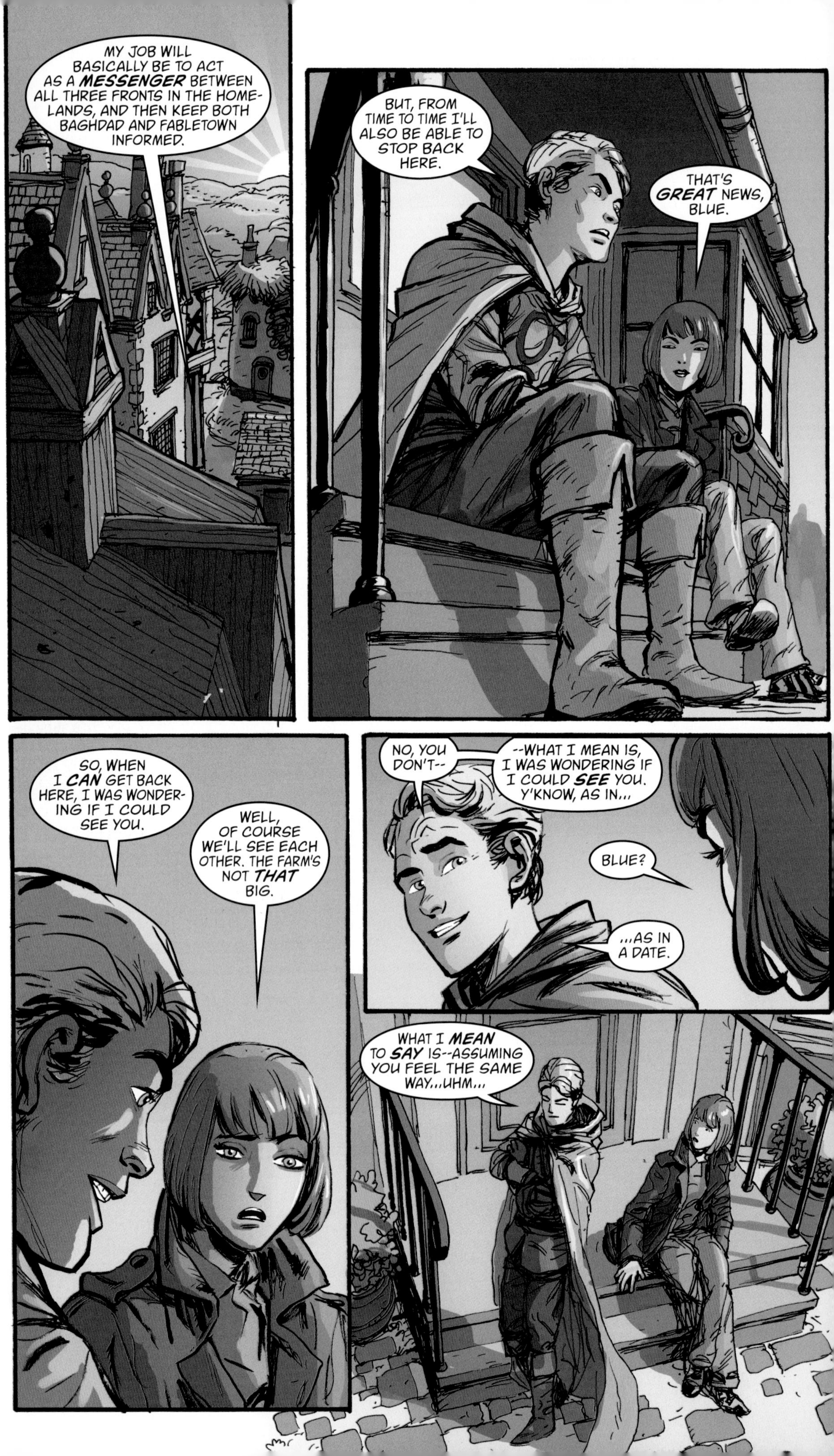

MY JOB WILL BASICALLY BE TO ACT AS A MESSENGER BETWEEN ALL THREE FRONTS IN THE HOME-LANDS, AND THEN KEEP BOTH BAGHDAD AND FABLETOWN INFORMED.
BUT, FROM TIME TO TIME I'LL ALSO BE ABLE TO STOP BACK HERE.
THAT'S GREAT NEWS, BLUE.
SO, WHEN I CAN GET BACK HERE, I WAS WONDER-ING IF I COULD SEE YOU.
WELL, OF COURSE WE'LL SEE EACH OTHER. THE FARM'S NOT THAT BIG.
NO, YOU DON'T--
--WHAT I MEAN IS, I WAS WONDERING IF I COULD SEE YOU. Y'KNOW, AS IN...
BLUE?
...AS IN A DATE.
WHAT I MEAN TO SAY IS--ASSUMING YOU FEEL THE SAME WAY...UHM...

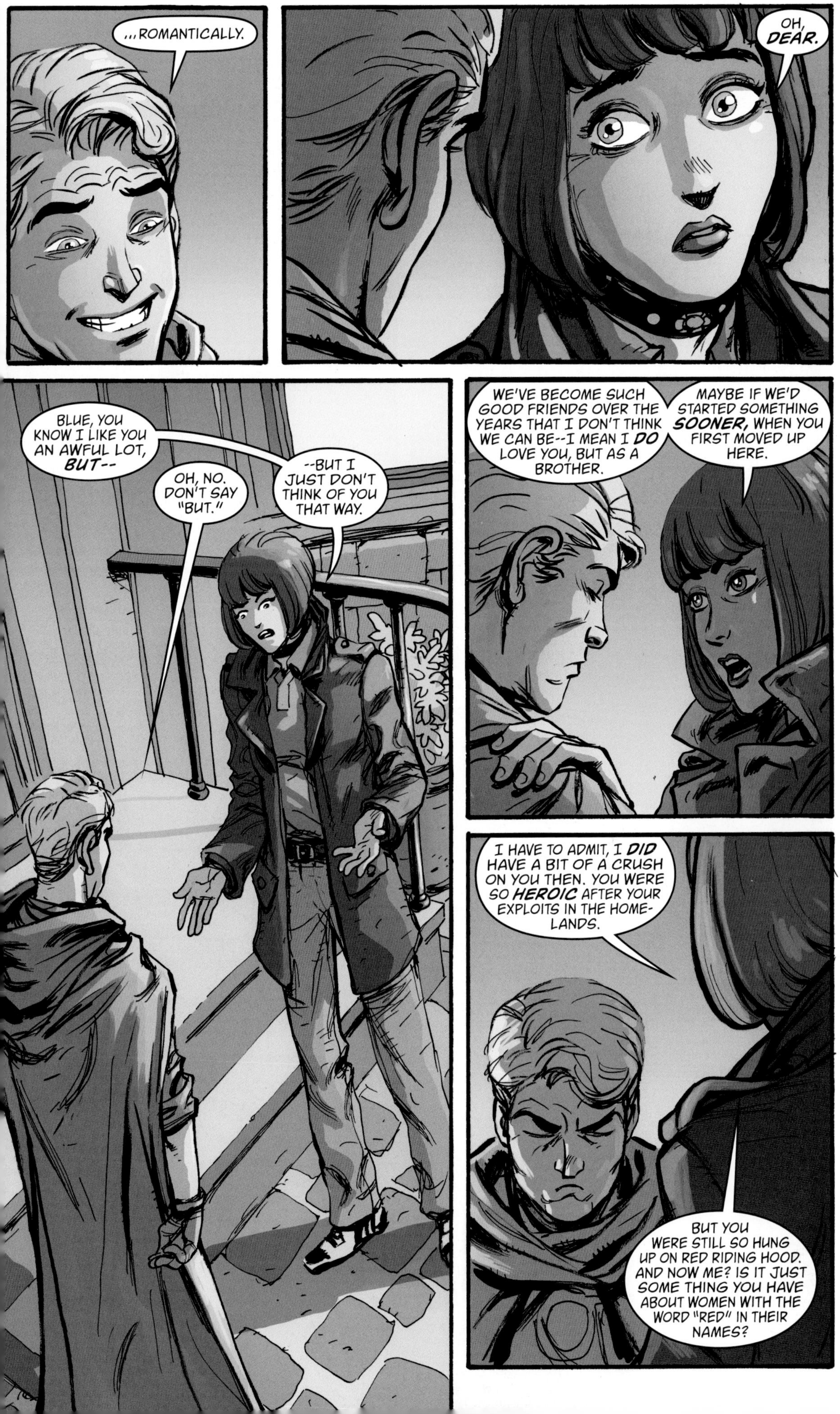

...ROMANTICALLY.
OH, DEAR.
BLUE, YOU KNOW I LIKE YOU AN AWFUL LOT, BUT--
OH, NO. DON'T SAY "BUT."
--BUT I JUST DON'T THINK OF YOU THAT WAY.
WE'VE BECOME SUCH GOOD FRIENDS OVER THE YEARS THAT I DON'T THINK WE CAN BE--I MEAN I DO LOVE YOU, BUT AS A BROTHER.
MAYBE IF WE'D STARTED SOMETHING SOONER, WHEN YOU FIRST MOVED UP HERE.
I HAVE TO ADMIT, I DID HAVE A BIT OF A CRUSH ON YOU THEN. YOU WERE SO HEROIC AFTER YOUR EXPLOITS IN THE HOME-LANDS.
BUT YOU WERE STILL SO HUNG UP ON RED RIDING HOOD. AND NOW ME? IS IT JUST SOME THING YOU HAVE ABOUT WOMEN WITH THE WORD "RED" IN THEIR NAMES?

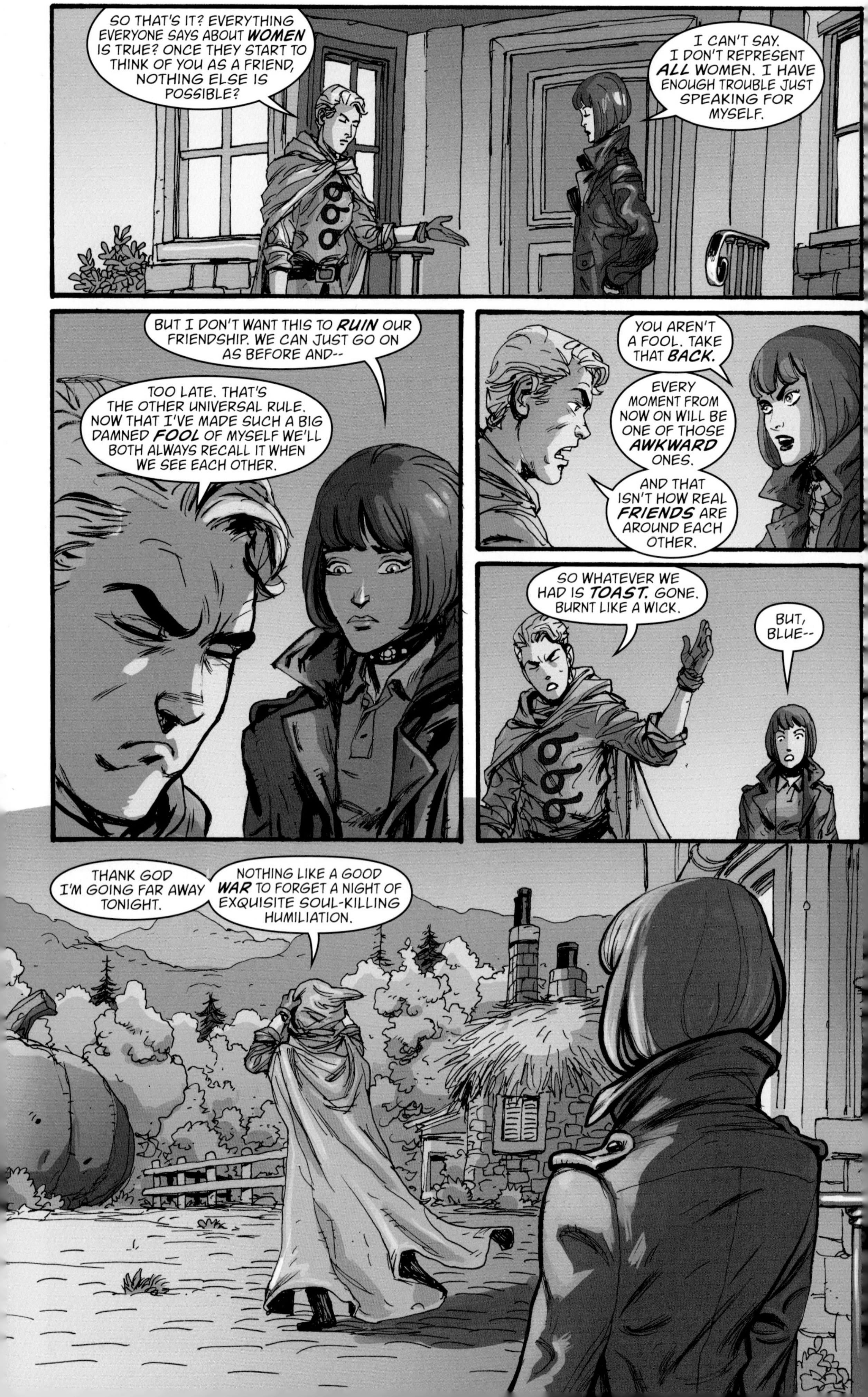
SO THAT'S IT? EVERYTHING EVERYONE SAYS ABOUT **WOMEN** IS TRUE? ONCE THEY START TO THINK OF YOU AS A FRIEND, NOTHING ELSE IS POSSIBLE?
I CAN'T SAY. I DON'T REPRESENT **ALL** WOMEN. I HAVE ENOUGH TROUBLE JUST SPEAKING FOR MYSELF.
BUT I DON'T WANT THIS TO **RUIN** OUR FRIENDSHIP. WE CAN JUST GO ON AS BEFORE AND--
TOO LATE. THAT'S THE OTHER UNIVERSAL RULE. NOW THAT I'VE MADE SUCH A BIG DAMNED **FOOL** OF MYSELF WE'LL BOTH ALWAYS RECALL IT WHEN WE SEE EACH OTHER.
YOU AREN'T A FOOL. TAKE THAT **BACK.**
EVERY MOMENT FROM NOW ON WILL BE ONE OF THOSE **AWKWARD** ONES.
AND THAT ISN'T HOW REAL **FRIENDS** ARE AROUND EACH OTHER.
SO WHATEVER WE HAD IS **TOAST.** GONE. BURNT LIKE A WICK.
BUT, BLUE--
THANK GOD I'M GOING FAR AWAY TONIGHT.
NOTHING LIKE A GOOD **WAR** TO FORGET A NIGHT OF EXQUISITE SOUL-KILLING HUMILIATION.

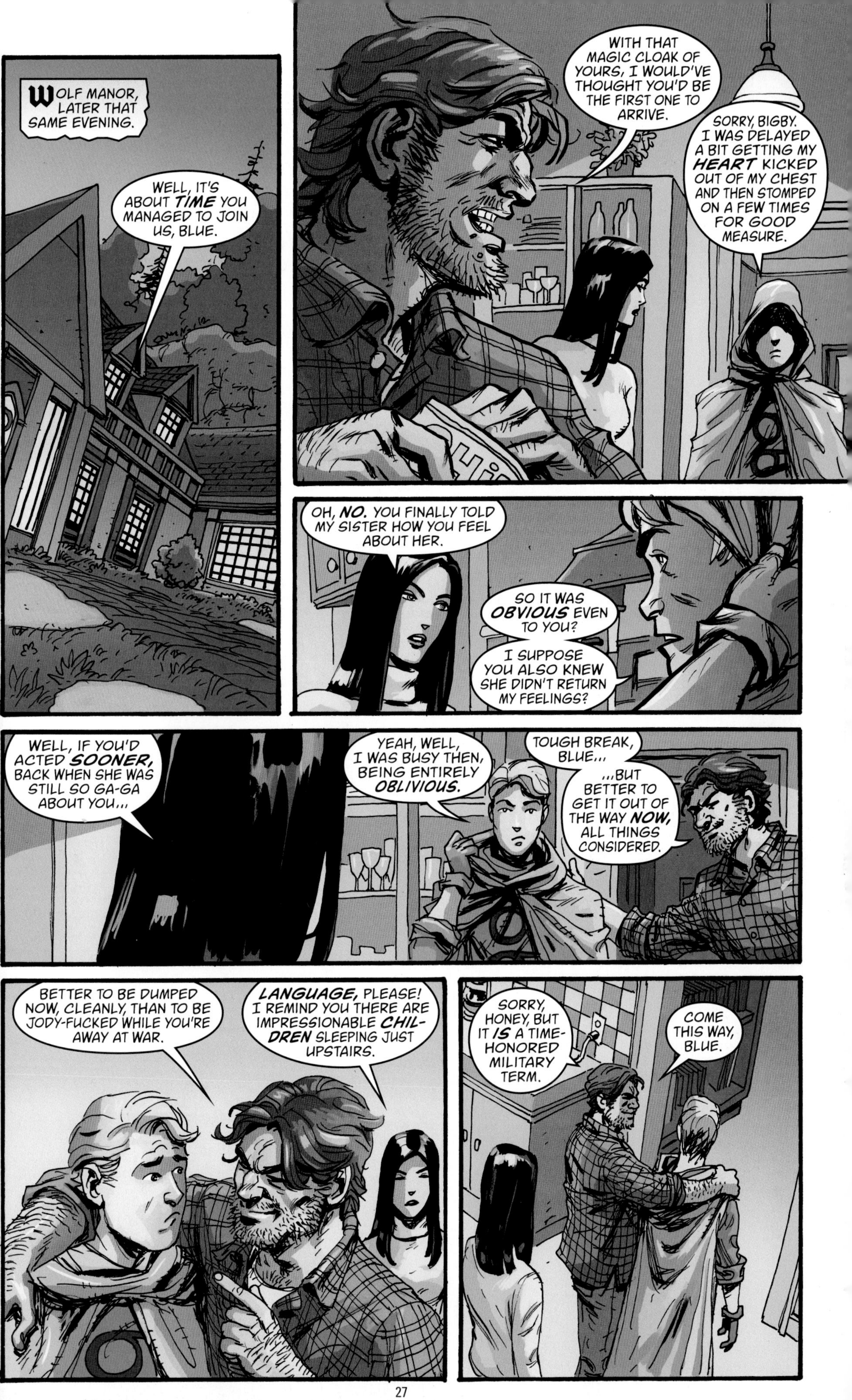
WOLF MANOR, LATER THAT SAME EVENING.
WELL, IT'S ABOUT TIME YOU MANAGED TO JOIN US, BLUE.
WITH THAT MAGIC CLOAK OF YOURS, I WOULD'VE THOUGHT YOU'D BE THE FIRST ONE TO ARRIVE.
SORRY, BIGBY. I WAS DELAYED A BIT GETTING MY HEART KICKED OUT OF MY CHEST AND THEN STOMPED ON A FEW TIMES FOR GOOD MEASURE.
OH, NO. YOU FINALLY TOLD MY SISTER HOW YOU FEEL ABOUT HER.
SO IT WAS OBVIOUS EVEN TO YOU?
I SUPPOSE YOU ALSO KNEW SHE DIDN'T RETURN MY FEELINGS?
WELL, IF YOU'D ACTED SOONER, BACK WHEN SHE WAS STILL SO GA-GA ABOUT YOU...
YEAH, WELL, I WAS BUSY THEN, BEING ENTIRELY OBLIVIOUS.
TOUGH BREAK, BLUE...
...BUT BETTER TO GET IT OUT OF THE WAY NOW, ALL THINGS CONSIDERED.
BETTER TO BE DUMPED NOW, CLEANLY, THAN TO BE JODY-FUCKED WHILE YOU'RE AWAY AT WAR.
LANGUAGE, PLEASE! I REMIND YOU THERE ARE IMPRESSIONABLE CHIL-DREN SLEEPING JUST UPSTAIRS.
SORRY, HONEY, BUT IT IS A TIME-HONORED MILITARY TERM.
COME THIS WAY, BLUE.

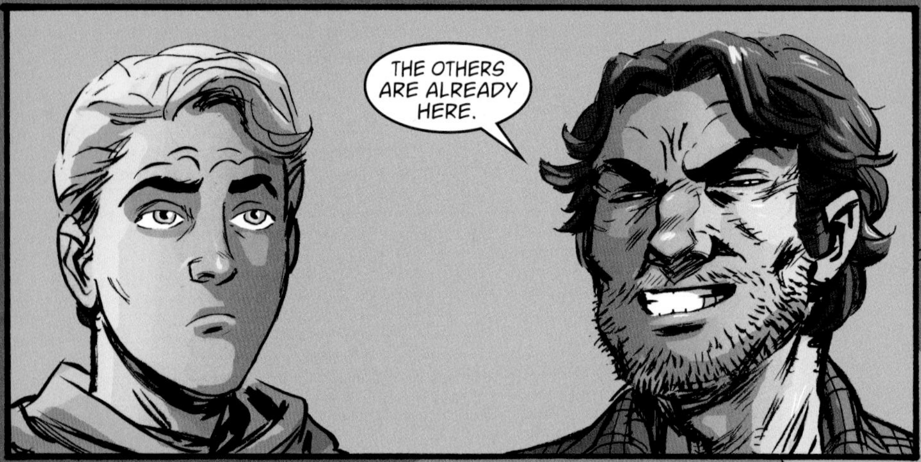
THE OTHERS ARE ALREADY HERE.

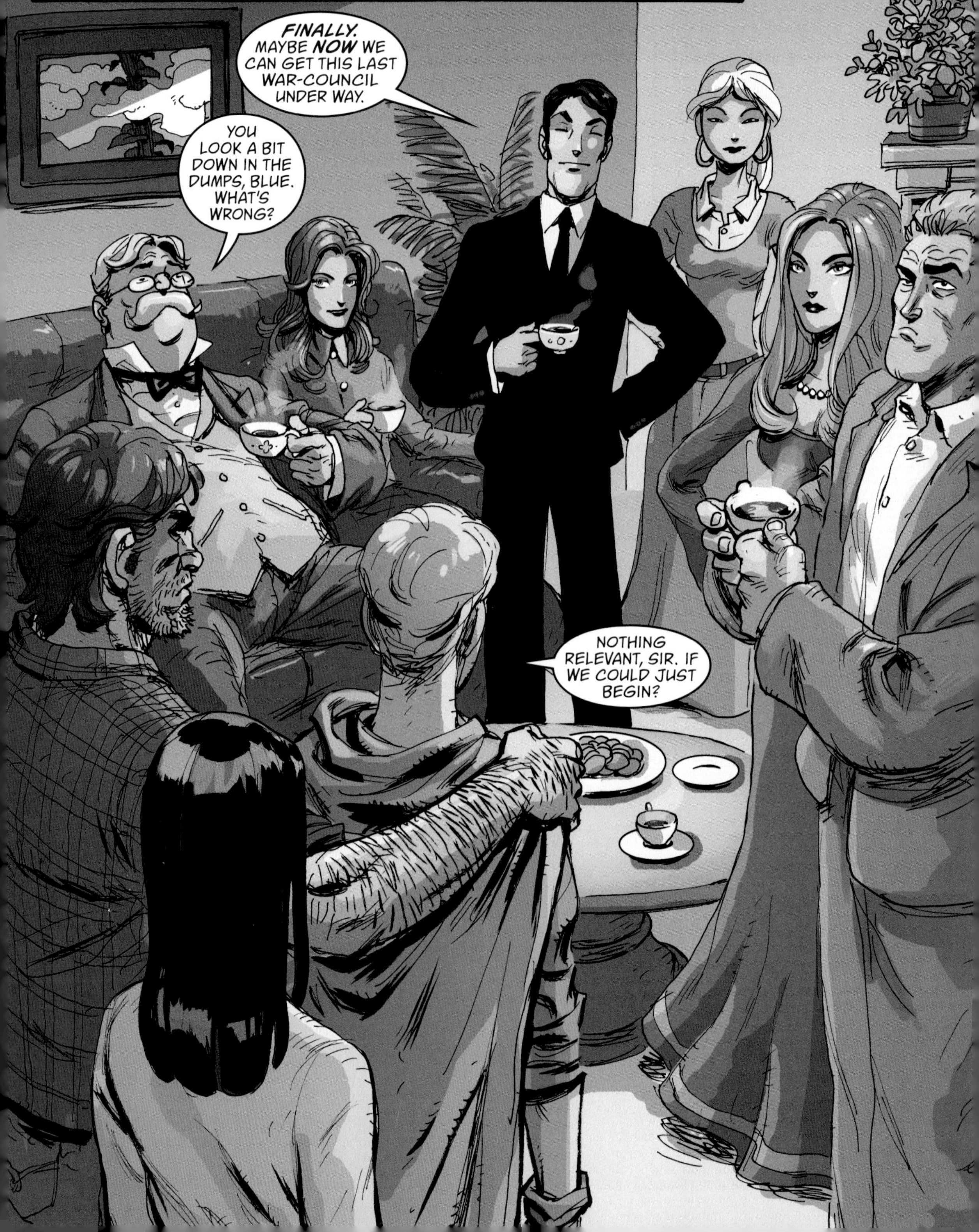
FINALLY. MAYBE *NOW* WE CAN GET THIS LAST WAR-COUNCIL UNDER WAY.
YOU LOOK A BIT DOWN IN THE DUMPS, BLUE. WHAT'S WRONG?
NOTHING RELEVANT, SIR. IF WE COULD JUST BEGIN?

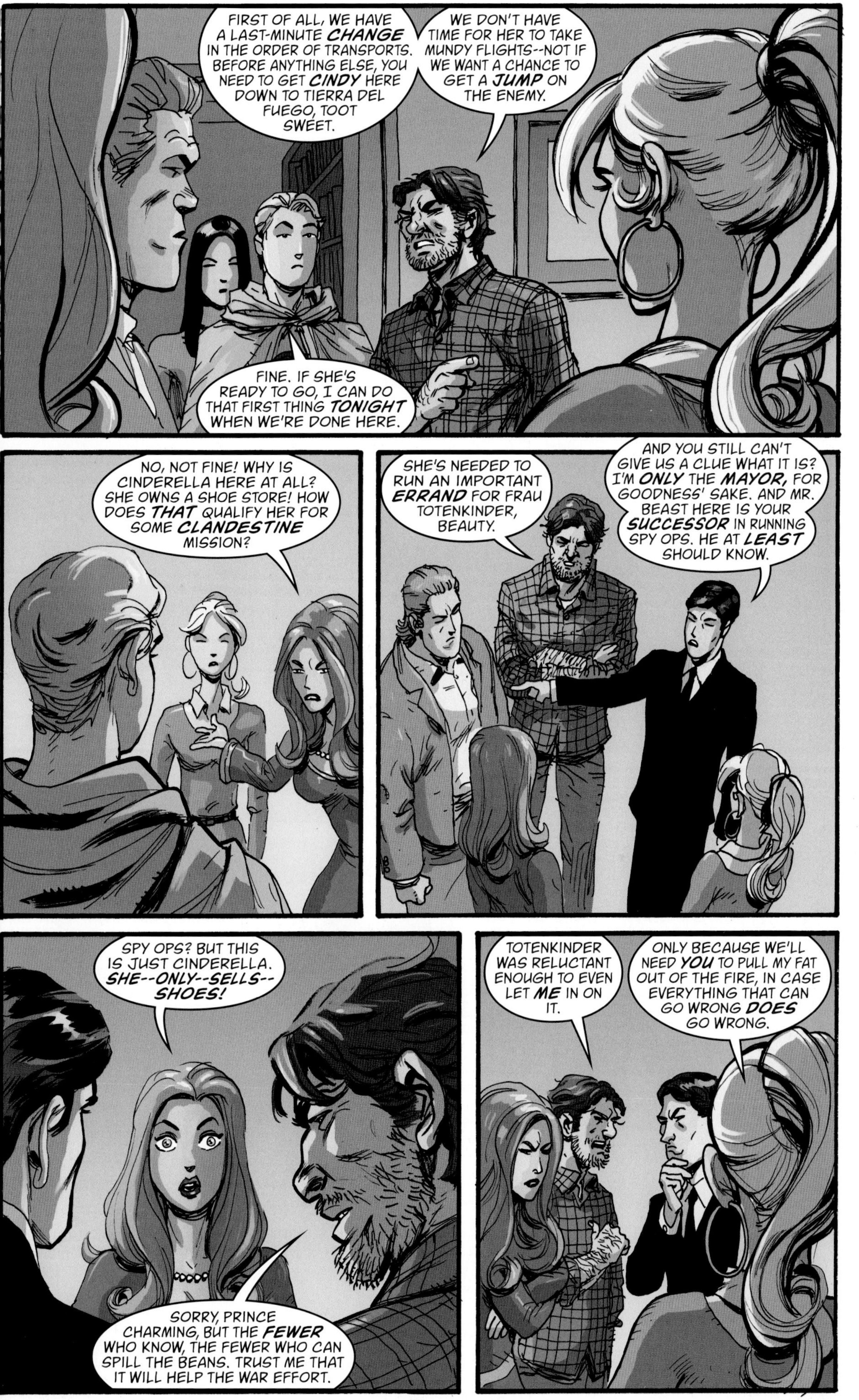
FIRST OF ALL, WE HAVE A LAST-MINUTE CHANGE IN THE ORDER OF TRANSPORTS. BEFORE ANYTHING ELSE, YOU NEED TO GET CINDY HERE DOWN TO TIERRA DEL FUEGO, TOOT SWEET.
WE DON'T HAVE TIME FOR HER TO TAKE MUNDY FLIGHTS--NOT IF WE WANT A CHANCE TO GET A JUMP ON THE ENEMY.
FINE. IF SHE'S READY TO GO, I CAN DO THAT FIRST THING TONIGHT WHEN WE'RE DONE HERE.
NO, NOT FINE! WHY IS CINDERELLA HERE AT ALL? SHE OWNS A SHOE STORE! HOW DOES THAT QUALIFY HER FOR SOME CLANDESTINE MISSION?
SHE'S NEEDED TO RUN AN IMPORTANT ERRAND FOR FRAU TOTENKINDER, BEAUTY.
AND YOU STILL CAN'T GIVE US A CLUE WHAT IT IS? I'M ONLY THE MAYOR, FOR GOODNESS' SAKE. AND MR. BEAST HERE IS YOUR SUCCESSOR IN RUNNING SPY OPS. HE AT LEAST SHOULD KNOW.
SPY OPS? BUT THIS IS JUST CINDERELLA. SHE--ONLY--SELLS--SHOES!
SORRY, PRINCE CHARMING, BUT THE FEWER WHO KNOW, THE FEWER WHO CAN SPILL THE BEANS. TRUST ME THAT IT WILL HELP THE WAR EFFORT.
TOTENKINDER WAS RELUCTANT ENOUGH TO EVEN LET ME IN ON IT.
ONLY BECAUSE WE'LL NEED YOU TO PULL MY FAT OUT OF THE FIRE, IN CASE EVERYTHING THAT CAN GO WRONG DOES GO WRONG.

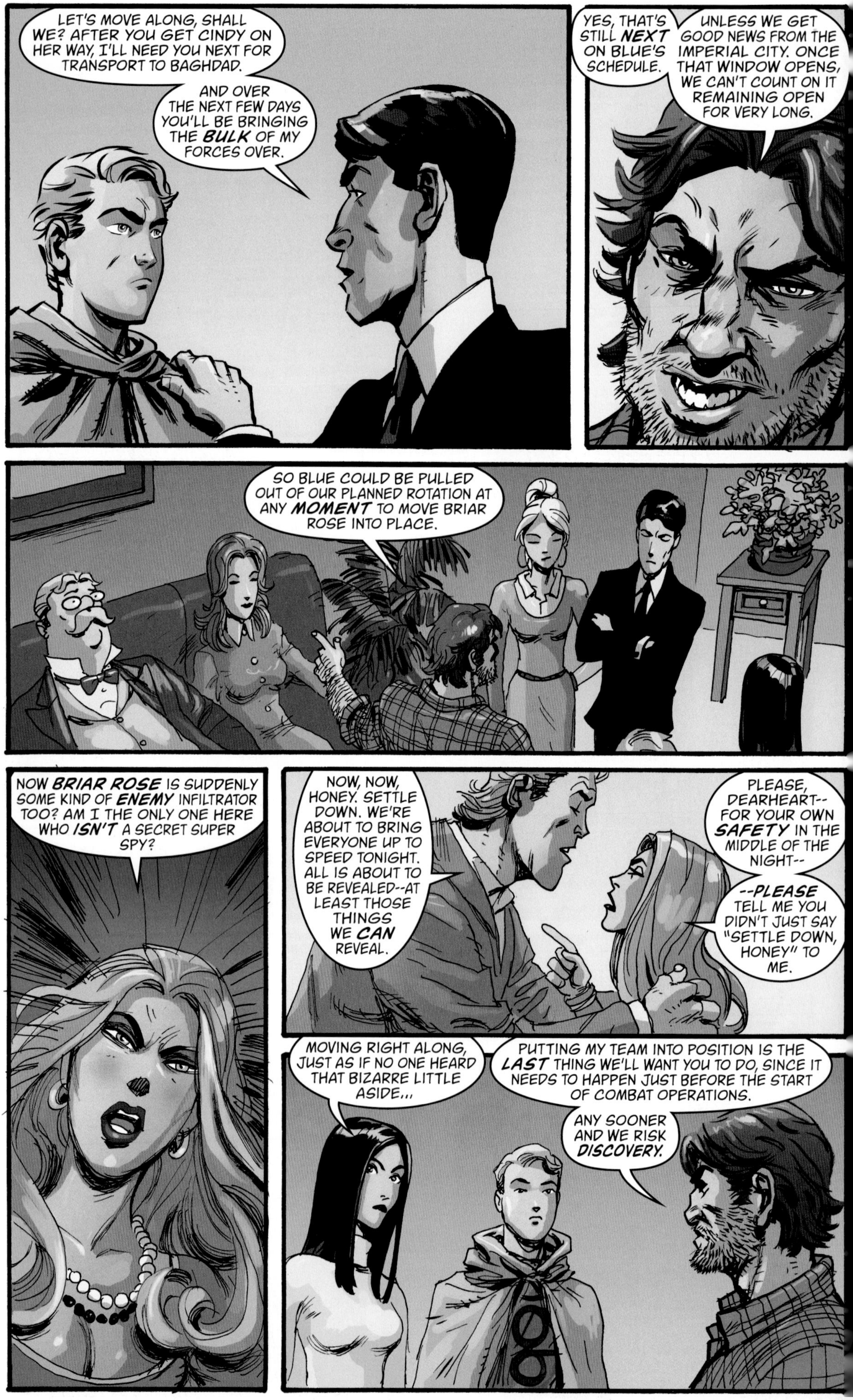
LET'S MOVE ALONG, SHALL WE? AFTER YOU GET CINDY ON HER WAY, I'LL NEED YOU NEXT FOR TRANSPORT TO BAGHDAD.
AND OVER THE NEXT FEW DAYS YOU'LL BE BRINGING THE **BULK** OF MY FORCES OVER.
YES, THAT'S STILL **NEXT** ON BLUE'S SCHEDULE.
UNLESS WE GET GOOD NEWS FROM THE IMPERIAL CITY. ONCE THAT WINDOW OPENS, WE CAN'T COUNT ON IT REMAINING OPEN FOR VERY LONG.
SO BLUE COULD BE PULLED OUT OF OUR PLANNED ROTATION AT ANY **MOMENT** TO MOVE BRIAR ROSE INTO PLACE.
NOW **BRIAR ROSE** IS SUDDENLY SOME KIND OF **ENEMY** INFILTRATOR TOO? AM I THE ONLY ONE HERE WHO **ISN'T** A SECRET SUPER SPY?
NOW, NOW, HONEY. SETTLE DOWN. WE'RE ABOUT TO BRING EVERYONE UP TO SPEED TONIGHT. ALL IS ABOUT TO BE REVEALED--AT LEAST THOSE THINGS WE **CAN** REVEAL.
PLEASE, DEARHEART--FOR YOUR OWN **SAFETY** IN THE MIDDLE OF THE NIGHT--
--**PLEASE** TELL ME YOU DIDN'T JUST SAY "SETTLE DOWN, HONEY" TO ME.
MOVING RIGHT ALONG, JUST AS IF NO ONE HEARD THAT BIZARRE LITTLE ASIDE...
PUTTING MY TEAM INTO POSITION IS THE **LAST** THING WE'LL WANT YOU TO DO, SINCE IT NEEDS TO HAPPEN JUST BEFORE THE START OF COMBAT OPERATIONS.
ANY SOONER AND WE RISK **DISCOVERY**.

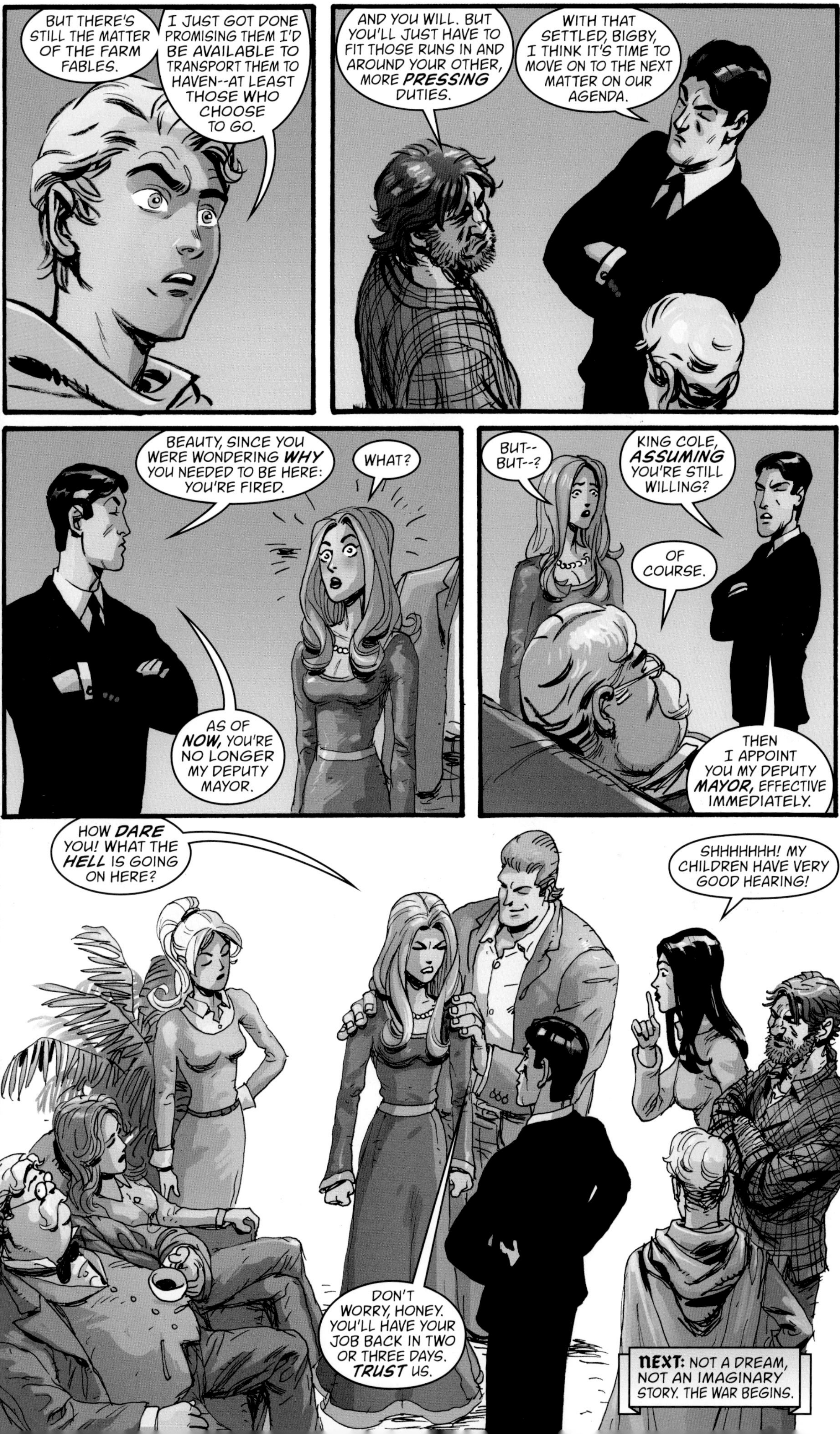
BUT THERE'S STILL THE MATTER OF THE FARM FABLES.
I JUST GOT DONE PROMISING THEM I'D BE AVAILABLE TO TRANSPORT THEM TO HAVEN--AT LEAST THOSE WHO CHOOSE TO GO.
AND YOU WILL. BUT YOU'LL JUST HAVE TO FIT THOSE RUNS IN AND AROUND YOUR OTHER, MORE PRESSING DUTIES.
WITH THAT SETTLED, BIGBY, I THINK IT'S TIME TO MOVE ON TO THE NEXT MATTER ON OUR AGENDA.
BEAUTY, SINCE YOU WERE WONDERING WHY YOU NEEDED TO BE HERE: YOU'RE FIRED.
WHAT?
AS OF NOW, YOU'RE NO LONGER MY DEPUTY MAYOR.
BUT-- BUT--?
KING COLE, ASSUMING YOU'RE STILL WILLING?
OF COURSE.
THEN I APPOINT YOU MY DEPUTY MAYOR, EFFECTIVE IMMEDIATELY.
HOW DARE YOU! WHAT THE HELL IS GOING ON HERE?
SHHHHHHH! MY CHILDREN HAVE VERY GOOD HEARING!
DON'T WORRY, HONEY. YOU'LL HAVE YOUR JOB BACK IN TWO OR THREE DAYS. TRUST US.
NEXT: NOT A DREAM, NOT AN IMAGINARY STORY. THE WAR BEGINS.

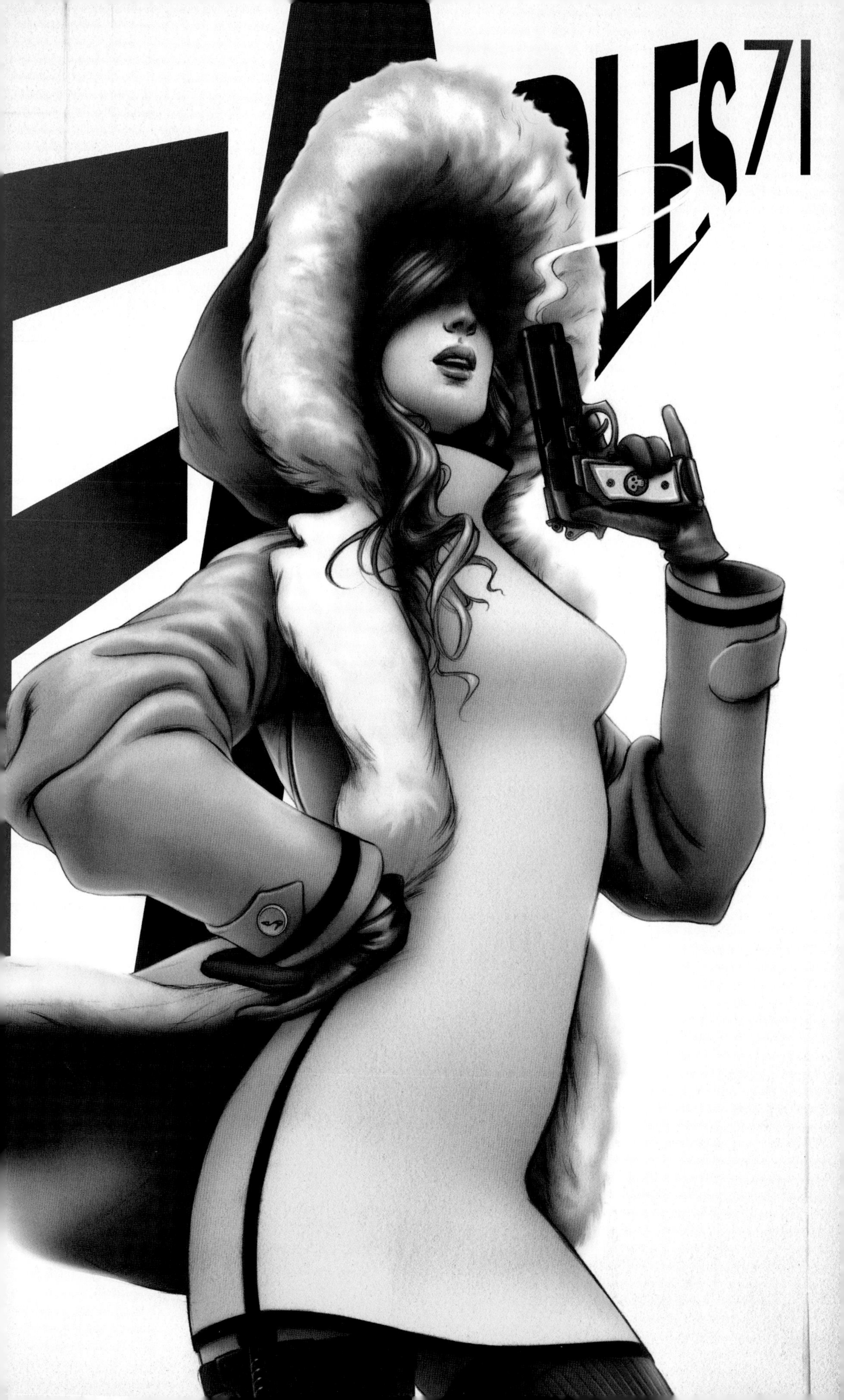
71

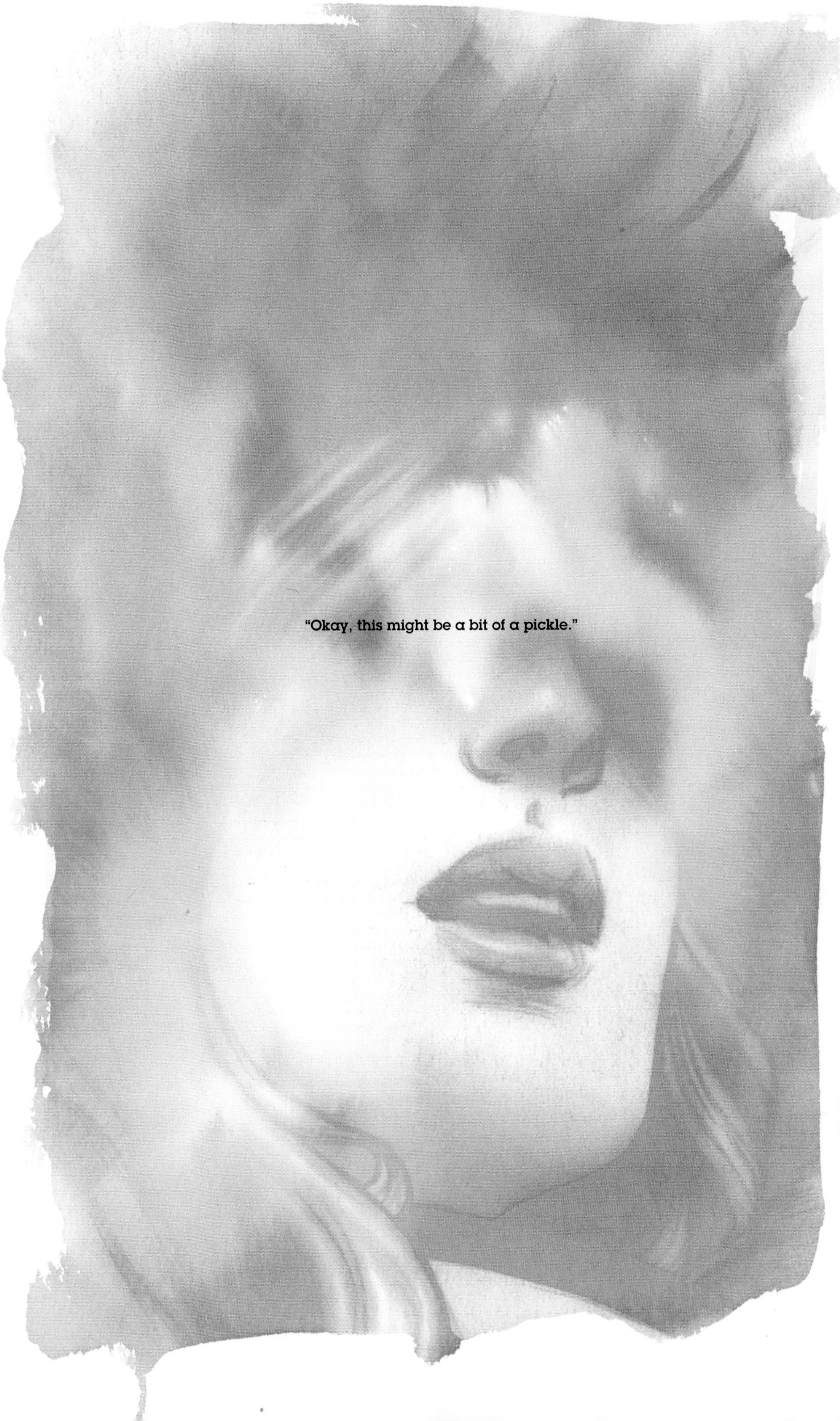
"Okay, this might be a bit of a pickle."

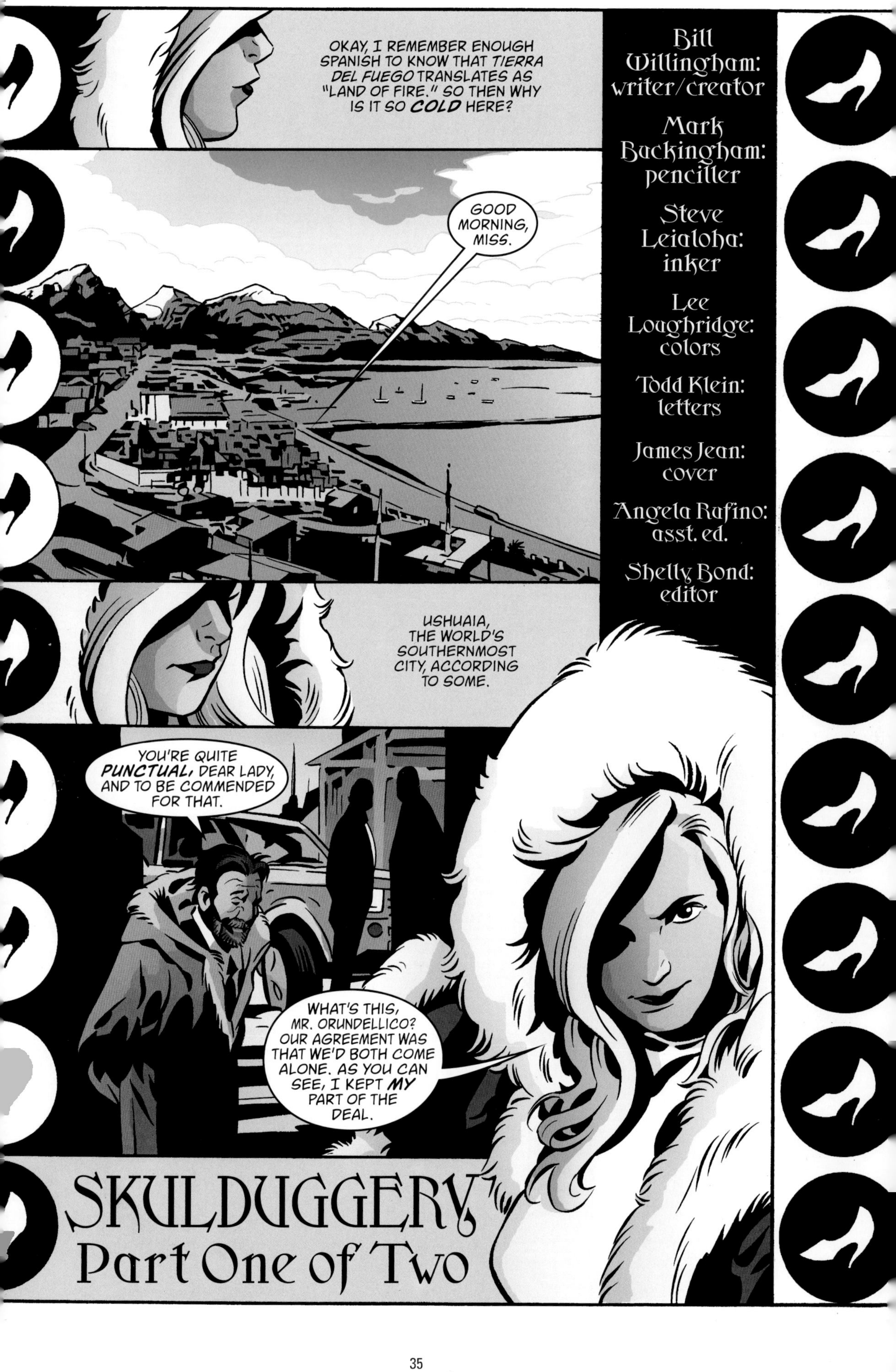
OKAY, I REMEMBER ENOUGH SPANISH TO KNOW THAT *TIERRA DEL FUEGO* TRANSLATES AS "LAND OF FIRE." SO THEN WHY IS IT SO **COLD** HERE?
GOOD MORNING, MISS.
USHUAIA, THE WORLD'S SOUTHERNMOST CITY, ACCORDING TO SOME.
YOU'RE QUITE **PUNCTUAL,** DEAR LADY, AND TO BE COMMENDED FOR THAT.
WHAT'S THIS, MR. ORUNDELLICO? OUR AGREEMENT WAS THAT WE'D BOTH COME ALONE. AS YOU CAN SEE, I KEPT **MY** PART OF THE DEAL.
Bill Willingham: writer/creator
Mark Buckingham: penciller
Steve Leialoha: inker
Lee Loughridge: colors
Todd Klein: letters
James Jean: cover
Angela Rufino: asst. ed.
Shelly Bond: editor
SKULDUGGERY
Part One of Two

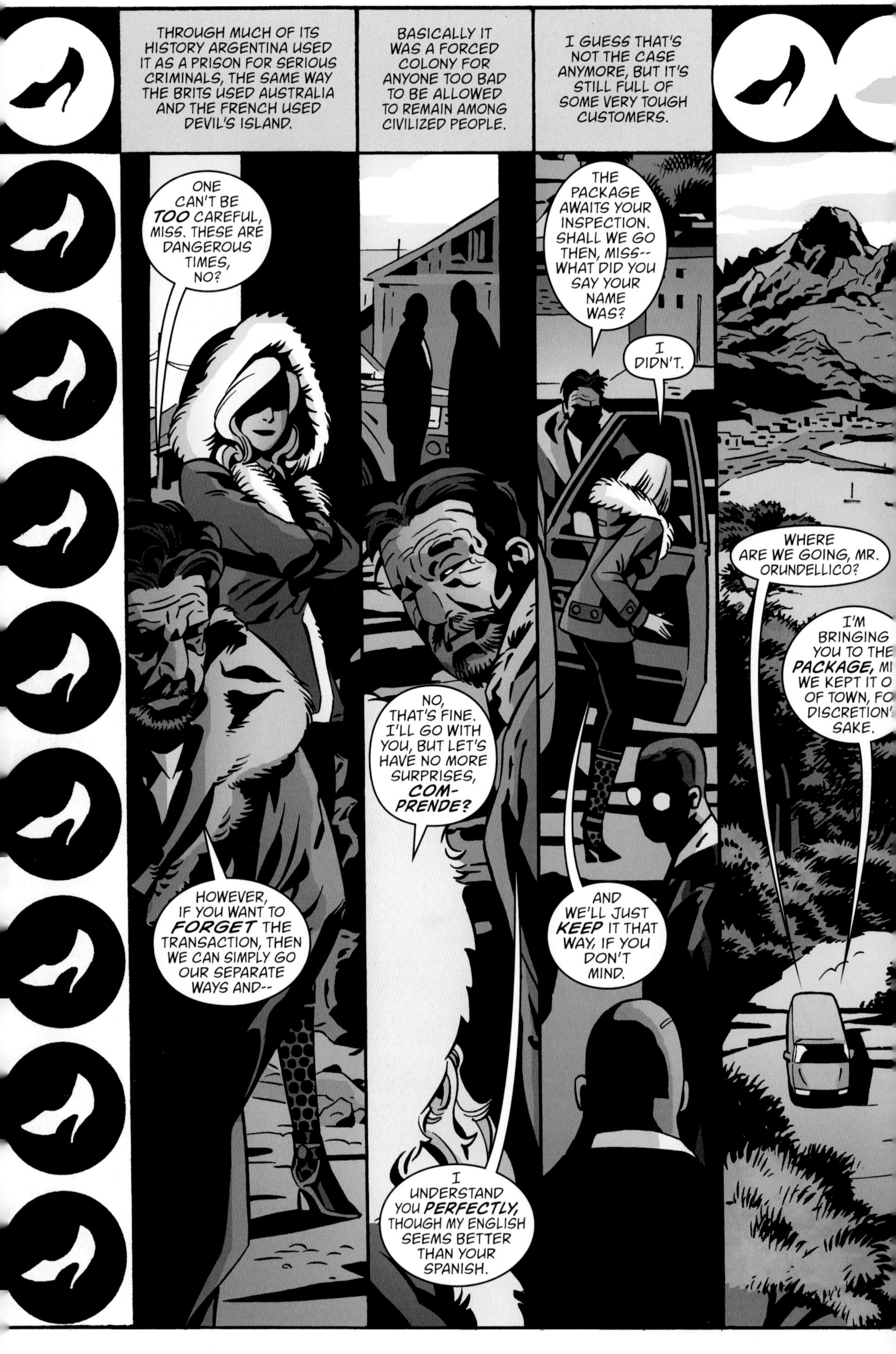
THROUGH MUCH OF ITS HISTORY ARGENTINA USED IT AS A PRISON FOR SERIOUS CRIMINALS, THE SAME WAY THE BRITS USED AUSTRALIA AND THE FRENCH USED DEVIL'S ISLAND.
BASICALLY IT WAS A FORCED COLONY FOR ANYONE TOO BAD TO BE ALLOWED TO REMAIN AMONG CIVILIZED PEOPLE.
I GUESS THAT'S NOT THE CASE ANYMORE, BUT IT'S STILL FULL OF SOME VERY TOUGH CUSTOMERS.
ONE CAN'T BE TOO CAREFUL, MISS. THESE ARE DANGEROUS TIMES, NO?
HOWEVER, IF YOU WANT TO FORGET THE TRANSACTION, THEN WE CAN SIMPLY GO OUR SEPARATE WAYS AND--
NO, THAT'S FINE. I'LL GO WITH YOU, BUT LET'S HAVE NO MORE SURPRISES, COMPRENDE?
I UNDERSTAND YOU PERFECTLY, THOUGH MY ENGLISH SEEMS BETTER THAN YOUR SPANISH.
THE PACKAGE AWAITS YOUR INSPECTION. SHALL WE GO THEN, MISS-- WHAT DID YOU SAY YOUR NAME WAS?
I DIDN'T.
AND WE'LL JUST KEEP IT THAT WAY, IF YOU DON'T MIND.
WHERE ARE WE GOING, MR. ORUNDELLICO?
I'M BRINGING YOU TO THE PACKAGE, MI WE KEPT IT O OF TOWN, FO DISCRETION' SAKE.

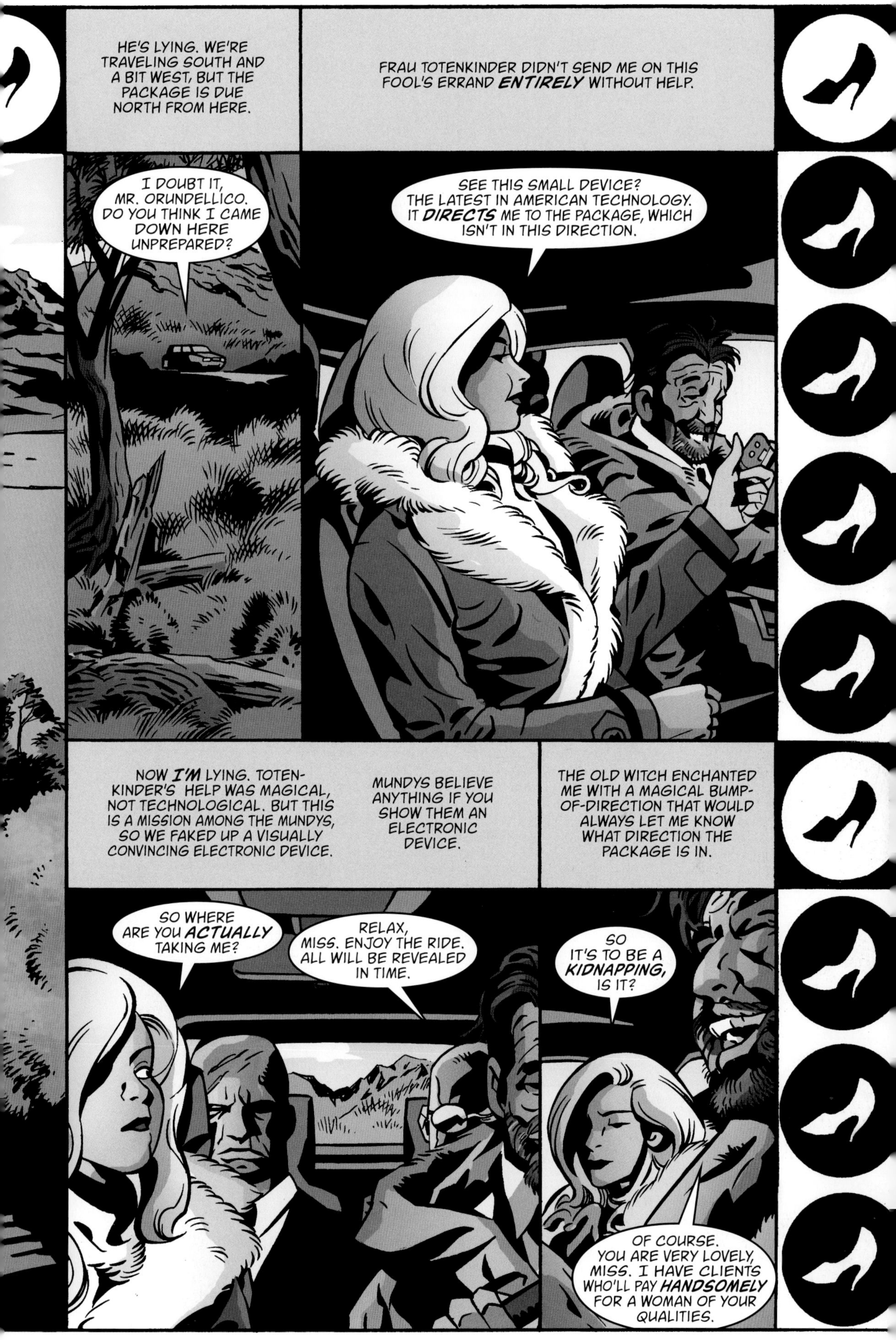

HE'S LYING. WE'RE TRAVELING SOUTH AND A BIT WEST, BUT THE PACKAGE IS DUE NORTH FROM HERE.
FRAU TOTENKINDER DIDN'T SEND ME ON THIS FOOL'S ERRAND ENTIRELY WITHOUT HELP.
I DOUBT IT, MR. ORUNDELLICO. DO YOU THINK I CAME DOWN HERE UNPREPARED?
SEE THIS SMALL DEVICE? THE LATEST IN AMERICAN TECHNOLOGY. IT DIRECTS ME TO THE PACKAGE, WHICH ISN'T IN THIS DIRECTION.
NOW I'M LYING. TOTEN-KINDER'S HELP WAS MAGICAL, NOT TECHNOLOGICAL. BUT THIS IS A MISSION AMONG THE MUNDYS, SO WE FAKED UP A VISUALLY CONVINCING ELECTRONIC DEVICE.
MUNDYS BELIEVE ANYTHING IF YOU SHOW THEM AN ELECTRONIC DEVICE.
THE OLD WITCH ENCHANTED ME WITH A MAGICAL BUMP-OF-DIRECTION THAT WOULD ALWAYS LET ME KNOW WHAT DIRECTION THE PACKAGE IS IN.
SO WHERE ARE YOU ACTUALLY TAKING ME?
RELAX, MISS. ENJOY THE RIDE. ALL WILL BE REVEALED IN TIME.
SO IT'S TO BE A KIDNAPPING, IS IT?
OF COURSE. YOU ARE VERY LOVELY, MISS. I HAVE CLIENTS WHO'LL PAY HANDSOMELY FOR A WOMAN OF YOUR QUALITIES.

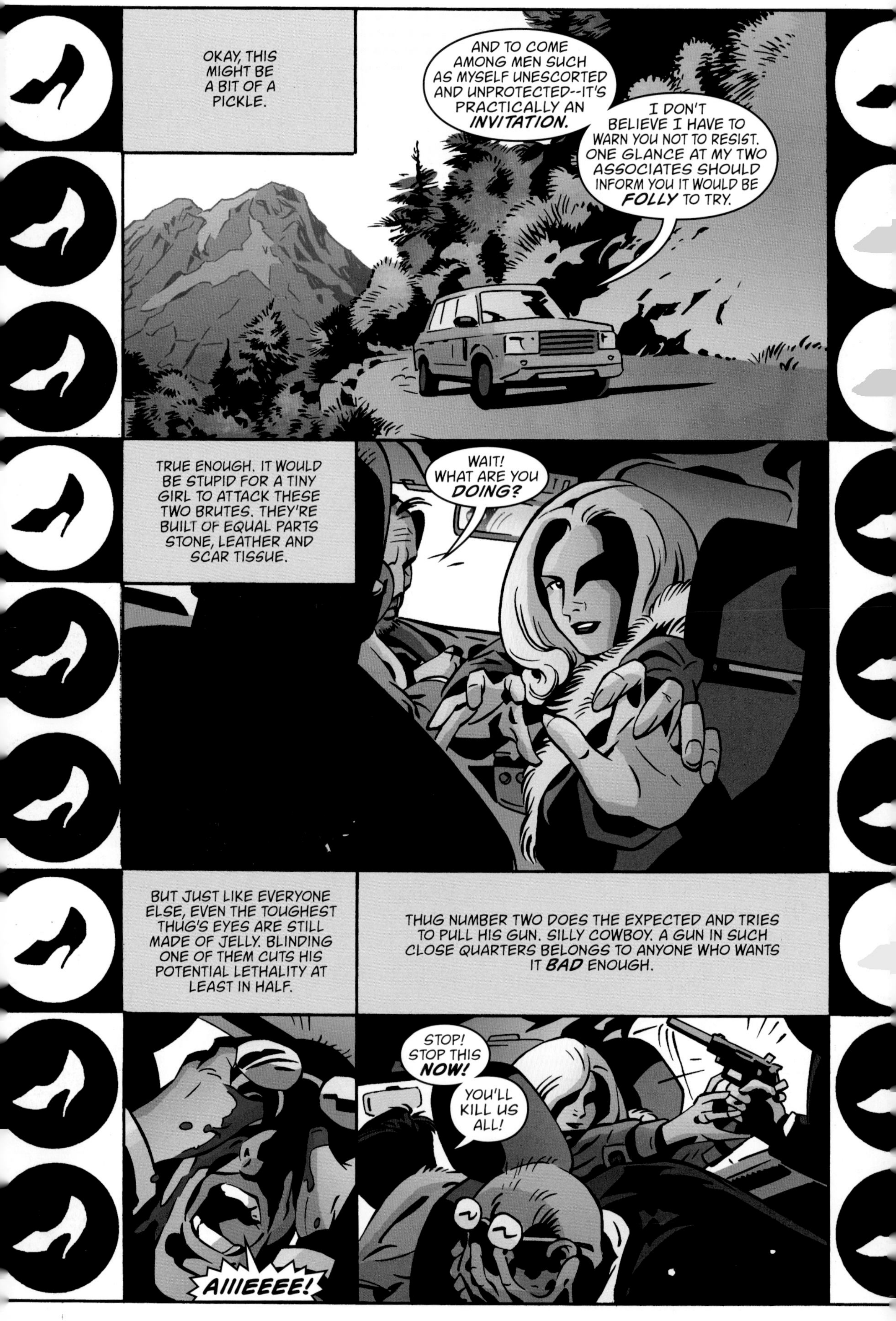

OKAY, THIS MIGHT BE A BIT OF A PICKLE.
AND TO COME AMONG MEN SUCH AS MYSELF UNESCORTED AND UNPROTECTED--IT'S PRACTICALLY AN INVITATION.
I DON'T BELIEVE I HAVE TO WARN YOU NOT TO RESIST. ONE GLANCE AT MY TWO ASSOCIATES SHOULD INFORM YOU IT WOULD BE FOLLY TO TRY.
TRUE ENOUGH. IT WOULD BE STUPID FOR A TINY GIRL TO ATTACK THESE TWO BRUTES. THEY'RE BUILT OF EQUAL PARTS STONE, LEATHER AND SCAR TISSUE.
WAIT! WHAT ARE YOU DOING?
BUT JUST LIKE EVERYONE ELSE, EVEN THE TOUGHEST THUG'S EYES ARE STILL MADE OF JELLY. BLINDING ONE OF THEM CUTS HIS POTENTIAL LETHALITY AT LEAST IN HALF.
AIIIEEEE!
THUG NUMBER TWO DOES THE EXPECTED AND TRIES TO PULL HIS GUN. SILLY COWBOY. A GUN IN SUCH CLOSE QUARTERS BELONGS TO ANYONE WHO WANTS IT BAD ENOUGH.
STOP! STOP THIS NOW!
YOU'LL KILL US ALL!

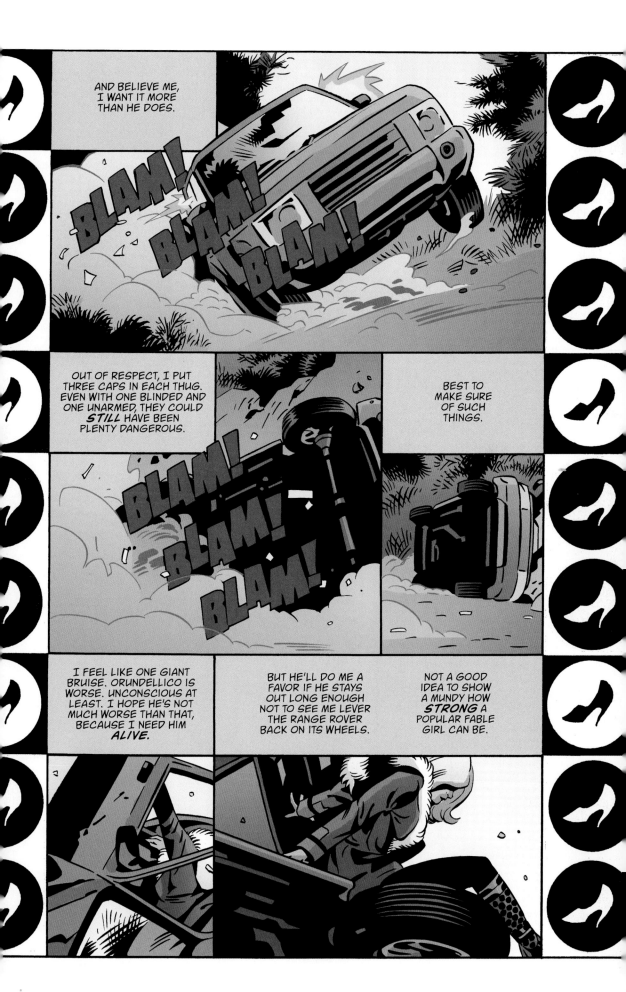

AND BELIEVE ME, I WANT IT MORE THAN HE DOES.

BLAM! BLAM! BLAM!

OUT OF RESPECT, I PUT THREE CAPS IN EACH THUG. EVEN WITH ONE BLINDED AND ONE UNARMED, THEY COULD *STILL* HAVE BEEN PLENTY DANGEROUS.

BEST TO MAKE SURE OF SUCH THINGS.

BLAM! BLAM! BLAM!

I FEEL LIKE ONE GIANT BRUISE. ORUNDELLICO IS WORSE. UNCONSCIOUS AT LEAST. I HOPE HE'S NOT MUCH WORSE THAN THAT, BECAUSE I NEED HIM *ALIVE*.

BUT HE'LL DO ME A FAVOR IF HE STAYS OUT LONG ENOUGH NOT TO SEE ME LEVER THE RANGE ROVER BACK ON ITS WHEELS.

NOT A GOOD IDEA TO SHOW A MUNDY HOW *STRONG* A POPULAR FABLE GIRL CAN BE.

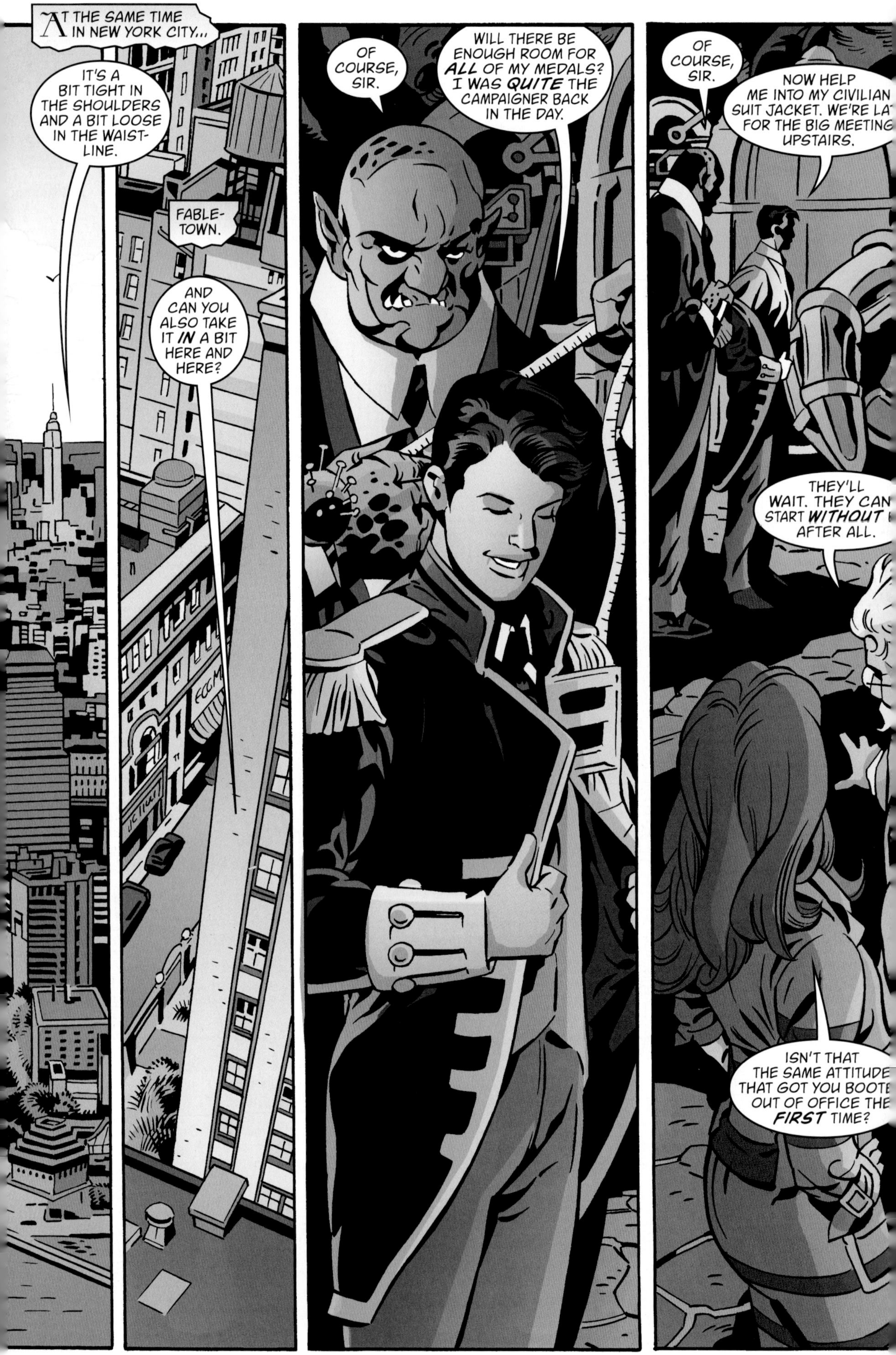
AT THE SAME TIME IN NEW YORK CITY...
IT'S A BIT TIGHT IN THE SHOULDERS AND A BIT LOOSE IN THE WAIST-LINE.
FABLE-TOWN.
AND CAN YOU ALSO TAKE IT *IN* A BIT HERE AND HERE?
OF COURSE, SIR.
WILL THERE BE ENOUGH ROOM FOR *ALL* OF MY MEDALS? I WAS *QUITE* THE CAMPAIGNER BACK IN THE DAY.
OF COURSE, SIR.
NOW HELP ME INTO MY CIVILIAN SUIT JACKET. WE'RE LA FOR THE BIG MEETING UPSTAIRS.
THEY'LL WAIT. THEY CAN START *WITHOUT* AFTER ALL.
ISN'T THAT THE SAME ATTITUDE THAT GOT YOU BOOTE OUT OF OFFICE THE *FIRST* TIME?

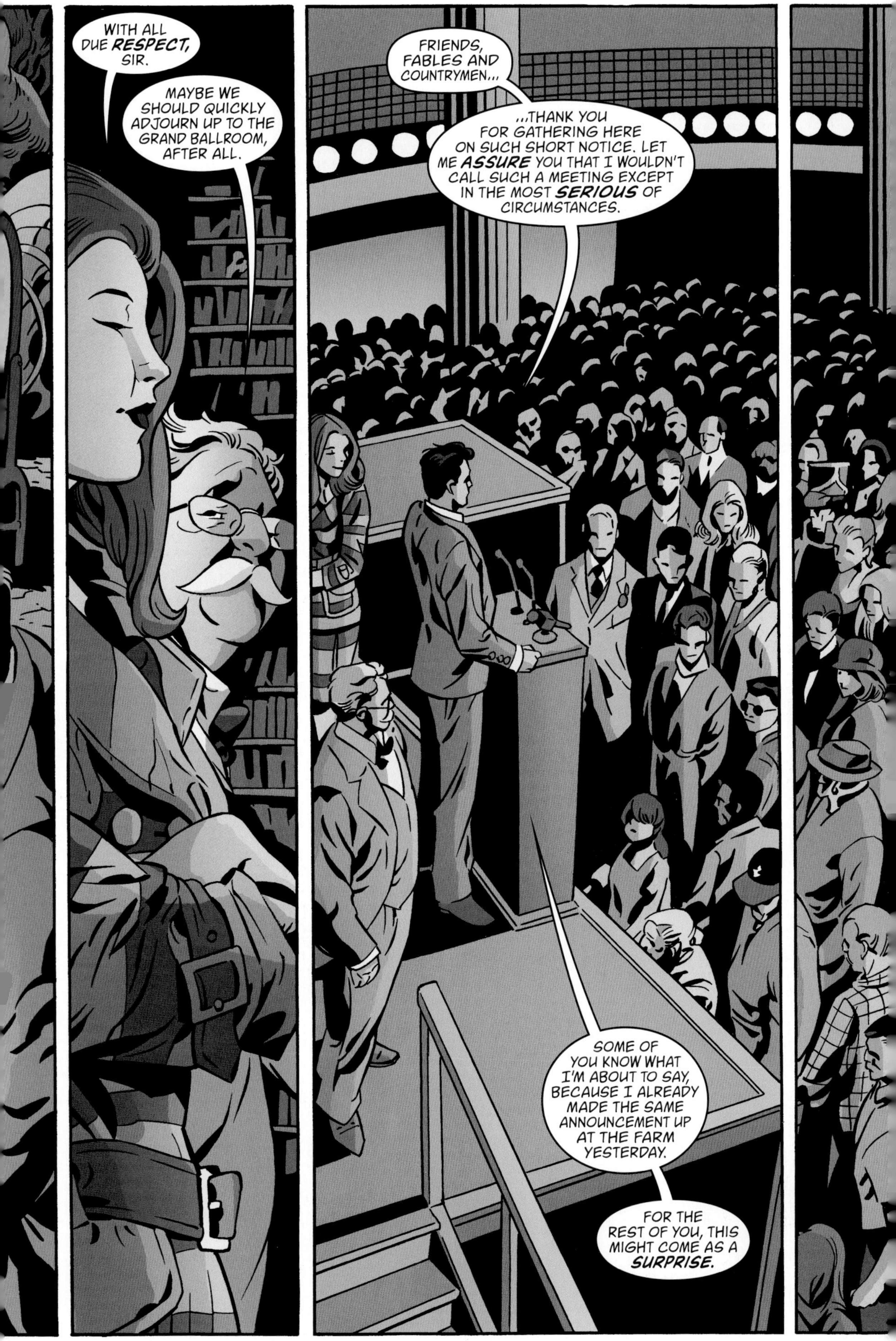

WITH ALL DUE **RESPECT,** SIR.
MAYBE WE SHOULD QUICKLY ADJOURN UP TO THE GRAND BALLROOM, AFTER ALL.
FRIENDS, FABLES AND COUNTRYMEN...
...THANK YOU FOR GATHERING HERE ON SUCH SHORT NOTICE. LET ME **ASSURE** YOU THAT I WOULDN'T CALL SUCH A MEETING EXCEPT IN THE MOST **SERIOUS** OF CIRCUMSTANCES.
SOME OF YOU KNOW WHAT I'M ABOUT TO SAY, BECAUSE I ALREADY MADE THE SAME ANNOUNCEMENT UP AT THE FARM YESTERDAY.
FOR THE REST OF YOU, THIS MIGHT COME AS A **SURPRISE.**

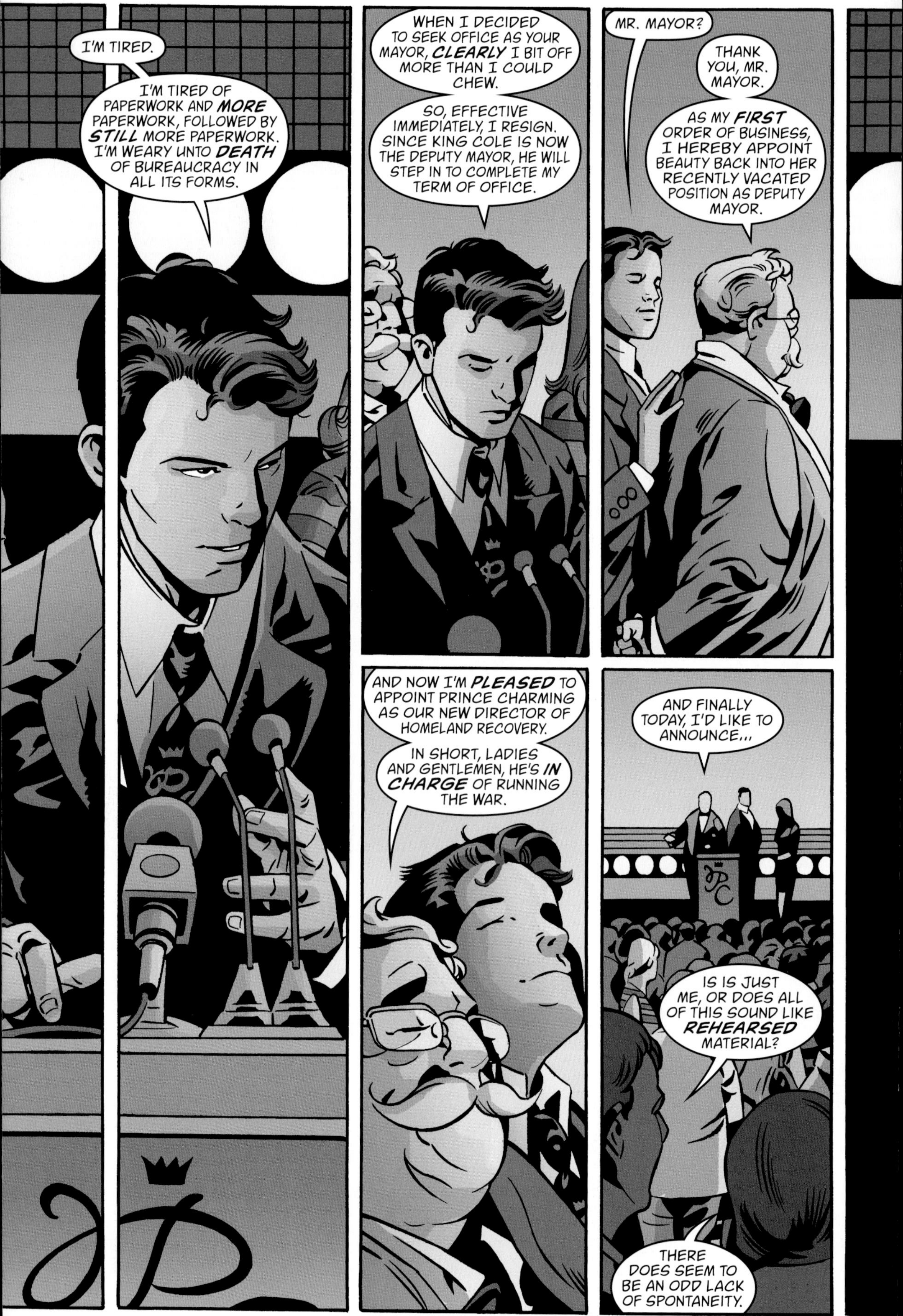

I'M TIRED.
I'M TIRED OF PAPERWORK AND MORE PAPERWORK, FOLLOWED BY STILL MORE PAPERWORK. I'M WEARY UNTO DEATH OF BUREAUCRACY IN ALL ITS FORMS.
WHEN I DECIDED TO SEEK OFFICE AS YOUR MAYOR, CLEARLY I BIT OFF MORE THAN I COULD CHEW.
SO, EFFECTIVE IMMEDIATELY, I RESIGN. SINCE KING COLE IS NOW THE DEPUTY MAYOR, HE WILL STEP IN TO COMPLETE MY TERM OF OFFICE.
MR. MAYOR?
THANK YOU, MR. MAYOR.
AS MY FIRST ORDER OF BUSINESS, I HEREBY APPOINT BEAUTY BACK INTO HER RECENTLY VACATED POSITION AS DEPUTY MAYOR.
AND NOW I'M PLEASED TO APPOINT PRINCE CHARMING AS OUR NEW DIRECTOR OF HOMELAND RECOVERY.
IN SHORT, LADIES AND GENTLEMEN, HE'S IN CHARGE OF RUNNING THE WAR.
AND FINALLY TODAY, I'D LIKE TO ANNOUNCE...
IS IS JUST ME, OR DOES ALL OF THIS SOUND LIKE REHEARSED MATERIAL?
THERE DOES SEEM TO BE AN ODD LACK OF SPONTANEITY.

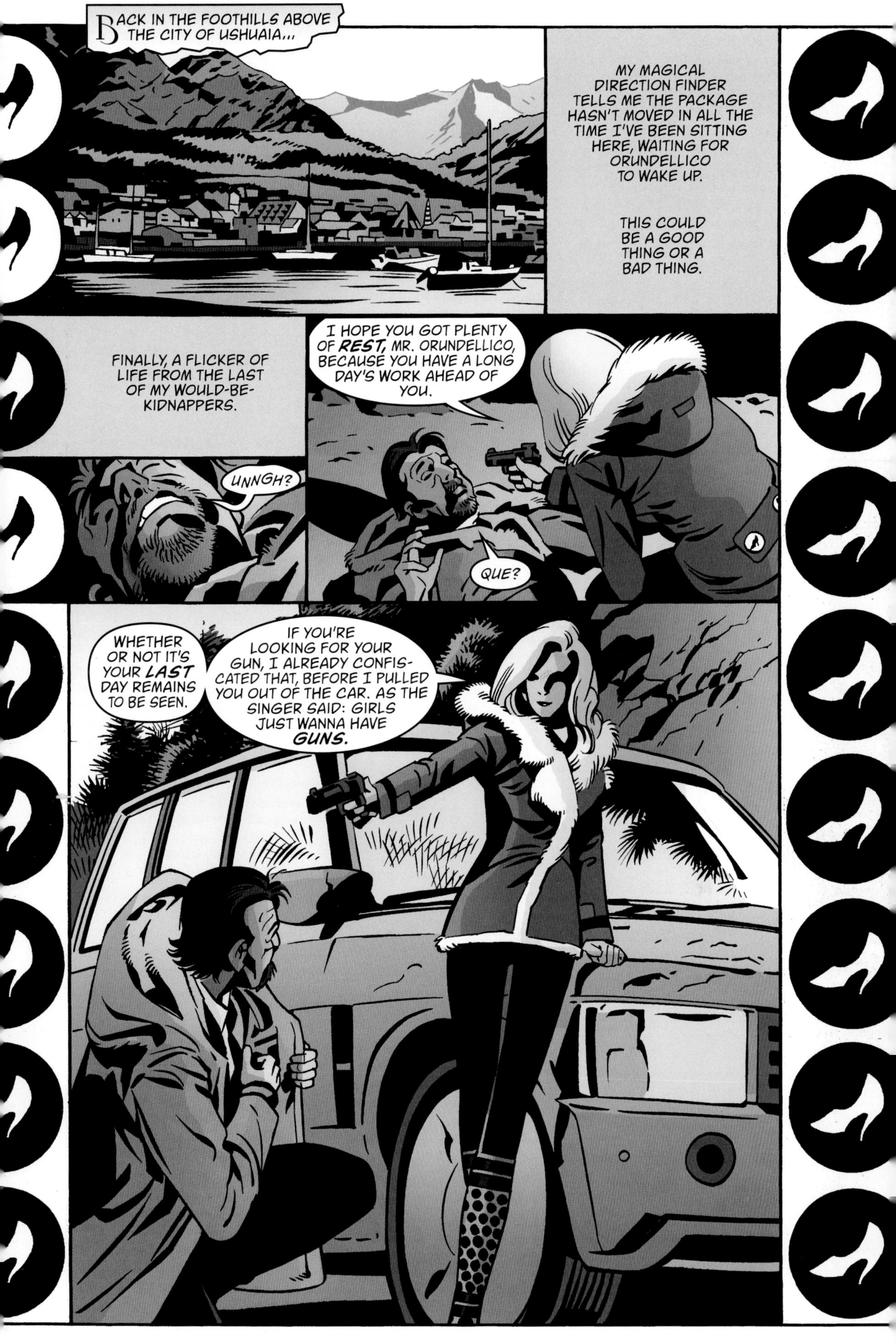
BACK IN THE FOOTHILLS ABOVE THE CITY OF USHUAIA...
MY MAGICAL DIRECTION FINDER TELLS ME THE PACKAGE HASN'T MOVED IN ALL THE TIME I'VE BEEN SITTING HERE, WAITING FOR ORUNDELLICO TO WAKE UP.
THIS COULD BE A GOOD THING OR A BAD THING.
FINALLY, A FLICKER OF LIFE FROM THE LAST OF MY WOULD-BE-KIDNAPPERS.
UNNGH?
I HOPE YOU GOT PLENTY OF REST, MR. ORUNDELLICO, BECAUSE YOU HAVE A LONG DAY'S WORK AHEAD OF YOU.
QUE?
WHETHER OR NOT IT'S YOUR LAST DAY REMAINS TO BE SEEN.
IF YOU'RE LOOKING FOR YOUR GUN, I ALREADY CONFIS-CATED THAT, BEFORE I PULLED YOU OUT OF THE CAR. AS THE SINGER SAID: GIRLS JUST WANNA HAVE GUNS.

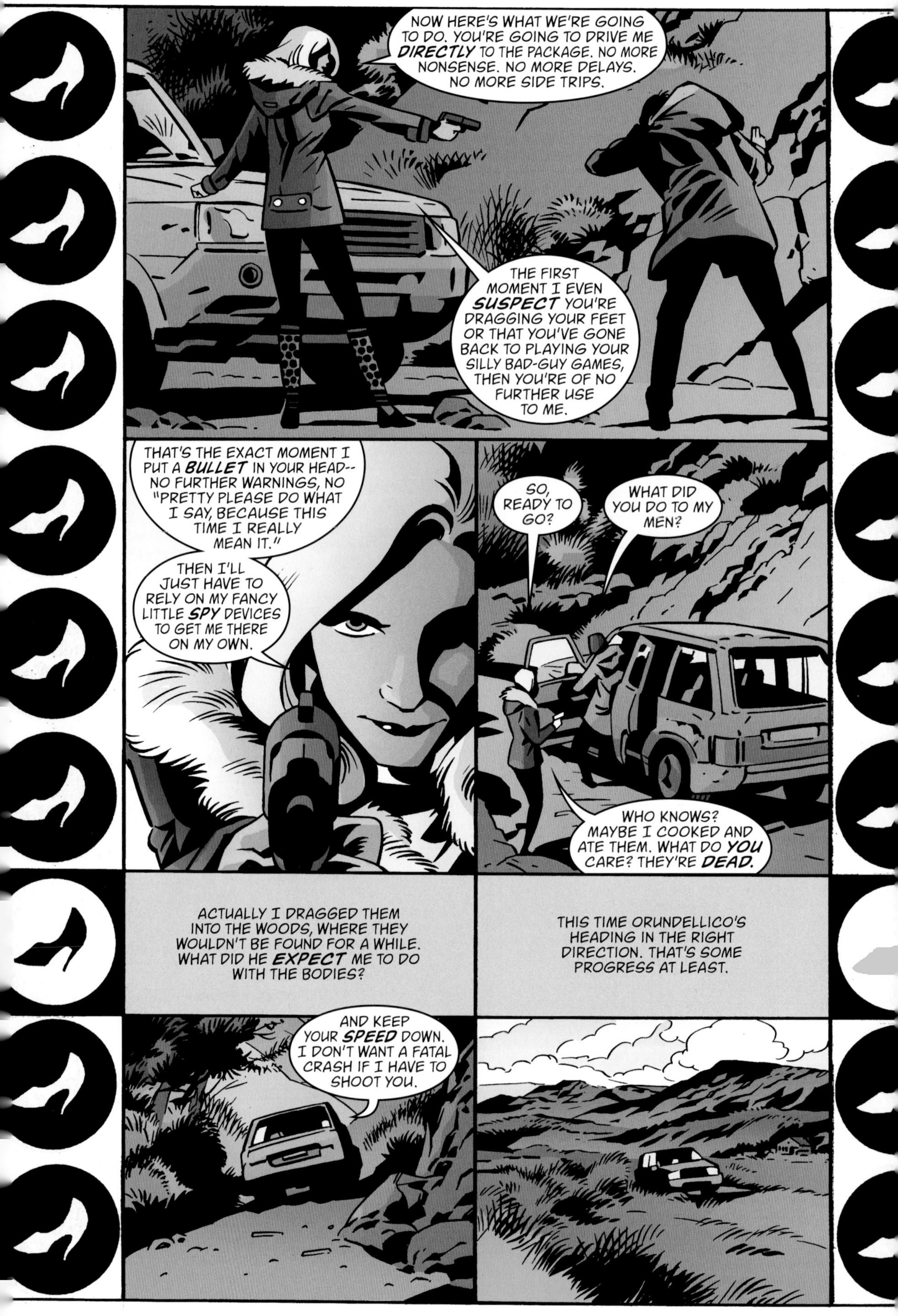
NOW HERE'S WHAT WE'RE GOING TO DO. YOU'RE GOING TO DRIVE ME DIRECTLY TO THE PACKAGE. NO MORE NONSENSE. NO MORE DELAYS. NO MORE SIDE TRIPS.
THE FIRST MOMENT I EVEN SUSPECT YOU'RE DRAGGING YOUR FEET OR THAT YOU'VE GONE BACK TO PLAYING YOUR SILLY BAD-GUY GAMES, THEN YOU'RE OF NO FURTHER USE TO ME.
THAT'S THE EXACT MOMENT I PUT A BULLET IN YOUR HEAD-- NO FURTHER WARNINGS, NO "PRETTY PLEASE DO WHAT I SAY, BECAUSE THIS TIME I REALLY MEAN IT."
THEN I'LL JUST HAVE TO RELY ON MY FANCY LITTLE SPY DEVICES TO GET ME THERE ON MY OWN.
SO, READY TO GO?
WHAT DID YOU DO TO MY MEN?
WHO KNOWS? MAYBE I COOKED AND ATE THEM. WHAT DO YOU CARE? THEY'RE DEAD.
ACTUALLY I DRAGGED THEM INTO THE WOODS, WHERE THEY WOULDN'T BE FOUND FOR A WHILE. WHAT DID HE EXPECT ME TO DO WITH THE BODIES?
THIS TIME ORUNDELLICO'S HEADING IN THE RIGHT DIRECTION. THAT'S SOME PROGRESS AT LEAST.
AND KEEP YOUR SPEED DOWN. I DON'T WANT A FATAL CRASH IF I HAVE TO SHOOT YOU.

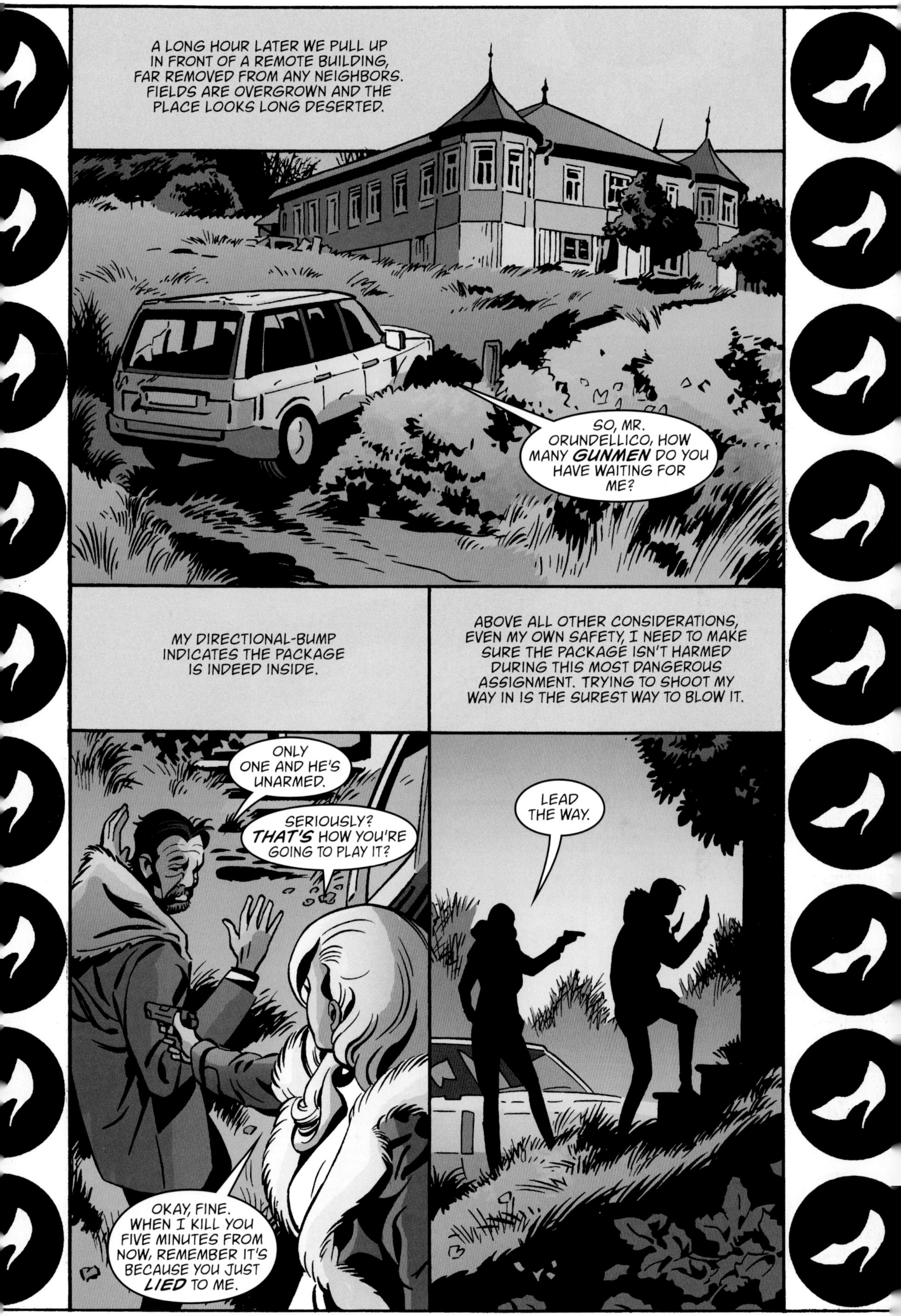
A LONG HOUR LATER WE PULL UP IN FRONT OF A REMOTE BUILDING, FAR REMOVED FROM ANY NEIGHBORS. FIELDS ARE OVERGROWN AND THE PLACE LOOKS LONG DESERTED.
SO, MR. ORUNDELLICO, HOW MANY GUNMEN DO YOU HAVE WAITING FOR ME?
MY DIRECTIONAL-BUMP INDICATES THE PACKAGE IS INDEED INSIDE.
ABOVE ALL OTHER CONSIDERATIONS, EVEN MY OWN SAFETY, I NEED TO MAKE SURE THE PACKAGE ISN'T HARMED DURING THIS MOST DANGEROUS ASSIGNMENT. TRYING TO SHOOT MY WAY IN IS THE SUREST WAY TO BLOW IT.
ONLY ONE AND HE'S UNARMED.
SERIOUSLY? THAT'S HOW YOU'RE GOING TO PLAY IT?
OKAY, FINE. WHEN I KILL YOU FIVE MINUTES FROM NOW, REMEMBER IT'S BECAUSE YOU JUST LIED TO ME.
LEAD THE WAY.

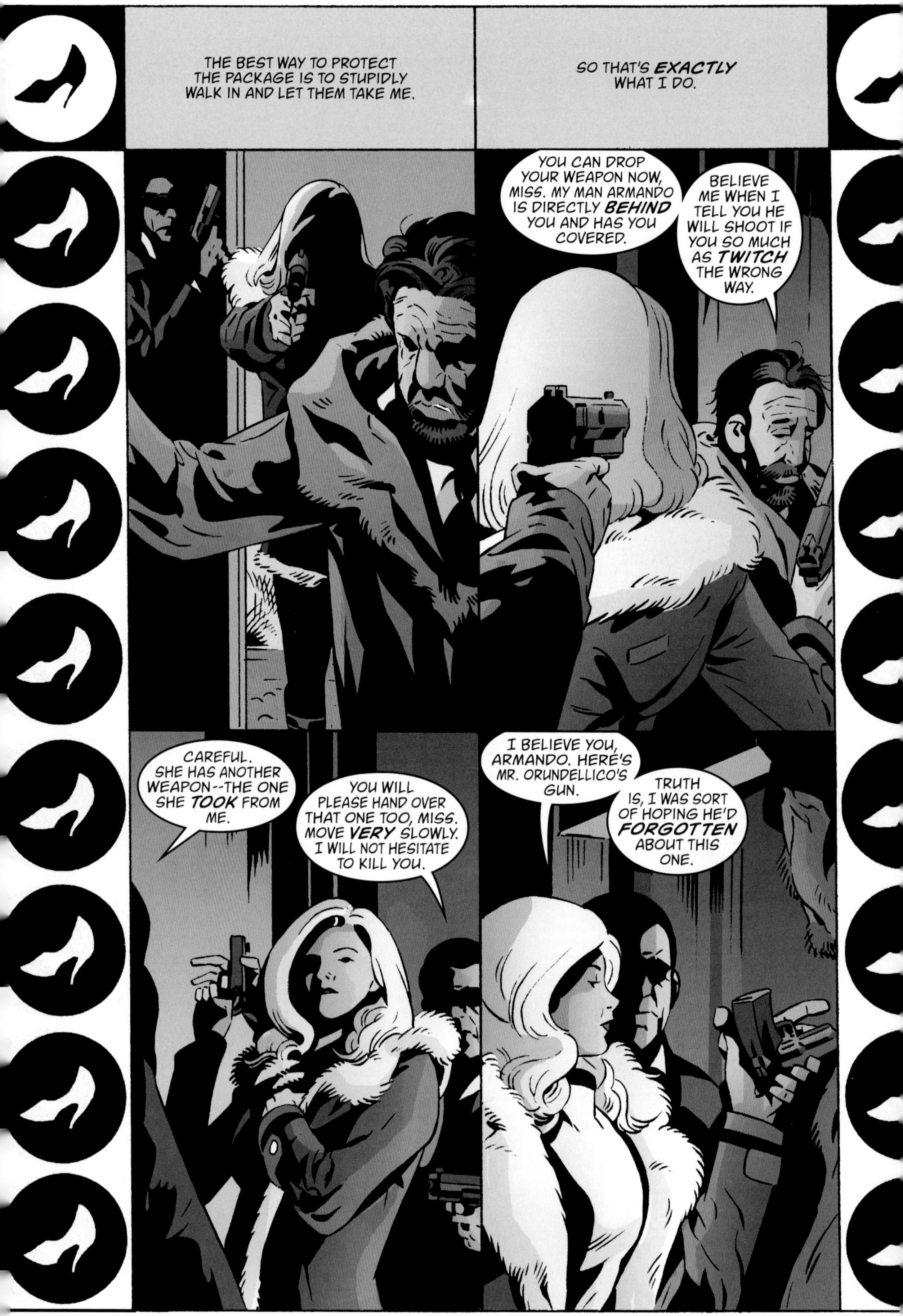
THE BEST WAY TO PROTECT THE PACKAGE IS TO STUPIDLY WALK IN AND LET THEM TAKE ME.
SO THAT'S EXACTLY WHAT I DO.
YOU CAN DROP YOUR WEAPON NOW, MISS. MY MAN ARMANDO IS DIRECTLY BEHIND YOU AND HAS YOU COVERED.
BELIEVE ME WHEN I TELL YOU HE WILL SHOOT IF YOU SO MUCH AS TWITCH THE WRONG WAY.
CAREFUL. SHE HAS ANOTHER WEAPON--THE ONE SHE TOOK FROM ME.
YOU WILL PLEASE HAND OVER THAT ONE TOO, MISS. MOVE VERY SLOWLY. I WILL NOT HESITATE TO KILL YOU.
I BELIEVE YOU, ARMANDO. HERE'S MR. ORUNDELLICO'S GUN.
TRUTH IS, I WAS SORT OF HOPING HE'D FORGOTTEN ABOUT THIS ONE.

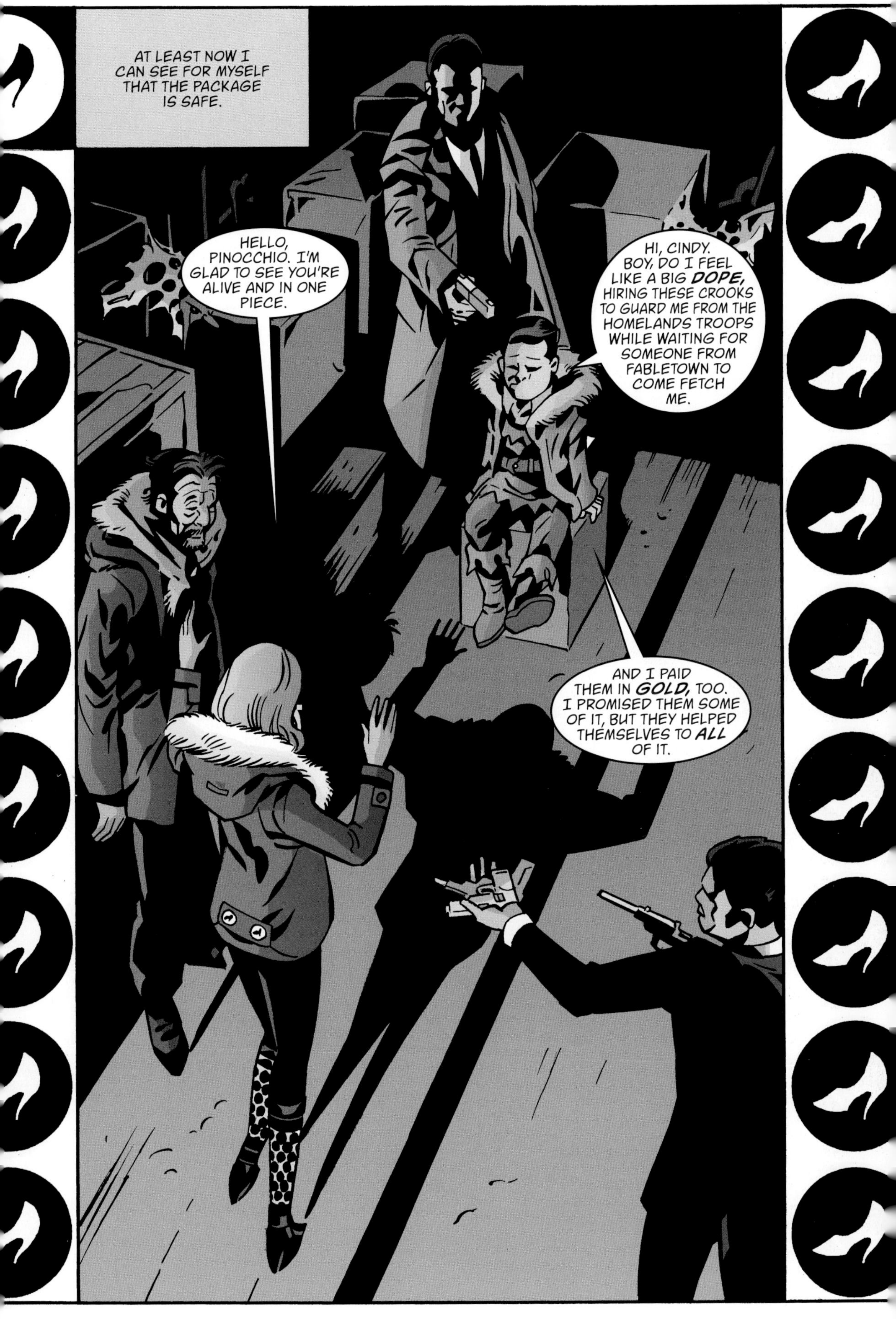
AT LEAST NOW I CAN SEE FOR MYSELF THAT THE PACKAGE IS SAFE.
HELLO, PINOCCHIO. I'M GLAD TO SEE YOU'RE ALIVE AND IN ONE PIECE.
HI, CINDY. BOY, DO I FEEL LIKE A BIG DOPE, HIRING THESE CROOKS TO GUARD ME FROM THE HOMELANDS TROOPS WHILE WAITING FOR SOMEONE FROM FABLETOWN TO COME FETCH ME.
AND I PAID THEM IN GOLD, TOO. I PROMISED THEM SOME OF IT, BUT THEY HELPED THEMSELVES TO ALL OF IT.

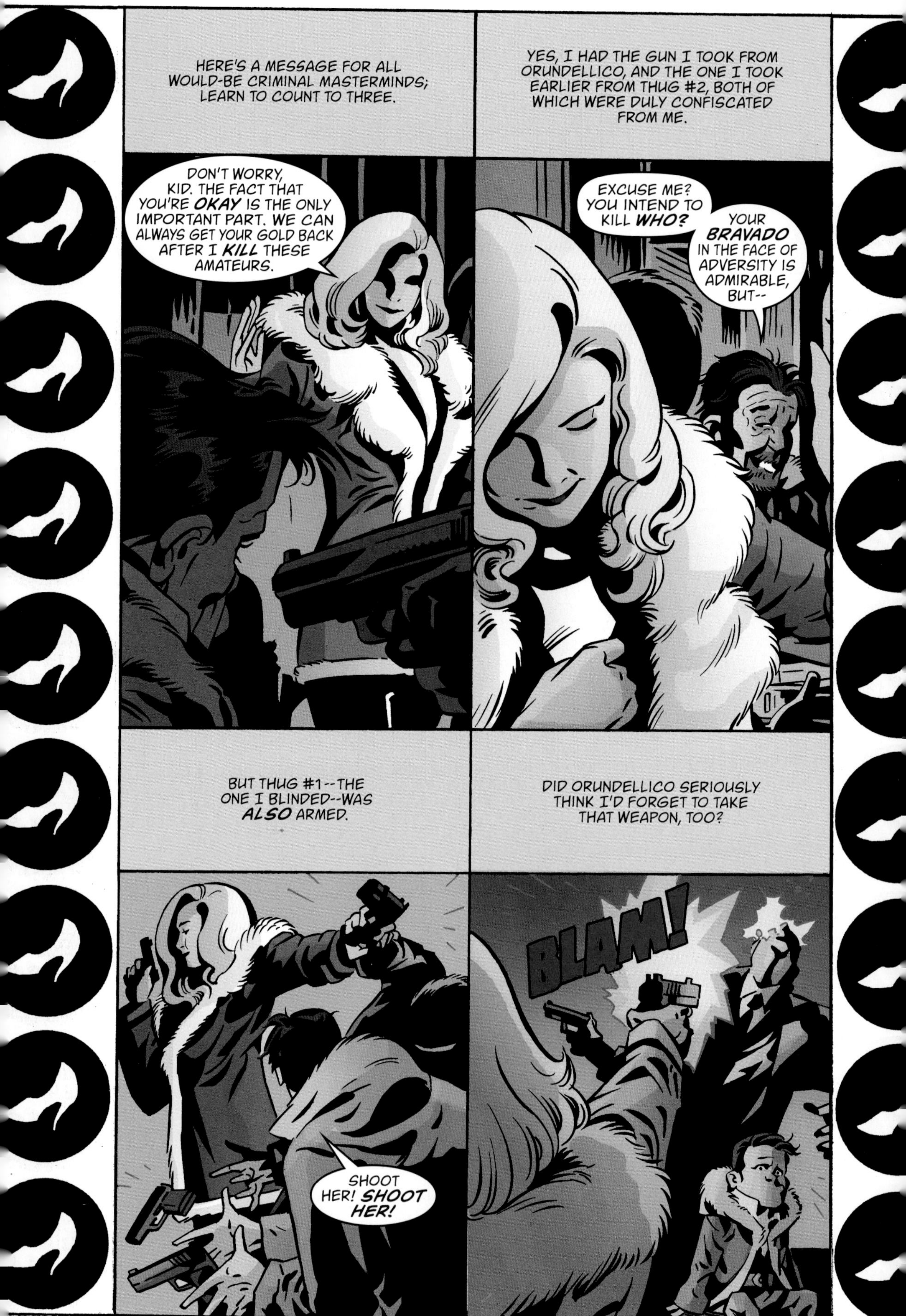
HERE'S A MESSAGE FOR ALL WOULD-BE CRIMINAL MASTERMINDS; LEARN TO COUNT TO THREE.
YES, I HAD THE GUN I TOOK FROM ORUNDELLICO, AND THE ONE I TOOK EARLIER FROM THUG #2, BOTH OF WHICH WERE DULY CONFISCATED FROM ME.
DON'T WORRY, KID. THE FACT THAT YOU'RE OKAY IS THE ONLY IMPORTANT PART. WE CAN ALWAYS GET YOUR GOLD BACK AFTER I KILL THESE AMATEURS.
EXCUSE ME? YOU INTEND TO KILL WHO?
YOUR BRAVADO IN THE FACE OF ADVERSITY IS ADMIRABLE, BUT--
BUT THUG #1--THE ONE I BLINDED--WAS ALSO ARMED.
DID ORUNDELLICO SERIOUSLY THINK I'D FORGET TO TAKE THAT WEAPON, TOO?
SHOOT HER! SHOOT HER!
BLAM!

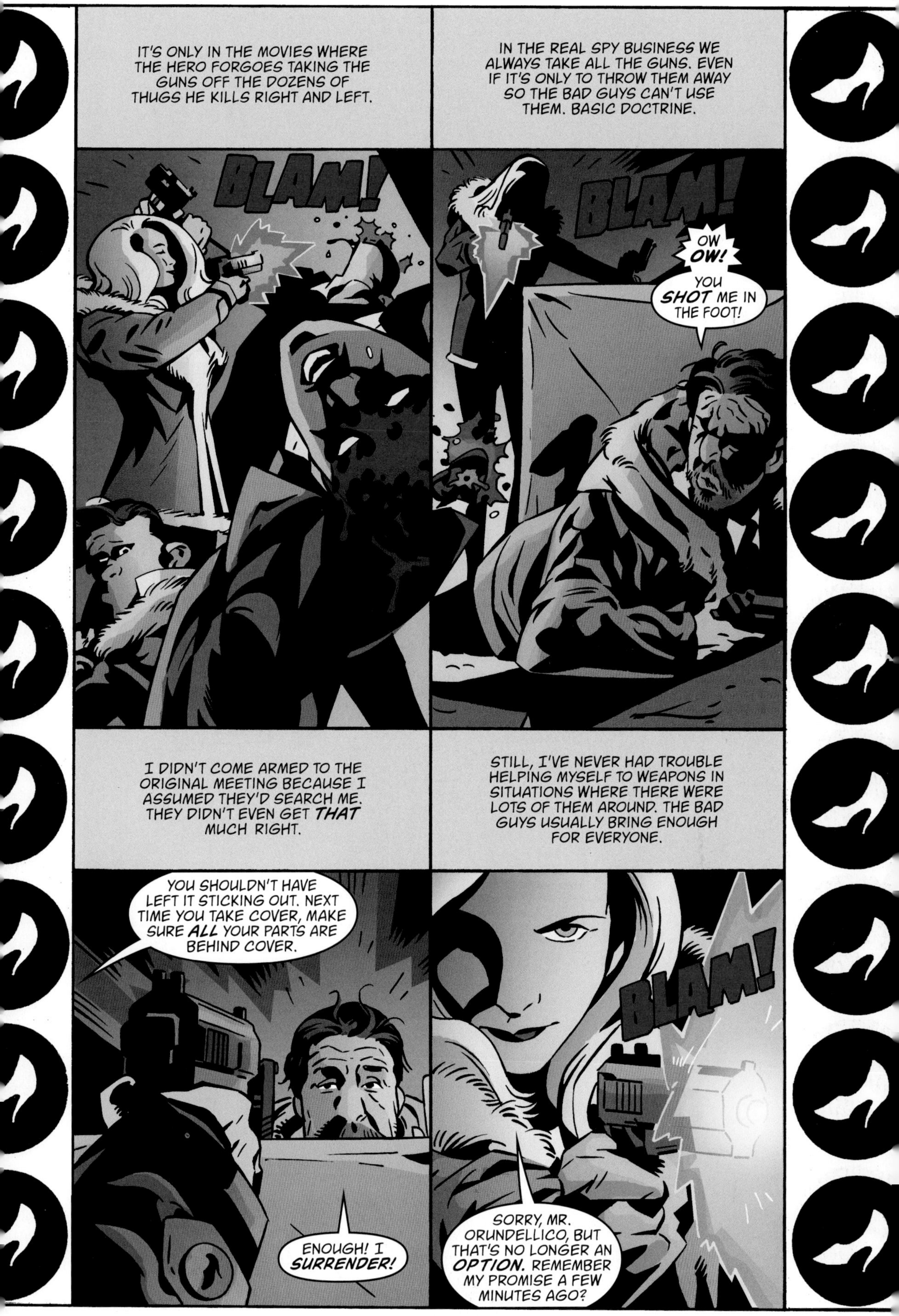
IT'S ONLY IN THE MOVIES WHERE THE HERO FORGOES TAKING THE GUNS OFF THE DOZENS OF THUGS HE KILLS RIGHT AND LEFT.
IN THE REAL SPY BUSINESS WE ALWAYS TAKE ALL THE GUNS. EVEN IF IT'S ONLY TO THROW THEM AWAY SO THE BAD GUYS CAN'T USE THEM. BASIC DOCTRINE.
BLAM!
BLAM!
OW *OW!*
YOU *SHOT* ME IN THE FOOT!
I DIDN'T COME ARMED TO THE ORIGINAL MEETING BECAUSE I ASSUMED THEY'D SEARCH ME. THEY DIDN'T EVEN GET *THAT* MUCH RIGHT.
STILL, I'VE NEVER HAD TROUBLE HELPING MYSELF TO WEAPONS IN SITUATIONS WHERE THERE WERE LOTS OF THEM AROUND. THE BAD GUYS USUALLY BRING ENOUGH FOR EVERYONE.
YOU SHOULDN'T HAVE LEFT IT STICKING OUT. NEXT TIME YOU TAKE COVER, MAKE SURE *ALL* YOUR PARTS ARE BEHIND COVER.
ENOUGH! I *SURRENDER!*
BLAM!
SORRY, MR. ORUNDELLICO, BUT THAT'S NO LONGER AN *OPTION.* REMEMBER MY PROMISE A FEW MINUTES AGO?

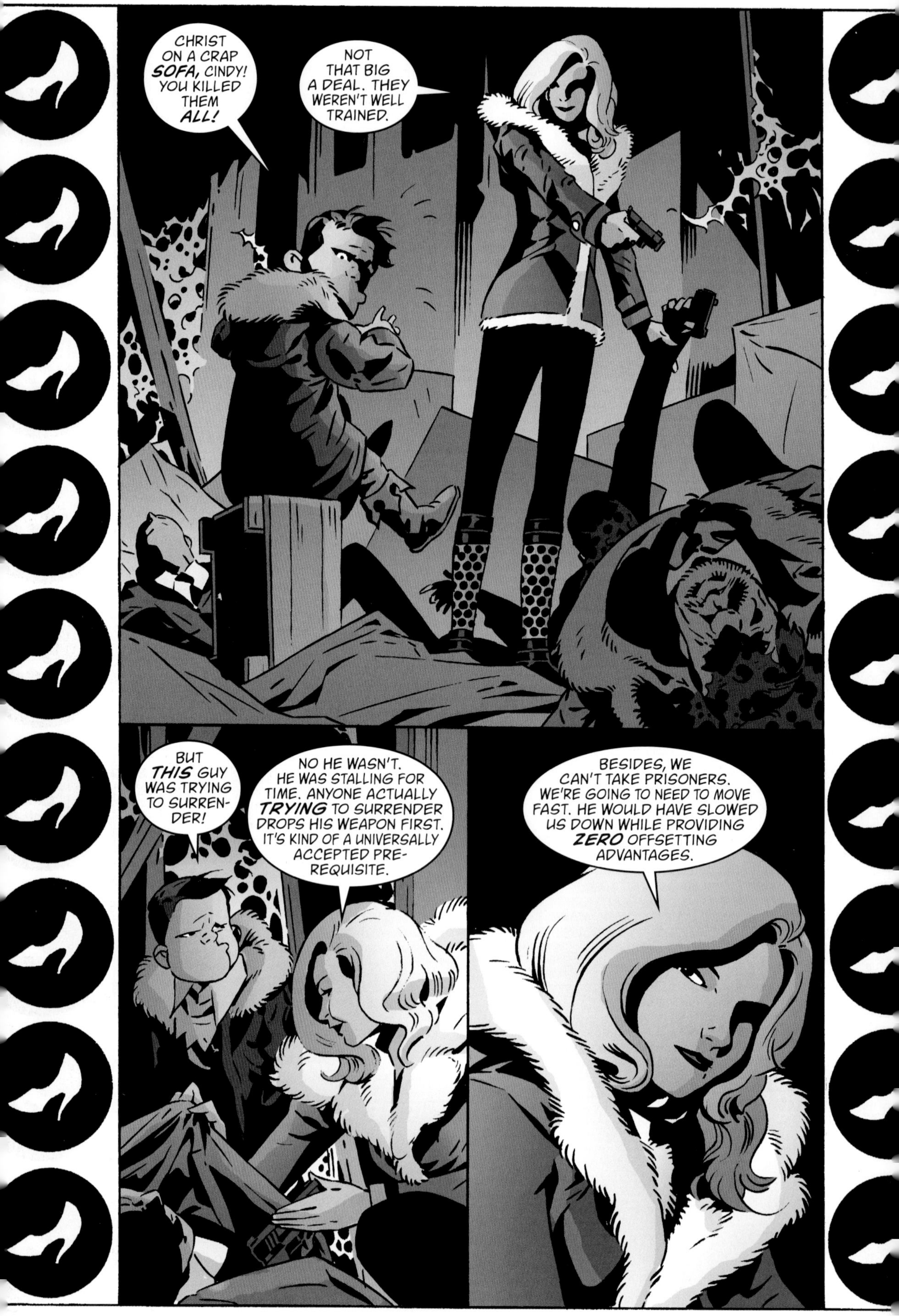
CHRIST ON A CRAP SOFA, CINDY! YOU KILLED THEM ALL!
NOT THAT BIG A DEAL. THEY WEREN'T WELL TRAINED.
BUT THIS GUY WAS TRYING TO SURREN-DER!
NO HE WASN'T. HE WAS STALLING FOR TIME. ANYONE ACTUALLY TRYING TO SURRENDER DROPS HIS WEAPON FIRST. IT'S KIND OF A UNIVERSALLY ACCEPTED PRE-REQUISITE.
BESIDES, WE CAN'T TAKE PRISONERS. WE'RE GOING TO NEED TO MOVE FAST. HE WOULD HAVE SLOWED US DOWN WHILE PROVIDING ZERO OFFSETTING ADVANTAGES.

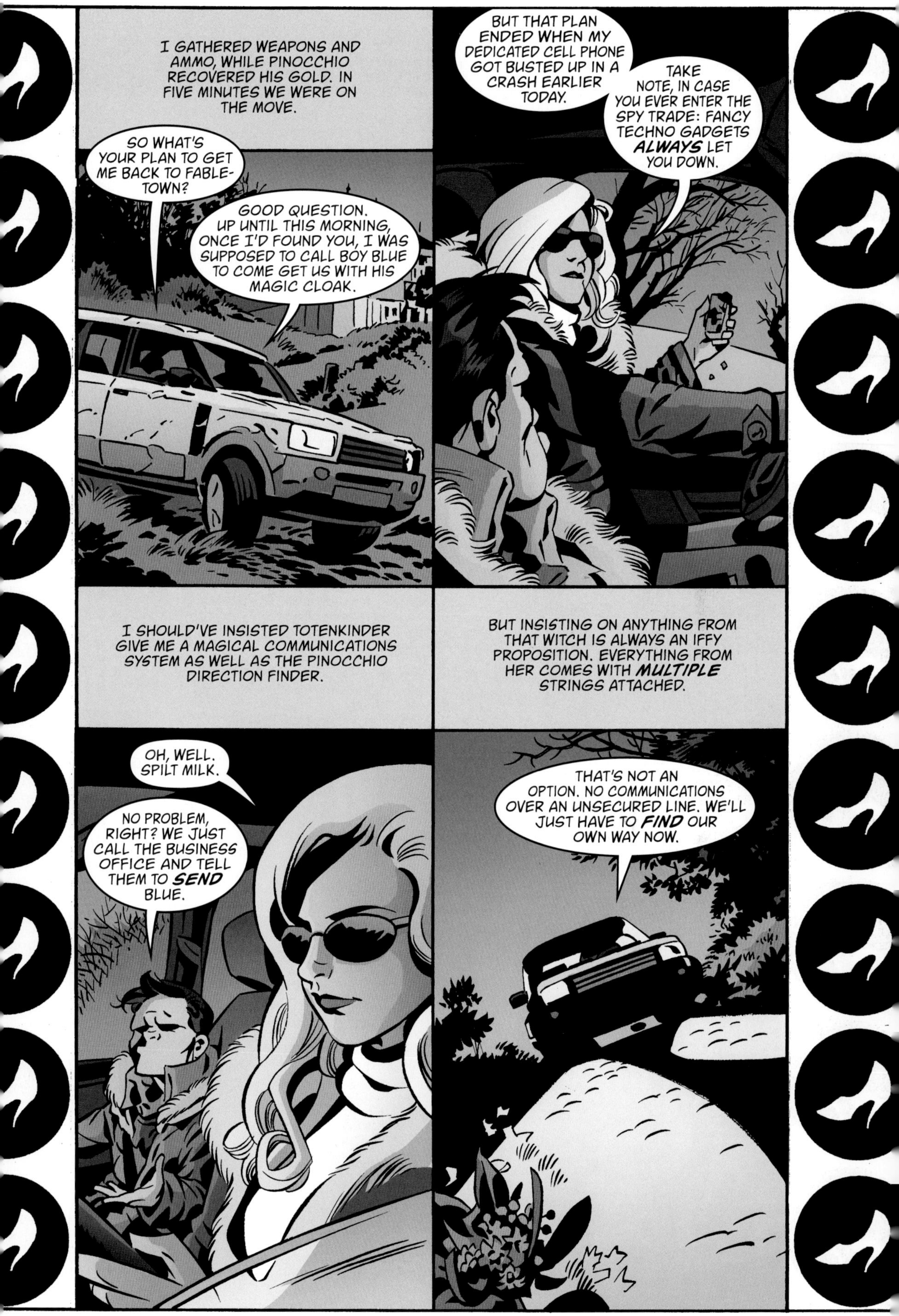
I GATHERED WEAPONS AND AMMO, WHILE PINOCCHIO RECOVERED HIS GOLD. IN FIVE MINUTES WE WERE ON THE MOVE.
SO WHAT'S YOUR PLAN TO GET ME BACK TO FABLE-TOWN?
GOOD QUESTION. UP UNTIL THIS MORNING, ONCE I'D FOUND YOU, I WAS SUPPOSED TO CALL BOY BLUE TO COME GET US WITH HIS MAGIC CLOAK.
BUT THAT PLAN ENDED WHEN MY DEDICATED CELL PHONE GOT BUSTED UP IN A CRASH EARLIER TODAY.
TAKE NOTE, IN CASE YOU EVER ENTER THE SPY TRADE: FANCY TECHNO GADGETS ***ALWAYS*** LET YOU DOWN.
I SHOULD'VE INSISTED TOTENKINDER GIVE ME A MAGICAL COMMUNICATIONS SYSTEM AS WELL AS THE PINOCCHIO DIRECTION FINDER.
BUT INSISTING ON ANYTHING FROM THAT WITCH IS ALWAYS AN IFFY PROPOSITION. EVERYTHING FROM HER COMES WITH ***MULTIPLE*** STRINGS ATTACHED.
OH, WELL. SPILT MILK.
NO PROBLEM, RIGHT? WE JUST CALL THE BUSINESS OFFICE AND TELL THEM TO ***SEND*** BLUE.
THAT'S NOT AN OPTION. NO COMMUNICATIONS OVER AN UNSECURED LINE. WE'LL JUST HAVE TO ***FIND*** OUR OWN WAY NOW.

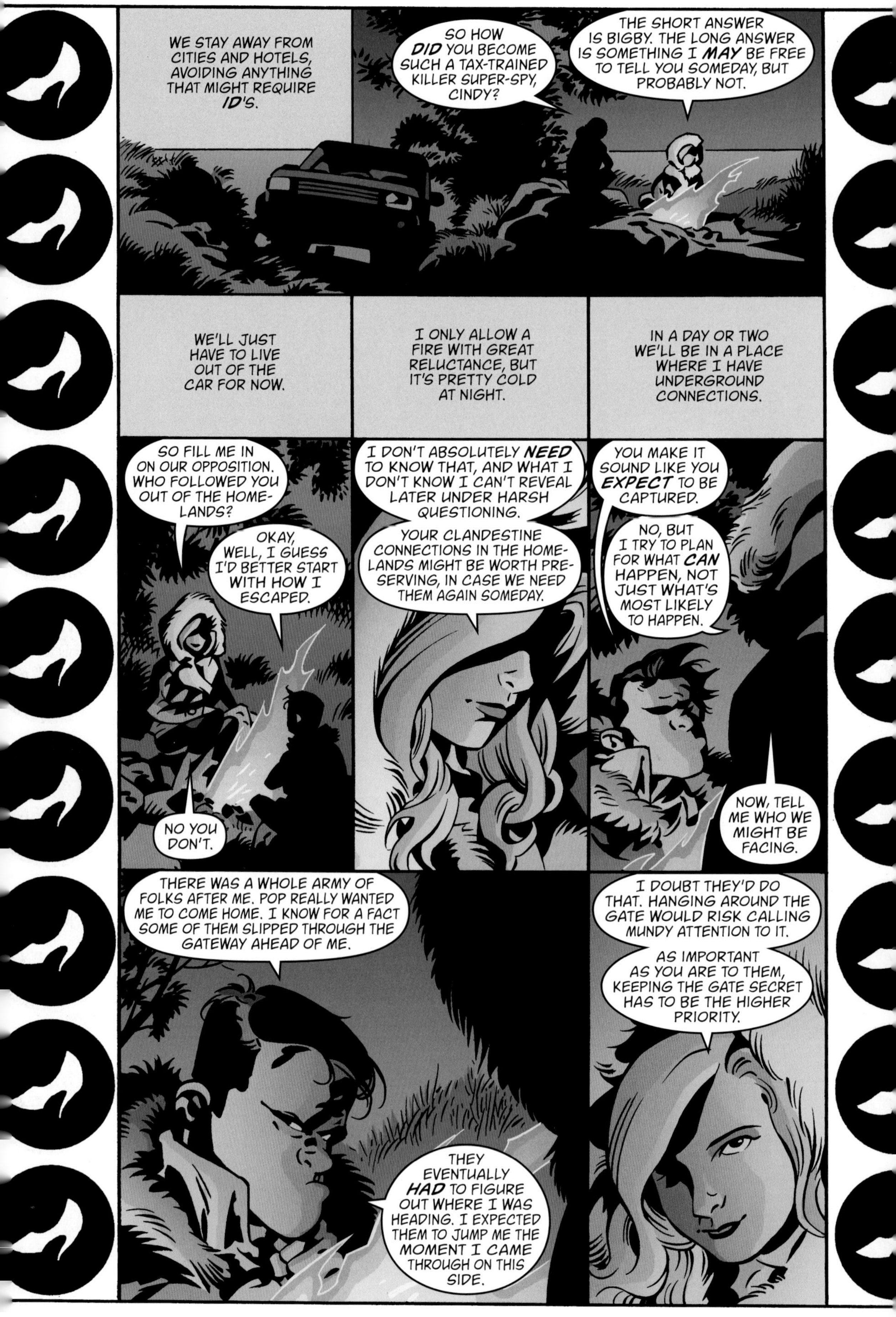

WE STAY AWAY FROM CITIES AND HOTELS, AVOIDING ANYTHING THAT MIGHT REQUIRE *ID*'S.
SO HOW *DID* YOU BECOME SUCH A TAX-TRAINED KILLER SUPER-SPY, CINDY?
THE SHORT ANSWER IS BIGBY. THE LONG ANSWER IS SOMETHING I *MAY* BE FREE TO TELL YOU SOMEDAY, BUT PROBABLY NOT.
WE'LL JUST HAVE TO LIVE OUT OF THE CAR FOR NOW.
I ONLY ALLOW A FIRE WITH GREAT RELUCTANCE, BUT IT'S PRETTY COLD AT NIGHT.
IN A DAY OR TWO WE'LL BE IN A PLACE WHERE I HAVE UNDERGROUND CONNECTIONS.
SO FILL ME IN ON OUR OPPOSITION. WHO FOLLOWED YOU OUT OF THE HOME-LANDS?
OKAY, WELL, I GUESS I'D BETTER START WITH HOW I ESCAPED.
NO YOU DON'T.
I DON'T ABSOLUTELY *NEED* TO KNOW THAT, AND WHAT I DON'T KNOW I CAN'T REVEAL LATER UNDER HARSH QUESTIONING.
YOUR CLANDESTINE CONNECTIONS IN THE HOME-LANDS MIGHT BE WORTH PRE-SERVING, IN CASE WE NEED THEM AGAIN SOMEDAY.
YOU MAKE IT SOUND LIKE YOU *EXPECT* TO BE CAPTURED.
NO, BUT I TRY TO PLAN FOR WHAT *CAN* HAPPEN, NOT JUST WHAT'S MOST LIKELY TO HAPPEN.
NOW, TELL ME WHO WE MIGHT BE FACING.
THERE WAS A WHOLE ARMY OF FOLKS AFTER ME. POP REALLY WANTED ME TO COME HOME. I KNOW FOR A FACT SOME OF THEM SLIPPED THROUGH THE GATEWAY AHEAD OF ME.
THEY EVENTUALLY *HAD* TO FIGURE OUT WHERE I WAS HEADING. I EXPECTED THEM TO JUMP ME THE MOMENT I CAME THROUGH ON THIS SIDE.
I DOUBT THEY'D DO THAT. HANGING AROUND THE GATE WOULD RISK CALLING MUNDY ATTENTION TO IT.
AS IMPORTANT AS YOU ARE TO THEM, KEEPING THE GATE SECRET HAS TO BE THE HIGHER PRIORITY.

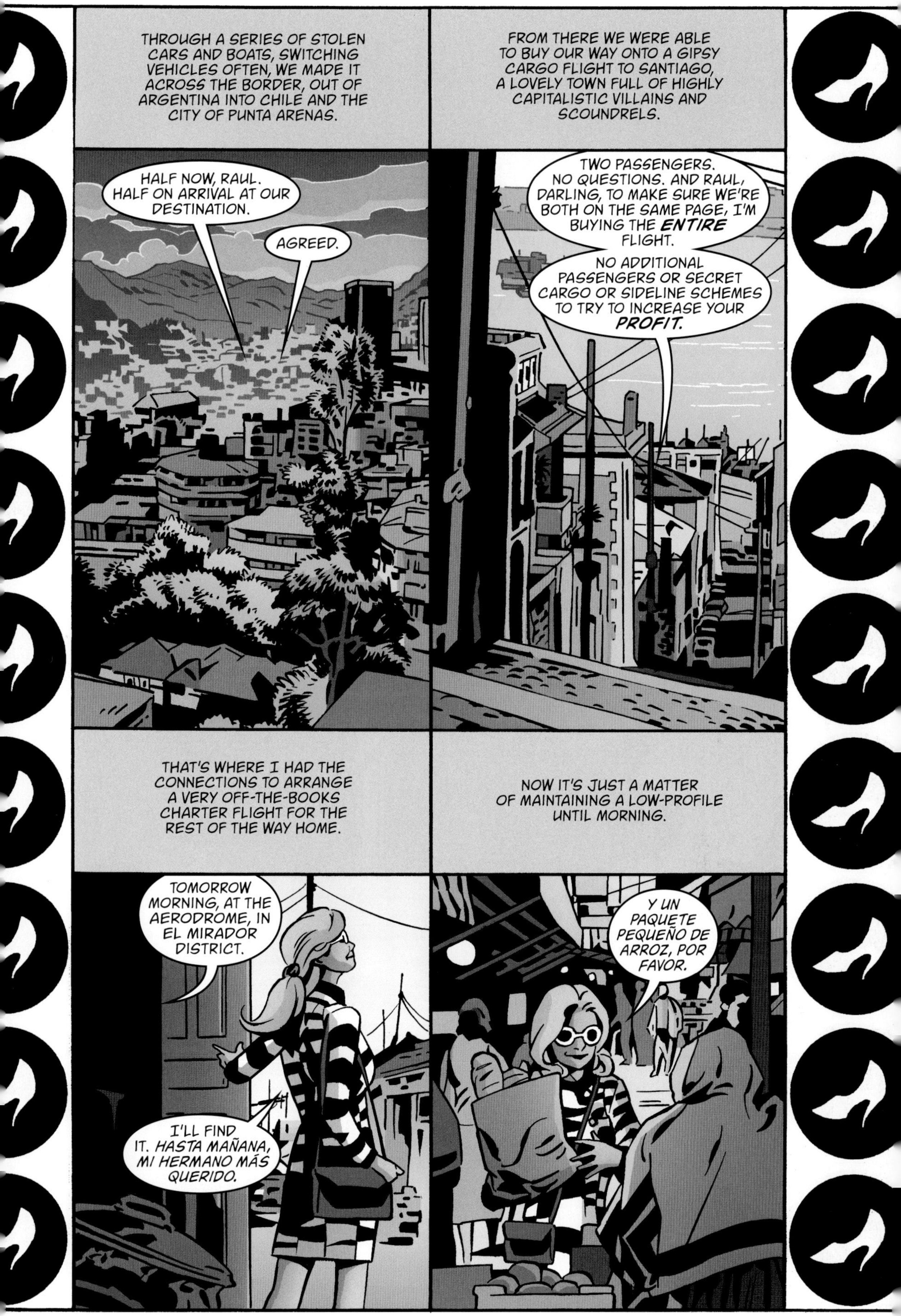
THROUGH A SERIES OF STOLEN CARS AND BOATS, SWITCHING VEHICLES OFTEN, WE MADE IT ACROSS THE BORDER, OUT OF ARGENTINA INTO CHILE AND THE CITY OF PUNTA ARENAS.
FROM THERE WE WERE ABLE TO BUY OUR WAY ONTO A GIPSY CARGO FLIGHT TO SANTIAGO, A LOVELY TOWN FULL OF HIGHLY CAPITALISTIC VILLAINS AND SCOUNDRELS.
HALF NOW, RAUL. HALF ON ARRIVAL AT OUR DESTINATION.
AGREED.
TWO PASSENGERS. NO QUESTIONS. AND RAUL, DARLING, TO MAKE SURE WE'RE BOTH ON THE SAME PAGE, I'M BUYING THE ***ENTIRE*** FLIGHT.
NO ADDITIONAL PASSENGERS OR SECRET CARGO OR SIDELINE SCHEMES TO TRY TO INCREASE YOUR ***PROFIT.***
THAT'S WHERE I HAD THE CONNECTIONS TO ARRANGE A VERY OFF-THE-BOOKS CHARTER FLIGHT FOR THE REST OF THE WAY HOME.
NOW IT'S JUST A MATTER OF MAINTAINING A LOW-PROFILE UNTIL MORNING.
TOMORROW MORNING, AT THE AERODROME, IN EL MIRADOR DISTRICT.
I'LL FIND IT. *HASTA MAÑANA, MI HERMANO MÁS QUERIDO.*
Y UN PAQUETE PEQUEÑO DE ARROZ, POR FAVOR.

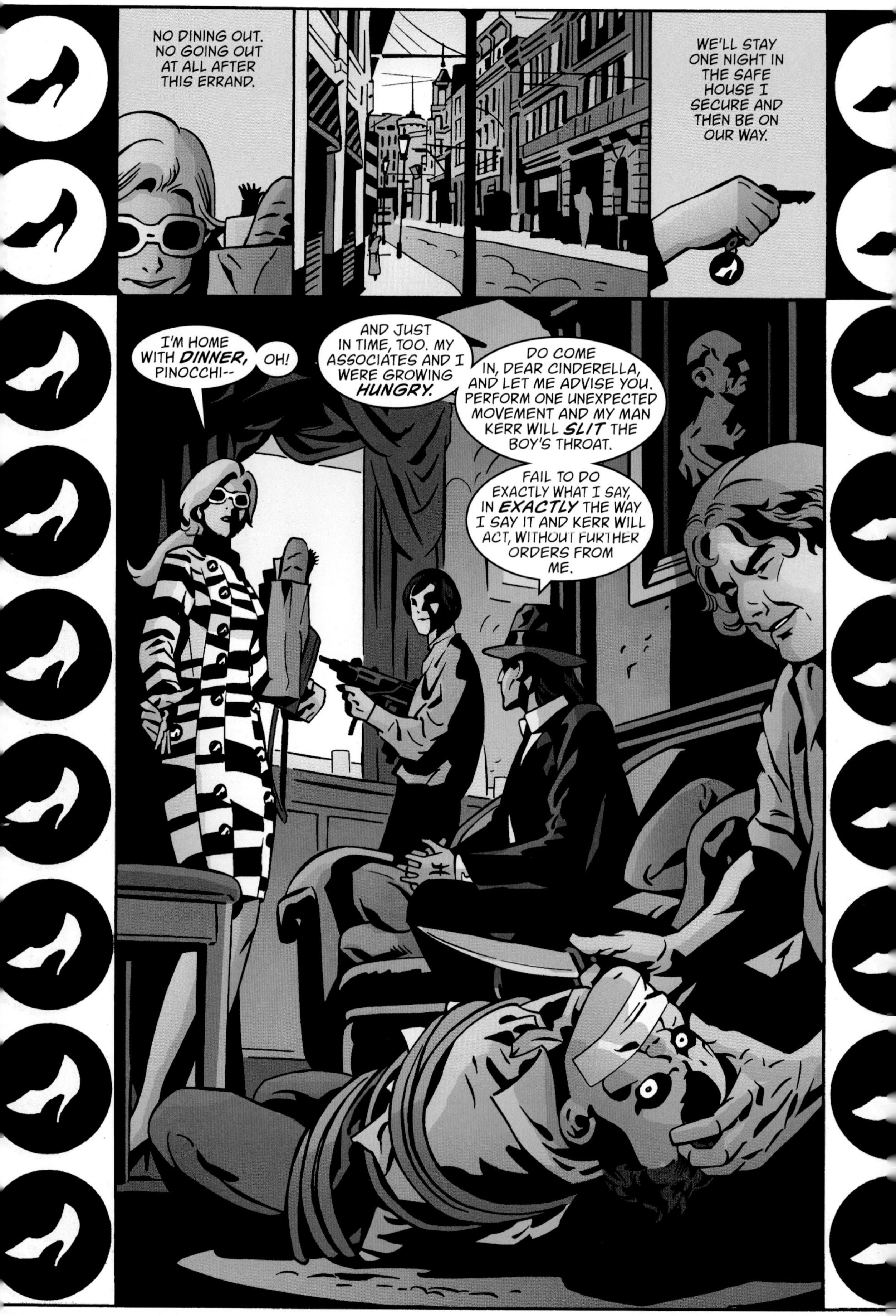
NO DINING OUT. NO GOING OUT AT ALL AFTER THIS ERRAND.
WE'LL STAY ONE NIGHT IN THE SAFE HOUSE I SECURE AND THEN BE ON OUR WAY.
I'M HOME WITH DINNER, PINOCCHI--
OH!
AND JUST IN TIME, TOO. MY ASSOCIATES AND I WERE GROWING HUNGRY.
DO COME IN, DEAR CINDERELLA, AND LET ME ADVISE YOU. PERFORM ONE UNEXPECTED MOVEMENT AND MY MAN KERR WILL SLIT THE BOY'S THROAT.
FAIL TO DO EXACTLY WHAT I SAY, IN EXACTLY THE WAY I SAY IT AND KERR WILL ACT, WITHOUT FURTHER ORDERS FROM ME.

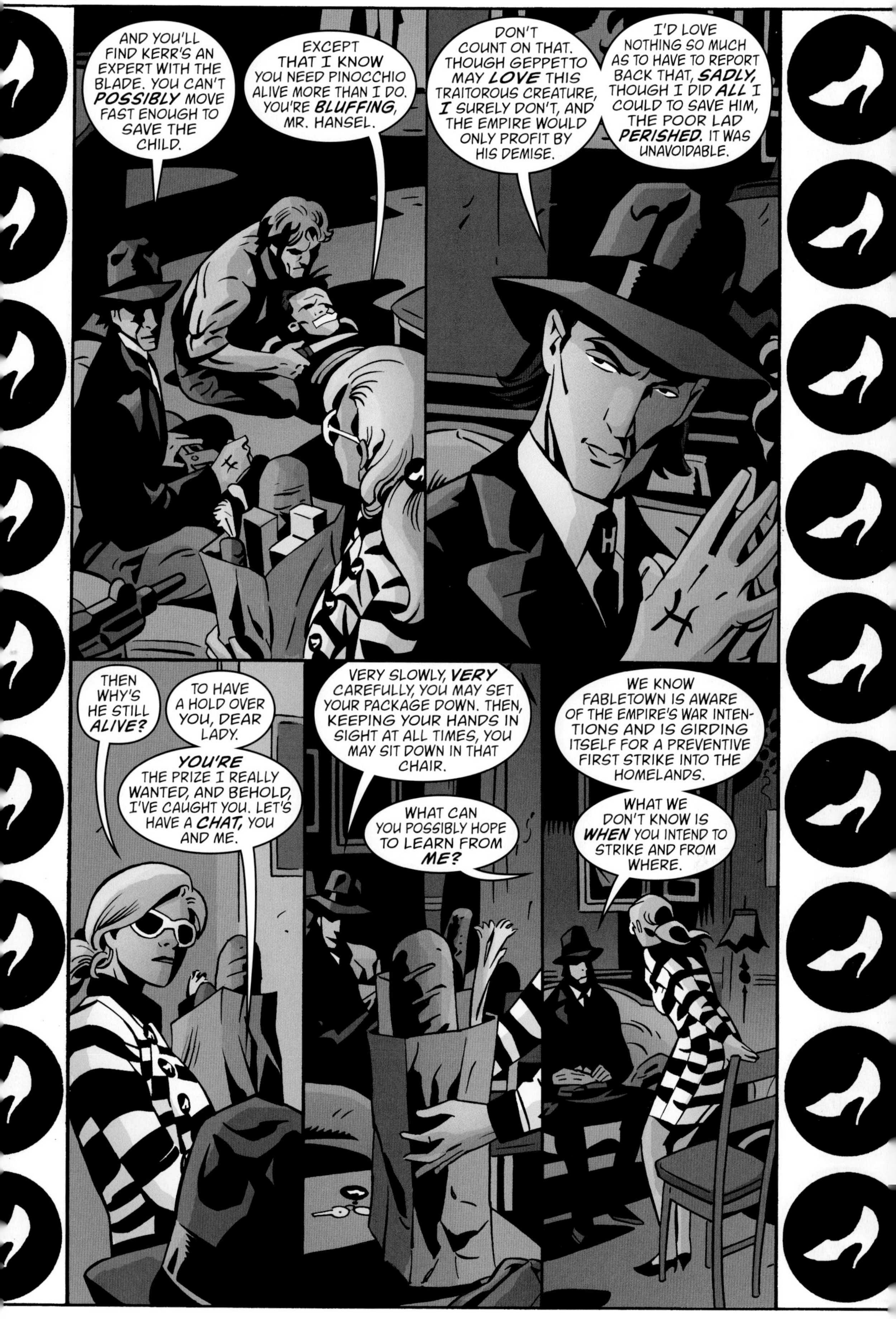
AND YOU'LL FIND KERR'S AN EXPERT WITH THE BLADE. YOU CAN'T POSSIBLY MOVE FAST ENOUGH TO SAVE THE CHILD.
EXCEPT THAT I KNOW YOU NEED PINOCCHIO ALIVE MORE THAN I DO. YOU'RE BLUFFING, MR. HANSEL.
DON'T COUNT ON THAT. THOUGH GEPPETTO MAY LOVE THIS TRAITOROUS CREATURE, I SURELY DON'T, AND THE EMPIRE WOULD ONLY PROFIT BY HIS DEMISE.
I'D LOVE NOTHING SO MUCH AS TO HAVE TO REPORT BACK THAT, SADLY, THOUGH I DID ALL I COULD TO SAVE HIM, THE POOR LAD PERISHED. IT WAS UNAVOIDABLE.
THEN WHY'S HE STILL ALIVE?
TO HAVE A HOLD OVER YOU, DEAR LADY.
YOU'RE THE PRIZE I REALLY WANTED, AND BEHOLD, I'VE CAUGHT YOU. LET'S HAVE A CHAT, YOU AND ME.
VERY SLOWLY, VERY CAREFULLY, YOU MAY SET YOUR PACKAGE DOWN. THEN, KEEPING YOUR HANDS IN SIGHT AT ALL TIMES, YOU MAY SIT DOWN IN THAT CHAIR.
WHAT CAN YOU POSSIBLY HOPE TO LEARN FROM ME?
WE KNOW FABLETOWN IS AWARE OF THE EMPIRE'S WAR INTENTIONS AND IS GIRDING ITSELF FOR A PREVENTIVE FIRST STRIKE INTO THE HOMELANDS.
WHAT WE DON'T KNOW IS WHEN YOU INTEND TO STRIKE AND FROM WHERE.

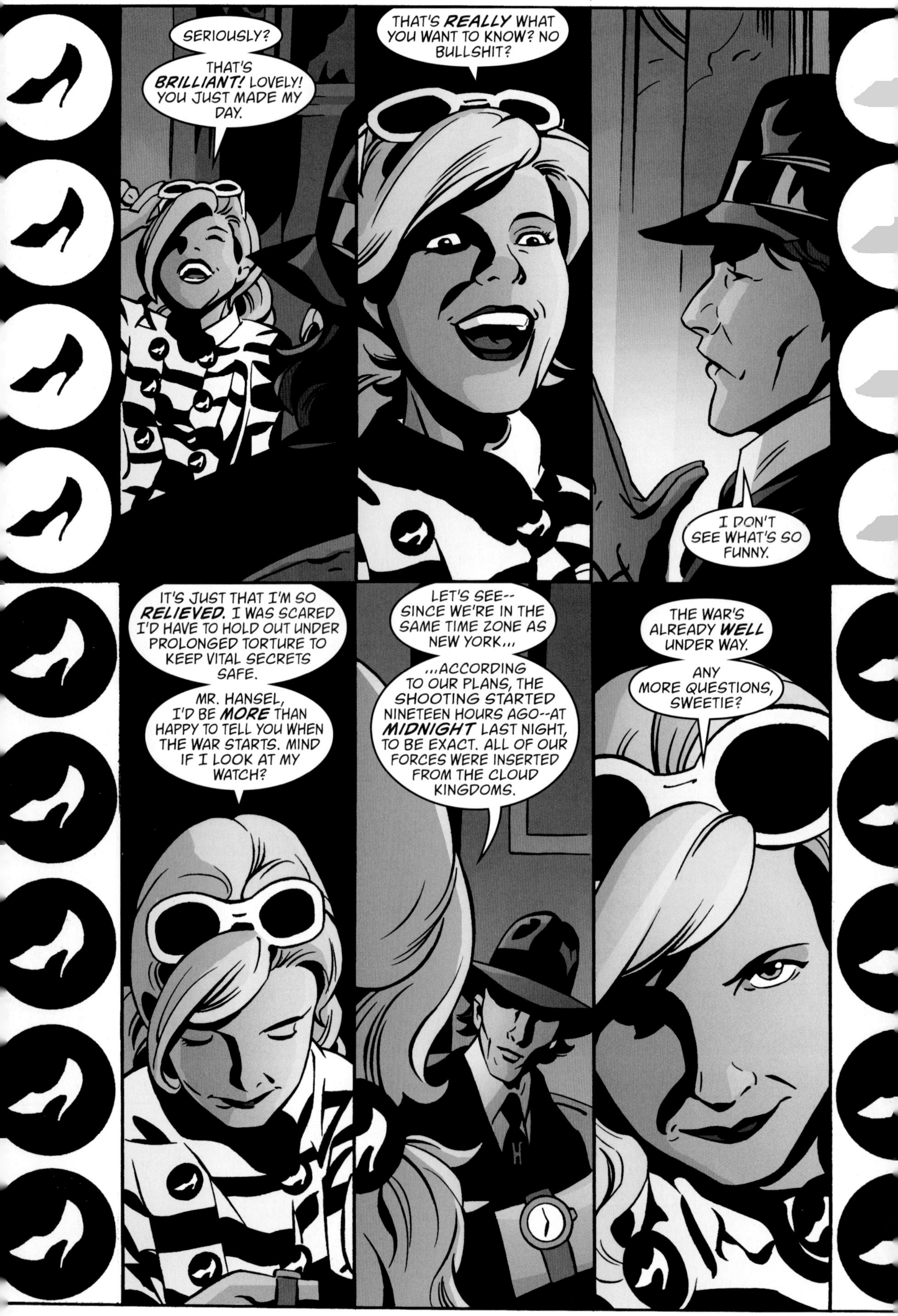
SERIOUSLY?
THAT'S **BRILLIANT!** LOVELY! YOU JUST MADE MY DAY.
THAT'S **REALLY** WHAT YOU WANT TO KNOW? NO BULLSHIT?
I DON'T SEE WHAT'S SO FUNNY.
IT'S JUST THAT I'M SO **RELIEVED.** I WAS SCARED I'D HAVE TO HOLD OUT UNDER PROLONGED TORTURE TO KEEP VITAL SECRETS SAFE.
MR. HANSEL, I'D BE **MORE** THAN HAPPY TO TELL YOU WHEN THE WAR STARTS. MIND IF I LOOK AT MY WATCH?
LET'S SEE-- SINCE WE'RE IN THE SAME TIME ZONE AS NEW YORK...
...ACCORDING TO OUR PLANS, THE SHOOTING STARTED NINETEEN HOURS AGO--AT **MIDNIGHT** LAST NIGHT, TO BE EXACT. ALL OF OUR FORCES WERE INSERTED FROM THE CLOUD KINGDOMS.
THE WAR'S ALREADY **WELL** UNDER WAY.
ANY MORE QUESTIONS, SWEETIE?

NEXT: MORE GRATUITOUS MAYHEM

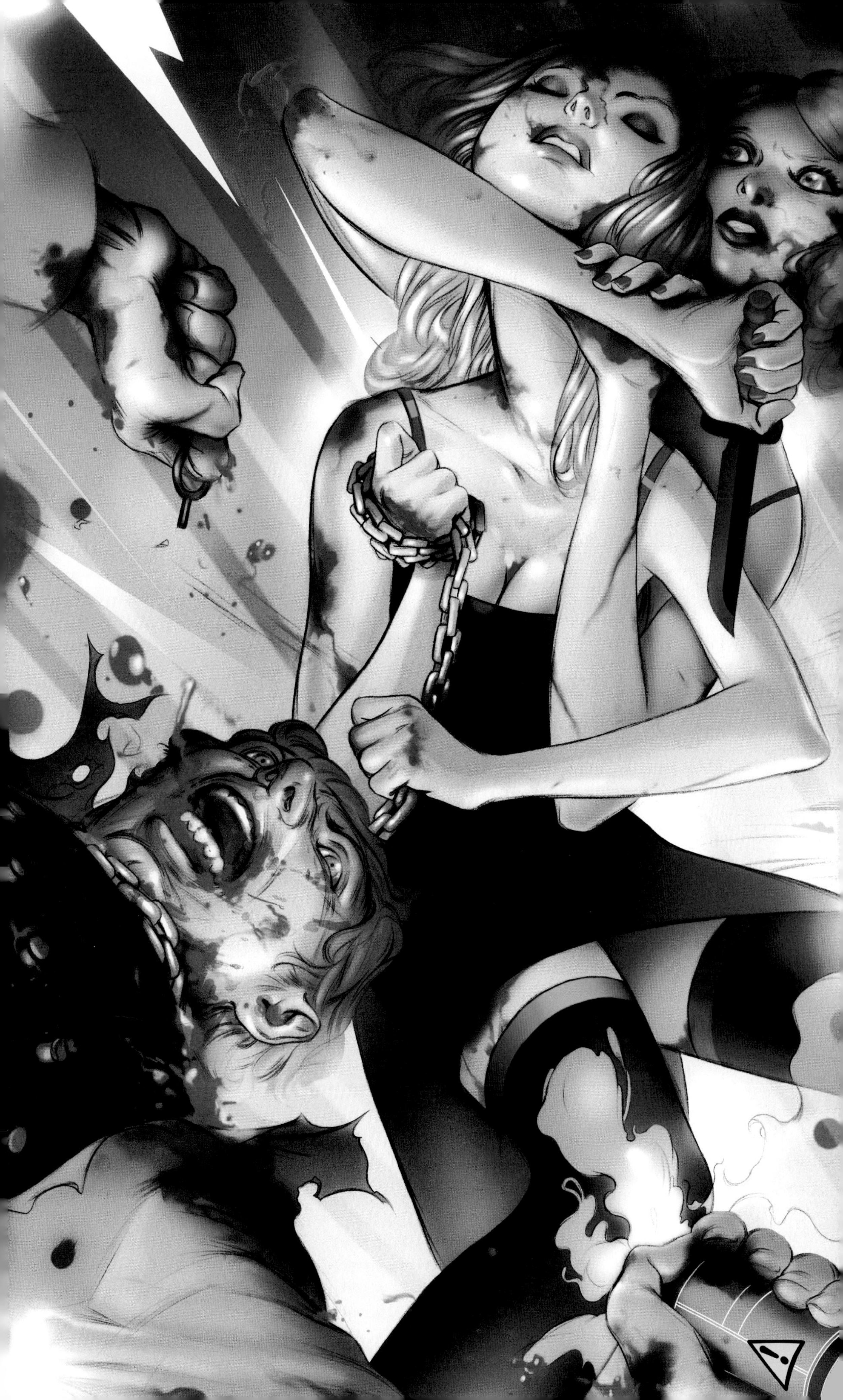

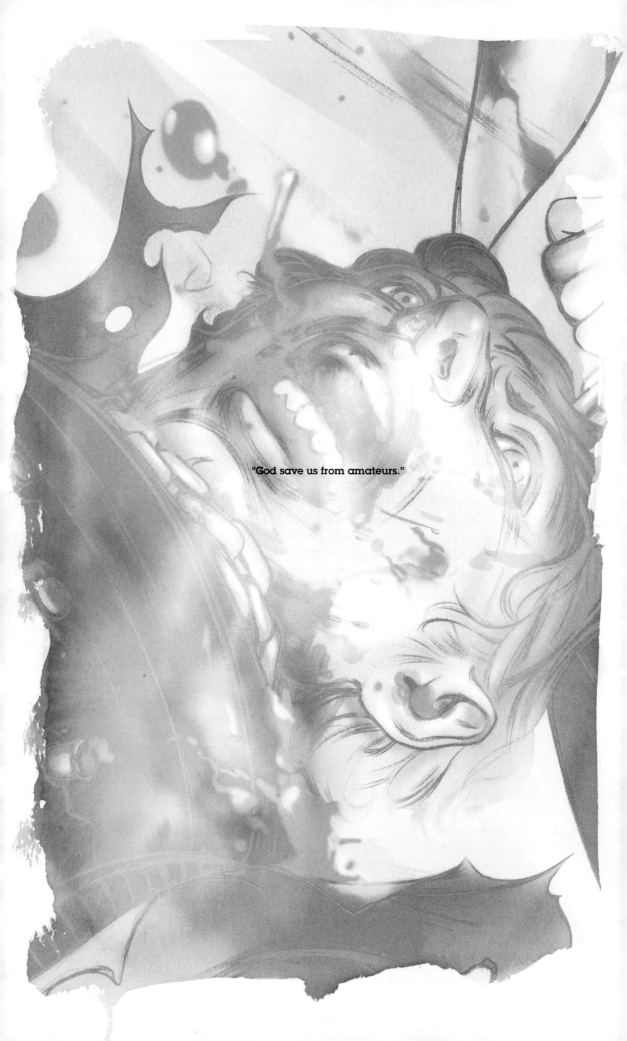

"God save us from amateurs."

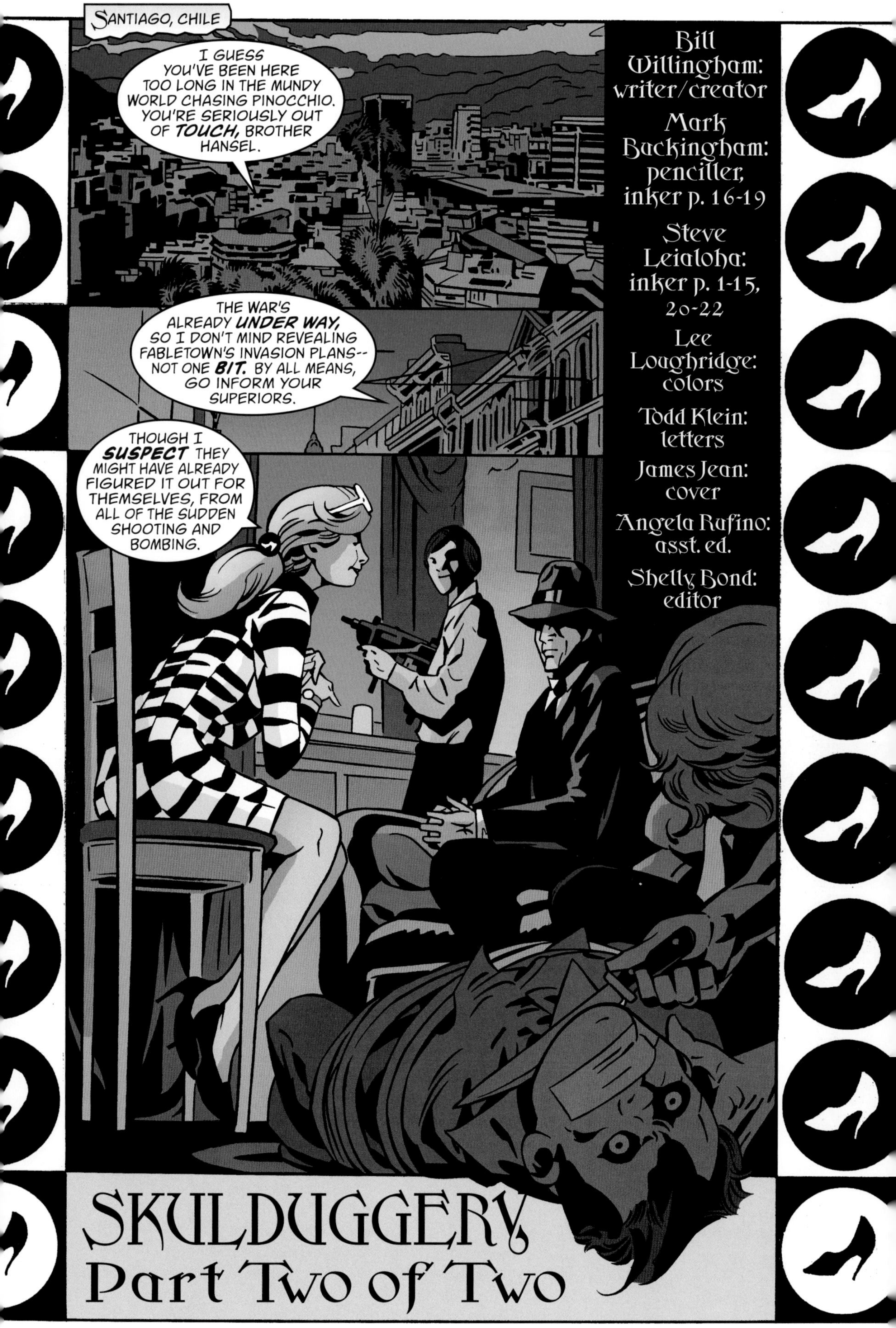
SANTIAGO, CHILE
I GUESS YOU'VE BEEN HERE TOO LONG IN THE MUNDY WORLD CHASING PINOCCHIO. YOU'RE SERIOUSLY OUT OF TOUCH, BROTHER HANSEL.
Bill Willingham: writer/creator
Mark Buckingham: penciller, inker p. 16-19
Steve Leialoha: inker p. 1-15, 20-22
Lee Loughridge: colors
Todd Klein: letters
James Jean: cover
Angela Rufino: asst. ed.
Shelly Bond: editor
THE WAR'S ALREADY UNDER WAY, SO I DON'T MIND REVEALING FABLETOWN'S INVASION PLANS--NOT ONE BIT. BY ALL MEANS, GO INFORM YOUR SUPERIORS.
THOUGH I SUSPECT THEY MIGHT HAVE ALREADY FIGURED IT OUT FOR THEMSELVES, FROM ALL OF THE SUDDEN SHOOTING AND BOMBING.
SKULDUGGERY
Part Two of Two

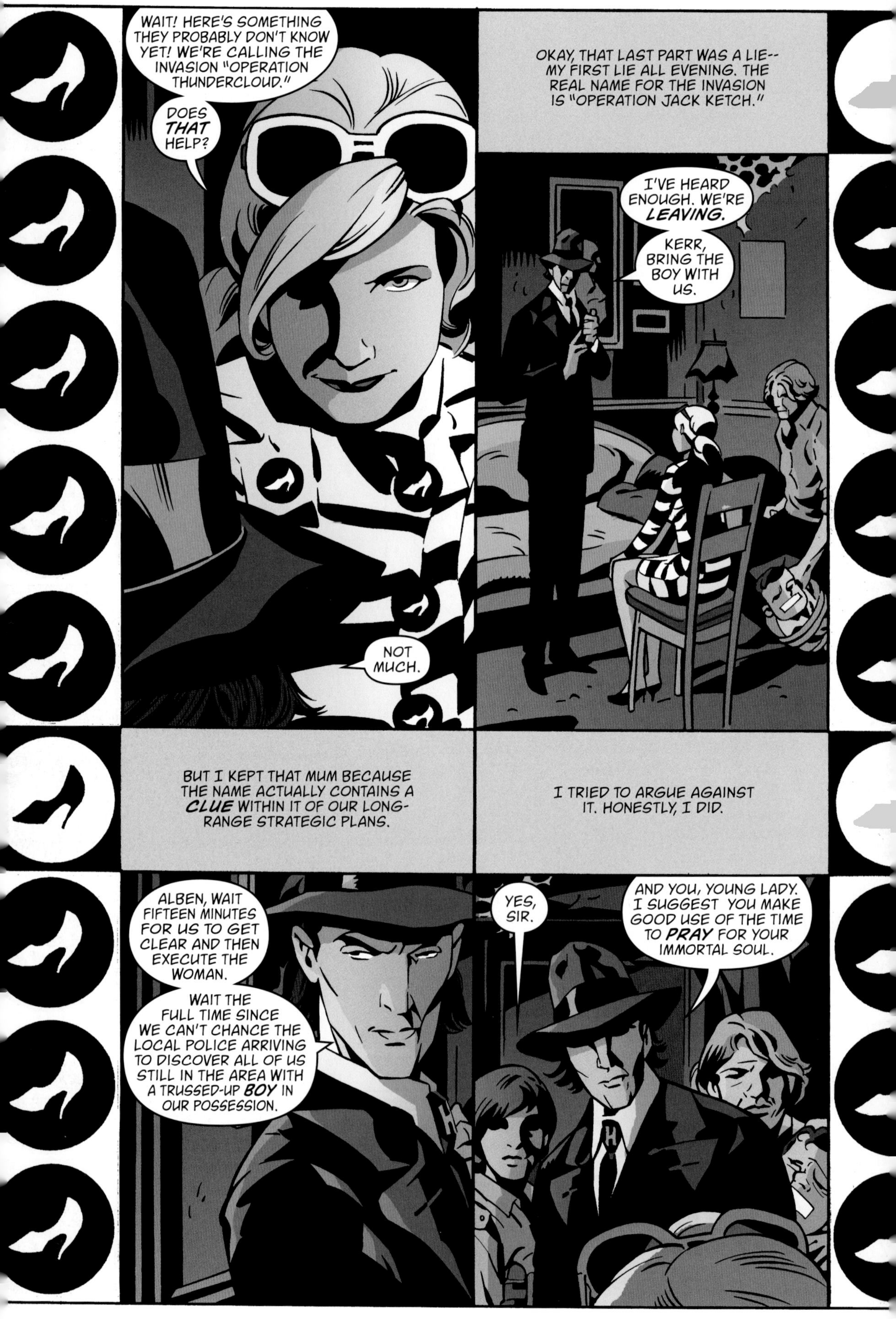
WAIT! HERE'S SOMETHING THEY PROBABLY DON'T KNOW YET! WE'RE CALLING THE INVASION "OPERATION THUNDERCLOUD."
DOES THAT HELP?
NOT MUCH.
OKAY, THAT LAST PART WAS A LIE-- MY FIRST LIE ALL EVENING. THE REAL NAME FOR THE INVASION IS "OPERATION JACK KETCH."
I'VE HEARD ENOUGH. WE'RE LEAVING.
KERR, BRING THE BOY WITH US.
BUT I KEPT THAT MUM BECAUSE THE NAME ACTUALLY CONTAINS A CLUE WITHIN IT OF OUR LONG-RANGE STRATEGIC PLANS.
I TRIED TO ARGUE AGAINST IT. HONESTLY, I DID.
ALBEN, WAIT FIFTEEN MINUTES FOR US TO GET CLEAR AND THEN EXECUTE THE WOMAN.
WAIT THE FULL TIME SINCE WE CAN'T CHANCE THE LOCAL POLICE ARRIVING TO DISCOVER ALL OF US STILL IN THE AREA WITH A TRUSSED-UP BOY IN OUR POSSESSION.
YES, SIR.
AND YOU, YOUNG LADY. I SUGGEST YOU MAKE GOOD USE OF THE TIME TO PRAY FOR YOUR IMMORTAL SOUL.

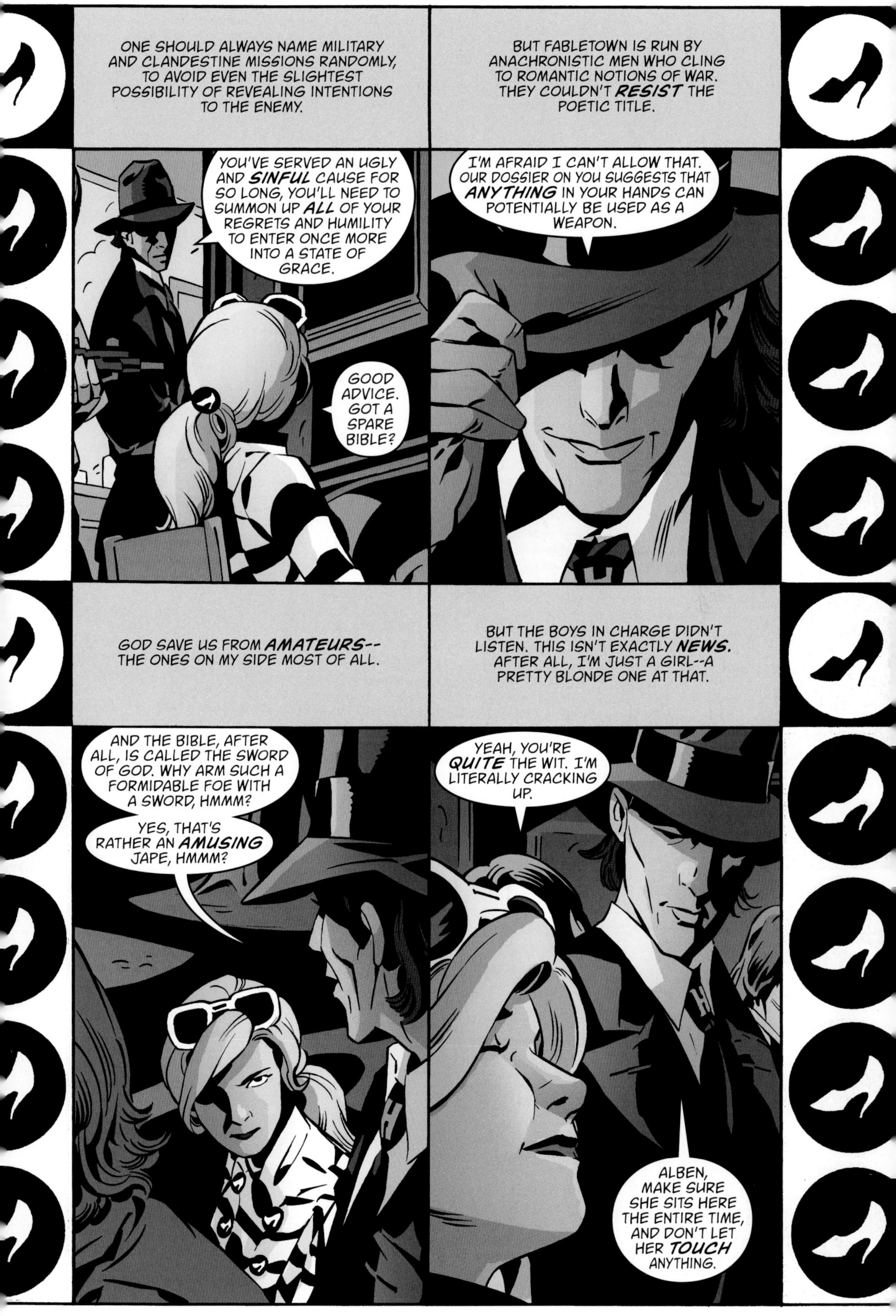
ONE SHOULD ALWAYS NAME MILITARY AND CLANDESTINE MISSIONS RANDOMLY, TO AVOID EVEN THE SLIGHTEST POSSIBILITY OF REVEALING INTENTIONS TO THE ENEMY.
BUT FABLETOWN IS RUN BY ANACHRONISTIC MEN WHO CLING TO ROMANTIC NOTIONS OF WAR. THEY COULDN'T *RESIST* THE POETIC TITLE.
YOU'VE SERVED AN UGLY AND *SINFUL* CAUSE FOR SO LONG, YOU'LL NEED TO SUMMON UP *ALL* OF YOUR REGRETS AND HUMILITY TO ENTER ONCE MORE INTO A STATE OF GRACE.
GOOD ADVICE. GOT A SPARE BIBLE?
I'M AFRAID I CAN'T ALLOW THAT. OUR DOSSIER ON YOU SUGGESTS THAT *ANYTHING* IN YOUR HANDS CAN POTENTIALLY BE USED AS A WEAPON.
GOD SAVE US FROM *AMATEURS*-- THE ONES ON MY SIDE MOST OF ALL.
BUT THE BOYS IN CHARGE DIDN'T LISTEN. THIS ISN'T EXACTLY *NEWS.* AFTER ALL, I'M JUST A GIRL--A PRETTY BLONDE ONE AT THAT.
AND THE BIBLE, AFTER ALL, IS CALLED THE SWORD OF GOD. WHY ARM SUCH A FORMIDABLE FOE WITH A SWORD, HMMM?
YES, THAT'S RATHER AN *AMUSING* JAPE, HMMM?
YEAH, YOU'RE *QUITE* THE WIT. I'M LITERALLY CRACKING UP.
ALBEN, MAKE SURE SHE SITS HERE THE ENTIRE TIME, AND DON'T LET HER *TOUCH* ANYTHING.

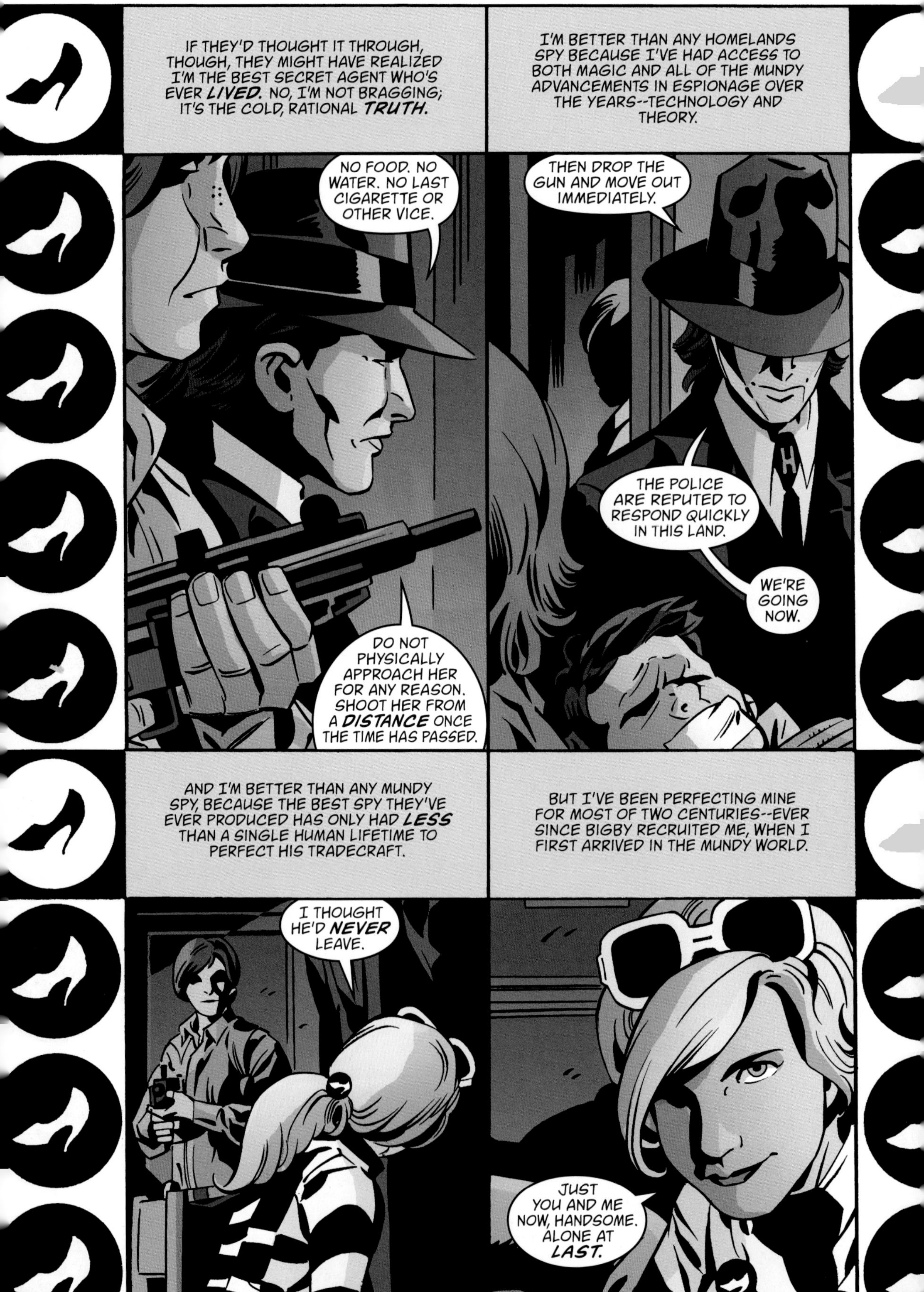
IF THEY'D THOUGHT IT THROUGH, THOUGH, THEY MIGHT HAVE REALIZED I'M THE BEST SECRET AGENT WHO'S EVER LIVED. NO, I'M NOT BRAGGING; IT'S THE COLD, RATIONAL TRUTH.
NO FOOD. NO WATER. NO LAST CIGARETTE OR OTHER VICE.
DO NOT PHYSICALLY APPROACH HER FOR ANY REASON. SHOOT HER FROM A DISTANCE ONCE THE TIME HAS PASSED.
I'M BETTER THAN ANY HOMELANDS SPY BECAUSE I'VE HAD ACCESS TO BOTH MAGIC AND ALL OF THE MUNDY ADVANCEMENTS IN ESPIONAGE OVER THE YEARS--TECHNOLOGY AND THEORY.
THEN DROP THE GUN AND MOVE OUT IMMEDIATELY.
THE POLICE ARE REPUTED TO RESPOND QUICKLY IN THIS LAND.
WE'RE GOING NOW.
AND I'M BETTER THAN ANY MUNDY SPY, BECAUSE THE BEST SPY THEY'VE EVER PRODUCED HAS ONLY HAD LESS THAN A SINGLE HUMAN LIFETIME TO PERFECT HIS TRADECRAFT.
I THOUGHT HE'D NEVER LEAVE.
BUT I'VE BEEN PERFECTING MINE FOR MOST OF TWO CENTURIES--EVER SINCE BIGBY RECRUITED ME, WHEN I FIRST ARRIVED IN THE MUNDY WORLD.
JUST YOU AND ME NOW, HANDSOME. ALONE AT LAST.

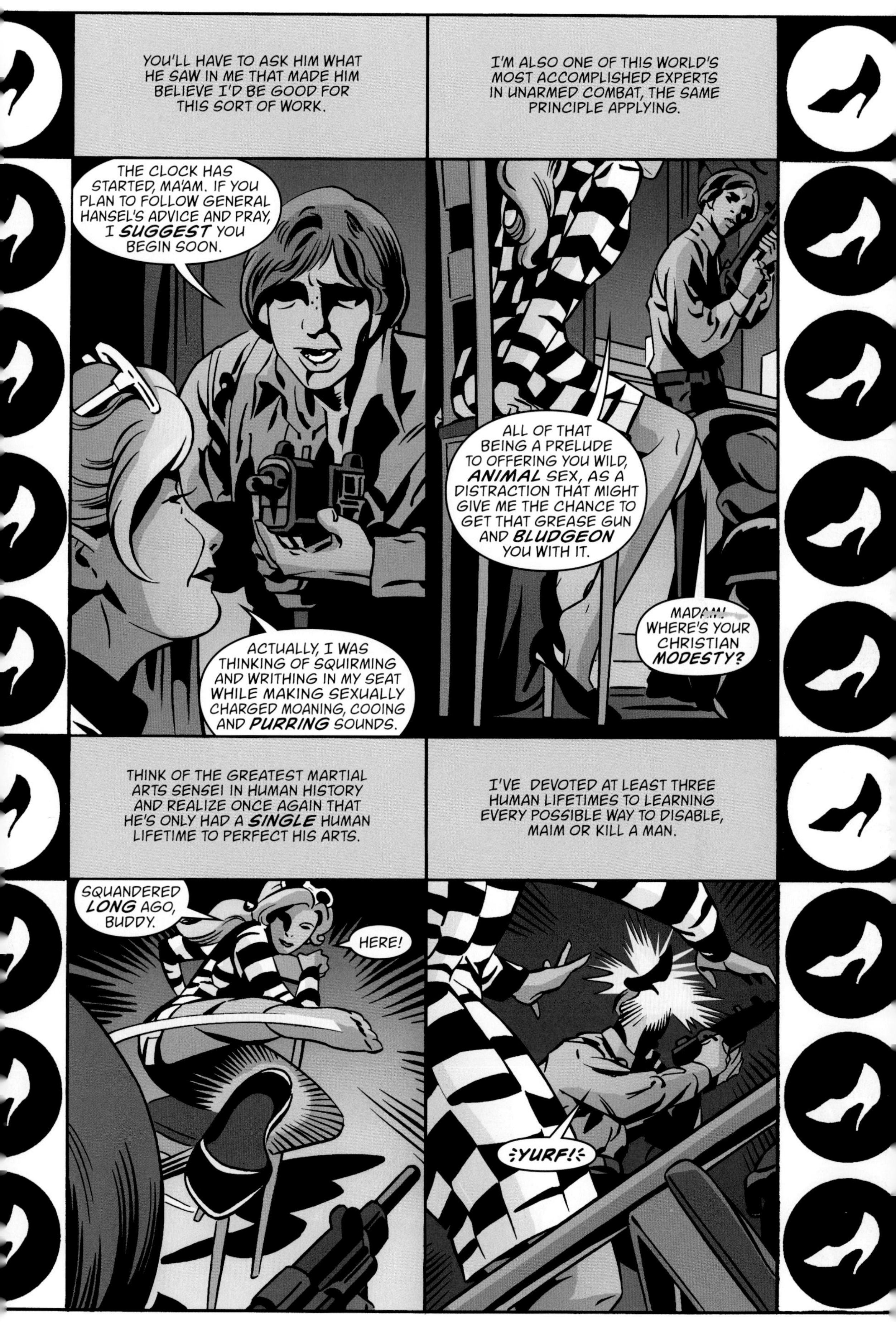
YOU'LL HAVE TO ASK HIM WHAT HE SAW IN ME THAT MADE HIM BELIEVE I'D BE GOOD FOR THIS SORT OF WORK.
I'M ALSO ONE OF THIS WORLD'S MOST ACCOMPLISHED EXPERTS IN UNARMED COMBAT, THE SAME PRINCIPLE APPLYING.
THE CLOCK HAS STARTED, MA'AM. IF YOU PLAN TO FOLLOW GENERAL HANSEL'S ADVICE AND PRAY, I SUGGEST YOU BEGIN SOON.
ACTUALLY, I WAS THINKING OF SQUIRMING AND WRITHING IN MY SEAT WHILE MAKING SEXUALLY CHARGED MOANING, COOING AND PURRING SOUNDS.
ALL OF THAT BEING A PRELUDE TO OFFERING YOU WILD, ANIMAL SEX, AS A DISTRACTION THAT MIGHT GIVE ME THE CHANCE TO GET THAT GREASE GUN AND BLUDGEON YOU WITH IT.
MADAM! WHERE'S YOUR CHRISTIAN MODESTY?
THINK OF THE GREATEST MARTIAL ARTS SENSEI IN HUMAN HISTORY AND REALIZE ONCE AGAIN THAT HE'S ONLY HAD A SINGLE HUMAN LIFETIME TO PERFECT HIS ARTS.
I'VE DEVOTED AT LEAST THREE HUMAN LIFETIMES TO LEARNING EVERY POSSIBLE WAY TO DISABLE, MAIM OR KILL A MAN.
SQUANDERED LONG AGO, BUDDY.
HERE!
YURF!

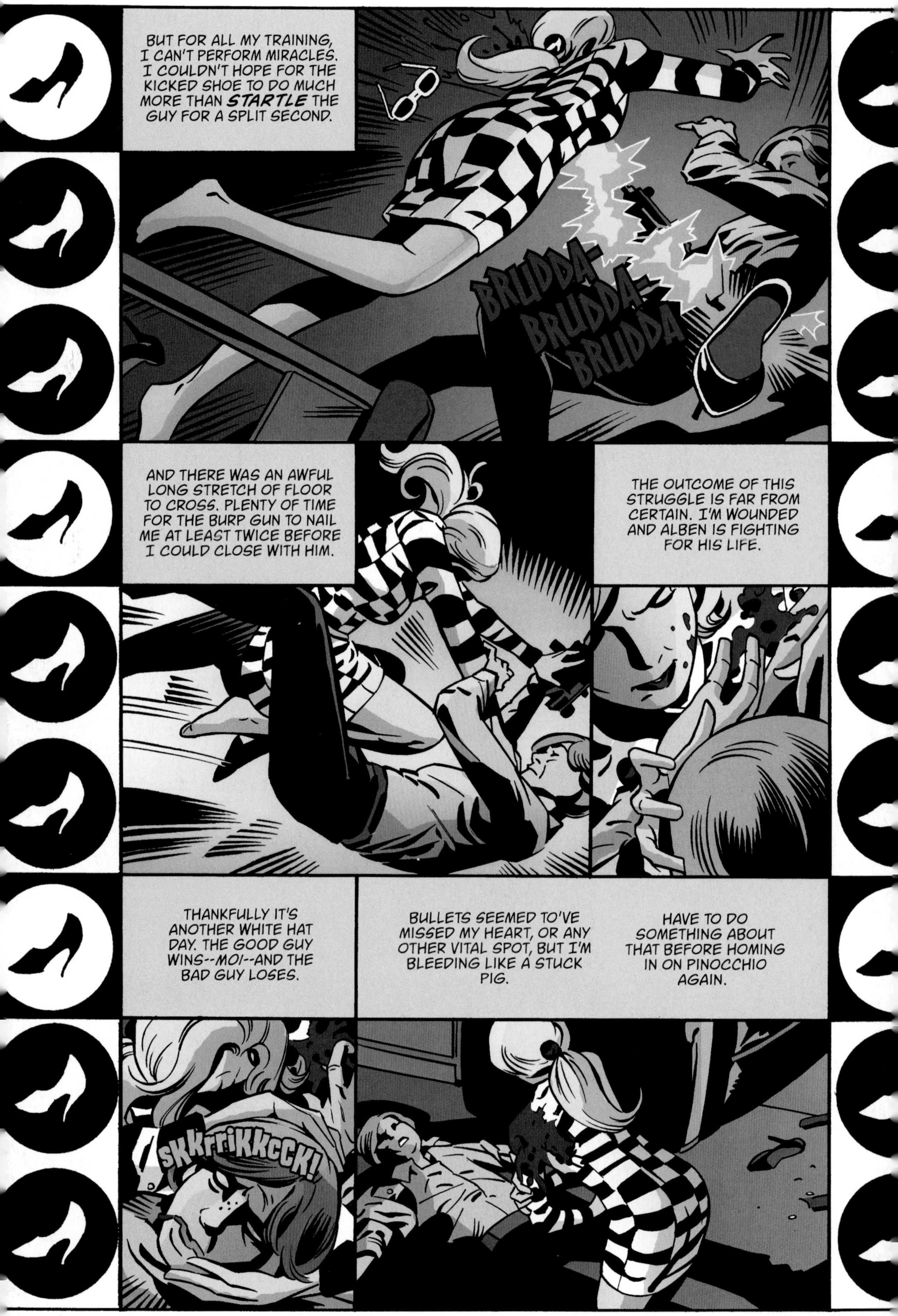
BUT FOR ALL MY TRAINING, I CAN'T PERFORM MIRACLES. I COULDN'T HOPE FOR THE KICKED SHOE TO DO MUCH MORE THAN STARTLE THE GUY FOR A SPLIT SECOND.
BRUDDA-BRUDDA-BRUDDA
AND THERE WAS AN AWFUL LONG STRETCH OF FLOOR TO CROSS. PLENTY OF TIME FOR THE BURP GUN TO NAIL ME AT LEAST TWICE BEFORE I COULD CLOSE WITH HIM.
THE OUTCOME OF THIS STRUGGLE IS FAR FROM CERTAIN. I'M WOUNDED AND ALBEN IS FIGHTING FOR HIS LIFE.
THANKFULLY IT'S ANOTHER WHITE HAT DAY. THE GOOD GUY WINS--MOI--AND THE BAD GUY LOSES.
SKKRRIKKCCK!
BULLETS SEEMED TO'VE MISSED MY HEART, OR ANY OTHER VITAL SPOT, BUT I'M BLEEDING LIKE A STUCK PIG.
HAVE TO DO SOMETHING ABOUT THAT BEFORE HOMING IN ON PINOCCHIO AGAIN.

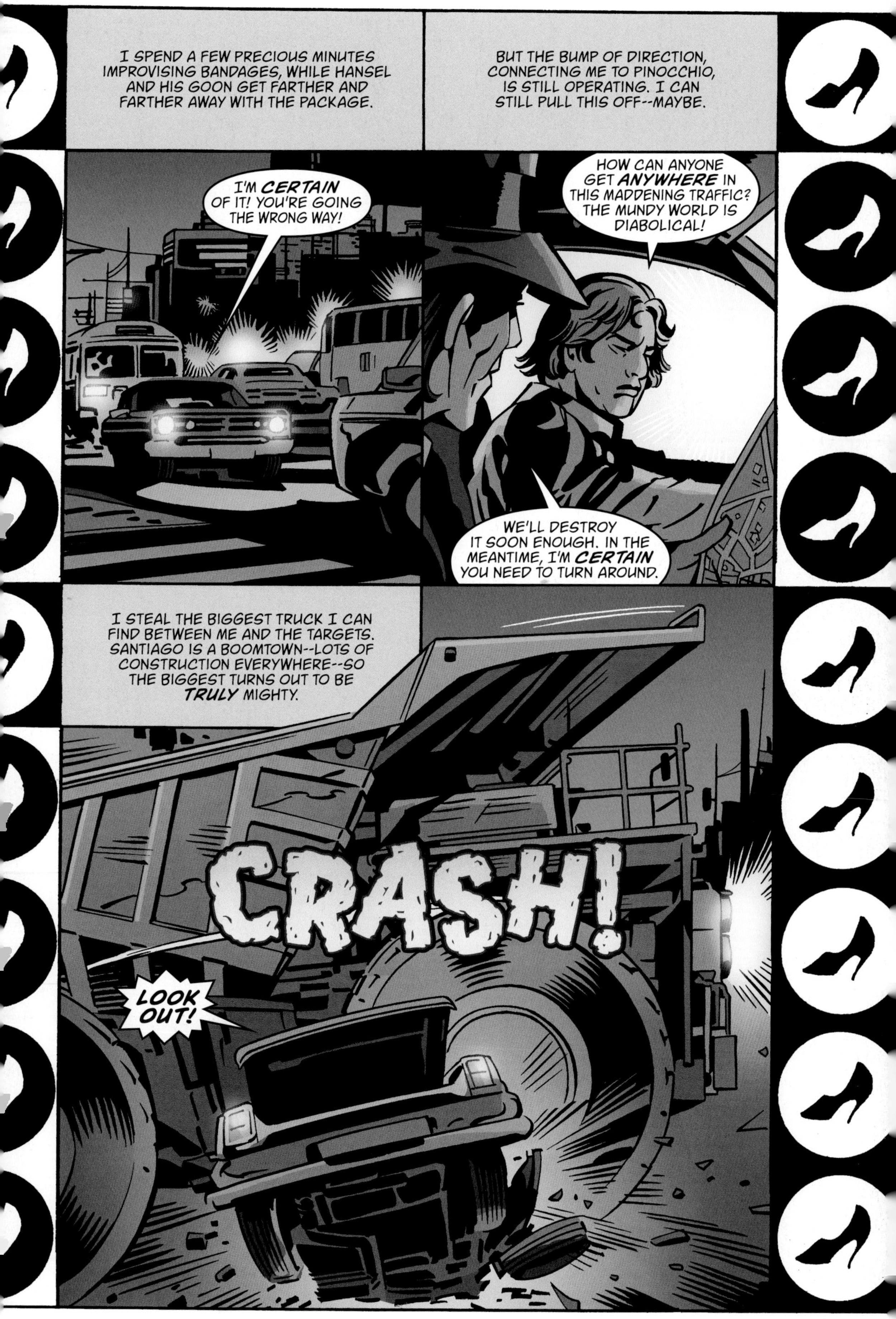

I SPEND A FEW PRECIOUS MINUTES IMPROVISING BANDAGES, WHILE HANSEL AND HIS GOON GET FARTHER AND FARTHER AWAY WITH THE PACKAGE.
BUT THE BUMP OF DIRECTION, CONNECTING ME TO PINOCCHIO, IS STILL OPERATING. I CAN STILL PULL THIS OFF--MAYBE.
I'M *CERTAIN* OF IT! YOU'RE GOING THE WRONG WAY!
HOW CAN ANYONE GET *ANYWHERE* IN THIS MADDENING TRAFFIC? THE MUNDY WORLD IS DIABOLICAL!
WE'LL DESTROY IT SOON ENOUGH. IN THE MEANTIME, I'M *CERTAIN* YOU NEED TO TURN AROUND.
I STEAL THE BIGGEST TRUCK I CAN FIND BETWEEN ME AND THE TARGETS. SANTIAGO IS A BOOMTOWN--LOTS OF CONSTRUCTION EVERYWHERE--SO THE BIGGEST TURNS OUT TO BE *TRULY* MIGHTY.
CRASH!
LOOK OUT!

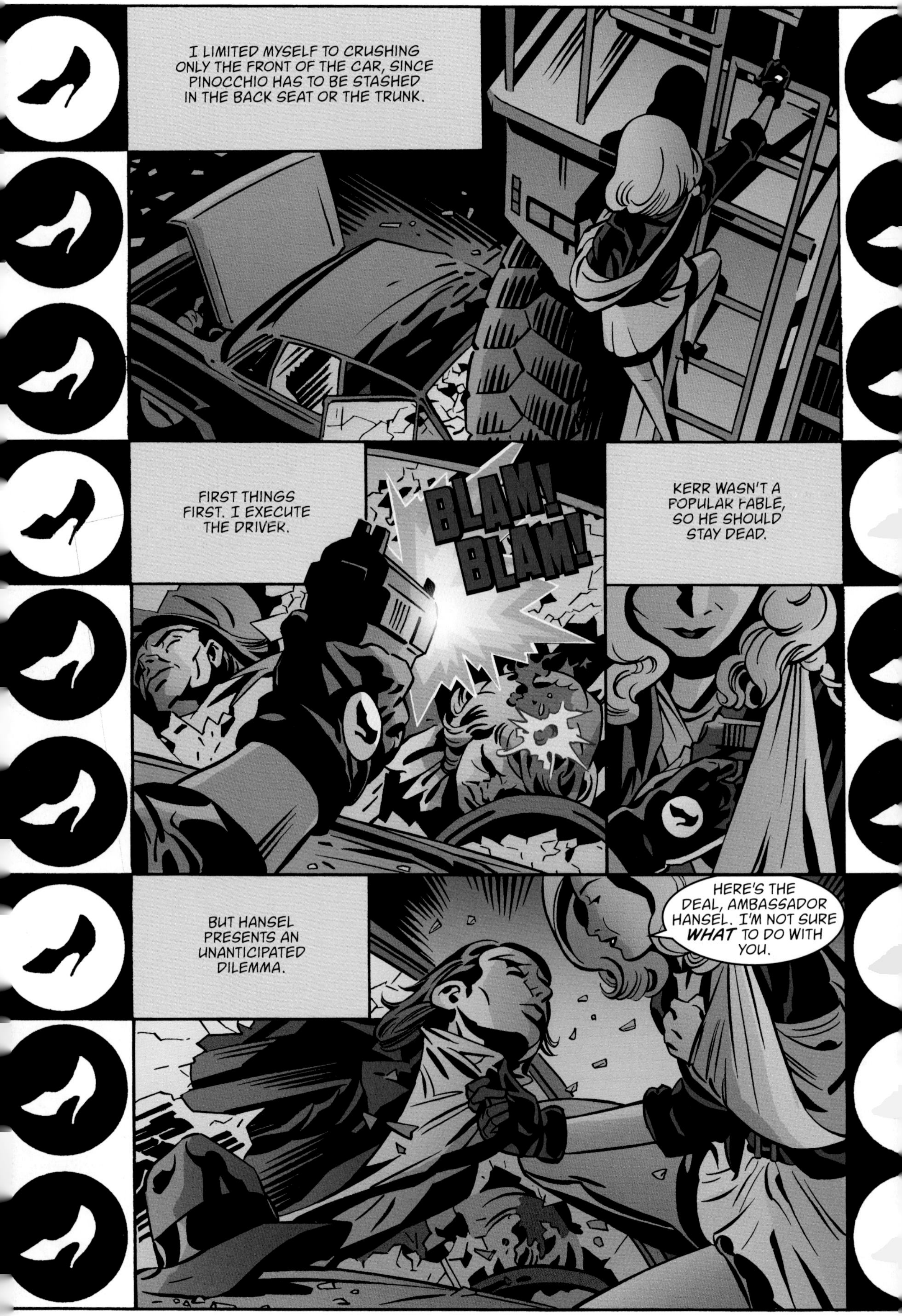

I LIMITED MYSELF TO CRUSHING ONLY THE FRONT OF THE CAR, SINCE PINOCCHIO HAS TO BE STASHED IN THE BACK SEAT OR THE TRUNK.
FIRST THINGS FIRST. I EXECUTE THE DRIVER.
BLAM! BLAM!
KERR WASN'T A POPULAR FABLE, SO HE SHOULD STAY DEAD.
BUT HANSEL PRESENTS AN UNANTICIPATED DILEMMA.
HERE'S THE DEAL, AMBASSADOR HANSEL. I'M NOT SURE **WHAT** TO DO WITH YOU.

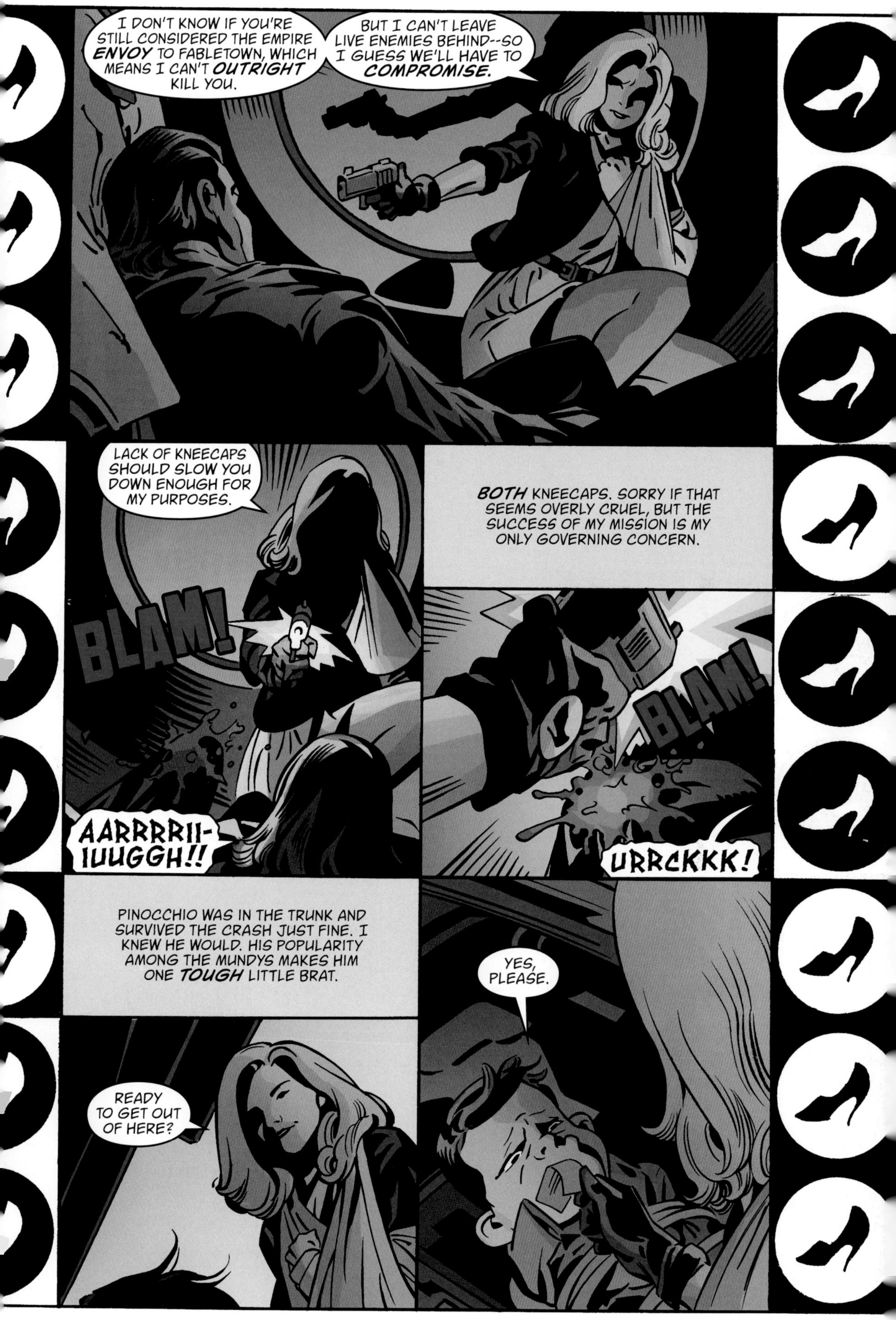
I DON'T KNOW IF YOU'RE STILL CONSIDERED THE EMPIRE *ENVOY* TO FABLETOWN, WHICH MEANS I CAN'T *OUTRIGHT* KILL YOU.
BUT I CAN'T LEAVE LIVE ENEMIES BEHIND--SO I GUESS WE'LL HAVE TO *COMPROMISE.*
LACK OF KNEECAPS SHOULD SLOW YOU DOWN ENOUGH FOR MY PURPOSES.
BLAM!
AARRRRII-IUUGGH!!
BOTH KNEECAPS. SORRY IF THAT SEEMS OVERLY CRUEL, BUT THE SUCCESS OF MY MISSION IS MY ONLY GOVERNING CONCERN.
BLAM!
URRCKKK!
PINOCCHIO WAS IN THE TRUNK AND SURVIVED THE CRASH JUST FINE. I KNEW HE WOULD. HIS POPULARITY AMONG THE MUNDYS MAKES HIM ONE *TOUGH* LITTLE BRAT.
READY TO GET OUT OF HERE?
YES, PLEASE.

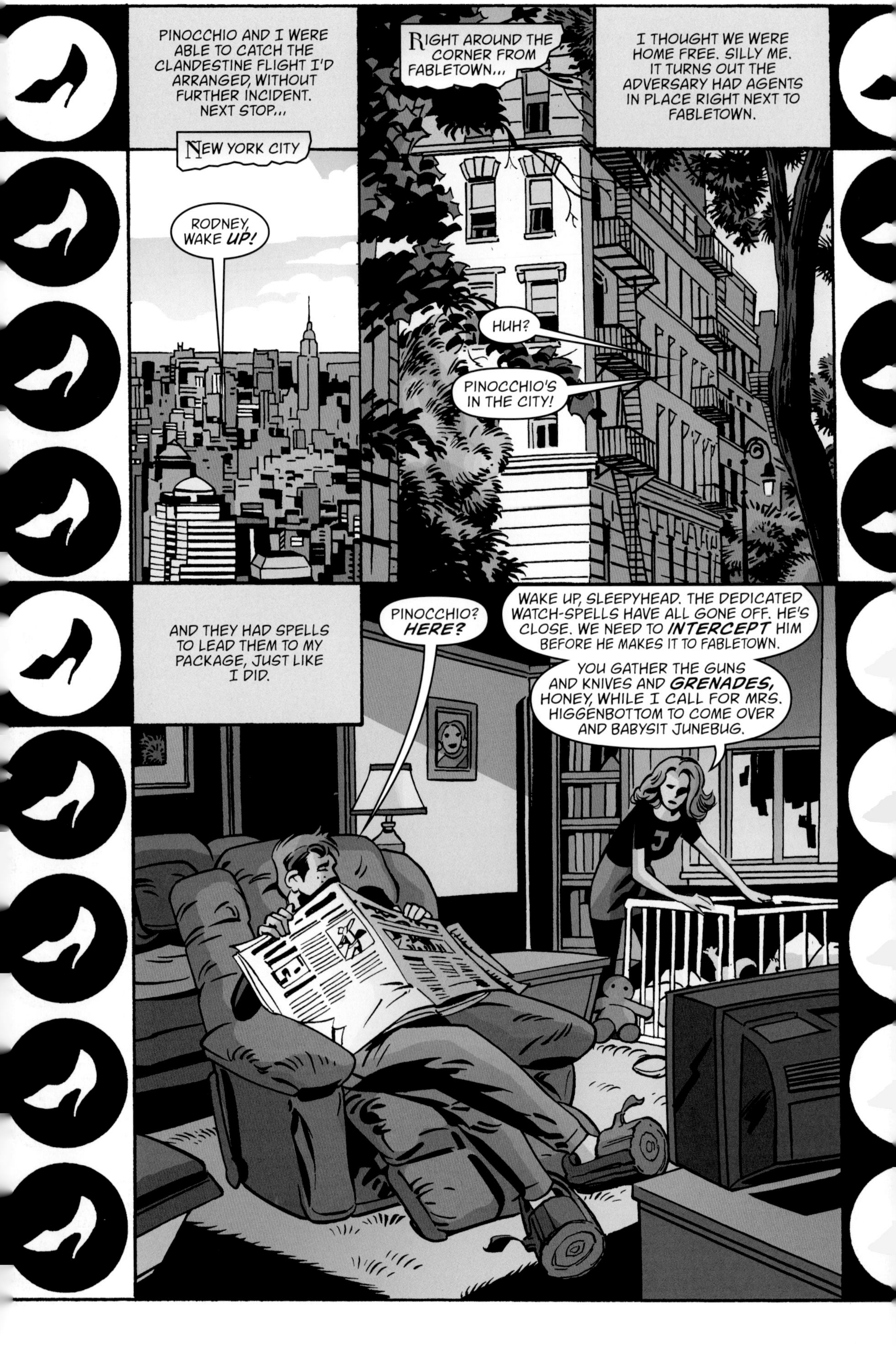
PINOCCHIO AND I WERE ABLE TO CATCH THE CLANDESTINE FLIGHT I'D ARRANGED, WITHOUT FURTHER INCIDENT. NEXT STOP...
NEW YORK CITY
RODNEY, WAKE *UP!*
RIGHT AROUND THE CORNER FROM FABLETOWN...
I THOUGHT WE WERE HOME FREE. SILLY ME. IT TURNS OUT THE ADVERSARY HAD AGENTS IN PLACE RIGHT NEXT TO FABLETOWN.
HUH?
PINOCCHIO'S IN THE CITY!
AND THEY HAD SPELLS TO LEAD THEM TO MY PACKAGE, JUST LIKE I DID.
PINOCCHIO? ***HERE?***
WAKE UP, SLEEPYHEAD. THE DEDICATED WATCH-SPELLS HAVE ALL GONE OFF. HE'S CLOSE. WE NEED TO ***INTERCEPT*** HIM BEFORE HE MAKES IT TO FABLETOWN.
YOU GATHER THE GUNS AND KNIVES AND ***GRENADES,*** HONEY, WHILE I CALL FOR MRS. HIGGENBOTTOM TO COME OVER AND BABYSIT JUNEBUG.

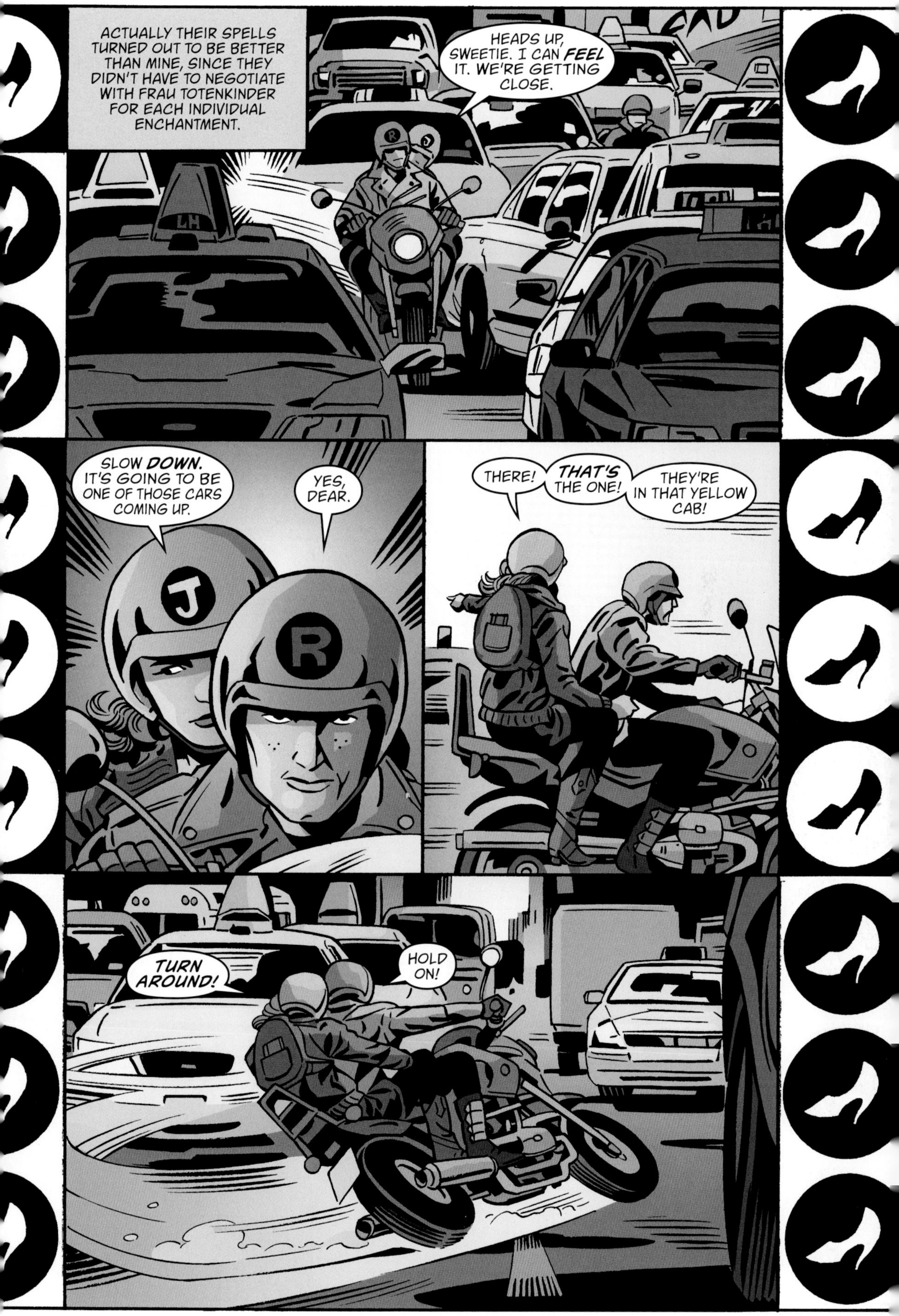
ACTUALLY THEIR SPELLS TURNED OUT TO BE BETTER THAN MINE, SINCE THEY DIDN'T HAVE TO NEGOTIATE WITH FRAU TOTENKINDER FOR EACH INDIVIDUAL ENCHANTMENT.
HEADS UP, SWEETIE. I CAN FEEL IT. WE'RE GETTING CLOSE.
SLOW DOWN. IT'S GOING TO BE ONE OF THOSE CARS COMING UP.
YES, DEAR.
THERE!
THAT'S THE ONE!
THEY'RE IN THAT YELLOW CAB!
TURN AROUND!
HOLD ON!

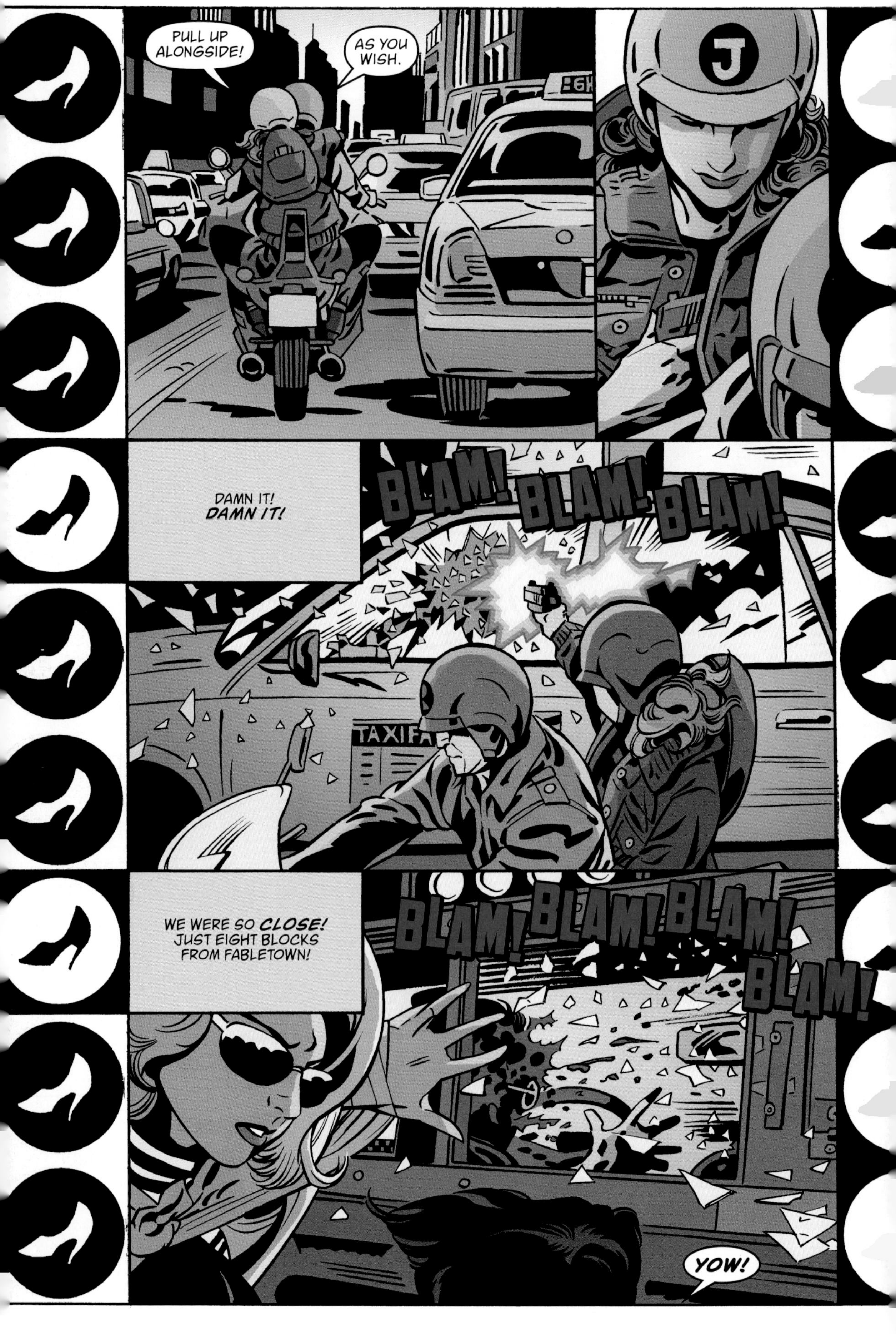
PULL UP ALONGSIDE!
AS YOU WISH.
DAMN IT! ***DAMN IT!***
BLAM! BLAM! BLAM!
TAXIFA
WE WERE SO ***CLOSE!*** JUST EIGHT BLOCKS FROM FABLETOWN!
BLAM! BLAM! BLAM! BLAM!
YOW!

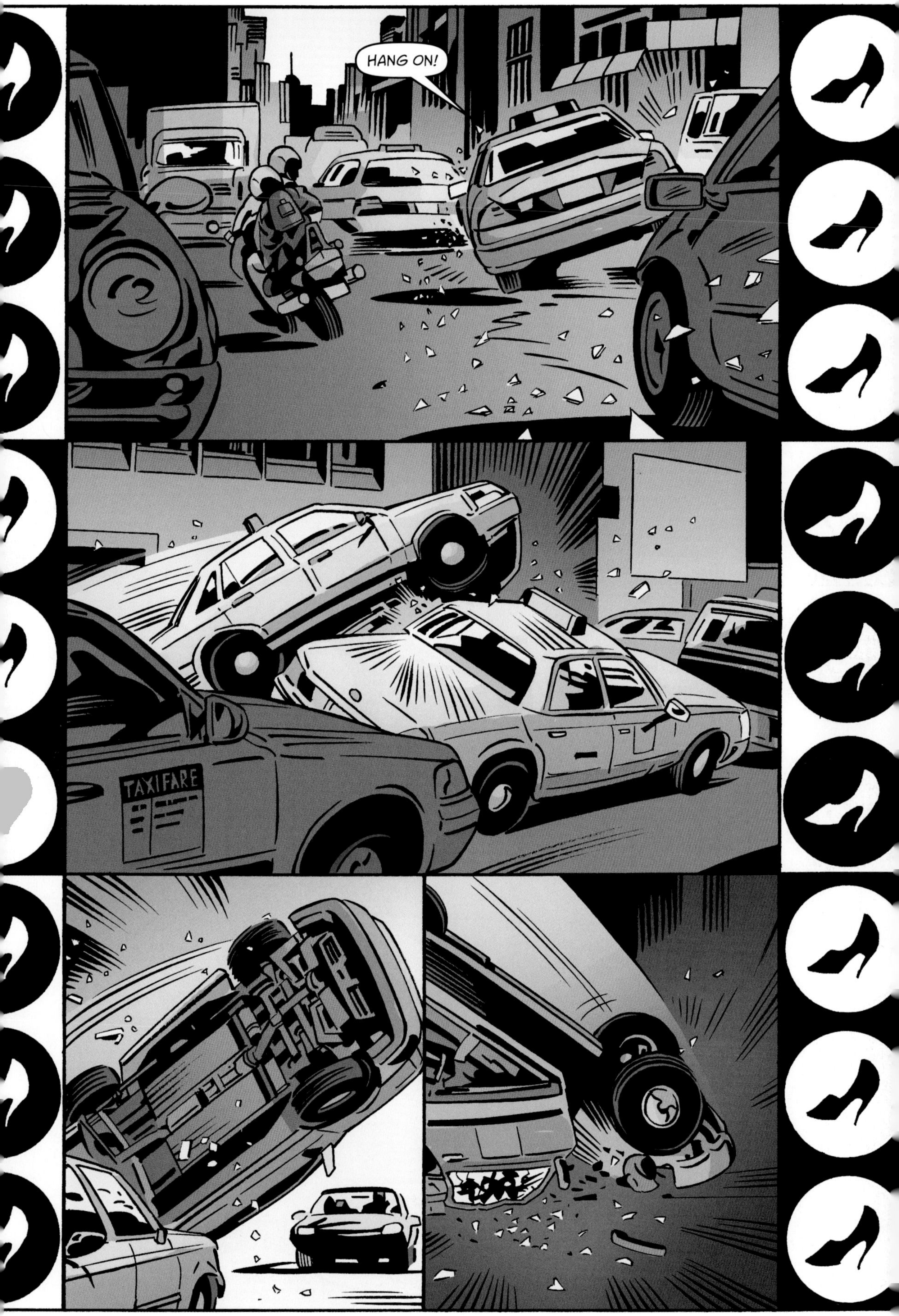
HANG ON!
TAXIFARE

SO DAMNED CLOSE.

ARE YOU STILL *ALIVE,* KID?

I.... THINK SO.

THEN, IF YOU'RE STILL IN ONE *PIECE,* TRY TO PULL YOURSELF OUT.

MAKE A RUN FOR FABLETOWN, WHILE I SEE WHAT WE'RE UP AGAINST *THIS* TIME, AND TRY TO HOLD THEM OFF.

THAT'S CINDERELLA. I RECOGNIZE HER FROM OUR SURVEILLANCE PHOTOS. SHE'S SUPPOSED TO BE *DEADLY.*

NOT SO MUCH NOW. SHE LOOKS PRETTY BEAT UP.

BEAT UP ENOUGH TO LET HER *LIVE?*

UNFORTUNATELY NOT. OUR INSTRUCTIONS IN JUST SUCH AN INSTANCE ARE *UNEQUIVOCAL.* WE KILL HER AND TAKE THE BOY.

SORRY, MISS. WE TAKE NO *JOY* IN THIS.

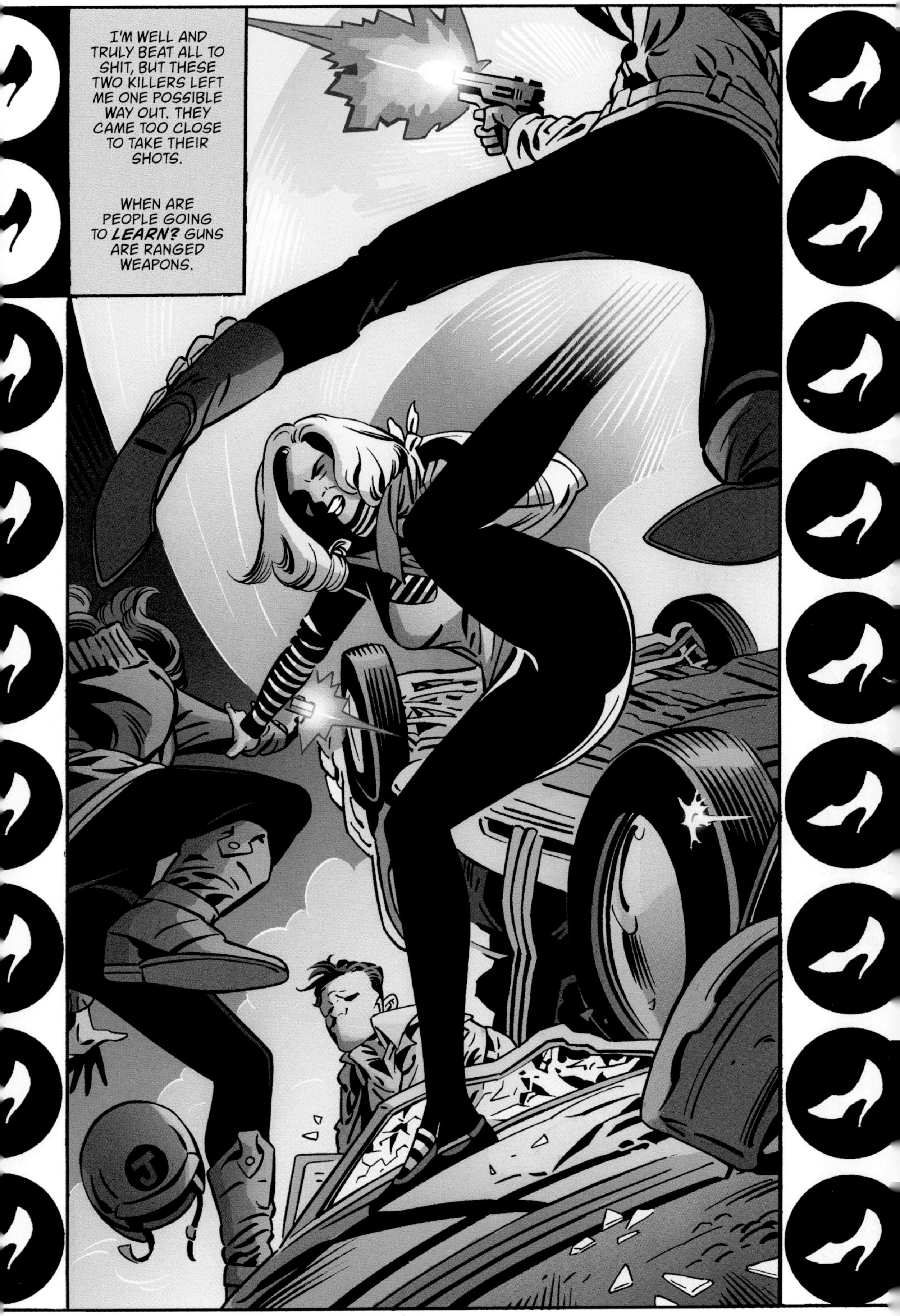
I'M WELL AND TRULY BEAT ALL TO SHIT, BUT THESE TWO KILLERS LEFT ME ONE POSSIBLE WAY OUT. THEY CAME TOO CLOSE TO TAKE THEIR SHOTS.
WHEN ARE PEOPLE GOING TO ***LEARN?*** GUNS ARE RANGED WEAPONS.

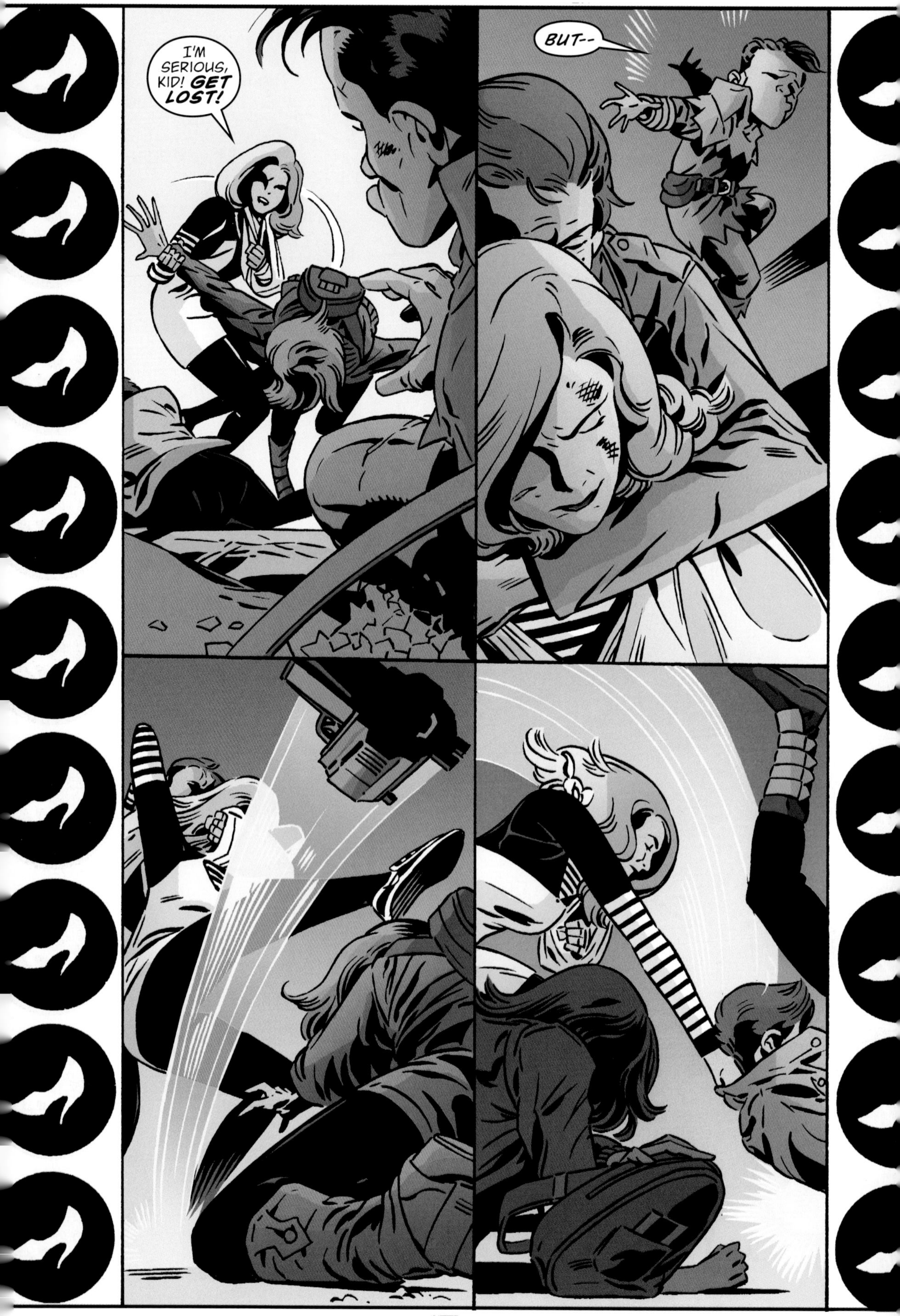

I'M SERIOUS, KID! **GET LOST!**
BUT--

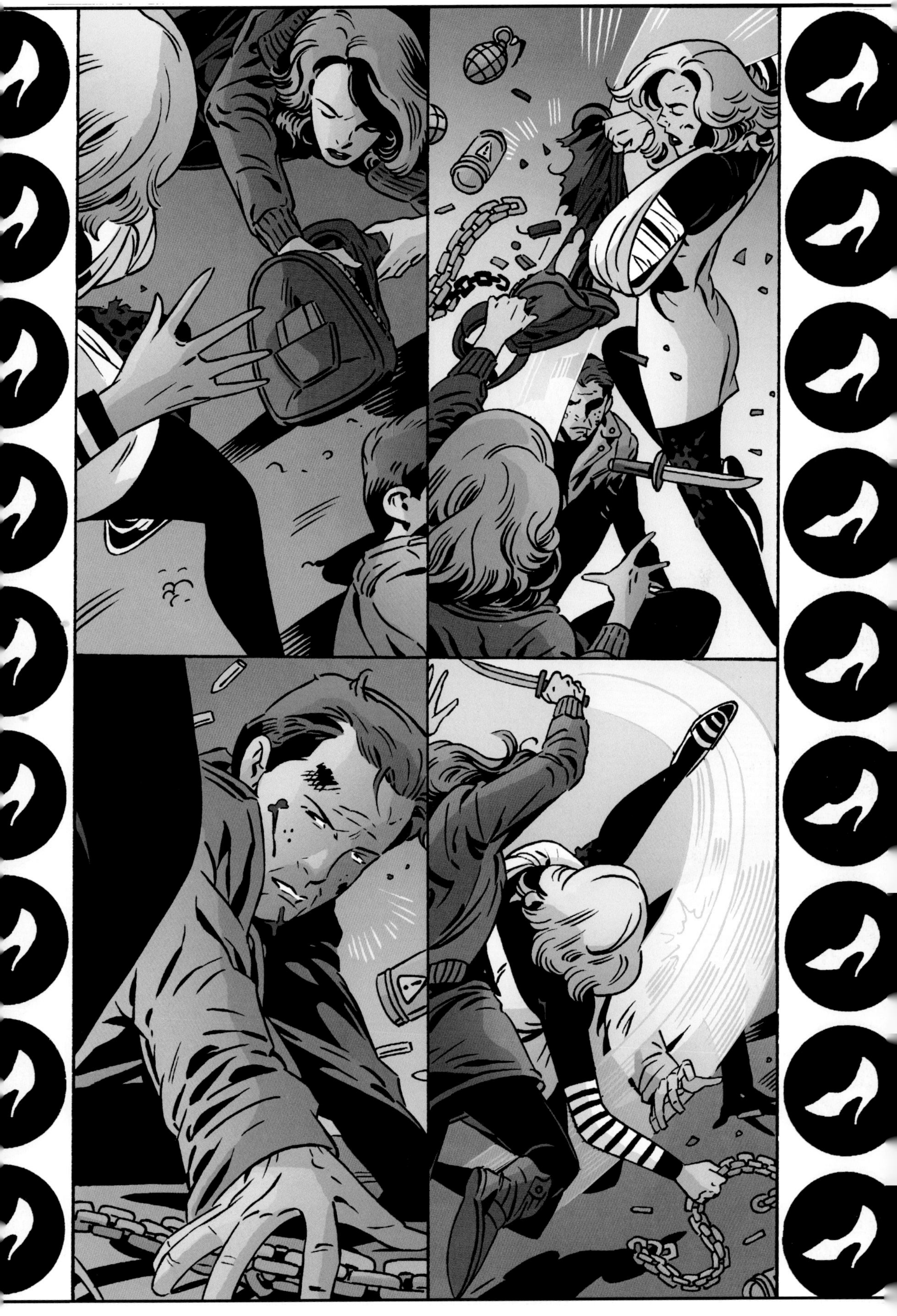

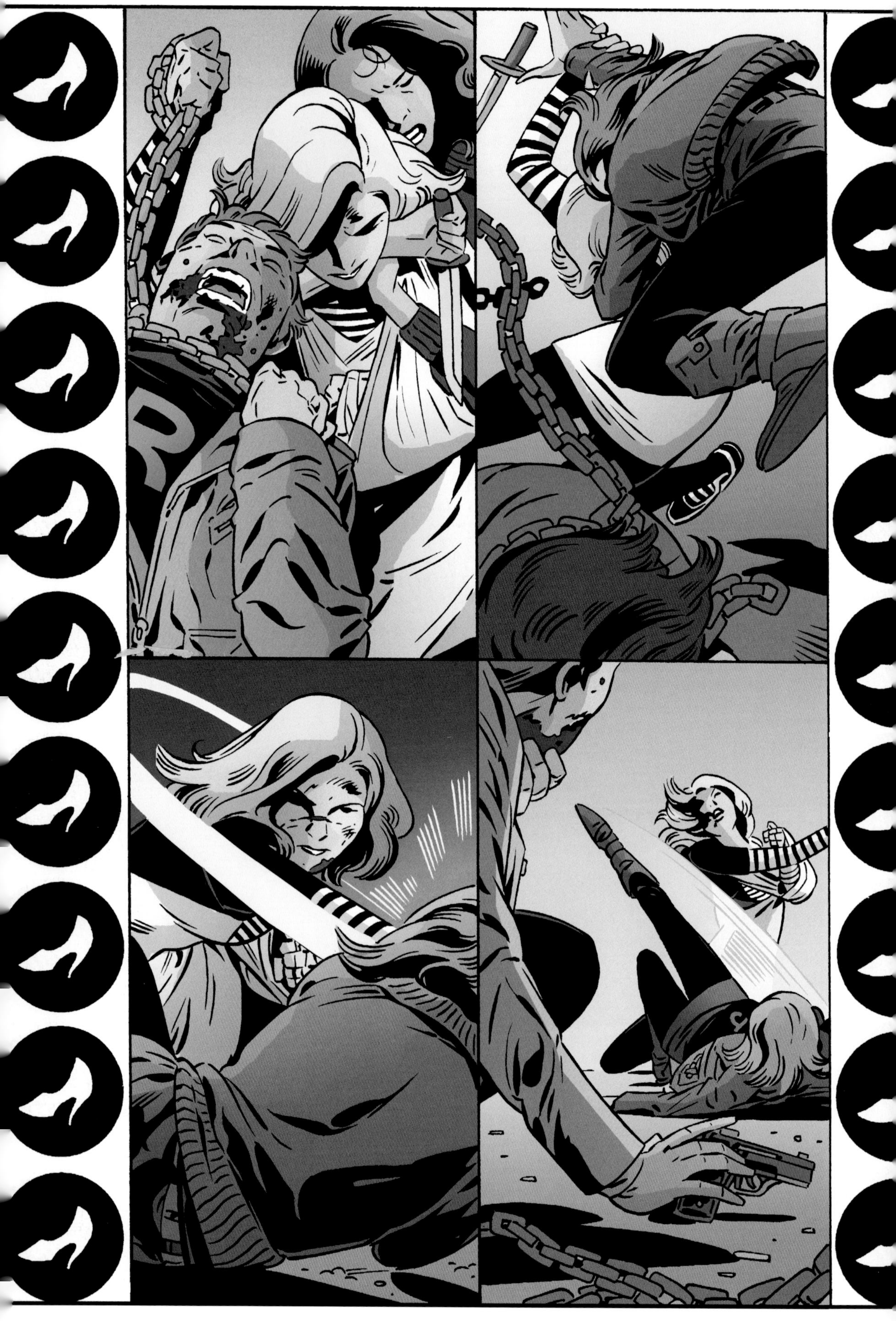

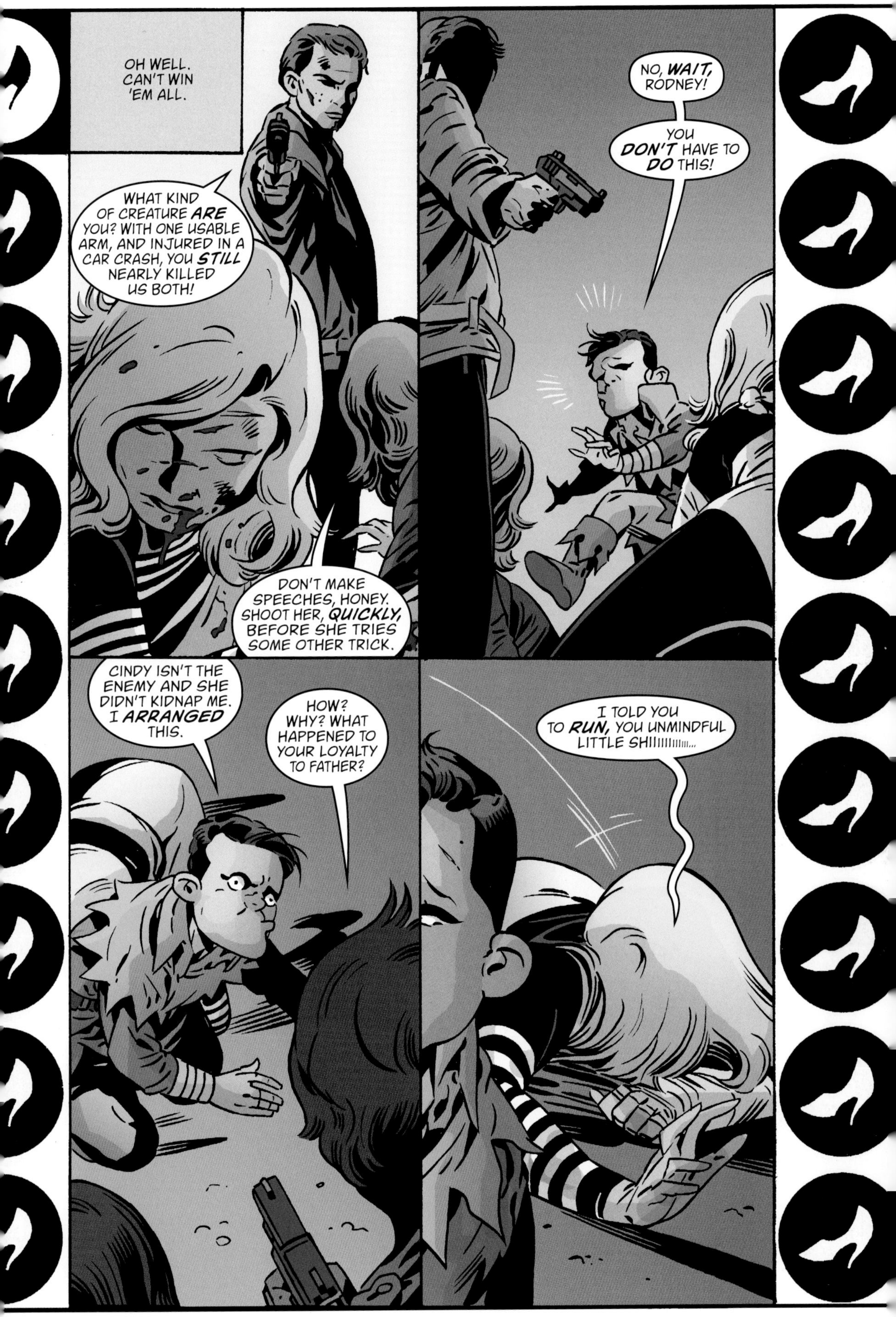

OH WELL. CAN'T WIN 'EM ALL.
WHAT KIND OF CREATURE **ARE** YOU? WITH ONE USABLE ARM, AND INJURED IN A CAR CRASH, YOU **STILL** NEARLY KILLED US BOTH!
DON'T MAKE SPEECHES, HONEY. SHOOT HER, **QUICKLY,** BEFORE SHE TRIES SOME OTHER TRICK.
NO, **WAIT,** RODNEY!
YOU **DON'T** HAVE TO **DO** THIS!
CINDY ISN'T THE ENEMY AND SHE DIDN'T KIDNAP ME. I **ARRANGED** THIS.
HOW? WHY? WHAT HAPPENED TO YOUR LOYALTY TO FATHER?
I TOLD YOU TO **RUN,** YOU UNMINDFUL LITTLE SHIIIIIIIIIIII...

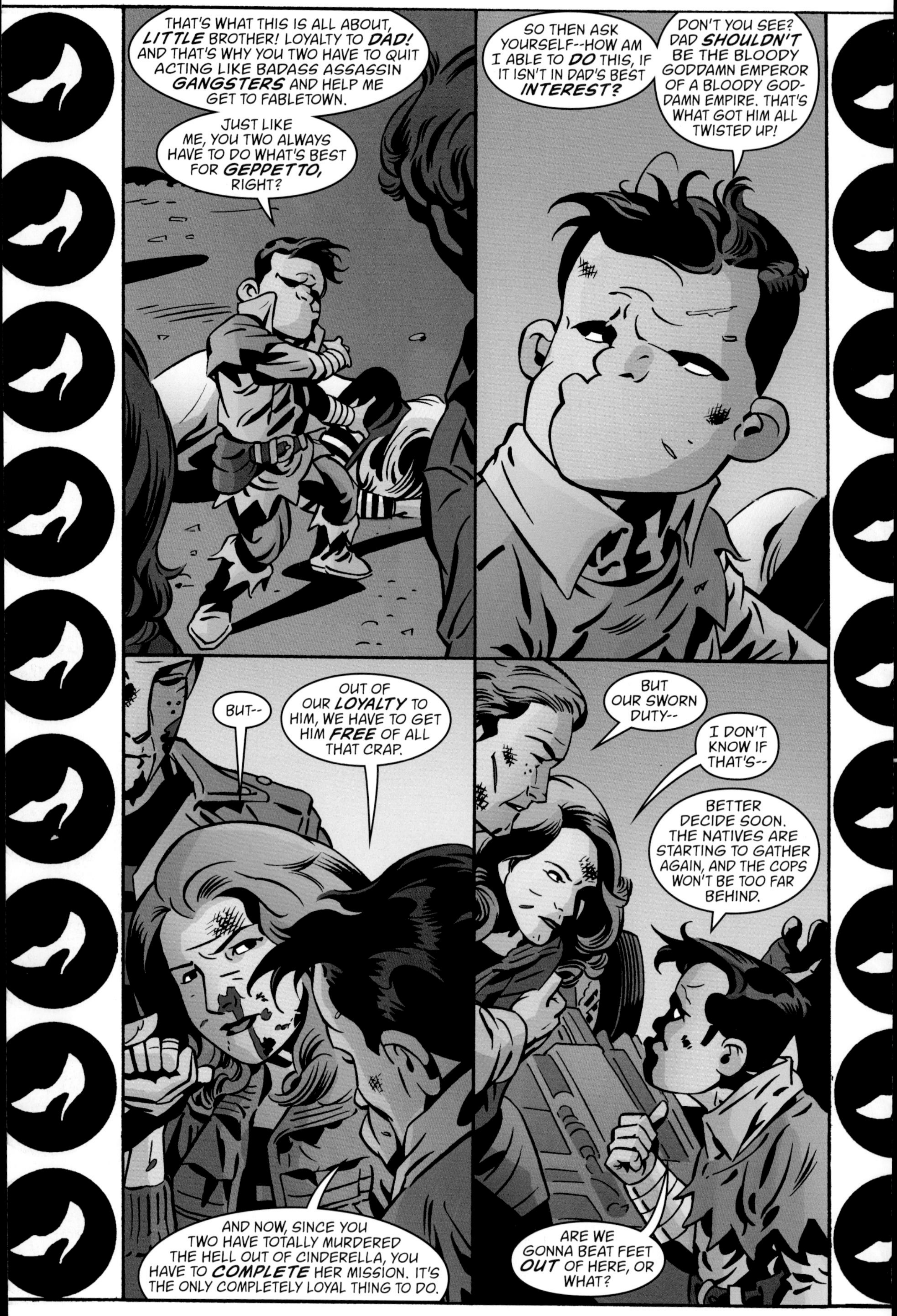
THAT'S WHAT THIS IS ALL ABOUT, LITTLE BROTHER! LOYALTY TO DAD! AND THAT'S WHY YOU TWO HAVE TO QUIT ACTING LIKE BADASS ASSASSIN GANGSTERS AND HELP ME GET TO FABLETOWN.
JUST LIKE ME, YOU TWO ALWAYS HAVE TO DO WHAT'S BEST FOR GEPPETTO, RIGHT?
SO THEN ASK YOURSELF--HOW AM I ABLE TO DO THIS, IF IT ISN'T IN DAD'S BEST INTEREST?
DON'T YOU SEE? DAD SHOULDN'T BE THE BLOODY GODDAMN EMPEROR OF A BLOODY GOD-DAMN EMPIRE. THAT'S WHAT GOT HIM ALL TWISTED UP!
BUT--
OUT OF OUR LOYALTY TO HIM, WE HAVE TO GET HIM FREE OF ALL THAT CRAP.
AND NOW, SINCE YOU TWO HAVE TOTALLY MURDERED THE HELL OUT OF CINDERELLA, YOU HAVE TO COMPLETE HER MISSION. IT'S THE ONLY COMPLETELY LOYAL THING TO DO.
BUT OUR SWORN DUTY--
I DON'T KNOW IF THAT'S--
BETTER DECIDE SOON. THE NATIVES ARE STARTING TO GATHER AGAIN, AND THE COPS WON'T BE TOO FAR BEHIND.
ARE WE GONNA BEAT FEET OUT OF HERE, OR WHAT?

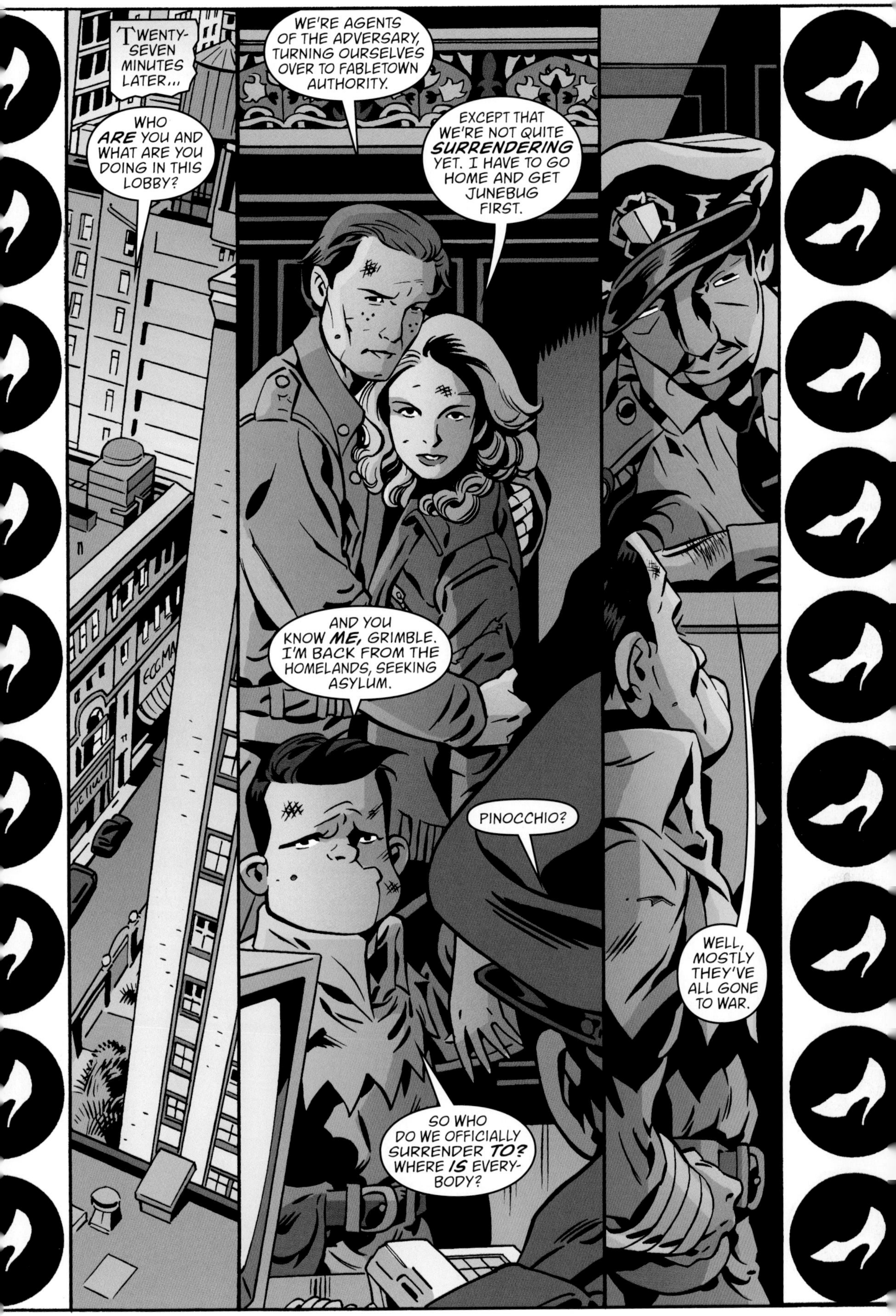
TWENTY-SEVEN MINUTES LATER...
WHO *ARE* YOU AND WHAT ARE YOU DOING IN THIS LOBBY?
WE'RE AGENTS OF THE ADVERSARY, TURNING OURSELVES OVER TO FABLETOWN AUTHORITY.
EXCEPT THAT WE'RE NOT QUITE *SURRENDERING* YET. I HAVE TO GO HOME AND GET JUNEBUG FIRST.
AND YOU KNOW *ME,* GRIMBLE. I'M BACK FROM THE HOMELANDS, SEEKING ASYLUM.
SO WHO DO WE OFFICIALLY SURRENDER *TO?* WHERE *IS* EVERY-BODY?
PINOCCHIO?
WELL, MOSTLY THEY'VE ALL GONE TO WAR.

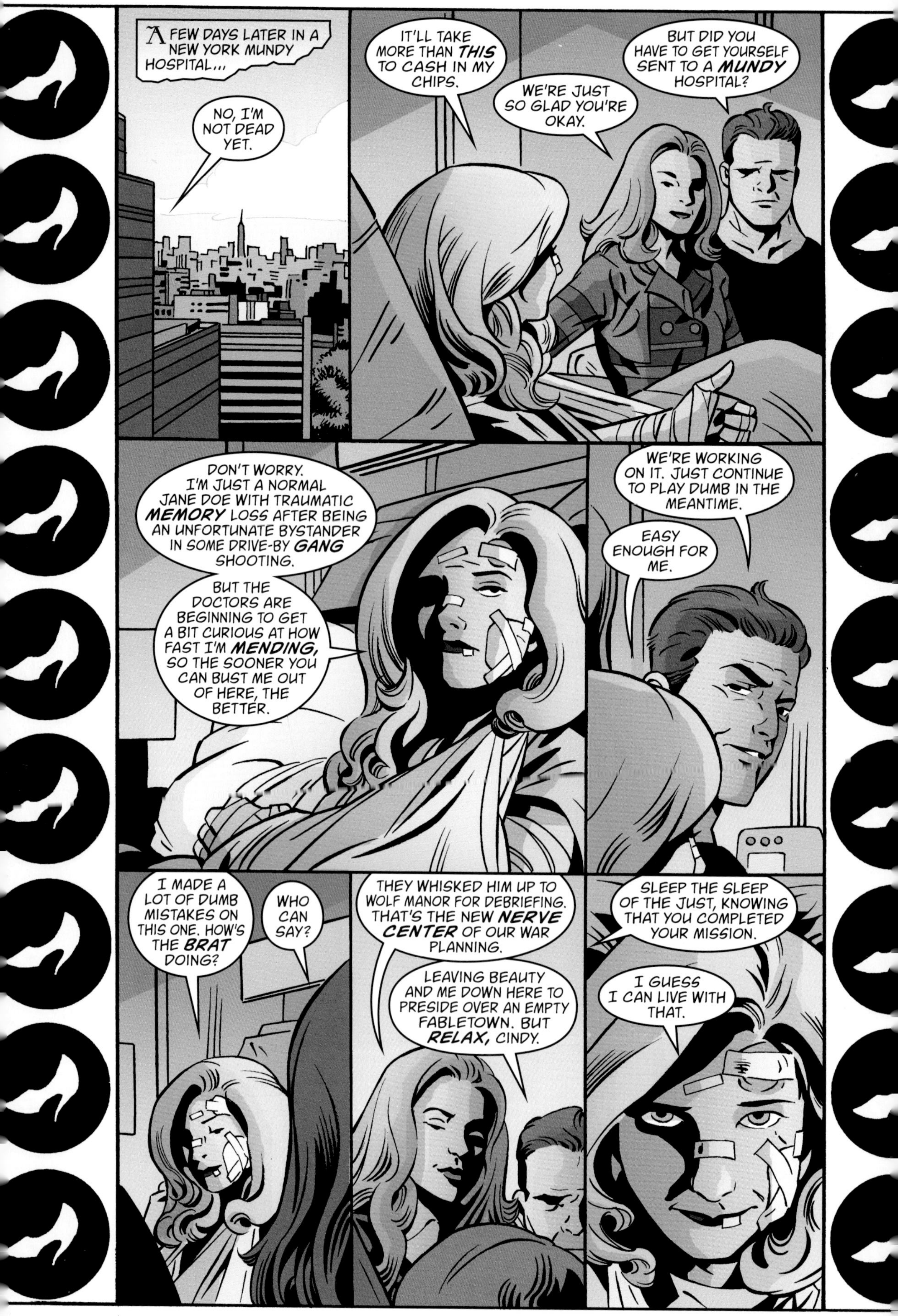
A FEW DAYS LATER IN A NEW YORK MUNDY HOSPITAL...
NO, I'M NOT DEAD YET.
IT'LL TAKE MORE THAN THIS TO CASH IN MY CHIPS.
WE'RE JUST SO GLAD YOU'RE OKAY.
BUT DID YOU HAVE TO GET YOURSELF SENT TO A MUNDY HOSPITAL?
DON'T WORRY. I'M JUST A NORMAL JANE DOE WITH TRAUMATIC MEMORY LOSS AFTER BEING AN UNFORTUNATE BYSTANDER IN SOME DRIVE-BY GANG SHOOTING.
BUT THE DOCTORS ARE BEGINNING TO GET A BIT CURIOUS AT HOW FAST I'M MENDING, SO THE SOONER YOU CAN BUST ME OUT OF HERE, THE BETTER.
WE'RE WORKING ON IT. JUST CONTINUE TO PLAY DUMB IN THE MEANTIME.
EASY ENOUGH FOR ME.
I MADE A LOT OF DUMB MISTAKES ON THIS ONE. HOW'S THE BRAT DOING?
WHO CAN SAY?
THEY WHISKED HIM UP TO WOLF MANOR FOR DEBRIEFING. THAT'S THE NEW NERVE CENTER OF OUR WAR PLANNING.
LEAVING BEAUTY AND ME DOWN HERE TO PRESIDE OVER AN EMPTY FABLETOWN. BUT RELAX, CINDY.
SLEEP THE SLEEP OF THE JUST, KNOWING THAT YOU COMPLETED YOUR MISSION.
I GUESS I CAN LIVE WITH THAT.

NEXT: THE BATTLESHIP

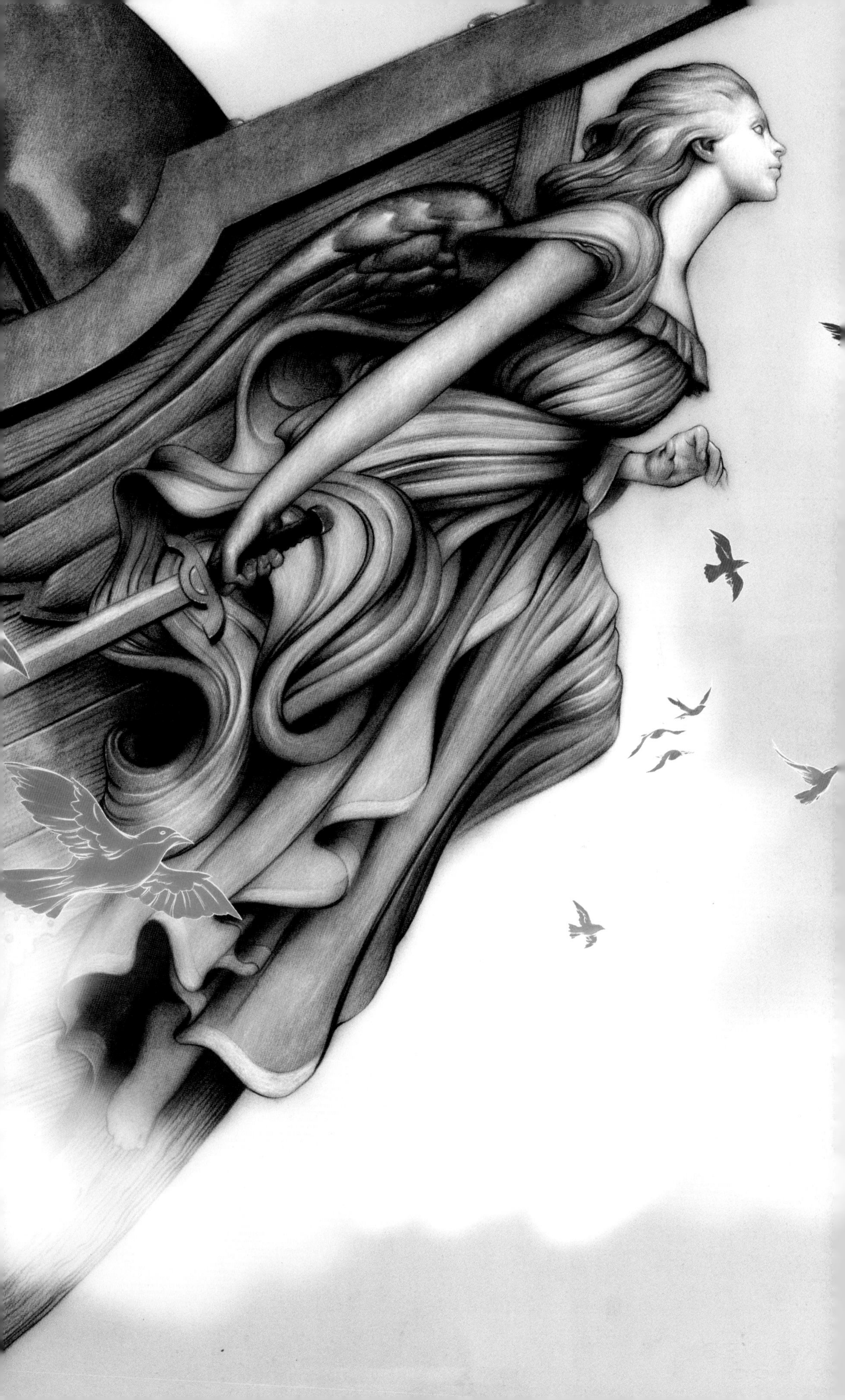

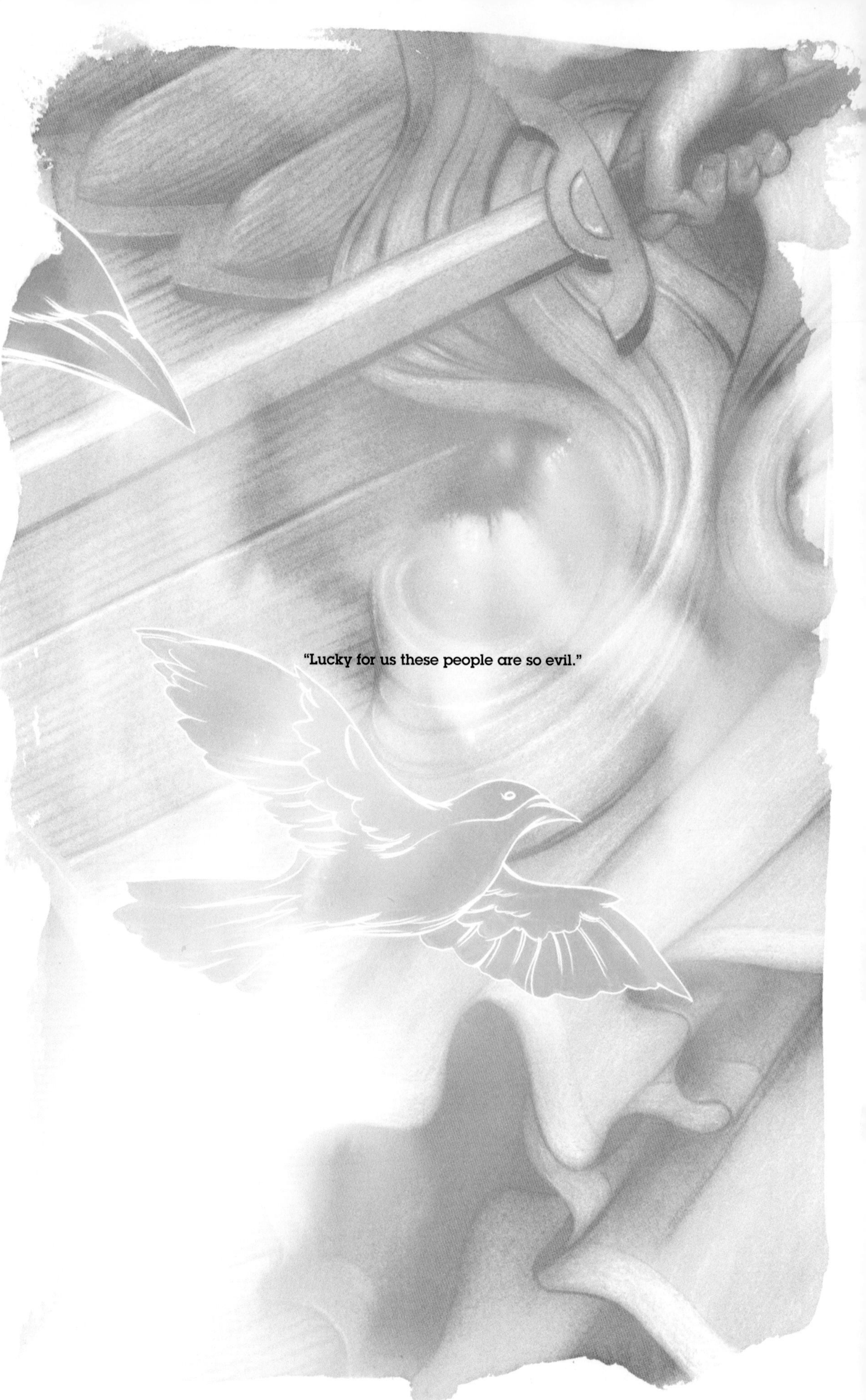

"Lucky for us these people are so evil."

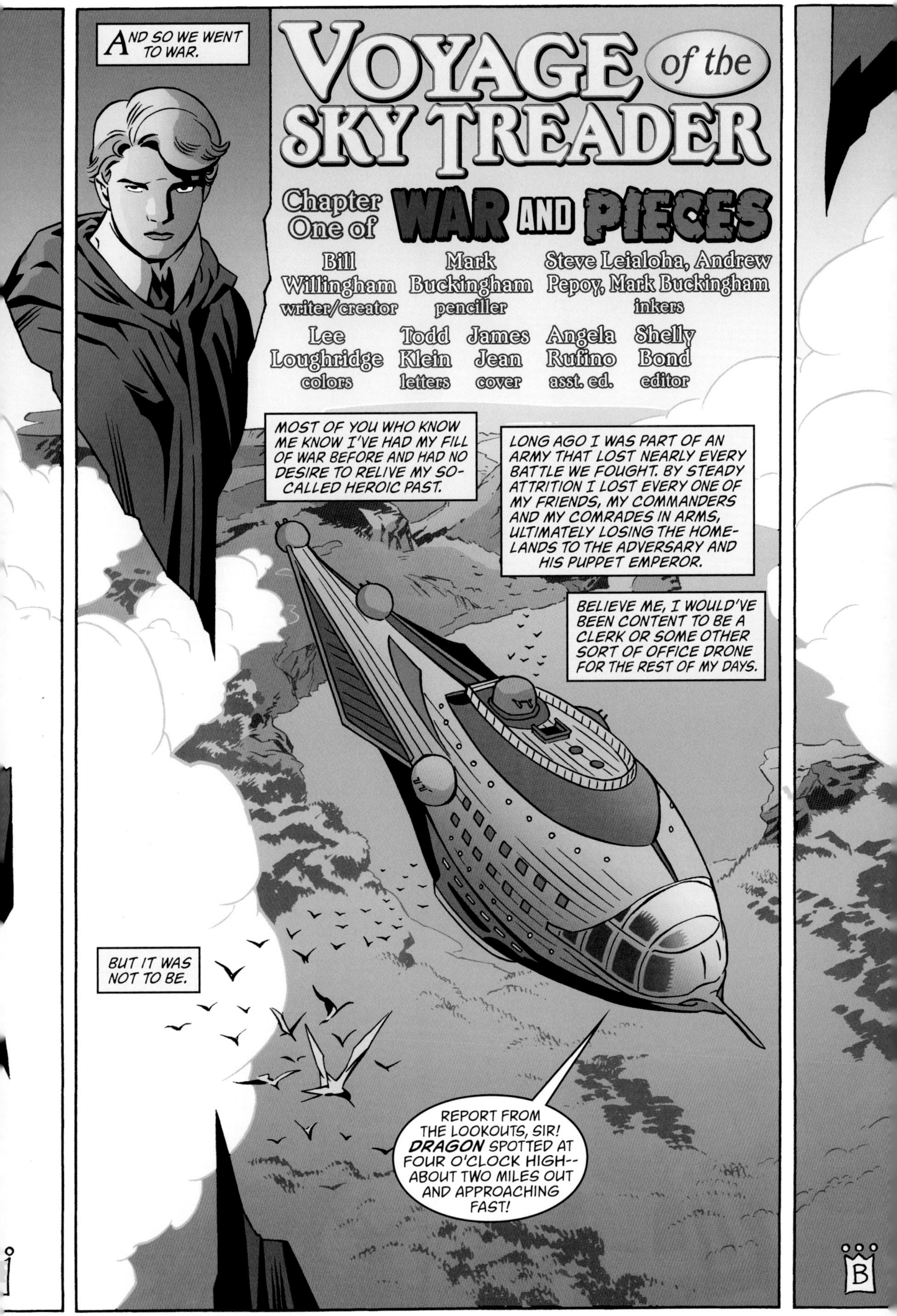
AND SO WE WENT TO WAR.
VOYAGE of the SKY TREADER
Chapter One of WAR AND PIECES
Bill Willingham writer/creator
Mark Buckingham penciller
Steve Leialoha, Andrew Pepoy, Mark Buckingham inkers
Lee Loughridge colors
Todd Klein letters
James Jean cover
Angela Rufino asst. ed.
Shelly Bond editor
MOST OF YOU WHO KNOW ME KNOW I'VE HAD MY FILL OF WAR BEFORE AND HAD NO DESIRE TO RELIVE MY SO-CALLED HEROIC PAST.
LONG AGO I WAS PART OF AN ARMY THAT LOST NEARLY EVERY BATTLE WE FOUGHT. BY STEADY ATTRITION I LOST EVERY ONE OF MY FRIENDS, MY COMMANDERS AND MY COMRADES IN ARMS, ULTIMATELY LOSING THE HOMELANDS TO THE ADVERSARY AND HIS PUPPET EMPEROR.
BELIEVE ME, I WOULD'VE BEEN CONTENT TO BE A CLERK OR SOME OTHER SORT OF OFFICE DRONE FOR THE REST OF MY DAYS.
BUT IT WAS NOT TO BE.
REPORT FROM THE LOOKOUTS, SIR! DRAGON SPOTTED AT FOUR O'CLOCK HIGH-- ABOUT TWO MILES OUT AND APPROACHING FAST!

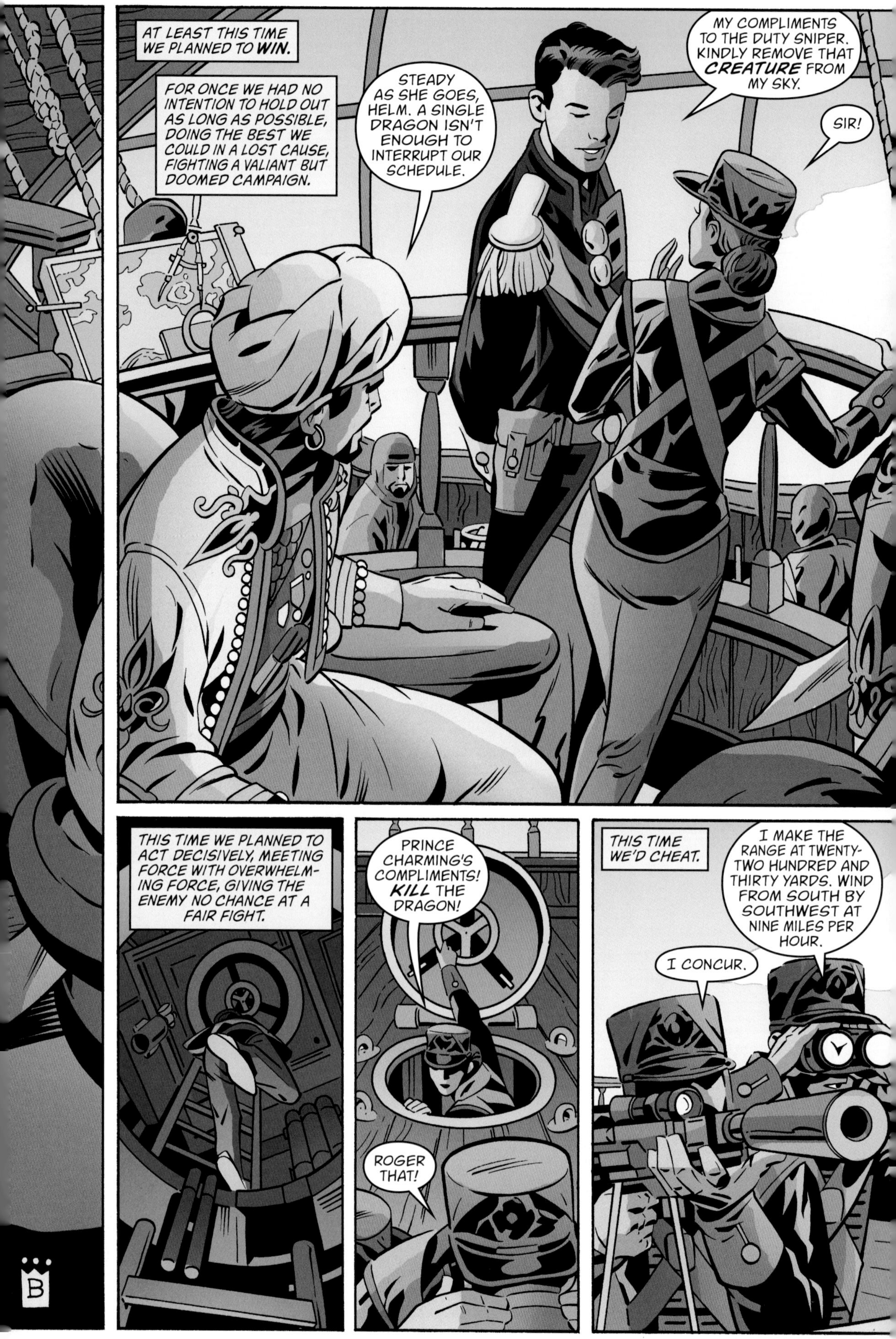
AT LEAST THIS TIME WE PLANNED TO **WIN**.
FOR ONCE WE HAD NO INTENTION TO HOLD OUT AS LONG AS POSSIBLE, DOING THE BEST WE COULD IN A LOST CAUSE, FIGHTING A VALIANT BUT DOOMED CAMPAIGN.
STEADY AS SHE GOES, HELM. A SINGLE DRAGON ISN'T ENOUGH TO INTERRUPT OUR SCHEDULE.
MY COMPLIMENTS TO THE DUTY SNIPER. KINDLY REMOVE THAT **CREATURE** FROM MY SKY.
SIR!
THIS TIME WE PLANNED TO ACT DECISIVELY, MEETING FORCE WITH OVERWHELMING FORCE, GIVING THE ENEMY NO CHANCE AT A FAIR FIGHT.
PRINCE CHARMING'S COMPLIMENTS! **KILL** THE DRAGON!
ROGER THAT!
THIS TIME WE'D CHEAT.
I MAKE THE RANGE AT TWENTY-TWO HUNDRED AND THIRTY YARDS. WIND FROM SOUTH BY SOUTHWEST AT NINE MILES PER HOUR.
I CONCUR.

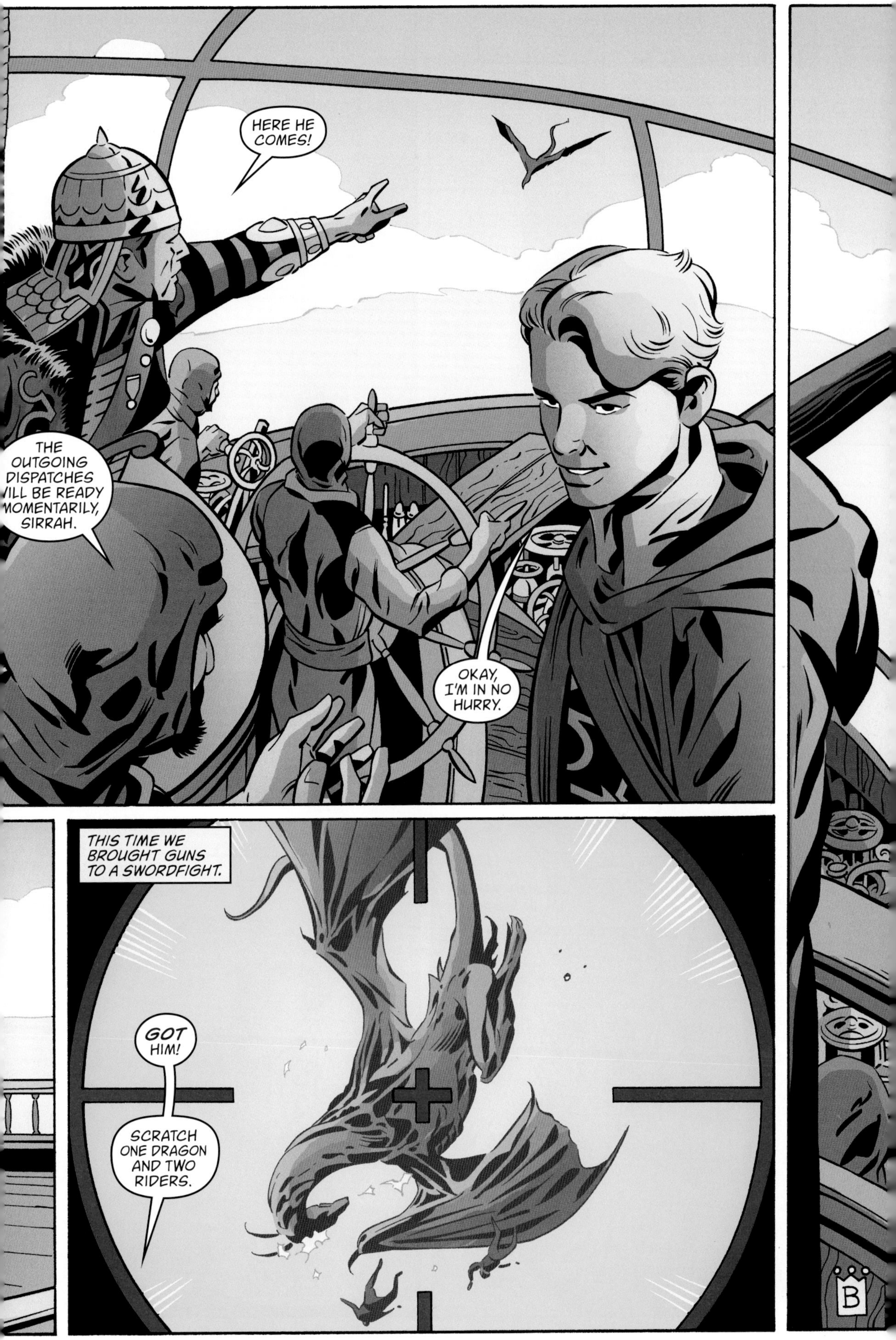
HERE HE COMES!
THE OUTGOING DISPATCHES WILL BE READY MOMENTARILY, SIRRAH.
OKAY, I'M IN NO HURRY.
THIS TIME WE BROUGHT GUNS TO A SWORDFIGHT.
GOT HIM!
SCRATCH ONE DRAGON AND TWO RIDERS.

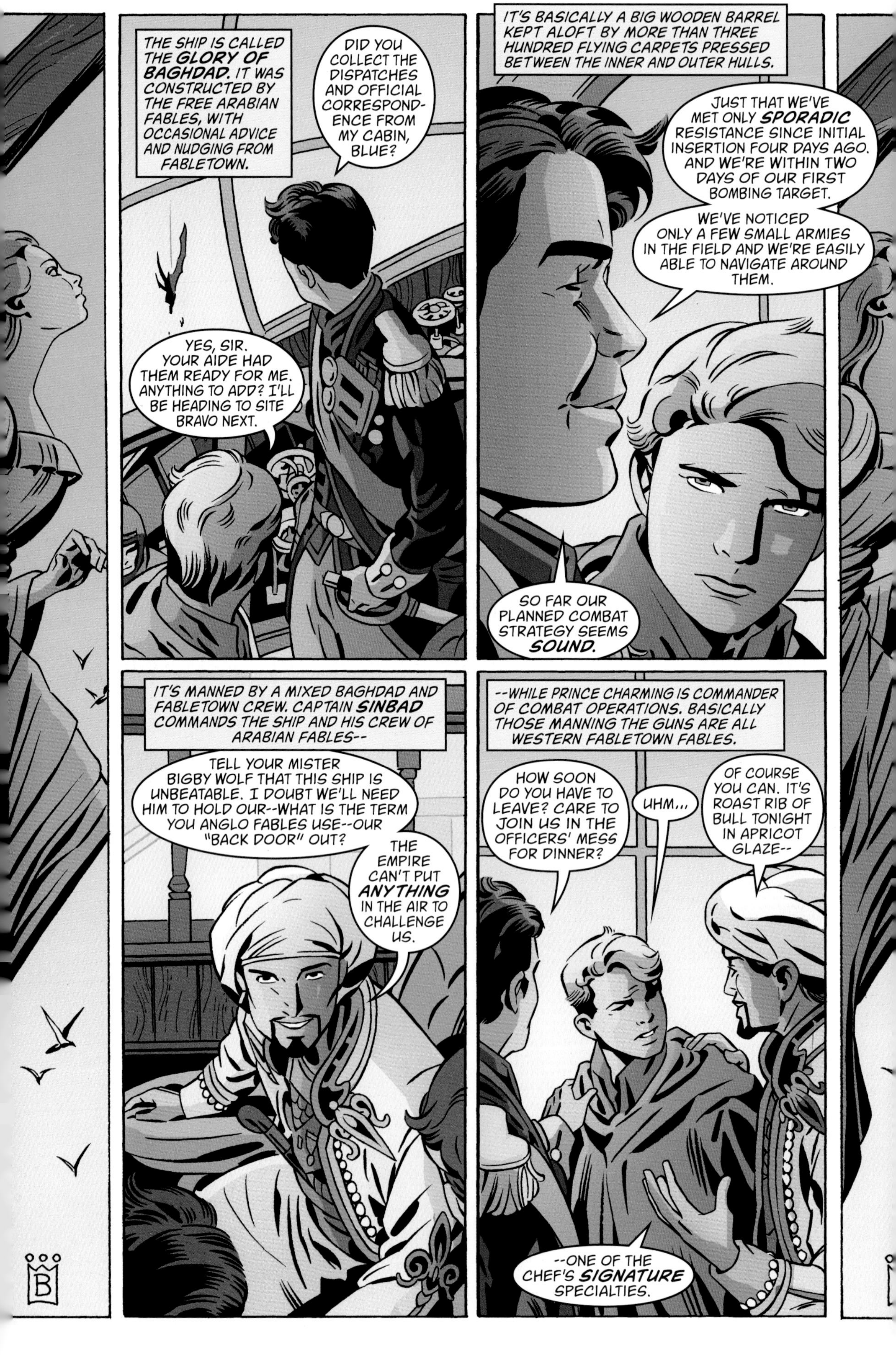
THE SHIP IS CALLED THE GLORY OF BAGHDAD. IT WAS CONSTRUCTED BY THE FREE ARABIAN FABLES, WITH OCCASIONAL ADVICE AND NUDGING FROM FABLETOWN.
DID YOU COLLECT THE DISPATCHES AND OFFICIAL CORRESPONDENCE FROM MY CABIN, BLUE?
YES, SIR. YOUR AIDE HAD THEM READY FOR ME. ANYTHING TO ADD? I'LL BE HEADING TO SITE BRAVO NEXT.
IT'S BASICALLY A BIG WOODEN BARREL KEPT ALOFT BY MORE THAN THREE HUNDRED FLYING CARPETS PRESSED BETWEEN THE INNER AND OUTER HULLS.
JUST THAT WE'VE MET ONLY SPORADIC RESISTANCE SINCE INITIAL INSERTION FOUR DAYS AGO. AND WE'RE WITHIN TWO DAYS OF OUR FIRST BOMBING TARGET.
WE'VE NOTICED ONLY A FEW SMALL ARMIES IN THE FIELD AND WE'RE EASILY ABLE TO NAVIGATE AROUND THEM.
SO FAR OUR PLANNED COMBAT STRATEGY SEEMS SOUND.
IT'S MANNED BY A MIXED BAGHDAD AND FABLETOWN CREW. CAPTAIN SINBAD COMMANDS THE SHIP AND HIS CREW OF ARABIAN FABLES--
TELL YOUR MISTER BIGBY WOLF THAT THIS SHIP IS UNBEATABLE. I DOUBT WE'LL NEED HIM TO HOLD OUR--WHAT IS THE TERM YOU ANGLO FABLES USE--OUR "BACK DOOR" OUT?
THE EMPIRE CAN'T PUT ANYTHING IN THE AIR TO CHALLENGE US.
--WHILE PRINCE CHARMING IS COMMANDER OF COMBAT OPERATIONS. BASICALLY THOSE MANNING THE GUNS ARE ALL WESTERN FABLETOWN FABLES.
HOW SOON DO YOU HAVE TO LEAVE? CARE TO JOIN US IN THE OFFICERS' MESS FOR DINNER?
UHM...
OF COURSE YOU CAN. IT'S ROAST RIB OF BULL TONIGHT IN APRICOT GLAZE--
--ONE OF THE CHEF'S SIGNATURE SPECIALTIES.

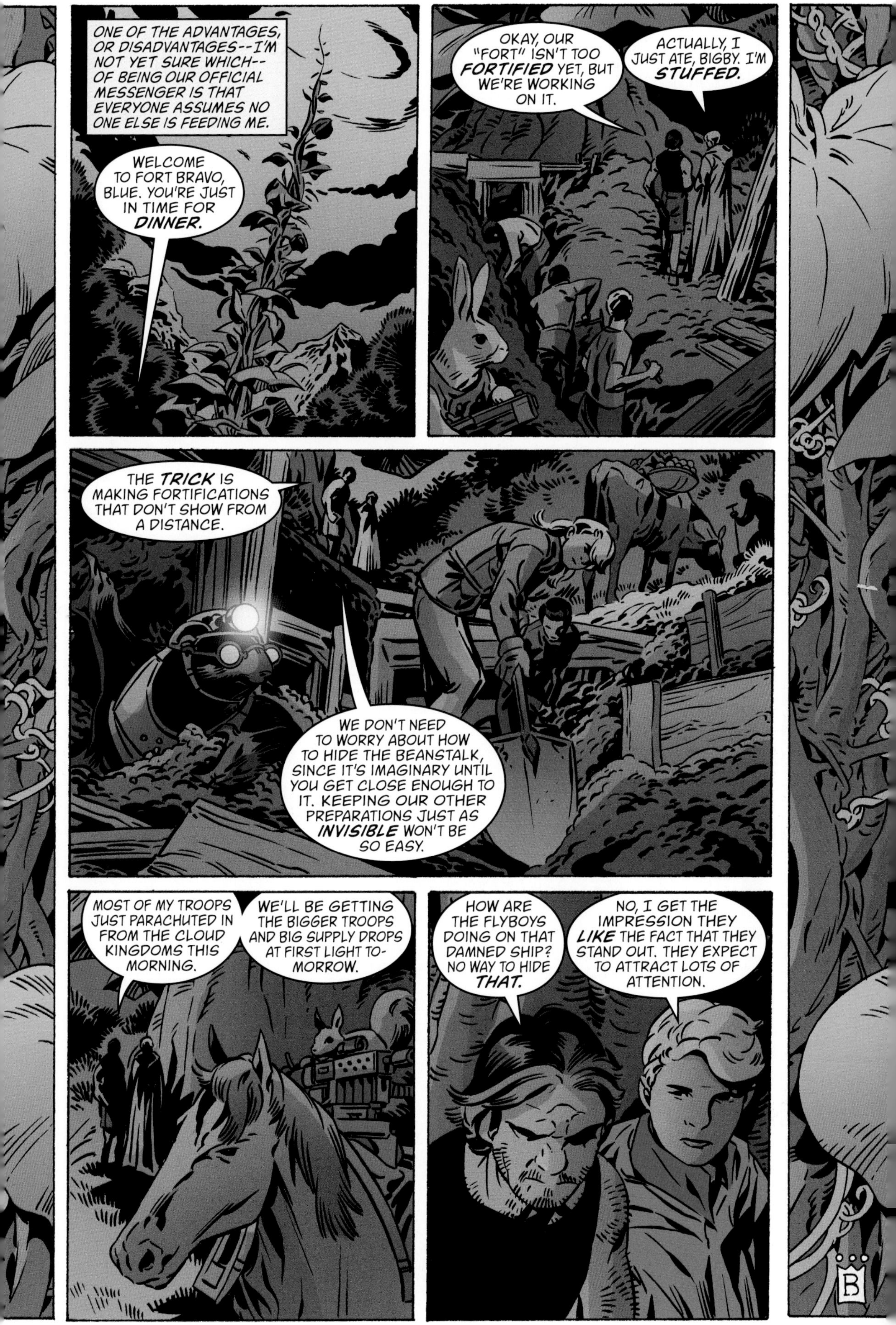
ONE OF THE ADVANTAGES, OR DISADVANTAGES--I'M NOT YET SURE WHICH--OF BEING OUR OFFICIAL MESSENGER IS THAT EVERYONE ASSUMES NO ONE ELSE IS FEEDING ME.
WELCOME TO FORT BRAVO, BLUE. YOU'RE JUST IN TIME FOR DINNER.
OKAY, OUR "FORT" ISN'T TOO FORTIFIED YET, BUT WE'RE WORKING ON IT.
ACTUALLY, I JUST ATE, BIGBY. I'M STUFFED.
THE TRICK IS MAKING FORTIFICATIONS THAT DON'T SHOW FROM A DISTANCE.
WE DON'T NEED TO WORRY ABOUT HOW TO HIDE THE BEANSTALK, SINCE IT'S IMAGINARY UNTIL YOU GET CLOSE ENOUGH TO IT. KEEPING OUR OTHER PREPARATIONS JUST AS INVISIBLE WON'T BE SO EASY.
MOST OF MY TROOPS JUST PARACHUTED IN FROM THE CLOUD KINGDOMS THIS MORNING.
WE'LL BE GETTING THE BIGGER TROOPS AND BIG SUPPLY DROPS AT FIRST LIGHT TO-MORROW.
HOW ARE THE FLYBOYS DOING ON THAT DAMNED SHIP? NO WAY TO HIDE THAT.
NO, I GET THE IMPRESSION THEY LIKE THE FACT THAT THEY STAND OUT. THEY EXPECT TO ATTRACT LOTS OF ATTENTION.

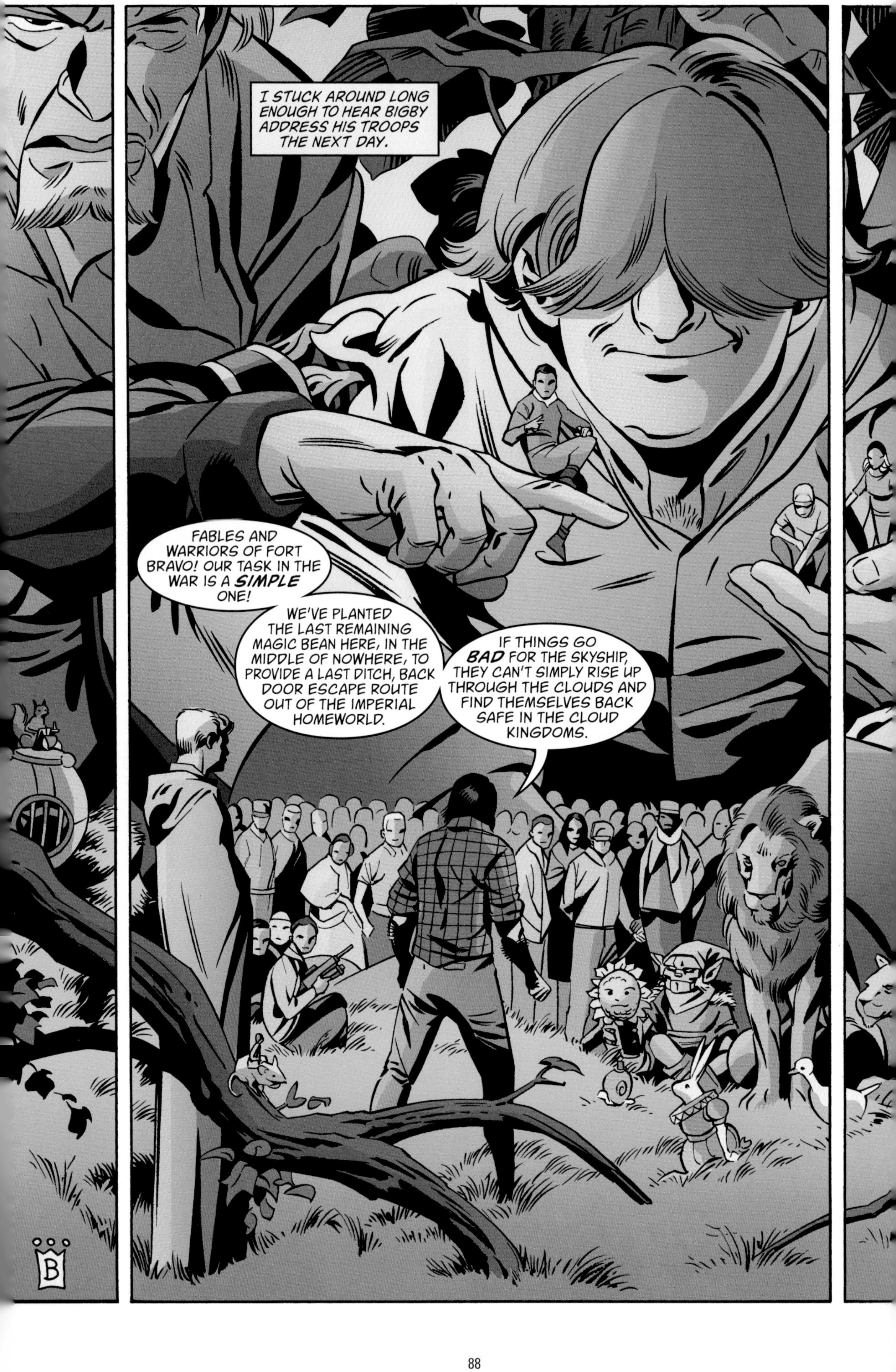
I STUCK AROUND LONG ENOUGH TO HEAR BIGBY ADDRESS HIS TROOPS THE NEXT DAY.
FABLES AND WARRIORS OF FORT BRAVO! OUR TASK IN THE WAR IS A *SIMPLE* ONE!
WE'VE PLANTED THE LAST REMAINING MAGIC BEAN HERE, IN THE MIDDLE OF NOWHERE, TO PROVIDE A LAST DITCH, BACK DOOR ESCAPE ROUTE OUT OF THE IMPERIAL HOMEWORLD.
IF THINGS GO *BAD* FOR THE SKYSHIP, THEY CAN'T SIMPLY RISE UP THROUGH THE CLOUDS AND FIND THEMSELVES BACK SAFE IN THE CLOUD KINGDOMS.

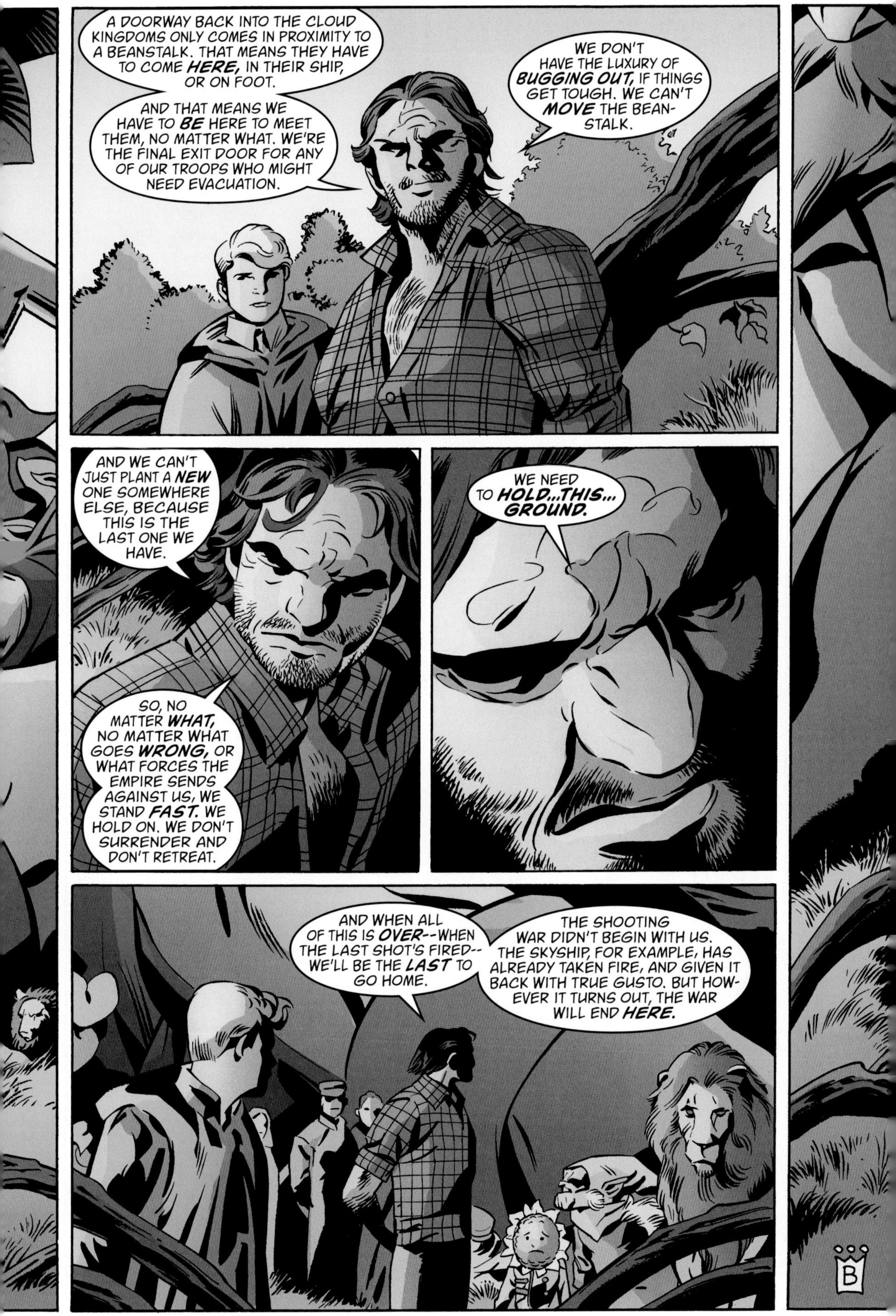
A DOORWAY BACK INTO THE CLOUD KINGDOMS ONLY COMES IN PROXIMITY TO A BEANSTALK. THAT MEANS THEY HAVE TO COME HERE, IN THEIR SHIP, OR ON FOOT.
AND THAT MEANS WE HAVE TO BE HERE TO MEET THEM, NO MATTER WHAT. WE'RE THE FINAL EXIT DOOR FOR ANY OF OUR TROOPS WHO MIGHT NEED EVACUATION.
WE DON'T HAVE THE LUXURY OF BUGGING OUT, IF THINGS GET TOUGH. WE CAN'T MOVE THE BEAN-STALK.
AND WE CAN'T JUST PLANT A NEW ONE SOMEWHERE ELSE, BECAUSE THIS IS THE LAST ONE WE HAVE.
SO, NO MATTER WHAT, NO MATTER WHAT GOES WRONG, OR WHAT FORCES THE EMPIRE SENDS AGAINST US, WE STAND FAST. WE HOLD ON. WE DON'T SURRENDER AND DON'T RETREAT.
WE NEED TO HOLD...THIS... GROUND.
AND WHEN ALL OF THIS IS OVER--WHEN THE LAST SHOT'S FIRED--WE'LL BE THE LAST TO GO HOME.
THE SHOOTING WAR DIDN'T BEGIN WITH US. THE SKYSHIP, FOR EXAMPLE, HAS ALREADY TAKEN FIRE, AND GIVEN IT BACK WITH TRUE GUSTO. BUT HOW-EVER IT TURNS OUT, THE WAR WILL END HERE.
B

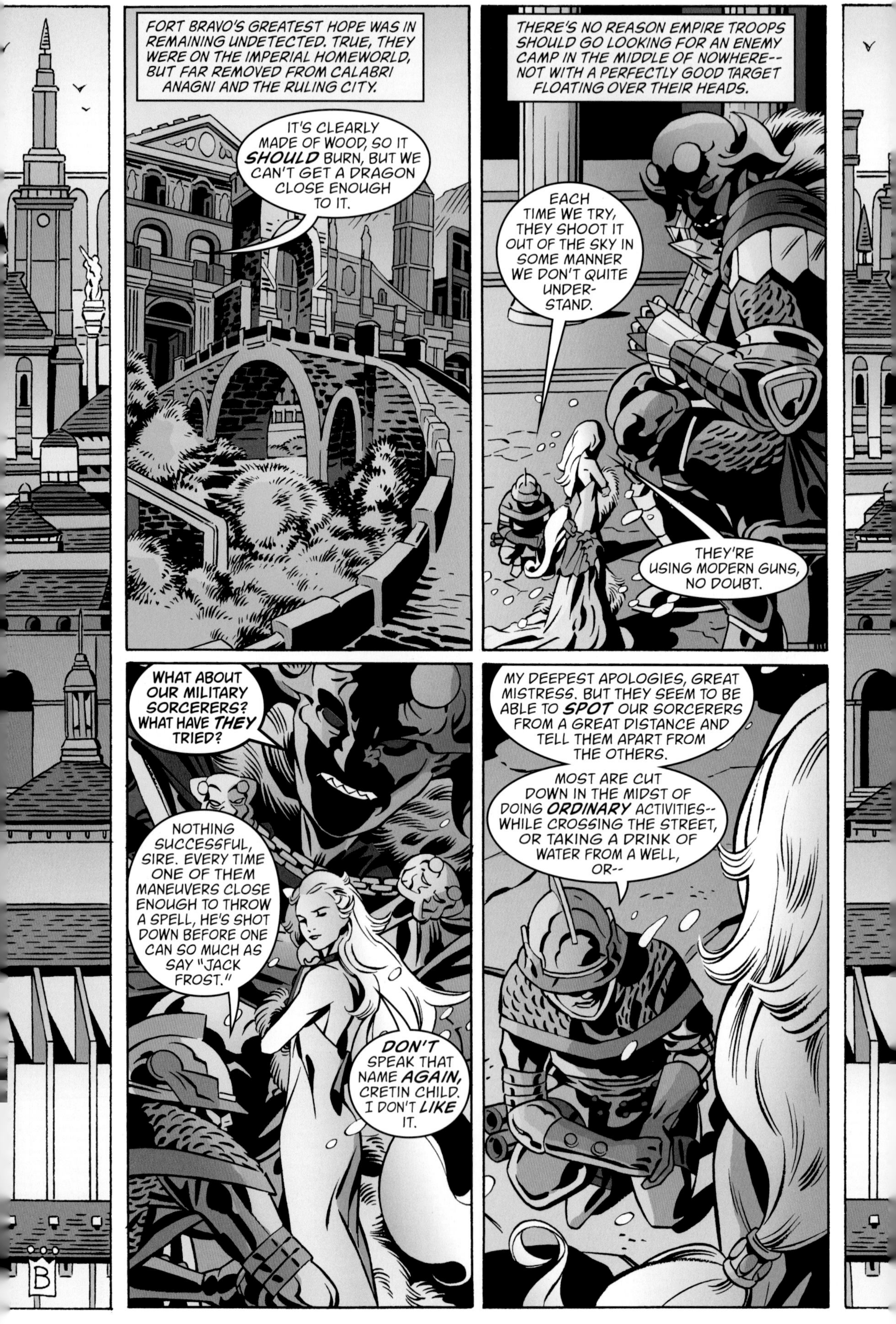
FORT BRAVO'S GREATEST HOPE WAS IN REMAINING UNDETECTED. TRUE, THEY WERE ON THE IMPERIAL HOMEWORLD, BUT FAR REMOVED FROM CALABRI ANAGNI AND THE RULING CITY.
IT'S CLEARLY MADE OF WOOD, SO IT SHOULD BURN, BUT WE CAN'T GET A DRAGON CLOSE ENOUGH TO IT.
THERE'S NO REASON EMPIRE TROOPS SHOULD GO LOOKING FOR AN ENEMY CAMP IN THE MIDDLE OF NOWHERE--NOT WITH A PERFECTLY GOOD TARGET FLOATING OVER THEIR HEADS.
EACH TIME WE TRY, THEY SHOOT IT OUT OF THE SKY IN SOME MANNER WE DON'T QUITE UNDER-STAND.
THEY'RE USING MODERN GUNS, NO DOUBT.
WHAT ABOUT OUR MILITARY SORCERERS? WHAT HAVE THEY TRIED?
NOTHING SUCCESSFUL, SIRE. EVERY TIME ONE OF THEM MANEUVERS CLOSE ENOUGH TO THROW A SPELL, HE'S SHOT DOWN BEFORE ONE CAN SO MUCH AS SAY "JACK FROST."
DON'T SPEAK THAT NAME AGAIN, CRETIN CHILD. I DON'T LIKE IT.
MY DEEPEST APOLOGIES, GREAT MISTRESS. BUT THEY SEEM TO BE ABLE TO SPOT OUR SORCERERS FROM A GREAT DISTANCE AND TELL THEM APART FROM THE OTHERS.
MOST ARE CUT DOWN IN THE MIDST OF DOING ORDINARY ACTIVITIES--WHILE CROSSING THE STREET, OR TAKING A DRINK OF WATER FROM A WELL, OR--
B

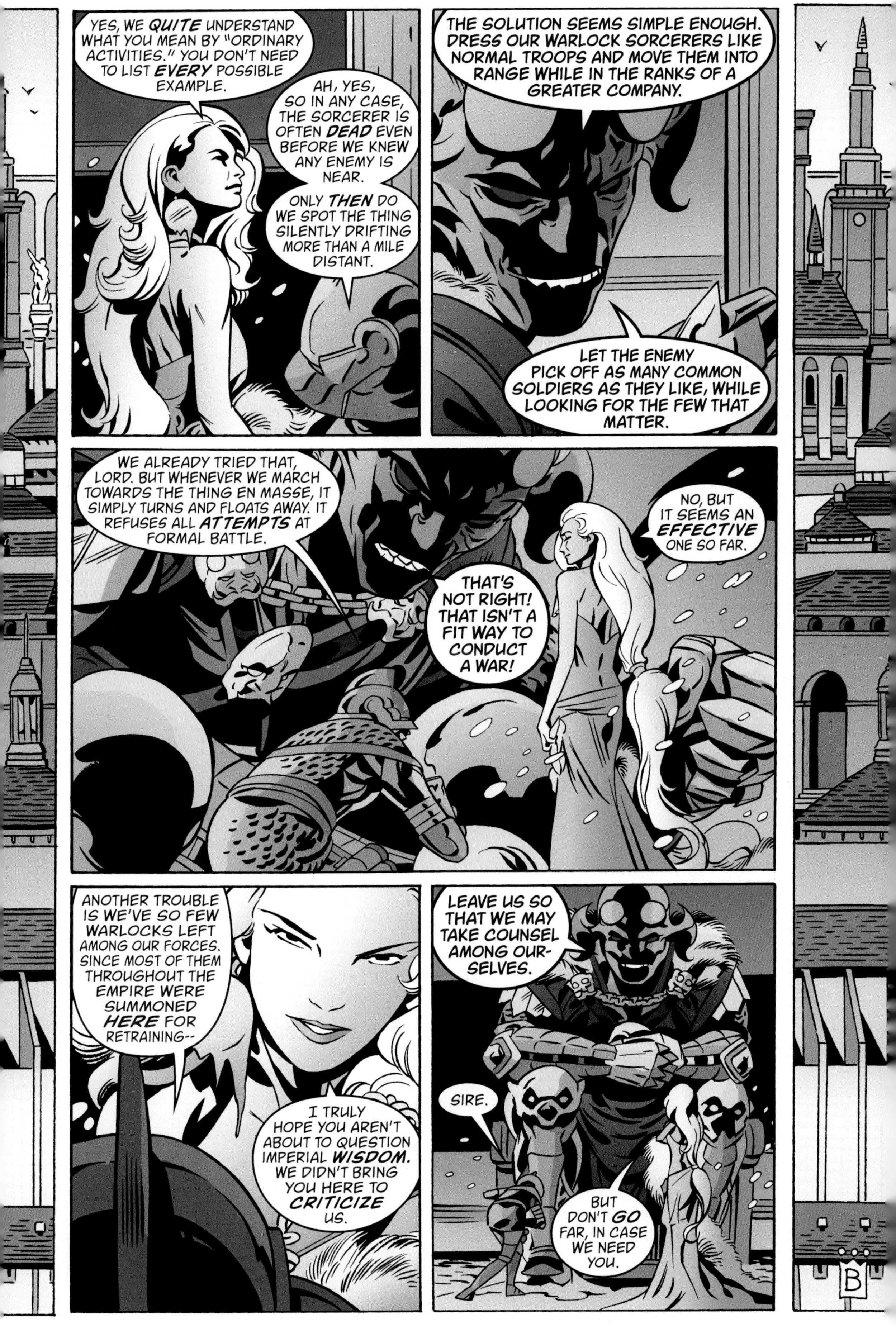
YES, WE QUITE UNDERSTAND WHAT YOU MEAN BY "ORDINARY ACTIVITIES." YOU DON'T NEED TO LIST EVERY POSSIBLE EXAMPLE.
AH, YES, SO IN ANY CASE, THE SORCERER IS OFTEN DEAD EVEN BEFORE WE KNEW ANY ENEMY IS NEAR.
ONLY THEN DO WE SPOT THE THING SILENTLY DRIFTING MORE THAN A MILE DISTANT.
THE SOLUTION SEEMS SIMPLE ENOUGH. DRESS OUR WARLOCK SORCERERS LIKE NORMAL TROOPS AND MOVE THEM INTO RANGE WHILE IN THE RANKS OF A GREATER COMPANY.
LET THE ENEMY PICK OFF AS MANY COMMON SOLDIERS AS THEY LIKE, WHILE LOOKING FOR THE FEW THAT MATTER.
WE ALREADY TRIED THAT, LORD. BUT WHENEVER WE MARCH TOWARDS THE THING EN MASSE, IT SIMPLY TURNS AND FLOATS AWAY. IT REFUSES ALL ATTEMPTS AT FORMAL BATTLE.
THAT'S NOT RIGHT! THAT ISN'T A FIT WAY TO CONDUCT A WAR!
NO, BUT IT SEEMS AN EFFECTIVE ONE SO FAR.
ANOTHER TROUBLE IS WE'VE SO FEW WARLOCKS LEFT AMONG OUR FORCES. SINCE MOST OF THEM THROUGHOUT THE EMPIRE WERE SUMMONED HERE FOR RETRAINING--
I TRULY HOPE YOU AREN'T ABOUT TO QUESTION IMPERIAL WISDOM. WE DIDN'T BRING YOU HERE TO CRITICIZE US.
LEAVE US SO THAT WE MAY TAKE COUNSEL AMONG OUR-SELVES.
SIRE.
BUT DON'T GO FAR, IN CASE WE NEED YOU.

FATHER GEPPETTO SHOULD BE HERE TO HEAR THESE BAD TIDINGS. I'M *TROUBLED* THAT HE IS NOT.

HE'S STILL IN MOURNING OVER THE LOSS OF THE GROVE AND SO MANY OF YOUR SIBLINGS. I'LL TRY TO FETCH HIM AGAIN TOMORROW, OR THE NEXT DAY.

BUT IN THE MEANTIME WE MUST FEND FOR OURSELVES. FOR BETTER OR WORSE, THE EMPIRE'S IN *OUR* HANDS ALONE FOR NOW.

SO WHAT DO WE DO ABOUT THIS UNTOUCHABLE *SHIP* IN THE SKY?

WE BURN IT OUT OF THE SKY, OF COURSE. BUT, INSTEAD OF SENDING ONE DRAGON AT A TIME, WE SEND ALL OF THEM AT *ONCE.*

AND AT THE SAME TIME WE SEND EVERY OTHER CREATURE OR SUBJECT THAT CAN FLY, ALL IN ONE VAST SWARM. IT WILL BE *COSTLY,* BUT--

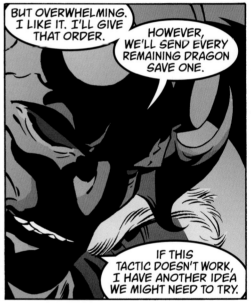

BUT OVERWHELMING. I LIKE IT. I'LL GIVE THAT ORDER.

HOWEVER, WE'LL SEND EVERY REMAINING DRAGON SAVE ONE.

IF THIS TACTIC DOESN'T WORK, I HAVE ANOTHER IDEA WE MIGHT NEED TO TRY.

AS YOU THINK BEST.

YOU SHOULDN'T HAVE TO STAY HERE FOR LONG BEFORE IT'S TIME TO *ACT,* BRIAR ROSE.

I HAVE NO IDEA WHAT SORTS OF THINGS THEY WERE PLOTTING IN OTHER PARTS OF THE IMPERIAL CITY, BUT WE HAD OUR OWN PLOTS AND PLANS GOING ON IN ONE SMALL CORNER OF IT.

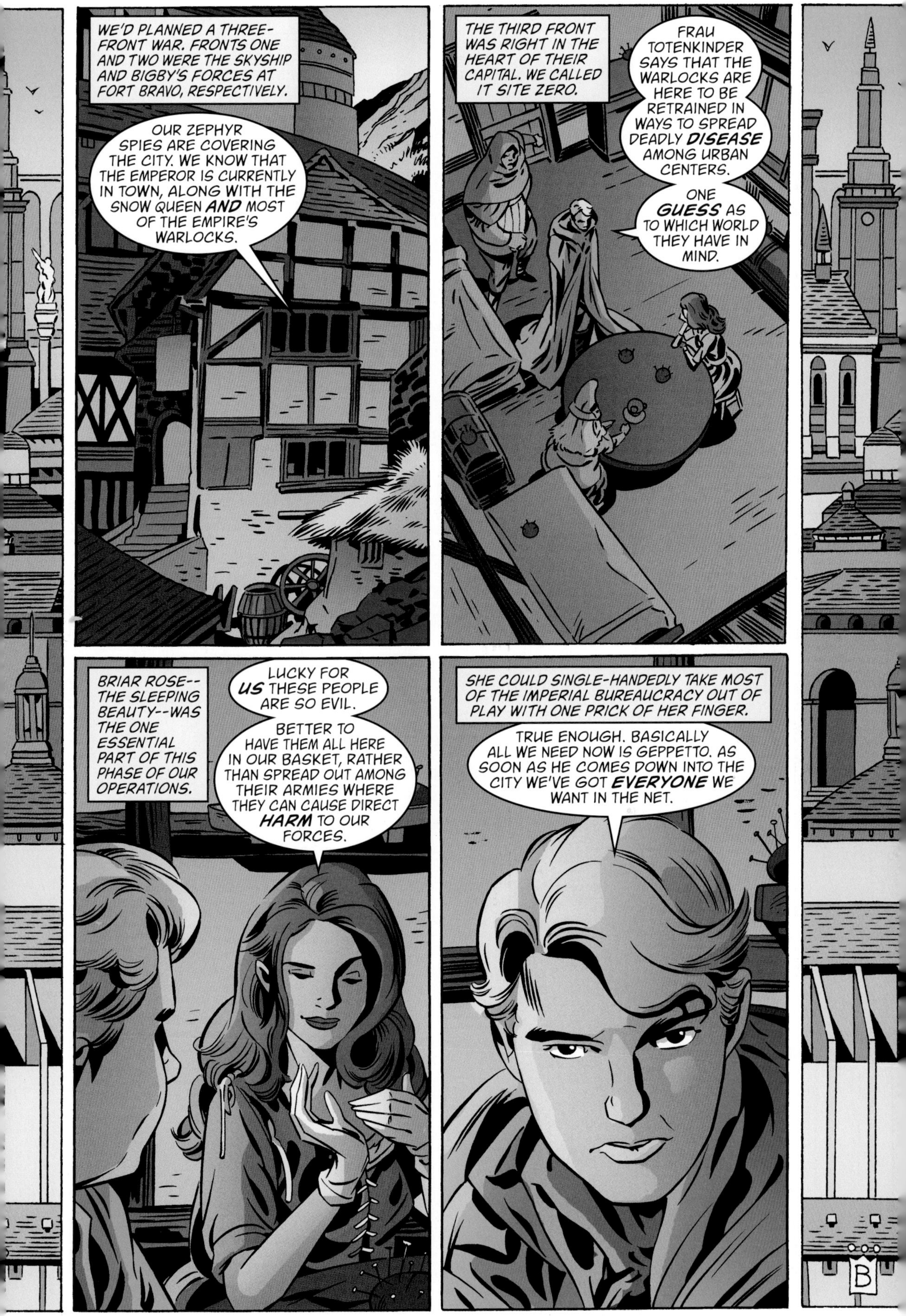

WE'D PLANNED A THREE-FRONT WAR. FRONTS ONE AND TWO WERE THE SKYSHIP AND BIGBY'S FORCES AT FORT BRAVO, RESPECTIVELY.
OUR ZEPHYR SPIES ARE COVERING THE CITY. WE KNOW THAT THE EMPEROR IS CURRENTLY IN TOWN, ALONG WITH THE SNOW QUEEN AND MOST OF THE EMPIRE'S WARLOCKS.
THE THIRD FRONT WAS RIGHT IN THE HEART OF THEIR CAPITAL. WE CALLED IT SITE ZERO.
FRAU TOTENKINDER SAYS THAT THE WARLOCKS ARE HERE TO BE RETRAINED IN WAYS TO SPREAD DEADLY DISEASE AMONG URBAN CENTERS.
ONE GUESS AS TO WHICH WORLD THEY HAVE IN MIND.
BRIAR ROSE--THE SLEEPING BEAUTY--WAS THE ONE ESSENTIAL PART OF THIS PHASE OF OUR OPERATIONS.
LUCKY FOR US THESE PEOPLE ARE SO EVIL.
BETTER TO HAVE THEM ALL HERE IN OUR BASKET, RATHER THAN SPREAD OUT AMONG THEIR ARMIES WHERE THEY CAN CAUSE DIRECT HARM TO OUR FORCES.
SHE COULD SINGLE-HANDEDLY TAKE MOST OF THE IMPERIAL BUREAUCRACY OUT OF PLAY WITH ONE PRICK OF HER FINGER.
TRUE ENOUGH. BASICALLY ALL WE NEED NOW IS GEPPETTO. AS SOON AS HE COMES DOWN INTO THE CITY WE'VE GOT EVERYONE WE WANT IN THE NET.

HAKIM IS HERE TO PROTECT BRIAR ROSE, IN CASE THE BAD GUYS FIND THIS HOVEL.

JUST SIT TIGHT UNTIL THEN. NEVER GO OUTSIDE. NEVER ANSWER THE DOOR. AND DON'T *ACT* UNTIL I GIVE YOU THE OFFICIAL GO-AHEAD.

UNLESS THEY DISCOVER US.

THAT'S RIGHT.

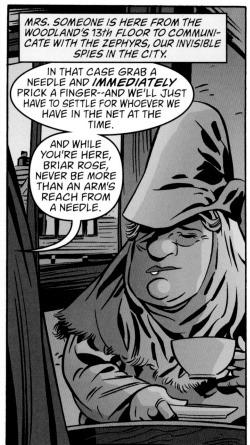

MRS. SOMEONE IS HERE FROM THE WOODLAND'S 13th FLOOR TO COMMUNI- CATE WITH THE ZEPHYRS, OUR INVISIBLE SPIES IN THE CITY.

IN THAT CASE GRAB A NEEDLE AND *IMMEDIATELY* PRICK A FINGER--AND WE'LL JUST HAVE TO SETTLE FOR WHOEVER WE HAVE IN THE NET AT THE TIME.

AND WHILE YOU'RE HERE, BRIAR ROSE, NEVER BE MORE THAN AN ARM'S REACH FROM A NEEDLE.

YES, BLUE, I'VE BEEN *FULLY* BRIEFED. I KNOW WHAT TO DO IF THEY FIND US HERE.

WHEN THAT HAPPENS REST ASSURED THAT I WILL PROVIDE THE *SECONDS* SHE NEEDS TO ACT. *NO ONE* WILL GET PAST ME WHILE I STILL LIVE.

FAIR ENOUGH, HAKIM. I'M OFF, THEN. ANYTHING YOU WANT ME TO BRING ON MY NEXT VISIT?

MORE BLANKETS. IT GETS COOL AT NIGHT HERE.

MORE MINT TEA.

MORE HAPPYTIME INDIVIDUALLY WRAPPED SNACK CAKES WITH THE *CHOCOLATE* CREAM FILLING.

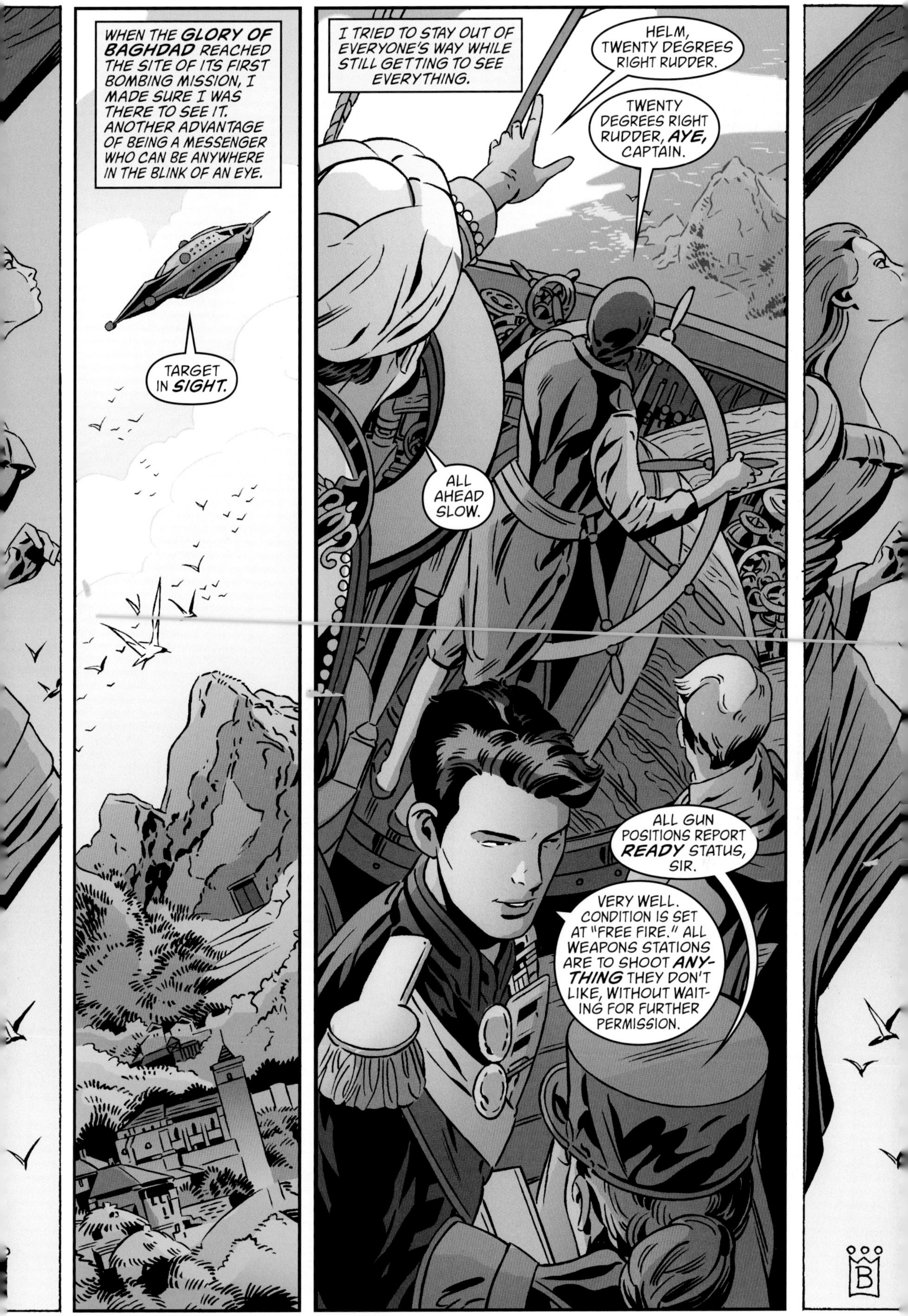
WHEN THE GLORY OF BAGHDAD REACHED THE SITE OF ITS FIRST BOMBING MISSION, I MADE SURE I WAS THERE TO SEE IT. ANOTHER ADVANTAGE OF BEING A MESSENGER WHO CAN BE ANYWHERE IN THE BLINK OF AN EYE.
TARGET IN SIGHT.
I TRIED TO STAY OUT OF EVERYONE'S WAY WHILE STILL GETTING TO SEE EVERYTHING.
HELM, TWENTY DEGREES RIGHT RUDDER.
TWENTY DEGREES RIGHT RUDDER, AYE, CAPTAIN.
ALL AHEAD SLOW.
ALL GUN POSITIONS REPORT READY STATUS, SIR.
VERY WELL. CONDITION IS SET AT "FREE FIRE." ALL WEAPONS STATIONS ARE TO SHOOT ANYTHING THEY DON'T LIKE, WITHOUT WAITING FOR FURTHER PERMISSION.

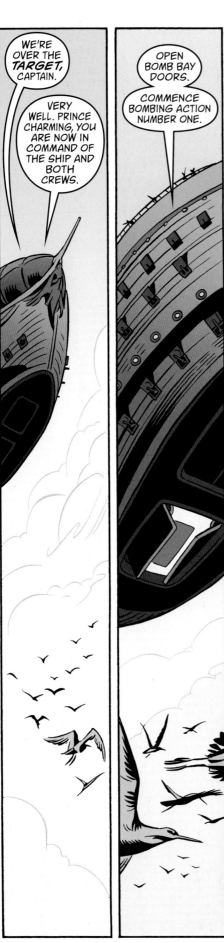

WE'RE OVER THE *TARGET,* CAPTAIN.

VERY WELL. PRINCE CHARMING, YOU ARE NOW IN COMMAND OF THE SHIP AND BOTH CREWS.

OPEN BOMB BAY DOORS.

COMMENCE BOMBING ACTION NUMBER ONE.

IN THE LONG RUN WE WEREN' ABLE TO PURCHASE OUR OW MASSIVE BUNKER-BUSTER BOMBS ON THE BLACK MARKE OR ANY OTHER MARKET. WE HAD TO BUILD OUR OWN.

BOMB IS AWAY!

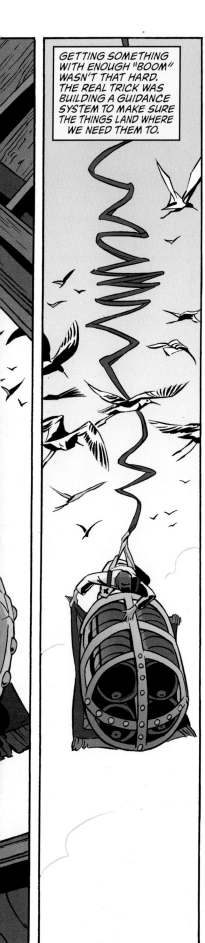

GETTING SOMETHING WITH ENOUGH "BOOM" WASN'T THAT HARD. THE REAL TRICK WAS BUILDING A GUIDANCE SYSTEM TO MAKE SURE THE THINGS LAND WHERE WE NEED THEM TO.

EVENTUALLY WE SETTLED ON WHAT WE ALREADY KNEW. WE DECIDED TO STEER THE BOMBS DOWN ONTO THE TARGET USING FLYING CARPETS AND A SINGLE VERY SCARED PILOT.

WE TESTED THE PROCESS FOR WEEKS IN THE ARABIAN DESERT.

IT WORKED. THE CARPETS WERE ABLE TO STEER THE FALLING BOMBS JUST ENOUGH TO MAKE SURE THEY FELL PRETTY MUCH WHERE WE WANTED THEM TO.

GO, YOU MOTHERLESS WHORE!

GO!

GRANTED, OUR METHOD OF RECOVERING THE PILOT ALIVE WAS A BIT PRIMITIVE--AND DECIDEDLY **NOT** COMFORTABLE--BUT IT WORKED, TOO.

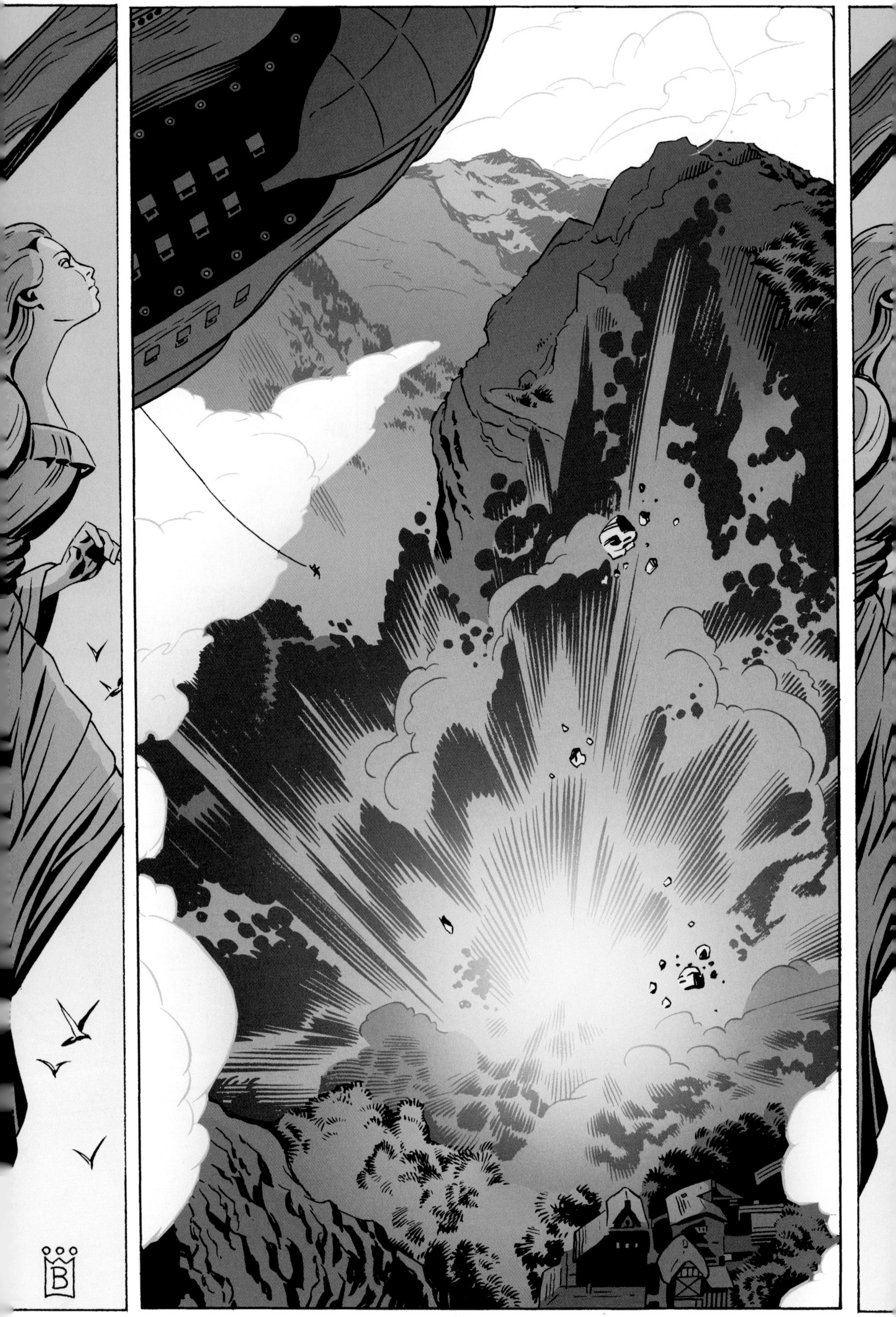

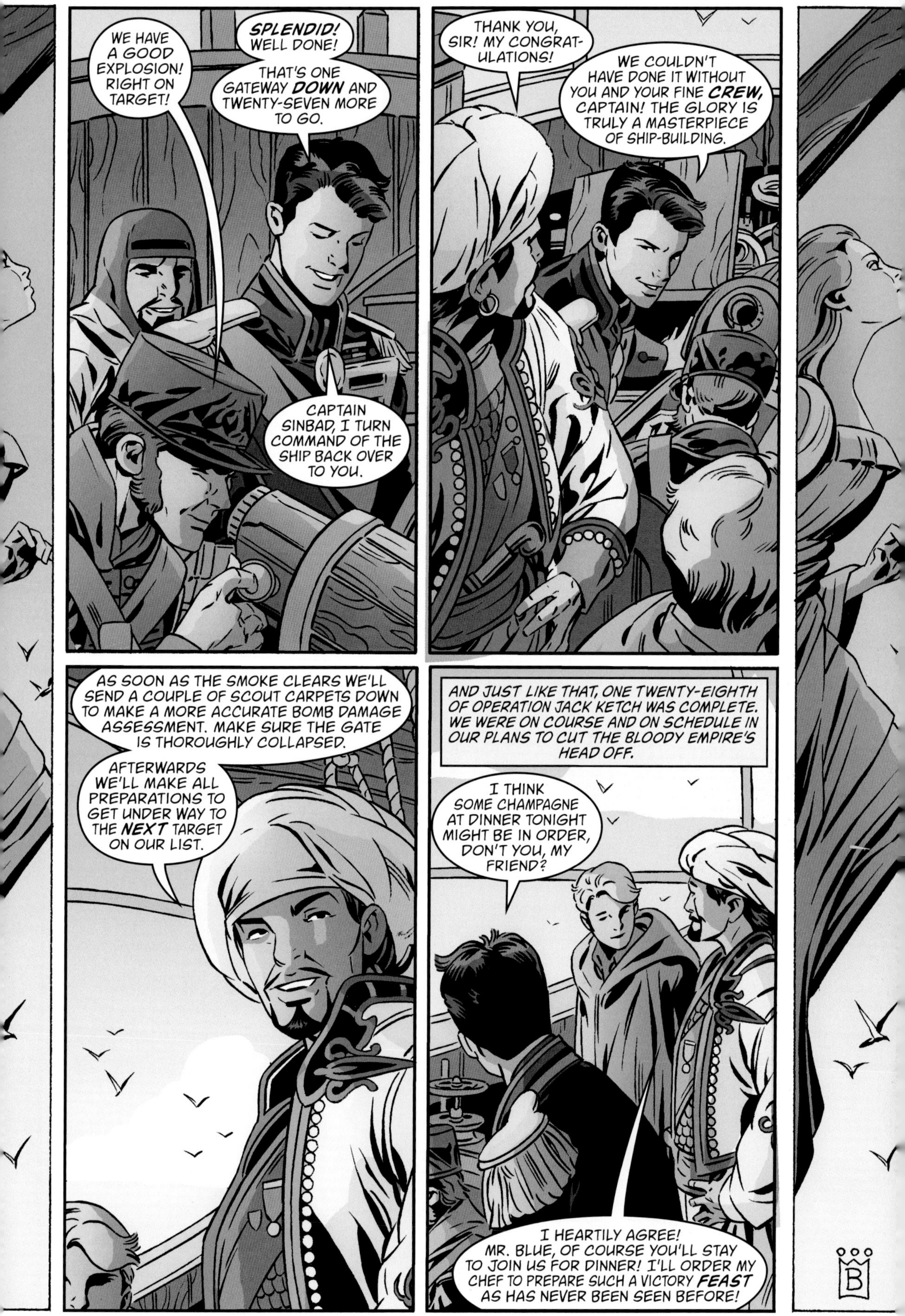
WE HAVE A GOOD EXPLOSION! RIGHT ON TARGET!
SPLENDID! WELL DONE!
THAT'S ONE GATEWAY DOWN AND TWENTY-SEVEN MORE TO GO.
CAPTAIN SINBAD, I TURN COMMAND OF THE SHIP BACK OVER TO YOU.
THANK YOU, SIR! MY CONGRAT-ULATIONS!
WE COULDN'T HAVE DONE IT WITHOUT YOU AND YOUR FINE CREW, CAPTAIN! THE GLORY IS TRULY A MASTERPIECE OF SHIP-BUILDING.
AS SOON AS THE SMOKE CLEARS WE'LL SEND A COUPLE OF SCOUT CARPETS DOWN TO MAKE A MORE ACCURATE BOMB DAMAGE ASSESSMENT. MAKE SURE THE GATE IS THOROUGHLY COLLAPSED.
AFTERWARDS WE'LL MAKE ALL PREPARATIONS TO GET UNDER WAY TO THE NEXT TARGET ON OUR LIST.
AND JUST LIKE THAT, ONE TWENTY-EIGHTH OF OPERATION JACK KETCH WAS COMPLETE. WE WERE ON COURSE AND ON SCHEDULE IN OUR PLANS TO CUT THE BLOODY EMPIRE'S HEAD OFF.
I THINK SOME CHAMPAGNE AT DINNER TONIGHT MIGHT BE IN ORDER, DON'T YOU, MY FRIEND?
I HEARTILY AGREE! MR. BLUE, OF COURSE YOU'LL STAY TO JOIN US FOR DINNER! I'LL ORDER MY CHEF TO PREPARE SUCH A VICTORY FEAST AS HAS NEVER BEEN SEEN BEFORE!

AT LEAST ONCE A DAY MY TELEPORTATION ROTATION TAKES ME BACK TO FABLETOWN.

HOW'S IT GOING OUT THERE, BLUE? HOW ARE WE DOING?

THE STATED REASON IS TO DROP OFF MESSAGES AND PICK UP BOTH RETURN DISPATCHES AND SUPPLIES FOR OUR TROOPS IN THE FIELD.

NOT BAD. SITE BRAVO REMAINS UNDISCOVERED BY THE ENEMY, AND THE GLORY HAS COMPLETED ITS *THIRD* BOMBING MISSION.

BUT THE REAL REASON IS TO MAKE SURE FABLETOWN HASN'T BEEN INVADED. YOU CAN'T TELL FROM OUT ON THE STREET, BUT WE'VE TURNED THE NEIGHBORHOOD INTO AN ARMED FORTRESS.

CASUALTIES?

NONE TO SPEAK OF SO FAR, BEAST. PRIVATE CEDARHEART SHOT HIMSELF IN THE ARM WHILE CLEANING HIS RIFLE, BUT NO ENEMY-INFLICTED CASUALTIES.

CEDARHEART? I SEEM TO RECALL WHEN HE CAME THROUGH HERE. WAS IT MERE *CLUMSINESS* OR WAS HE TRYING FOR A COWARD'S DISCHARGE?

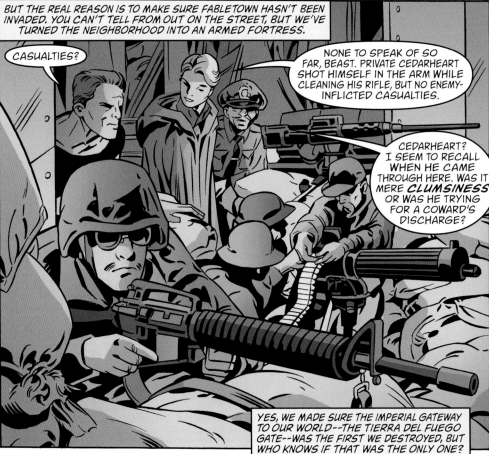

YES, WE MADE SURE THE IMPERIAL GATEWAY TO OUR WORLD--THE TIERRA DEL FUEGO GATE--WAS THE FIRST WE DESTROYED, BUT WHO KNOWS IF THAT WAS THE ONLY ONE?

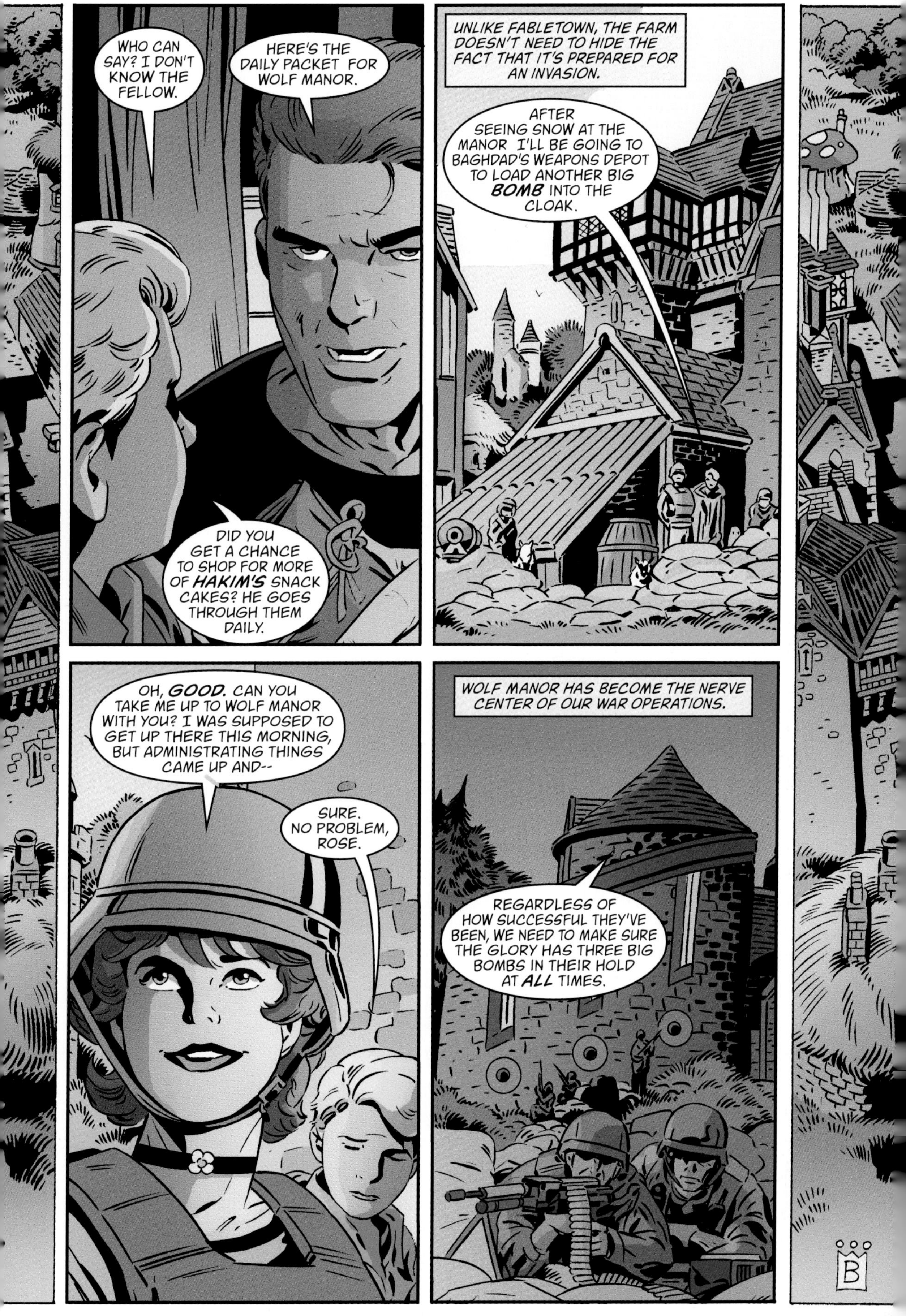
WHO CAN SAY? I DON'T KNOW THE FELLOW.
HERE'S THE DAILY PACKET FOR WOLF MANOR.
DID YOU GET A CHANCE TO SHOP FOR MORE OF HAKIM'S SNACK CAKES? HE GOES THROUGH THEM DAILY.
UNLIKE FABLETOWN, THE FARM DOESN'T NEED TO HIDE THE FACT THAT IT'S PREPARED FOR AN INVASION.
AFTER SEEING SNOW AT THE MANOR I'LL BE GOING TO BAGHDAD'S WEAPONS DEPOT TO LOAD ANOTHER BIG BOMB INTO THE CLOAK.
OH, GOOD. CAN YOU TAKE ME UP TO WOLF MANOR WITH YOU? I WAS SUPPOSED TO GET UP THERE THIS MORNING, BUT ADMINISTRATING THINGS CAME UP AND--
SURE. NO PROBLEM, ROSE.
WOLF MANOR HAS BECOME THE NERVE CENTER OF OUR WAR OPERATIONS.
REGARDLESS OF HOW SUCCESSFUL THEY'VE BEEN, WE NEED TO MAKE SURE THE GLORY HAS THREE BIG BOMBS IN THEIR HOLD AT ALL TIMES.

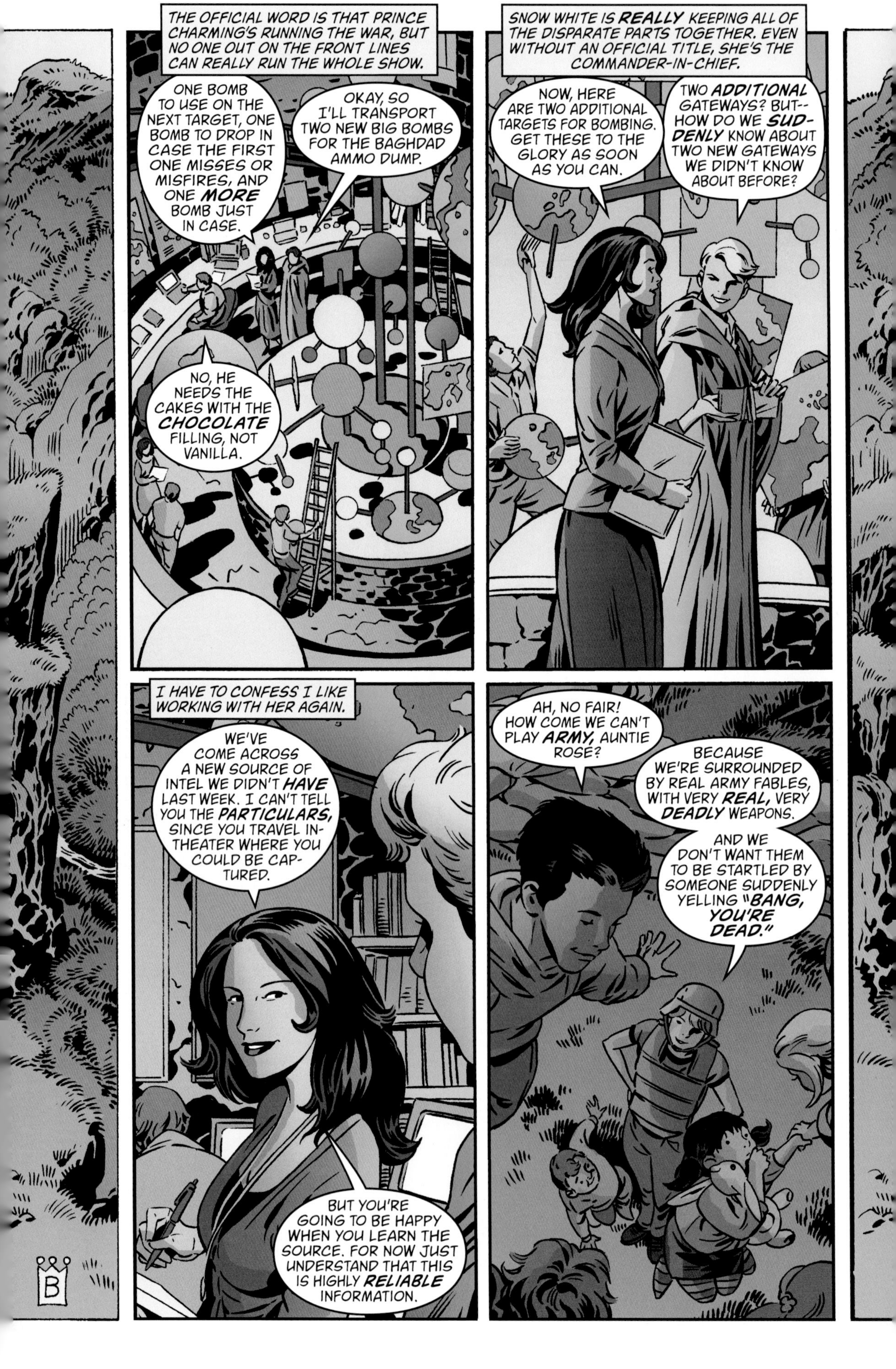
THE OFFICIAL WORD IS THAT PRINCE CHARMING'S RUNNING THE WAR, BUT NO ONE OUT ON THE FRONT LINES CAN REALLY RUN THE WHOLE SHOW.
ONE BOMB TO USE ON THE NEXT TARGET, ONE BOMB TO DROP IN CASE THE FIRST ONE MISSES OR MISFIRES, AND ONE MORE BOMB JUST IN CASE.
OKAY, SO I'LL TRANSPORT TWO NEW BIG BOMBS FOR THE BAGHDAD AMMO DUMP.
NO, HE NEEDS THE CAKES WITH THE CHOCOLATE FILLING, NOT VANILLA.
SNOW WHITE IS REALLY KEEPING ALL OF THE DISPARATE PARTS TOGETHER. EVEN WITHOUT AN OFFICIAL TITLE, SHE'S THE COMMANDER-IN-CHIEF.
NOW, HERE ARE TWO ADDITIONAL TARGETS FOR BOMBING. GET THESE TO THE GLORY AS SOON AS YOU CAN.
TWO ADDITIONAL GATEWAYS? BUT--HOW DO WE SUDDENLY KNOW ABOUT TWO NEW GATEWAYS WE DIDN'T KNOW ABOUT BEFORE?
I HAVE TO CONFESS I LIKE WORKING WITH HER AGAIN.
WE'VE COME ACROSS A NEW SOURCE OF INTEL WE DIDN'T HAVE LAST WEEK. I CAN'T TELL YOU THE PARTICULARS, SINCE YOU TRAVEL IN-THEATER WHERE YOU COULD BE CAPTURED.
BUT YOU'RE GOING TO BE HAPPY WHEN YOU LEARN THE SOURCE. FOR NOW JUST UNDERSTAND THAT THIS IS HIGHLY RELIABLE INFORMATION.
AH, NO FAIR! HOW COME WE CAN'T PLAY ARMY, AUNTIE ROSE?
BECAUSE WE'RE SURROUNDED BY REAL ARMY FABLES, WITH VERY REAL, VERY DEADLY WEAPONS.
AND WE DON'T WANT THEM TO BE STARTLED BY SOMEONE SUDDENLY YELLING "BANG, YOU'RE DEAD."

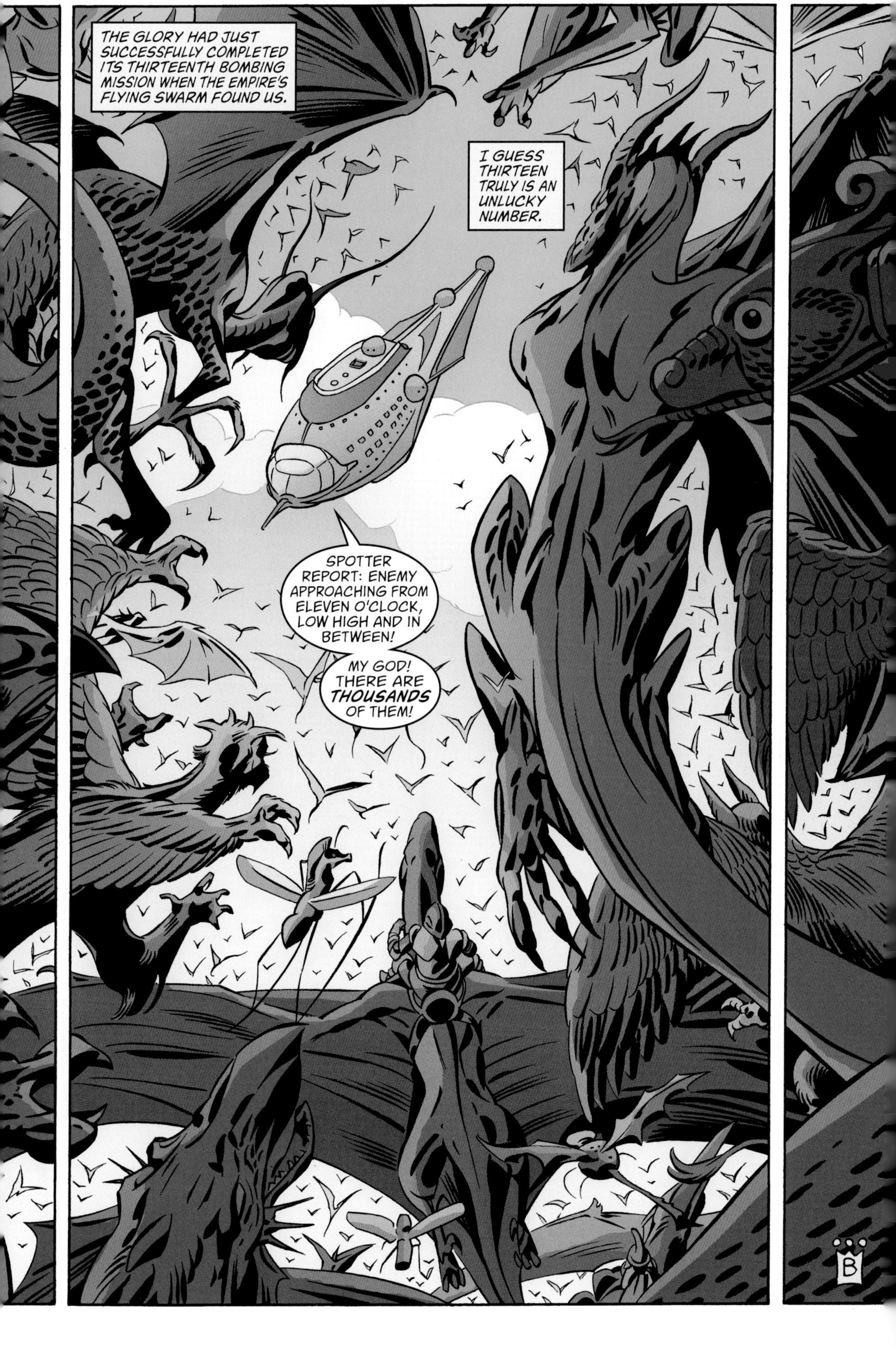

THE GLORY HAD JUST SUCCESSFULLY COMPLETED ITS THIRTEENTH BOMBING MISSION WHEN THE EMPIRE'S FLYING SWARM FOUND US.
I GUESS THIRTEEN TRULY IS AN UNLUCKY NUMBER.
SPOTTER REPORT: ENEMY APPROACHING FROM ELEVEN O'CLOCK, LOW HIGH AND IN BETWEEN!
MY GOD! THERE ARE THOUSANDS OF THEM!

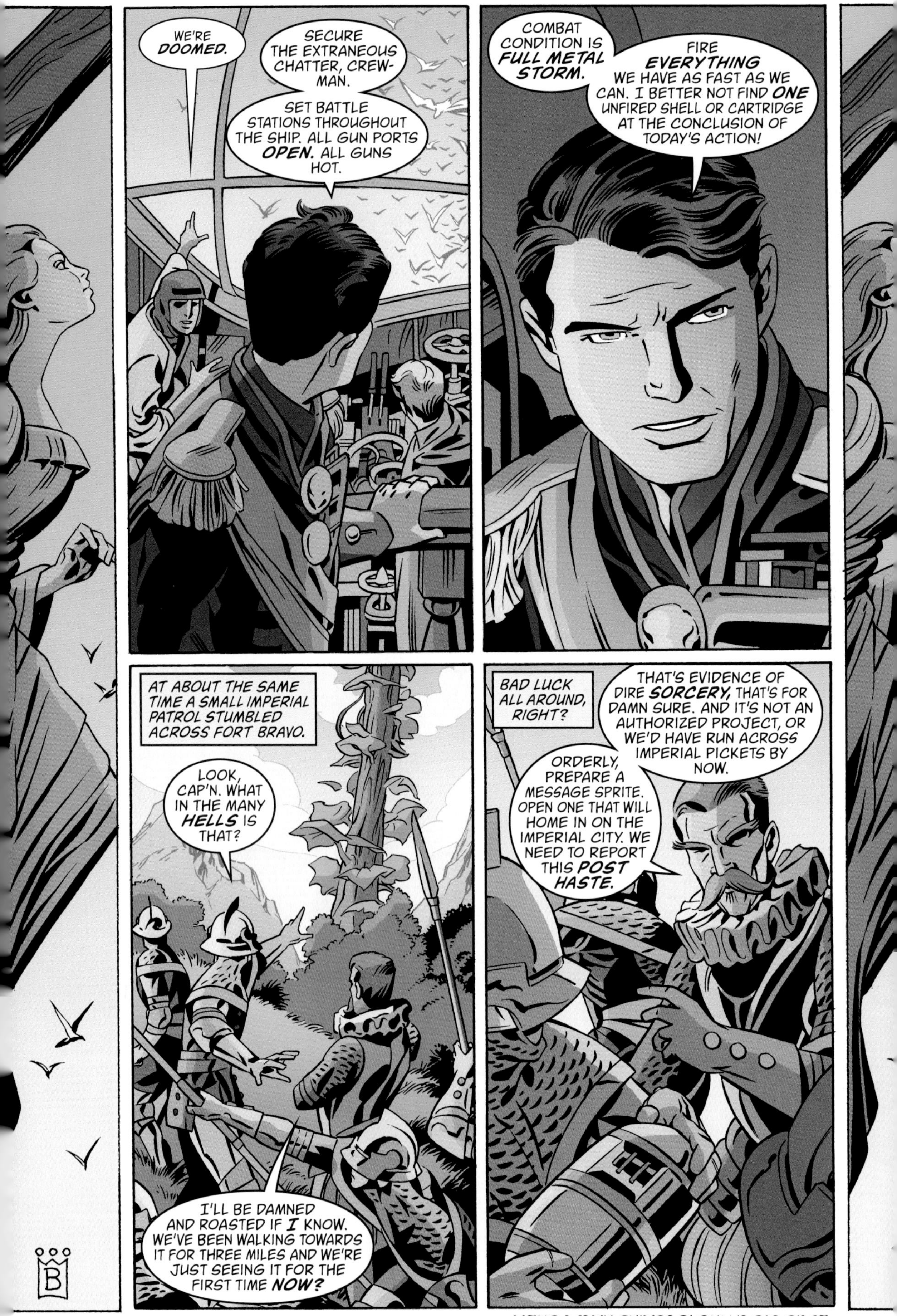
WE'RE DOOMED.
SECURE THE EXTRANEOUS CHATTER, CREW-MAN.
SET BATTLE STATIONS THROUGHOUT THE SHIP. ALL GUN PORTS OPEN. ALL GUNS HOT.
COMBAT CONDITION IS FULL METAL STORM.
FIRE EVERYTHING WE HAVE AS FAST AS WE CAN. I BETTER NOT FIND ONE UNFIRED SHELL OR CARTRIDGE AT THE CONCLUSION OF TODAY'S ACTION!
AT ABOUT THE SAME TIME A SMALL IMPERIAL PATROL STUMBLED ACROSS FORT BRAVO.
LOOK, CAP'N. WHAT IN THE MANY HELLS IS THAT?
I'LL BE DAMNED AND ROASTED IF I KNOW. WE'VE BEEN WALKING TOWARDS IT FOR THREE MILES AND WE'RE JUST SEEING IT FOR THE FIRST TIME NOW?
BAD LUCK ALL AROUND, RIGHT?
THAT'S EVIDENCE OF DIRE SORCERY, THAT'S FOR DAMN SURE. AND IT'S NOT AN AUTHORIZED PROJECT, OR WE'D HAVE RUN ACROSS IMPERIAL PICKETS BY NOW.
ORDERLY, PREPARE A MESSAGE SPRITE. OPEN ONE THAT WILL HOME IN ON THE IMPERIAL CITY. WE NEED TO REPORT THIS POST HASTE.
NEXT: MANY THINGS BLOW UP BIG TIME.

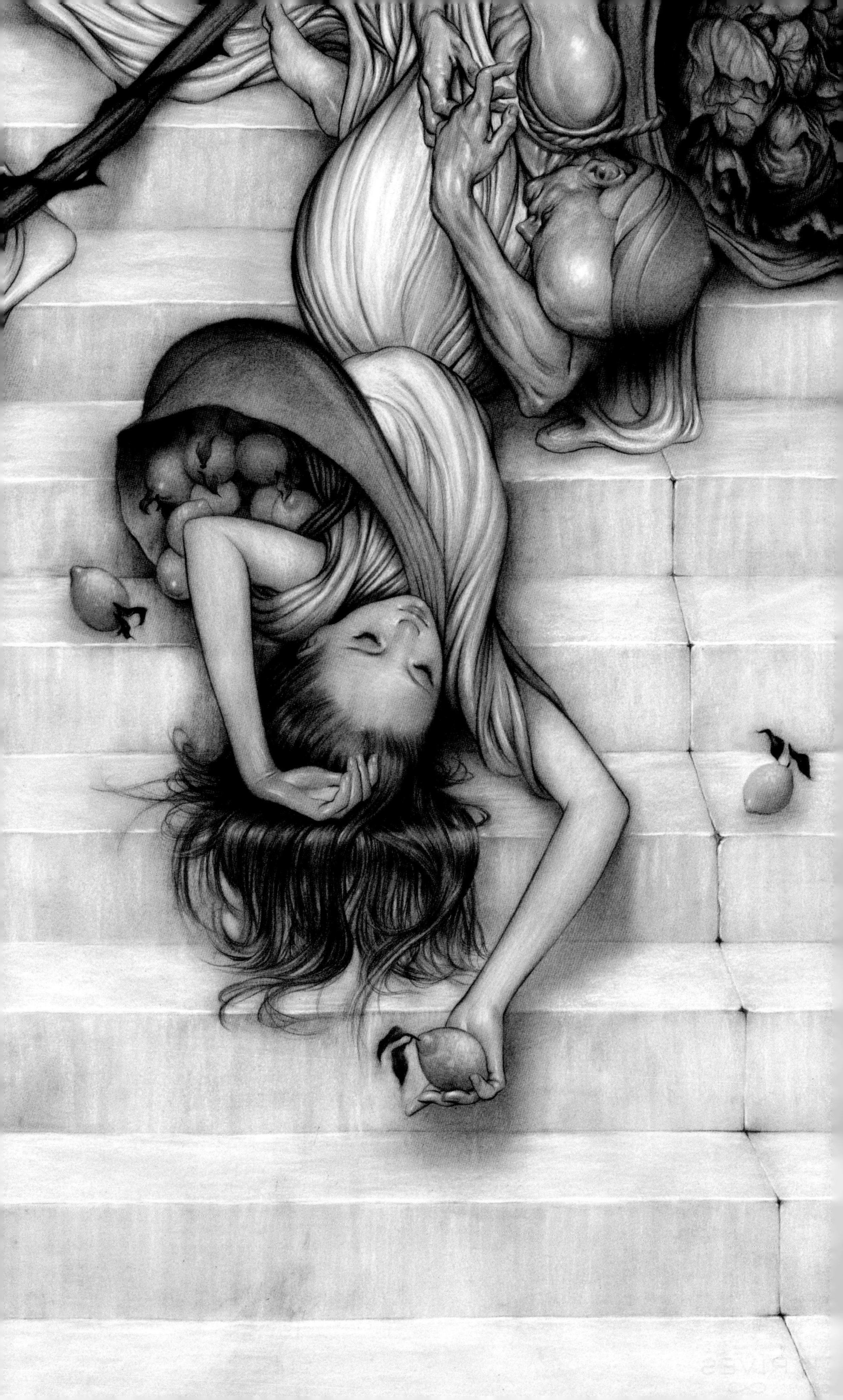

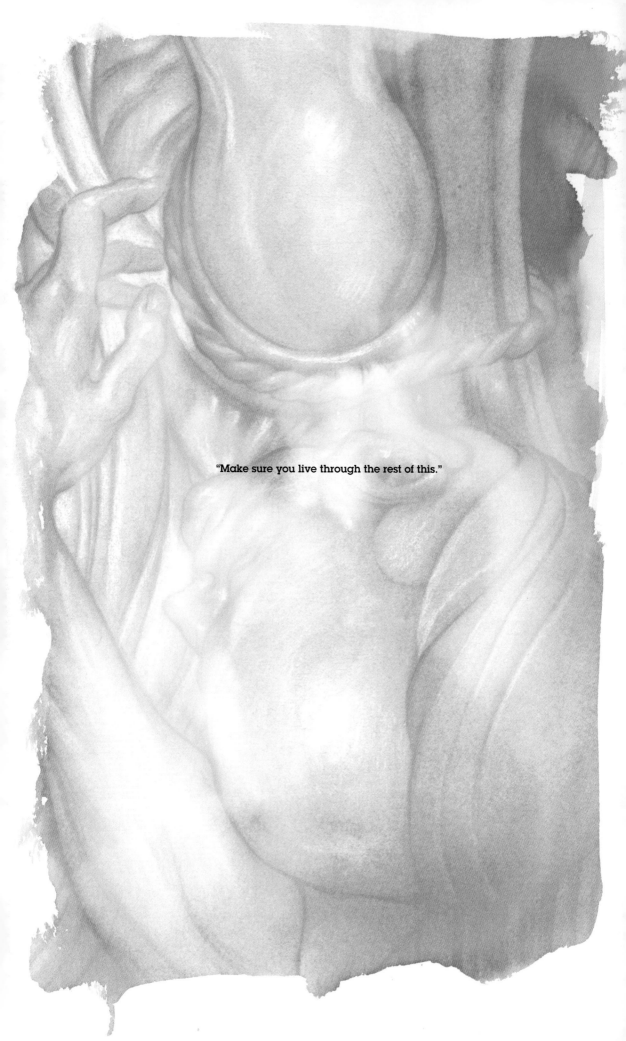

"Make sure you live through the rest of this."

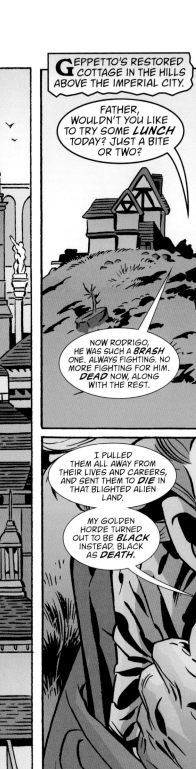

GEPPETTO'S RESTORED COTTAGE IN THE HILLS ABOVE THE IMPERIAL CITY.

FATHER, WOULDN'T YOU LIKE TO TRY SOME *LUNCH* TODAY? JUST A BITE OR TWO?

NOW RODRIGO, HE WAS SUCH A *BRASH* ONE. ALWAYS FIGHTING. NO MORE FIGHTING FOR HIM. *DEAD* NOW, ALONG WITH THE REST.

AND REMEMBER ANTONIO OCTAVIUS? HE DIDN'T LIKE THE MILITARY SO MUCH, BUT HE SERVED IN ORDER TO ADVANCE IN THE *GOVERNMENT*. SCHOLARLY BOY, HE WAS.

ALWAYS HAD HIS NOSE IN A *BOOK*. ROSE UP ALL THE WAY TO LIEUTENANT GOVERNOR OF THE SEVENTH MILITARY DISTRICT OF...

WAS IT KARSE OR KURREWYN? I FORGET. ONE OF THE *K* WORLDS ANYWAY.

GONE NOW, ALONG WITH THE OTHERS.

PLEASE, FATHER. TRY JUST ONE *SIP*.

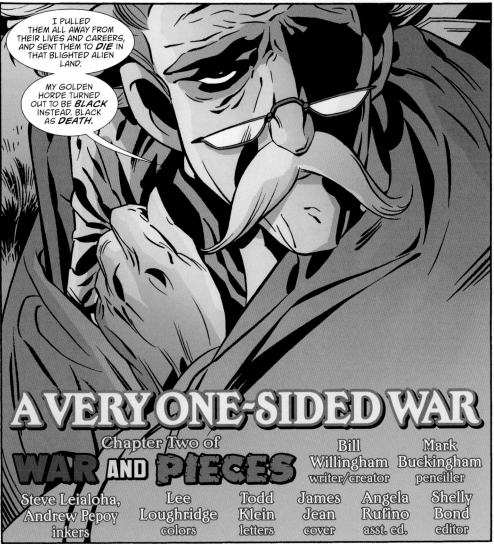

I PULLED THEM ALL AWAY FROM THEIR LIVES AND CAREERS, AND SENT THEM TO *DIE* IN THAT BLIGHTED ALIEN LAND.

MY GOLDEN HORDE TURNED OUT TO BE *BLACK* INSTEAD. BLACK AS *DEATH*.

A VERY ONE-SIDED WAR
Chapter Two of
WAR AND PIECES

Bill Willingham
writer/creator

Mark Buckingham
penciller

Steve Leialoha, Andrew Pepoy
inkers

Lee Loughridge
colors

Todd Klein
letters

James Jean
cover

Angela Rufino
asst. ed.

Shelly Bond
editor

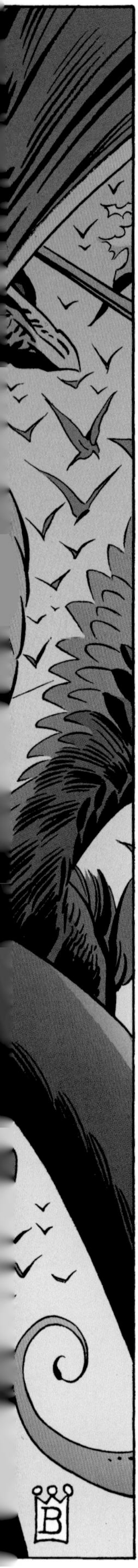
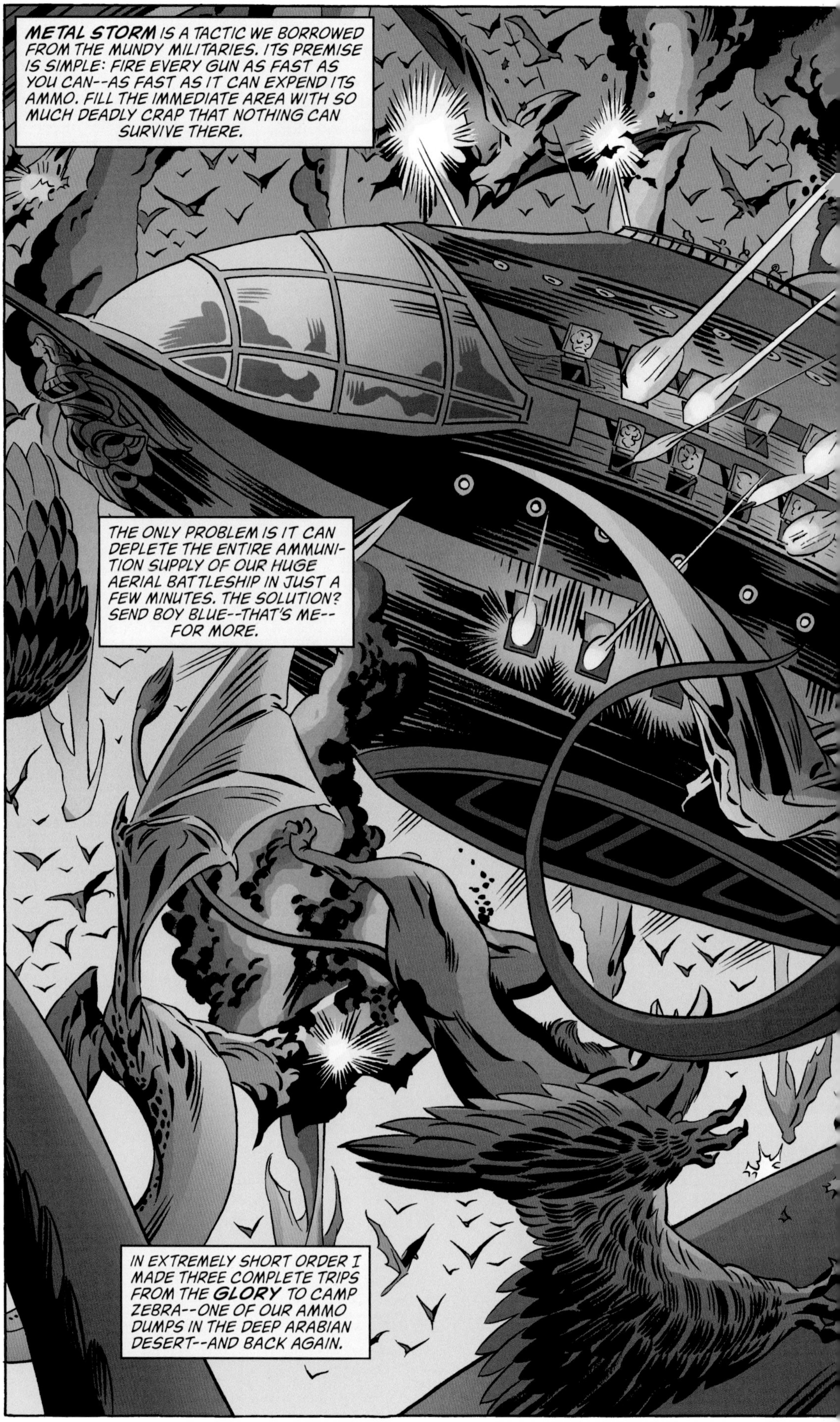
METAL STORM IS A TACTIC WE BORROWED FROM THE MUNDY MILITARIES. ITS PREMISE IS SIMPLE: FIRE EVERY GUN AS FAST AS YOU CAN--AS FAST AS IT CAN EXPEND ITS AMMO. FILL THE IMMEDIATE AREA WITH SO MUCH DEADLY CRAP THAT NOTHING CAN SURVIVE THERE.
THE ONLY PROBLEM IS IT CAN DEPLETE THE ENTIRE AMMUNITION SUPPLY OF OUR HUGE AERIAL BATTLESHIP IN JUST A FEW MINUTES. THE SOLUTION? SEND BOY BLUE--THAT'S ME--FOR MORE.
IN EXTREMELY SHORT ORDER I MADE THREE COMPLETE TRIPS FROM THE GLORY TO CAMP ZEBRA--ONE OF OUR AMMO DUMPS IN THE DEEP ARABIAN DESERT--AND BACK AGAIN.

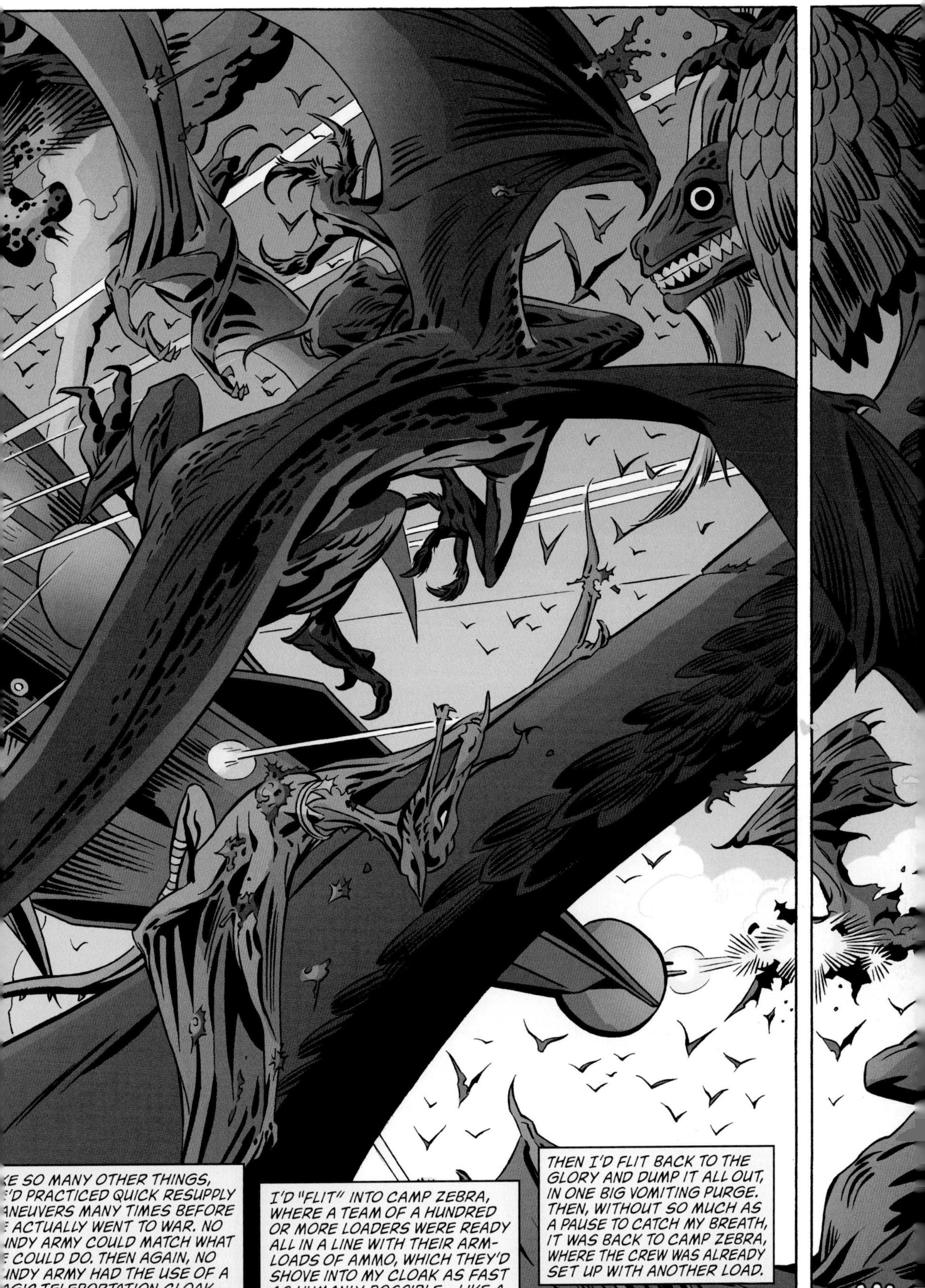
KE SO MANY OTHER THINGS, 'D PRACTICED QUICK RESUPPLY ANEUVERS MANY TIMES BEFORE E ACTUALLY WENT TO WAR. NO UNDY ARMY COULD MATCH WHAT E COULD DO. THEN AGAIN, NO UNDY ARMY HAD THE USE OF A AGIC TELEPORTATION CLOAK.
I'D "FLIT" INTO CAMP ZEBRA, WHERE A TEAM OF A HUNDRED OR MORE LOADERS WERE READY ALL IN A LINE WITH THEIR ARM-LOADS OF AMMO, WHICH THEY'D SHOVE INTO MY CLOAK AS FAST AS HUMANLY POSSIBLE--LIKE A WELL-TRAINED RACING PIT CREW.
THEN I'D FLIT BACK TO THE GLORY AND DUMP IT ALL OUT, IN ONE BIG VOMITING PURGE. THEN, WITHOUT SO MUCH AS A PAUSE TO CATCH MY BREATH, IT WAS BACK TO CAMP ZEBRA, WHERE THE CREW WAS ALREADY SET UP WITH ANOTHER LOAD.
REPEAT AS NECESSARY.

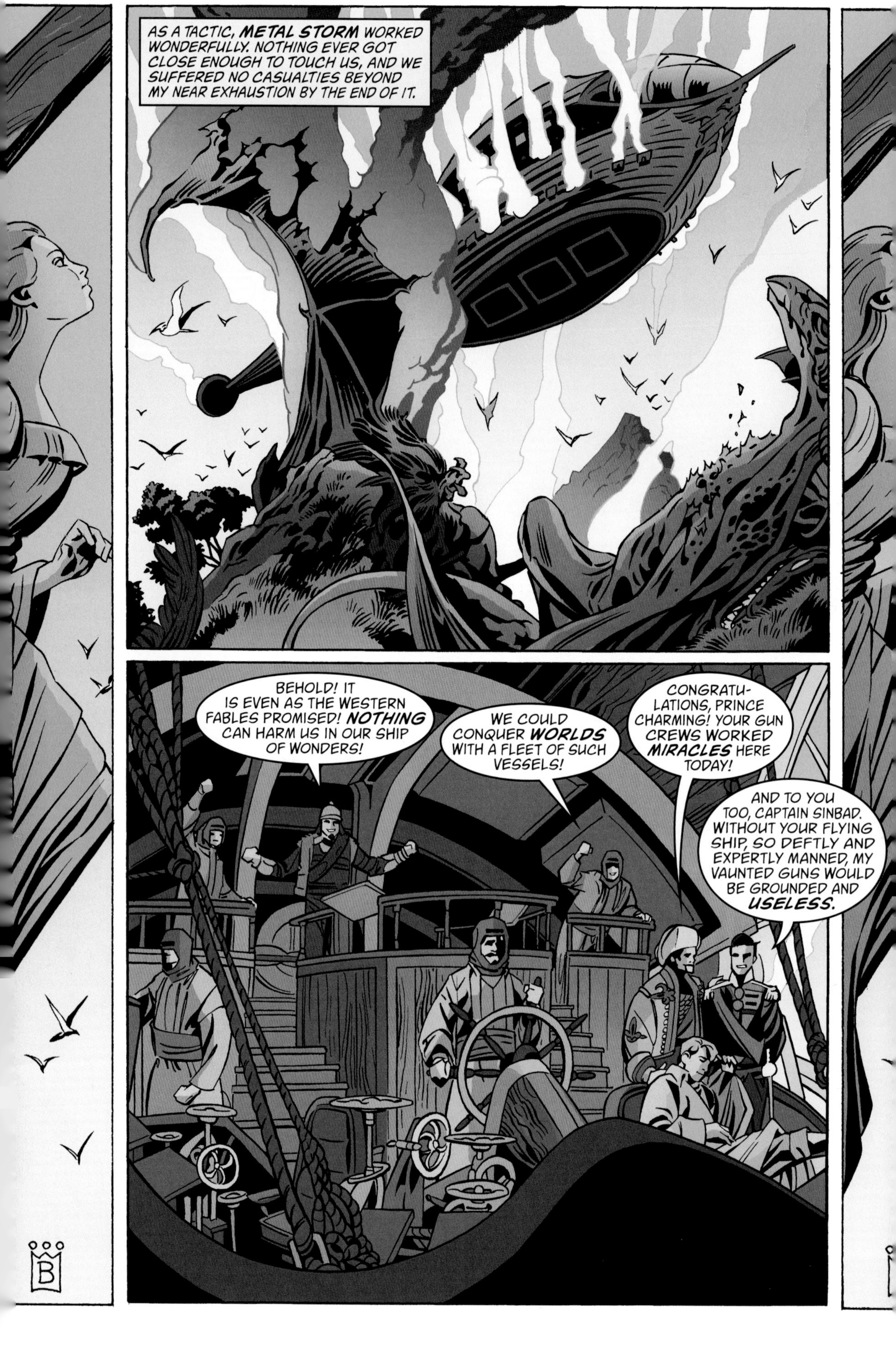
AS A TACTIC, **METAL STORM** WORKED WONDERFULLY. NOTHING EVER GOT CLOSE ENOUGH TO TOUCH US, AND WE SUFFERED NO CASUALTIES BEYOND MY NEAR EXHAUSTION BY THE END OF IT.
BEHOLD! IT IS EVEN AS THE WESTERN FABLES PROMISED! ***NOTHING*** CAN HARM US IN OUR SHIP OF WONDERS!
WE COULD CONQUER ***WORLDS*** WITH A FLEET OF SUCH VESSELS!
CONGRATULATIONS, PRINCE CHARMING! YOUR GUN CREWS WORKED ***MIRACLES*** HERE TODAY!
AND TO YOU TOO, CAPTAIN SINBAD. WITHOUT YOUR FLYING SHIP, SO DEFTLY AND EXPERTLY MANNED, MY VAUNTED GUNS WOULD BE GROUNDED AND ***USELESS***.

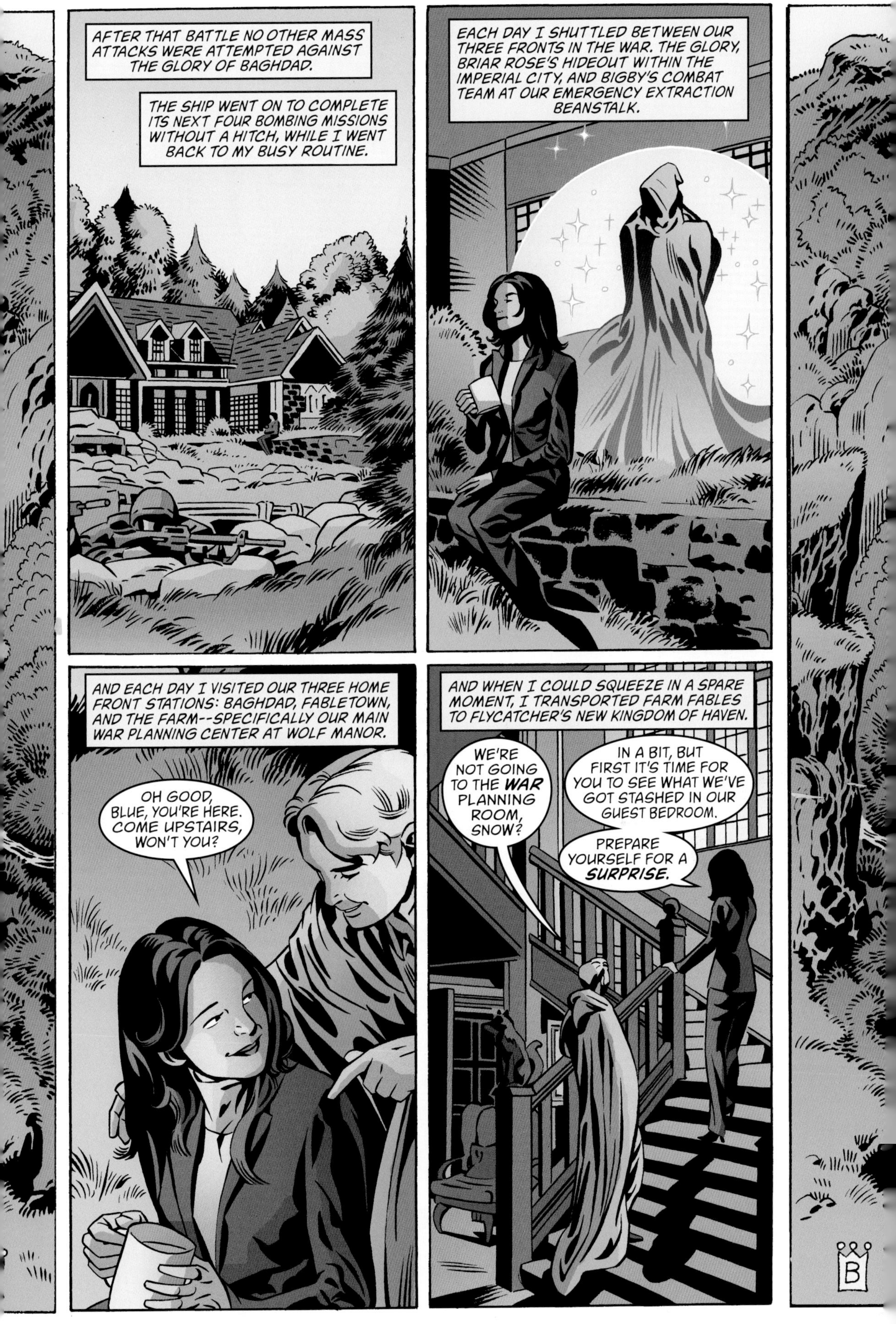
AFTER THAT BATTLE NO OTHER MASS ATTACKS WERE ATTEMPTED AGAINST THE GLORY OF BAGHDAD.
THE SHIP WENT ON TO COMPLETE ITS NEXT FOUR BOMBING MISSIONS WITHOUT A HITCH, WHILE I WENT BACK TO MY BUSY ROUTINE.
EACH DAY I SHUTTLED BETWEEN OUR THREE FRONTS IN THE WAR. THE GLORY, BRIAR ROSE'S HIDEOUT WITHIN THE IMPERIAL CITY, AND BIGBY'S COMBAT TEAM AT OUR EMERGENCY EXTRACTION BEANSTALK.
AND EACH DAY I VISITED OUR THREE HOME FRONT STATIONS: BAGHDAD, FABLETOWN, AND THE FARM--SPECIFICALLY OUR MAIN WAR PLANNING CENTER AT WOLF MANOR.
OH GOOD, BLUE, YOU'RE HERE. COME UPSTAIRS, WON'T YOU?
AND WHEN I COULD SQUEEZE IN A SPARE MOMENT, I TRANSPORTED FARM FABLES TO FLYCATCHER'S NEW KINGDOM OF HAVEN.
WE'RE NOT GOING TO THE **WAR** PLANNING ROOM, SNOW?
IN A BIT, BUT FIRST IT'S TIME FOR YOU TO SEE WHAT WE'VE GOT STASHED IN OUR GUEST BEDROOM.
PREPARE YOURSELF FOR A **SURPRISE**.

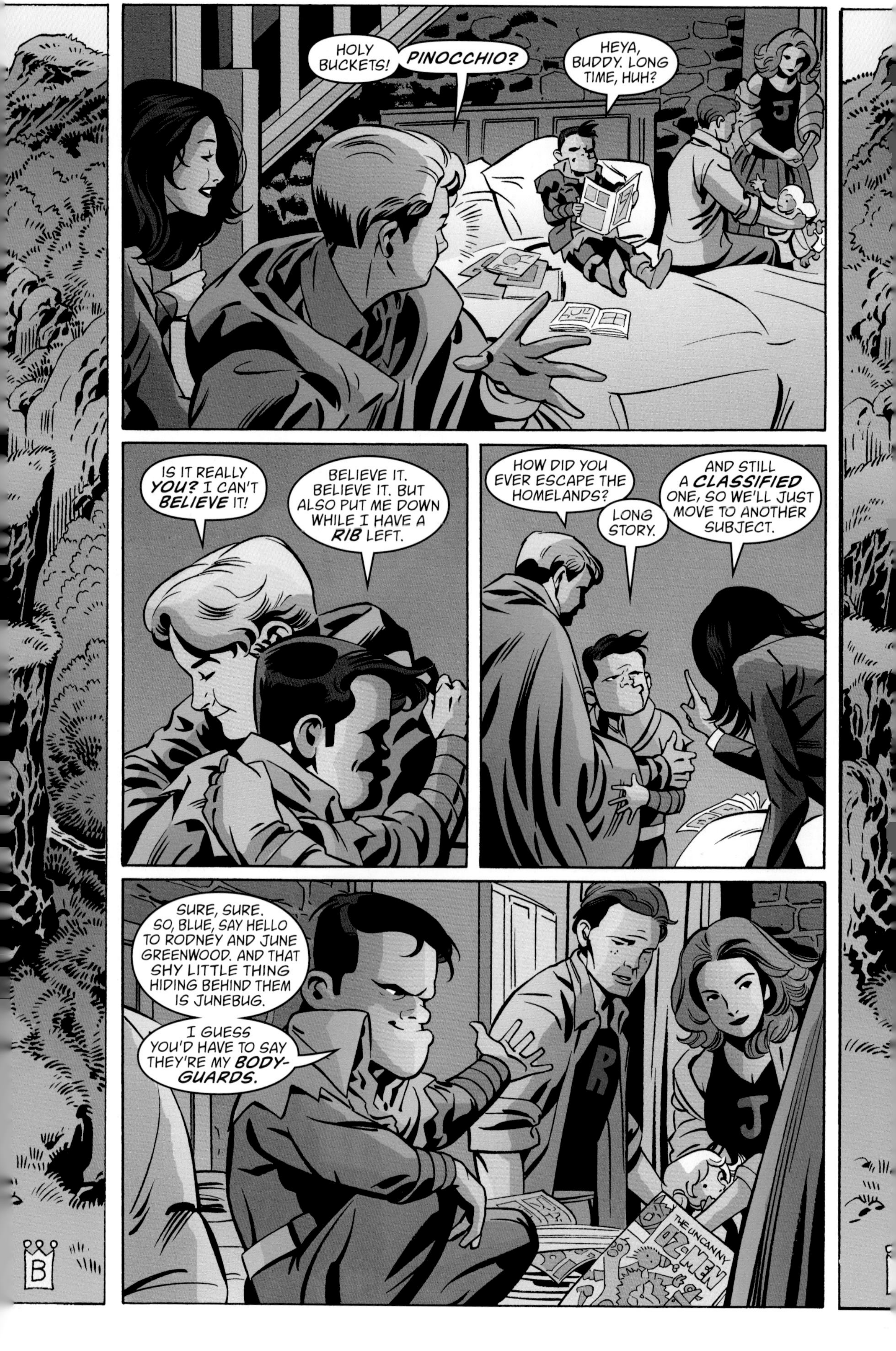
HOLY BUCKETS! PINOCCHIO?
HEYA, BUDDY. LONG TIME, HUH?
IS IT REALLY YOU? I CAN'T BELIEVE IT!
BELIEVE IT. BELIEVE IT. BUT ALSO PUT ME DOWN WHILE I HAVE A RIB LEFT.
HOW DID YOU EVER ESCAPE THE HOMELANDS?
LONG STORY.
AND STILL A CLASSIFIED ONE, SO WE'LL JUST MOVE TO ANOTHER SUBJECT.
SURE, SURE. SO, BLUE, SAY HELLO TO RODNEY AND JUNE GREENWOOD. AND THAT SHY LITTLE THING HIDING BEHIND THEM IS JUNEBUG.
I GUESS YOU'D HAVE TO SAY THEY'RE MY BODY-GUARDS.
THE UNCANNY OZ MEN

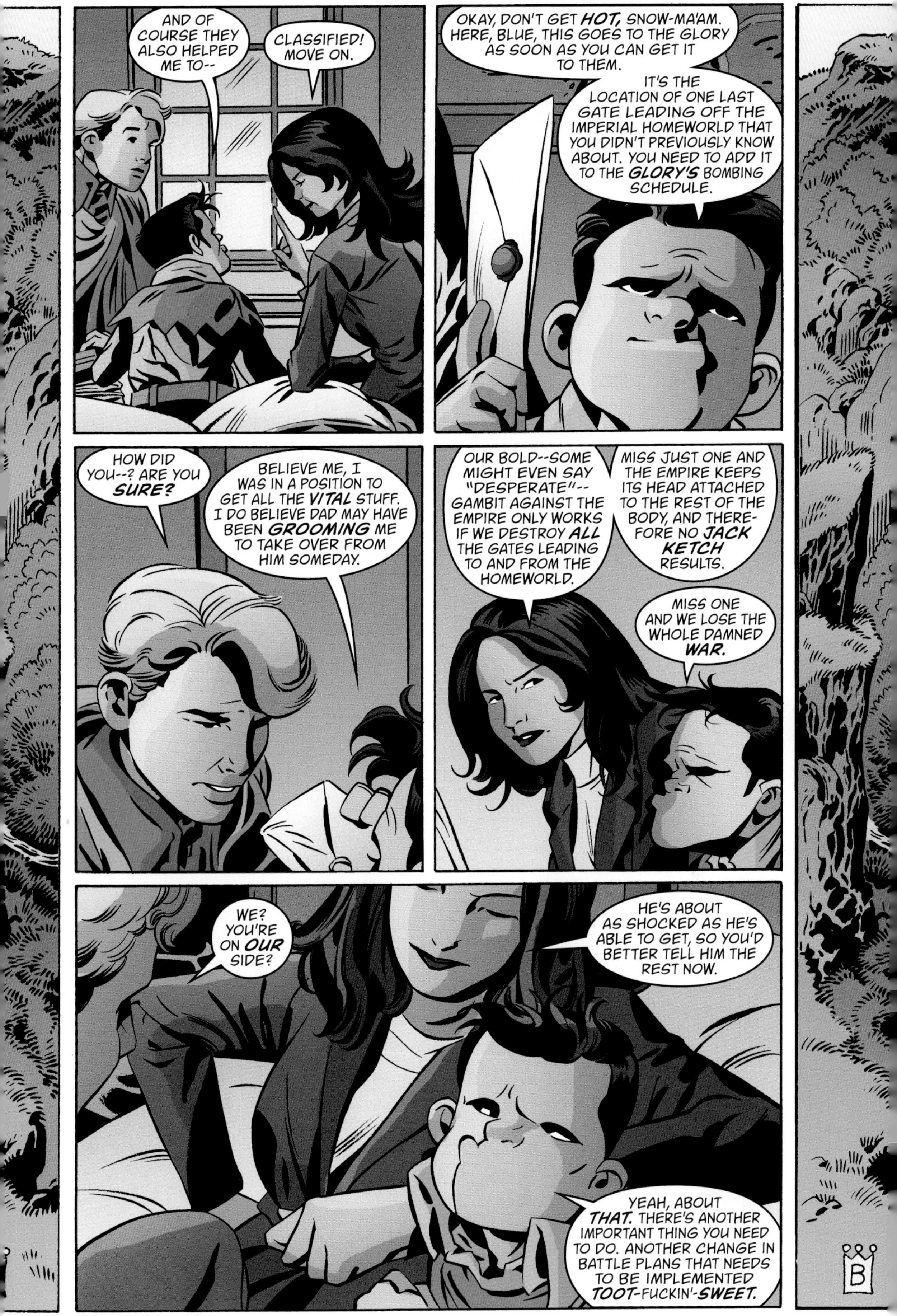
AND OF COURSE THEY ALSO HELPED ME TO--
CLASSIFIED! MOVE ON.
OKAY, DON'T GET HOT, SNOW-MA'AM. HERE, BLUE, THIS GOES TO THE GLORY AS SOON AS YOU CAN GET IT TO THEM.
IT'S THE LOCATION OF ONE LAST GATE LEADING OFF THE IMPERIAL HOMEWORLD THAT YOU DIDN'T PREVIOUSLY KNOW ABOUT. YOU NEED TO ADD IT TO THE GLORY'S BOMBING SCHEDULE.
HOW DID YOU--? ARE YOU SURE?
BELIEVE ME, I WAS IN A POSITION TO GET ALL THE VITAL STUFF. I DO BELIEVE DAD MAY HAVE BEEN GROOMING ME TO TAKE OVER FROM HIM SOMEDAY.
OUR BOLD--SOME MIGHT EVEN SAY "DESPERATE"--GAMBIT AGAINST THE EMPIRE ONLY WORKS IF WE DESTROY ALL THE GATES LEADING TO AND FROM THE HOMEWORLD.
MISS JUST ONE AND THE EMPIRE KEEPS ITS HEAD ATTACHED TO THE REST OF THE BODY, AND THEREFORE NO JACK KETCH RESULTS.
MISS ONE AND WE LOSE THE WHOLE DAMNED WAR.
WE? YOU'RE ON OUR SIDE?
HE'S ABOUT AS SHOCKED AS HE'S ABLE TO GET, SO YOU'D BETTER TELL HIM THE REST NOW.
YEAH, ABOUT THAT. THERE'S ANOTHER IMPORTANT THING YOU NEED TO DO. ANOTHER CHANGE IN BATTLE PLANS THAT NEEDS TO BE IMPLEMENTED TOOT-FUCKIN'-SWEET.
B

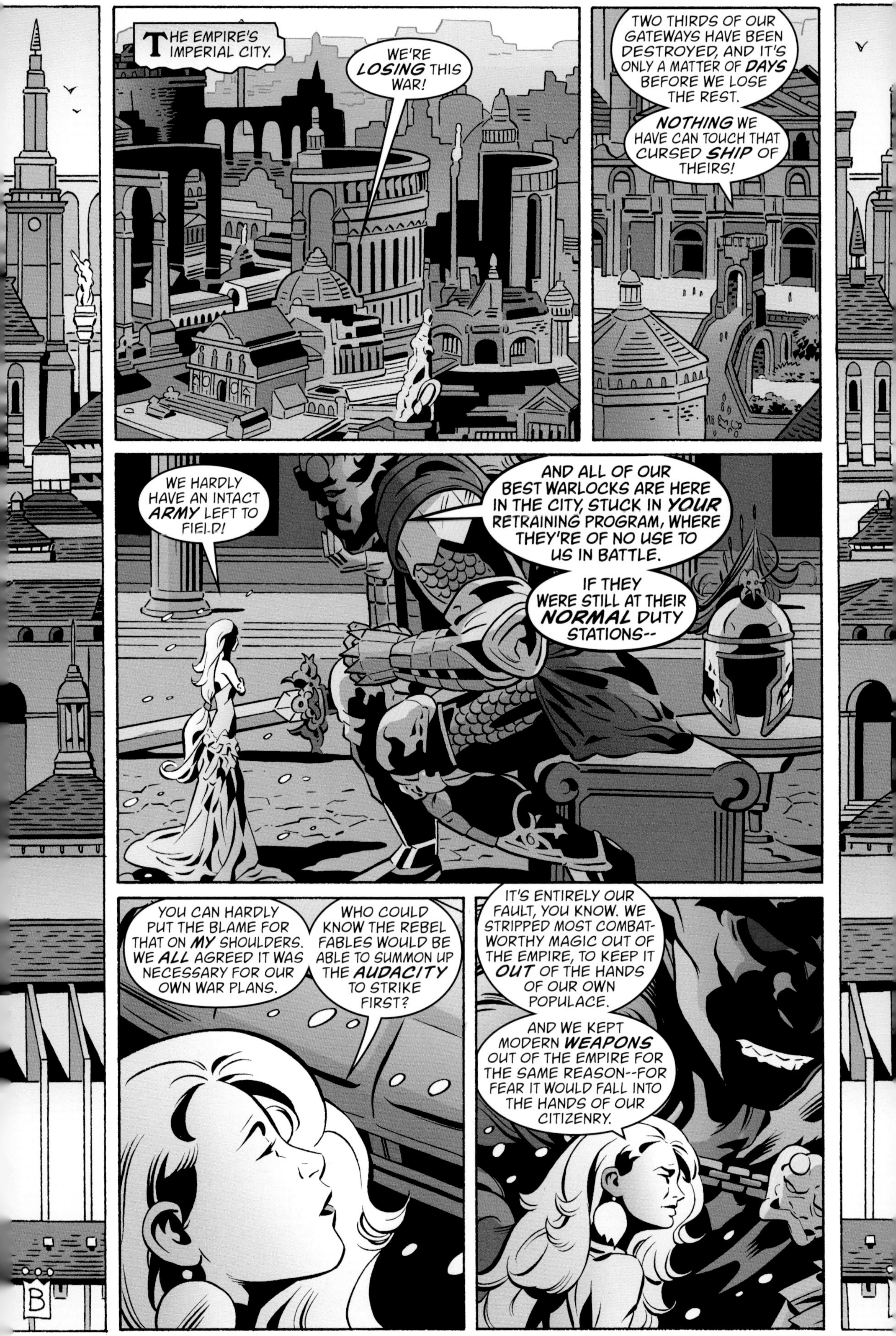
THE EMPIRE'S IMPERIAL CITY.
WE'RE LOSING THIS WAR!
TWO THIRDS OF OUR GATEWAYS HAVE BEEN DESTROYED, AND IT'S ONLY A MATTER OF DAYS BEFORE WE LOSE THE REST.
NOTHING WE HAVE CAN TOUCH THAT CURSED SHIP OF THEIRS!
WE HARDLY HAVE AN INTACT ARMY LEFT TO FIELD!
AND ALL OF OUR BEST WARLOCKS ARE HERE IN THE CITY, STUCK IN YOUR RETRAINING PROGRAM, WHERE THEY'RE OF NO USE TO US IN BATTLE.
IF THEY WERE STILL AT THEIR NORMAL DUTY STATIONS--
YOU CAN HARDLY PUT THE BLAME FOR THAT ON MY SHOULDERS. WE ALL AGREED IT WAS NECESSARY FOR OUR OWN WAR PLANS.
WHO COULD KNOW THE REBEL FABLES WOULD BE ABLE TO SUMMON UP THE AUDACITY TO STRIKE FIRST?
IT'S ENTIRELY OUR FAULT, YOU KNOW. WE STRIPPED MOST COMBAT-WORTHY MAGIC OUT OF THE EMPIRE, TO KEEP IT OUT OF THE HANDS OF OUR OWN POPULACE.
AND WE KEPT MODERN WEAPONS OUT OF THE EMPIRE FOR THE SAME REASON--FOR FEAR IT WOULD FALL INTO THE HANDS OF OUR CITIZENRY.
B

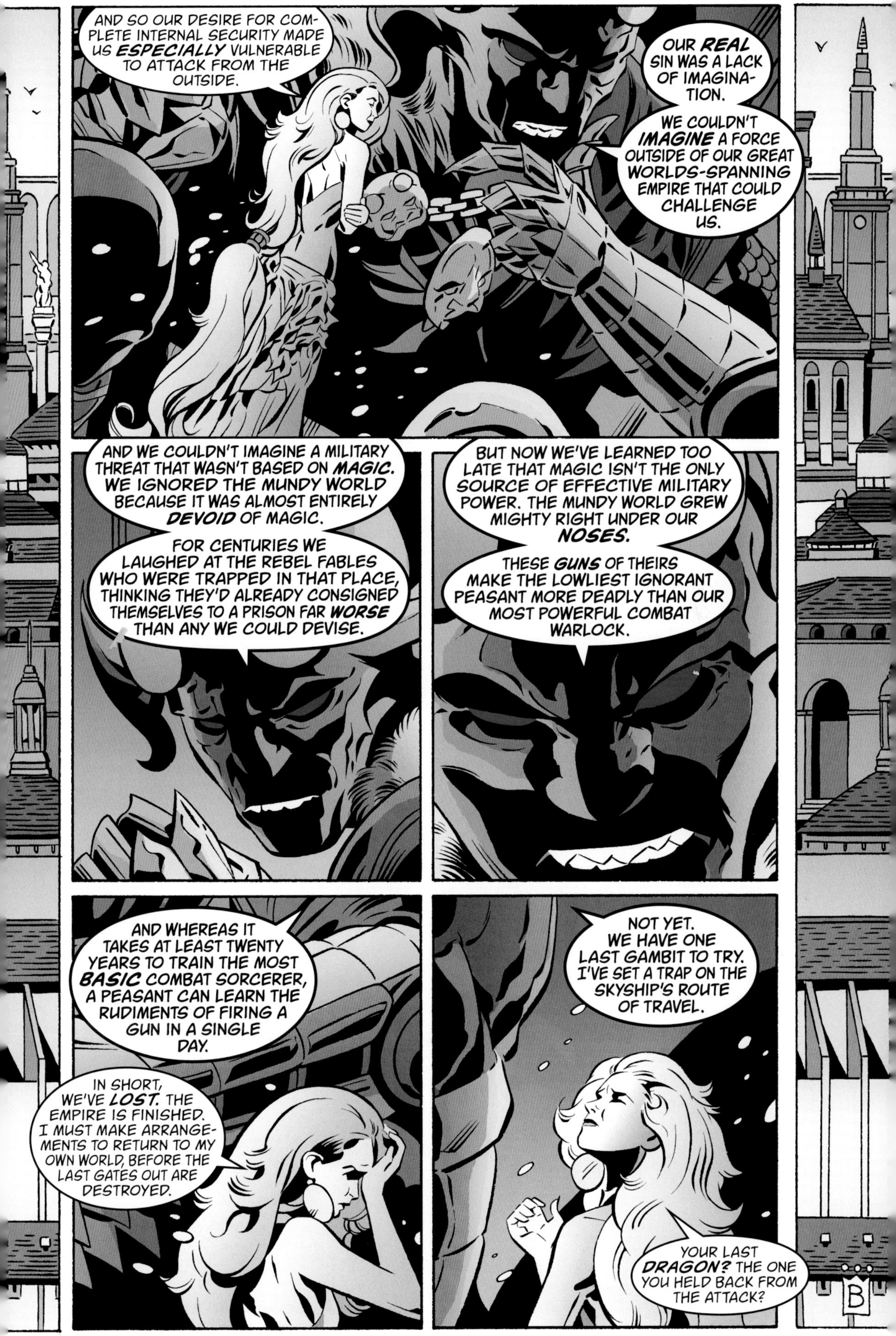
AND SO OUR DESIRE FOR COMPLETE INTERNAL SECURITY MADE US ESPECIALLY VULNERABLE TO ATTACK FROM THE OUTSIDE.
OUR REAL SIN WAS A LACK OF IMAGINATION.
WE COULDN'T IMAGINE A FORCE OUTSIDE OF OUR GREAT WORLDS-SPANNING EMPIRE THAT COULD CHALLENGE US.
AND WE COULDN'T IMAGINE A MILITARY THREAT THAT WASN'T BASED ON MAGIC. WE IGNORED THE MUNDY WORLD BECAUSE IT WAS ALMOST ENTIRELY DEVOID OF MAGIC.
FOR CENTURIES WE LAUGHED AT THE REBEL FABLES WHO WERE TRAPPED IN THAT PLACE, THINKING THEY'D ALREADY CONSIGNED THEMSELVES TO A PRISON FAR WORSE THAN ANY WE COULD DEVISE.
BUT NOW WE'VE LEARNED TOO LATE THAT MAGIC ISN'T THE ONLY SOURCE OF EFFECTIVE MILITARY POWER. THE MUNDY WORLD GREW MIGHTY RIGHT UNDER OUR NOSES.
THESE GUNS OF THEIRS MAKE THE LOWLIEST IGNORANT PEASANT MORE DEADLY THAN OUR MOST POWERFUL COMBAT WARLOCK.
AND WHEREAS IT TAKES AT LEAST TWENTY YEARS TO TRAIN THE MOST BASIC COMBAT SORCERER, A PEASANT CAN LEARN THE RUDIMENTS OF FIRING A GUN IN A SINGLE DAY.
IN SHORT, WE'VE LOST. THE EMPIRE IS FINISHED. I MUST MAKE ARRANGEMENTS TO RETURN TO MY OWN WORLD, BEFORE THE LAST GATES OUT ARE DESTROYED.
NOT YET. WE HAVE ONE LAST GAMBIT TO TRY. I'VE SET A TRAP ON THE SKYSHIP'S ROUTE OF TRAVEL.
YOUR LAST DRAGON? THE ONE YOU HELD BACK FROM THE ATTACK?

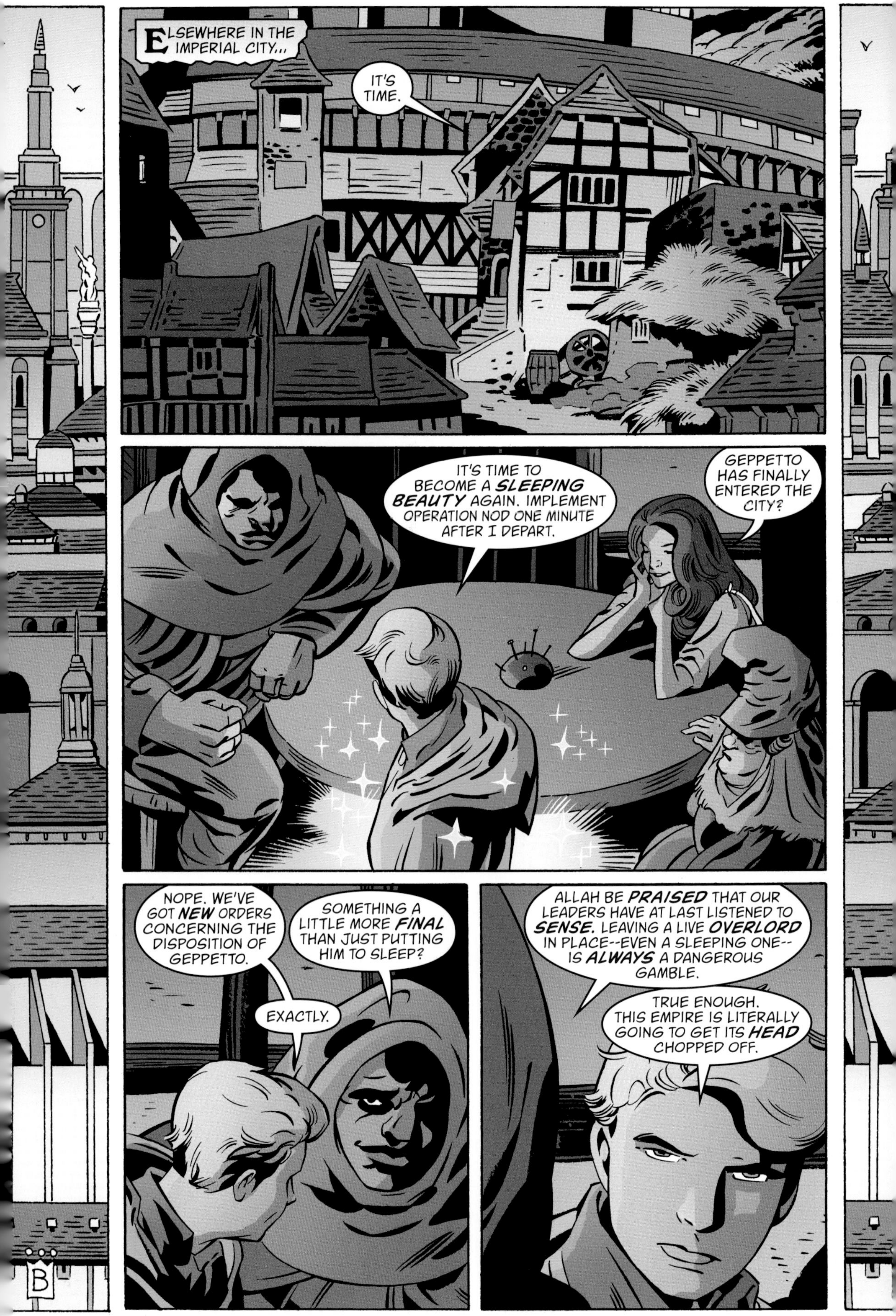
ELSEWHERE IN THE IMPERIAL CITY...
IT'S TIME.
IT'S TIME TO BECOME A **SLEEPING BEAUTY** AGAIN. IMPLEMENT OPERATION NOD ONE MINUTE AFTER I DEPART.
GEPPETTO HAS FINALLY ENTERED THE CITY?
NOPE. WE'VE GOT **NEW** ORDERS CONCERNING THE DISPOSITION OF GEPPETTO.
SOMETHING A LITTLE MORE **FINAL** THAN JUST PUTTING HIM TO SLEEP?
EXACTLY.
ALLAH BE **PRAISED** THAT OUR LEADERS HAVE AT LAST LISTENED TO **SENSE.** LEAVING A LIVE **OVERLORD** IN PLACE--EVEN A SLEEPING ONE--IS **ALWAYS** A DANGEROUS GAMBLE.
TRUE ENOUGH. THIS EMPIRE IS LITERALLY GOING TO GET ITS **HEAD** CHOPPED OFF.
B

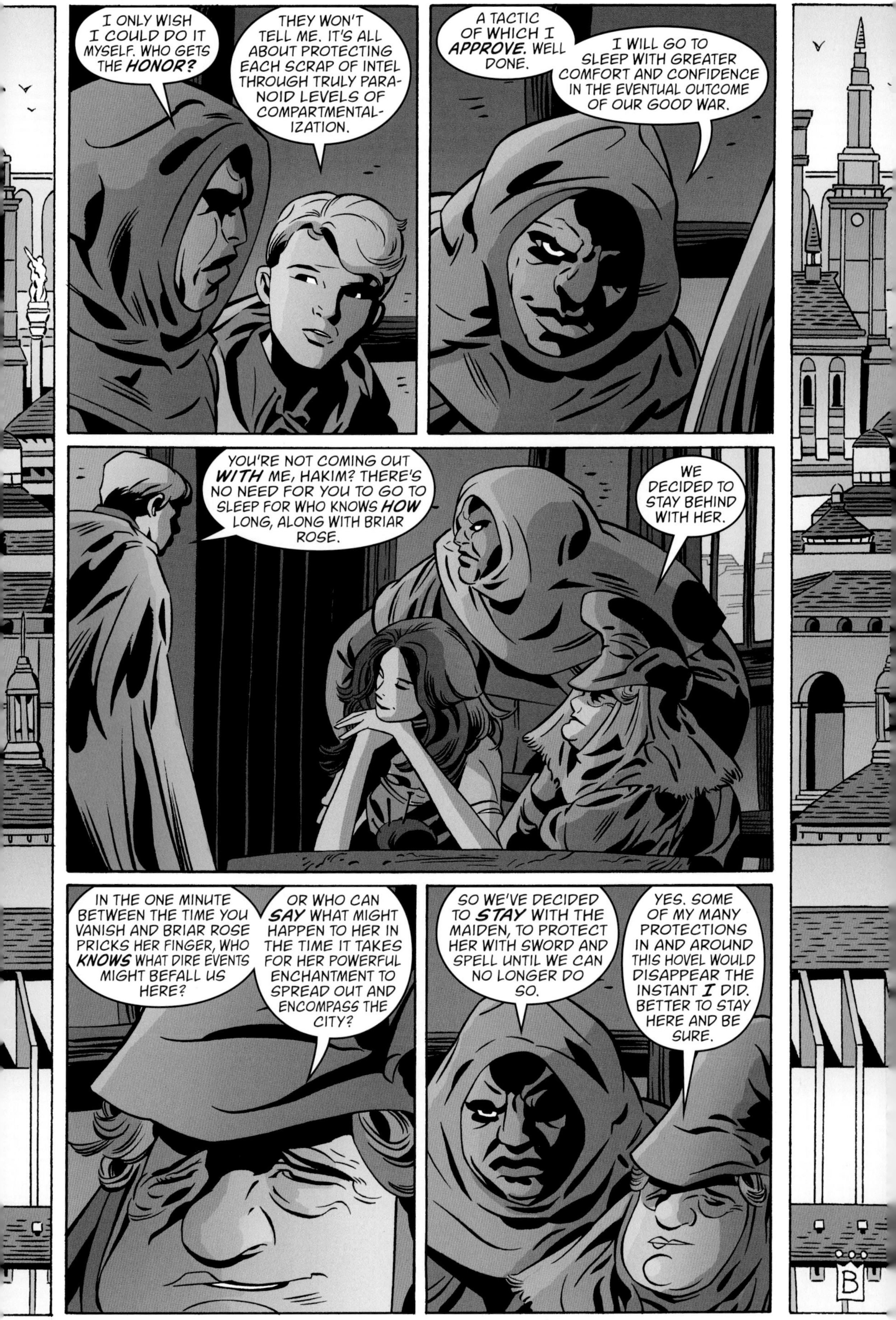
I ONLY WISH I COULD DO IT MYSELF. WHO GETS THE HONOR?
THEY WON'T TELL ME. IT'S ALL ABOUT PROTECTING EACH SCRAP OF INTEL THROUGH TRULY PARA-NOID LEVELS OF COMPARTMENTAL-IZATION.
A TACTIC OF WHICH I APPROVE. WELL DONE.
I WILL GO TO SLEEP WITH GREATER COMFORT AND CONFIDENCE IN THE EVENTUAL OUTCOME OF OUR GOOD WAR.
YOU'RE NOT COMING OUT WITH ME, HAKIM? THERE'S NO NEED FOR YOU TO GO TO SLEEP FOR WHO KNOWS HOW LONG, ALONG WITH BRIAR ROSE.
WE DECIDED TO STAY BEHIND WITH HER.
IN THE ONE MINUTE BETWEEN THE TIME YOU VANISH AND BRIAR ROSE PRICKS HER FINGER, WHO KNOWS WHAT DIRE EVENTS MIGHT BEFALL US HERE?
OR WHO CAN SAY WHAT MIGHT HAPPEN TO HER IN THE TIME IT TAKES FOR HER POWERFUL ENCHANTMENT TO SPREAD OUT AND ENCOMPASS THE CITY?
SO WE'VE DECIDED TO STAY WITH THE MAIDEN, TO PROTECT HER WITH SWORD AND SPELL UNTIL WE CAN NO LONGER DO SO.
YES. SOME OF MY MANY PROTECTIONS IN AND AROUND THIS HOVEL WOULD DISAPPEAR THE INSTANT I DID. BETTER TO STAY HERE AND BE SURE.
B

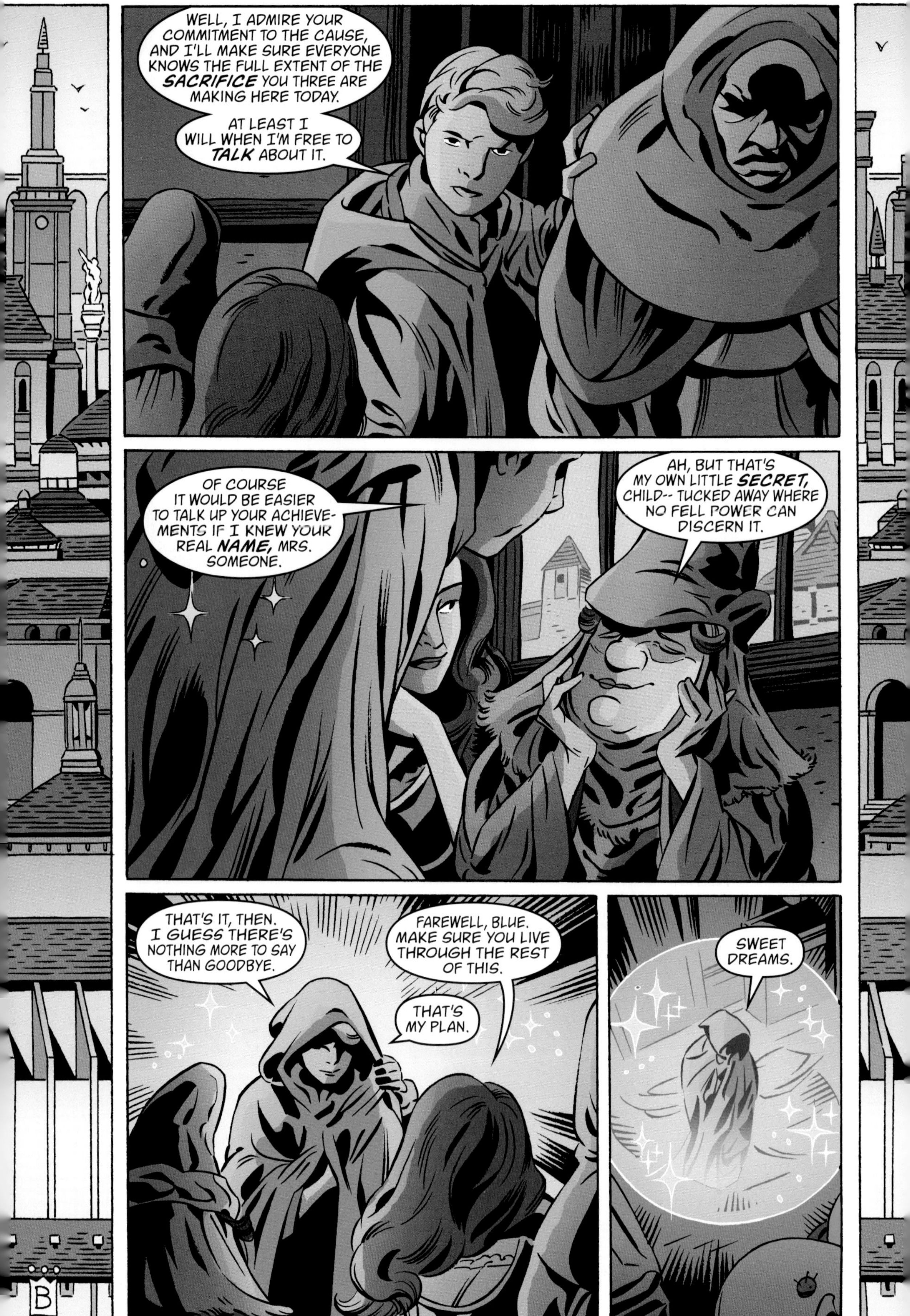
WELL, I ADMIRE YOUR COMMITMENT TO THE CAUSE, AND I'LL MAKE SURE EVERYONE KNOWS THE FULL EXTENT OF THE SACRIFICE YOU THREE ARE MAKING HERE TODAY.
AT LEAST I WILL WHEN I'M FREE TO TALK ABOUT IT.
OF COURSE IT WOULD BE EASIER TO TALK UP YOUR ACHIEVEMENTS IF I KNEW YOUR REAL NAME, MRS. SOMEONE.
AH, BUT THAT'S MY OWN LITTLE SECRET, CHILD-- TUCKED AWAY WHERE NO FELL POWER CAN DISCERN IT.
THAT'S IT, THEN. I GUESS THERE'S NOTHING MORE TO SAY THAN GOODBYE.
FAREWELL, BLUE. MAKE SURE YOU LIVE THROUGH THE REST OF THIS.
THAT'S MY PLAN.
SWEET DREAMS.

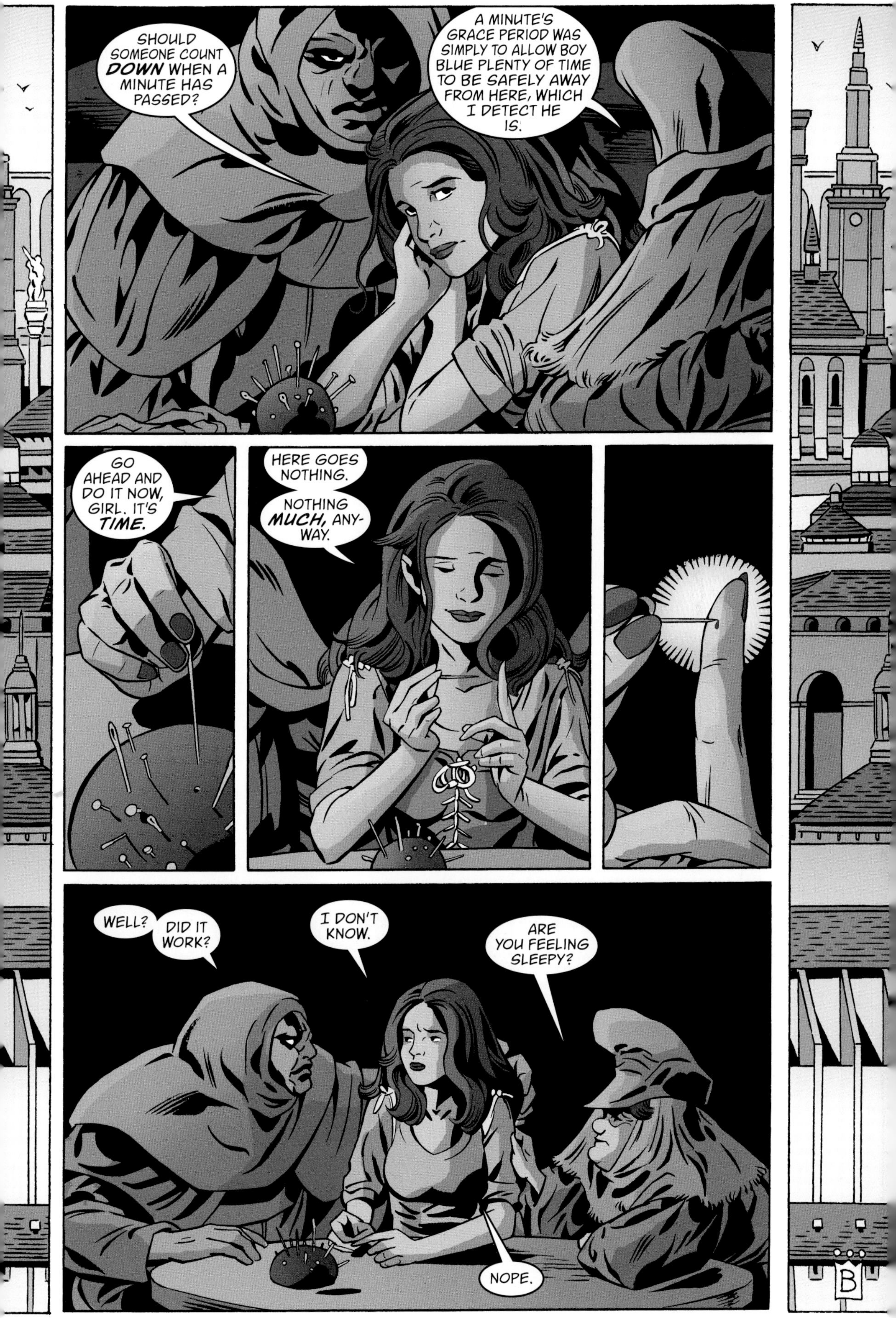
SHOULD SOMEONE COUNT DOWN WHEN A MINUTE HAS PASSED?
A MINUTE'S GRACE PERIOD WAS SIMPLY TO ALLOW BOY BLUE PLENTY OF TIME TO BE SAFELY AWAY FROM HERE, WHICH I DETECT HE IS.
GO AHEAD AND DO IT NOW, GIRL. IT'S TIME.
HERE GOES NOTHING.
NOTHING MUCH, ANY-WAY.
WELL?
DID IT WORK?
I DON'T KNOW.
ARE YOU FEELING SLEEPY?
NOPE.
B

NOT A--
≶YAWN≶
--BIT.

OH, HERE WE GO.

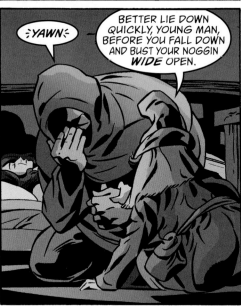

≶YAWN≶

BETTER LIE DOWN QUICKLY, YOUNG MAN, BEFORE YOU FALL DOWN AND BUST YOUR NOGGIN *WIDE* OPEN.

ZZZZZZZZZZZ

ONE OF THE BIGGEST AND MOST VITAL PARTS OF OUR WAR PLANS WAS THE GAMBIT TO TAKE OUT THE EMPIRE'S ENTIRE RULING CITY WITHOUT FIRING A SHOT.

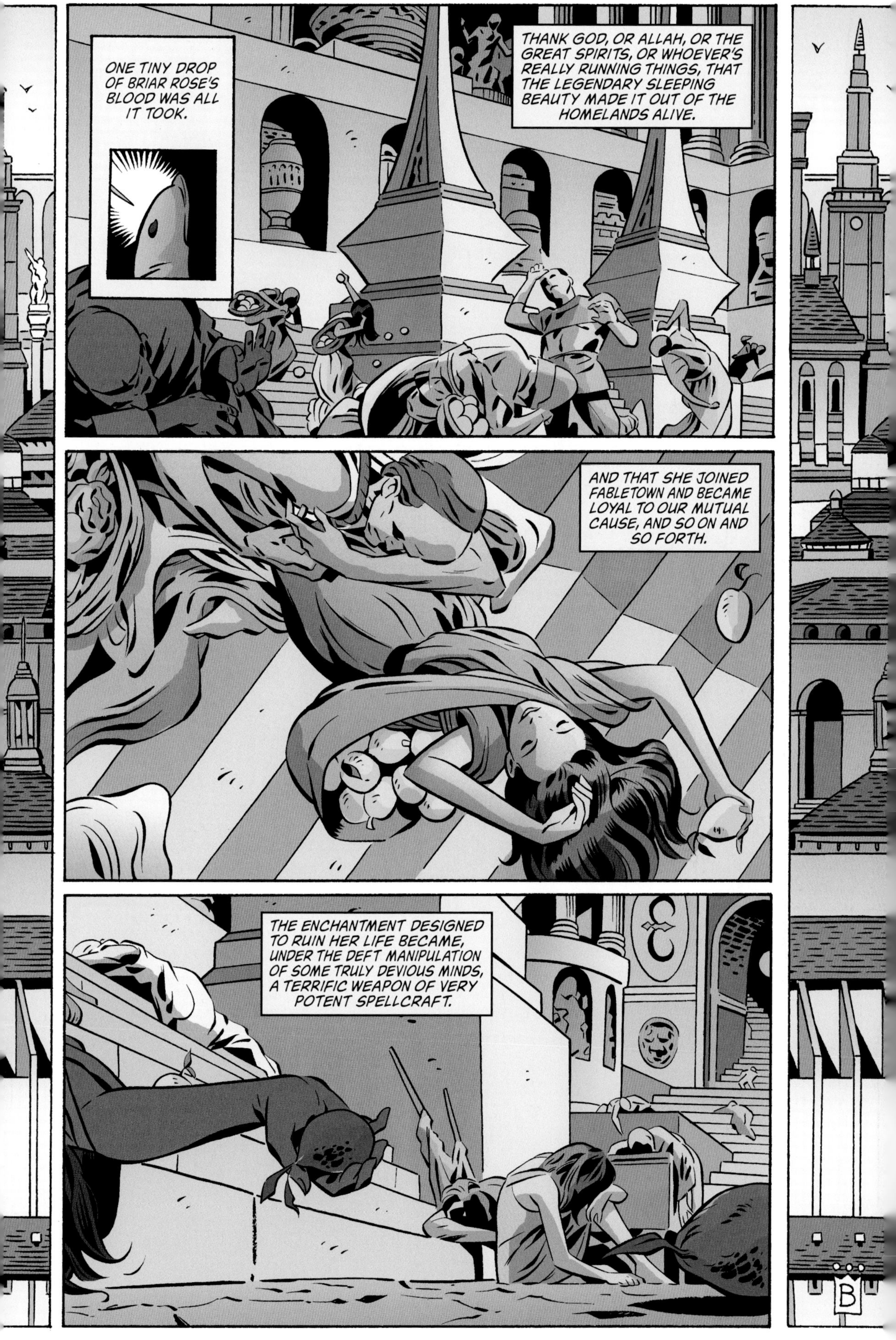
ONE TINY DROP OF BRIAR ROSE'S BLOOD WAS ALL IT TOOK.
THANK GOD, OR ALLAH, OR THE GREAT SPIRITS, OR WHOEVER'S REALLY RUNNING THINGS, THAT THE LEGENDARY SLEEPING BEAUTY MADE IT OUT OF THE HOMELANDS ALIVE.
AND THAT SHE JOINED FABLETOWN AND BECAME LOYAL TO OUR MUTUAL CAUSE, AND SO ON AND SO FORTH.
THE ENCHANTMENT DESIGNED TO RUIN HER LIFE BECAME, UNDER THE DEFT MANIPULATION OF SOME TRULY DEVIOUS MINDS, A TERRIFIC WEAPON OF VERY POTENT SPELLCRAFT.

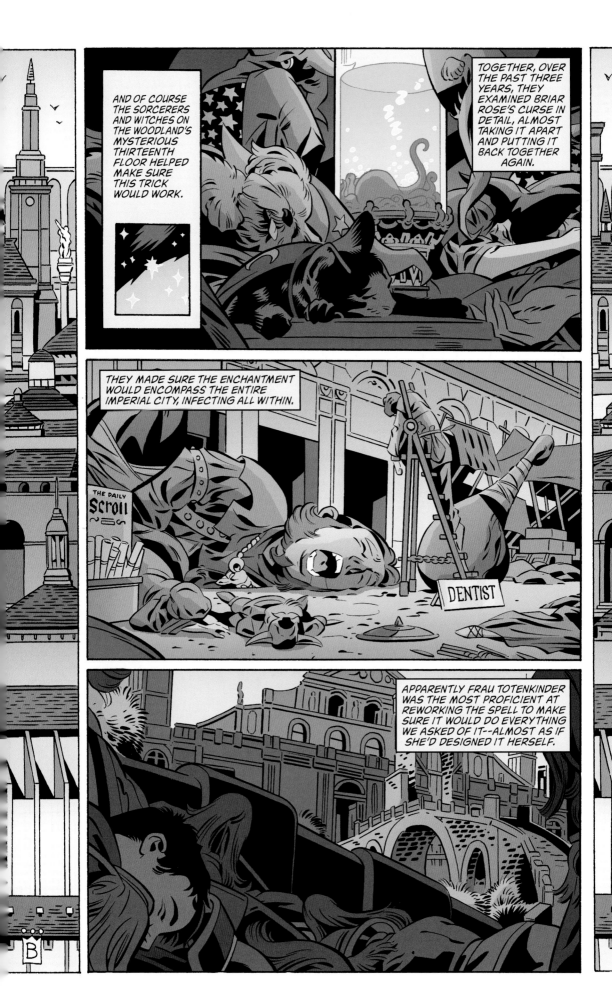

AND OF COURSE THE SORCERERS AND WITCHES ON THE WOODLAND'S MYSTERIOUS THIRTEENTH FLOOR HELPED MAKE SURE THIS TRICK WOULD WORK.

TOGETHER, OVER THE PAST THREE YEARS, THEY EXAMINED BRIAR ROSE'S CURSE IN DETAIL, ALMOST TAKING IT APART AND PUTTING IT BACK TOGETHER AGAIN.

THEY MADE SURE THE ENCHANTMENT WOULD ENCOMPASS THE ENTIRE IMPERIAL CITY, INFECTING ALL WITHIN.

THE DAILY SCROLL

DENTIST

APPARENTLY FRAU TOTENKINDER WAS THE MOST PROFICIENT AT REWORKING THE SPELL TO MAKE SURE IT WOULD DO EVERYTHING WE ASKED OF IT--ALMOST AS IF SHE'D DESIGNED IT HERSELF.

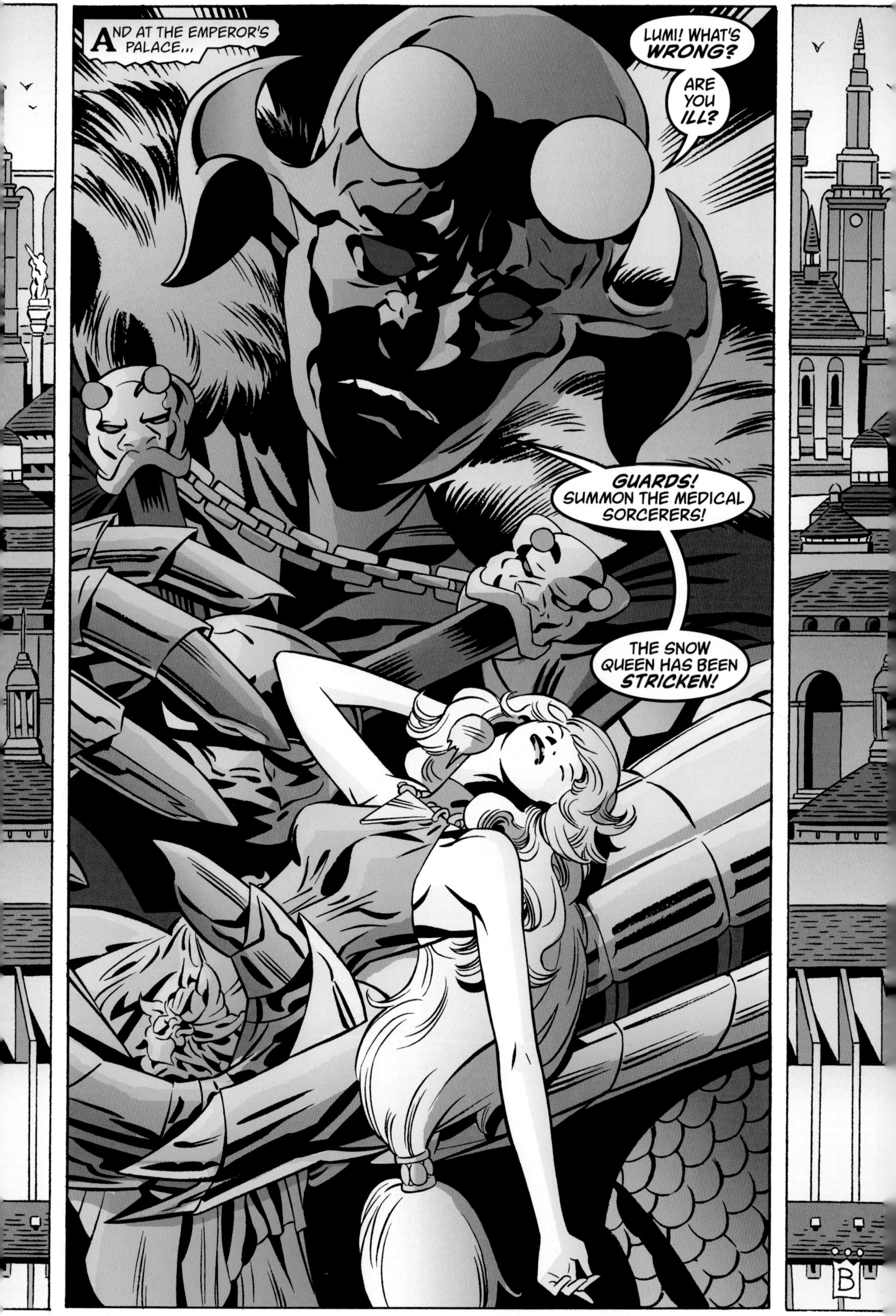
AND AT THE EMPEROR'S PALACE...
LUMI! WHAT'S WRONG?
ARE YOU ILL?
GUARDS! SUMMON THE MEDICAL SORCERERS!
THE SNOW QUEEN HAS BEEN STRICKEN!
B

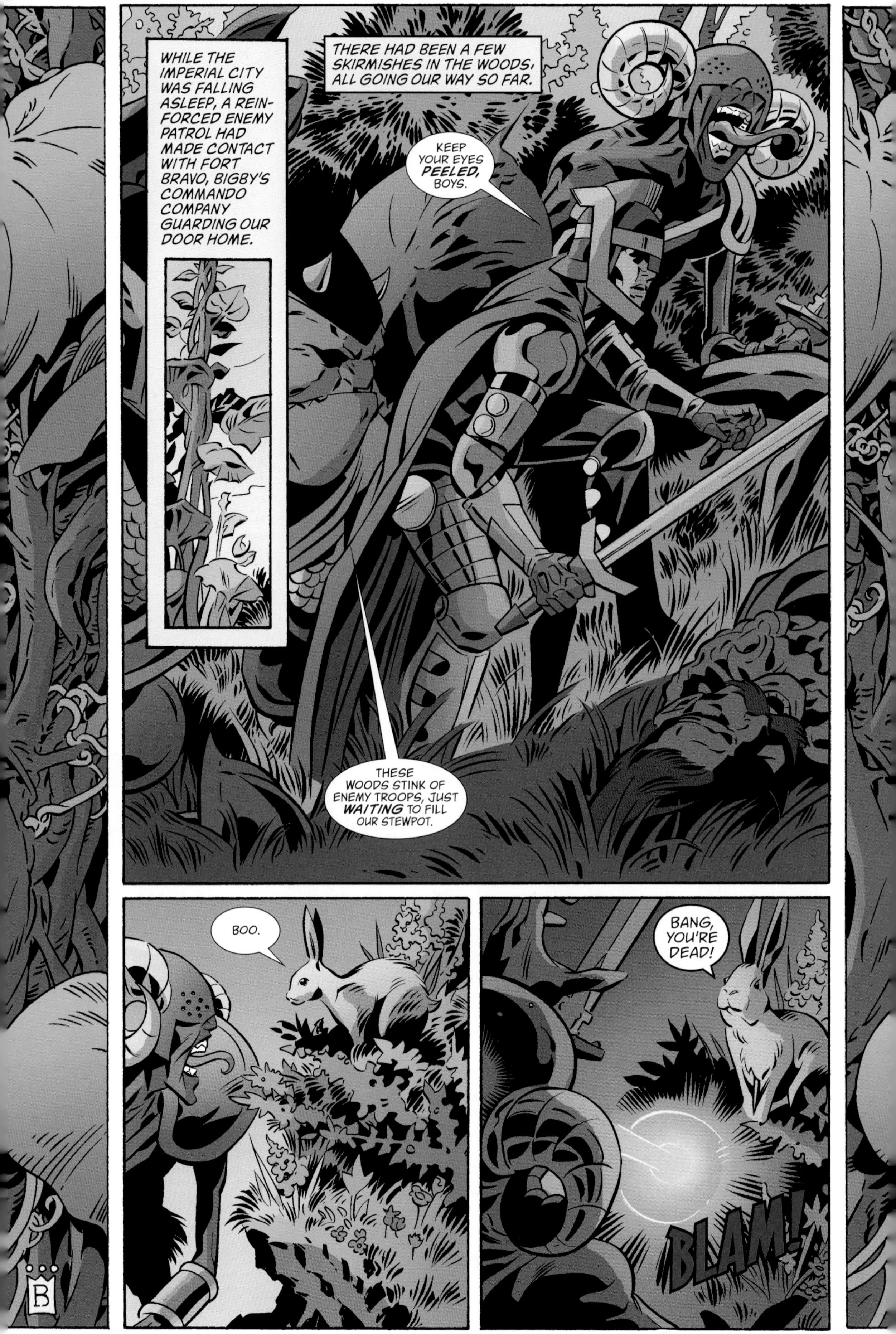
WHILE THE IMPERIAL CITY WAS FALLING ASLEEP, A REIN-FORCED ENEMY PATROL HAD MADE CONTACT WITH FORT BRAVO, BIGBY'S COMMANDO COMPANY GUARDING OUR DOOR HOME.
THERE HAD BEEN A FEW SKIRMISHES IN THE WOODS, ALL GOING OUR WAY SO FAR.
KEEP YOUR EYES **PEELED,** BOYS.
THESE WOODS STINK OF ENEMY TROOPS, JUST **WAITING** TO FILL OUR STEWPOT.
BOO.
BANG, YOU'RE DEAD!
BLAM!

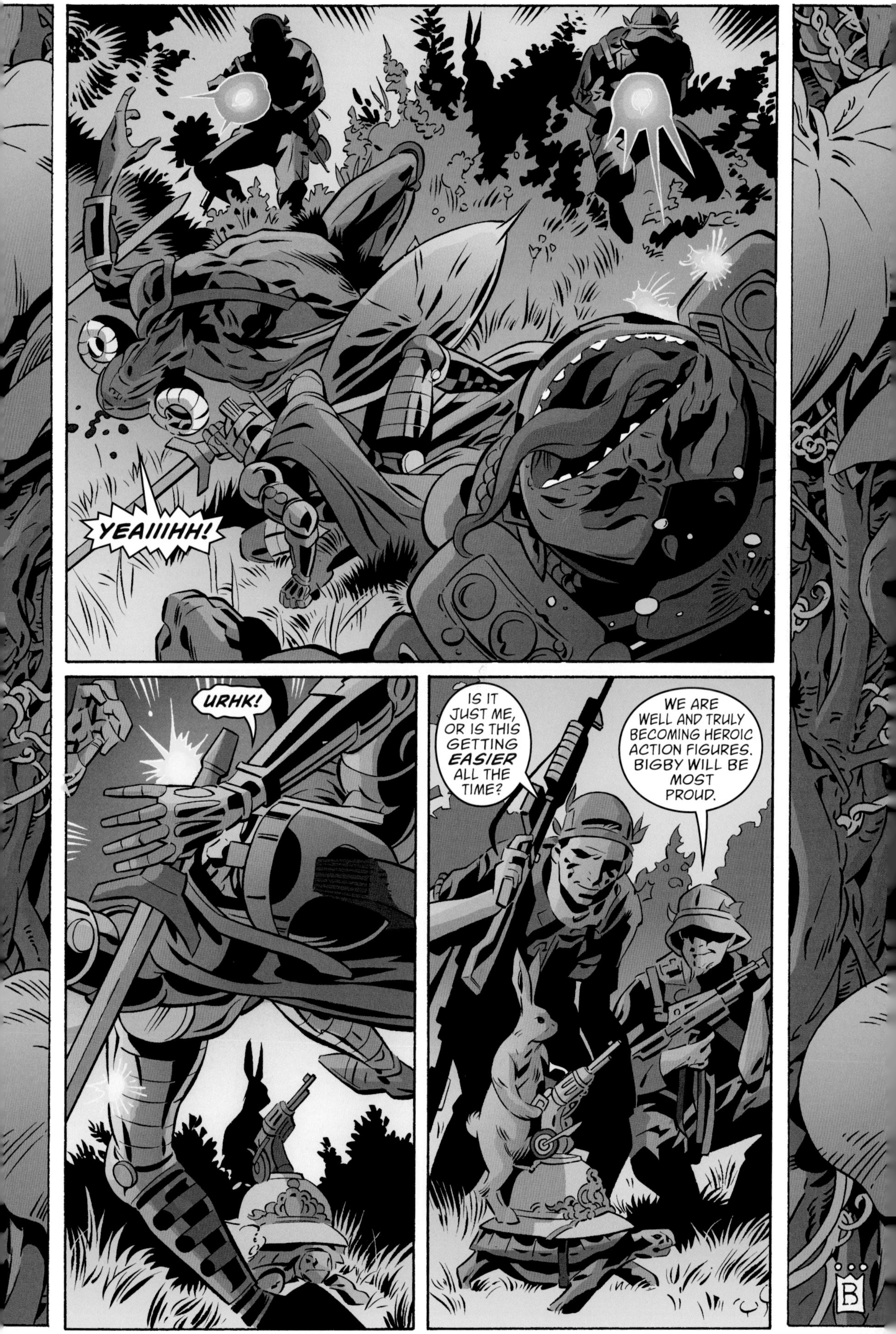
YEAIIIHH!
URHK!
IS IT JUST ME, OR IS THIS GETTING *EASIER* ALL THE TIME?
WE ARE WELL AND TRULY BECOMING HEROIC ACTION FIGURES. BIGBY WILL BE MOST PROUD.

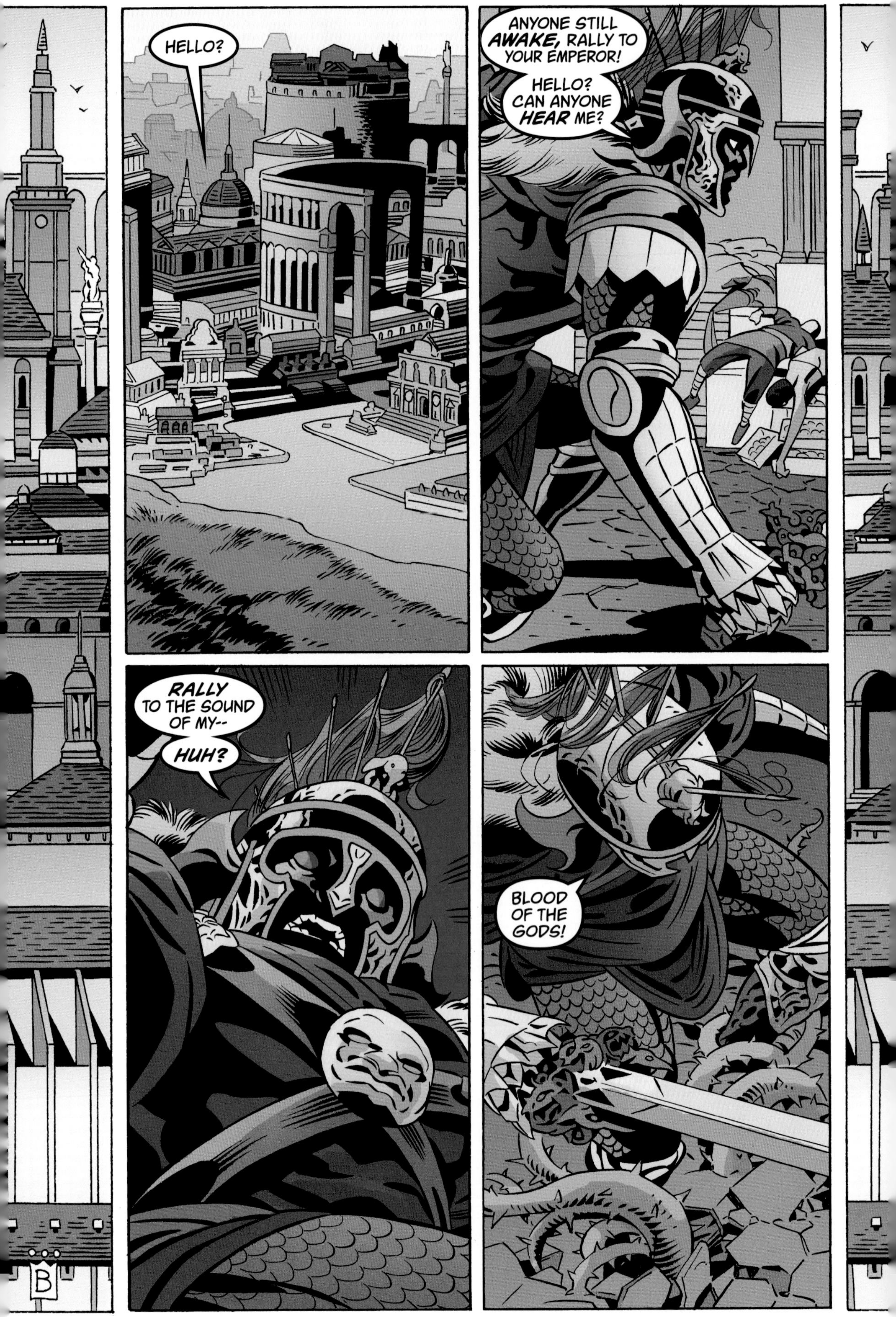
HELLO?
ANYONE STILL AWAKE, RALLY TO YOUR EMPEROR!
HELLO? CAN ANYONE HEAR ME?
RALLY TO THE SOUND OF MY--
HUH?
BLOOD OF THE GODS!
B

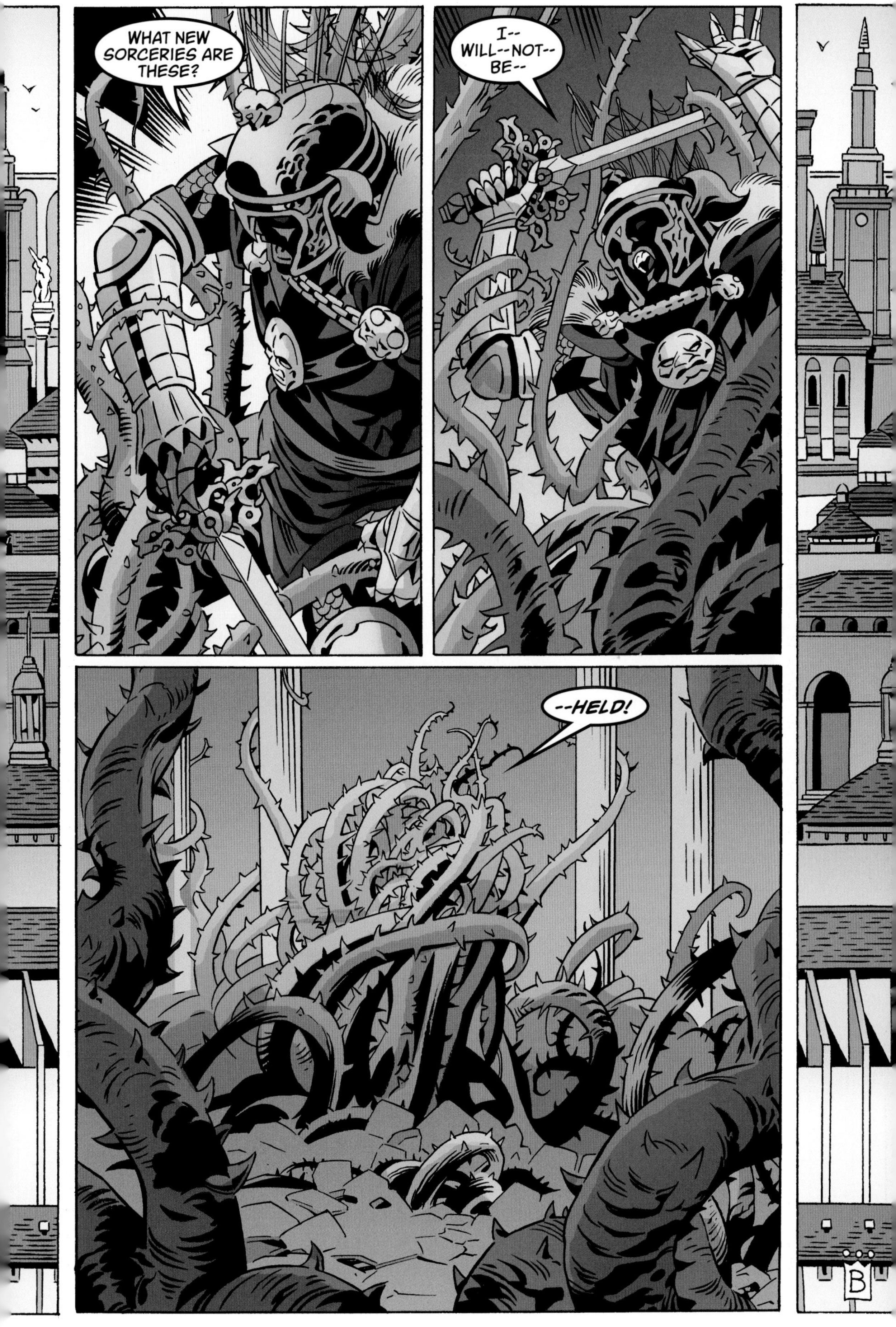
WHAT NEW SORCERIES ARE THESE?
I-- WILL--NOT-- BE--
--HELD!
B

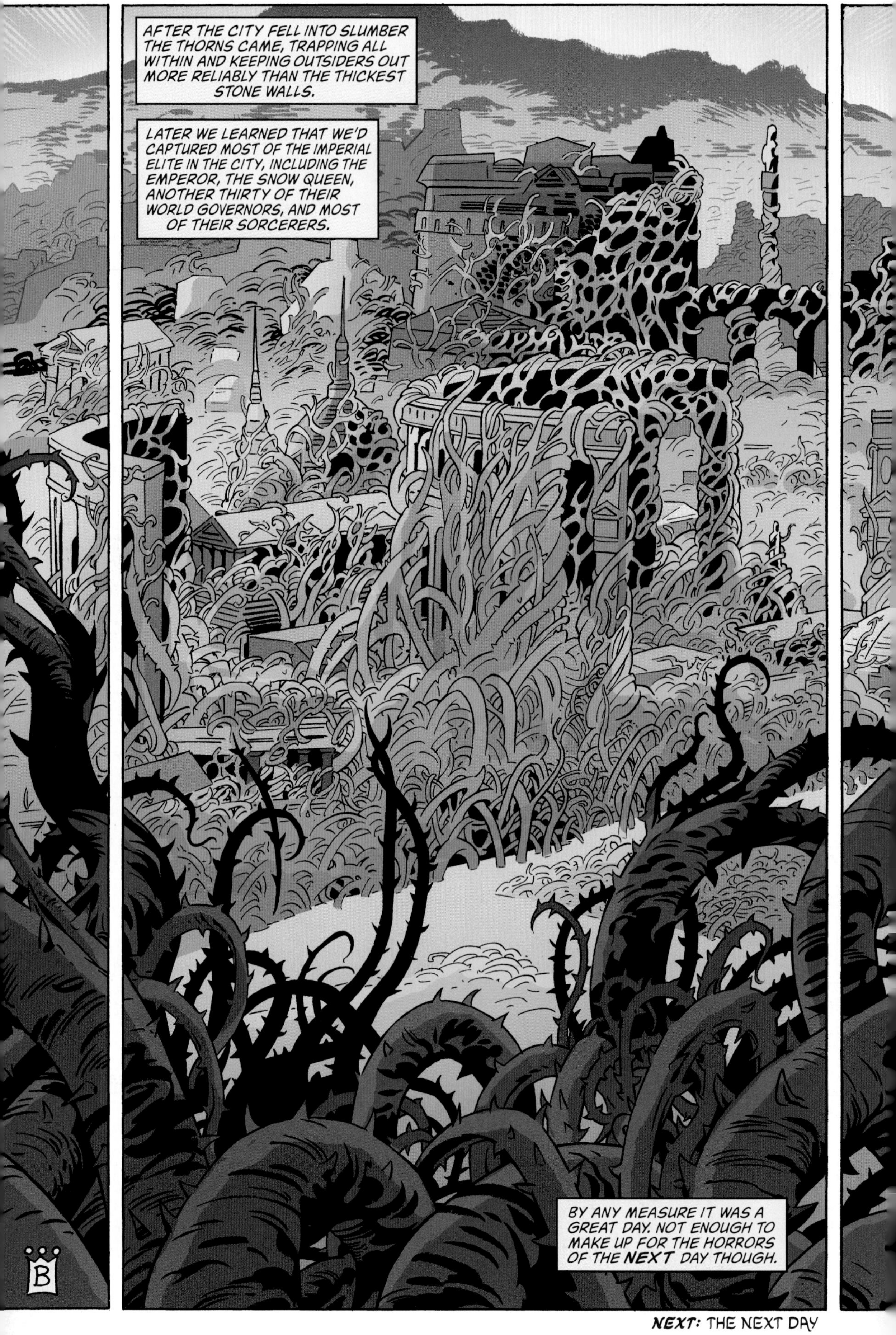
AFTER THE CITY FELL INTO SLUMBER THE THORNS CAME, TRAPPING ALL WITHIN AND KEEPING OUTSIDERS OUT MORE RELIABLY THAN THE THICKEST STONE WALLS.
LATER WE LEARNED THAT WE'D CAPTURED MOST OF THE IMPERIAL ELITE IN THE CITY, INCLUDING THE EMPEROR, THE SNOW QUEEN, ANOTHER THIRTY OF THEIR WORLD GOVERNORS, AND MOST OF THEIR SORCERERS.
BY ANY MEASURE IT WAS A GREAT DAY. NOT ENOUGH TO MAKE UP FOR THE HORRORS OF THE **NEXT** DAY THOUGH.

NEXT: THE NEXT DAY

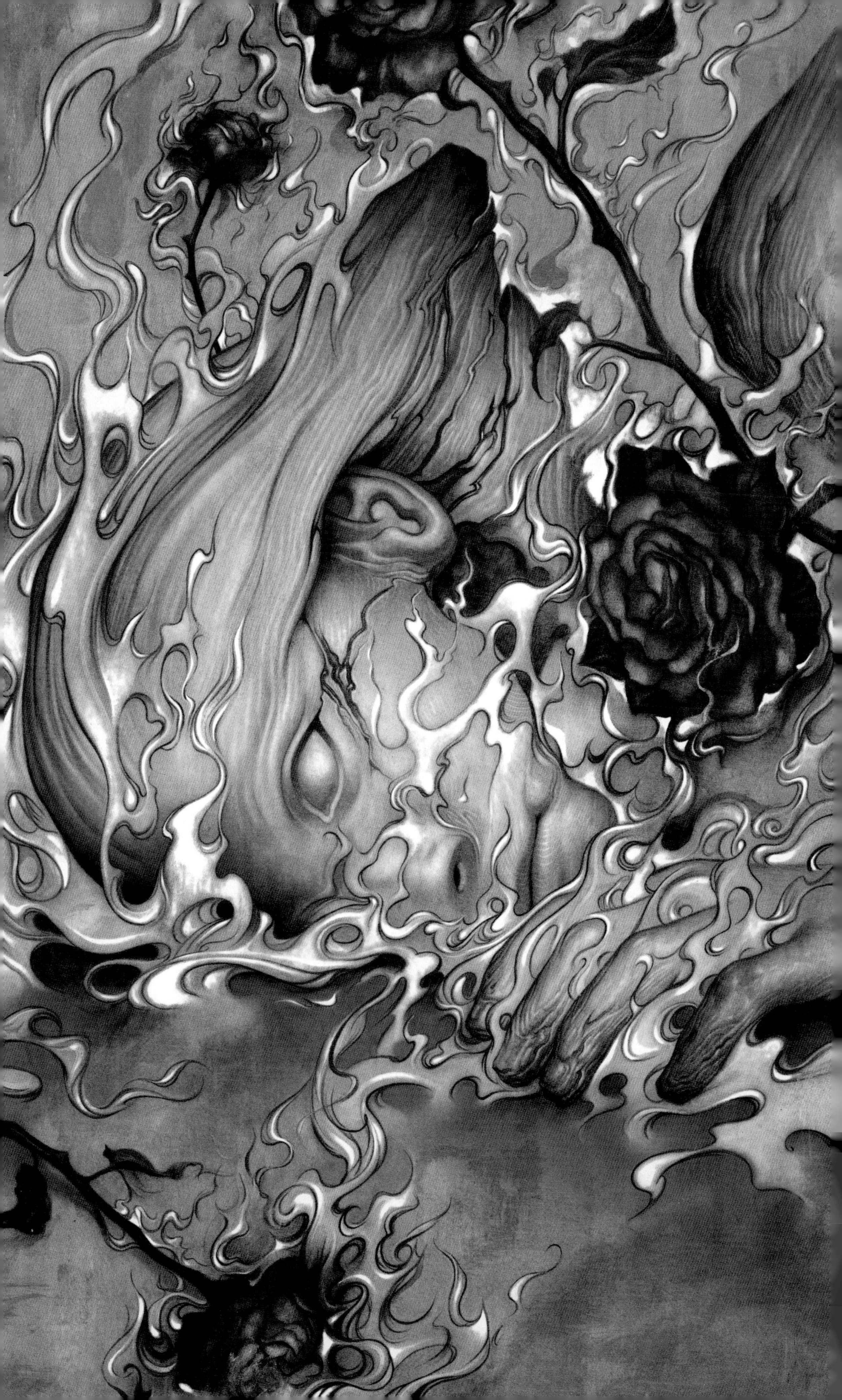

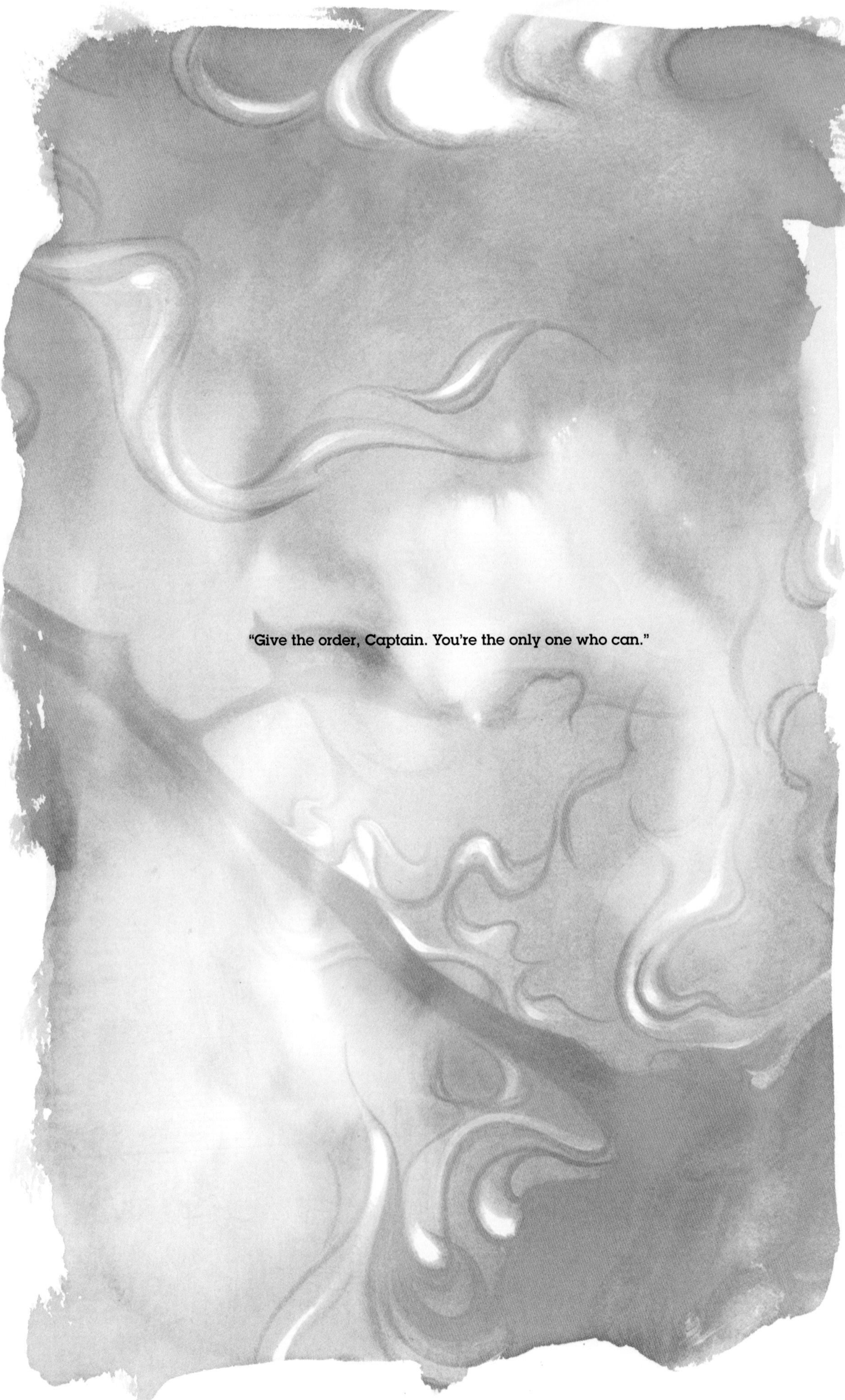

"Give the order, Captain. You're the only one who can."

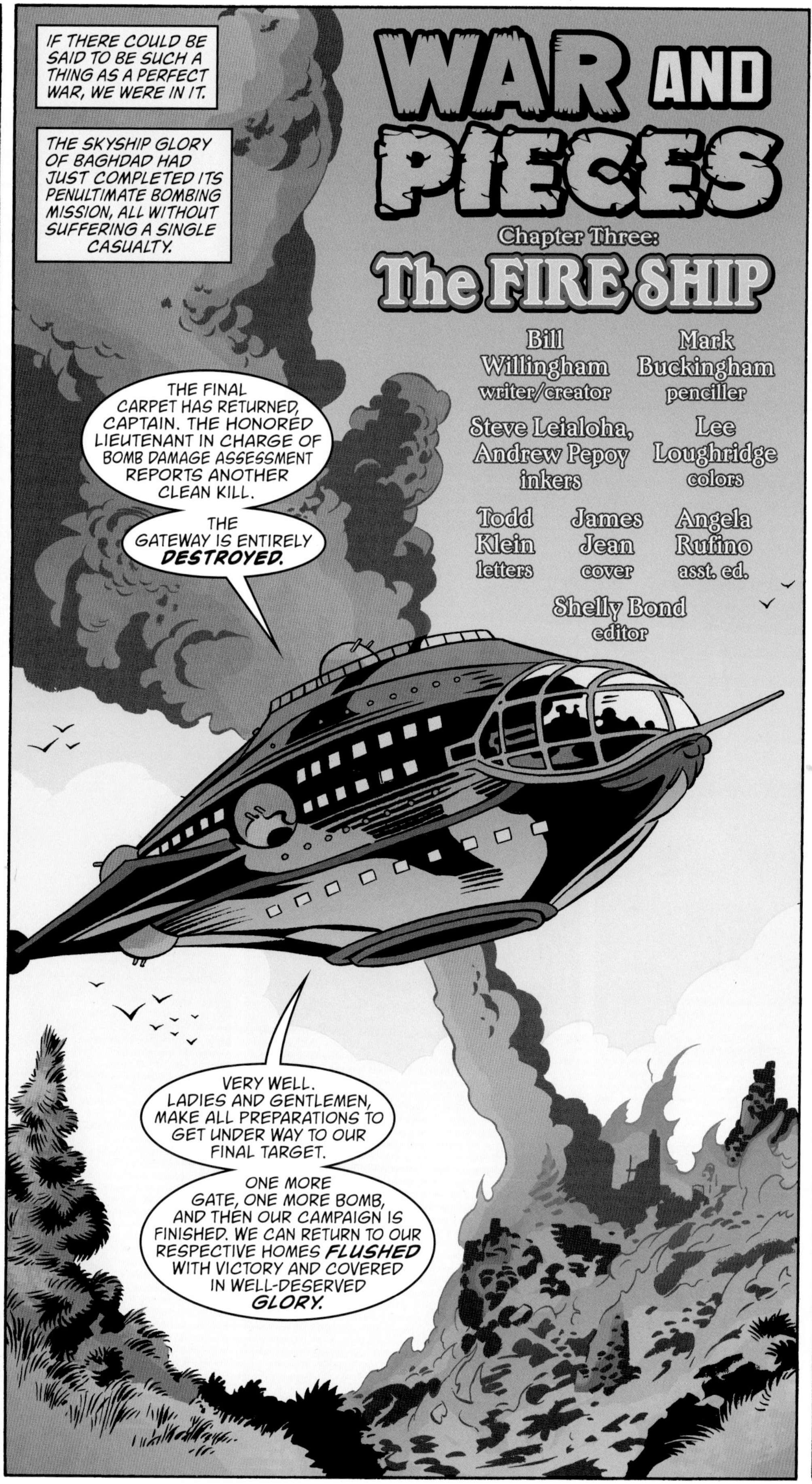

IF THERE COULD BE SAID TO BE SUCH A THING AS A PERFECT WAR, WE WERE IN IT.
THE SKYSHIP GLORY OF BAGHDAD HAD JUST COMPLETED ITS PENULTIMATE BOMBING MISSION, ALL WITHOUT SUFFERING A SINGLE CASUALTY.
WAR AND PIECES
Chapter Three:
The FIRE SHIP
Bill Willingham writer/creator
Mark Buckingham penciller
Steve Leialoha, Andrew Pepoy inkers
Lee Loughridge colors
Todd Klein letters
James Jean cover
Angela Rufino asst. ed.
Shelly Bond editor
THE FINAL CARPET HAS RETURNED, CAPTAIN. THE HONORED LIEUTENANT IN CHARGE OF BOMB DAMAGE ASSESSMENT REPORTS ANOTHER CLEAN KILL.
THE GATEWAY IS ENTIRELY DESTROYED.
VERY WELL. LADIES AND GENTLEMEN, MAKE ALL PREPARATIONS TO GET UNDER WAY TO OUR FINAL TARGET.
ONE MORE GATE, ONE MORE BOMB, AND THEN OUR CAMPAIGN IS FINISHED. WE CAN RETURN TO OUR RESPECTIVE HOMES FLUSHED WITH VICTORY AND COVERED IN WELL-DESERVED GLORY.

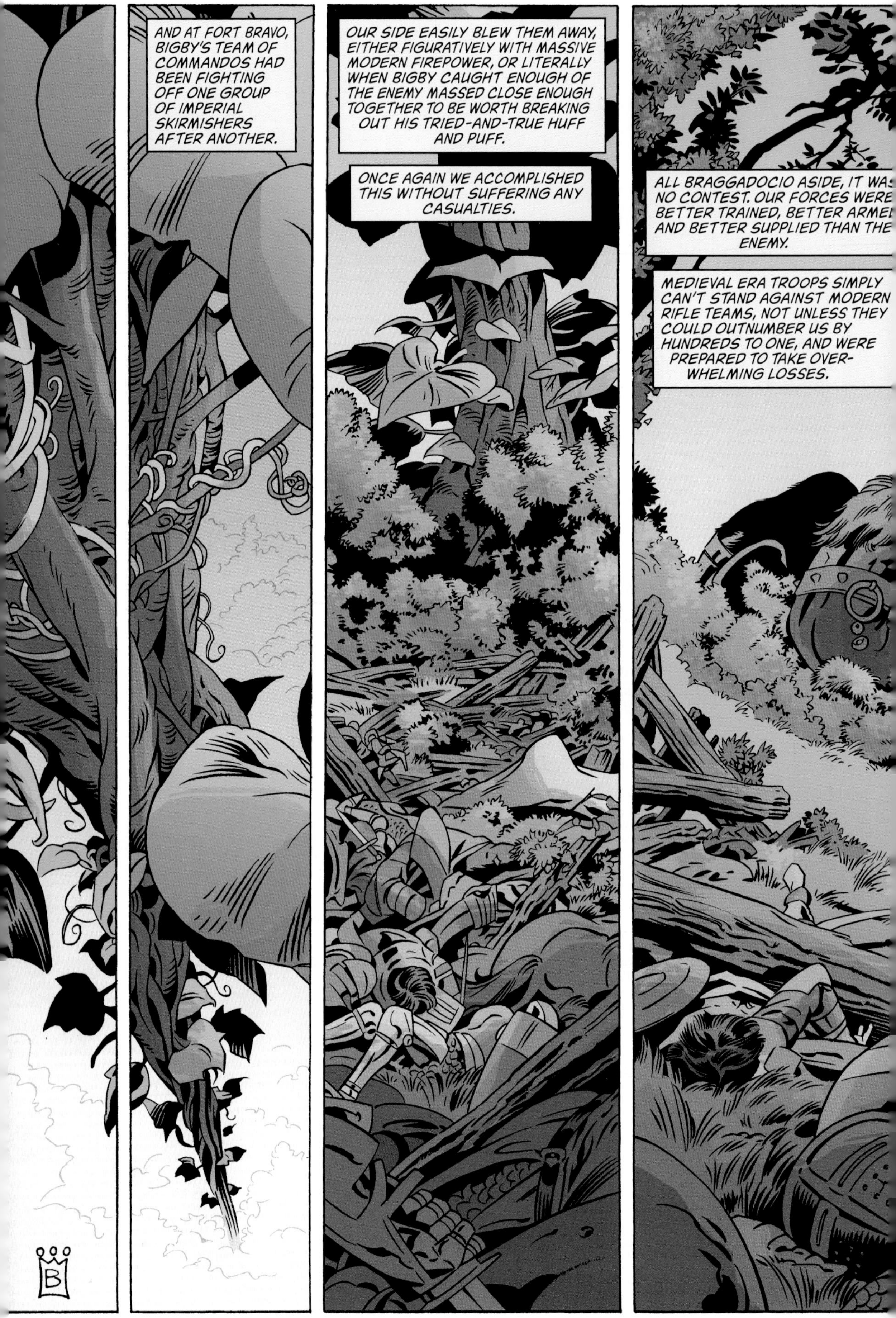
AND AT FORT BRAVO, BIGBY'S TEAM OF COMMANDOS HAD BEEN FIGHTING OFF ONE GROUP OF IMPERIAL SKIRMISHERS AFTER ANOTHER.
OUR SIDE EASILY BLEW THEM AWAY, EITHER FIGURATIVELY WITH MASSIVE MODERN FIREPOWER, OR LITERALLY WHEN BIGBY CAUGHT ENOUGH OF THE ENEMY MASSED CLOSE ENOUGH TOGETHER TO BE WORTH BREAKING OUT HIS TRIED-AND-TRUE HUFF AND PUFF.
ONCE AGAIN WE ACCOMPLISHED THIS WITHOUT SUFFERING ANY CASUALTIES.
ALL BRAGGADOCIO ASIDE, IT WAS NO CONTEST. OUR FORCES WERE BETTER TRAINED, BETTER ARMED AND BETTER SUPPLIED THAN THE ENEMY.
MEDIEVAL ERA TROOPS SIMPLY CAN'T STAND AGAINST MODERN RIFLE TEAMS, NOT UNLESS THEY COULD OUTNUMBER US BY HUNDREDS TO ONE, AND WERE PREPARED TO TAKE OVER-WHELMING LOSSES.

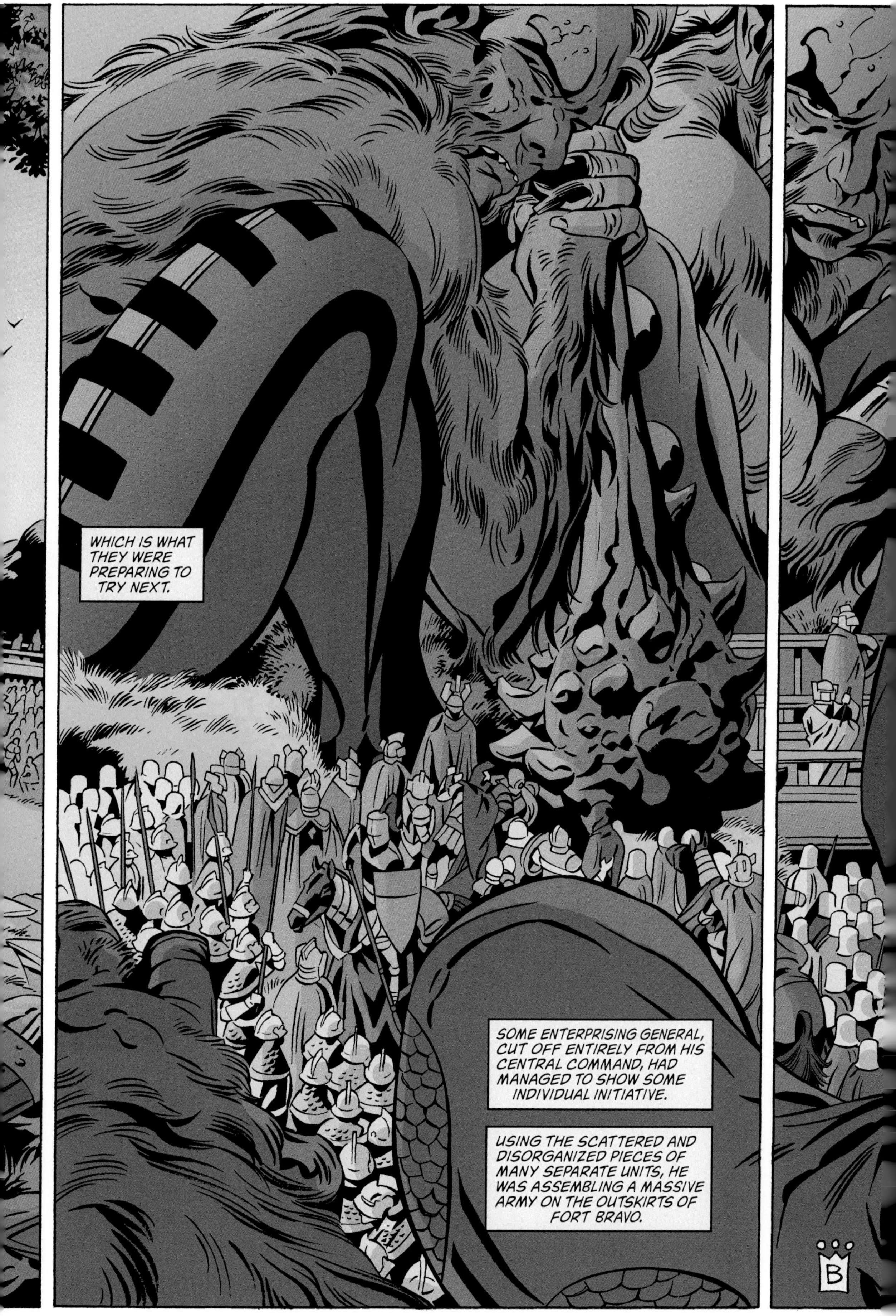
WHICH IS WHAT THEY WERE PREPARING TO TRY NEXT.
SOME ENTERPRISING GENERAL, CUT OFF ENTIRELY FROM HIS CENTRAL COMMAND, HAD MANAGED TO SHOW SOME INDIVIDUAL INITIATIVE.
USING THE SCATTERED AND DISORGANIZED PIECES OF MANY SEPARATE UNITS, HE WAS ASSEMBLING A MASSIVE ARMY ON THE OUTSKIRTS OF FORT BRAVO.

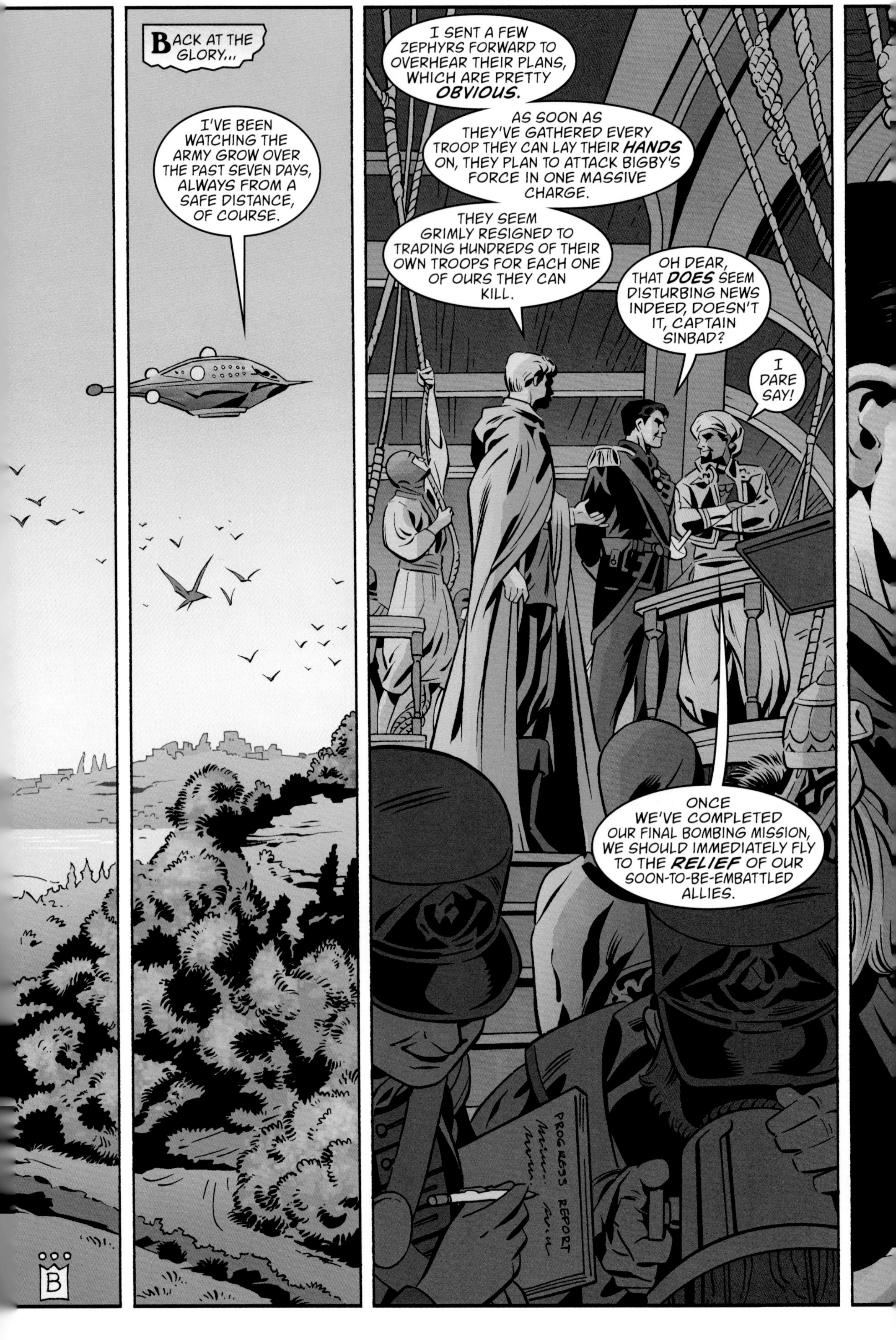

BACK AT THE GLORY...
I'VE BEEN WATCHING THE ARMY GROW OVER THE PAST SEVEN DAYS, ALWAYS FROM A SAFE DISTANCE, OF COURSE.
I SENT A FEW ZEPHYRS FORWARD TO OVERHEAR THEIR PLANS, WHICH ARE PRETTY ***OBVIOUS.***
AS SOON AS THEY'VE GATHERED EVERY TROOP THEY CAN LAY THEIR ***HANDS*** ON, THEY PLAN TO ATTACK BIGBY'S FORCE IN ONE MASSIVE CHARGE.
THEY SEEM GRIMLY RESIGNED TO TRADING HUNDREDS OF THEIR OWN TROOPS FOR EACH ONE OF OURS THEY CAN KILL.
OH DEAR, THAT ***DOES*** SEEM DISTURBING NEWS INDEED, DOESN'T IT, CAPTAIN SINBAD?
I DARE SAY!
ONCE WE'VE COMPLETED OUR FINAL BOMBING MISSION, WE SHOULD IMMEDIATELY FLY TO THE ***RELIEF*** OF OUR SOON-TO-BE-EMBATTLED ALLIES.
PROGRESS REPORT

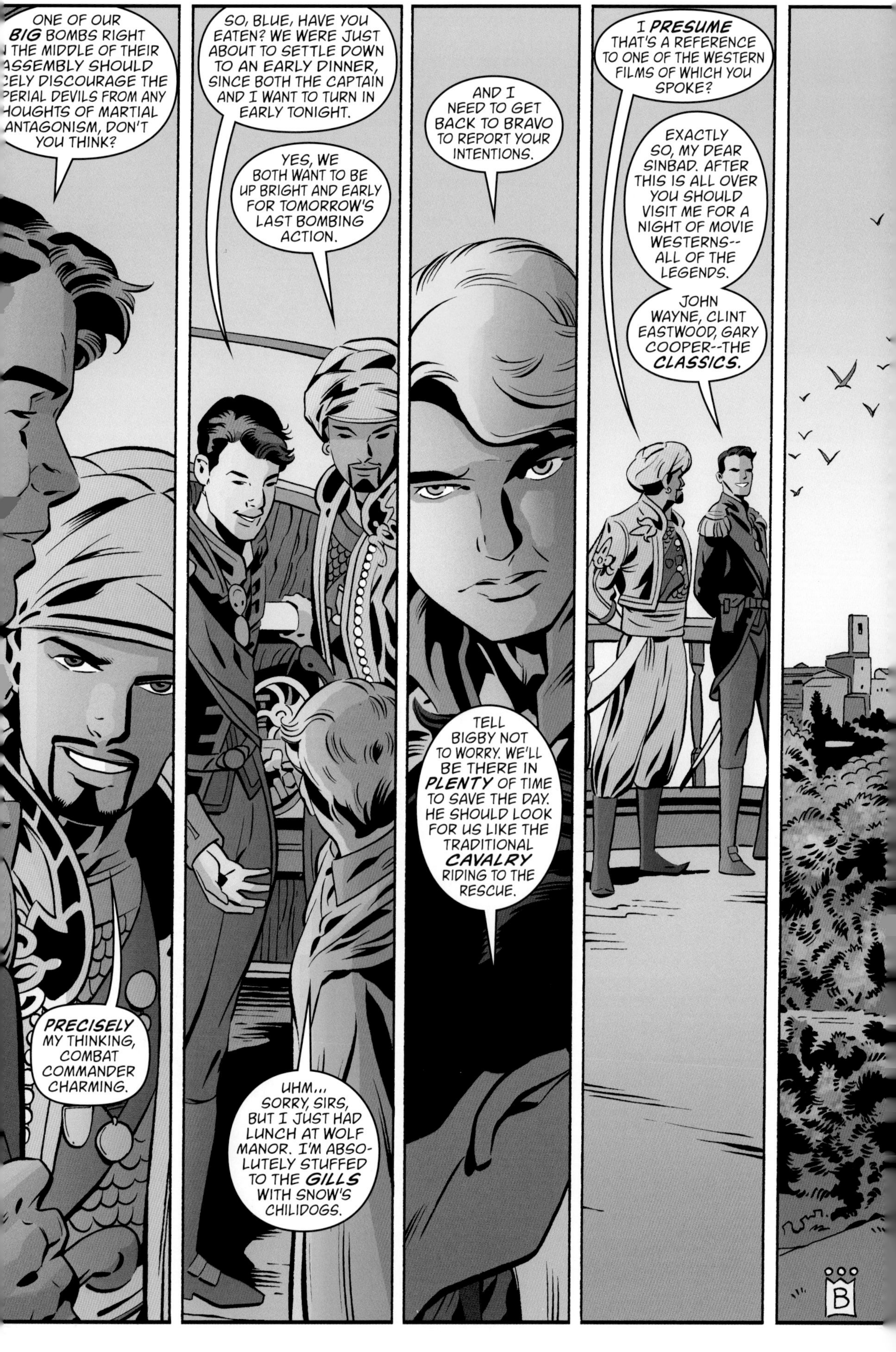
ONE OF OUR BIG BOMBS RIGHT IN THE MIDDLE OF THEIR ASSEMBLY SHOULD ...CELY DISCOURAGE THE ...PERIAL DEVILS FROM ANY ...HOUGHTS OF MARTIAL ANTAGONISM, DON'T YOU THINK?
PRECISELY MY THINKING, COMBAT COMMANDER CHARMING.
SO, BLUE, HAVE YOU EATEN? WE WERE JUST ABOUT TO SETTLE DOWN TO AN EARLY DINNER, SINCE BOTH THE CAPTAIN AND I WANT TO TURN IN EARLY TONIGHT.
YES, WE BOTH WANT TO BE UP BRIGHT AND EARLY FOR TOMORROW'S LAST BOMBING ACTION.
UHM... SORRY, SIRS, BUT I JUST HAD LUNCH AT WOLF MANOR. I'M ABSO- LUTELY STUFFED TO THE GILLS WITH SNOW'S CHILIDOGS.
AND I NEED TO GET BACK TO BRAVO TO REPORT YOUR INTENTIONS.
TELL BIGBY NOT TO WORRY. WE'LL BE THERE IN PLENTY OF TIME TO SAVE THE DAY. HE SHOULD LOOK FOR US LIKE THE TRADITIONAL CAVALRY RIDING TO THE RESCUE.
I PRESUME THAT'S A REFERENCE TO ONE OF THE WESTERN FILMS OF WHICH YOU SPOKE?
EXACTLY SO, MY DEAR SINBAD. AFTER THIS IS ALL OVER YOU SHOULD VISIT ME FOR A NIGHT OF MOVIE WESTERNS-- ALL OF THE LEGENDS.
JOHN WAYNE, CLINT EASTWOOD, GARY COOPER--THE CLASSICS.
B

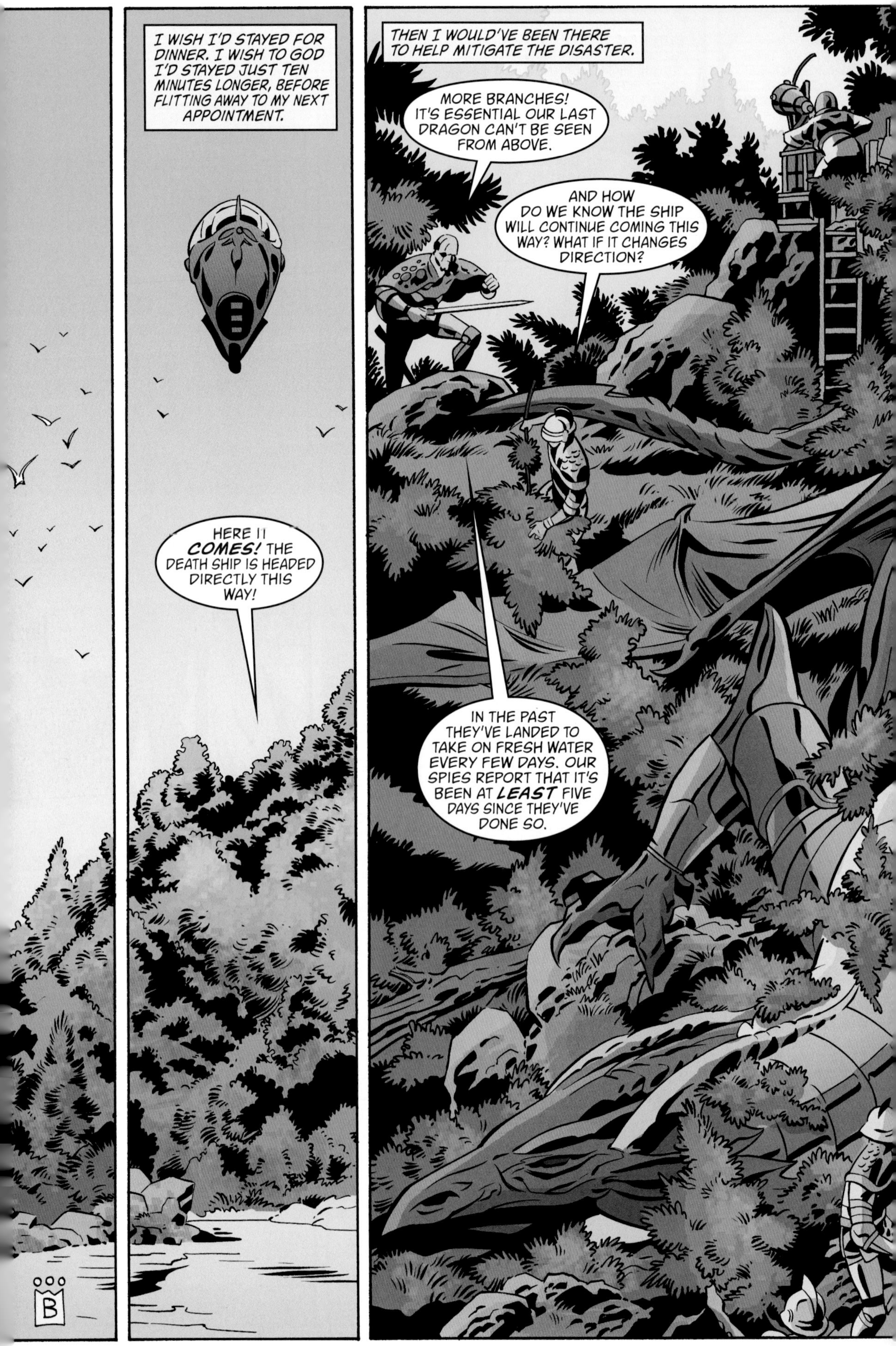
I WISH I'D STAYED FOR DINNER. I WISH TO GOD I'D STAYED JUST TEN MINUTES LONGER, BEFORE FLITTING AWAY TO MY NEXT APPOINTMENT.
HERE IT COMES! THE DEATH SHIP IS HEADED DIRECTLY THIS WAY!
THEN I WOULD'VE BEEN THERE TO HELP MITIGATE THE DISASTER.
MORE BRANCHES! IT'S ESSENTIAL OUR LAST DRAGON CAN'T BE SEEN FROM ABOVE.
AND HOW DO WE KNOW THE SHIP WILL CONTINUE COMING THIS WAY? WHAT IF IT CHANGES DIRECTION?
IN THE PAST THEY'VE LANDED TO TAKE ON FRESH WATER EVERY FEW DAYS. OUR SPIES REPORT THAT IT'S BEEN AT LEAST FIVE DAYS SINCE THEY'VE DONE SO.

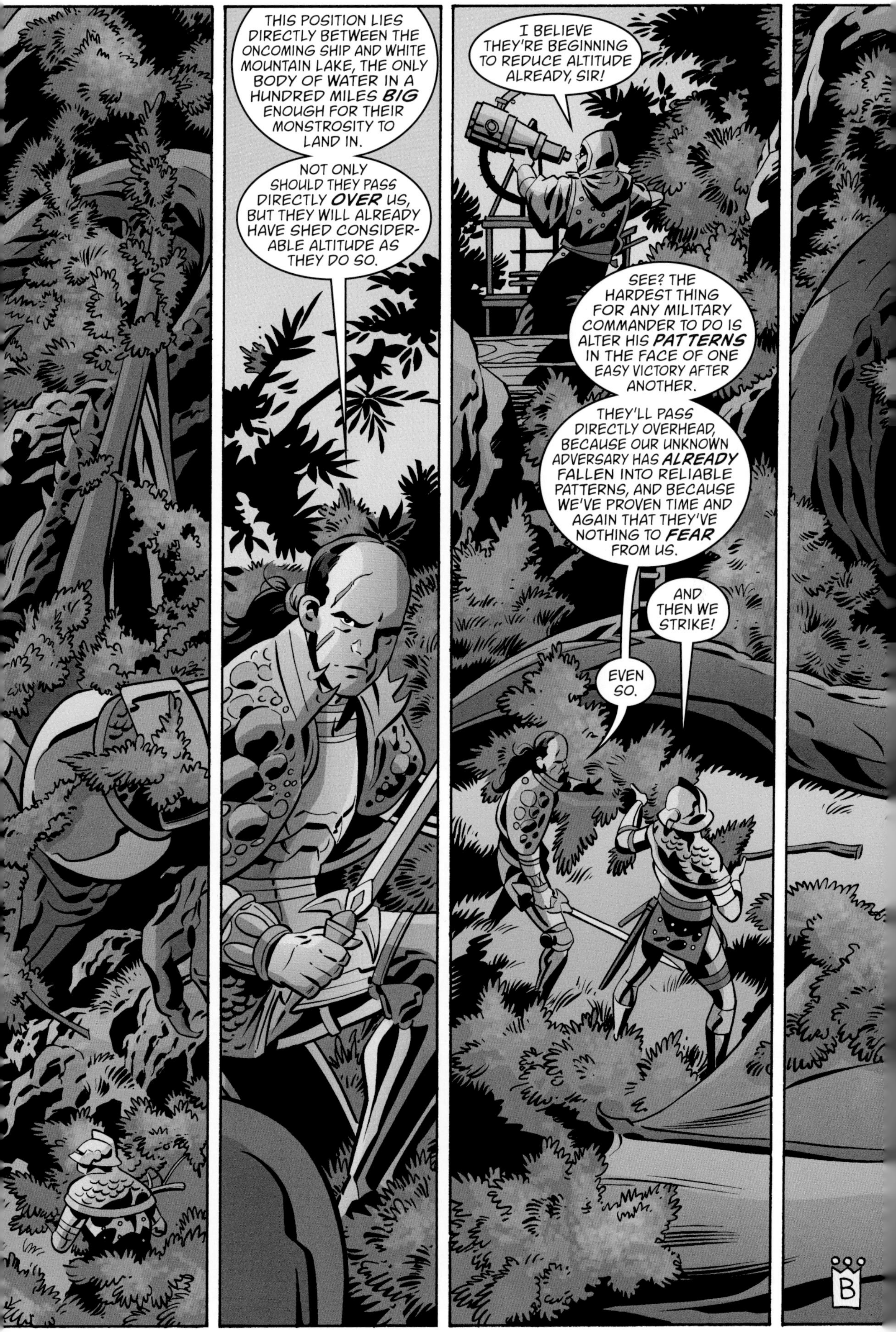
THIS POSITION LIES DIRECTLY BETWEEN THE ONCOMING SHIP AND WHITE MOUNTAIN LAKE, THE ONLY BODY OF WATER IN A HUNDRED MILES BIG ENOUGH FOR THEIR MONSTROSITY TO LAND IN.
NOT ONLY SHOULD THEY PASS DIRECTLY OVER US, BUT THEY WILL ALREADY HAVE SHED CONSIDER-ABLE ALTITUDE AS THEY DO SO.
I BELIEVE THEY'RE BEGINNING TO REDUCE ALTITUDE ALREADY, SIR!
SEE? THE HARDEST THING FOR ANY MILITARY COMMANDER TO DO IS ALTER HIS PATTERNS IN THE FACE OF ONE EASY VICTORY AFTER ANOTHER.
THEY'LL PASS DIRECTLY OVERHEAD, BECAUSE OUR UNKNOWN ADVERSARY HAS ALREADY FALLEN INTO RELIABLE PATTERNS, AND BECAUSE WE'VE PROVEN TIME AND AGAIN THAT THEY'VE NOTHING TO FEAR FROM US.
EVEN SO.
AND THEN WE STRIKE!

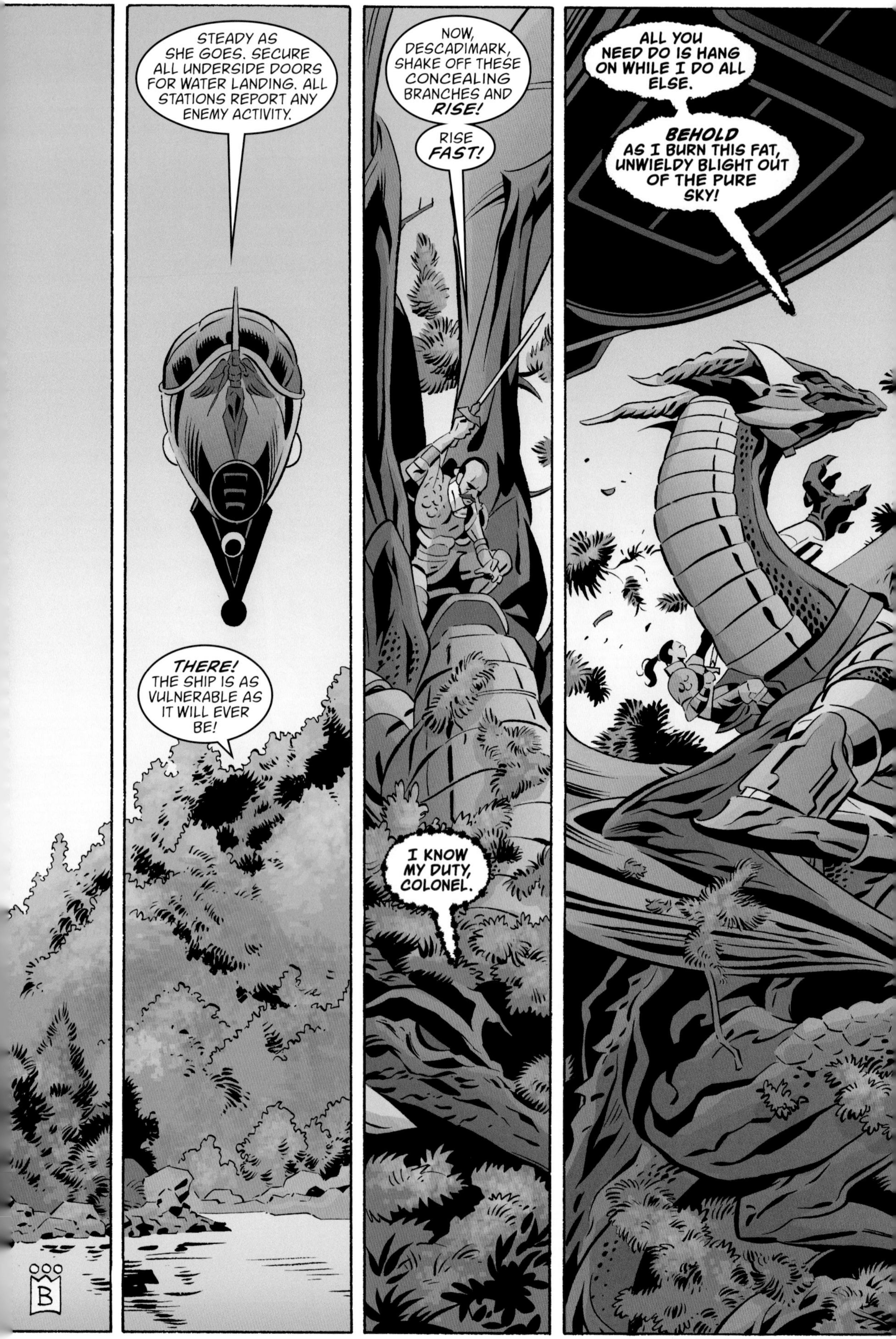
STEADY AS SHE GOES. SECURE ALL UNDERSIDE DOORS FOR WATER LANDING. ALL STATIONS REPORT ANY ENEMY ACTIVITY.
THERE! THE SHIP IS AS VULNERABLE AS IT WILL EVER BE!
NOW, DESCADIMARK, SHAKE OFF THESE CONCEALING BRANCHES AND RISE!
RISE FAST!
I KNOW MY DUTY, COLONEL.
ALL YOU NEED DO IS HANG ON WHILE I DO ALL ELSE.
BEHOLD AS I BURN THIS FAT, UNWIELDY BLIGHT OUT OF THE PURE SKY!

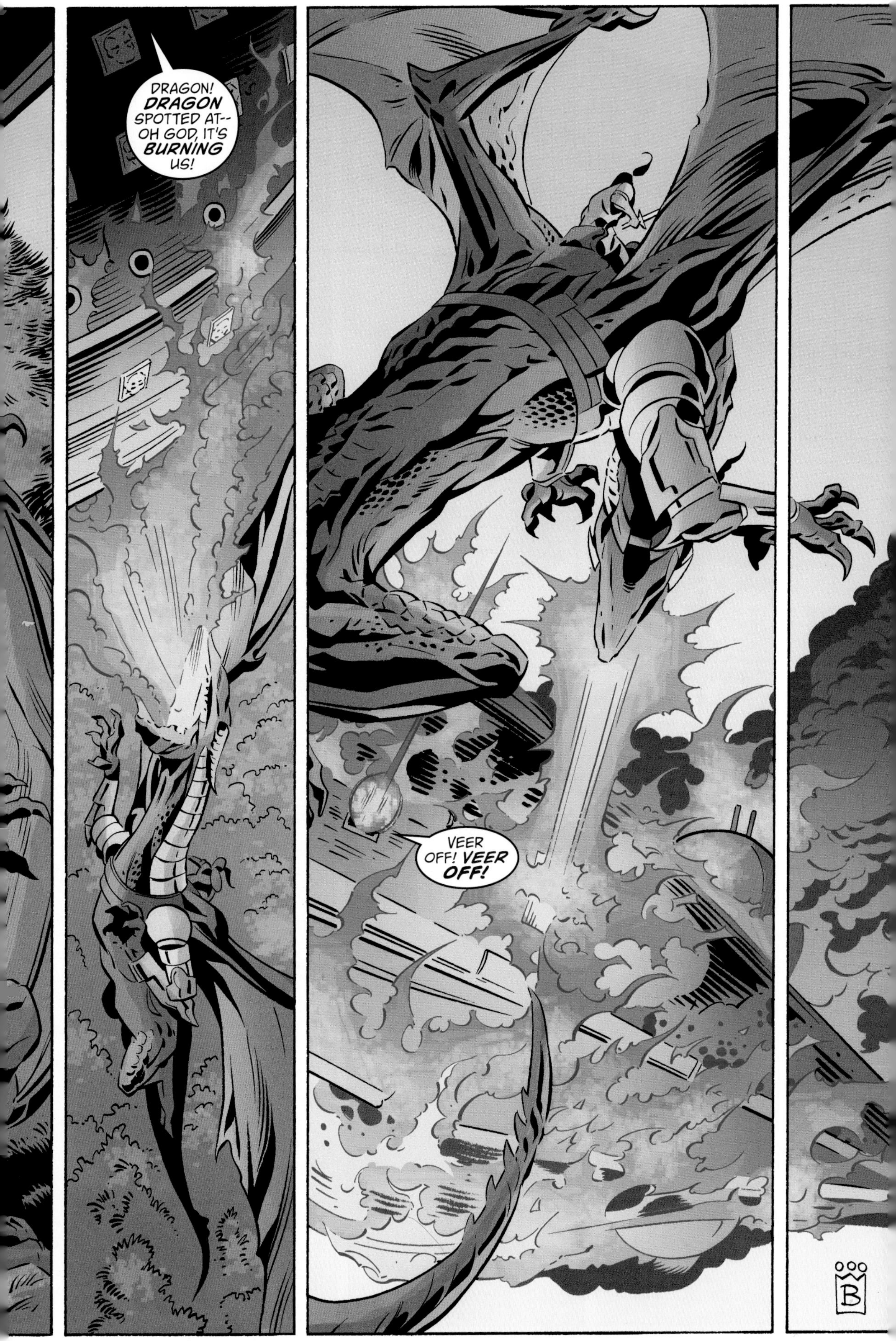
DRAGON! **DRAGON** SPOTTED AT-- OH GOD, IT'S **BURNING** US!
VEER OFF! **VEER OFF!**

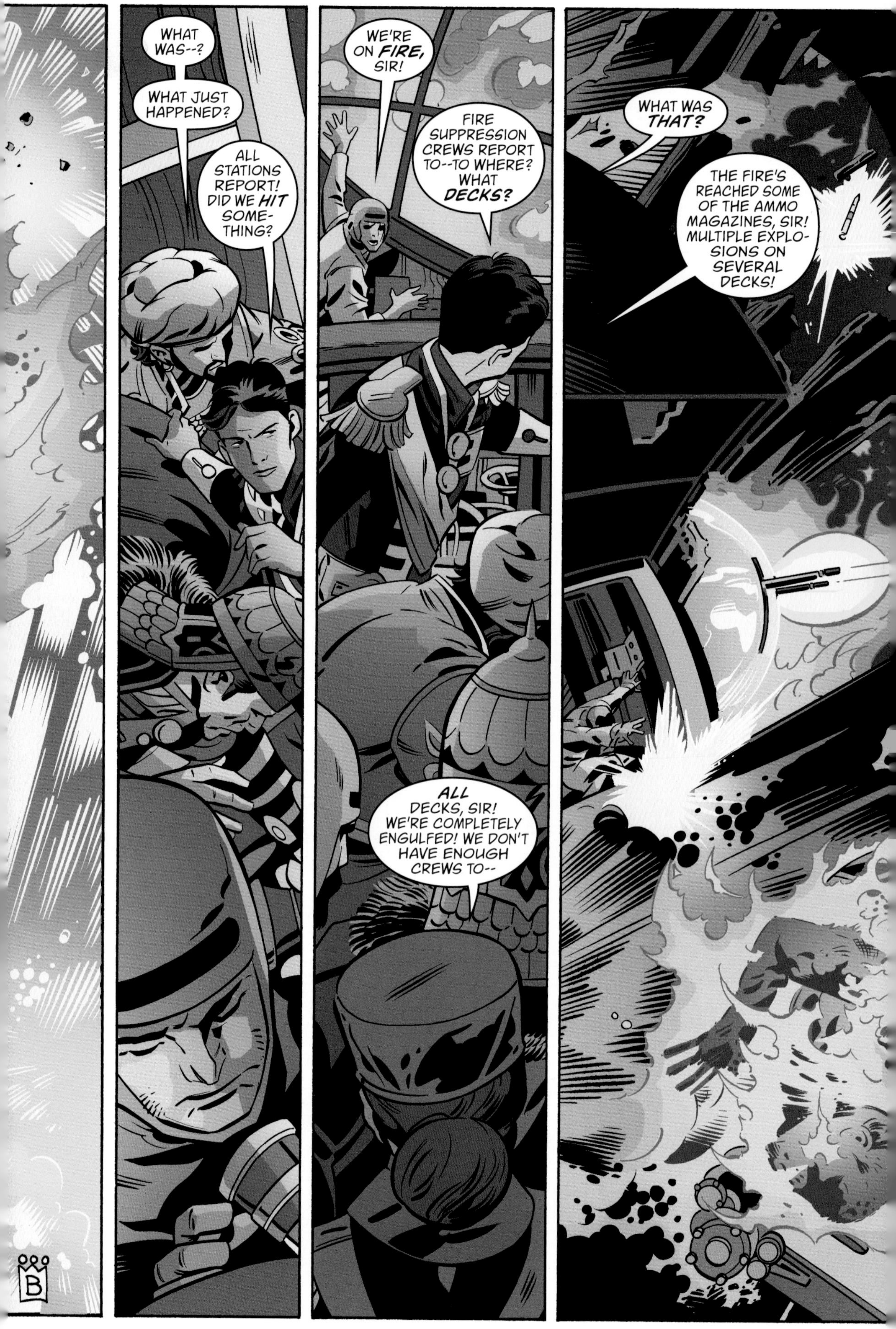

WHAT WAS--?
WHAT JUST HAPPENED?
ALL STATIONS REPORT! DID WE HIT SOME-THING?
WE'RE ON FIRE, SIR!
FIRE SUPPRESSION CREWS REPORT TO--TO WHERE? WHAT DECKS?
ALL DECKS, SIR! WE'RE COMPLETELY ENGULFED! WE DON'T HAVE ENOUGH CREWS TO--
WHAT WAS THAT?
THE FIRE'S REACHED SOME OF THE AMMO MAGAZINES, SIR! MULTIPLE EXPLO-SIONS ON SEVERAL DECKS!

WE NEED TO FIGHT THE FIRES AND RESTORE--

I BELIEVE THAT TIME HAS PASSED, CAPTAIN. THE SHIP IS **LOST**, MY FRIEND. IT'S TIME TO GIVE THE ORDER.

GIVE THE **ORDER**, CAPTAIN. YOU'RE THE ONLY ONE WHO CAN.

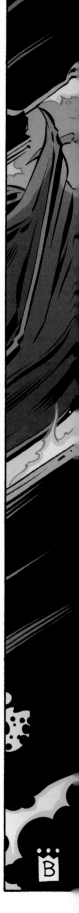

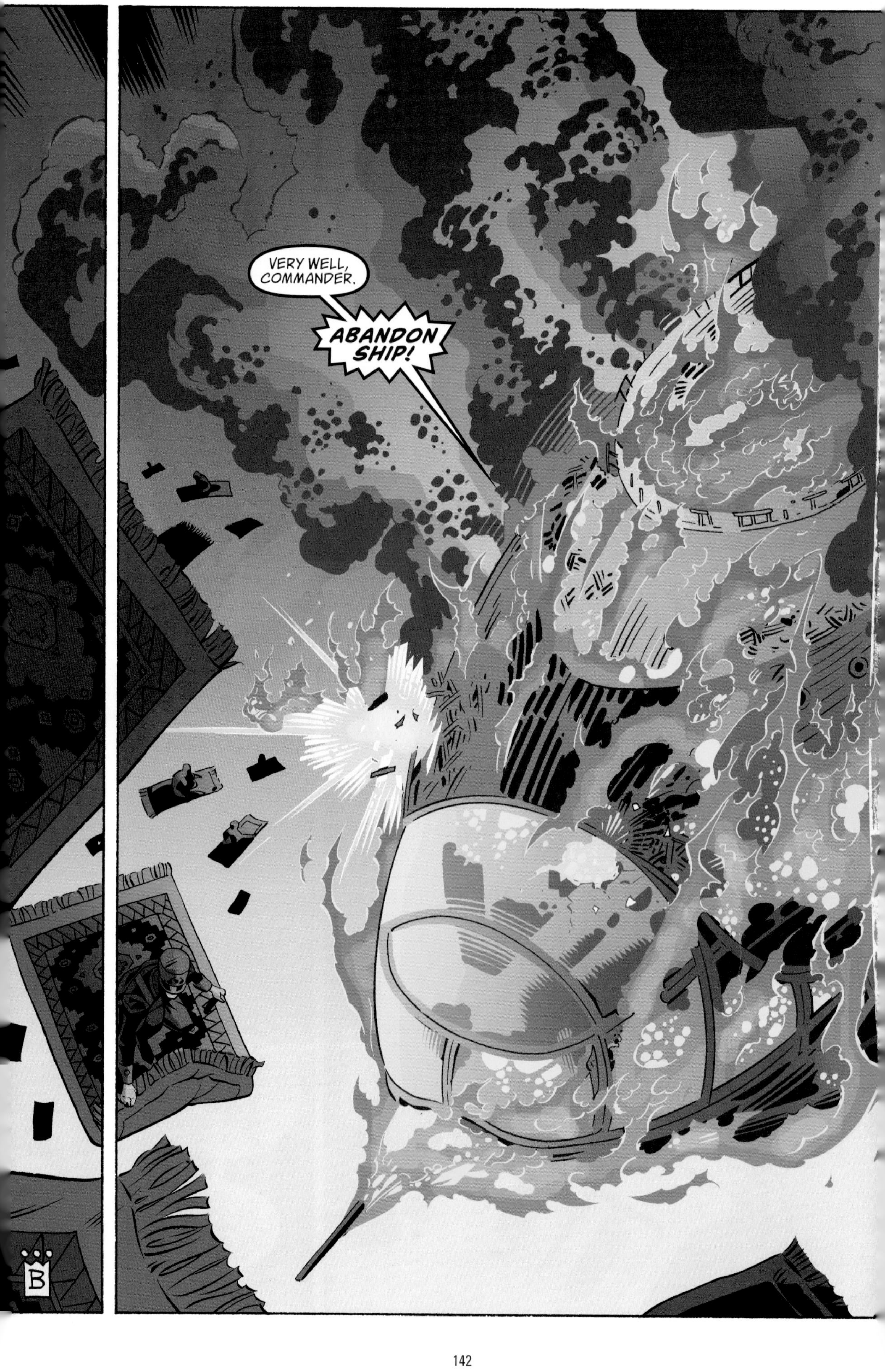
VERY WELL, COMMANDER.
ABANDON SHIP!

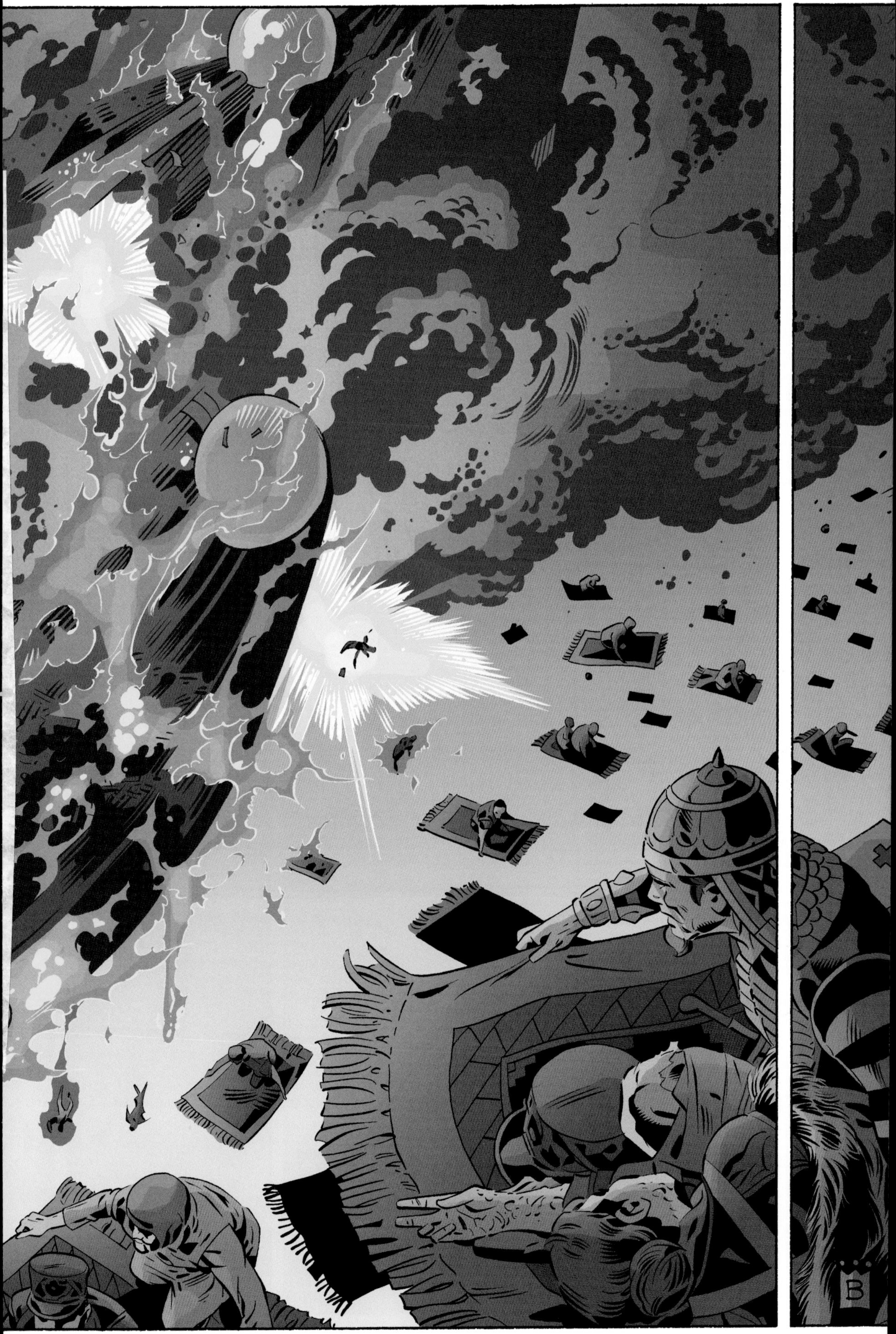

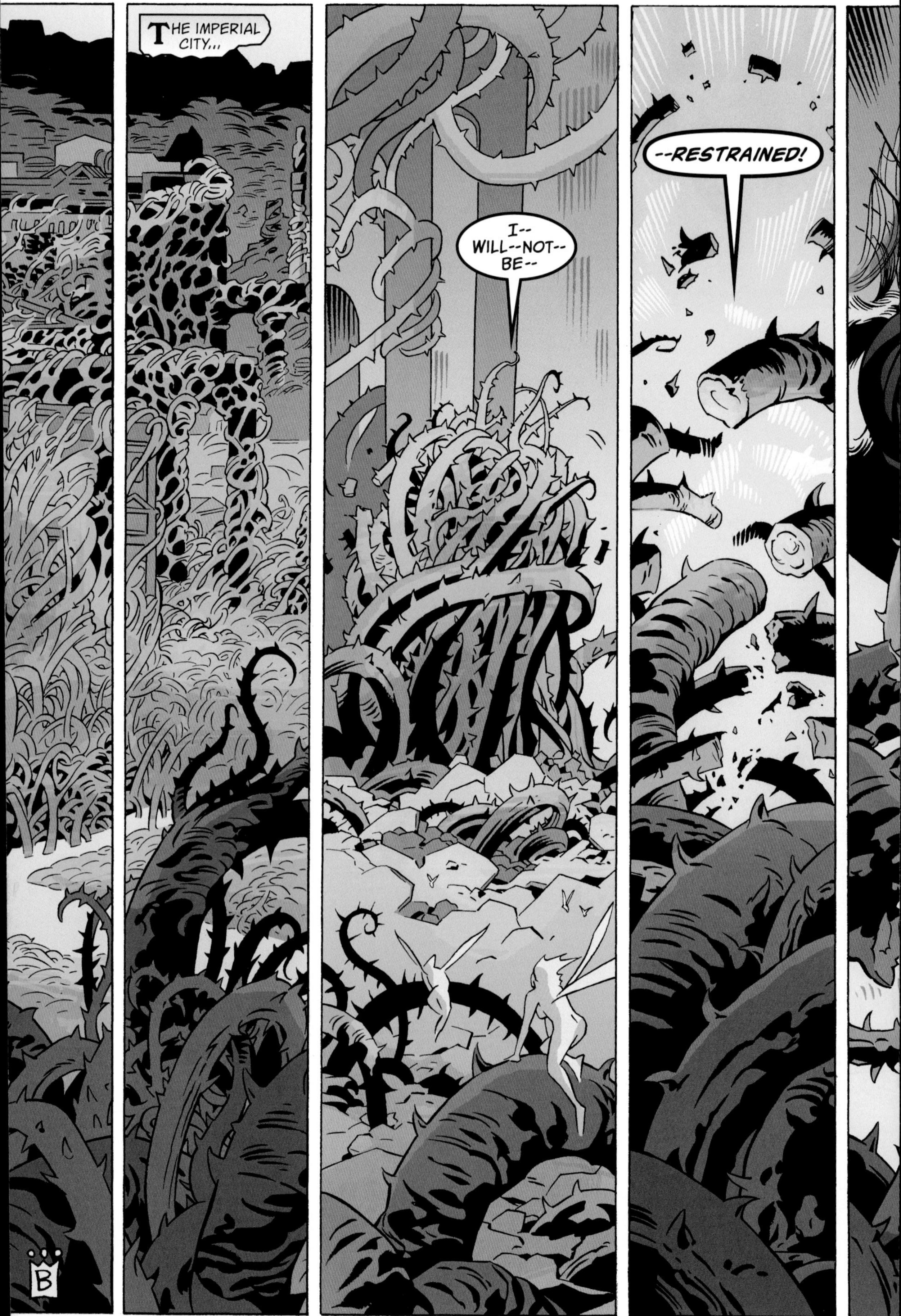
THE IMPERIAL CITY...
I--WILL--NOT--BE--
--RESTRAINED!

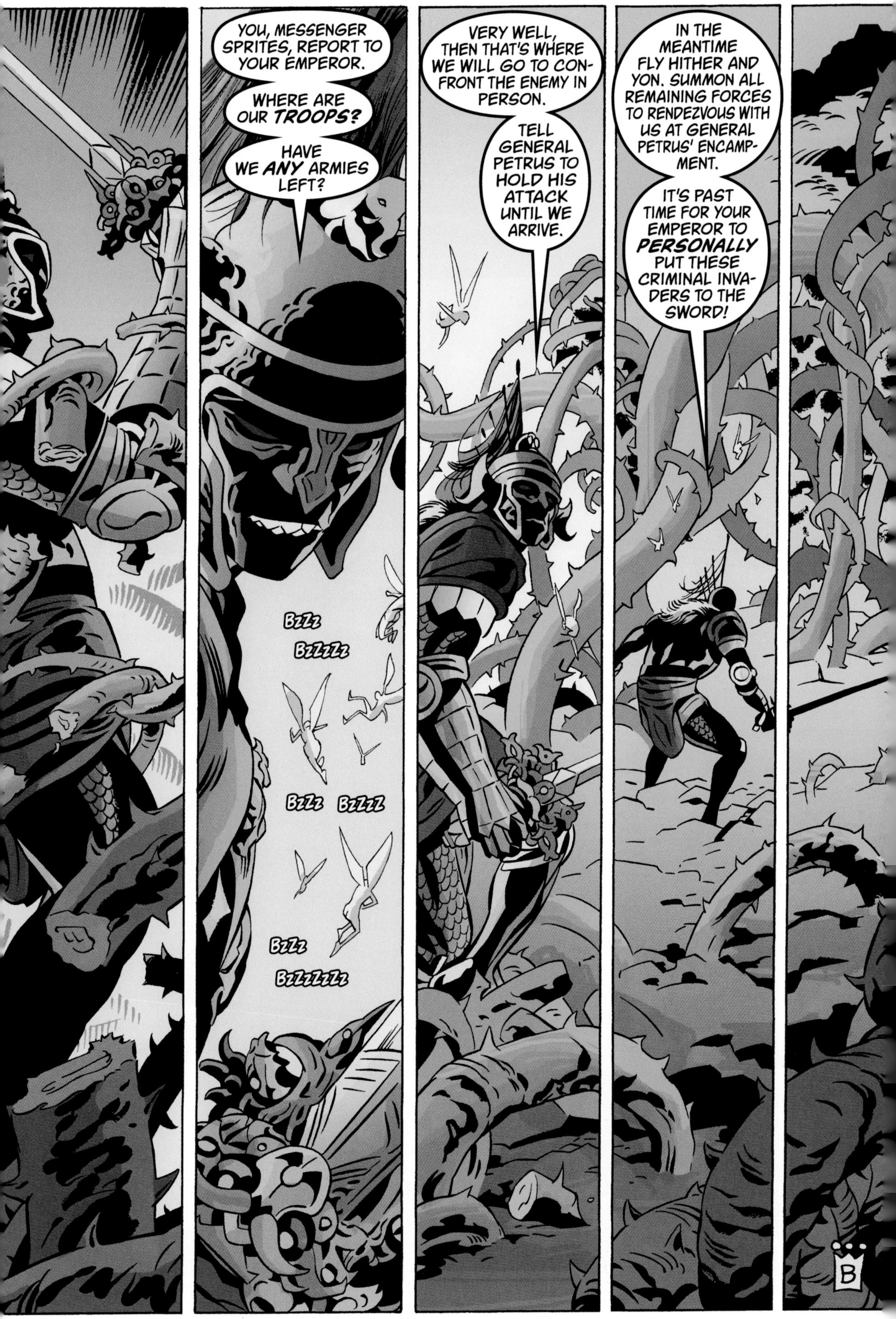
YOU, MESSENGER SPRITES, REPORT TO YOUR EMPEROR.
WHERE ARE OUR TROOPS?
HAVE WE ANY ARMIES LEFT?
BzZz
BzZzZz
BzZz BzZzZ
BzZz
BzZzZzZz
VERY WELL, THEN THAT'S WHERE WE WILL GO TO CONFRONT THE ENEMY IN PERSON.
TELL GENERAL PETRUS TO HOLD HIS ATTACK UNTIL WE ARRIVE.
IN THE MEANTIME FLY HITHER AND YON. SUMMON ALL REMAINING FORCES TO RENDEZVOUS WITH US AT GENERAL PETRUS' ENCAMPMENT.
IT'S PAST TIME FOR YOUR EMPEROR TO PERSONALLY PUT THESE CRIMINAL INVADERS TO THE SWORD!
B

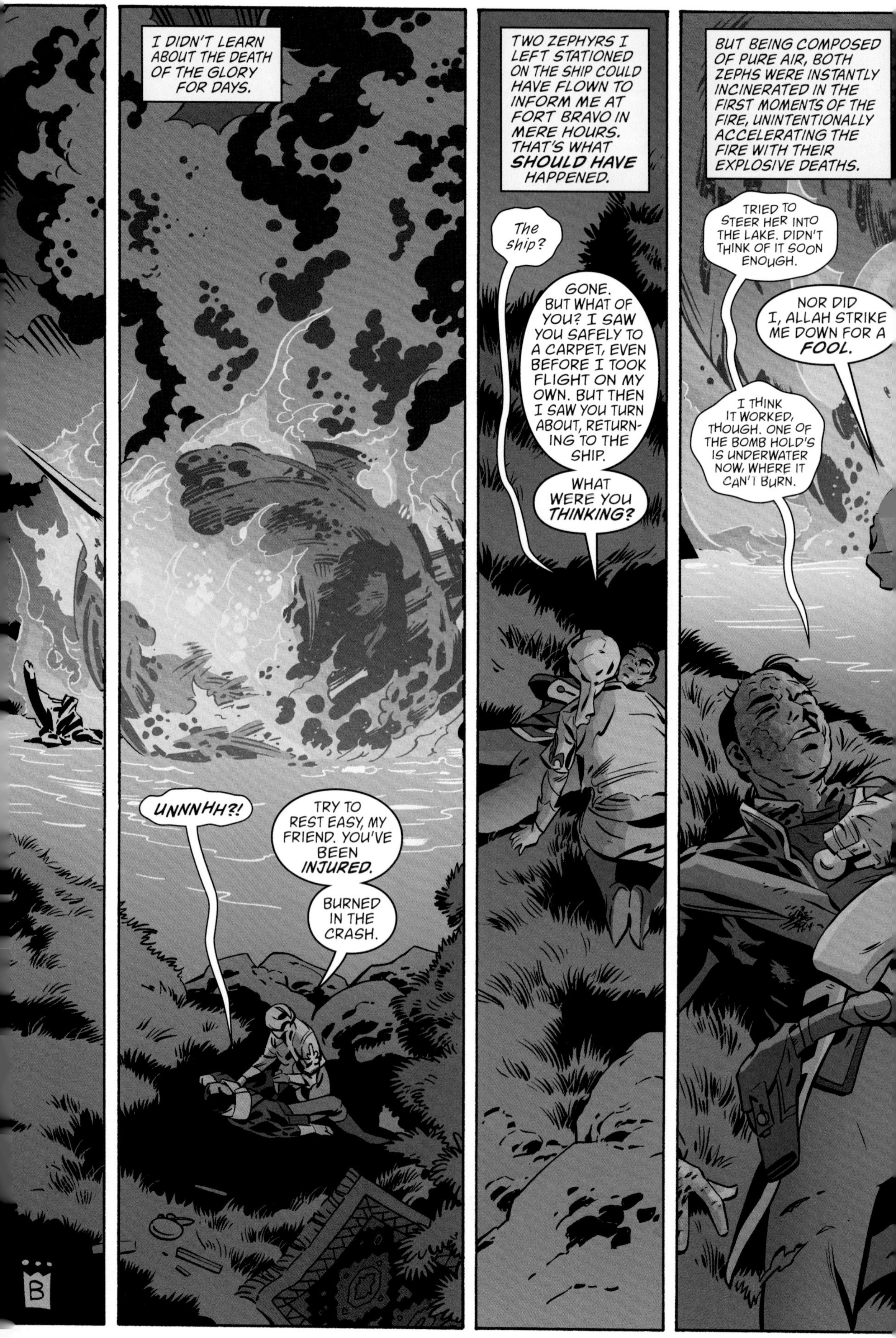

I DIDN'T LEARN ABOUT THE DEATH OF THE GLORY FOR DAYS.
UNNNHH?!
TRY TO REST EASY, MY FRIEND. YOU'VE BEEN INJURED.
BURNED IN THE CRASH.
TWO ZEPHYRS I LEFT STATIONED ON THE SHIP COULD HAVE FLOWN TO INFORM ME AT FORT BRAVO IN MERE HOURS. THAT'S WHAT SHOULD HAVE HAPPENED.
The ship?
GONE. BUT WHAT OF YOU? I SAW YOU SAFELY TO A CARPET, EVEN BEFORE I TOOK FLIGHT ON MY OWN. BUT THEN I SAW YOU TURN ABOUT, RETURNING TO THE SHIP.
WHAT WERE YOU THINKING?
BUT BEING COMPOSED OF PURE AIR, BOTH ZEPHS WERE INSTANTLY INCINERATED IN THE FIRST MOMENTS OF THE FIRE, UNINTENTIONALLY ACCELERATING THE FIRE WITH THEIR EXPLOSIVE DEATHS.
TRIED TO STEER HER INTO THE LAKE. DIDN'T THINK OF IT SOON ENOUGH.
NOR DID I, ALLAH STRIKE ME DOWN FOR A FOOL.
I THINK IT WORKED, THOUGH. ONE OF THE BOMB HOLD'S IS UNDERWATER NOW, WHERE IT CAN'T BURN.

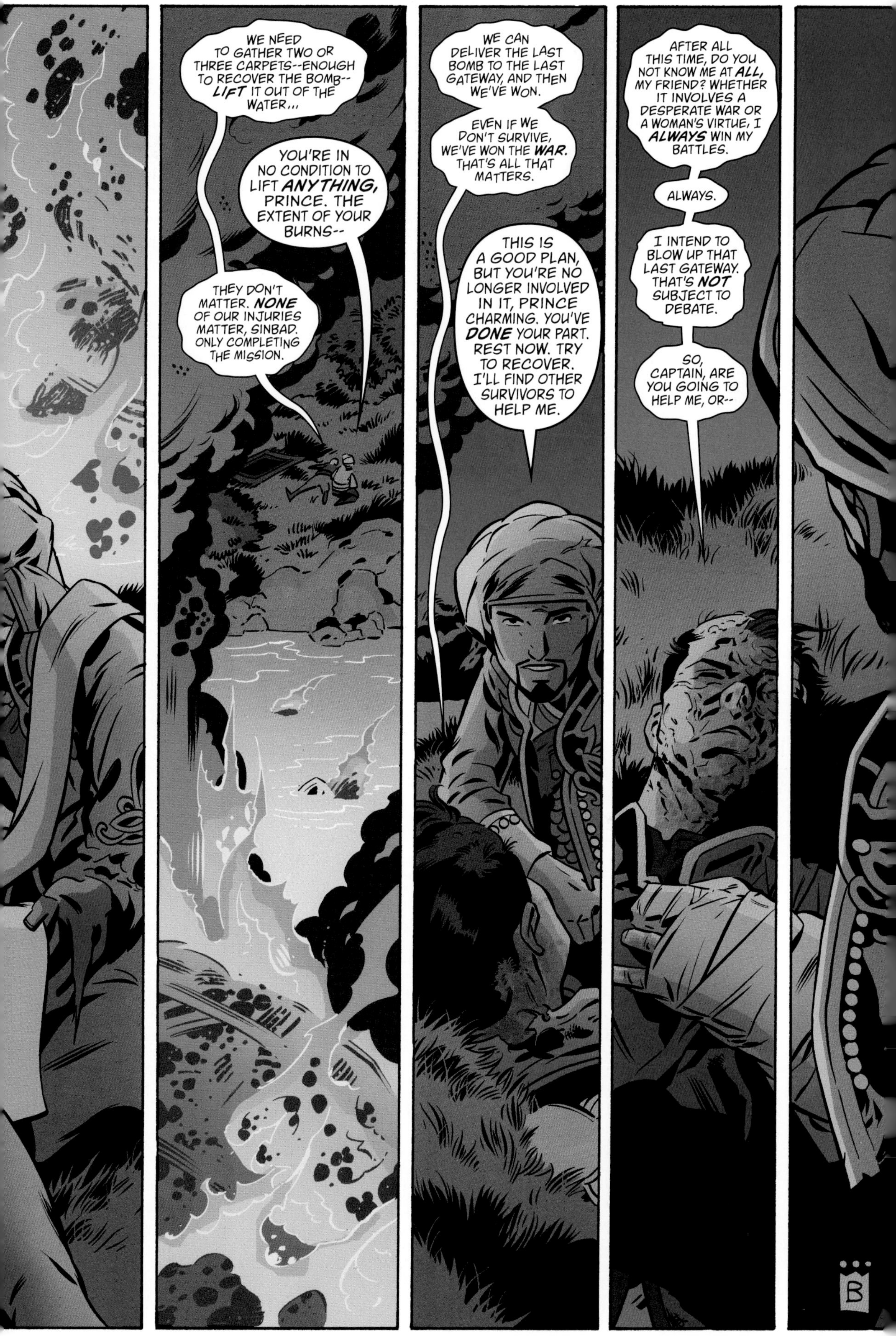
WE NEED TO GATHER TWO OR THREE CARPETS--ENOUGH TO RECOVER THE BOMB--LIFT IT OUT OF THE WATER...
YOU'RE IN NO CONDITION TO LIFT ANYTHING, PRINCE. THE EXTENT OF YOUR BURNS--
THEY DON'T MATTER. NONE OF OUR INJURIES MATTER, SINBAD. ONLY COMPLETING THE MISSION.
WE CAN DELIVER THE LAST BOMB TO THE LAST GATEWAY, AND THEN WE'VE WON.
EVEN IF WE DON'T SURVIVE, WE'VE WON THE WAR. THAT'S ALL THAT MATTERS.
THIS IS A GOOD PLAN, BUT YOU'RE NO LONGER INVOLVED IN IT, PRINCE CHARMING. YOU'VE DONE YOUR PART. REST NOW. TRY TO RECOVER. I'LL FIND OTHER SURVIVORS TO HELP ME.
AFTER ALL THIS TIME, DO YOU NOT KNOW ME AT ALL, MY FRIEND? WHETHER IT INVOLVES A DESPERATE WAR OR A WOMAN'S VIRTUE, I ALWAYS WIN MY BATTLES.
ALWAYS.
I INTEND TO BLOW UP THAT LAST GATEWAY. THAT'S NOT SUBJECT TO DEBATE.
SO, CAPTAIN, ARE YOU GOING TO HELP ME, OR--

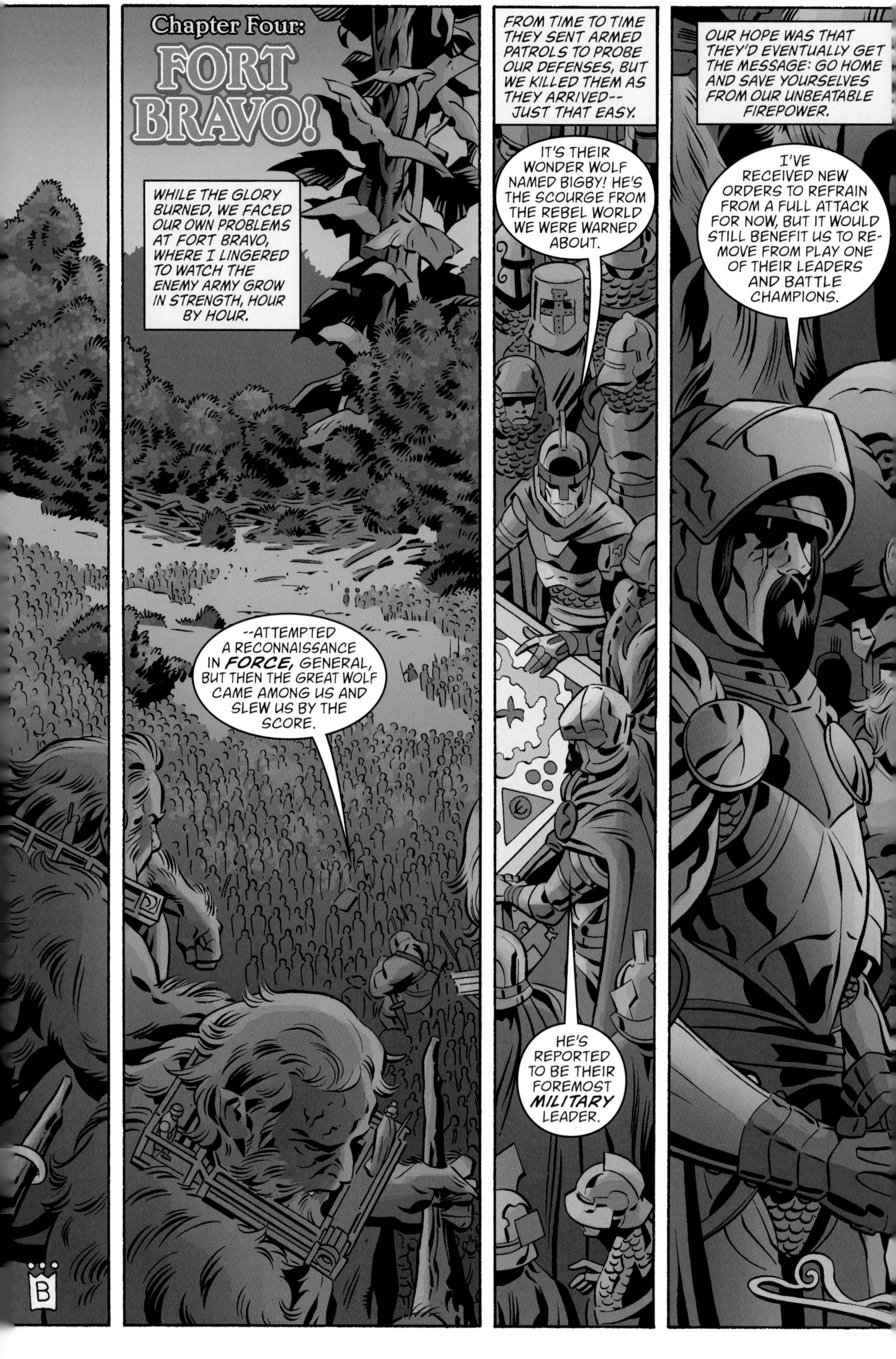

Chapter Four:
FORT BRAVO!
WHILE THE GLORY BURNED, WE FACED OUR OWN PROBLEMS AT FORT BRAVO, WHERE I LINGERED TO WATCH THE ENEMY ARMY GROW IN STRENGTH, HOUR BY HOUR.
--ATTEMPTED A RECONNAISSANCE IN FORCE, GENERAL, BUT THEN THE GREAT WOLF CAME AMONG US AND SLEW US BY THE SCORE.
FROM TIME TO TIME THEY SENT ARMED PATROLS TO PROBE OUR DEFENSES, BUT WE KILLED THEM AS THEY ARRIVED-- JUST THAT EASY.
IT'S THEIR WONDER WOLF NAMED BIGBY! HE'S THE SCOURGE FROM THE REBEL WORLD WE WERE WARNED ABOUT.
HE'S REPORTED TO BE THEIR FOREMOST MILITARY LEADER.
OUR HOPE WAS THAT THEY'D EVENTUALLY GET THE MESSAGE: GO HOME AND SAVE YOURSELVES FROM OUR UNBEATABLE FIREPOWER.
I'VE RECEIVED NEW ORDERS TO REFRAIN FROM A FULL ATTACK FOR NOW, BUT IT WOULD STILL BENEFIT US TO RE-MOVE FROM PLAY ONE OF THEIR LEADERS AND BATTLE CHAMPIONS.

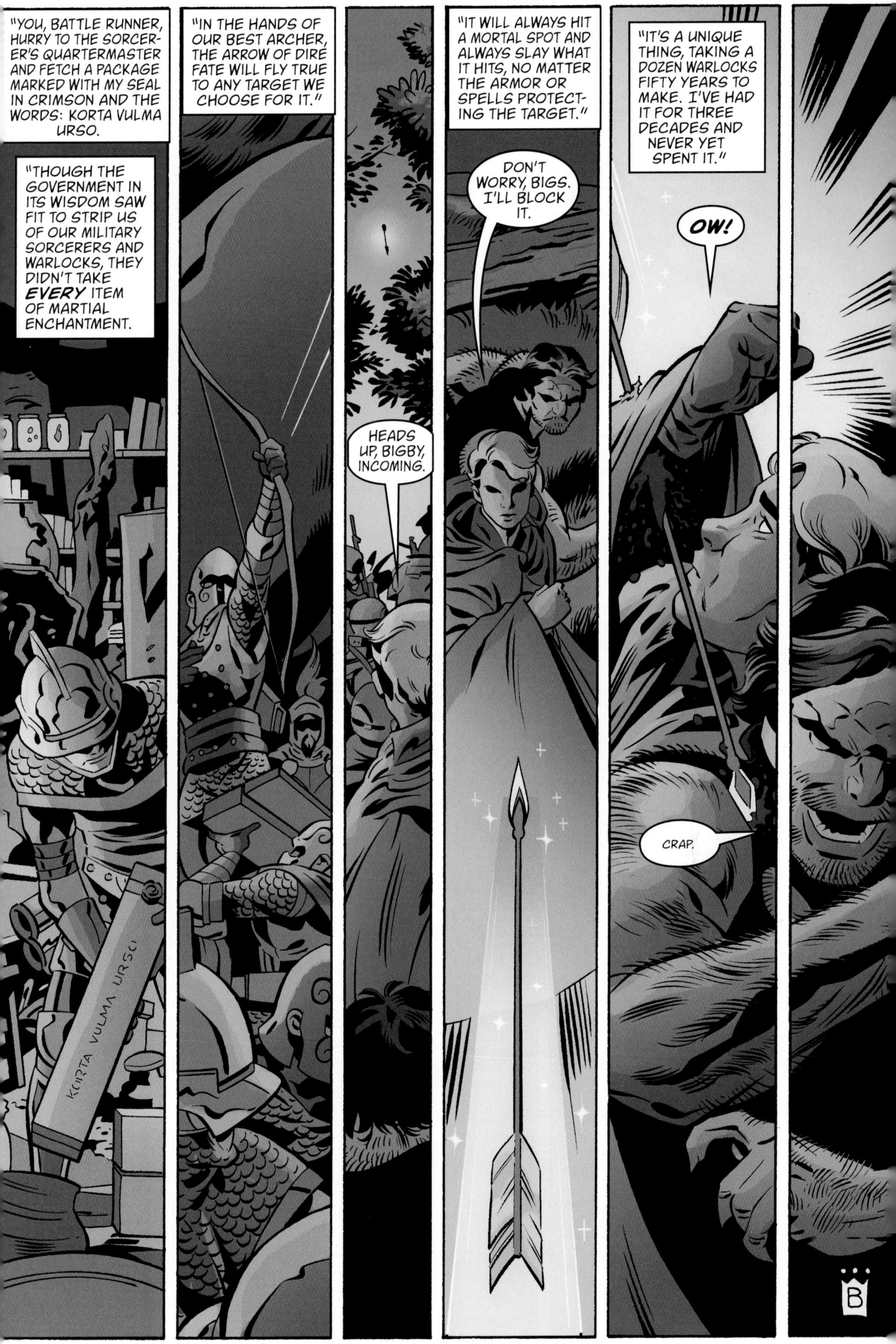
"YOU, BATTLE RUNNER, HURRY TO THE SORCERER'S QUARTERMASTER AND FETCH A PACKAGE MARKED WITH MY SEAL IN CRIMSON AND THE WORDS: KORTA VULMA URSO.
"THOUGH THE GOVERNMENT IN ITS WISDOM SAW FIT TO STRIP US OF OUR MILITARY SORCERERS AND WARLOCKS, THEY DIDN'T TAKE **EVERY** ITEM OF MARTIAL ENCHANTMENT.
KORTA VULMA URSO
"IN THE HANDS OF OUR BEST ARCHER, THE ARROW OF DIRE FATE WILL FLY TRUE TO ANY TARGET WE CHOOSE FOR IT."
HEADS UP, BIGBY, INCOMING.
"IT WILL ALWAYS HIT A MORTAL SPOT AND ALWAYS SLAY WHAT IT HITS, NO MATTER THE ARMOR OR SPELLS PROTECTING THE TARGET."
DON'T WORRY, BIGS. I'LL BLOCK IT.
"IT'S A UNIQUE THING, TAKING A DOZEN WARLOCKS FIFTY YEARS TO MAKE. I'VE HAD IT FOR THREE DECADES AND NEVER YET SPENT IT."
OW!
CRAP.
B

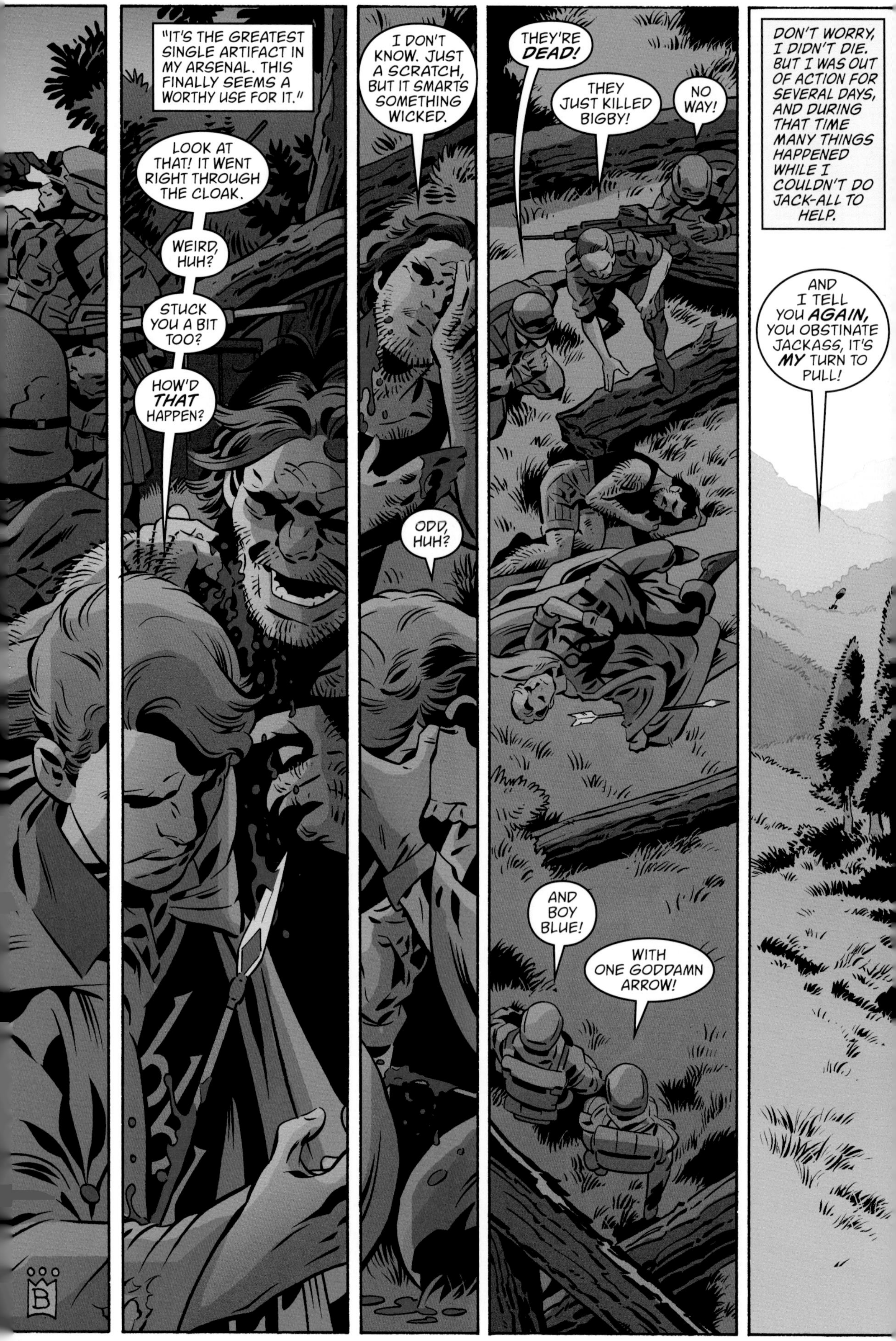
"IT'S THE GREATEST SINGLE ARTIFACT IN MY ARSENAL. THIS FINALLY SEEMS A WORTHY USE FOR IT."
LOOK AT THAT! IT WENT RIGHT THROUGH THE CLOAK.
WEIRD, HUH?
STUCK YOU A BIT TOO?
HOW'D *THAT* HAPPEN?
I DON'T KNOW. JUST A SCRATCH, BUT IT SMARTS SOMETHING WICKED.
ODD, HUH?
THEY'RE *DEAD!*
THEY JUST KILLED BIGBY!
NO WAY!
AND BOY BLUE!
WITH ONE GODDAMN ARROW!
DON'T WORRY, I DIDN'T DIE. BUT I WAS OUT OF ACTION FOR SEVERAL DAYS, AND DURING THAT TIME MANY THINGS HAPPENED WHILE I COULDN'T DO JACK-ALL TO HELP.
AND I TELL YOU *AGAIN,* YOU OBSTINATE JACKASS, IT'S *MY* TURN TO PULL!

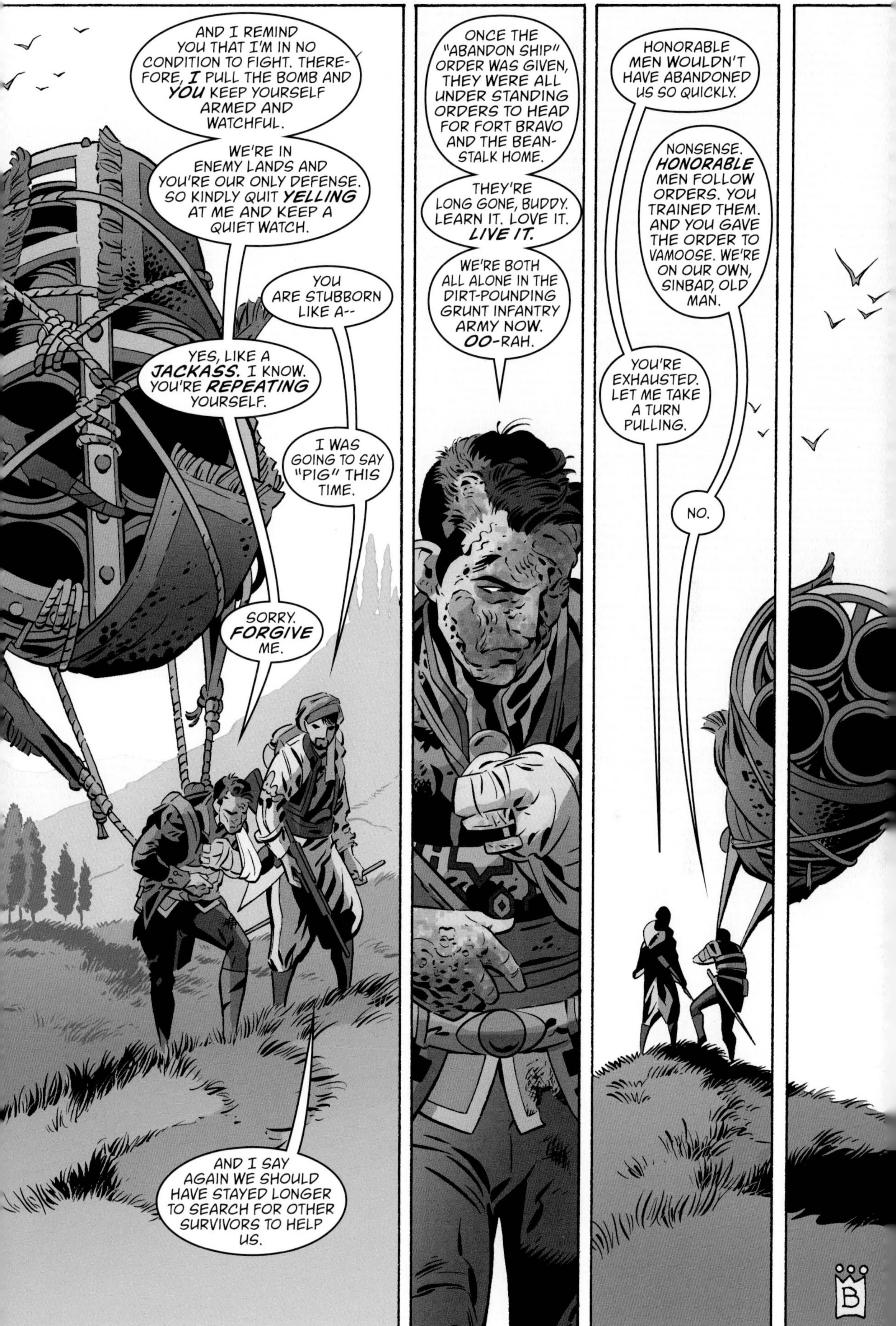
AND I REMIND YOU THAT I'M IN NO CONDITION TO FIGHT. THEREFORE, I PULL THE BOMB AND YOU KEEP YOURSELF ARMED AND WATCHFUL.
WE'RE IN ENEMY LANDS AND YOU'RE OUR ONLY DEFENSE. SO KINDLY QUIT YELLING AT ME AND KEEP A QUIET WATCH.
YOU ARE STUBBORN LIKE A--
YES, LIKE A JACKASS. I KNOW. YOU'RE REPEATING YOURSELF.
I WAS GOING TO SAY "PIG" THIS TIME.
SORRY. FORGIVE ME.
AND I SAY AGAIN WE SHOULD HAVE STAYED LONGER TO SEARCH FOR OTHER SURVIVORS TO HELP US.
ONCE THE "ABANDON SHIP" ORDER WAS GIVEN, THEY WERE ALL UNDER STANDING ORDERS TO HEAD FOR FORT BRAVO AND THE BEANSTALK HOME.
THEY'RE LONG GONE, BUDDY. LEARN IT. LOVE IT. LIVE IT.
WE'RE BOTH ALL ALONE IN THE DIRT-POUNDING GRUNT INFANTRY ARMY NOW. OO-RAH.
HONORABLE MEN WOULDN'T HAVE ABANDONED US SO QUICKLY.
NONSENSE. HONORABLE MEN FOLLOW ORDERS. YOU TRAINED THEM. AND YOU GAVE THE ORDER TO VAMOOSE. WE'RE ON OUR OWN, SINBAD, OLD MAN.
YOU'RE EXHAUSTED. LET ME TAKE A TURN PULLING.
NO.

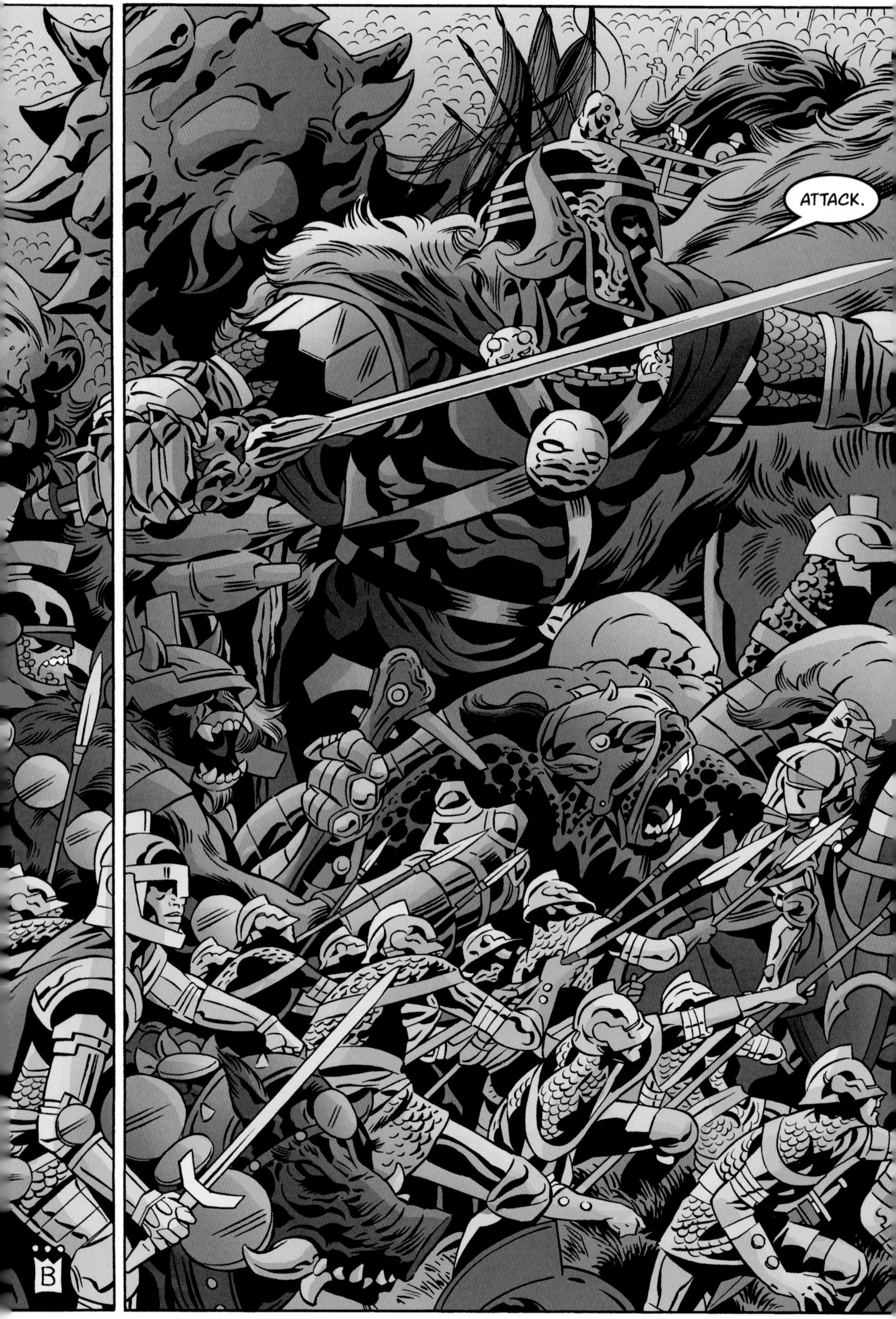
ATTACK.

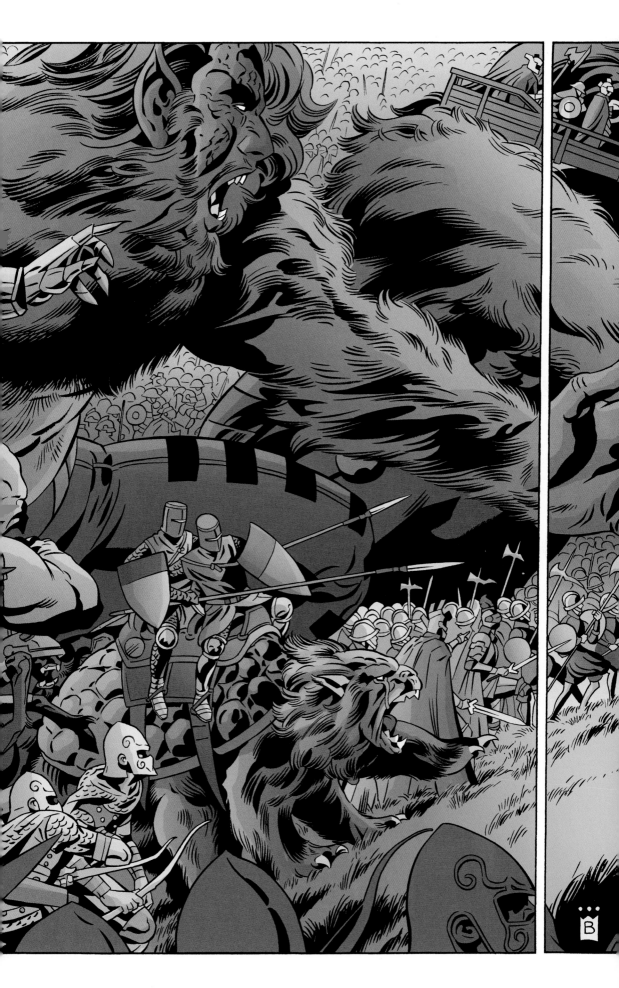

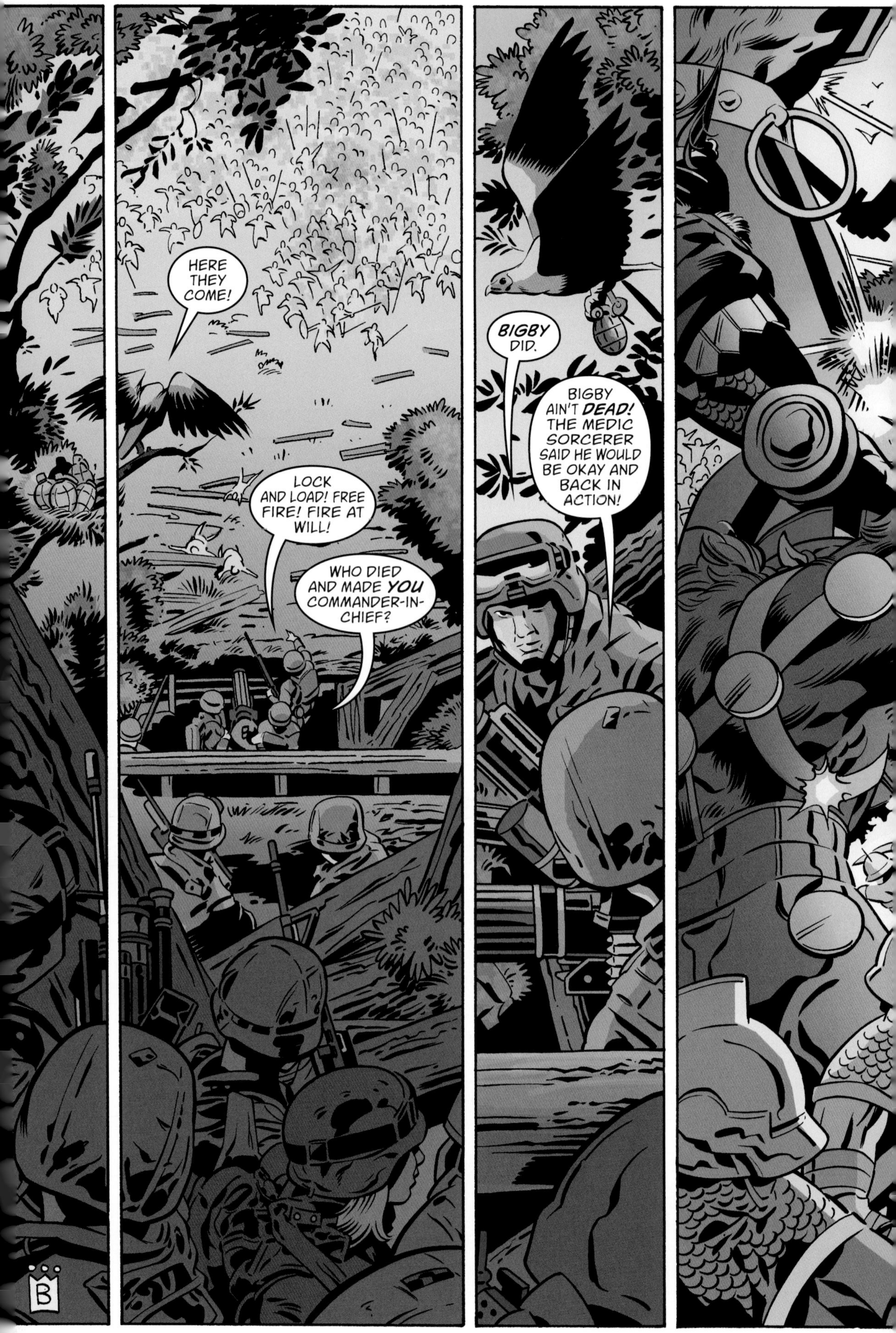

HERE THEY COME!
LOCK AND LOAD! FREE FIRE! FIRE AT WILL!
WHO DIED AND MADE **YOU** COMMANDER-IN-CHIEF?
BIGBY DID.
BIGBY AIN'T **DEAD!** THE MEDIC SORCERER SAID HE WOULD BE OKAY AND BACK IN ACTION!

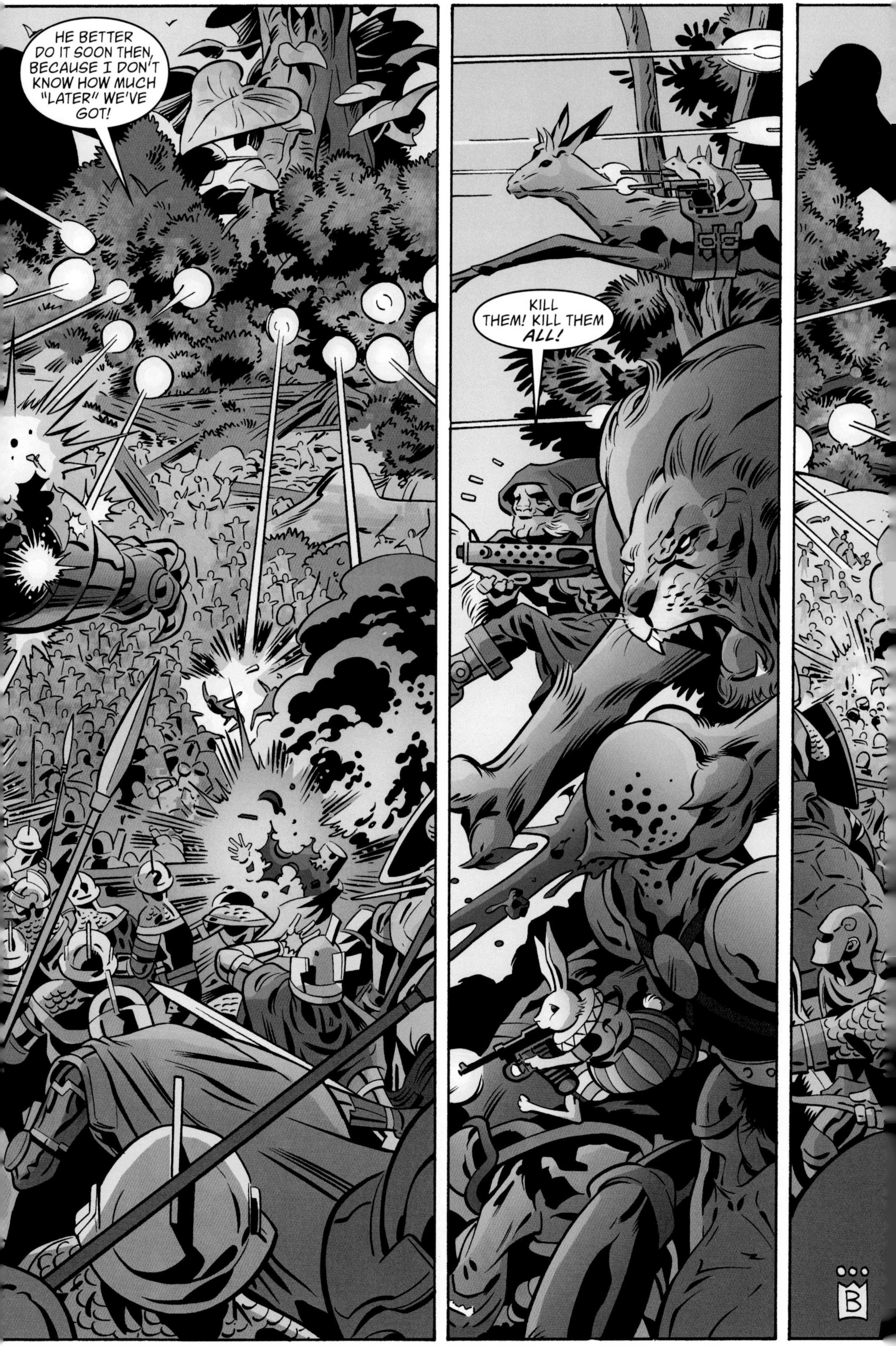
HE BETTER DO IT SOON THEN, BECAUSE I DON'T KNOW HOW MUCH "LATER" WE'VE GOT!
KILL THEM! KILL THEM ALL!

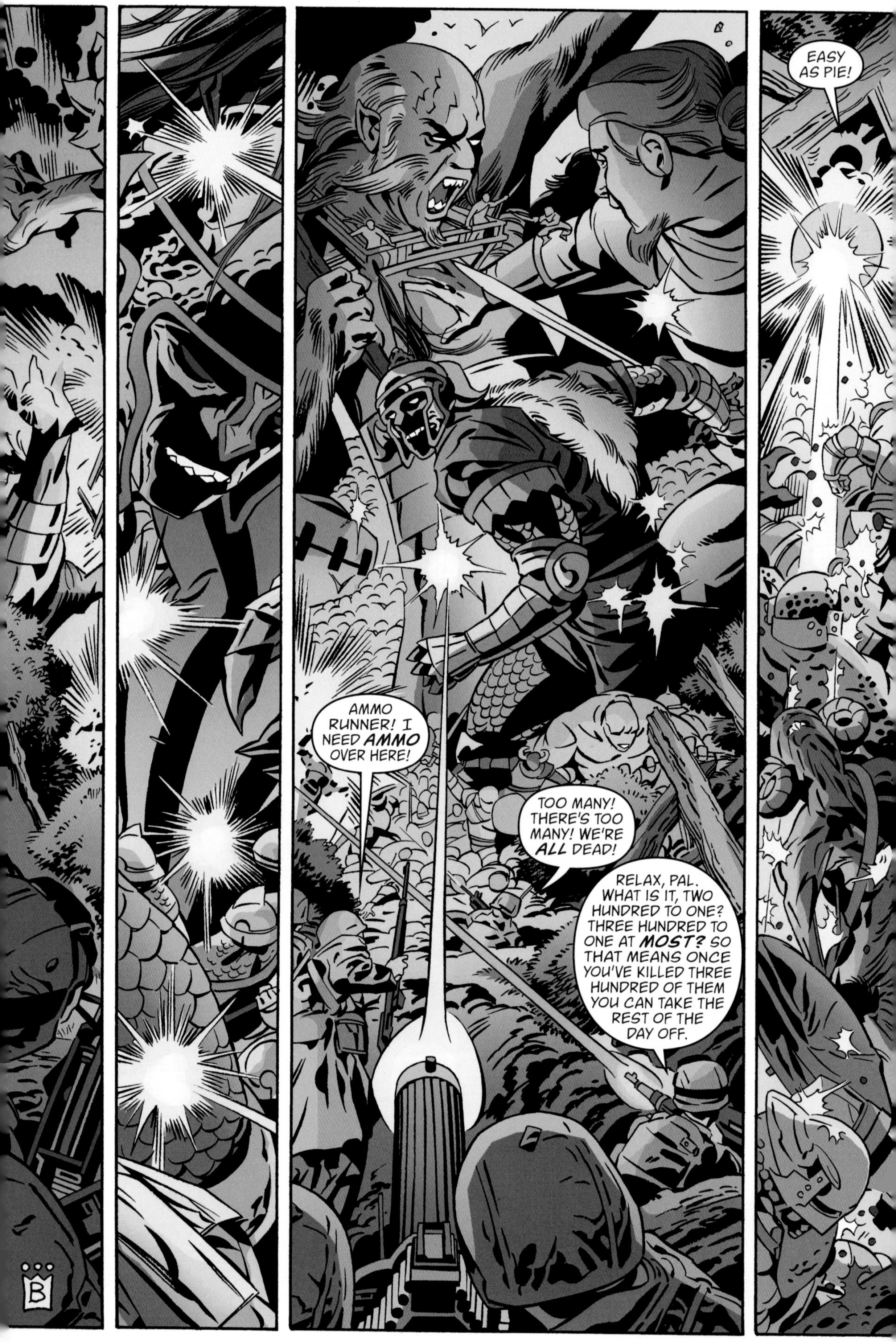
AMMO RUNNER! I NEED **AMMO** OVER HERE!
TOO MANY! THERE'S TOO MANY! WE'RE **ALL** DEAD!
RELAX, PAL. WHAT IS IT, TWO HUNDRED TO ONE? THREE HUNDRED TO ONE AT **MOST?** SO THAT MEANS ONCE YOU'VE KILLED THREE HUNDRED OF THEM YOU CAN TAKE THE REST OF THE DAY OFF.
EASY AS PIE!

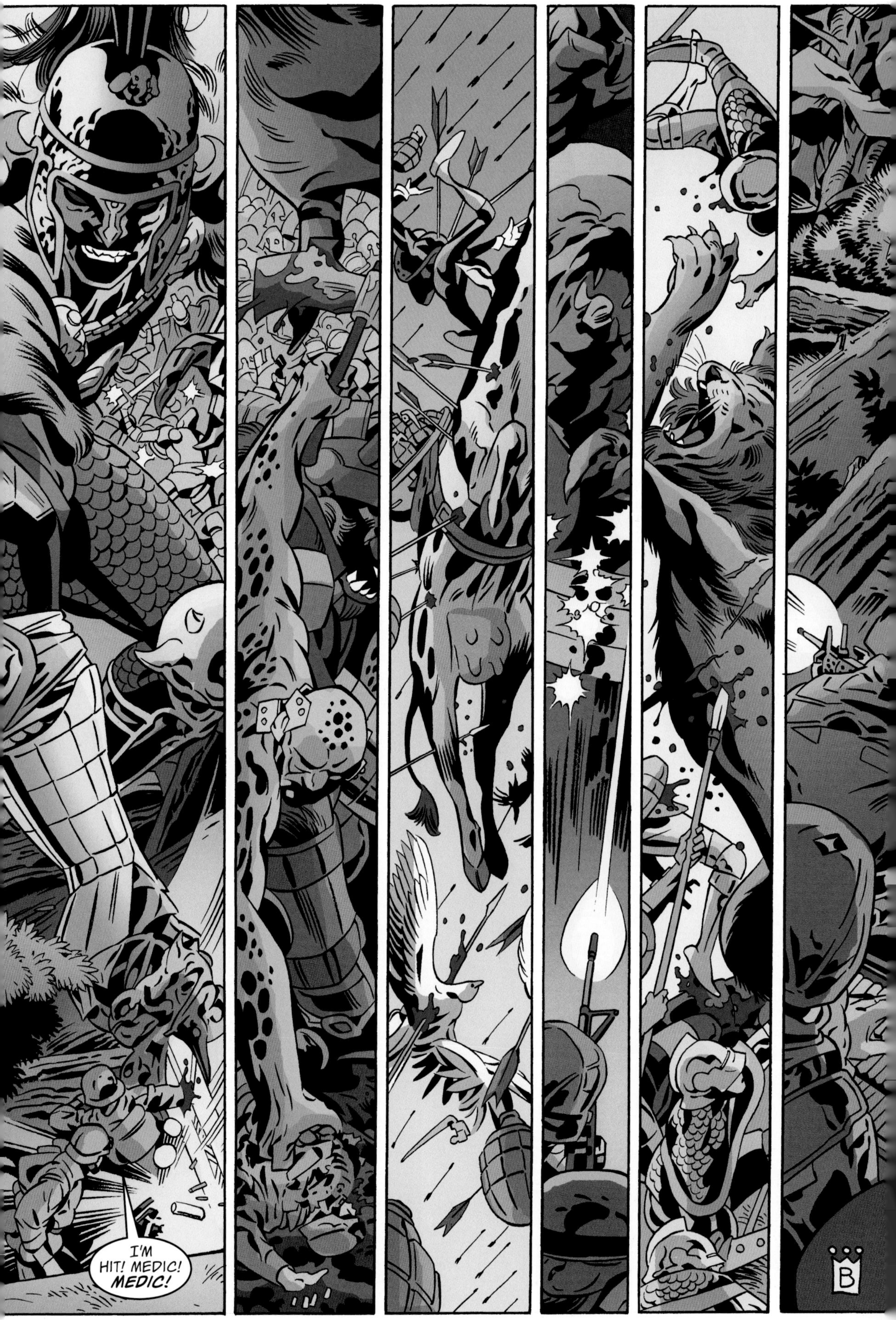
I'M HIT! MEDIC! MEDIC!

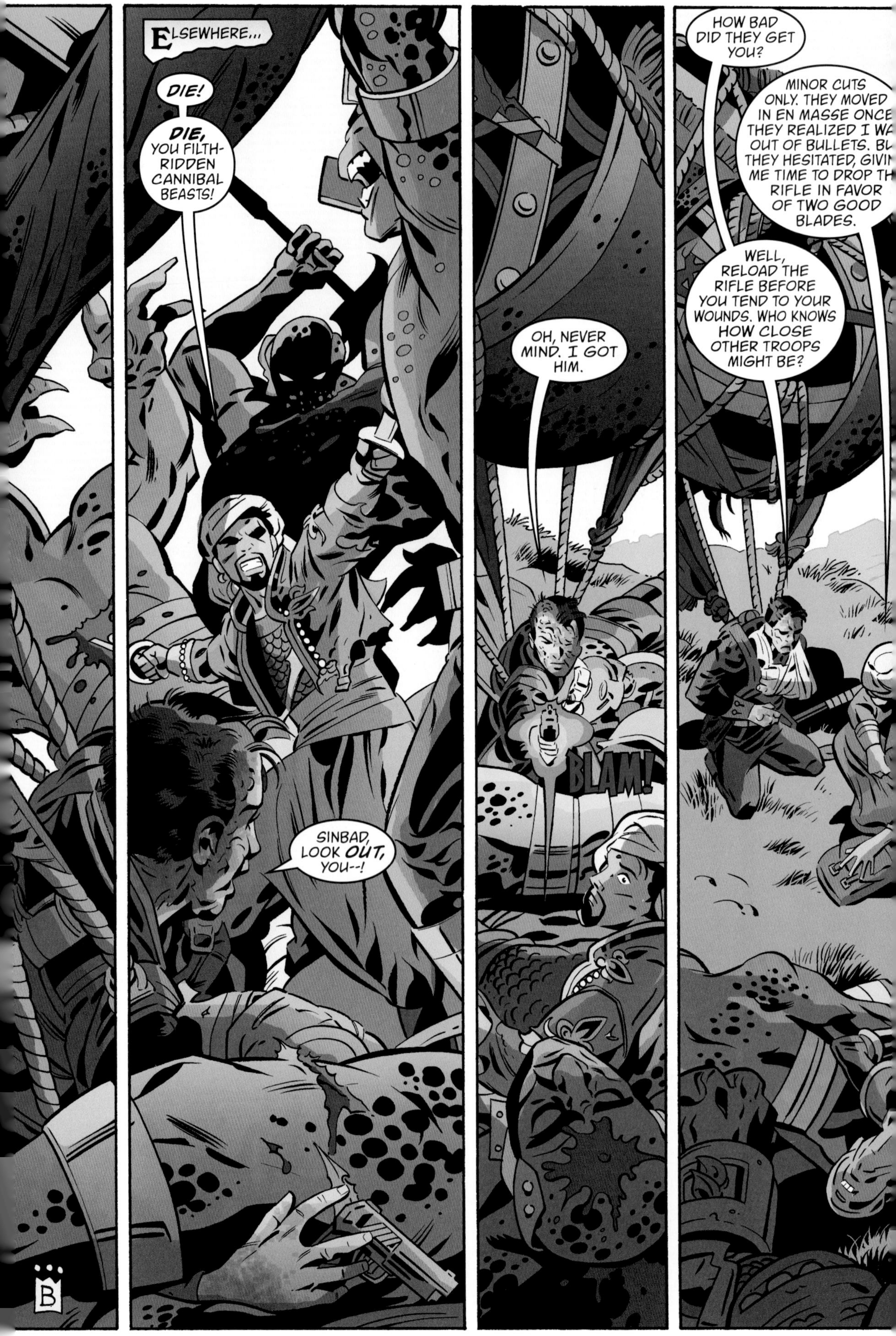
ELSEWHERE...
DIE!
DIE, YOU FILTH-RIDDEN CANNIBAL BEASTS!
SINBAD, LOOK OUT, YOU--!
OH, NEVER MIND. I GOT HIM.
BLAM!
HOW BAD DID THEY GET YOU?
MINOR CUTS ONLY. THEY MOVED IN EN MASSE ONCE THEY REALIZED I WA OUT OF BULLETS. BU THEY HESITATED, GIVIN ME TIME TO DROP TH RIFLE IN FAVOR OF TWO GOOD BLADES.
WELL, RELOAD THE RIFLE BEFORE YOU TEND TO YOUR WOUNDS. WHO KNOWS HOW CLOSE OTHER TROOPS MIGHT BE?

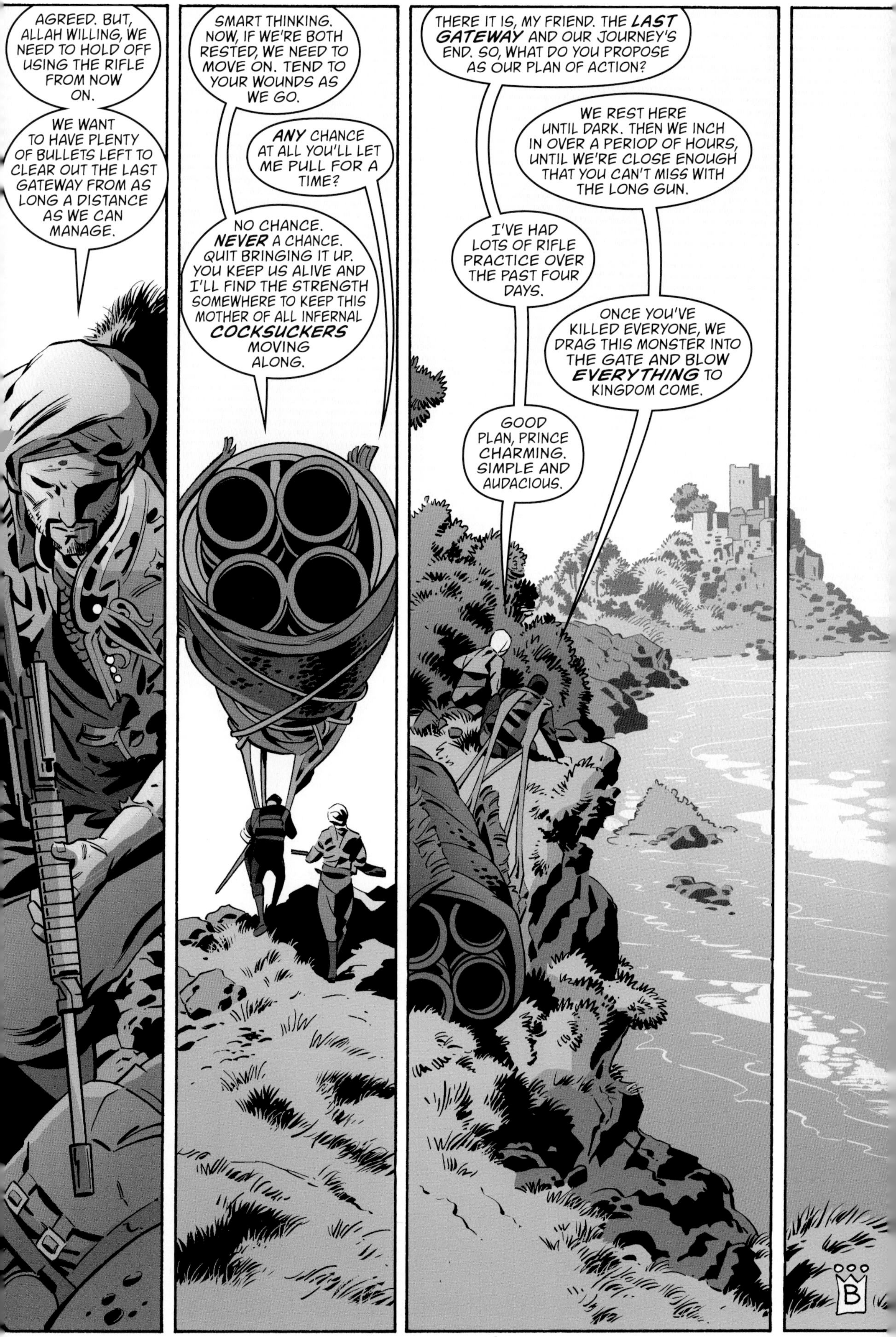

AGREED. BUT, ALLAH WILLING, WE NEED TO HOLD OFF USING THE RIFLE FROM NOW ON.
WE WANT TO HAVE PLENTY OF BULLETS LEFT TO CLEAR OUT THE LAST GATEWAY FROM AS LONG A DISTANCE AS WE CAN MANAGE.
SMART THINKING. NOW, IF WE'RE BOTH RESTED, WE NEED TO MOVE ON. TEND TO YOUR WOUNDS AS WE GO.
ANY CHANCE AT ALL YOU'LL LET ME PULL FOR A TIME?
NO CHANCE. NEVER A CHANCE. QUIT BRINGING IT UP. YOU KEEP US ALIVE AND I'LL FIND THE STRENGTH SOMEWHERE TO KEEP THIS MOTHER OF ALL INFERNAL COCKSUCKERS MOVING ALONG.
THERE IT IS, MY FRIEND. THE LAST GATEWAY AND OUR JOURNEY'S END. SO, WHAT DO YOU PROPOSE AS OUR PLAN OF ACTION?
WE REST HERE UNTIL DARK. THEN WE INCH IN OVER A PERIOD OF HOURS, UNTIL WE'RE CLOSE ENOUGH THAT YOU CAN'T MISS WITH THE LONG GUN.
I'VE HAD LOTS OF RIFLE PRACTICE OVER THE PAST FOUR DAYS.
ONCE YOU'VE KILLED EVERYONE, WE DRAG THIS MONSTER INTO THE GATE AND BLOW EVERYTHING TO KINGDOM COME.
GOOD PLAN, PRINCE CHARMING. SIMPLE AND AUDACIOUS.

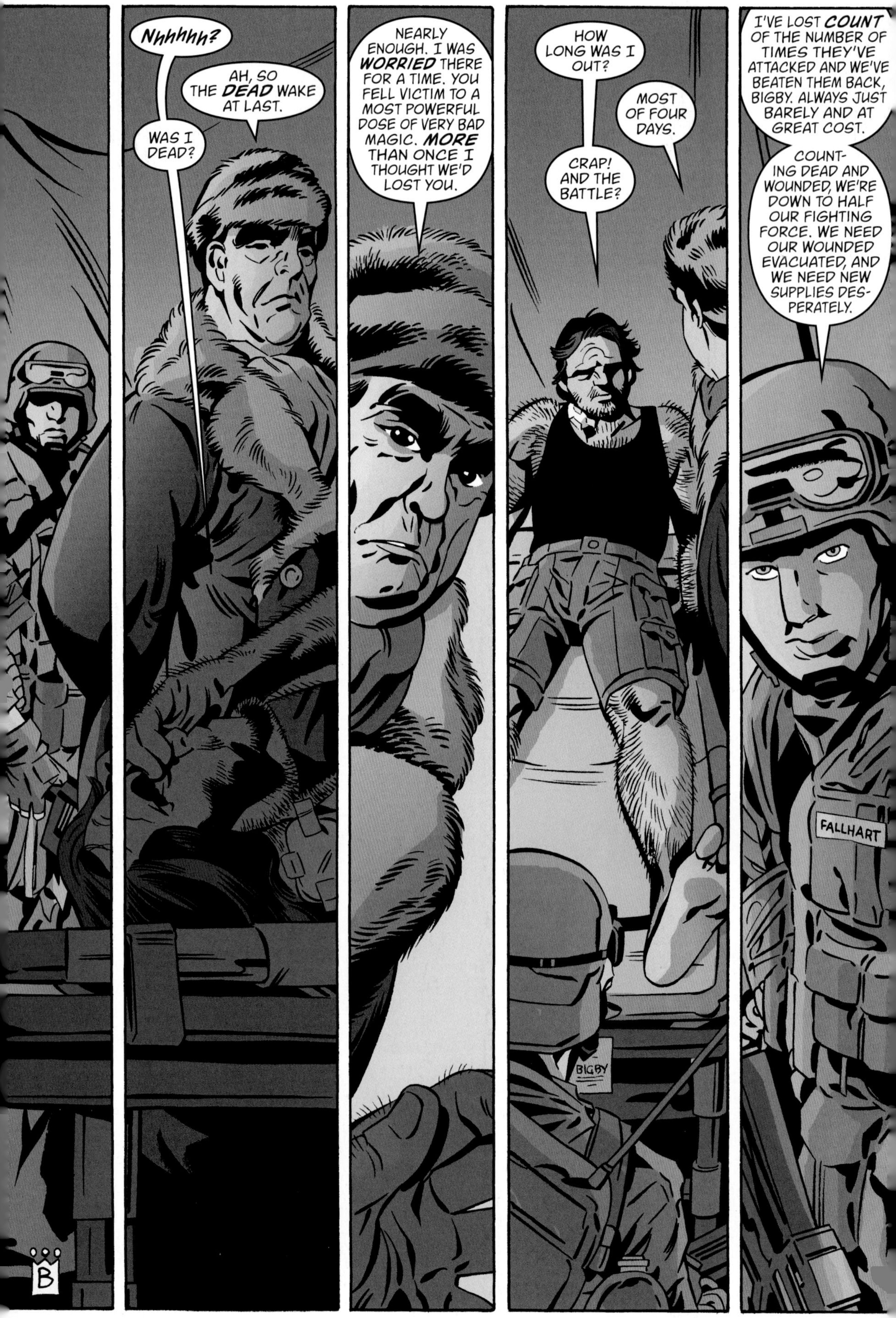

NHHHHH?
AH, SO THE DEAD WAKE AT LAST.
WAS I DEAD?
NEARLY ENOUGH. I WAS WORRIED THERE FOR A TIME. YOU FELL VICTIM TO A MOST POWERFUL DOSE OF VERY BAD MAGIC. MORE THAN ONCE I THOUGHT WE'D LOST YOU.
HOW LONG WAS I OUT?
MOST OF FOUR DAYS.
CRAP! AND THE BATTLE?
BIGBY
I'VE LOST COUNT OF THE NUMBER OF TIMES THEY'VE ATTACKED AND WE'VE BEATEN THEM BACK, BIGBY. ALWAYS JUST BARELY AND AT GREAT COST.
COUNTING DEAD AND WOUNDED, WE'RE DOWN TO HALF OUR FIGHTING FORCE. WE NEED OUR WOUNDED EVACUATED, AND WE NEED NEW SUPPLIES DESPERATELY.
FALLHART

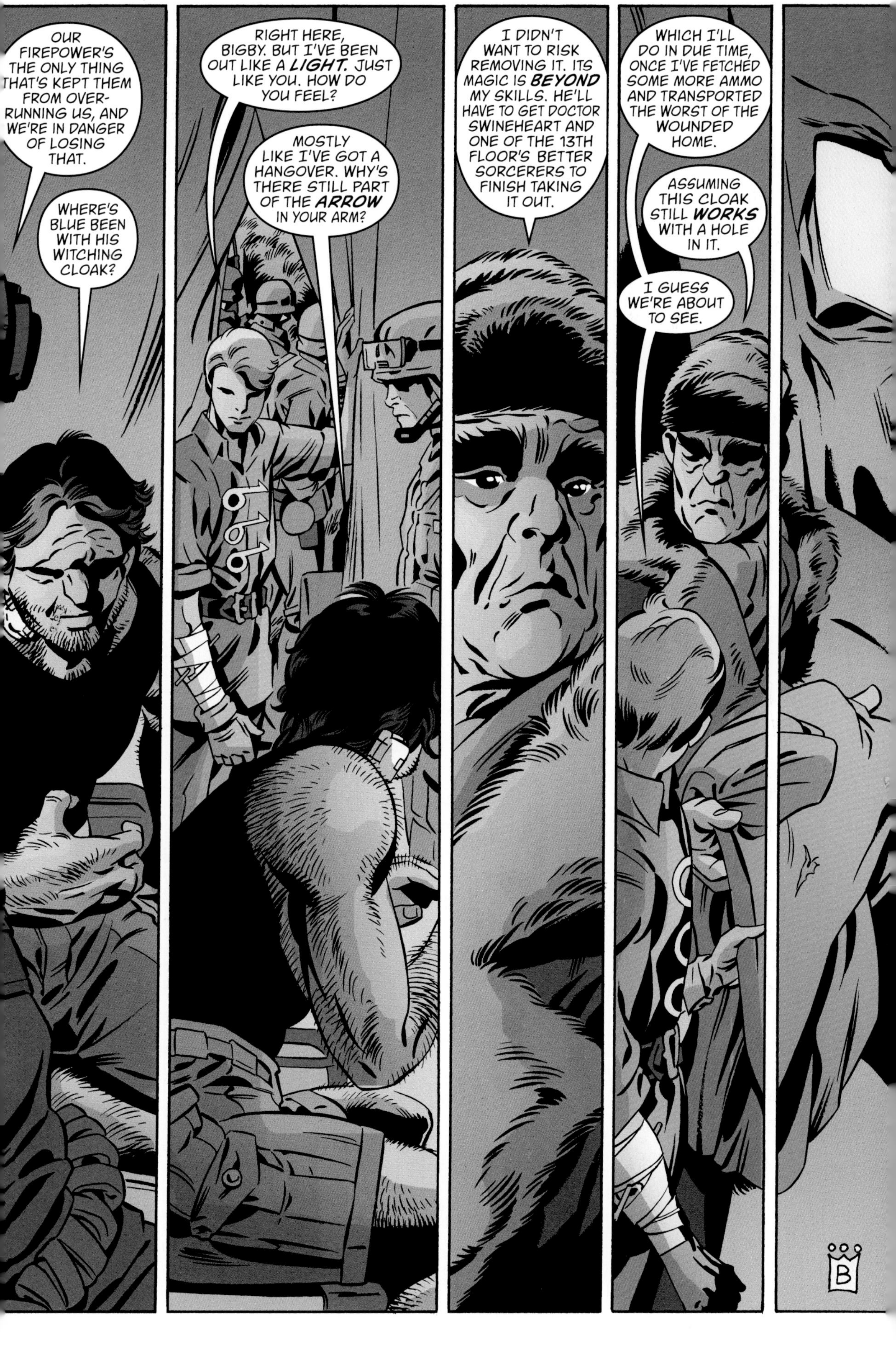
OUR FIREPOWER'S THE ONLY THING THAT'S KEPT THEM FROM OVER-RUNNING US, AND WE'RE IN DANGER OF LOSING THAT.
WHERE'S BLUE BEEN WITH HIS WITCHING CLOAK?
RIGHT HERE, BIGBY. BUT I'VE BEEN OUT LIKE A LIGHT. JUST LIKE YOU. HOW DO YOU FEEL?
MOSTLY LIKE I'VE GOT A HANGOVER. WHY'S THERE STILL PART OF THE ARROW IN YOUR ARM?
I DIDN'T WANT TO RISK REMOVING IT. ITS MAGIC IS BEYOND MY SKILLS. HE'LL HAVE TO GET DOCTOR SWINEHEART AND ONE OF THE 13TH FLOOR'S BETTER SORCERERS TO FINISH TAKING IT OUT.
WHICH I'LL DO IN DUE TIME, ONCE I'VE FETCHED SOME MORE AMMO AND TRANSPORTED THE WORST OF THE WOUNDED HOME.
ASSUMING THIS CLOAK STILL WORKS WITH A HOLE IN IT.
I GUESS WE'RE ABOUT TO SEE.

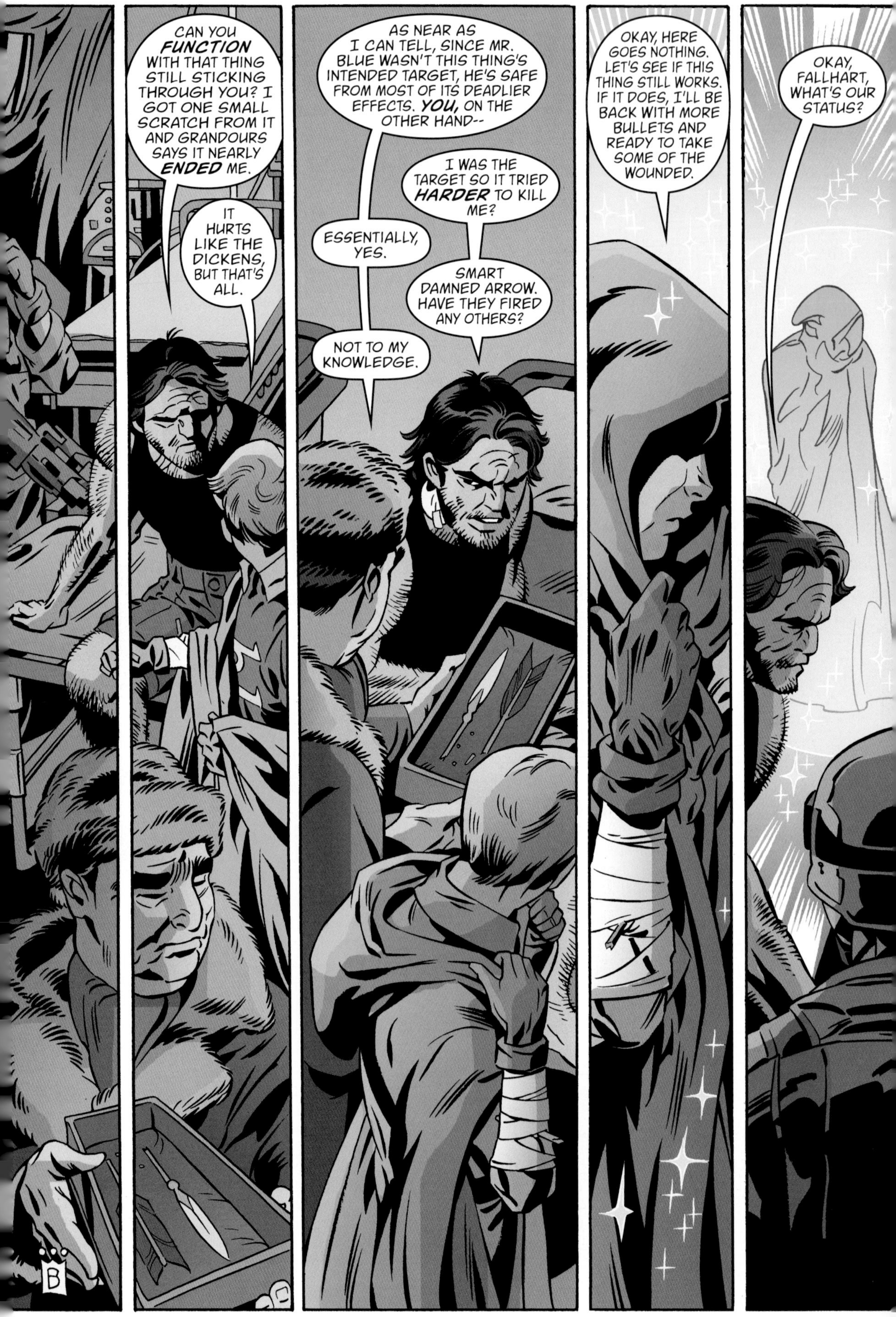
CAN YOU FUNCTION WITH THAT THING STILL STICKING THROUGH YOU? I GOT ONE SMALL SCRATCH FROM IT AND GRANDOURS SAYS IT NEARLY ENDED ME.
IT HURTS LIKE THE DICKENS, BUT THAT'S ALL.
AS NEAR AS I CAN TELL, SINCE MR. BLUE WASN'T THIS THING'S INTENDED TARGET, HE'S SAFE FROM MOST OF ITS DEADLIER EFFECTS. YOU, ON THE OTHER HAND--
I WAS THE TARGET SO IT TRIED HARDER TO KILL ME?
ESSENTIALLY, YES.
SMART DAMNED ARROW. HAVE THEY FIRED ANY OTHERS?
NOT TO MY KNOWLEDGE.
OKAY, HERE GOES NOTHING. LET'S SEE IF THIS THING STILL WORKS. IF IT DOES, I'LL BE BACK WITH MORE BULLETS AND READY TO TAKE SOME OF THE WOUNDED.
OKAY, FALLHART, WHAT'S OUR STATUS?

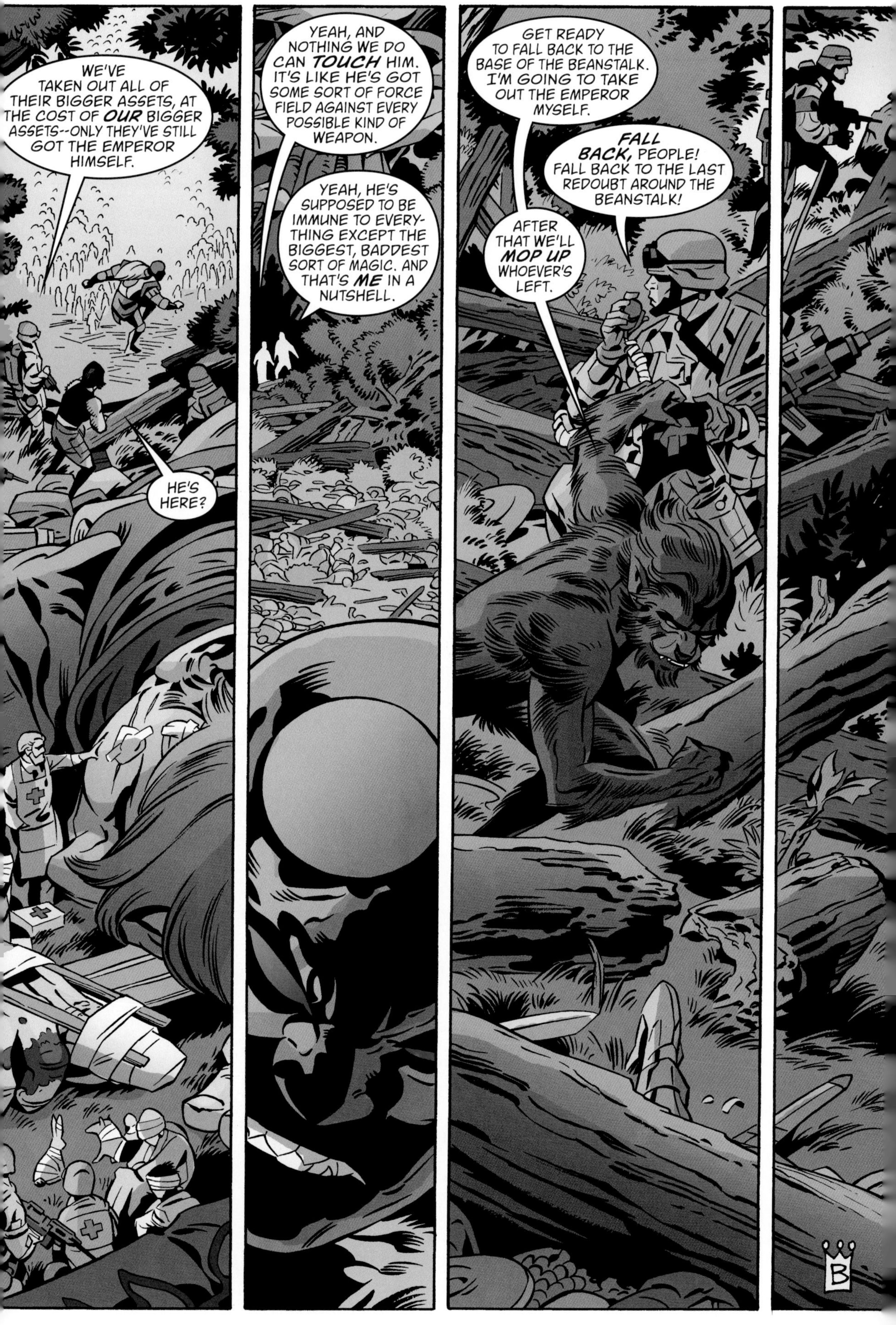
WE'VE TAKEN OUT ALL OF THEIR BIGGER ASSETS, AT THE COST OF OUR BIGGER ASSETS--ONLY THEY'VE STILL GOT THE EMPEROR HIMSELF.
HE'S HERE?
YEAH, AND NOTHING WE DO CAN TOUCH HIM. IT'S LIKE HE'S GOT SOME SORT OF FORCE FIELD AGAINST EVERY POSSIBLE KIND OF WEAPON.
YEAH, HE'S SUPPOSED TO BE IMMUNE TO EVERYTHING EXCEPT THE BIGGEST, BADDEST SORT OF MAGIC. AND THAT'S ME IN A NUTSHELL.
GET READY TO FALL BACK TO THE BASE OF THE BEANSTALK. I'M GOING TO TAKE OUT THE EMPEROR MYSELF.
AFTER THAT WE'LL MOP UP WHOEVER'S LEFT.
FALL BACK, PEOPLE! FALL BACK TO THE LAST REDOUBT AROUND THE BEANSTALK!

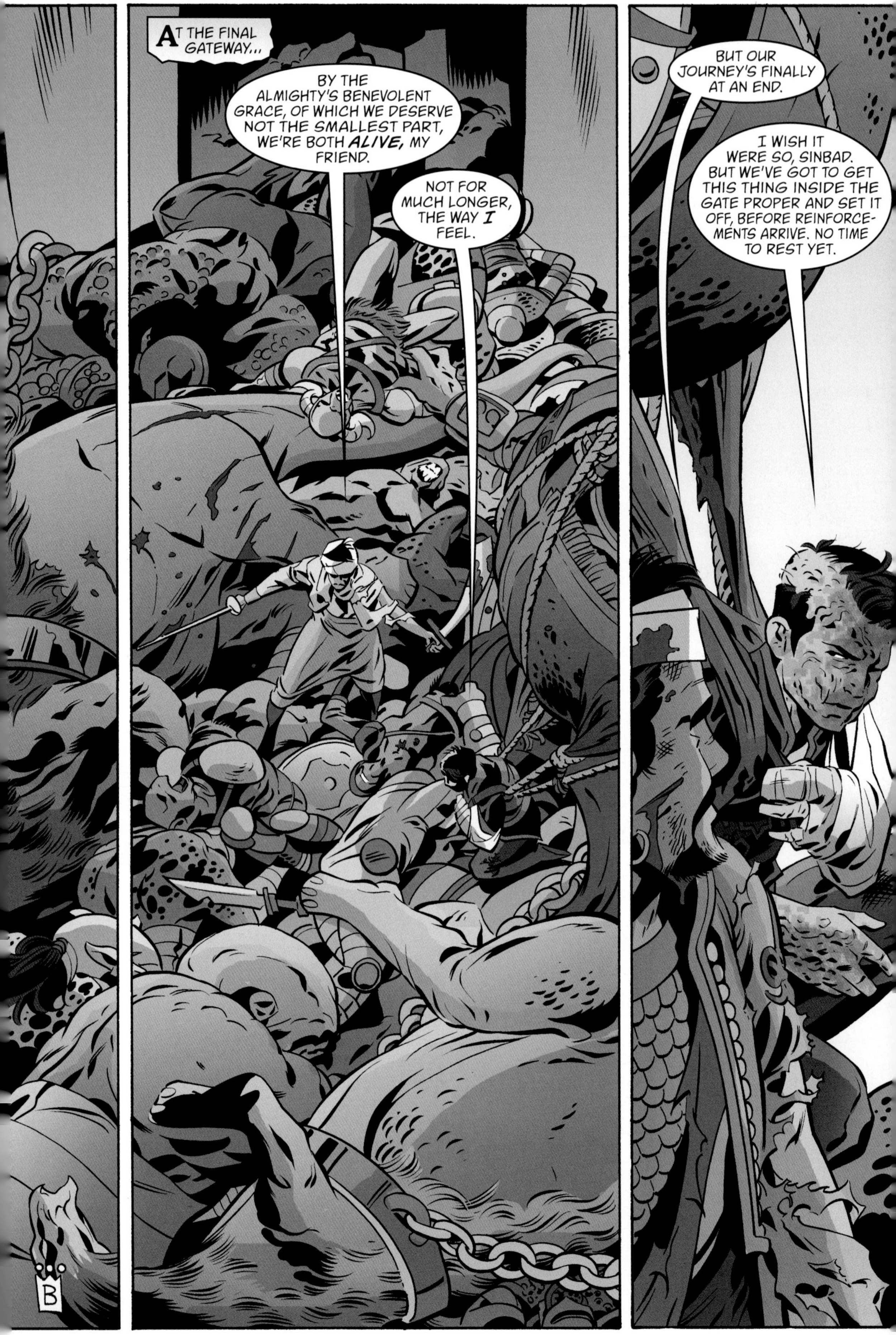
AT THE FINAL GATEWAY...
BY THE ALMIGHTY'S BENEVOLENT GRACE, OF WHICH WE DESERVE NOT THE SMALLEST PART, WE'RE BOTH ALIVE, MY FRIEND.
NOT FOR MUCH LONGER, THE WAY I FEEL.
BUT OUR JOURNEY'S FINALLY AT AN END.
I WISH IT WERE SO, SINBAD. BUT WE'VE GOT TO GET THIS THING INSIDE THE GATE PROPER AND SET IT OFF, BEFORE REINFORCEMENTS ARRIVE. NO TIME TO REST YET.

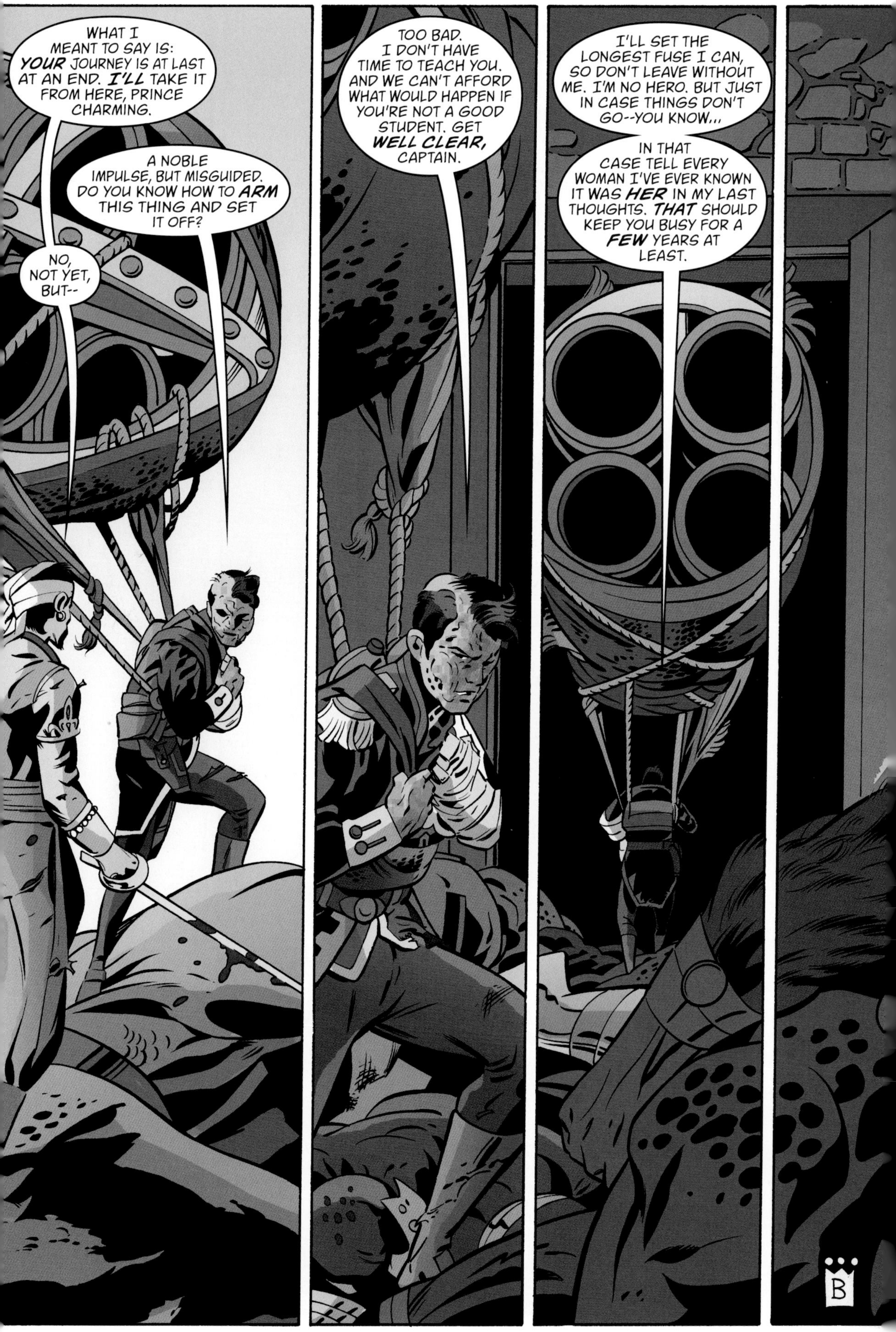
WHAT I MEANT TO SAY IS: YOUR JOURNEY IS AT LAST AT AN END. I'LL TAKE IT FROM HERE, PRINCE CHARMING.
A NOBLE IMPULSE, BUT MISGUIDED. DO YOU KNOW HOW TO ARM THIS THING AND SET IT OFF?
NO, NOT YET, BUT--
TOO BAD. I DON'T HAVE TIME TO TEACH YOU. AND WE CAN'T AFFORD WHAT WOULD HAPPEN IF YOU'RE NOT A GOOD STUDENT. GET WELL CLEAR, CAPTAIN.
I'LL SET THE LONGEST FUSE I CAN, SO DON'T LEAVE WITHOUT ME. I'M NO HERO. BUT JUST IN CASE THINGS DON'T GO--YOU KNOW...
IN THAT CASE TELL EVERY WOMAN I'VE EVER KNOWN IT WAS HER IN MY LAST THOUGHTS. THAT SHOULD KEEP YOU BUSY FOR A FEW YEARS AT LEAST.

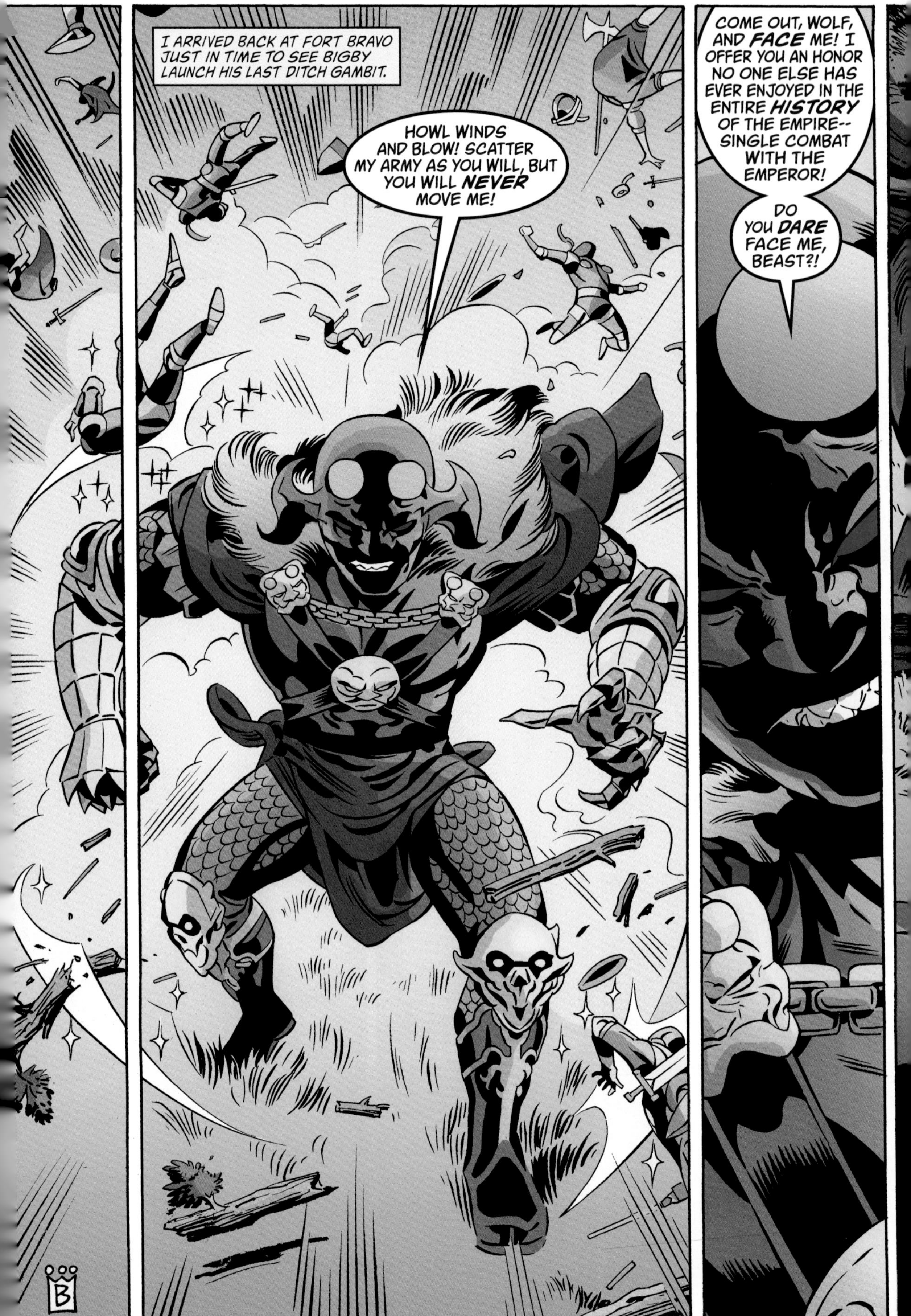
I ARRIVED BACK AT FORT BRAVO JUST IN TIME TO SEE BIGBY LAUNCH HIS LAST DITCH GAMBIT.
HOWL WINDS AND BLOW! SCATTER MY ARMY AS YOU WILL, BUT YOU WILL NEVER MOVE ME!
COME OUT, WOLF, AND FACE ME! I OFFER YOU AN HONOR NO ONE ELSE HAS EVER ENJOYED IN THE ENTIRE HISTORY OF THE EMPIRE-- SINGLE COMBAT WITH THE EMPEROR!
DO YOU DARE FACE ME, BEAST?!

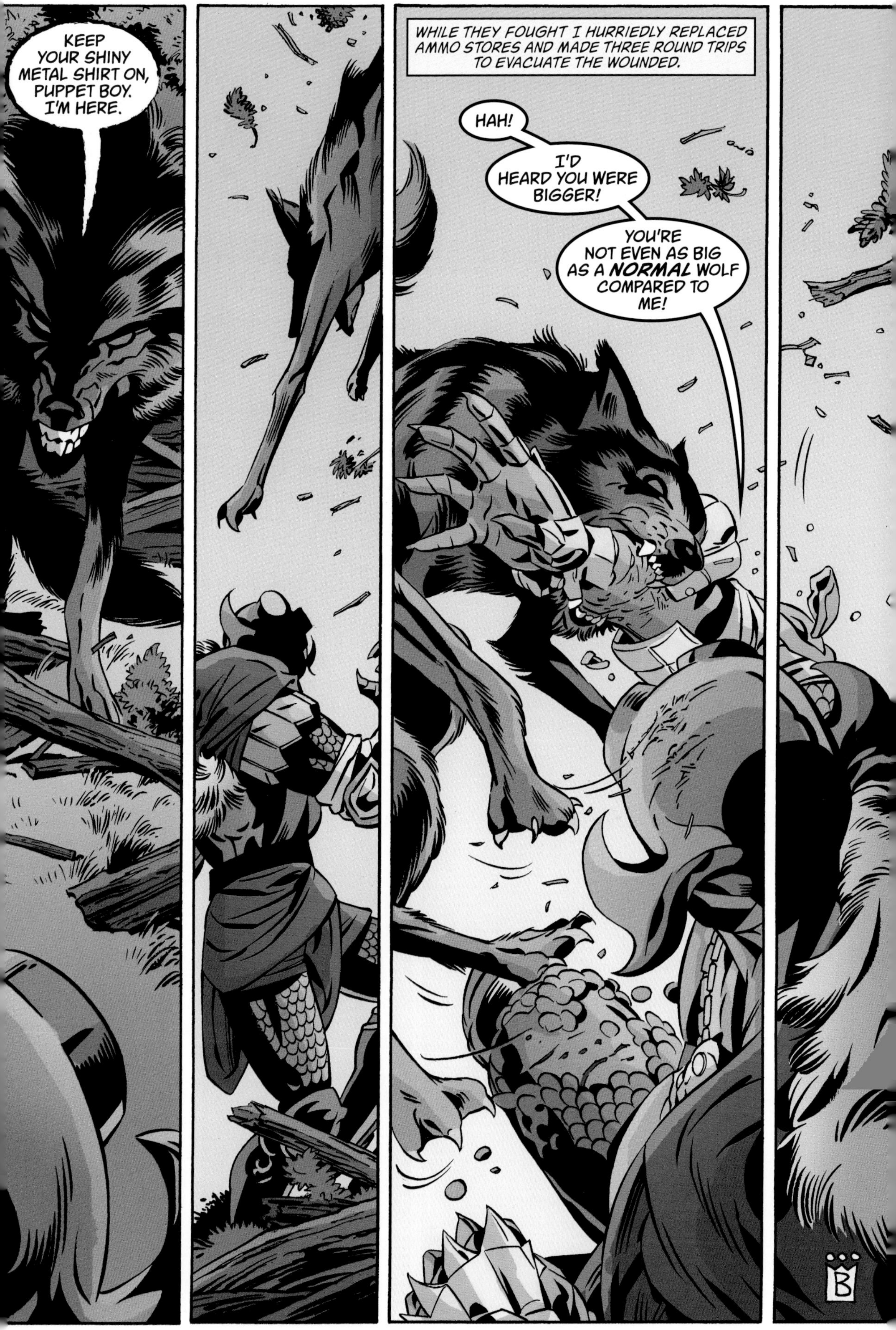
KEEP YOUR SHINY METAL SHIRT ON, PUPPET BOY. I'M HERE.
WHILE THEY FOUGHT I HURRIEDLY REPLACED AMMO STORES AND MADE THREE ROUND TRIPS TO EVACUATE THE WOUNDED.
HAH!
I'D HEARD YOU WERE BIGGER!
YOU'RE NOT EVEN AS BIG AS A **NORMAL** WOLF COMPARED TO ME!

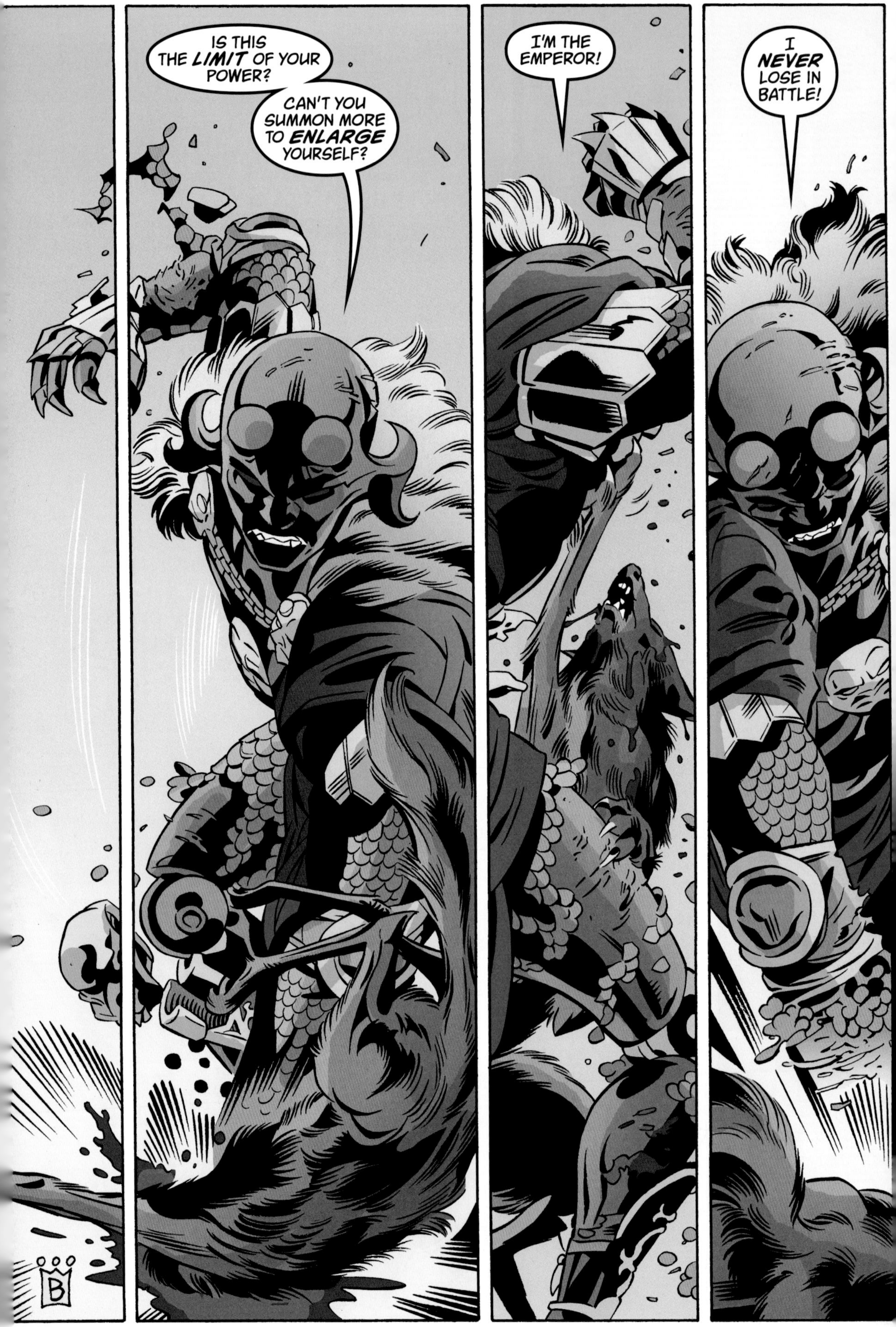
IS THIS THE LIMIT OF YOUR POWER?
CAN'T YOU SUMMON MORE TO ENLARGE YOURSELF?
I'M THE EMPEROR!
I NEVER LOSE IN BATTLE!

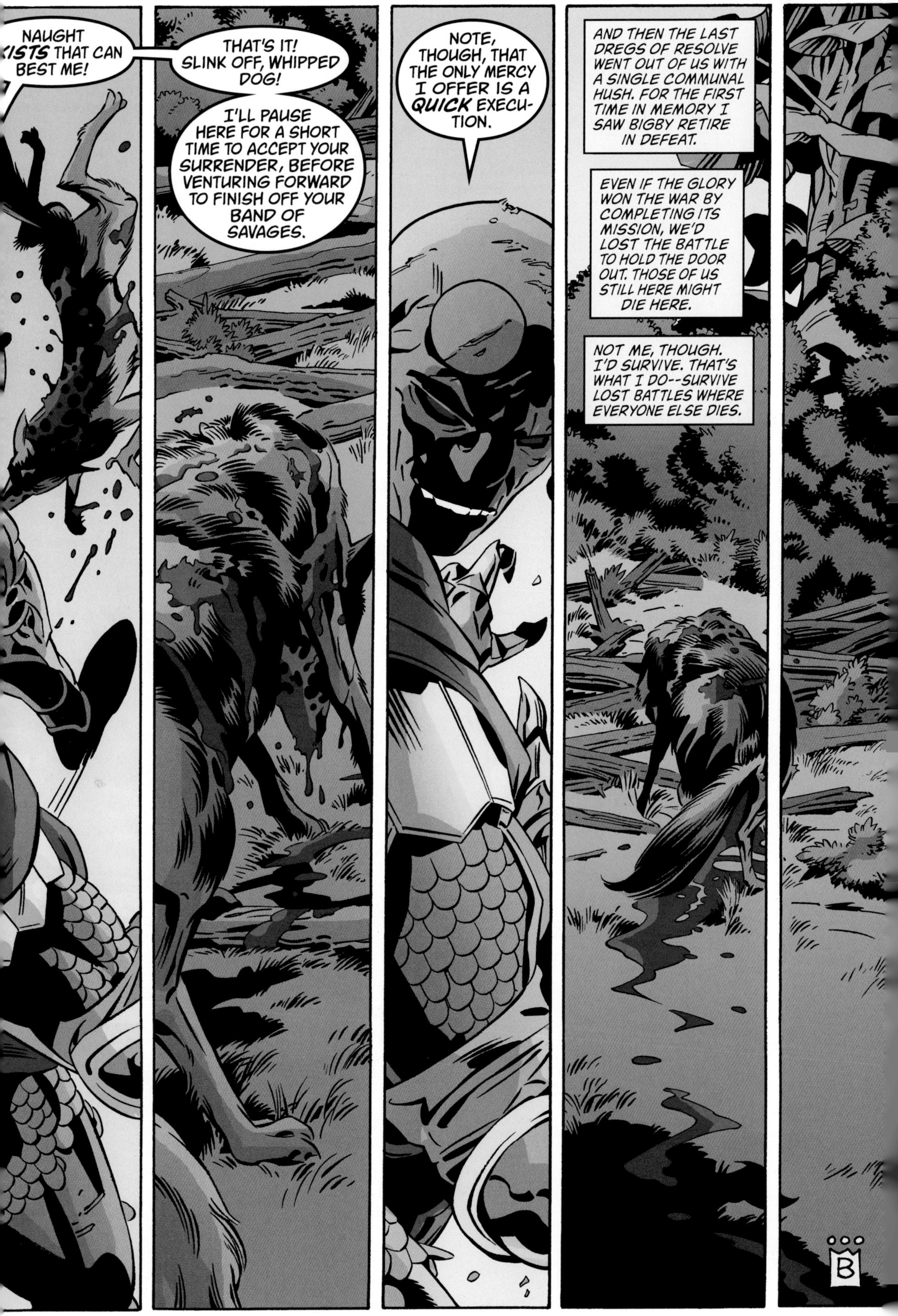
NAUGHT XISTS THAT CAN BEST ME!
THAT'S IT! SLINK OFF, WHIPPED DOG!
I'LL PAUSE HERE FOR A SHORT TIME TO ACCEPT YOUR SURRENDER, BEFORE VENTURING FORWARD TO FINISH OFF YOUR BAND OF SAVAGES.
NOTE, THOUGH, THAT THE ONLY MERCY I OFFER IS A QUICK EXECUTION.
AND THEN THE LAST DREGS OF RESOLVE WENT OUT OF US WITH A SINGLE COMMUNAL HUSH. FOR THE FIRST TIME IN MEMORY I SAW BIGBY RETIRE IN DEFEAT.
EVEN IF THE GLORY WON THE WAR BY COMPLETING ITS MISSION, WE'D LOST THE BATTLE TO HOLD THE DOOR OUT. THOSE OF US STILL HERE MIGHT DIE HERE.
NOT ME, THOUGH. I'D SURVIVE. THAT'S WHAT I DO--SURVIVE LOST BATTLES WHERE EVERYONE ELSE DIES.

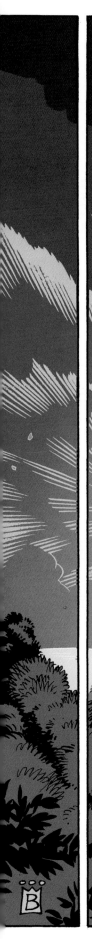

NO, OF COURSE I HAVEN'T GIVEN UP YET. I DON'T DO THAT. I JUST NEED TO REVISE MY METHOD. I'M GOING TO FIGHT THE EMPEROR ONE ON ONE AGAIN, BUT IN HUMAN FORM.

AND THIS TIME I'M GOING TO BORROW A TACTIC THE *MOUSE POLICE* USED IN THE BATTLE OF FABLE-TOWN.

170

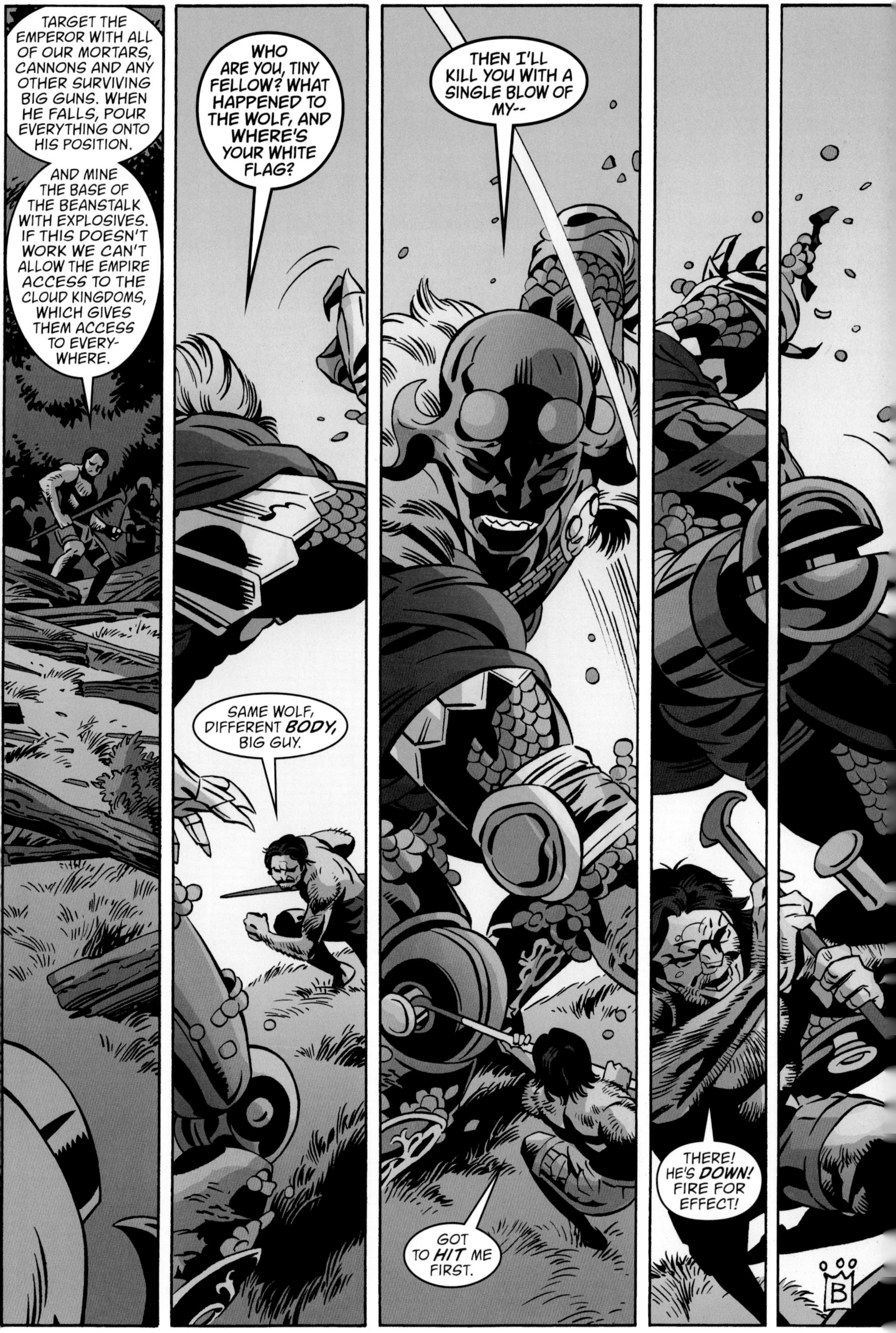
TARGET THE EMPEROR WITH ALL OF OUR MORTARS, CANNONS AND ANY OTHER SURVIVING BIG GUNS. WHEN HE FALLS, POUR EVERYTHING ONTO HIS POSITION.
AND MINE THE BASE OF THE BEANSTALK WITH EXPLOSIVES. IF THIS DOESN'T WORK WE CAN'T ALLOW THE EMPIRE ACCESS TO THE CLOUD KINGDOMS, WHICH GIVES THEM ACCESS TO EVERY-WHERE.
WHO ARE YOU, TINY FELLOW? WHAT HAPPENED TO THE WOLF, AND WHERE'S YOUR WHITE FLAG?
SAME WOLF, DIFFERENT **BODY,** BIG GUY.
THEN I'LL KILL YOU WITH A SINGLE BLOW OF MY--
GOT TO ***HIT*** ME FIRST.
THERE! HE'S ***DOWN!*** FIRE FOR EFFECT!

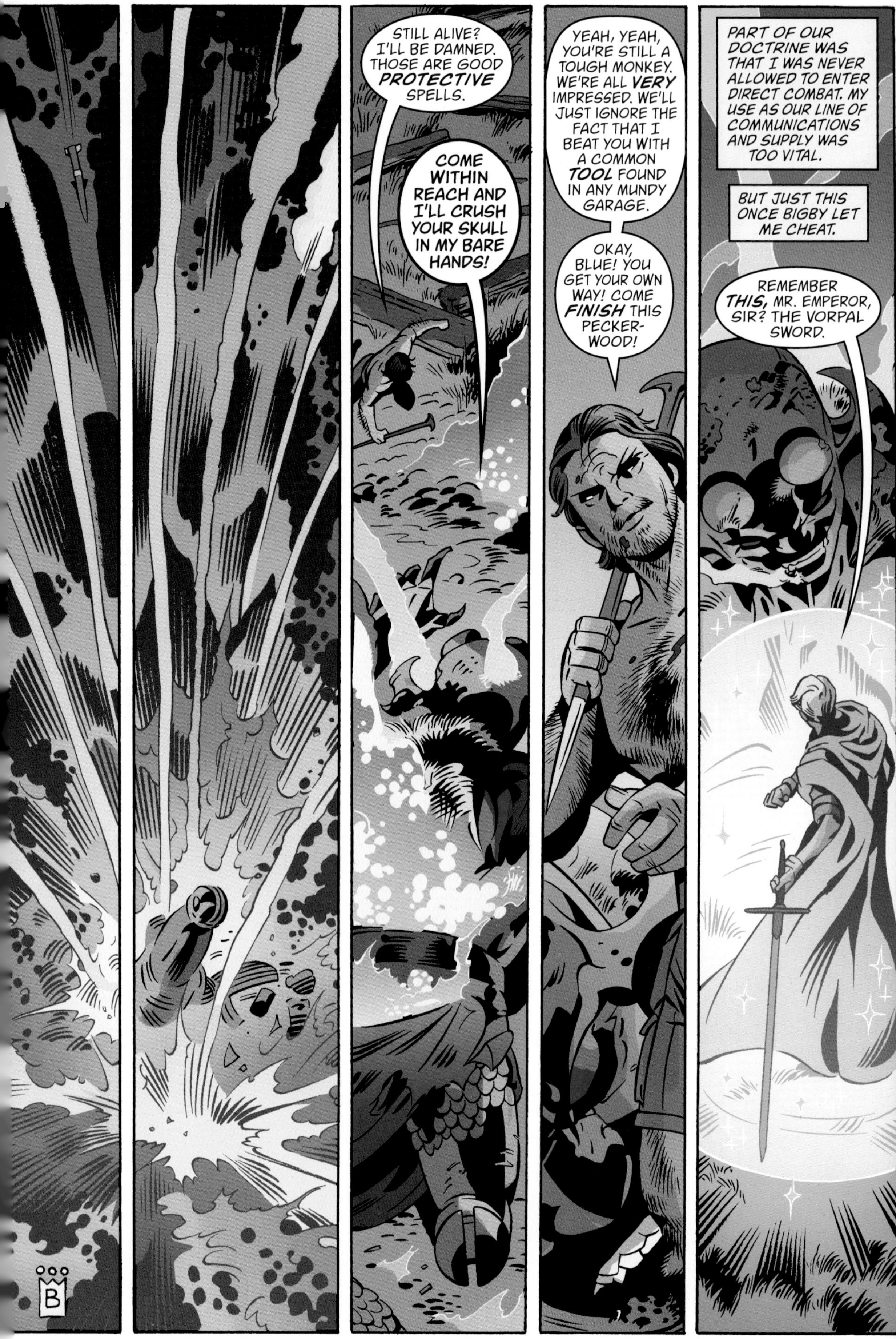
STILL ALIVE? I'LL BE DAMNED. THOSE ARE GOOD PROTECTIVE SPELLS.
COME WITHIN REACH AND I'LL CRUSH YOUR SKULL IN MY BARE HANDS!
YEAH, YEAH, YOU'RE STILL A TOUGH MONKEY. WE'RE ALL VERY IMPRESSED. WE'LL JUST IGNORE THE FACT THAT I BEAT YOU WITH A COMMON TOOL FOUND IN ANY MUNDY GARAGE.
OKAY, BLUE! YOU GET YOUR OWN WAY! COME FINISH THIS PECKER-WOOD!
PART OF OUR DOCTRINE WAS THAT I WAS NEVER ALLOWED TO ENTER DIRECT COMBAT. MY USE AS OUR LINE OF COMMUNICATIONS AND SUPPLY WAS TOO VITAL.
BUT JUST THIS ONCE BIGBY LET ME CHEAT.
REMEMBER THIS, MR. EMPEROR, SIR? THE VORPAL SWORD.

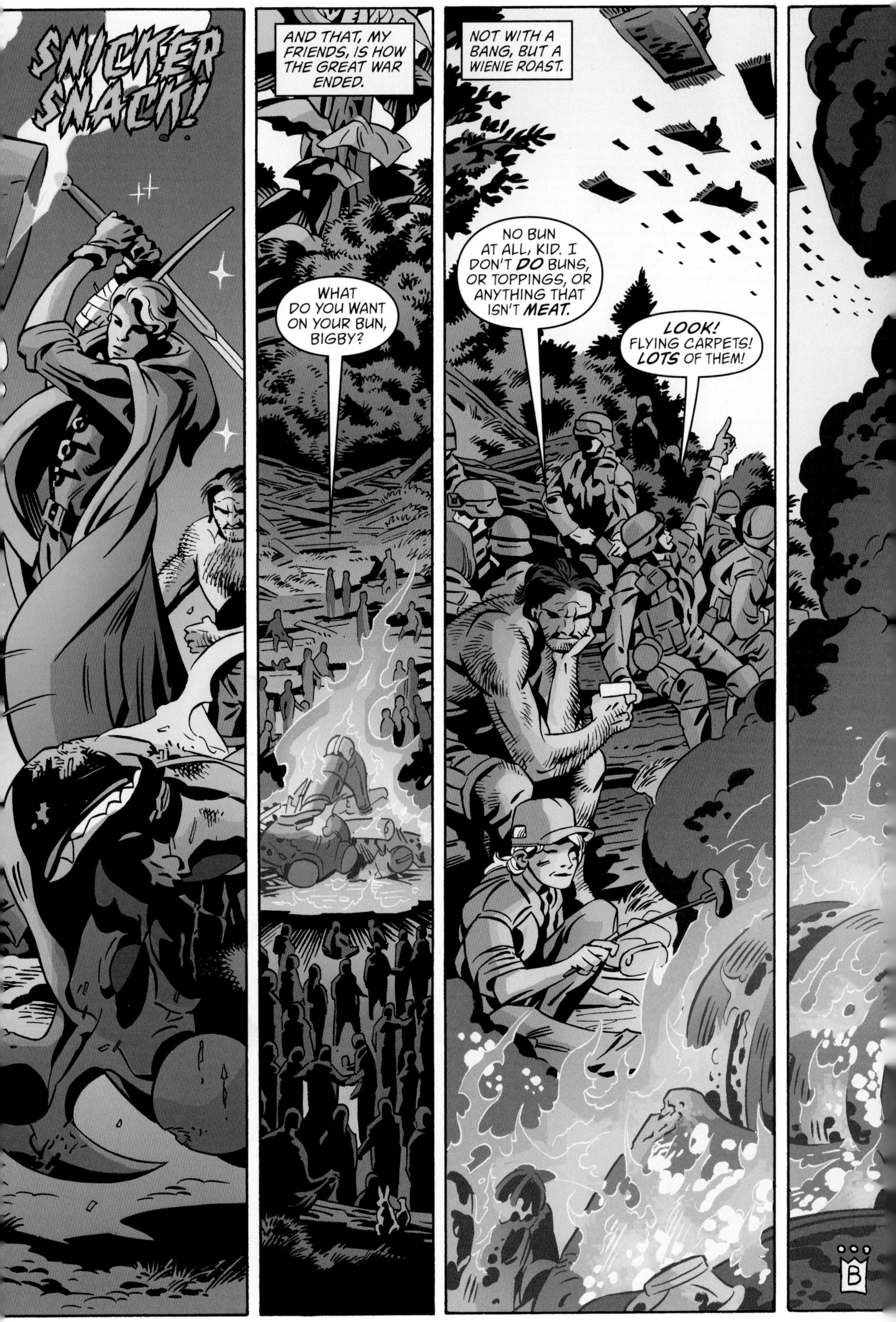
SNICKER SNACK!
AND THAT, MY FRIENDS, IS HOW THE GREAT WAR ENDED.
WHAT DO YOU WANT ON YOUR BUN, BIGBY?
NOT WITH A BANG, BUT A WIENIE ROAST.
NO BUN AT ALL, KID. I DON'T DO BUNS, OR TOPPINGS, OR ANYTHING THAT ISN'T MEAT.
LOOK! FLYING CARPETS! LOTS OF THEM!

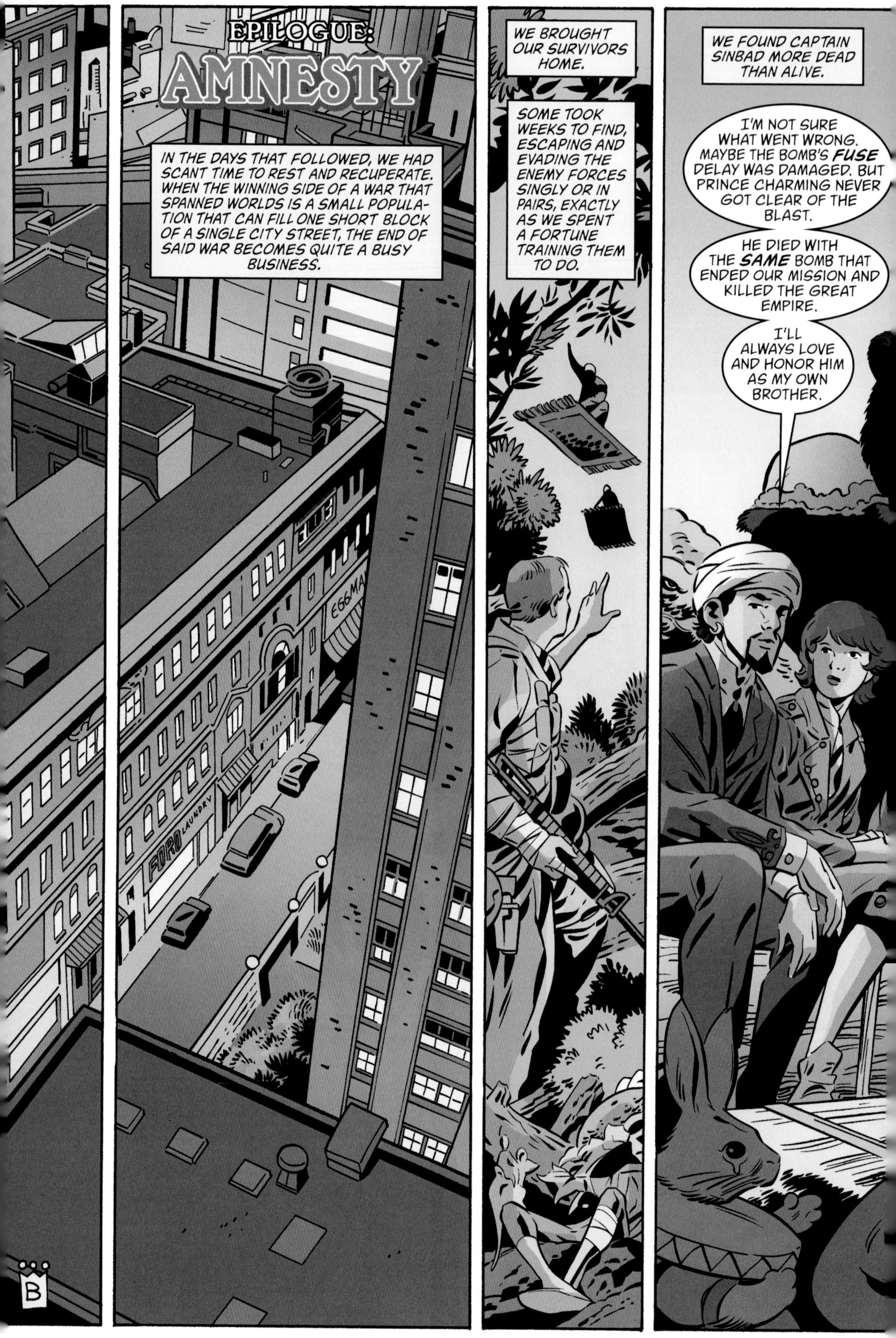
EPILOGUE:
AMNESTY
IN THE DAYS THAT FOLLOWED, WE HAD SCANT TIME TO REST AND RECUPERATE. WHEN THE WINNING SIDE OF A WAR THAT SPANNED WORLDS IS A SMALL POPULATION THAT CAN FILL ONE SHORT BLOCK OF A SINGLE CITY STREET, THE END OF SAID WAR BECOMES QUITE A BUSY BUSINESS.
FORD LAUNDRY
WE BROUGHT OUR SURVIVORS HOME.
SOME TOOK WEEKS TO FIND, ESCAPING AND EVADING THE ENEMY FORCES SINGLY OR IN PAIRS, EXACTLY AS WE SPENT A FORTUNE TRAINING THEM TO DO.
WE FOUND CAPTAIN SINBAD MORE DEAD THAN ALIVE.
I'M NOT SURE WHAT WENT WRONG. MAYBE THE BOMB'S FUSE DELAY WAS DAMAGED. BUT PRINCE CHARMING NEVER GOT CLEAR OF THE BLAST.
HE DIED WITH THE SAME BOMB THAT ENDED OUR MISSION AND KILLED THE GREAT EMPIRE.
I'LL ALWAYS LOVE AND HONOR HIM AS MY OWN BROTHER.

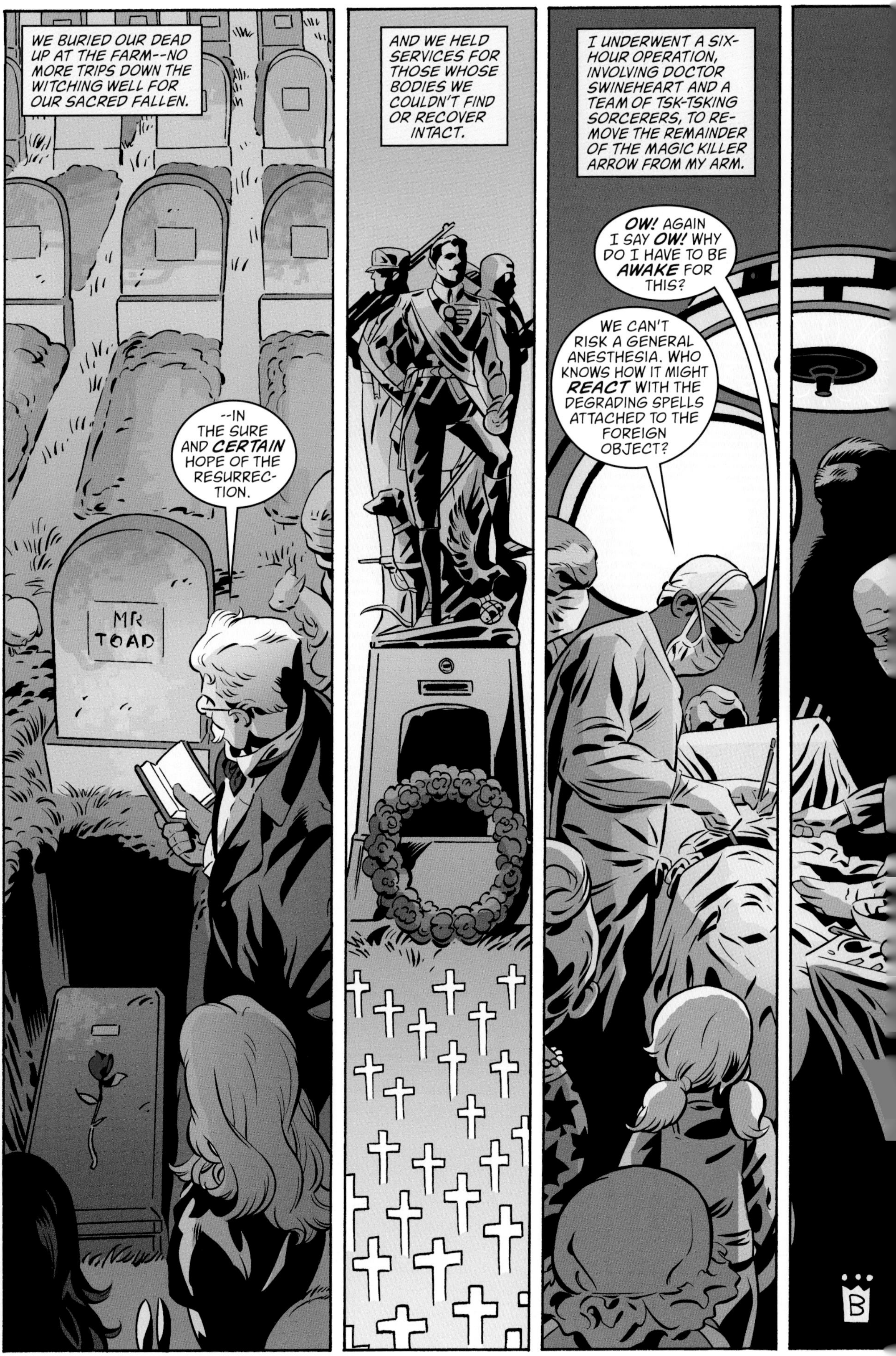
WE BURIED OUR DEAD UP AT THE FARM--NO MORE TRIPS DOWN THE WITCHING WELL FOR OUR SACRED FALLEN.
--IN THE SURE AND **CERTAIN** HOPE OF THE RESURRECTION.
MR TOAD
AND WE HELD SERVICES FOR THOSE WHOSE BODIES WE COULDN'T FIND OR RECOVER INTACT.
I UNDERWENT A SIX-HOUR OPERATION, INVOLVING DOCTOR SWINEHEART AND A TEAM OF TSK-TSKING SORCERERS, TO REMOVE THE REMAINDER OF THE MAGIC KILLER ARROW FROM MY ARM.
OW! AGAIN I SAY **OW!** WHY DO I HAVE TO BE **AWAKE** FOR THIS?
WE CAN'T RISK A GENERAL ANESTHESIA. WHO KNOWS HOW IT MIGHT **REACT** WITH THE DEGRADING SPELLS ATTACHED TO THE FOREIGN OBJECT?

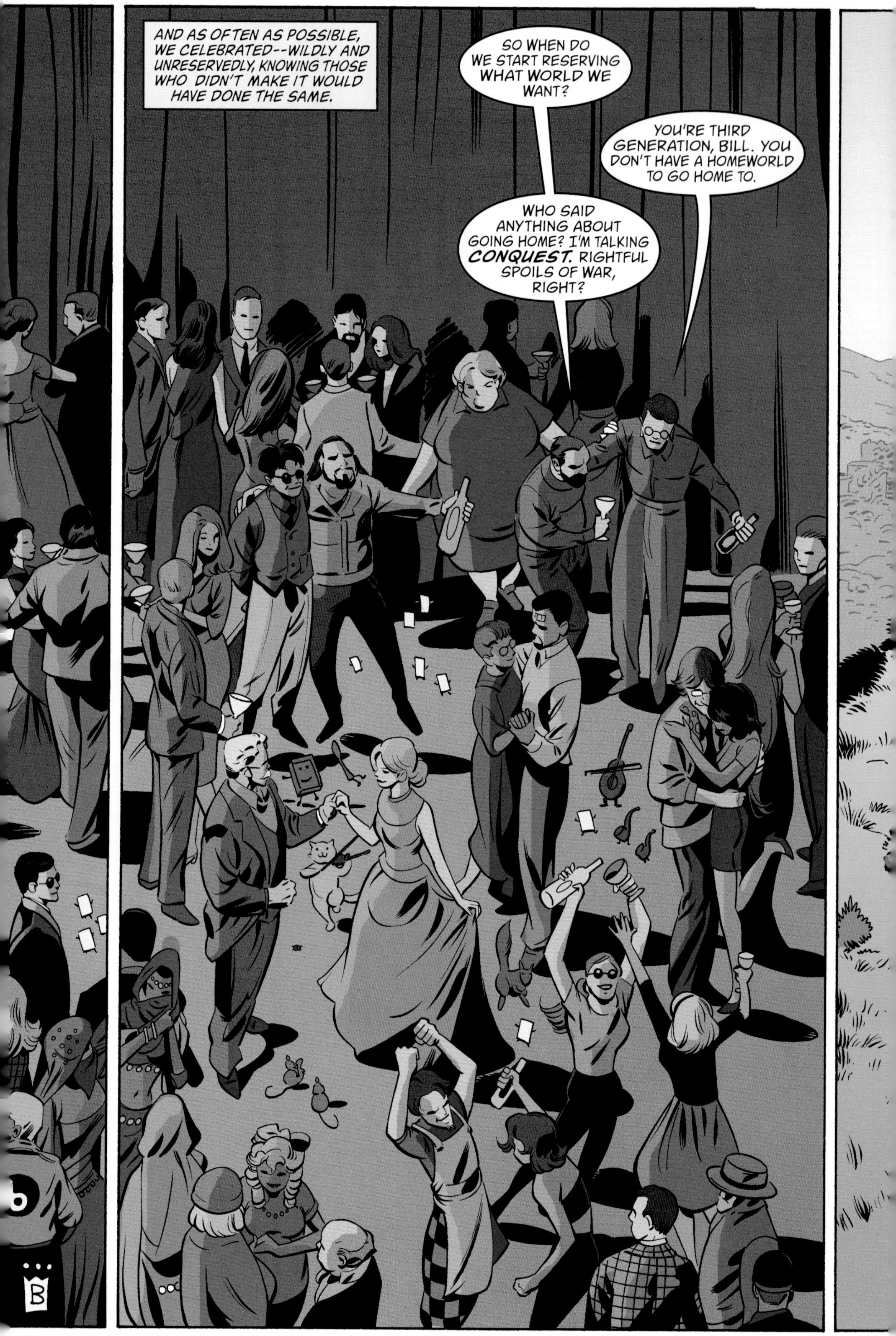
AND AS OFTEN AS POSSIBLE, WE CELEBRATED--WILDLY AND UNRESERVEDLY, KNOWING THOSE WHO DIDN'T MAKE IT WOULD HAVE DONE THE SAME.
SO WHEN DO WE START RESERVING WHAT WORLD WE WANT?
YOU'RE THIRD GENERATION, BILL. YOU DON'T HAVE A HOMEWORLD TO GO HOME TO.
WHO SAID ANYTHING ABOUT GOING HOME? I'M TALKING CONQUEST. RIGHTFUL SPOILS OF WAR, RIGHT?

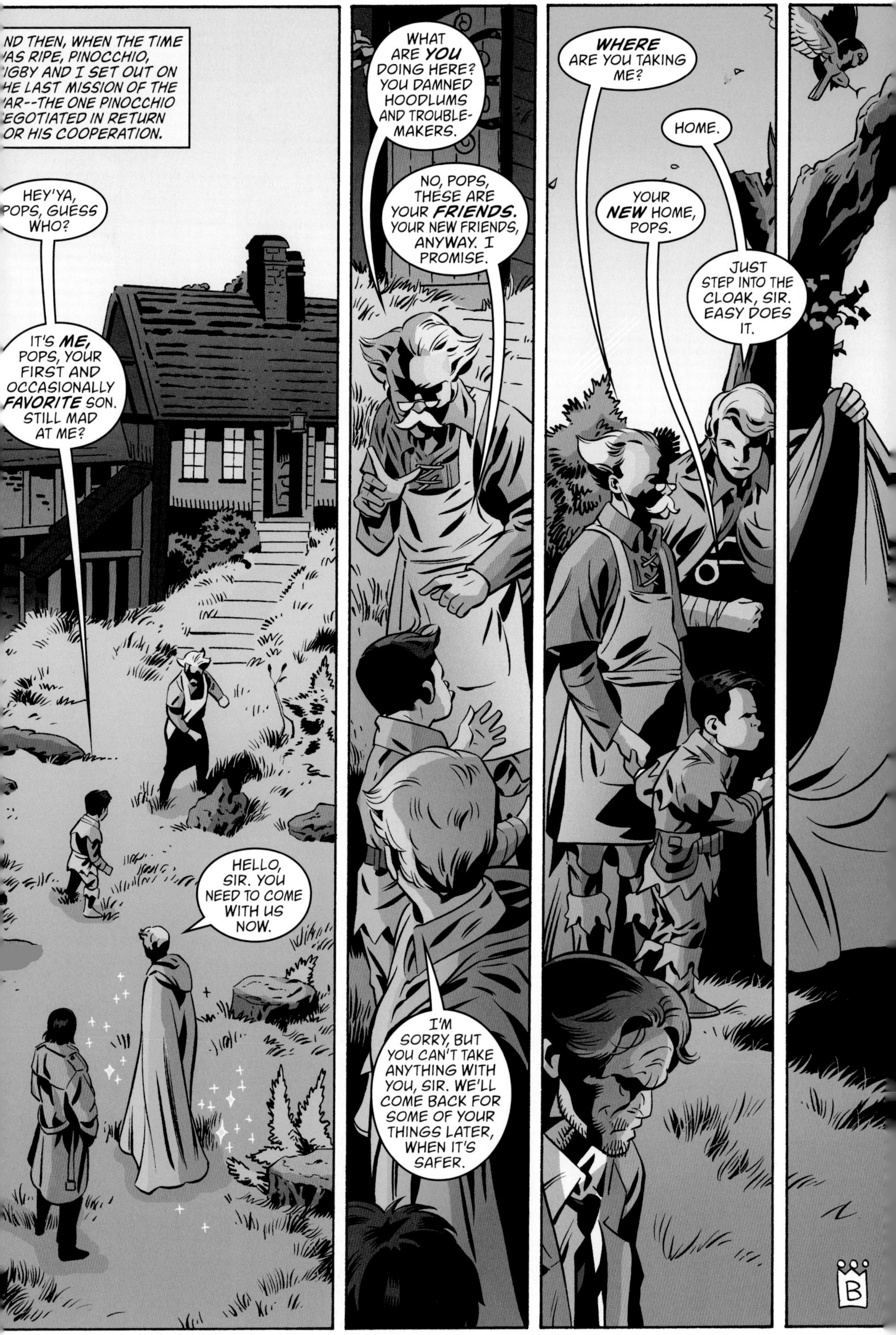

ND THEN, WHEN THE TIME
VAS RIPE, PINOCCHIO,
IGBY AND I SET OUT ON
HE LAST MISSION OF THE
VAR--THE ONE PINOCCHIO
EGOTIATED IN RETURN
OR HIS COOPERATION.
HEY'YA, POPS, GUESS WHO?
IT'S ME, POPS, YOUR FIRST AND OCCASIONALLY FAVORITE SON. STILL MAD AT ME?
HELLO, SIR. YOU NEED TO COME WITH US NOW.
WHAT ARE YOU DOING HERE? YOU DAMNED HOODLUMS AND TROUBLE-MAKERS.
NO, POPS, THESE ARE YOUR FRIENDS. YOUR NEW FRIENDS, ANYWAY. I PROMISE.
I'M SORRY, BUT YOU CAN'T TAKE ANYTHING WITH YOU, SIR. WE'LL COME BACK FOR SOME OF YOUR THINGS LATER, WHEN IT'S SAFER.
WHERE ARE YOU TAKING ME?
HOME.
YOUR NEW HOME, POPS.
JUST STEP INTO THE CLOAK, SIR. EASY DOES IT.

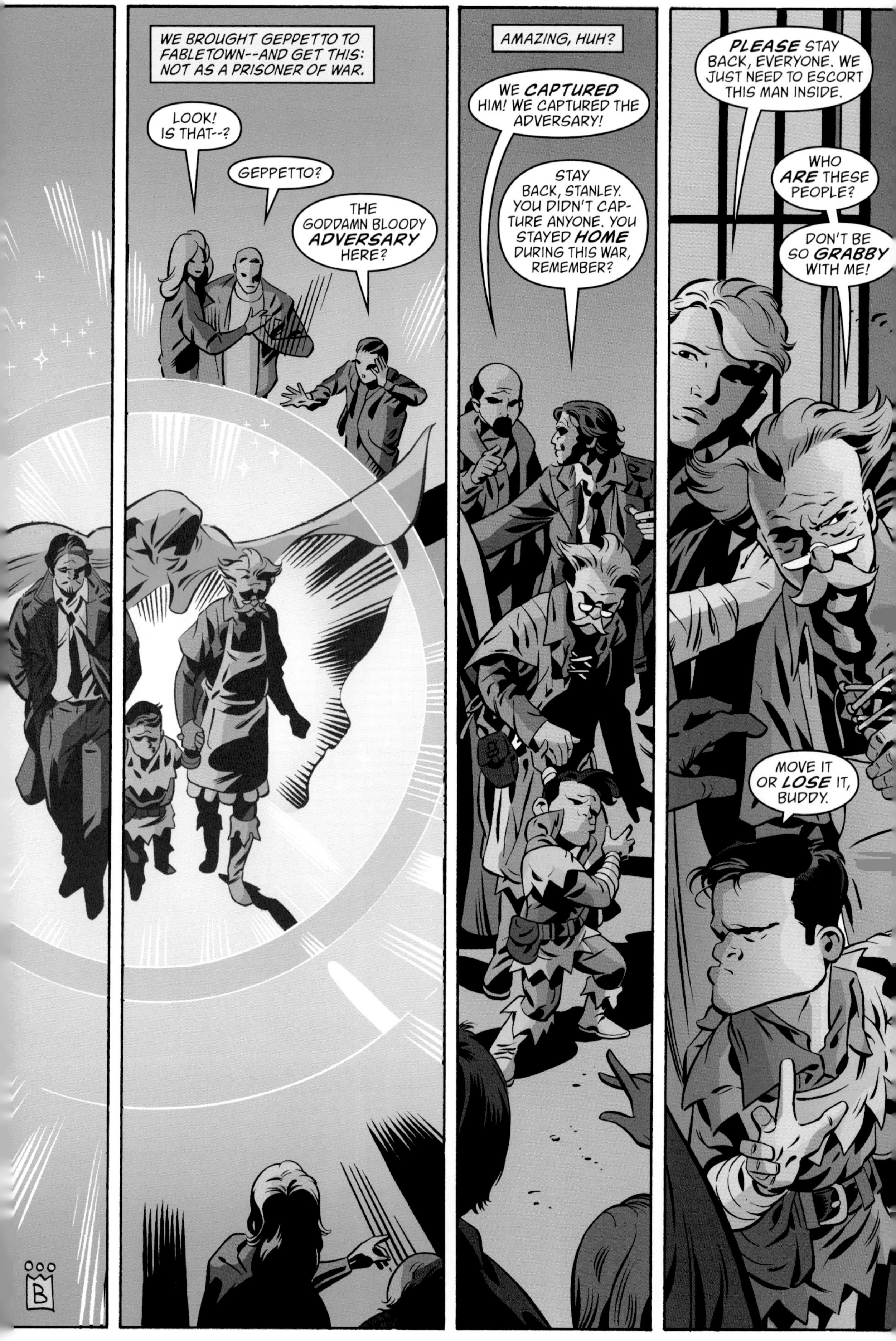
WE BROUGHT GEPPETTO TO FABLETOWN--AND GET THIS: NOT AS A PRISONER OF WAR.
LOOK! IS THAT--?
GEPPETTO?
THE GODDAMN BLOODY ADVERSARY HERE?
AMAZING, HUH?
WE CAPTURED HIM! WE CAPTURED THE ADVERSARY!
STAY BACK, STANLEY. YOU DIDN'T CAPTURE ANYONE. YOU STAYED HOME DURING THIS WAR, REMEMBER?
PLEASE STAY BACK, EVERYONE. WE JUST NEED TO ESCORT THIS MAN INSIDE.
WHO ARE THESE PEOPLE?
DON'T BE SO GRABBY WITH ME!
MOVE IT OR LOSE IT, BUDDY.

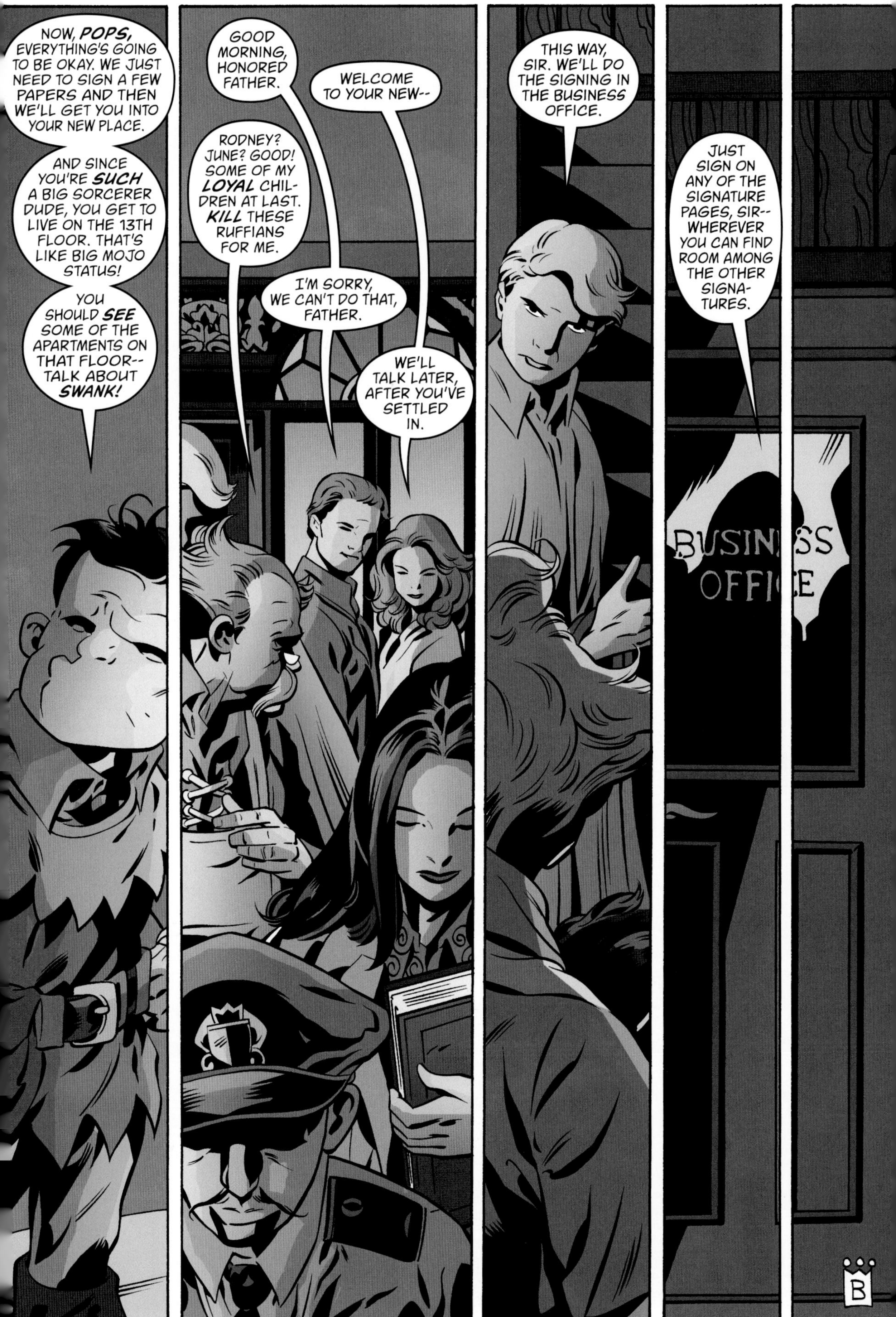
NOW, POPS, EVERYTHING'S GOING TO BE OKAY. WE JUST NEED TO SIGN A FEW PAPERS AND THEN WE'LL GET YOU INTO YOUR NEW PLACE.
AND SINCE YOU'RE SUCH A BIG SORCERER DUDE, YOU GET TO LIVE ON THE 13TH FLOOR. THAT'S LIKE BIG MOJO STATUS!
YOU SHOULD SEE SOME OF THE APARTMENTS ON THAT FLOOR-- TALK ABOUT SWANK!
GOOD MORNING, HONORED FATHER.
WELCOME TO YOUR NEW--
RODNEY? JUNE? GOOD! SOME OF MY LOYAL CHILDREN AT LAST. KILL THESE RUFFIANS FOR ME.
I'M SORRY, WE CAN'T DO THAT, FATHER.
WE'LL TALK LATER, AFTER YOU'VE SETTLED IN.
THIS WAY, SIR. WE'LL DO THE SIGNING IN THE BUSINESS OFFICE.
BUSINESS OFFICE
JUST SIGN ON ANY OF THE SIGNATURE PAGES, SIR-- WHEREVER YOU CAN FIND ROOM AMONG THE OTHER SIGNATURES.

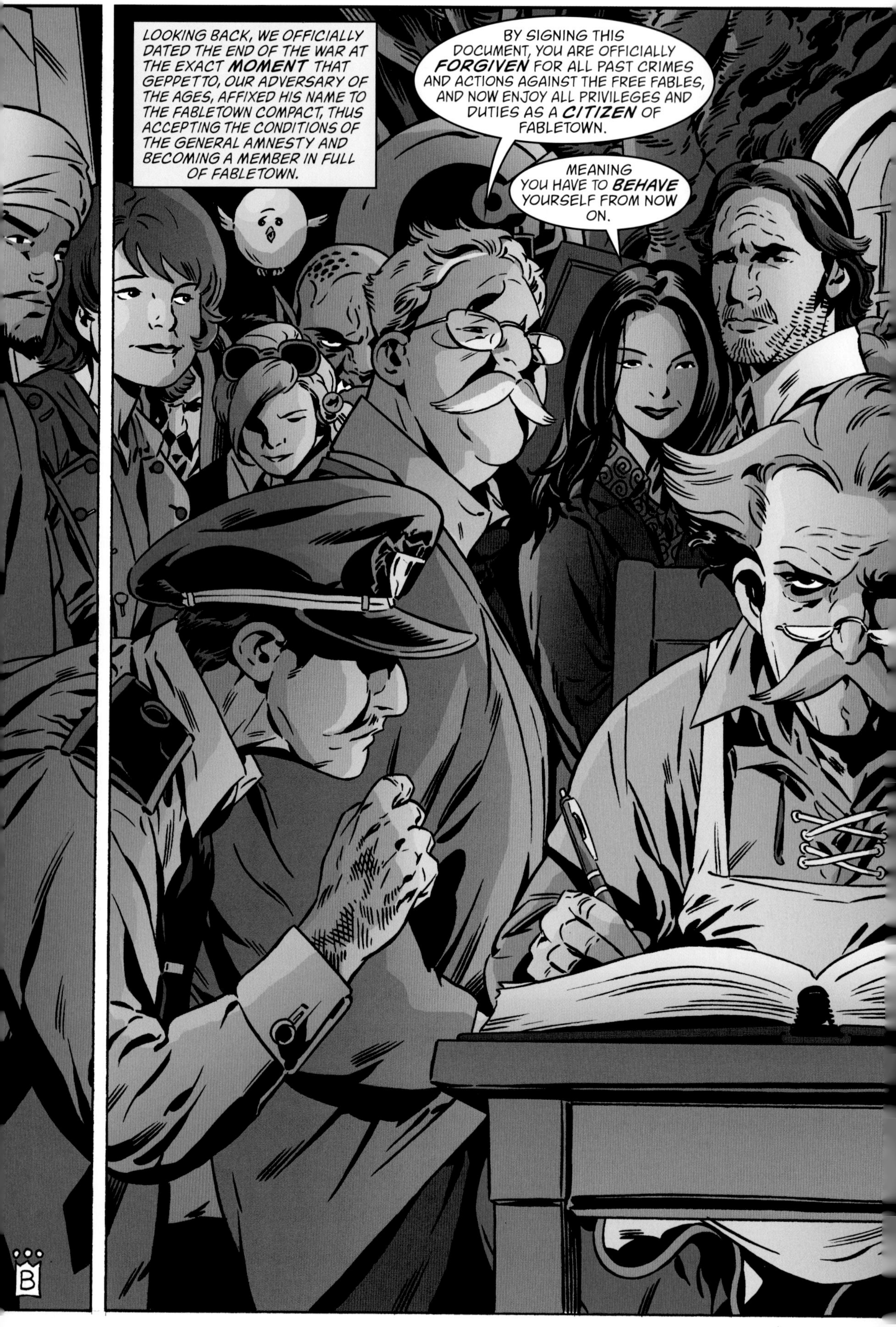
LOOKING BACK, WE OFFICIALLY DATED THE END OF THE WAR AT THE EXACT **MOMENT** THAT GEPPETTO, OUR ADVERSARY OF THE AGES, AFFIXED HIS NAME TO THE FABLETOWN COMPACT, THUS ACCEPTING THE CONDITIONS OF THE GENERAL AMNESTY AND BECOMING A MEMBER IN FULL OF FABLETOWN.
BY SIGNING THIS DOCUMENT, YOU ARE OFFICIALLY **FORGIVEN** FOR ALL PAST CRIMES AND ACTIONS AGAINST THE FREE FABLES, AND NOW ENJOY ALL PRIVILEGES AND DUTIES AS A **CITIZEN** OF FABLETOWN.
MEANING YOU HAVE TO **BEHAVE** YOURSELF FROM NOW ON.

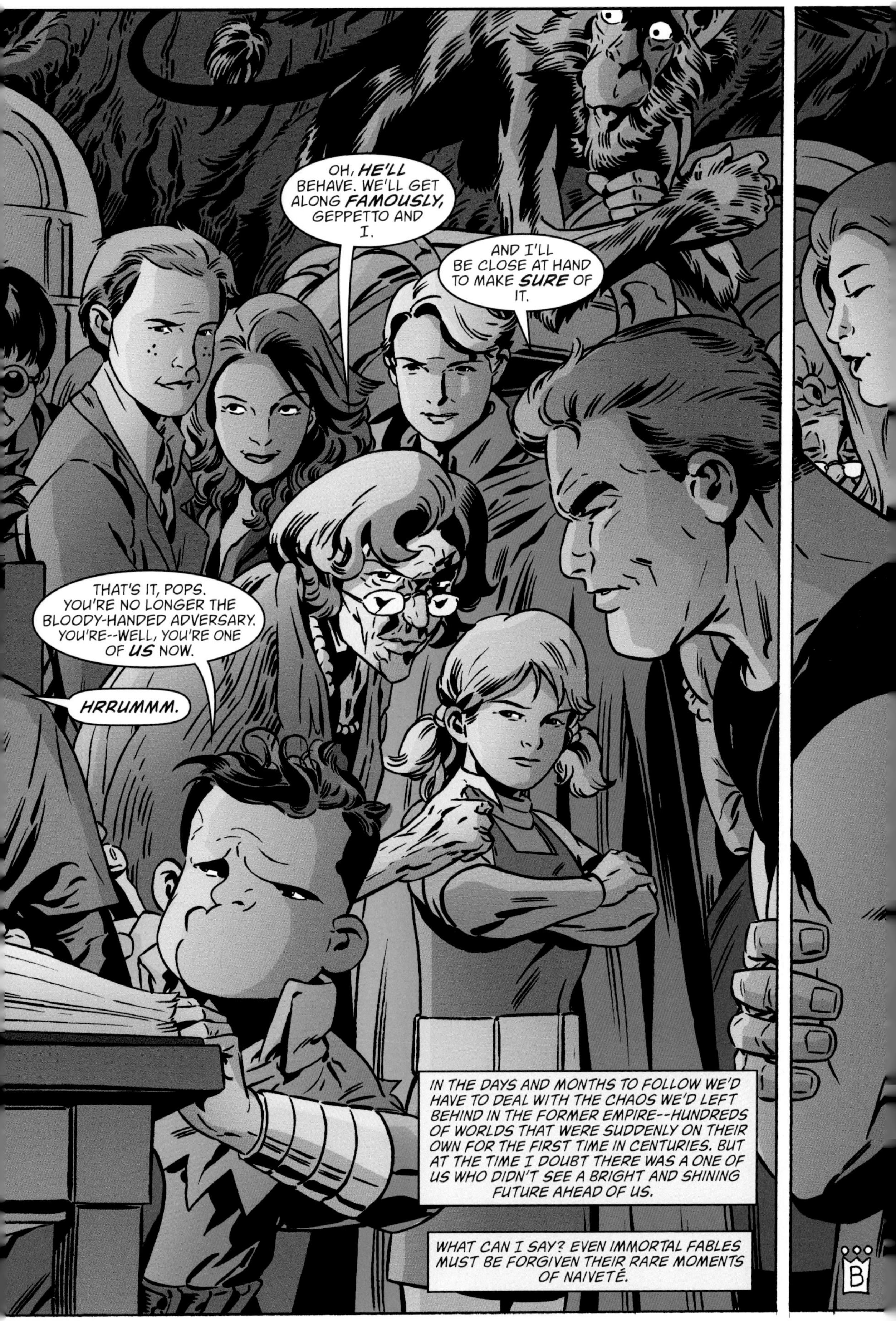
OH, HE'LL BEHAVE. WE'LL GET ALONG FAMOUSLY, GEPPETTO AND I.
AND I'LL BE CLOSE AT HAND TO MAKE SURE OF IT.
THAT'S IT, POPS. YOU'RE NO LONGER THE BLOODY-HANDED ADVERSARY. YOU'RE--WELL, YOU'RE ONE OF US NOW.
HRRUMMM.
IN THE DAYS AND MONTHS TO FOLLOW WE'D HAVE TO DEAL WITH THE CHAOS WE'D LEFT BEHIND IN THE FORMER EMPIRE--HUNDREDS OF WORLDS THAT WERE SUDDENLY ON THEIR OWN FOR THE FIRST TIME IN CENTURIES. BUT AT THE TIME I DOUBT THERE WAS A ONE OF US WHO DIDN'T SEE A BRIGHT AND SHINING FUTURE AHEAD OF US.
WHAT CAN I SAY? EVEN IMMORTAL FABLES MUST BE FORGIVEN THEIR RARE MOMENTS OF NAIVETÉ.

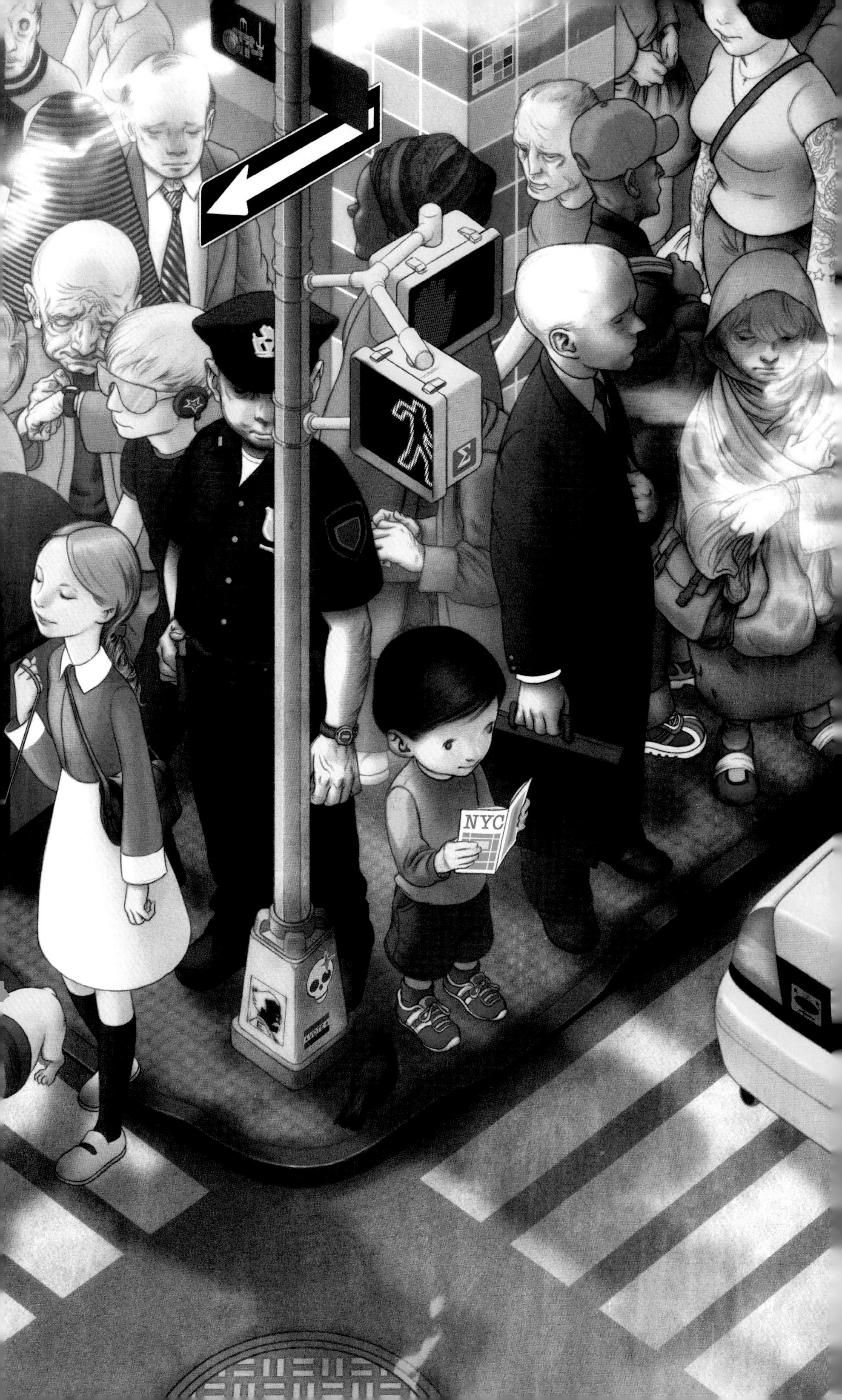
NYC
VOTE

"No kind man could ever do what I've done."

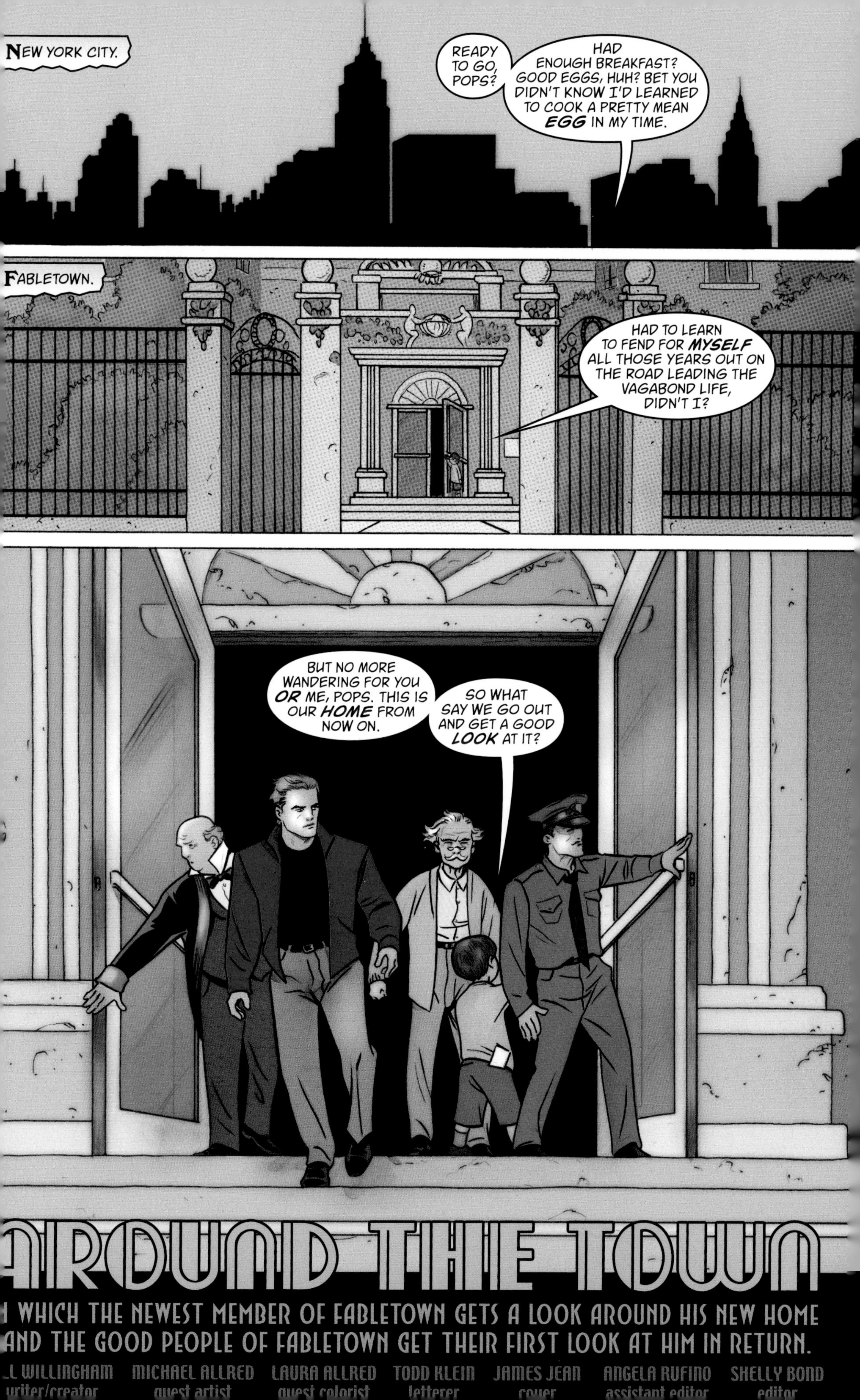
NEW YORK CITY.
READY TO GO, POPS?
HAD ENOUGH BREAKFAST? GOOD EGGS, HUH? BET YOU DIDN'T KNOW I'D LEARNED TO COOK A PRETTY MEAN EGG IN MY TIME.
FABLETOWN.
HAD TO LEARN TO FEND FOR MYSELF ALL THOSE YEARS OUT ON THE ROAD LEADING THE VAGABOND LIFE, DIDN'T I?
BUT NO MORE WANDERING FOR YOU OR ME, POPS. THIS IS OUR HOME FROM NOW ON.
SO WHAT SAY WE GO OUT AND GET A GOOD LOOK AT IT?

AROUND THE TOWN

IN WHICH THE NEWEST MEMBER OF FABLETOWN GETS A LOOK AROUND HIS NEW HOME AND THE GOOD PEOPLE OF FABLETOWN GET THEIR FIRST LOOK AT HIM IN RETURN.

L WILLINGHAM writer/creator · MICHAEL ALLRED guest artist · LAURA ALLRED guest colorist · TODD KLEIN letterer · JAMES JEAN cover · ANGELA RUFINO assistant editor · SHELLY BOND editor

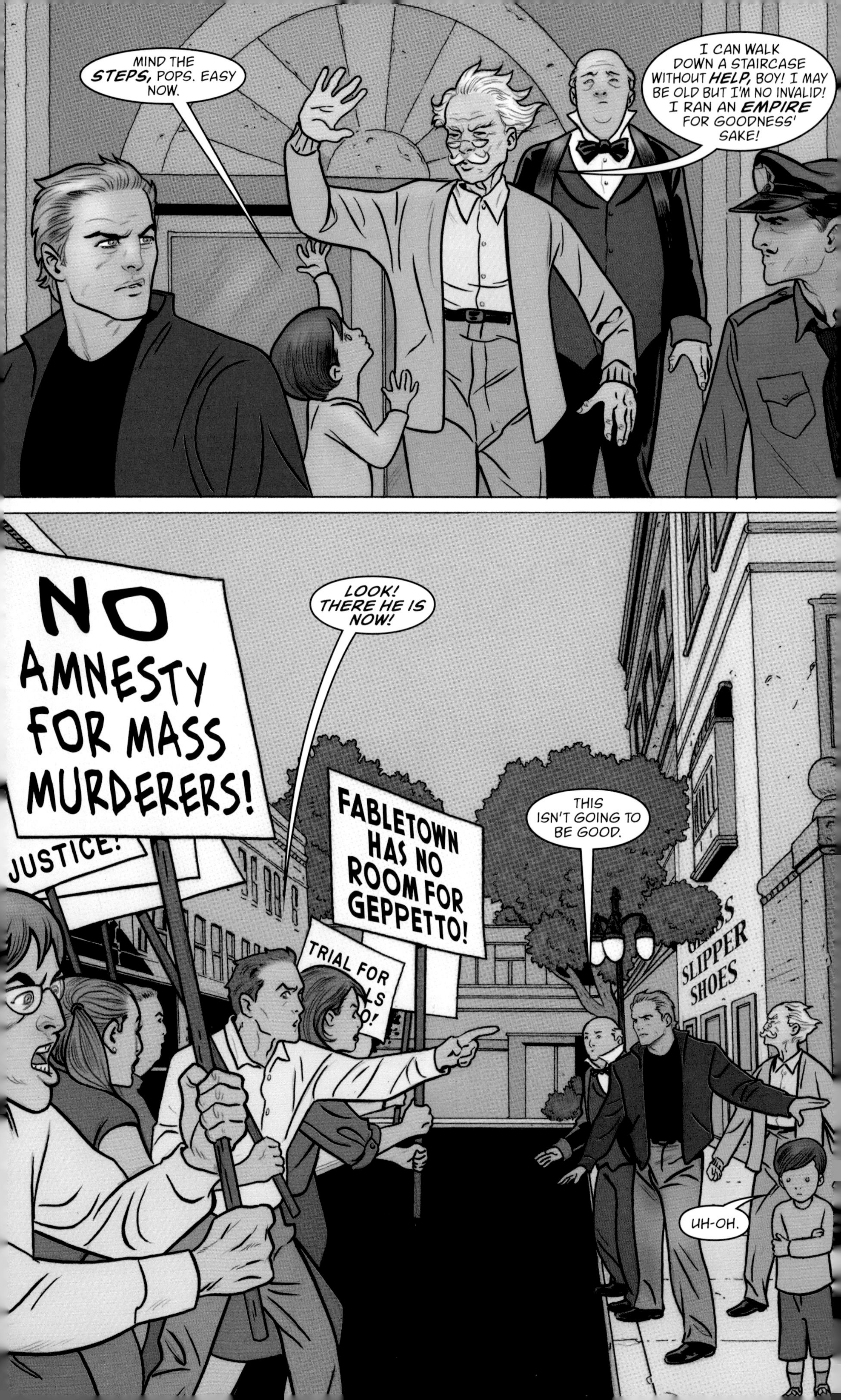
MIND THE *STEPS,* POPS. EASY NOW.
I CAN WALK DOWN A STAIRCASE WITHOUT *HELP,* BOY! I MAY BE OLD BUT I'M NO INVALID! I RAN AN *EMPIRE* FOR GOODNESS' SAKE!
NO AMNESTY FOR MASS MURDERERS!
JUSTICE!
LOOK! THERE HE IS NOW!
FABLETOWN HAS NO ROOM FOR GEPPETTO!
TRIAL FOR
THIS ISN'T GOING TO BE GOOD.
SLIPPER SHOES
UH-OH.

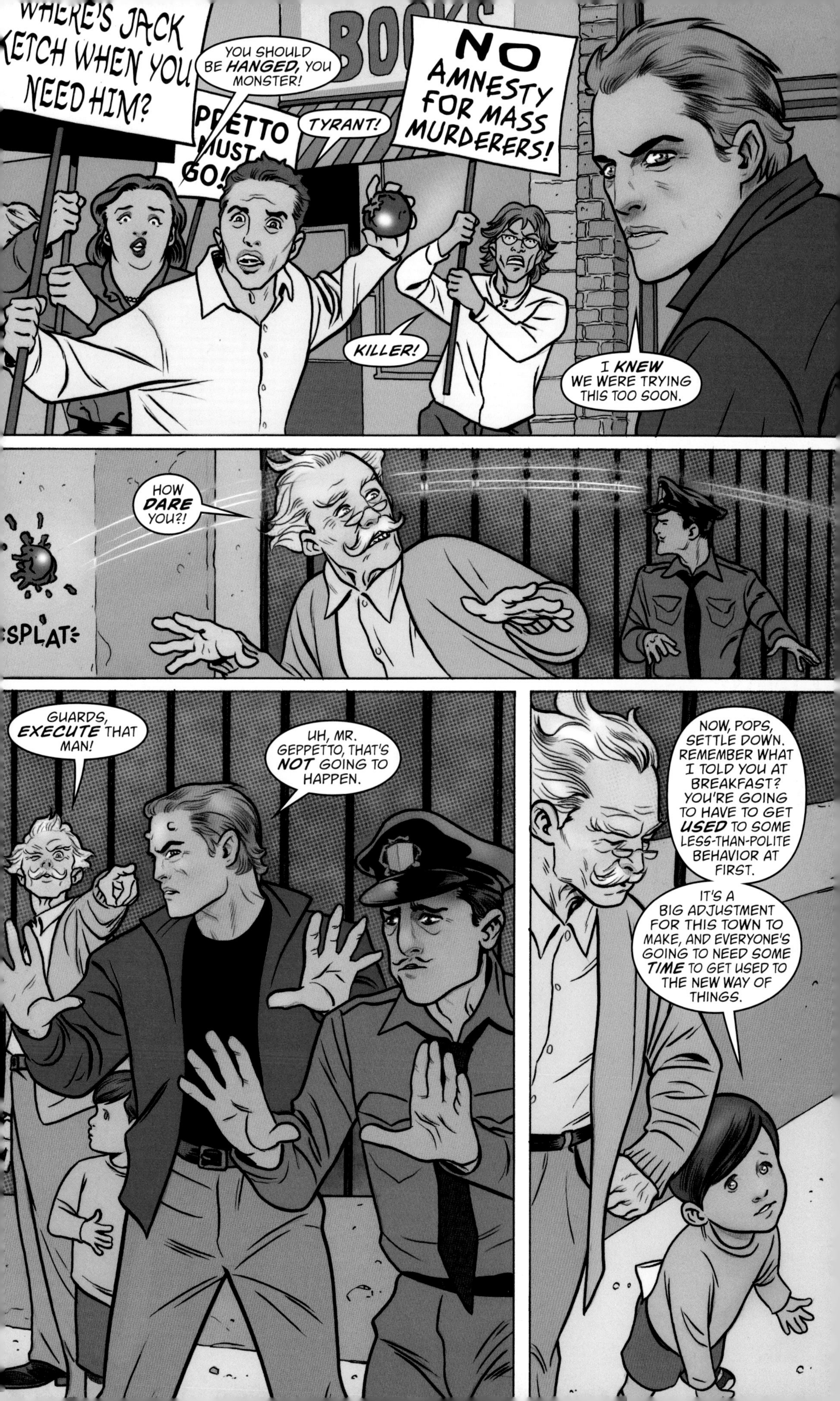

WHERE'S JACK KETCH WHEN YOU NEED HIM?
YOU SHOULD BE HANGED, YOU MONSTER!
BOOKS
PPETTO MUST GO!
TYRANT!
NO AMNESTY FOR MASS MURDERERS!
KILLER!
I KNEW WE WERE TRYING THIS TOO SOON.
HOW DARE YOU?!
SPLAT
GUARDS, EXECUTE THAT MAN!
UH, MR. GEPPETTO, THAT'S NOT GOING TO HAPPEN.
NOW, POPS, SETTLE DOWN. REMEMBER WHAT I TOLD YOU AT BREAKFAST? YOU'RE GOING TO HAVE TO GET USED TO SOME LESS-THAN-POLITE BEHAVIOR AT FIRST.
IT'S A BIG ADJUSTMENT FOR THIS TOWN TO MAKE, AND EVERYONE'S GOING TO NEED SOME TIME TO GET USED TO THE NEW WAY OF THINGS.

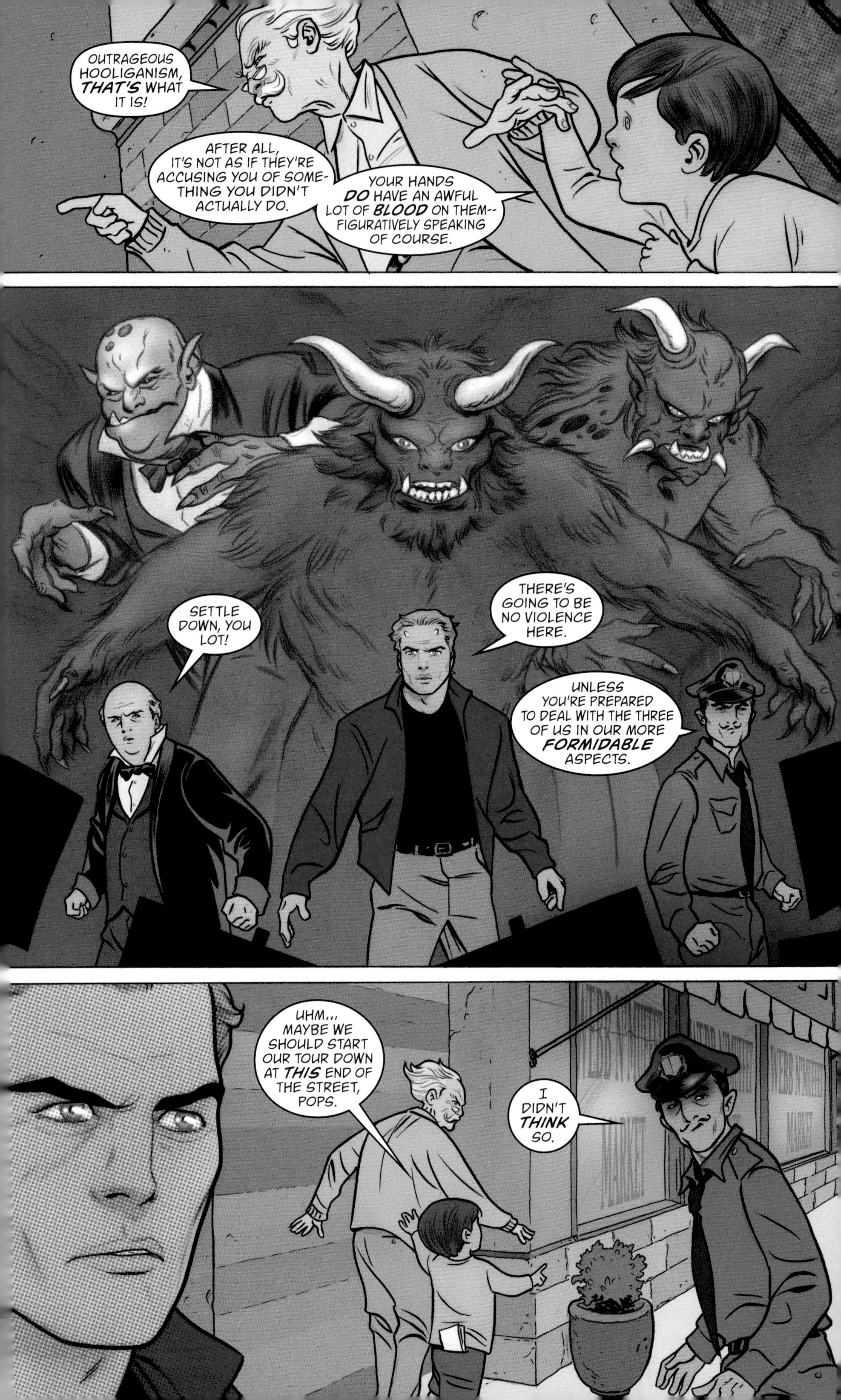
OUTRAGEOUS HOOLIGANISM, ***THAT'S*** WHAT IT IS!
AFTER ALL, IT'S NOT AS IF THEY'RE ACCUSING YOU OF SOMETHING YOU DIDN'T ACTUALLY DO.
YOUR HANDS ***DO*** HAVE AN AWFUL LOT OF ***BLOOD*** ON THEM-- FIGURATIVELY SPEAKING OF COURSE.
SETTLE DOWN, YOU LOT!
THERE'S GOING TO BE NO VIOLENCE HERE.
UNLESS YOU'RE PREPARED TO DEAL WITH THE THREE OF US IN OUR MORE ***FORMIDABLE*** ASPECTS.
UHM... MAYBE WE SHOULD START OUR TOUR DOWN AT ***THIS*** END OF THE STREET, POPS.
I DIDN'T ***THINK*** SO.

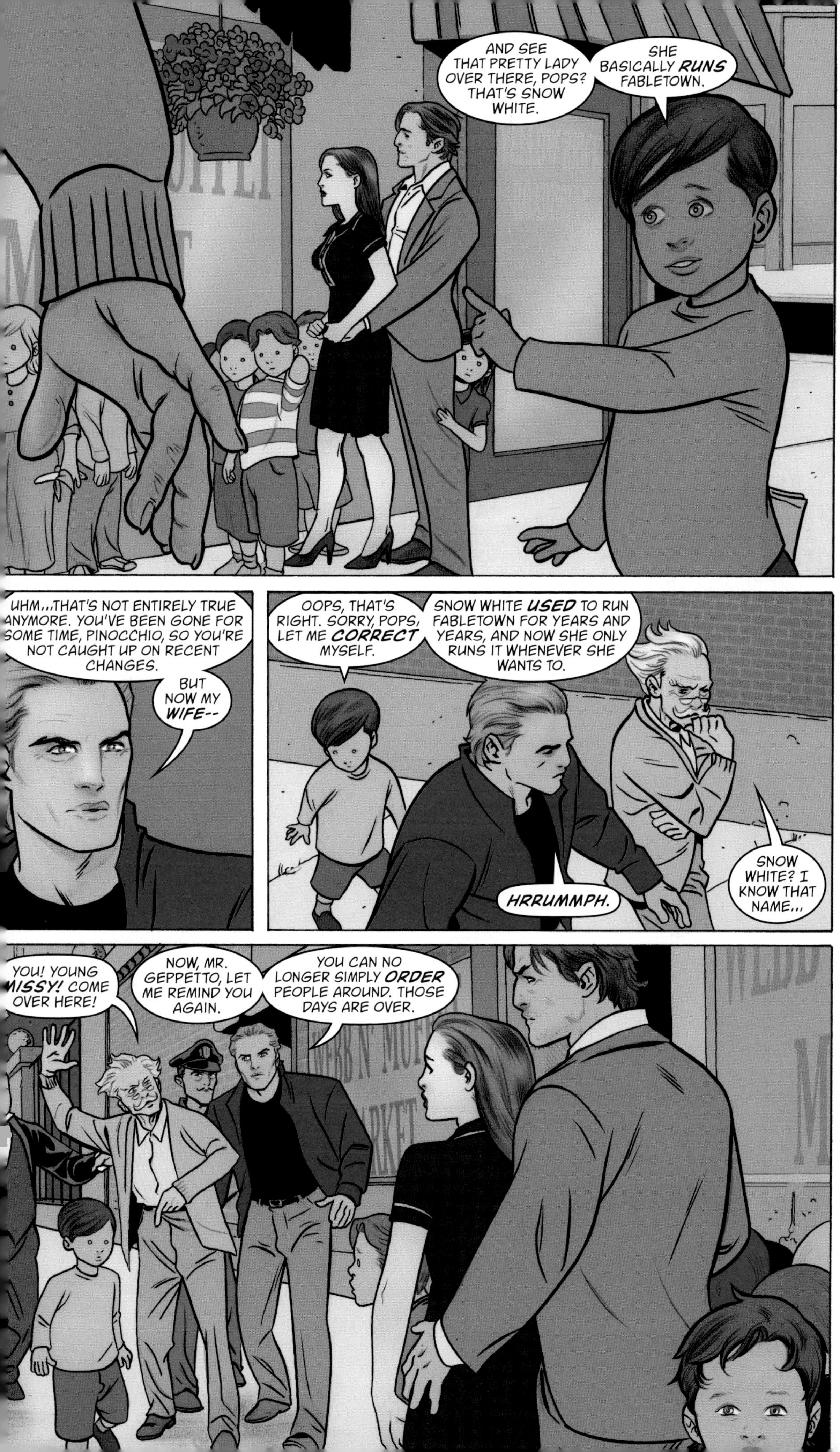

AND SEE THAT PRETTY LADY OVER THERE, POPS? THAT'S SNOW WHITE.
SHE BASICALLY RUNS FABLETOWN.
UHM...THAT'S NOT ENTIRELY TRUE ANYMORE. YOU'VE BEEN GONE FOR SOME TIME, PINOCCHIO, SO YOU'RE NOT CAUGHT UP ON RECENT CHANGES.
BUT NOW MY WIFE--
OOPS, THAT'S RIGHT. SORRY, POPS, LET ME CORRECT MYSELF.
SNOW WHITE USED TO RUN FABLETOWN FOR YEARS AND YEARS, AND NOW SHE ONLY RUNS IT WHENEVER SHE WANTS TO.
HRRUMMPH.
SNOW WHITE? I KNOW THAT NAME...
YOU! YOUNG MISSY! COME OVER HERE!
NOW, MR. GEPPETTO, LET ME REMIND YOU AGAIN.
YOU CAN NO LONGER SIMPLY ORDER PEOPLE AROUND. THOSE DAYS ARE OVER.

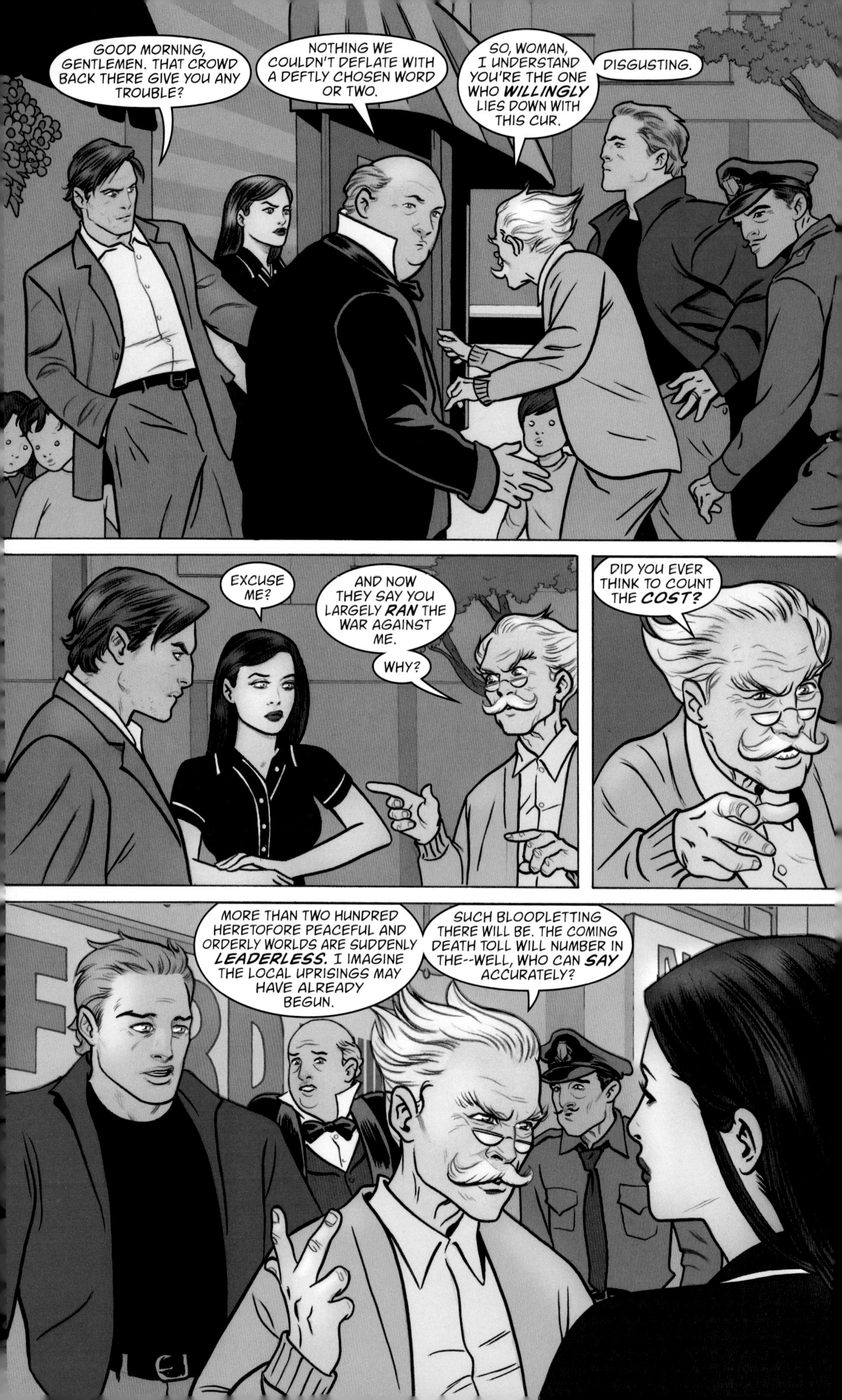
GOOD MORNING, GENTLEMEN. THAT CROWD BACK THERE GIVE YOU ANY TROUBLE?
NOTHING WE COULDN'T DEFLATE WITH A DEFTLY CHOSEN WORD OR TWO.
SO, WOMAN, I UNDERSTAND YOU'RE THE ONE WHO *WILLINGLY* LIES DOWN WITH THIS CUR.
DISGUSTING.
EXCUSE ME?
AND NOW THEY SAY YOU LARGELY *RAN* THE WAR AGAINST ME.
WHY?
DID YOU EVER THINK TO COUNT THE *COST?*
MORE THAN TWO HUNDRED HERETOFORE PEACEFUL AND ORDERLY WORLDS ARE SUDDENLY *LEADERLESS.* I IMAGINE THE LOCAL UPRISINGS MAY HAVE ALREADY BEGUN.
SUCH BLOODLETTING THERE WILL BE. THE COMING DEATH TOLL WILL NUMBER IN THE--WELL, WHO CAN *SAY* ACCURATELY?

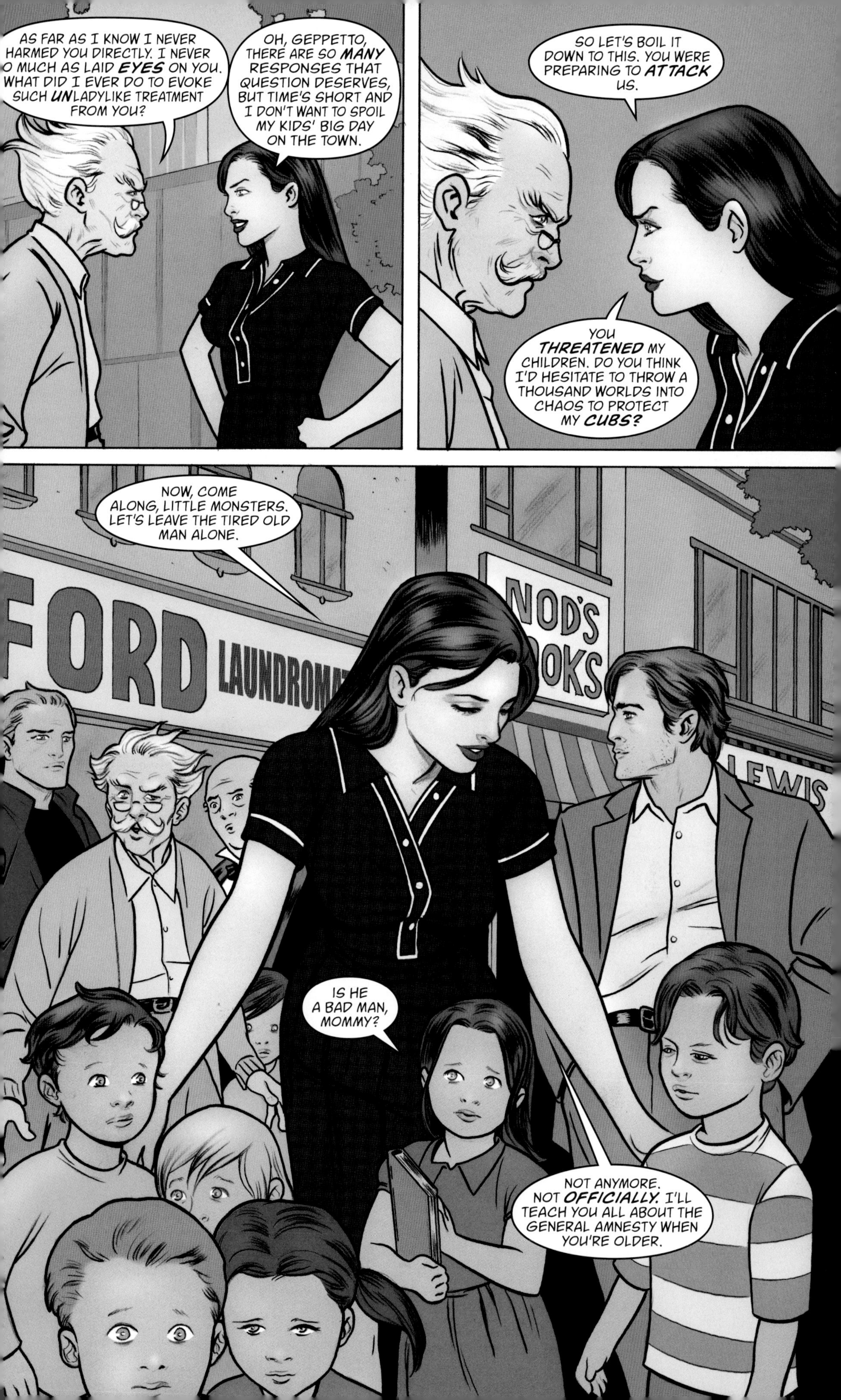
AS FAR AS I KNOW I NEVER HARMED YOU DIRECTLY. I NEVER SO MUCH AS LAID EYES ON YOU. WHAT DID I EVER DO TO EVOKE SUCH UNLADYLIKE TREATMENT FROM YOU?
OH, GEPPETTO, THERE ARE SO MANY RESPONSES THAT QUESTION DESERVES, BUT TIME'S SHORT AND I DON'T WANT TO SPOIL MY KIDS' BIG DAY ON THE TOWN.
SO LET'S BOIL IT DOWN TO THIS. YOU WERE PREPARING TO ATTACK US.
YOU THREATENED MY CHILDREN. DO YOU THINK I'D HESITATE TO THROW A THOUSAND WORLDS INTO CHAOS TO PROTECT MY CUBS?
NOW, COME ALONG, LITTLE MONSTERS. LET'S LEAVE THE TIRED OLD MAN ALONE.
FORD
LAUNDROMA
NOD'S
OKS
LEWIS
IS HE A BAD MAN, MOMMY?
NOT ANYMORE. NOT OFFICIALLY. I'LL TEACH YOU ALL ABOUT THE GENERAL AMNESTY WHEN YOU'RE OLDER.

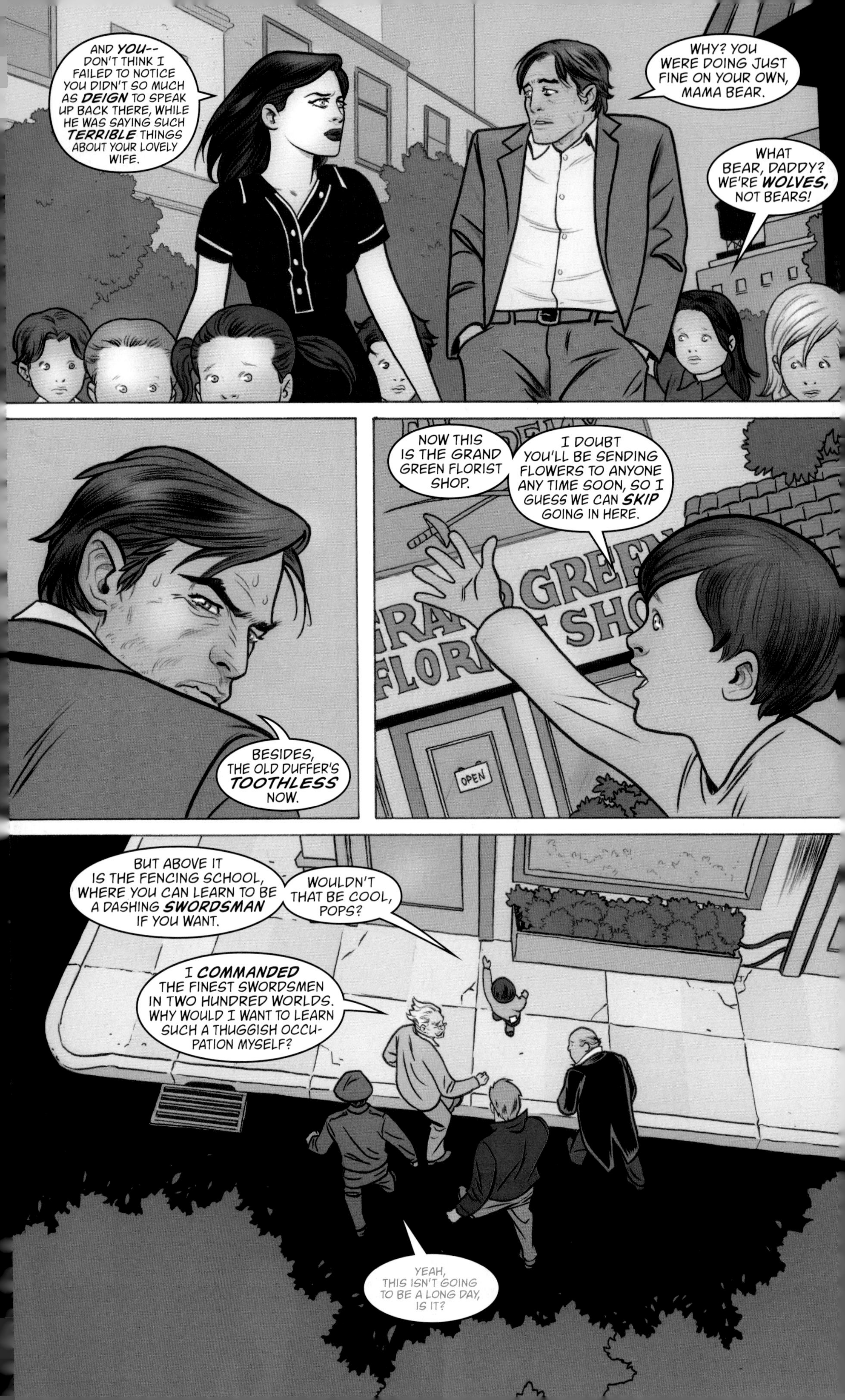
AND YOU--
DON'T THINK I FAILED TO NOTICE YOU DIDN'T SO MUCH AS DEIGN TO SPEAK UP BACK THERE, WHILE HE WAS SAYING SUCH TERRIBLE THINGS ABOUT YOUR LOVELY WIFE.
WHY? YOU WERE DOING JUST FINE ON YOUR OWN, MAMA BEAR.
WHAT BEAR, DADDY? WE'RE WOLVES, NOT BEARS!
BESIDES, THE OLD DUFFER'S TOOTHLESS NOW.
NOW THIS IS THE GRAND GREEN FLORIST SHOP.
I DOUBT YOU'LL BE SENDING FLOWERS TO ANYONE ANY TIME SOON, SO I GUESS WE CAN SKIP GOING IN HERE.
GRAND GREEN FLORIST SHOP
OPEN
BUT ABOVE IT IS THE FENCING SCHOOL, WHERE YOU CAN LEARN TO BE A DASHING SWORDSMAN IF YOU WANT.
WOULDN'T THAT BE COOL, POPS?
I COMMANDED THE FINEST SWORDSMEN IN TWO HUNDRED WORLDS. WHY WOULD I WANT TO LEARN SUCH A THUGGISH OCCUPATION MYSELF?
YEAH, THIS ISN'T GOING TO BE A LONG DAY, IS IT?

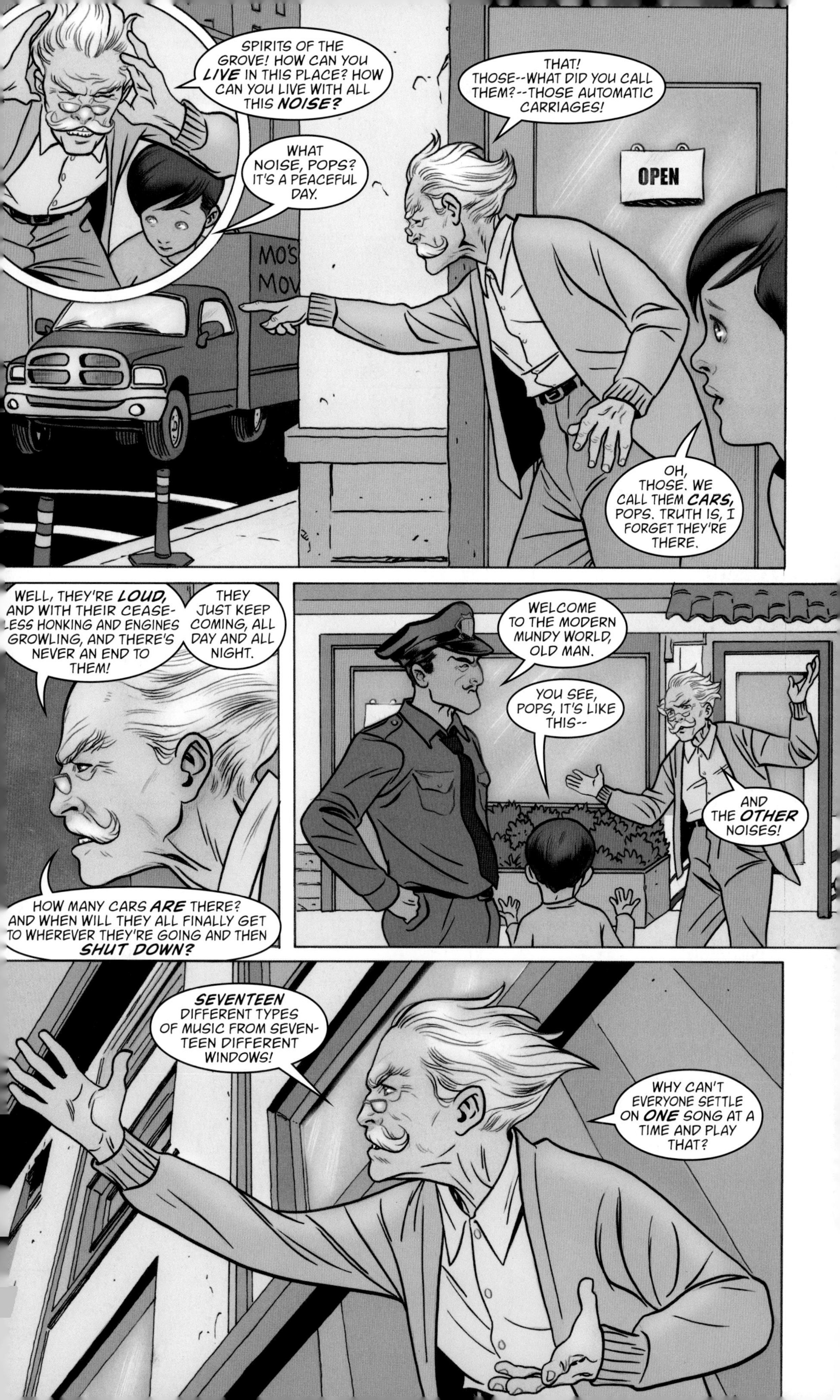
SPIRITS OF THE GROVE! HOW CAN YOU *LIVE* IN THIS PLACE? HOW CAN YOU LIVE WITH ALL THIS *NOISE?*
WHAT NOISE, POPS? IT'S A PEACEFUL DAY.
MO'S MOV
THAT! THOSE--WHAT DID YOU CALL THEM?--THOSE AUTOMATIC CARRIAGES!
OPEN
OH, THOSE. WE CALL THEM *CARS,* POPS. TRUTH IS, I FORGET THEY'RE THERE.
WELL, THEY'RE *LOUD,* AND WITH THEIR CEASE-LESS HONKING AND ENGINES GROWLING, AND THERE'S NEVER AN END TO THEM!
THEY JUST KEEP COMING, ALL DAY AND ALL NIGHT.
HOW MANY CARS *ARE* THERE? AND WHEN WILL THEY ALL FINALLY GET TO WHEREVER THEY'RE GOING AND THEN *SHUT DOWN?*
WELCOME TO THE MODERN MUNDY WORLD, OLD MAN.
YOU SEE, POPS, IT'S LIKE THIS--
AND THE *OTHER* NOISES!
SEVENTEEN DIFFERENT TYPES OF MUSIC FROM SEVEN-TEEN DIFFERENT WINDOWS!
WHY CAN'T EVERYONE SETTLE ON *ONE* SONG AT A TIME AND PLAY THAT?

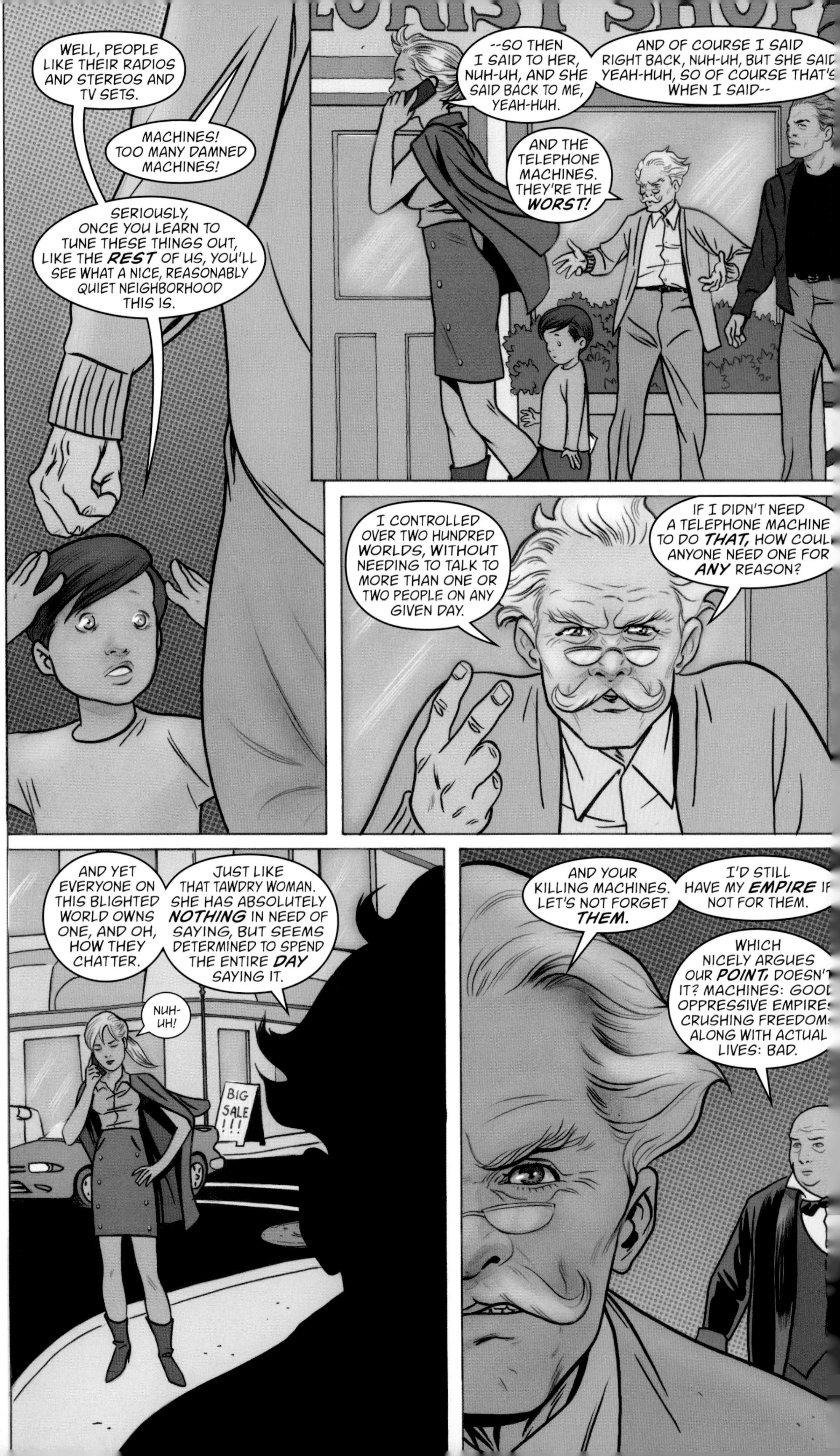

WELL, PEOPLE LIKE THEIR RADIOS AND STEREOS AND TV SETS.
MACHINES! TOO MANY DAMNED MACHINES!
SERIOUSLY, ONCE YOU LEARN TO TUNE THESE THINGS OUT, LIKE THE **REST** OF US, YOU'LL SEE WHAT A NICE, REASONABLY QUIET NEIGHBORHOOD THIS IS.
--SO THEN I SAID TO HER, NUH-UH, AND SHE SAID BACK TO ME, YEAH-HUH.
AND OF COURSE I SAID RIGHT BACK, NUH-UH, BUT SHE SAID YEAH-HUH, SO OF COURSE THAT'S WHEN I SAID--
AND THE TELEPHONE MACHINES. THEY'RE THE **WORST!**
I CONTROLLED OVER TWO HUNDRED WORLDS, WITHOUT NEEDING TO TALK TO MORE THAN ONE OR TWO PEOPLE ON ANY GIVEN DAY.
IF I DIDN'T NEED A TELEPHONE MACHINE TO DO **THAT,** HOW COULD ANYONE NEED ONE FOR **ANY** REASON?
AND YET EVERYONE ON THIS BLIGHTED WORLD OWNS ONE, AND OH, HOW THEY CHATTER.
JUST LIKE THAT TAWDRY WOMAN. SHE HAS ABSOLUTELY **NOTHING** IN NEED OF SAYING, BUT SEEMS DETERMINED TO SPEND THE ENTIRE **DAY** SAYING IT.
NUH-UH!
BIG SALE !!!
AND YOUR KILLING MACHINES. LET'S NOT FORGET **THEM.**
I'D STILL HAVE MY **EMPIRE** IF NOT FOR THEM.
WHICH NICELY ARGUES OUR **POINT,** DOESN'T IT? MACHINES: GOOD. OPPRESSIVE EMPIRES CRUSHING FREEDOMS ALONG WITH ACTUAL LIVES: BAD.

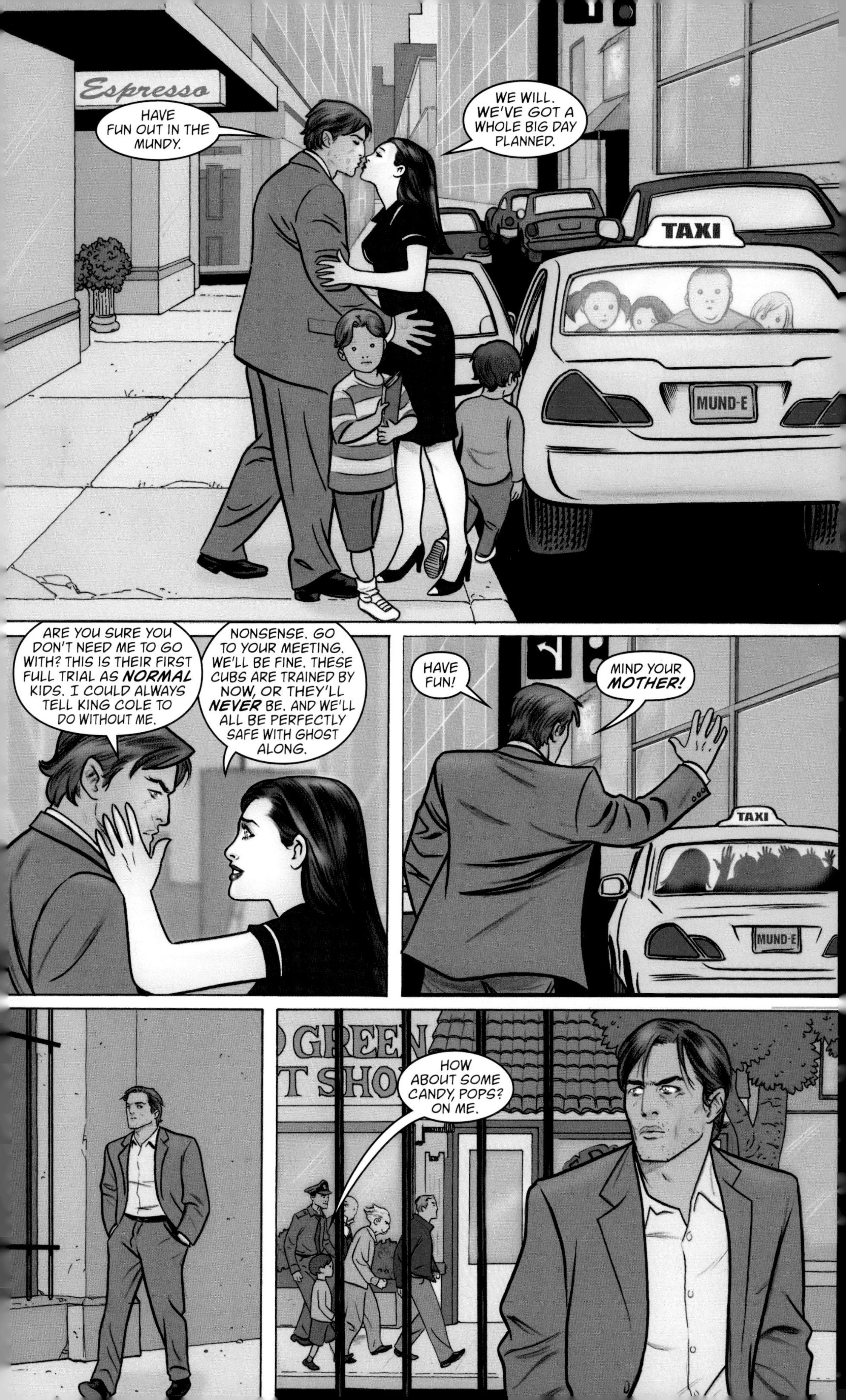
Espresso
HAVE FUN OUT IN THE MUNDY.
WE WILL. WE'VE GOT A WHOLE BIG DAY PLANNED.
TAXI
MUND-E
ARE YOU SURE YOU DON'T NEED ME TO GO WITH? THIS IS THEIR FIRST FULL TRIAL AS **NORMAL** KIDS. I COULD ALWAYS TELL KING COLE TO DO WITHOUT ME.
NONSENSE. GO TO YOUR MEETING. WE'LL BE FINE. THESE CUBS ARE TRAINED BY NOW, OR THEY'LL **NEVER** BE. AND WE'LL ALL BE PERFECTLY SAFE WITH GHOST ALONG.
HAVE FUN!
MIND YOUR **MOTHER!**
TAXI
MUND-E
HOW ABOUT SOME CANDY, POPS? ON ME.

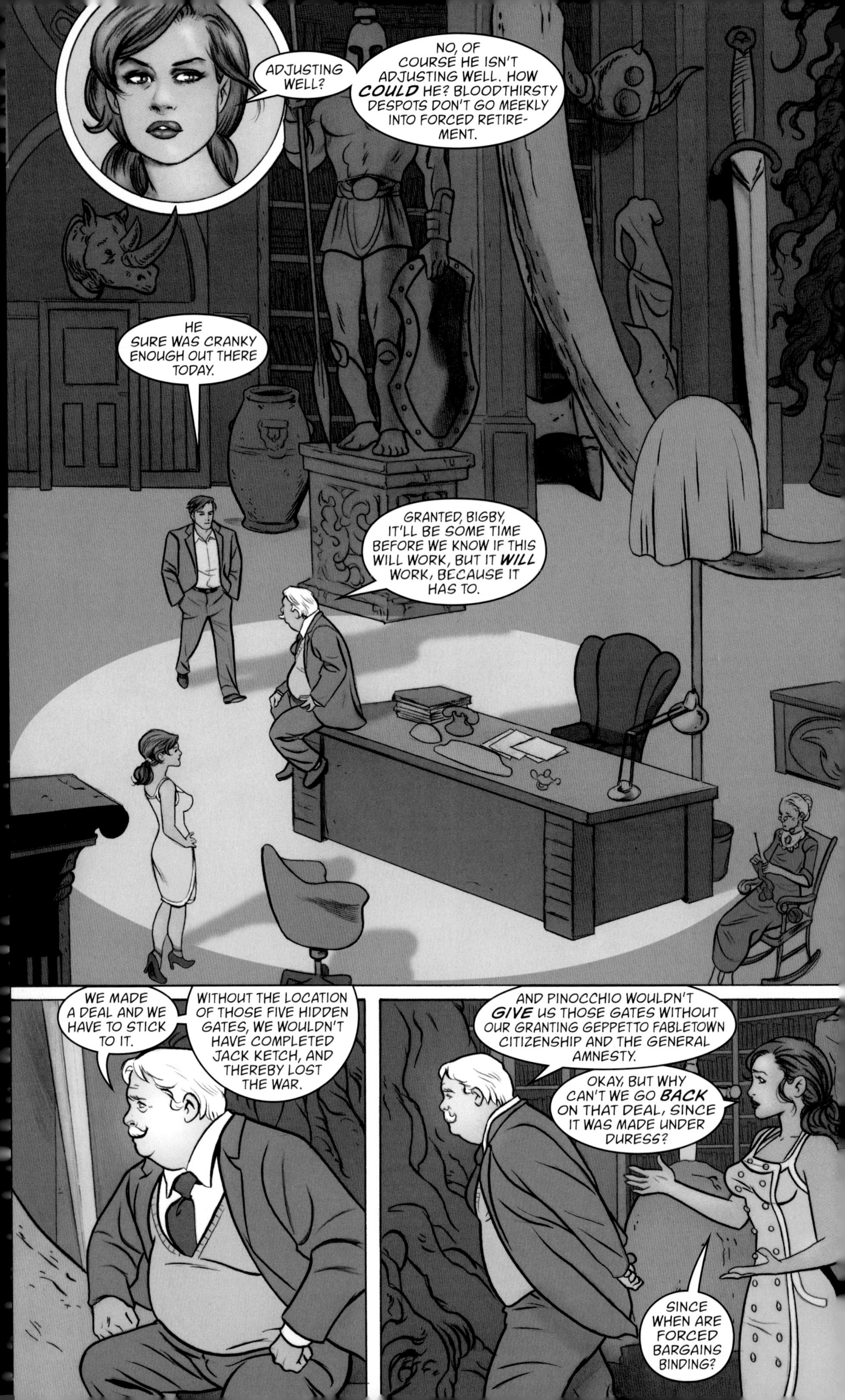
ADJUSTING WELL?
NO, OF COURSE HE ISN'T ADJUSTING WELL. HOW COULD HE? BLOODTHIRSTY DESPOTS DON'T GO MEEKLY INTO FORCED RETIREMENT.
HE SURE WAS CRANKY ENOUGH OUT THERE TODAY.
GRANTED, BIGBY, IT'LL BE SOME TIME BEFORE WE KNOW IF THIS WILL WORK, BUT IT WILL WORK, BECAUSE IT HAS TO.
WE MADE A DEAL AND WE HAVE TO STICK TO IT.
WITHOUT THE LOCATION OF THOSE FIVE HIDDEN GATES, WE WOULDN'T HAVE COMPLETED JACK KETCH, AND THEREBY LOST THE WAR.
AND PINOCCHIO WOULDN'T GIVE US THOSE GATES WITHOUT OUR GRANTING GEPPETTO FABLETOWN CITIZENSHIP AND THE GENERAL AMNESTY.
OKAY, BUT WHY CAN'T WE GO BACK ON THAT DEAL, SINCE IT WAS MADE UNDER DURESS?
SINCE WHEN ARE FORCED BARGAINS BINDING?

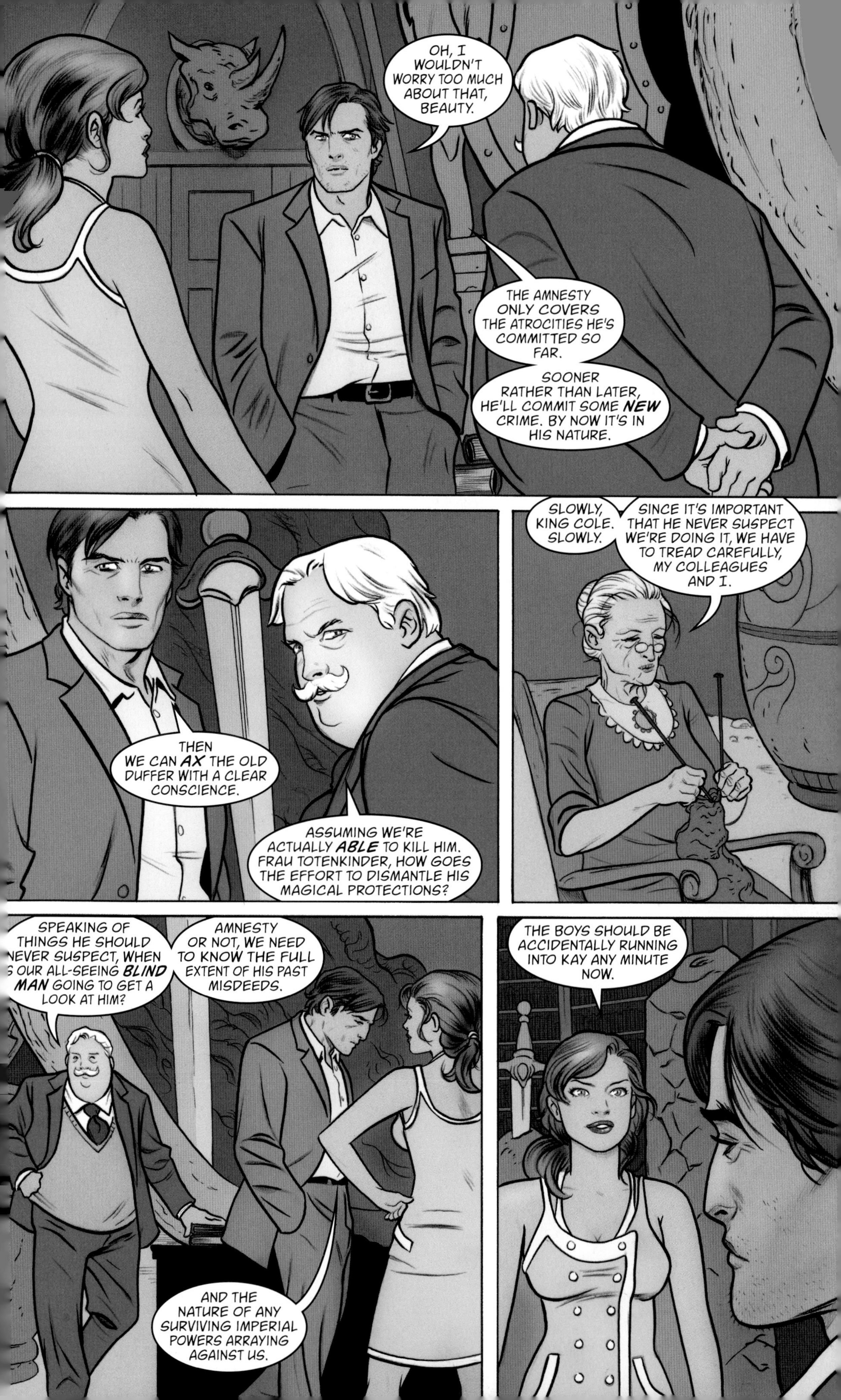
OH, I WOULDN'T WORRY TOO MUCH ABOUT THAT, BEAUTY.
THE AMNESTY ONLY COVERS THE ATROCITIES HE'S COMMITTED SO FAR.
SOONER RATHER THAN LATER, HE'LL COMMIT SOME NEW CRIME. BY NOW IT'S IN HIS NATURE.
THEN WE CAN AX THE OLD DUFFER WITH A CLEAR CONSCIENCE.
ASSUMING WE'RE ACTUALLY ABLE TO KILL HIM. FRAU TOTENKINDER, HOW GOES THE EFFORT TO DISMANTLE HIS MAGICAL PROTECTIONS?
SLOWLY, KING COLE. SLOWLY.
SINCE IT'S IMPORTANT THAT HE NEVER SUSPECT WE'RE DOING IT, WE HAVE TO TREAD CAREFULLY, MY COLLEAGUES AND I.
SPEAKING OF THINGS HE SHOULD NEVER SUSPECT, WHEN OUR ALL-SEEING BLIND MAN GOING TO GET A LOOK AT HIM?
AMNESTY OR NOT, WE NEED TO KNOW THE FULL EXTENT OF HIS PAST MISDEEDS.
AND THE NATURE OF ANY SURVIVING IMPERIAL POWERS ARRAYING AGAINST US.
THE BOYS SHOULD BE ACCIDENTALLY RUNNING INTO KAY ANY MINUTE NOW.

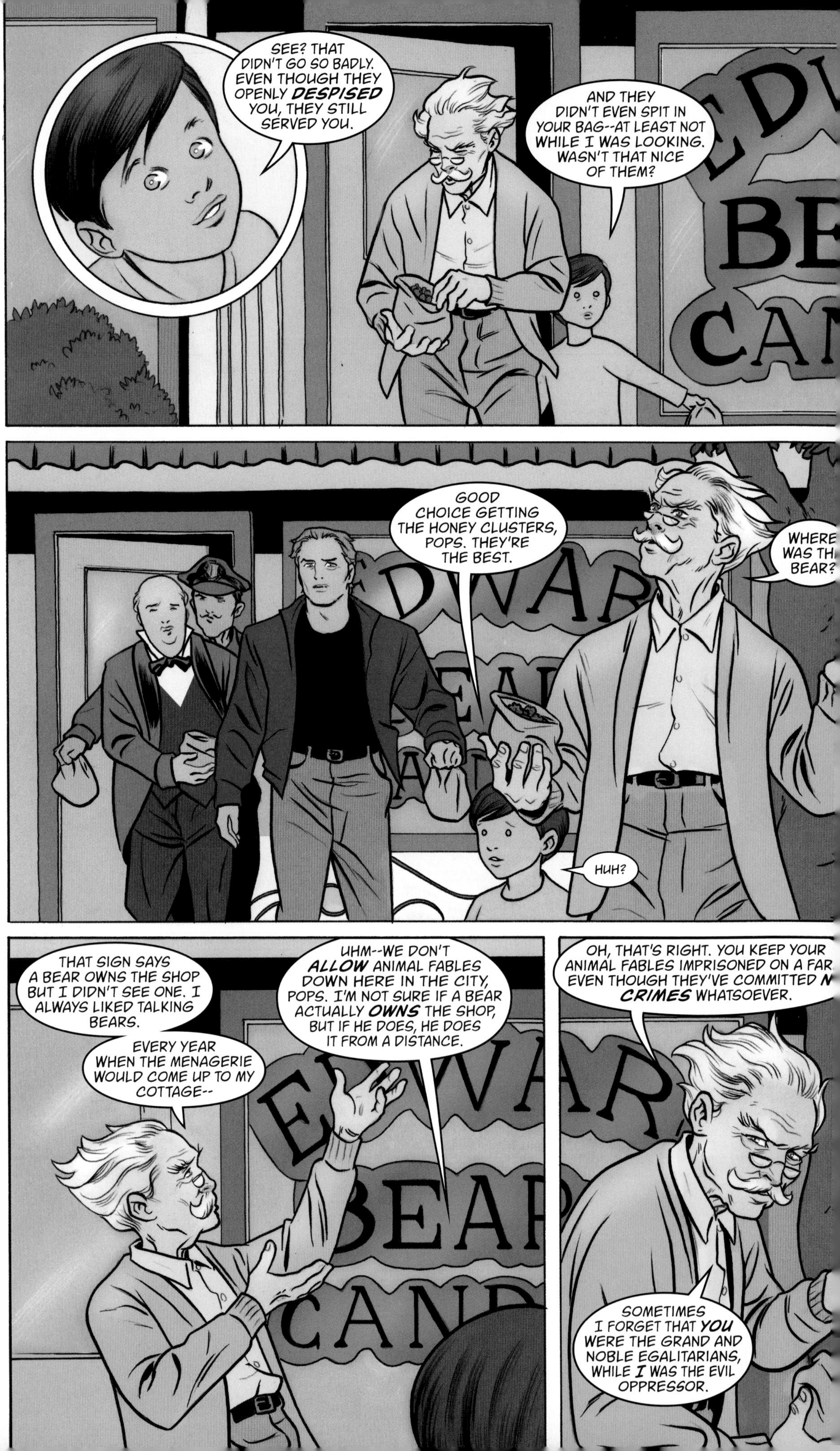
SEE? THAT DIDN'T GO SO BADLY. EVEN THOUGH THEY OPENLY DESPISED YOU, THEY STILL SERVED YOU.
AND THEY DIDN'T EVEN SPIT IN YOUR BAG--AT LEAST NOT WHILE I WAS LOOKING. WASN'T THAT NICE OF THEM?
EDW
BE
CAN
GOOD CHOICE GETTING THE HONEY CLUSTERS, POPS. THEY'RE THE BEST.
EDWAR
WHERE WAS TH BEAR?
HUH?
THAT SIGN SAYS A BEAR OWNS THE SHOP BUT I DIDN'T SEE ONE. I ALWAYS LIKED TALKING BEARS.
EVERY YEAR WHEN THE MENAGERIE WOULD COME UP TO MY COTTAGE--
UHM--WE DON'T ALLOW ANIMAL FABLES DOWN HERE IN THE CITY, POPS. I'M NOT SURE IF A BEAR ACTUALLY OWNS THE SHOP, BUT IF HE DOES, HE DOES IT FROM A DISTANCE.
EDWAR
BEAR
CAND
OH, THAT'S RIGHT. YOU KEEP YOUR ANIMAL FABLES IMPRISONED ON A FAR EVEN THOUGH THEY'VE COMMITTED N CRIMES WHATSOEVER.
SOMETIMES I FORGET THAT YOU WERE THE GRAND AND NOBLE EGALITARIANS, WHILE I WAS THE EVIL OPPRESSOR.

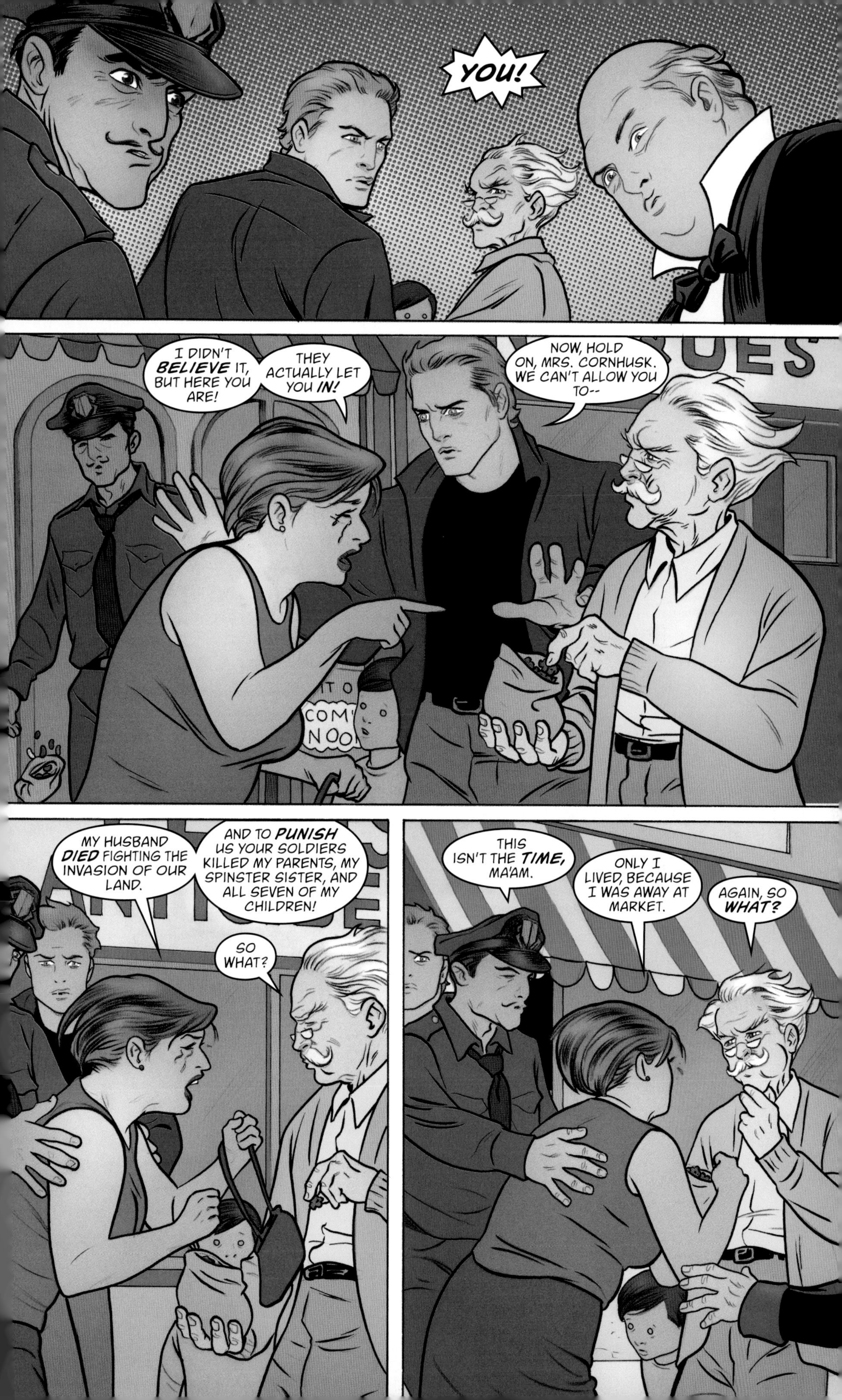

YOU!
I DIDN'T BELIEVE IT, BUT HERE YOU ARE!
THEY ACTUALLY LET YOU IN!
NOW, HOLD ON, MRS. CORNHUSK. WE CAN'T ALLOW YOU TO--
MY HUSBAND DIED FIGHTING THE INVASION OF OUR LAND.
AND TO PUNISH US YOUR SOLDIERS KILLED MY PARENTS, MY SPINSTER SISTER, AND ALL SEVEN OF MY CHILDREN!
SO WHAT?
THIS ISN'T THE TIME, MA'AM.
ONLY I LIVED, BECAUSE I WAS AWAY AT MARKET.
AGAIN, SO WHAT?

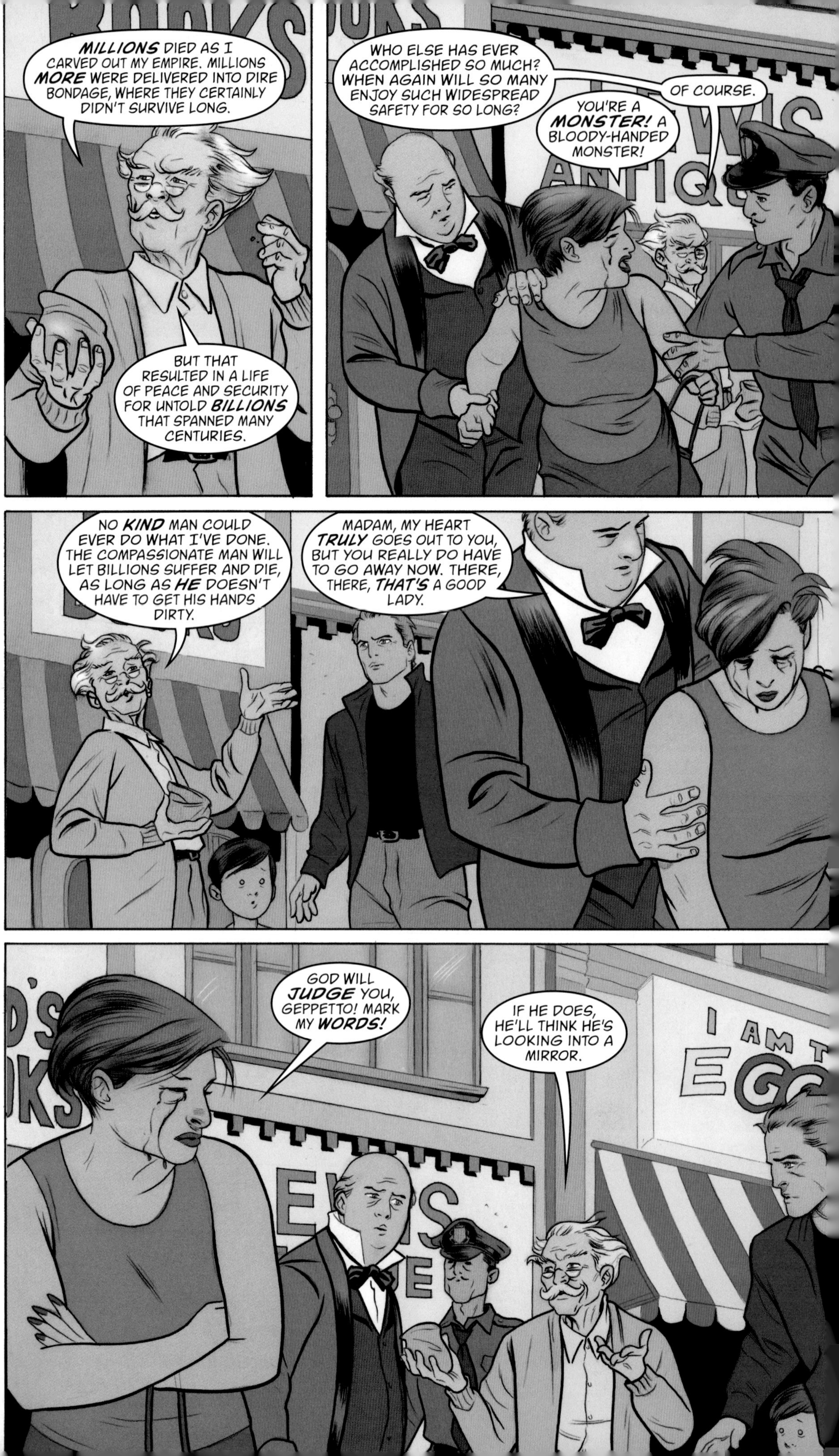
MILLIONS DIED AS I CARVED OUT MY EMPIRE. MILLIONS MORE WERE DELIVERED INTO DIRE BONDAGE, WHERE THEY CERTAINLY DIDN'T SURVIVE LONG.
BUT THAT RESULTED IN A LIFE OF PEACE AND SECURITY FOR UNTOLD BILLIONS THAT SPANNED MANY CENTURIES.
WHO ELSE HAS EVER ACCOMPLISHED SO MUCH? WHEN AGAIN WILL SO MANY ENJOY SUCH WIDESPREAD SAFETY FOR SO LONG?
OF COURSE.
YOU'RE A MONSTER! A BLOODY-HANDED MONSTER!
NO KIND MAN COULD EVER DO WHAT I'VE DONE. THE COMPASSIONATE MAN WILL LET BILLIONS SUFFER AND DIE, AS LONG AS HE DOESN'T HAVE TO GET HIS HANDS DIRTY.
MADAM, MY HEART TRULY GOES OUT TO YOU, BUT YOU REALLY DO HAVE TO GO AWAY NOW. THERE, THERE, THAT'S A GOOD LADY.
GOD WILL JUDGE YOU, GEPPETTO! MARK MY WORDS!
IF HE DOES, HE'LL THINK HE'S LOOKING INTO A MIRROR.

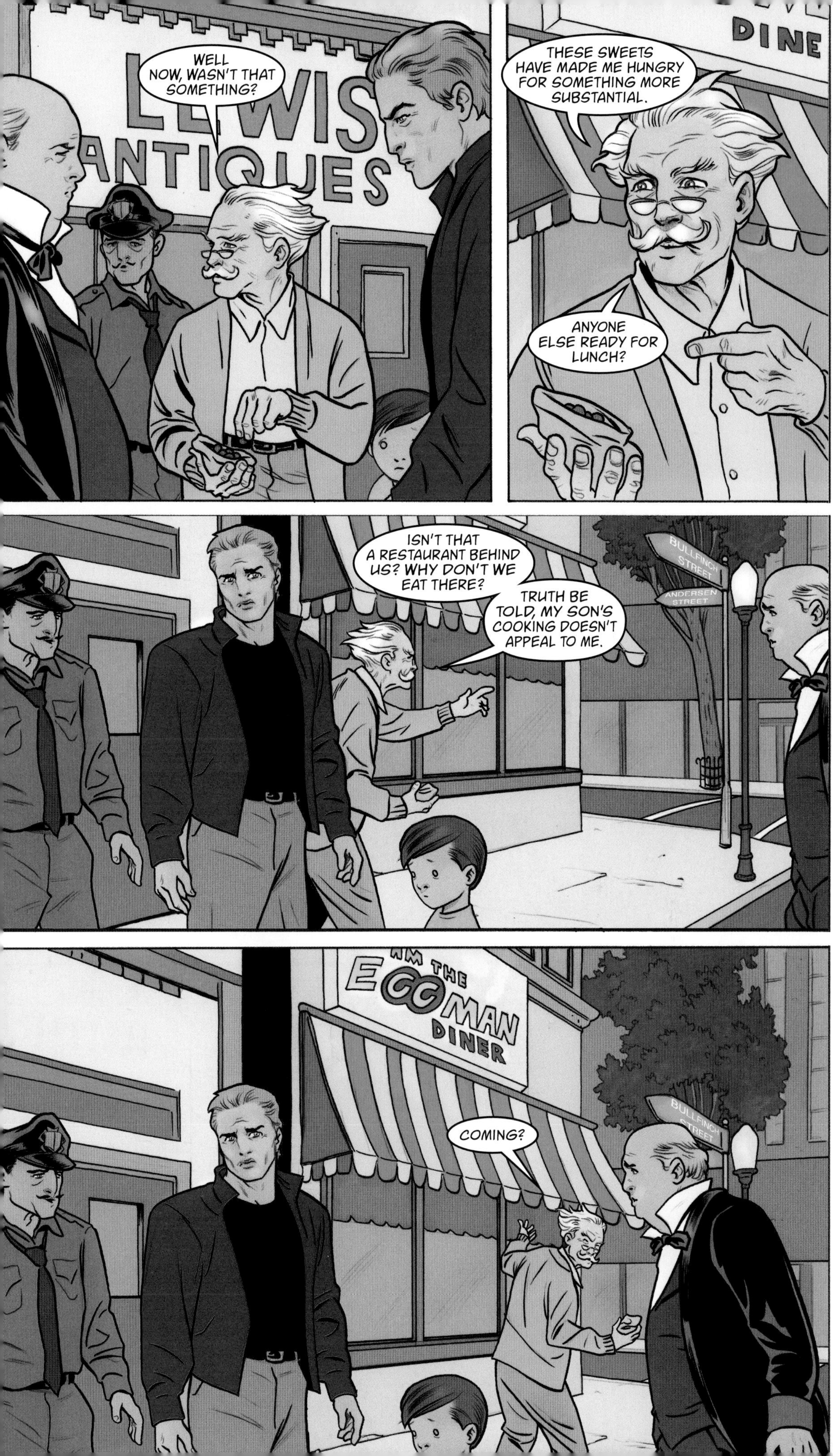
LEWIS ANTIQUES
WELL NOW, WASN'T THAT SOMETHING?
DINE
THESE SWEETS HAVE MADE ME HUNGRY FOR SOMETHING MORE SUBSTANTIAL.
ANYONE ELSE READY FOR LUNCH?
ISN'T THAT A RESTAURANT BEHIND US? WHY DON'T WE EAT THERE?
TRUTH BE TOLD, MY SON'S COOKING DOESN'T APPEAL TO ME.
BULLFINCH STREET
ANDERSEN STREET
EGG MAN DINER
COMING?
BULLFINCH STREET

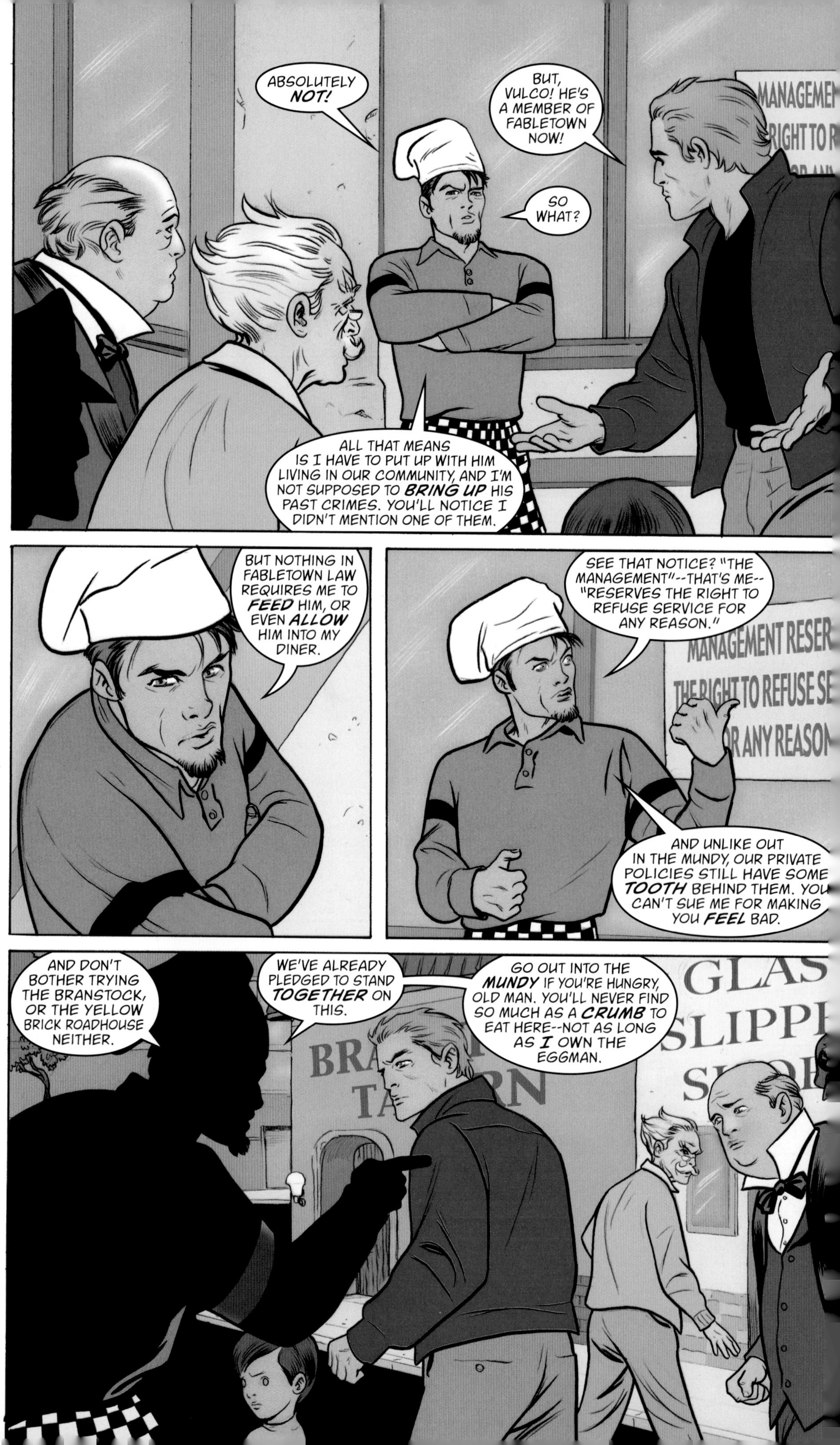
ABSOLUTELY NOT!
BUT, VULCO! HE'S A MEMBER OF FABLETOWN NOW!
SO WHAT?
ALL THAT MEANS IS I HAVE TO PUT UP WITH HIM LIVING IN OUR COMMUNITY, AND I'M NOT SUPPOSED TO BRING UP HIS PAST CRIMES. YOU'LL NOTICE I DIDN'T MENTION ONE OF THEM.
BUT NOTHING IN FABLETOWN LAW REQUIRES ME TO FEED HIM, OR EVEN ALLOW HIM INTO MY DINER.
SEE THAT NOTICE? "THE MANAGEMENT"--THAT'S ME--"RESERVES THE RIGHT TO REFUSE SERVICE FOR ANY REASON."
AND UNLIKE OUT IN THE MUNDY, OUR PRIVATE POLICIES STILL HAVE SOME TOOTH BEHIND THEM. YOU CAN'T SUE ME FOR MAKING YOU FEEL BAD.
AND DON'T BOTHER TRYING THE BRANSTOCK, OR THE YELLOW BRICK ROADHOUSE NEITHER.
WE'VE ALREADY PLEDGED TO STAND TOGETHER ON THIS.
GO OUT INTO THE MUNDY IF YOU'RE HUNGRY, OLD MAN. YOU'LL NEVER FIND SO MUCH AS A CRUMB TO EAT HERE--NOT AS LONG AS I OWN THE EGGMAN.

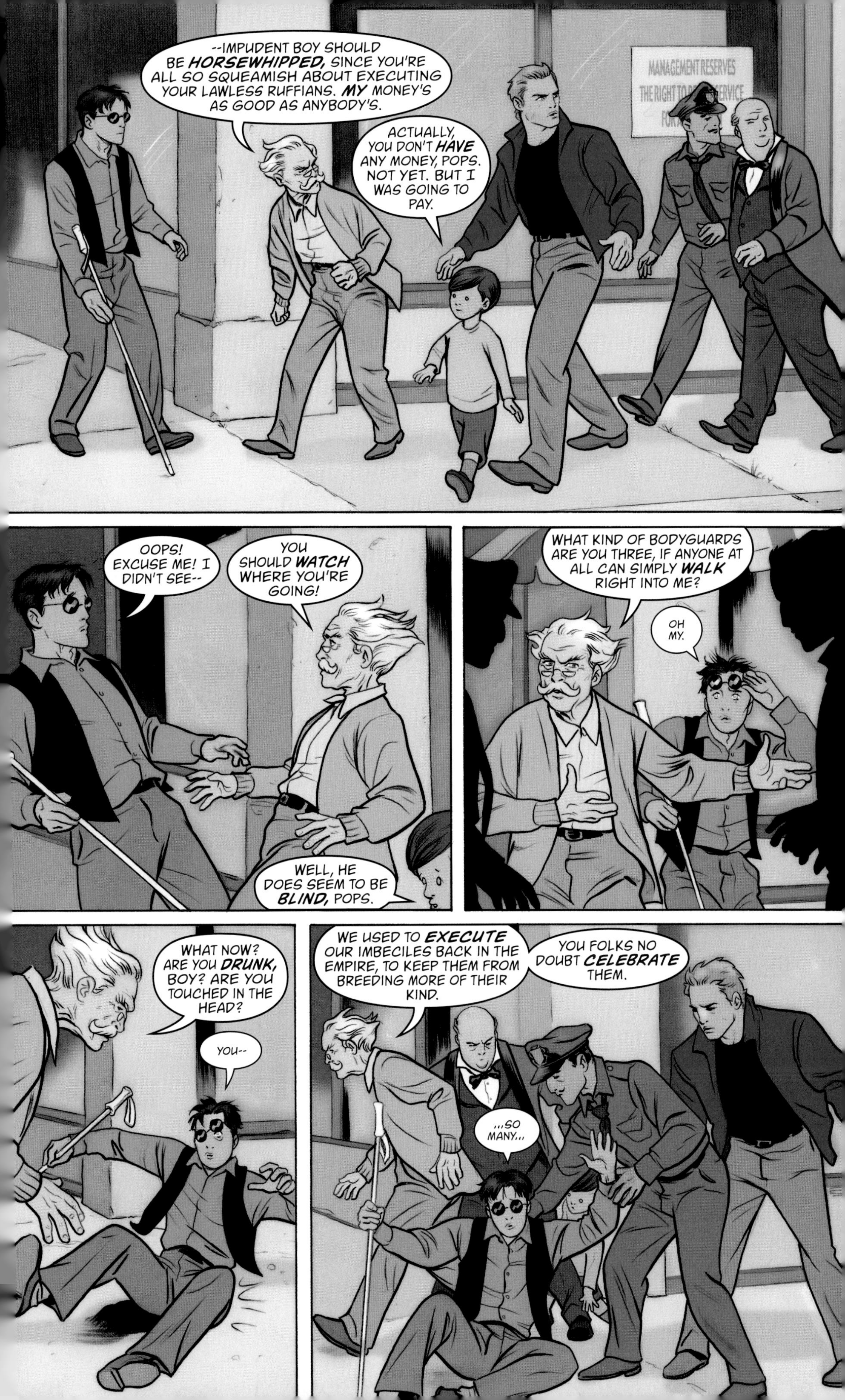
--IMPUDENT BOY SHOULD BE HORSEWHIPPED, SINCE YOU'RE ALL SO SQUEAMISH ABOUT EXECUTING YOUR LAWLESS RUFFIANS. MY MONEY'S AS GOOD AS ANYBODY'S.
ACTUALLY, YOU DON'T HAVE ANY MONEY, POPS. NOT YET. BUT I WAS GOING TO PAY.
MANAGEMENT RESERVES THE RIGHT TO
OOPS! EXCUSE ME! I DIDN'T SEE--
YOU SHOULD WATCH WHERE YOU'RE GOING!
WELL, HE DOES SEEM TO BE BLIND, POPS.
WHAT KIND OF BODYGUARDS ARE YOU THREE, IF ANYONE AT ALL CAN SIMPLY WALK RIGHT INTO ME?
OH MY.
WHAT NOW? ARE YOU DRUNK, BOY? ARE YOU TOUCHED IN THE HEAD?
YOU--
WE USED TO EXECUTE OUR IMBECILES BACK IN THE EMPIRE, TO KEEP THEM FROM BREEDING MORE OF THEIR KIND.
YOU FOLKS NO DOUBT CELEBRATE THEM.
...SO MANY...

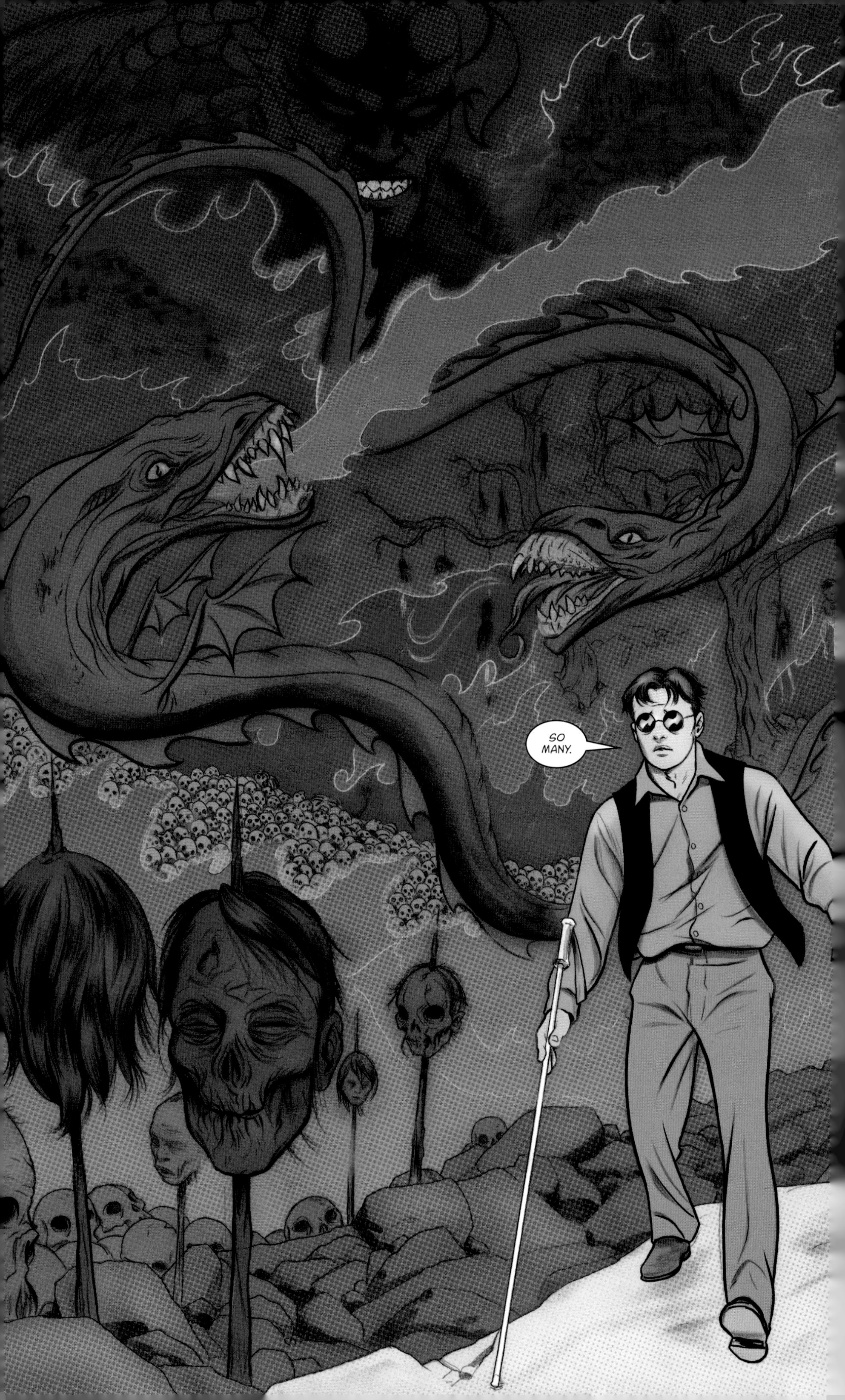
SO MANY.

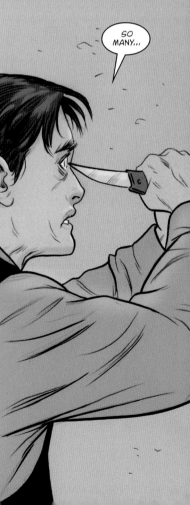

SO MANY...

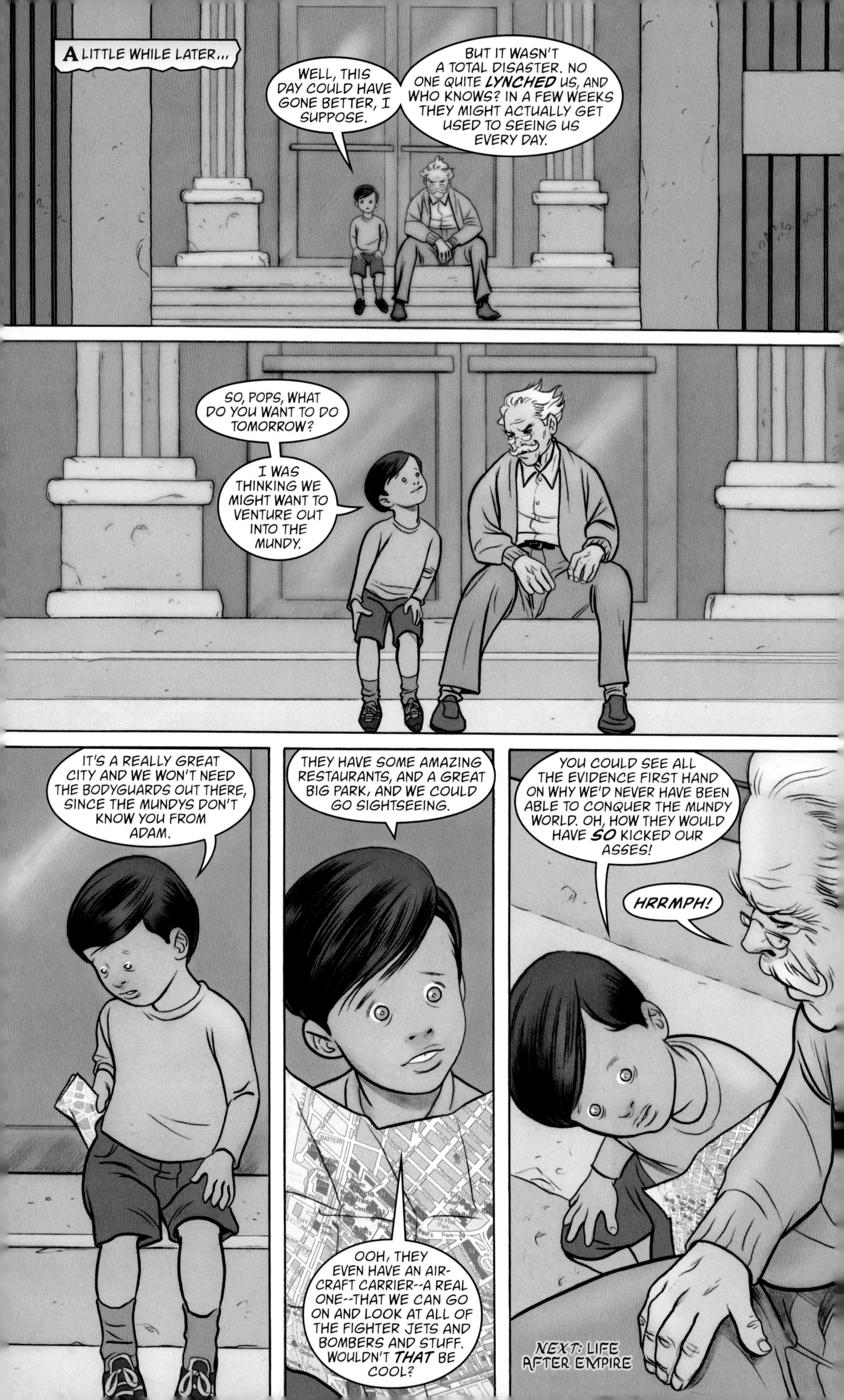
A LITTLE WHILE LATER...
WELL, THIS DAY COULD HAVE GONE BETTER, I SUPPOSE.
BUT IT WASN'T A TOTAL DISASTER. NO ONE QUITE LYNCHED US, AND WHO KNOWS? IN A FEW WEEKS THEY MIGHT ACTUALLY GET USED TO SEEING US EVERY DAY.
SO, POPS, WHAT DO YOU WANT TO DO TOMORROW?
I WAS THINKING WE MIGHT WANT TO VENTURE OUT INTO THE MUNDY.
IT'S A REALLY GREAT CITY AND WE WON'T NEED THE BODYGUARDS OUT THERE, SINCE THE MUNDYS DON'T KNOW YOU FROM ADAM.
THEY HAVE SOME AMAZING RESTAURANTS, AND A GREAT BIG PARK, AND WE COULD GO SIGHTSEEING.
OOH, THEY EVEN HAVE AN AIR-CRAFT CARRIER--A REAL ONE--THAT WE CAN GO ON AND LOOK AT ALL OF THE FIGHTER JETS AND BOMBERS AND STUFF. WOULDN'T THAT BE COOL?
YOU COULD SEE ALL THE EVIDENCE FIRST HAND ON WHY WE'D NEVER HAVE BEEN ABLE TO CONQUER THE MUNDY WORLD. OH, HOW THEY WOULD HAVE SO KICKED OUR ASSES!
HRRMPH!
NEXT: LIFE AFTER EMPIRE

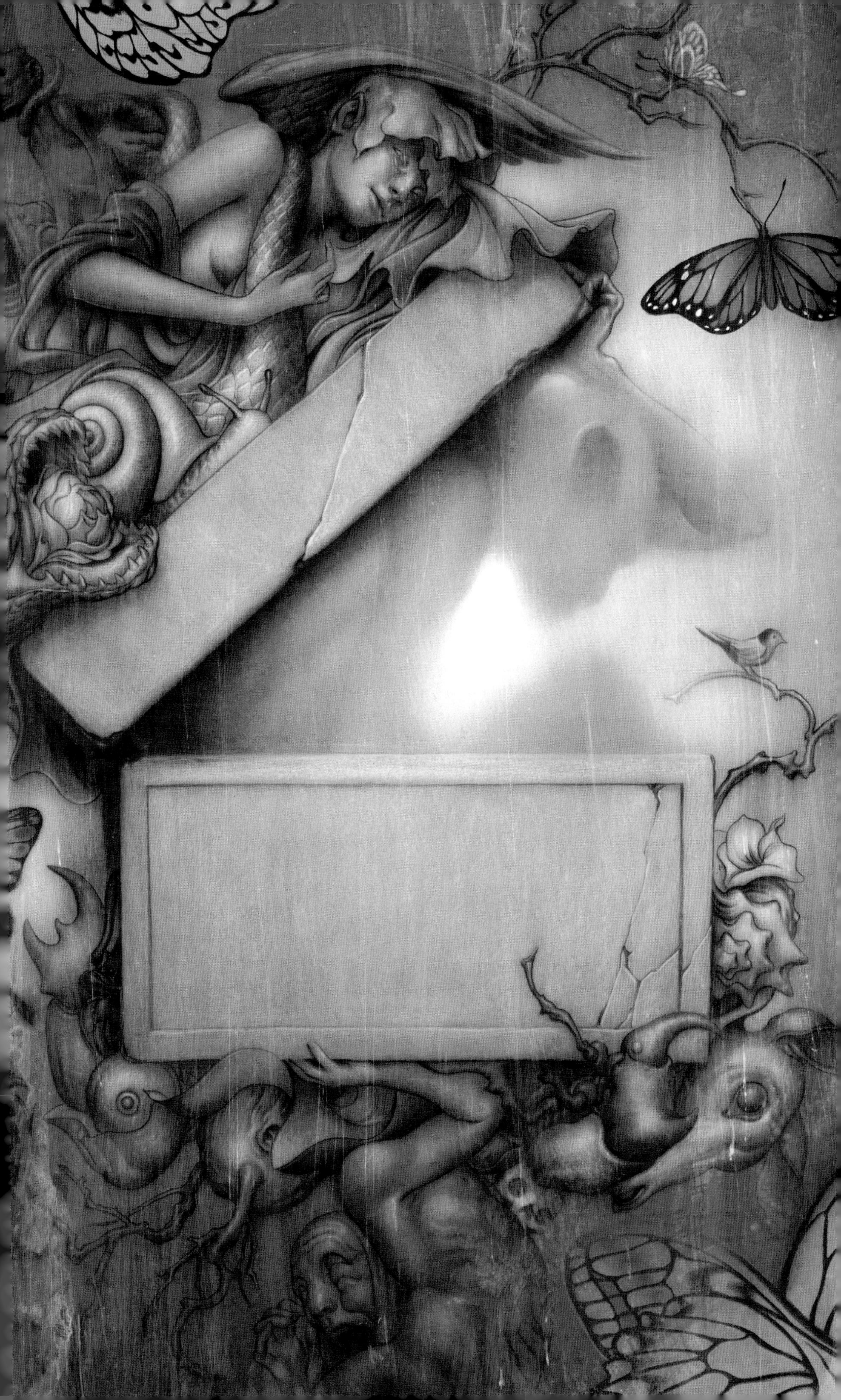

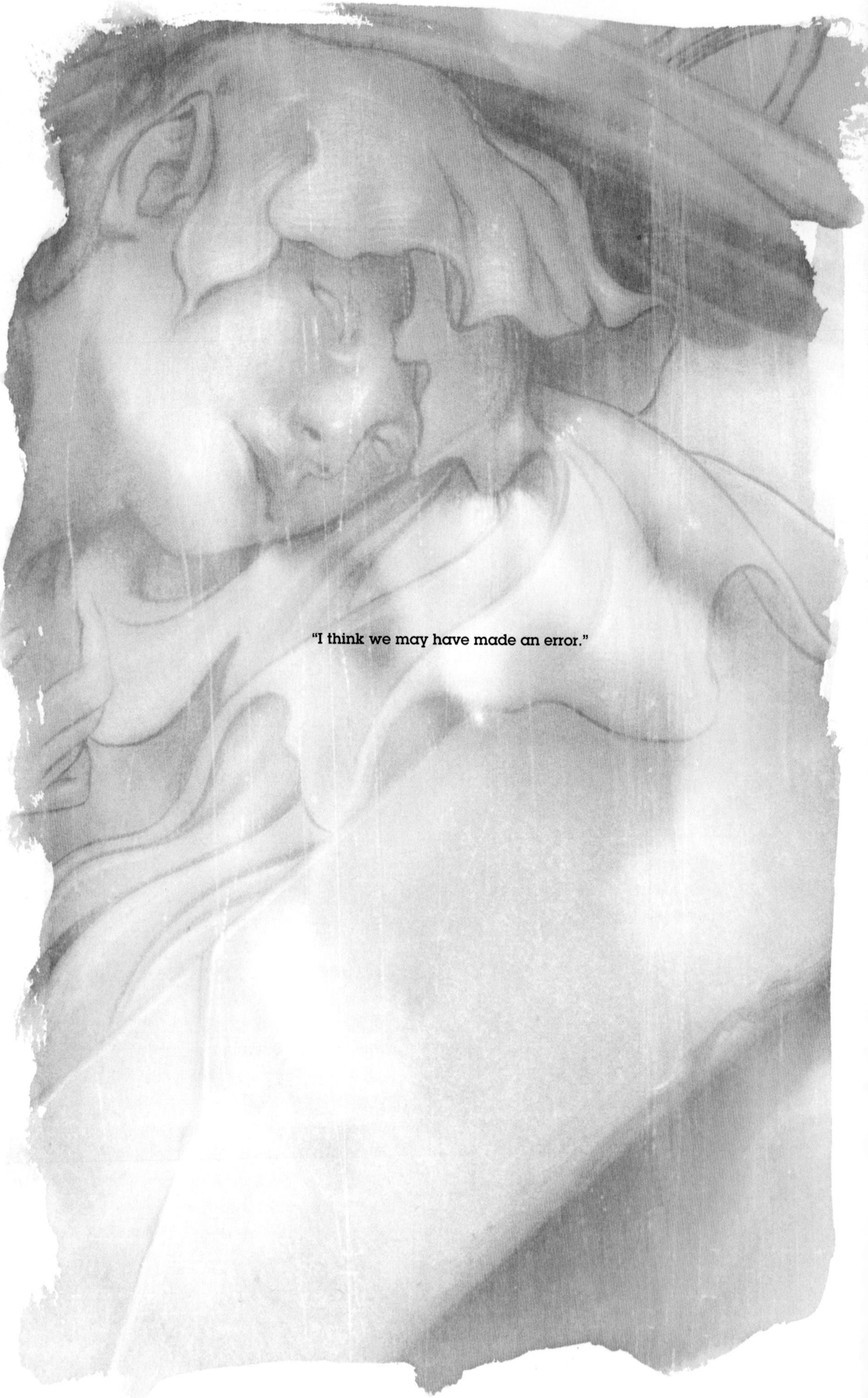
"I think we may have made an error."

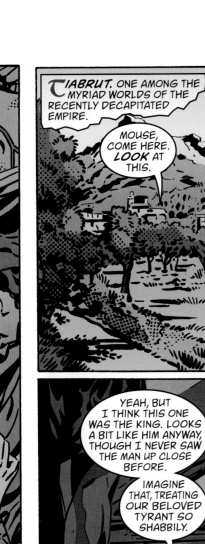

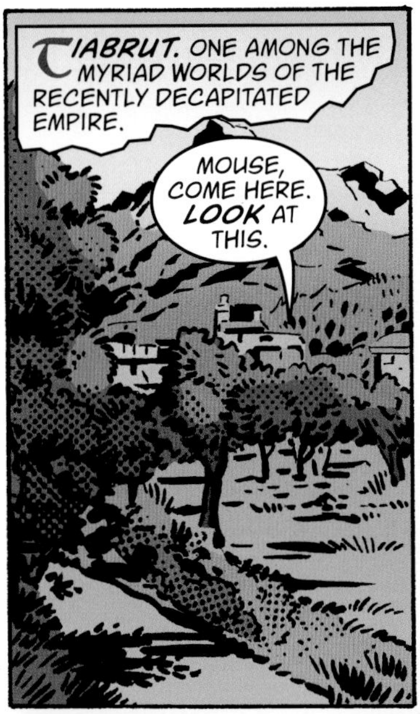
TIABRUT. ONE AMONG THE MYRIAD WORLDS OF THE RECENTLY DECAPITATED EMPIRE.
MOUSE, COME HERE. LOOK AT THIS.

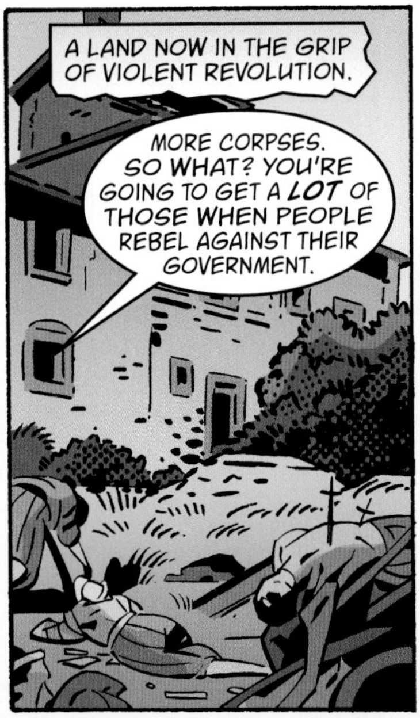
A LAND NOW IN THE GRIP OF VIOLENT REVOLUTION.
MORE CORPSES. SO WHAT? YOU'RE GOING TO GET A LOT OF THOSE WHEN PEOPLE REBEL AGAINST THEIR GOVERNMENT.

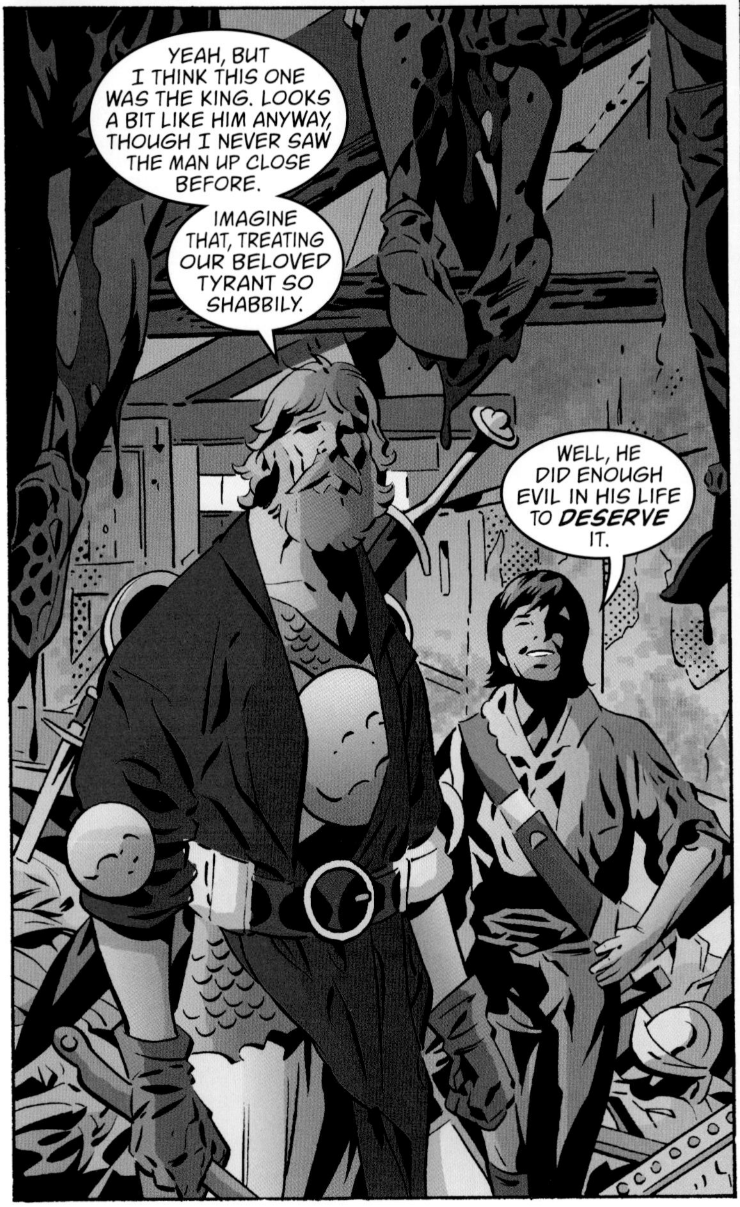
YEAH, BUT I THINK THIS ONE WAS THE KING. LOOKS A BIT LIKE HIM ANYWAY, THOUGH I NEVER SAW THE MAN UP CLOSE BEFORE.
IMAGINE THAT, TREATING OUR BELOVED TYRANT SO SHABBILY.
WELL, HE DID ENOUGH EVIL IN HIS LIFE TO DESERVE IT.

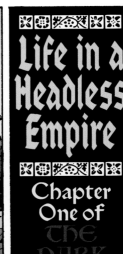

Life in a Headless Empire

Chapter One of THE DARK AGES

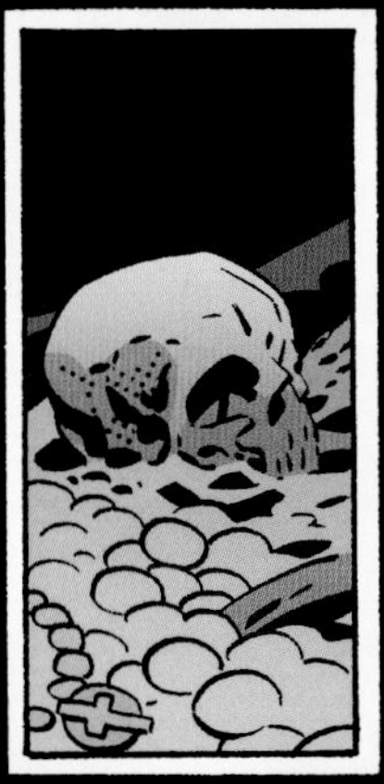

Bill Willingham writer/creator

Mark Buckingham penciller

Andrew Pepoy inker

Lee Loughridge colors

Todd Klein letters

James Jean cover

Angela Rufino associate editor

Shelly Bond editor

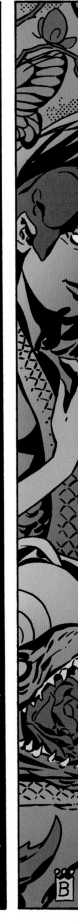

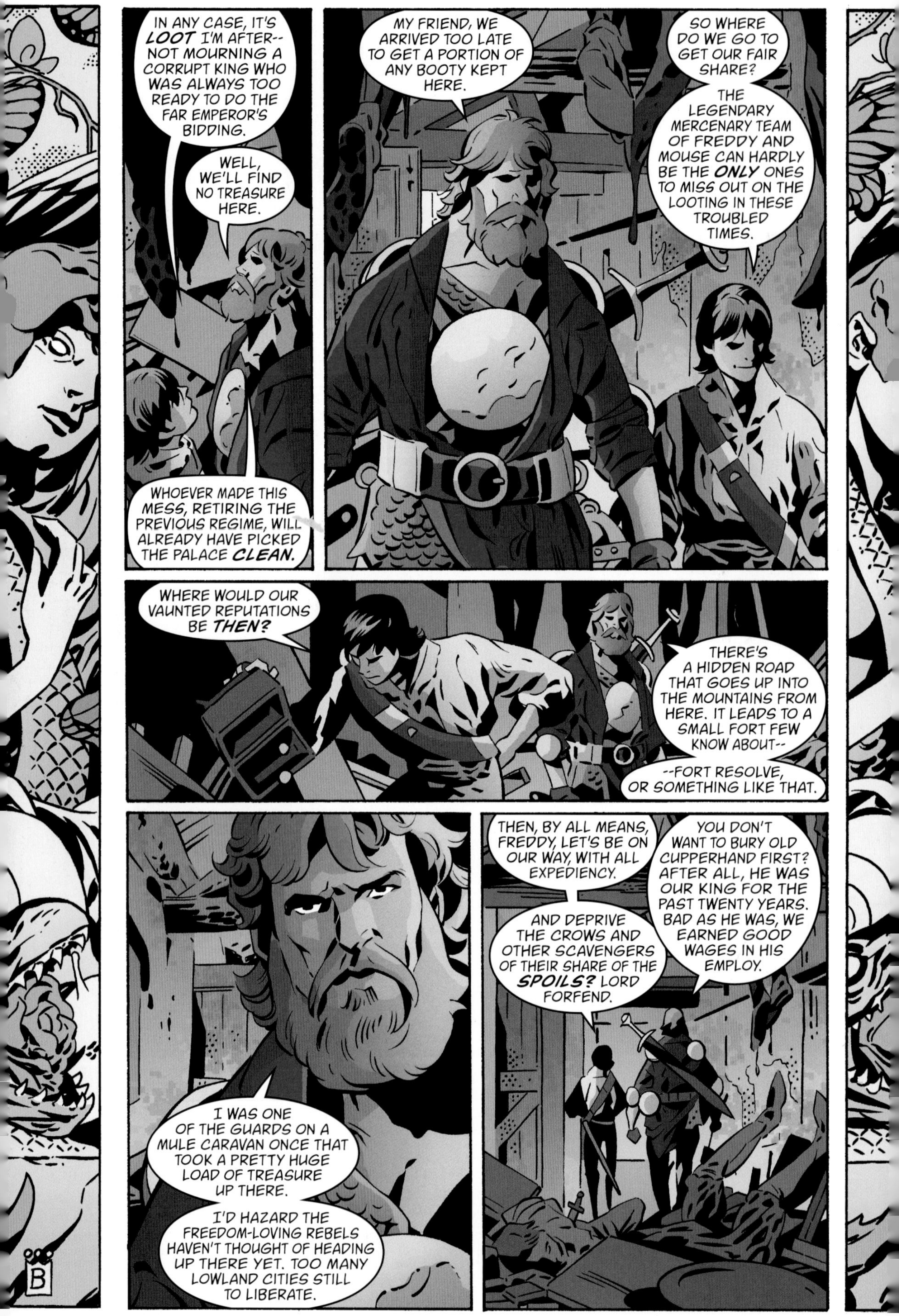
IN ANY CASE, IT'S LOOT I'M AFTER-- NOT MOURNING A CORRUPT KING WHO WAS ALWAYS TOO READY TO DO THE FAR EMPEROR'S BIDDING.
WELL, WE'LL FIND NO TREASURE HERE.
WHOEVER MADE THIS MESS, RETIRING THE PREVIOUS REGIME, WILL ALREADY HAVE PICKED THE PALACE CLEAN.
MY FRIEND, WE ARRIVED TOO LATE TO GET A PORTION OF ANY BOOTY KEPT HERE.
SO WHERE DO WE GO TO GET OUR FAIR SHARE?
THE LEGENDARY MERCENARY TEAM OF FREDDY AND MOUSE CAN HARDLY BE THE ONLY ONES TO MISS OUT ON THE LOOTING IN THESE TROUBLED TIMES.
WHERE WOULD OUR VAUNTED REPUTATIONS BE THEN?
THERE'S A HIDDEN ROAD THAT GOES UP INTO THE MOUNTAINS FROM HERE. IT LEADS TO A SMALL FORT FEW KNOW ABOUT--
--FORT RESOLVE, OR SOMETHING LIKE THAT.
I WAS ONE OF THE GUARDS ON A MULE CARAVAN ONCE THAT TOOK A PRETTY HUGE LOAD OF TREASURE UP THERE.
I'D HAZARD THE FREEDOM-LOVING REBELS HAVEN'T THOUGHT OF HEADING UP THERE YET. TOO MANY LOWLAND CITIES STILL TO LIBERATE.
THEN, BY ALL MEANS, FREDDY, LET'S BE ON OUR WAY, WITH ALL EXPEDIENCY.
YOU DON'T WANT TO BURY OLD CUPPERHAND FIRST? AFTER ALL, HE WAS OUR KING FOR THE PAST TWENTY YEARS. BAD AS HE WAS, WE EARNED GOOD WAGES IN HIS EMPLOY.
AND DEPRIVE THE CROWS AND OTHER SCAVENGERS OF THEIR SHARE OF THE SPOILS? LORD FORFEND.

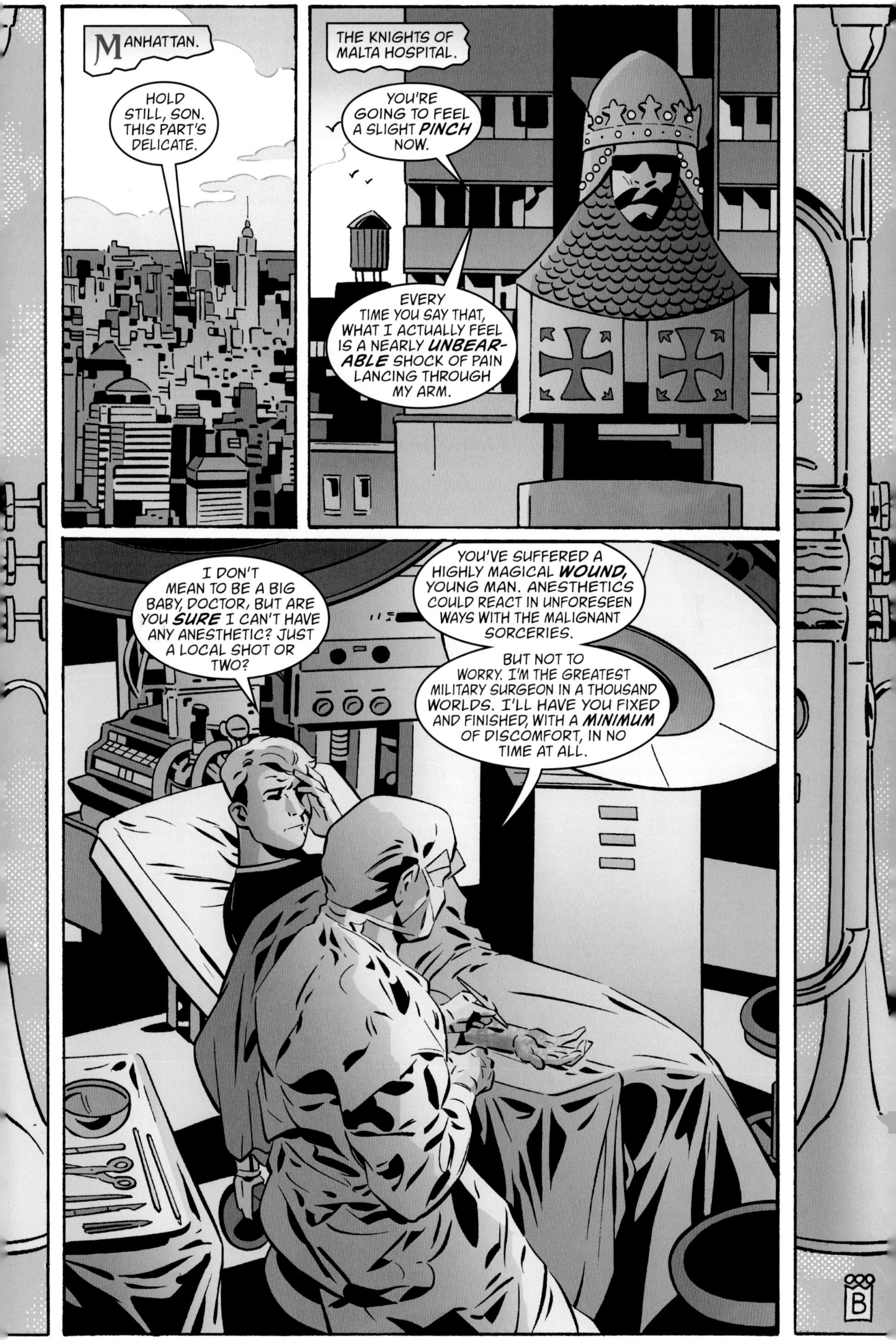
MANHATTAN.
HOLD STILL, SON. THIS PART'S DELICATE.
THE KNIGHTS OF MALTA HOSPITAL.
YOU'RE GOING TO FEEL A SLIGHT PINCH NOW.
EVERY TIME YOU SAY THAT, WHAT I ACTUALLY FEEL IS A NEARLY UNBEARABLE SHOCK OF PAIN LANCING THROUGH MY ARM.
I DON'T MEAN TO BE A BIG BABY, DOCTOR, BUT ARE YOU SURE I CAN'T HAVE ANY ANESTHETIC? JUST A LOCAL SHOT OR TWO?
YOU'VE SUFFERED A HIGHLY MAGICAL WOUND, YOUNG MAN. ANESTHETICS COULD REACT IN UNFORESEEN WAYS WITH THE MALIGNANT SORCERIES.
BUT NOT TO WORRY. I'M THE GREATEST MILITARY SURGEON IN A THOUSAND WORLDS. I'LL HAVE YOU FIXED AND FINISHED, WITH A MINIMUM OF DISCOMFORT, IN NO TIME AT ALL.

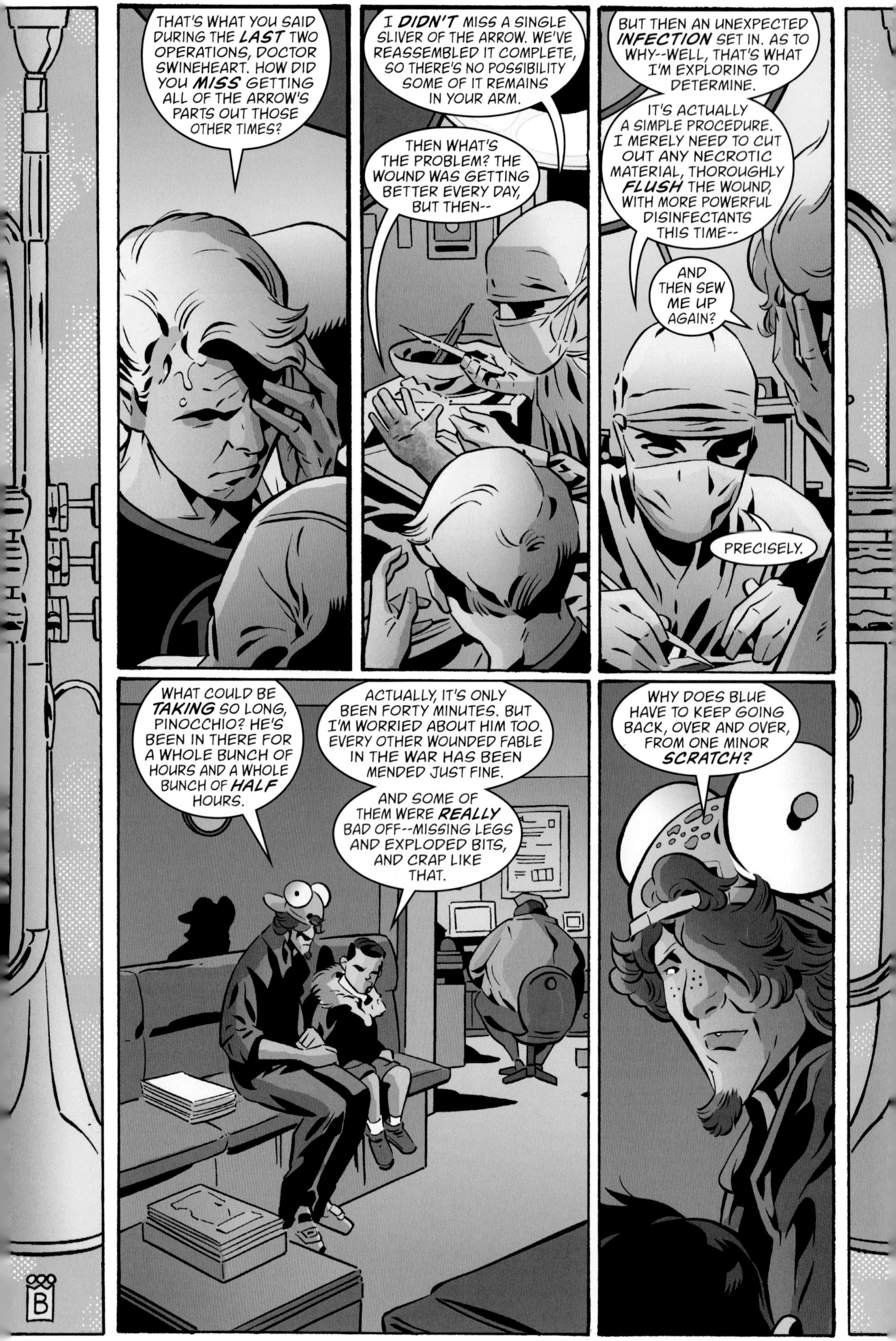
THAT'S WHAT YOU SAID DURING THE LAST TWO OPERATIONS, DOCTOR SWINEHEART. HOW DID YOU MISS GETTING ALL OF THE ARROW'S PARTS OUT THOSE OTHER TIMES?
I DIDN'T MISS A SINGLE SLIVER OF THE ARROW. WE'VE REASSEMBLED IT COMPLETE, SO THERE'S NO POSSIBILITY SOME OF IT REMAINS IN YOUR ARM.
THEN WHAT'S THE PROBLEM? THE WOUND WAS GETTING BETTER EVERY DAY, BUT THEN--
BUT THEN AN UNEXPECTED INFECTION SET IN. AS TO WHY--WELL, THAT'S WHAT I'M EXPLORING TO DETERMINE.
IT'S ACTUALLY A SIMPLE PROCEDURE. I MERELY NEED TO CUT OUT ANY NECROTIC MATERIAL, THOROUGHLY FLUSH THE WOUND, WITH MORE POWERFUL DISINFECTANTS THIS TIME--
AND THEN SEW ME UP AGAIN?
PRECISELY.
WHAT COULD BE TAKING SO LONG, PINOCCHIO? HE'S BEEN IN THERE FOR A WHOLE BUNCH OF HOURS AND A WHOLE BUNCH OF HALF HOURS.
ACTUALLY, IT'S ONLY BEEN FORTY MINUTES. BUT I'M WORRIED ABOUT HIM TOO. EVERY OTHER WOUNDED FABLE IN THE WAR HAS BEEN MENDED JUST FINE.
AND SOME OF THEM WERE REALLY BAD OFF--MISSING LEGS AND EXPLODED BITS, AND CRAP LIKE THAT.
WHY DOES BLUE HAVE TO KEEP GOING BACK, OVER AND OVER, FROM ONE MINOR SCRATCH?

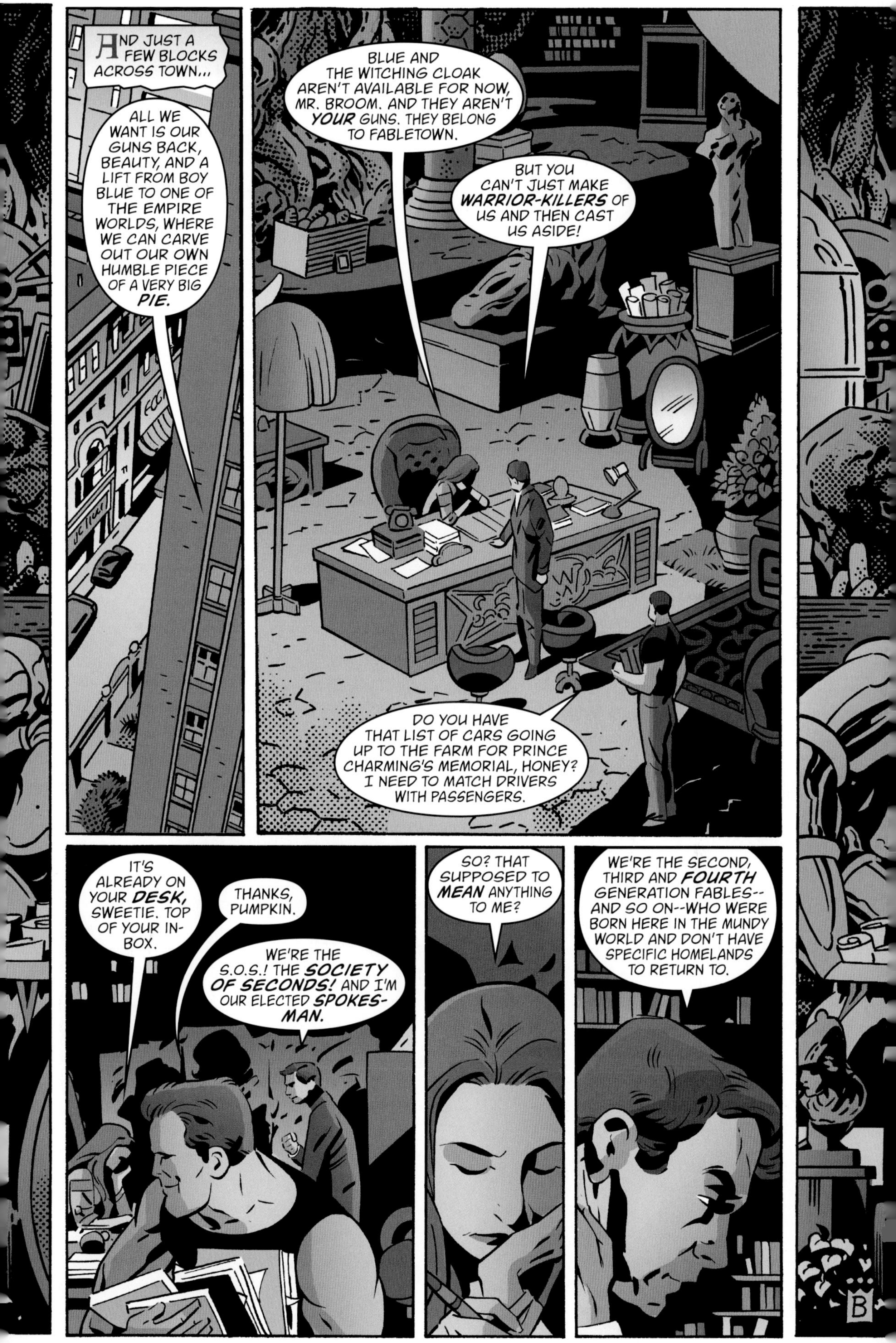

AND JUST A FEW BLOCKS ACROSS TOWN...
ALL WE WANT IS OUR GUNS BACK, BEAUTY, AND A LIFT FROM BOY BLUE TO ONE OF THE EMPIRE WORLDS, WHERE WE CAN CARVE OUT OUR OWN HUMBLE PIECE OF A VERY BIG PIE.
BLUE AND THE WITCHING CLOAK AREN'T AVAILABLE FOR NOW, MR. BROOM. AND THEY AREN'T YOUR GUNS. THEY BELONG TO FABLETOWN.
BUT YOU CAN'T JUST MAKE WARRIOR-KILLERS OF US AND THEN CAST US ASIDE!
DO YOU HAVE THAT LIST OF CARS GOING UP TO THE FARM FOR PRINCE CHARMING'S MEMORIAL, HONEY? I NEED TO MATCH DRIVERS WITH PASSENGERS.
IT'S ALREADY ON YOUR DESK, SWEETIE. TOP OF YOUR IN-BOX.
THANKS, PUMPKIN.
WE'RE THE S.O.S.! THE SOCIETY OF SECONDS! AND I'M OUR ELECTED SPOKES-MAN.
SO? THAT SUPPOSED TO MEAN ANYTHING TO ME?
WE'RE THE SECOND, THIRD AND FOURTH GENERATION FABLES--AND SO ON--WHO WERE BORN HERE IN THE MUNDY WORLD AND DON'T HAVE SPECIFIC HOMELANDS TO RETURN TO.

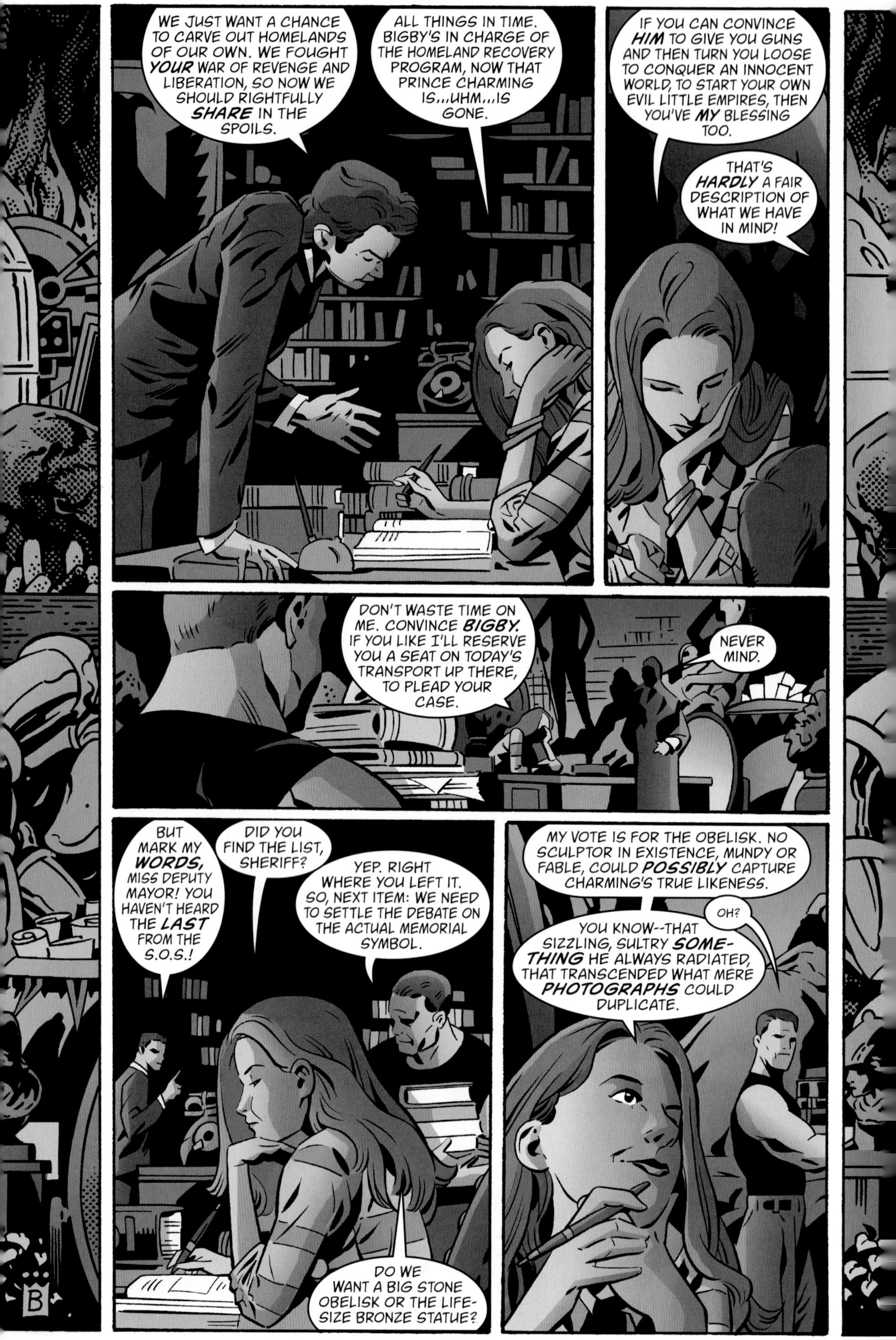
WE JUST WANT A CHANCE TO CARVE OUT HOMELANDS OF OUR OWN. WE FOUGHT YOUR WAR OF REVENGE AND LIBERATION, SO NOW WE SHOULD RIGHTFULLY SHARE IN THE SPOILS.
ALL THINGS IN TIME. BIGBY'S IN CHARGE OF THE HOMELAND RECOVERY PROGRAM, NOW THAT PRINCE CHARMING IS...UHM...IS GONE.
IF YOU CAN CONVINCE HIM TO GIVE YOU GUNS AND THEN TURN YOU LOOSE TO CONQUER AN INNOCENT WORLD, TO START YOUR OWN EVIL LITTLE EMPIRES, THEN YOU'VE MY BLESSING TOO.
THAT'S HARDLY A FAIR DESCRIPTION OF WHAT WE HAVE IN MIND!
DON'T WASTE TIME ON ME. CONVINCE BIGBY. IF YOU LIKE I'LL RESERVE YOU A SEAT ON TODAY'S TRANSPORT UP THERE, TO PLEAD YOUR CASE.
NEVER MIND.
BUT MARK MY WORDS, MISS DEPUTY MAYOR! YOU HAVEN'T HEARD THE LAST FROM THE S.O.S.!
DID YOU FIND THE LIST, SHERIFF?
YEP. RIGHT WHERE YOU LEFT IT. SO, NEXT ITEM: WE NEED TO SETTLE THE DEBATE ON THE ACTUAL MEMORIAL SYMBOL.
DO WE WANT A BIG STONE OBELISK OR THE LIFE-SIZE BRONZE STATUE?
MY VOTE IS FOR THE OBELISK. NO SCULPTOR IN EXISTENCE, MUNDY OR FABLE, COULD POSSIBLY CAPTURE CHARMING'S TRUE LIKENESS.
YOU KNOW--THAT SIZZLING, SULTRY SOME-THING HE ALWAYS RADIATED, THAT TRANSCENDED WHAT MERE PHOTOGRAPHS COULD DUPLICATE.
OH?

BACK IN THE WORLD OF TIABRUT...

YOU'RE NOT GOING TO MAKE ME FEEL GUILTY ABOUT SERVING IN KING CUPPERHAND'S ARMY, FREDDY, NO MATTER *HOW* VILE HE WAS.

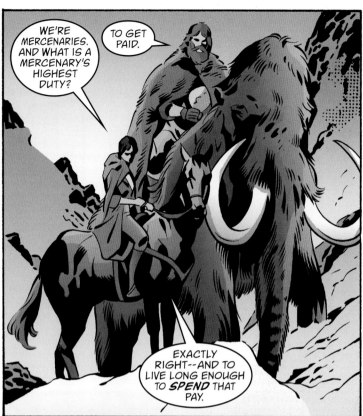

WE'RE MERCENARIES. AND WHAT IS A MERCENARY'S HIGHEST DUTY?

TO GET PAID.

EXACTLY RIGHT--AND TO LIVE LONG ENOUGH TO *SPEND* THAT PAY.

NOW, WE HAD A CHOICE TO FIGHT WITH THE KING OR AGAINST HIM.

BUT SINCE THE KING HAD THE BACKING OF THE EMPIRE, THOSE WHO FOUGHT AGAINST HIM TENDED TO DIE--IN QUITE *REMARKABLE* NUMBERS.

I KNOW YOU KNOW THIS BECAUSE YOU'VE *REMARKED* UPON IT MORE THAN ONCE.

HOWEVER, THOSE WHO FOUGHT *WITH* THE KING GENERALLY SURVIVED TO SPEND THEIR PAY.

CASE CLOSED, MY HIRSUTE FRIEND. WE WERE LEGALLY AND MORALLY IN THE RIGHT.

LOOK THERE. I THINK I SPY THE FORT AHEAD. LOOSEN YOUR SWORD, MOUSE. WE MAY HAVE TO *FIGHT* OUR WAY IN.

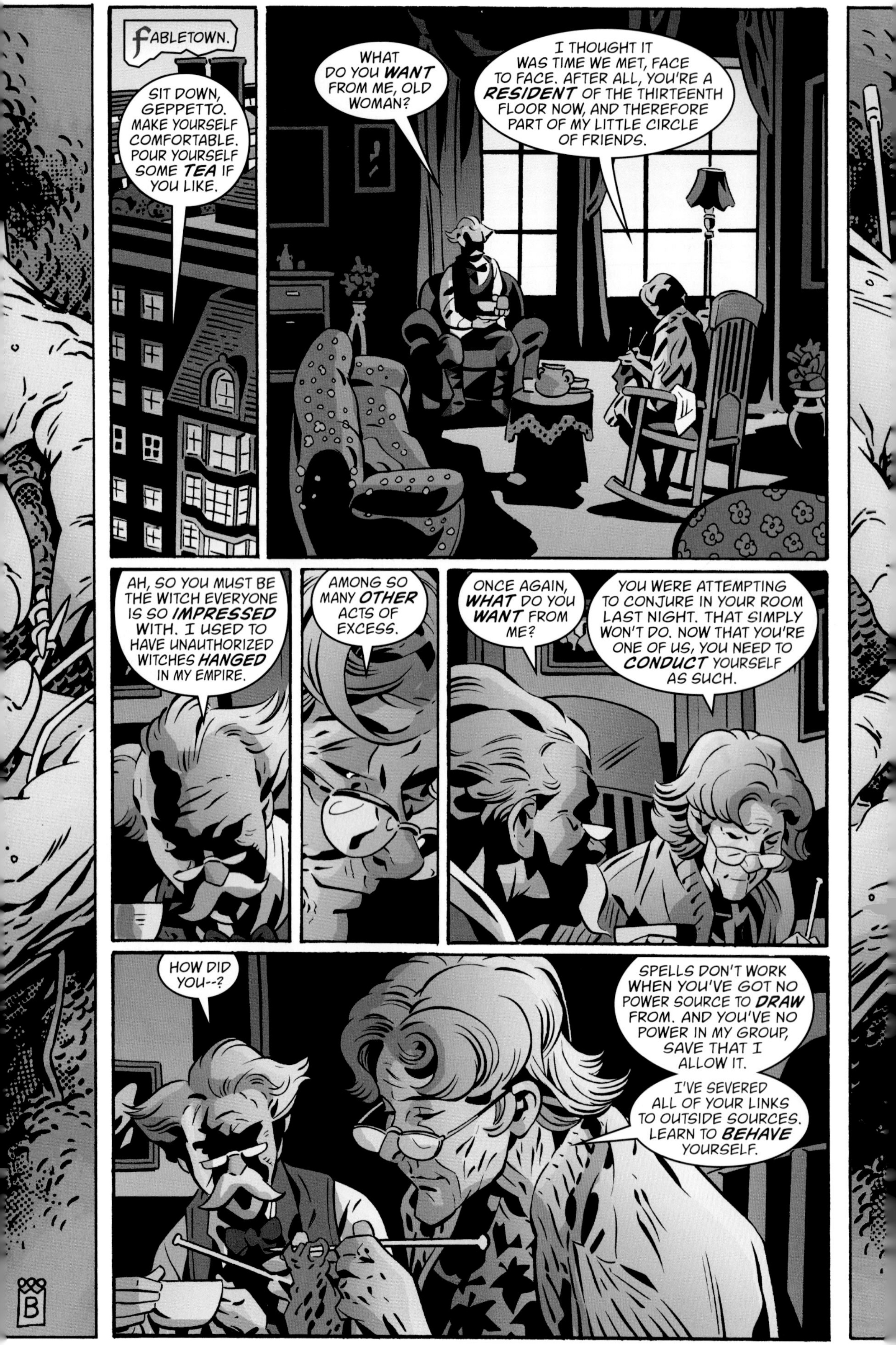
FABLETOWN.
SIT DOWN, GEPPETTO. MAKE YOURSELF COMFORTABLE. POUR YOURSELF SOME TEA IF YOU LIKE.
WHAT DO YOU WANT FROM ME, OLD WOMAN?
I THOUGHT IT WAS TIME WE MET, FACE TO FACE. AFTER ALL, YOU'RE A RESIDENT OF THE THIRTEENTH FLOOR NOW, AND THEREFORE PART OF MY LITTLE CIRCLE OF FRIENDS.
AH, SO YOU MUST BE THE WITCH EVERYONE IS SO IMPRESSED WITH. I USED TO HAVE UNAUTHORIZED WITCHES HANGED IN MY EMPIRE.
AMONG SO MANY OTHER ACTS OF EXCESS.
ONCE AGAIN, WHAT DO YOU WANT FROM ME?
YOU WERE ATTEMPTING TO CONJURE IN YOUR ROOM LAST NIGHT. THAT SIMPLY WON'T DO. NOW THAT YOU'RE ONE OF US, YOU NEED TO CONDUCT YOURSELF AS SUCH.
HOW DID YOU--?
SPELLS DON'T WORK WHEN YOU'VE GOT NO POWER SOURCE TO DRAW FROM. AND YOU'VE NO POWER IN MY GROUP, SAVE THAT I ALLOW IT.
I'VE SEVERED ALL OF YOUR LINKS TO OUTSIDE SOURCES. LEARN TO BEHAVE YOURSELF.

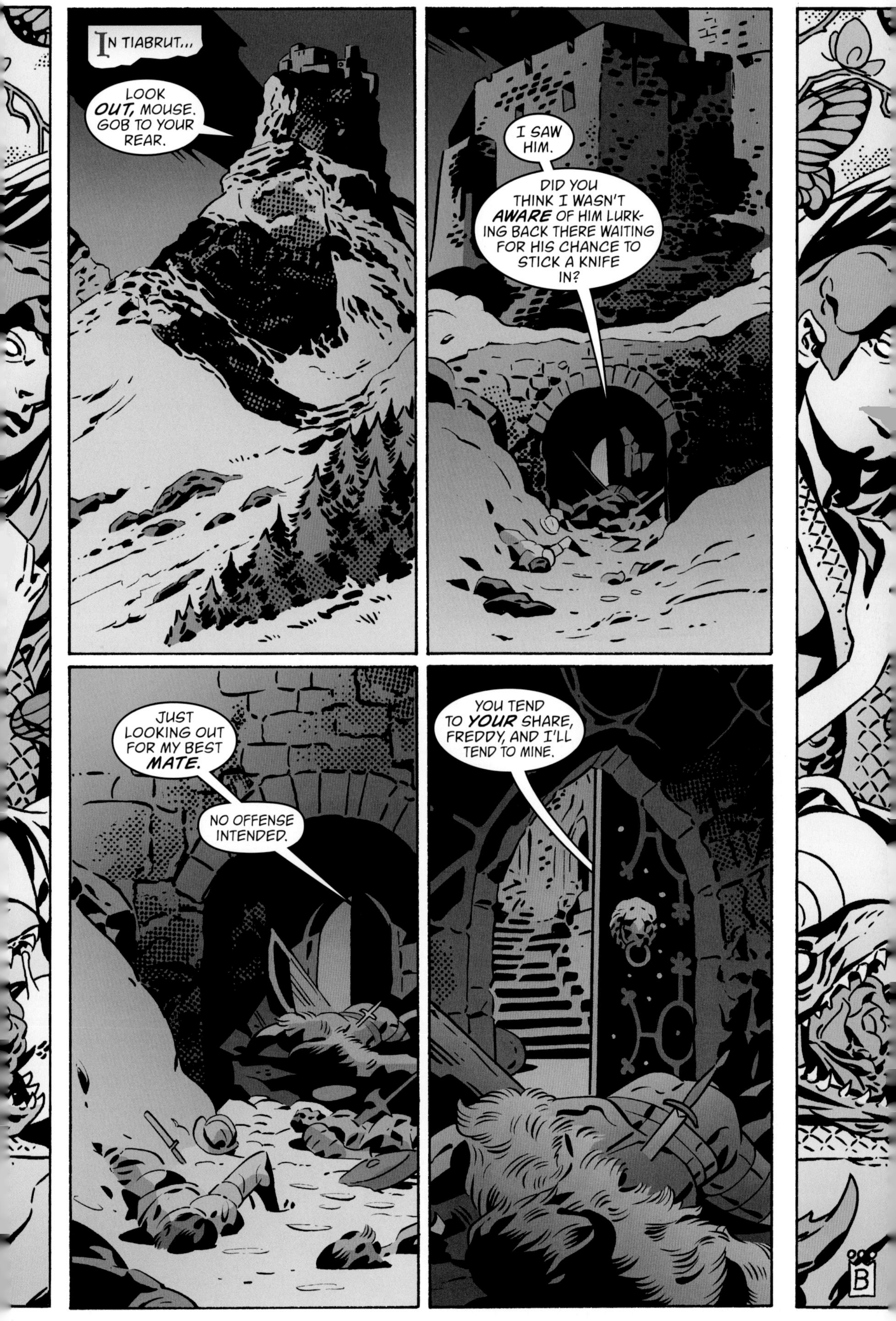
IN TIABRUT...
LOOK OUT, MOUSE. GOB TO YOUR REAR.
I SAW HIM.
DID YOU THINK I WASN'T AWARE OF HIM LURK-ING BACK THERE WAITING FOR HIS CHANCE TO STICK A KNIFE IN?
JUST LOOKING OUT FOR MY BEST MATE.
NO OFFENSE INTENDED.
YOU TEND TO YOUR SHARE, FREDDY, AND I'LL TEND TO MINE.

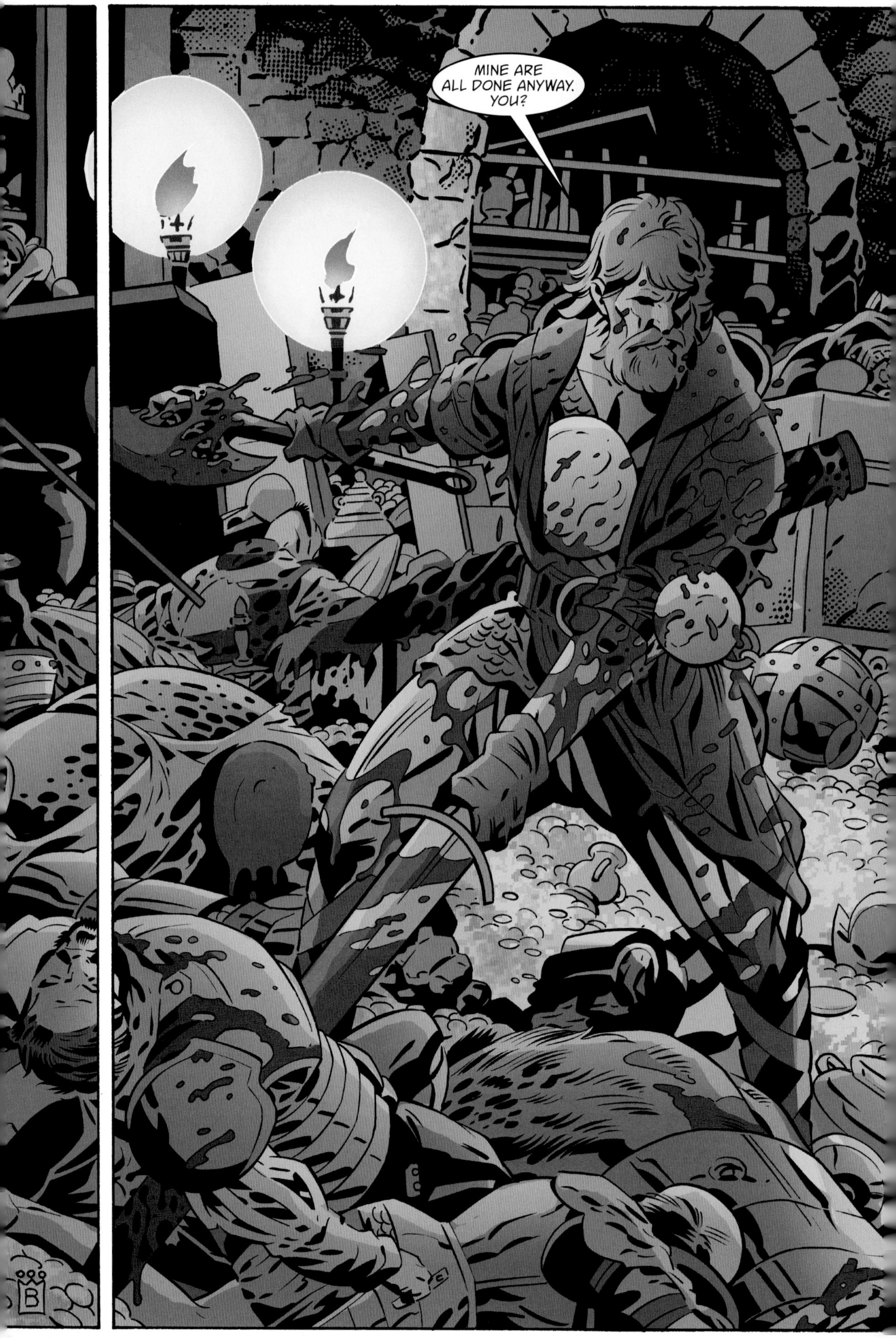
MINE ARE ALL DONE ANYWAY. YOU?

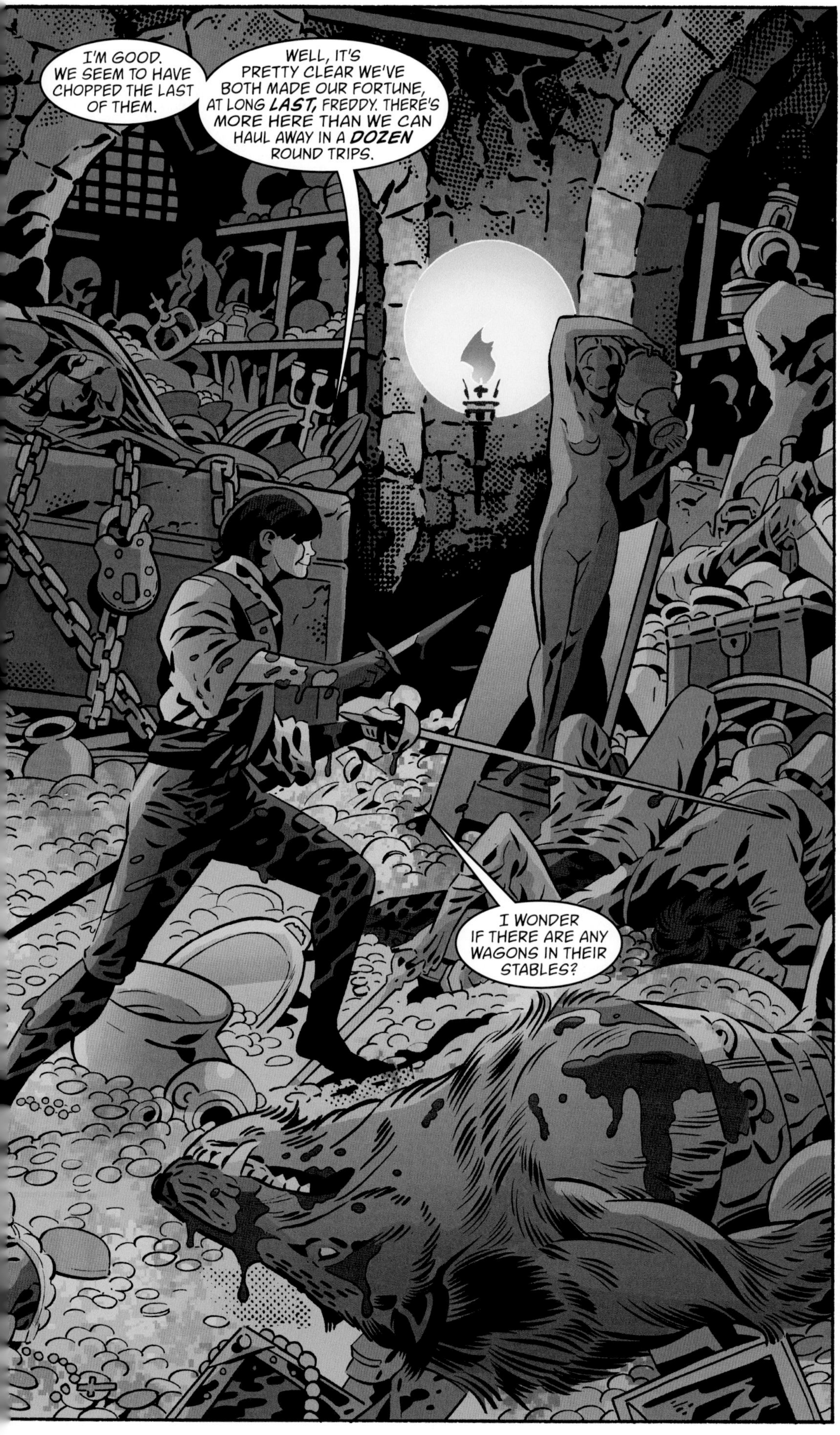
I'M GOOD. WE SEEM TO HAVE CHOPPED THE LAST OF THEM.
WELL, IT'S PRETTY CLEAR WE'VE BOTH MADE OUR FORTUNE, AT LONG *LAST,* FREDDY. THERE'S MORE HERE THAN WE CAN HAUL AWAY IN A *DOZEN* ROUND TRIPS.
I WONDER IF THERE ARE ANY WAGONS IN THEIR STABLES?
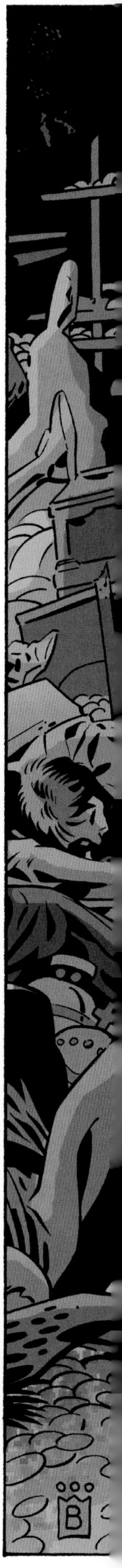

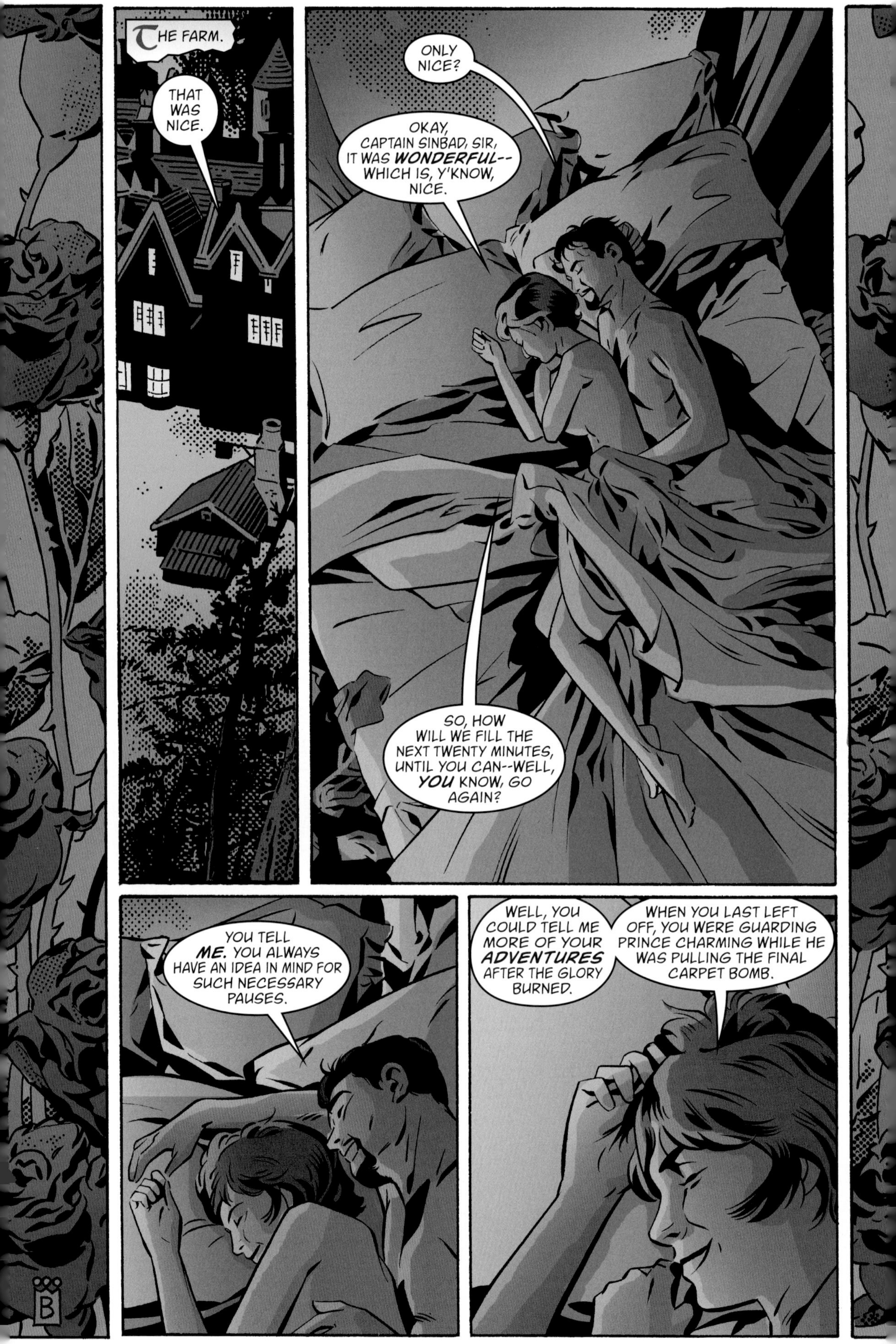
THE FARM.
THAT WAS NICE.
ONLY NICE?
OKAY, CAPTAIN SINBAD, SIR, IT WAS WONDERFUL-- WHICH IS, Y'KNOW, NICE.
SO, HOW WILL WE FILL THE NEXT TWENTY MINUTES, UNTIL YOU CAN--WELL, YOU KNOW, GO AGAIN?
YOU TELL ME. YOU ALWAYS HAVE AN IDEA IN MIND FOR SUCH NECESSARY PAUSES.
WELL, YOU COULD TELL ME MORE OF YOUR ADVENTURES AFTER THE GLORY BURNED.
WHEN YOU LAST LEFT OFF, YOU WERE GUARDING PRINCE CHARMING WHILE HE WAS PULLING THE FINAL CARPET BOMB.

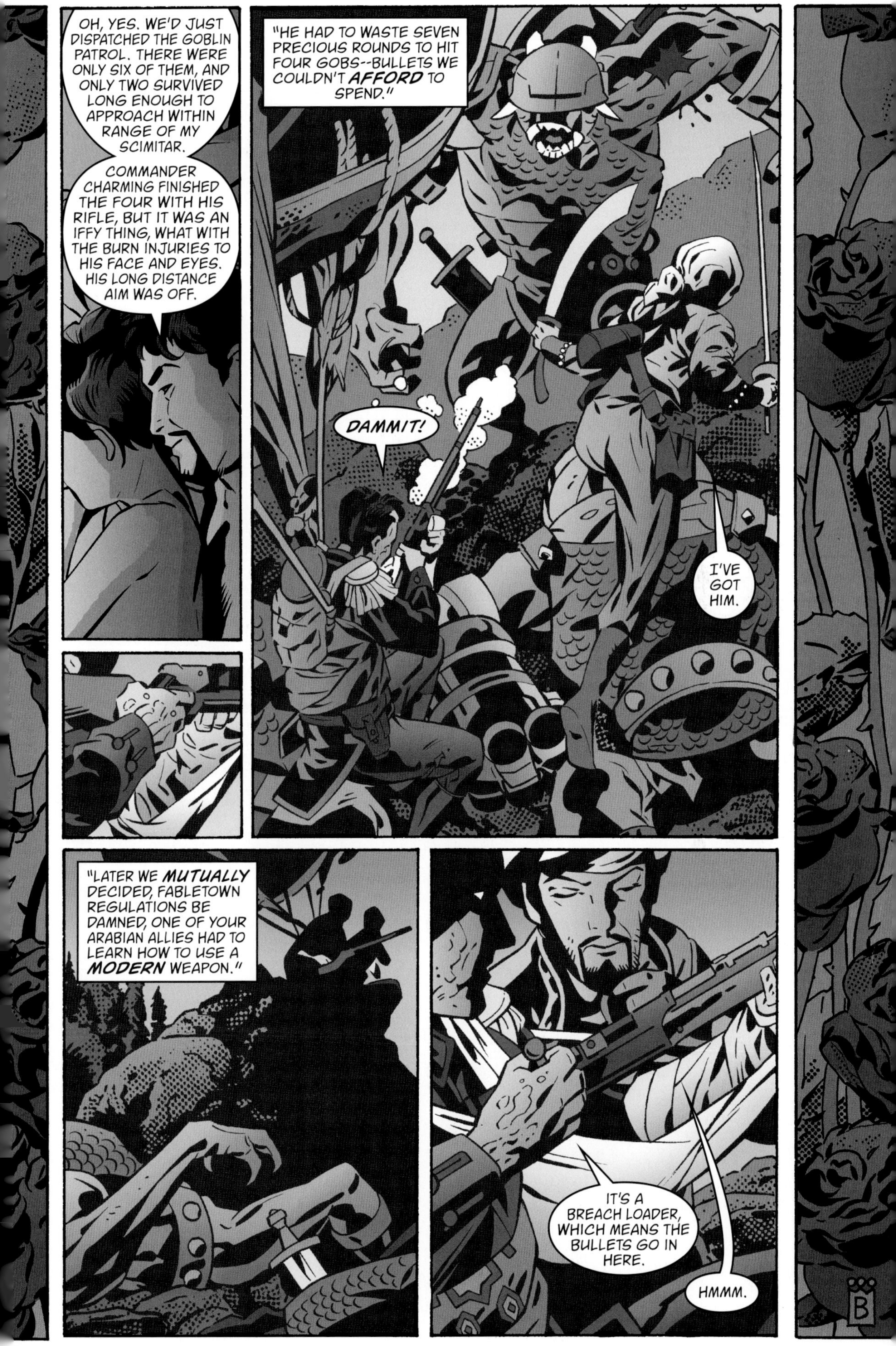
OH, YES. WE'D JUST DISPATCHED THE GOBLIN PATROL. THERE WERE ONLY SIX OF THEM, AND ONLY TWO SURVIVED LONG ENOUGH TO APPROACH WITHIN RANGE OF MY SCIMITAR.
COMMANDER CHARMING FINISHED THE FOUR WITH HIS RIFLE, BUT IT WAS AN IFFY THING, WHAT WITH THE BURN INJURIES TO HIS FACE AND EYES. HIS LONG DISTANCE AIM WAS OFF.
"HE HAD TO WASTE SEVEN PRECIOUS ROUNDS TO HIT FOUR GOBS--BULLETS WE COULDN'T **AFFORD** TO SPEND."
DAMMIT!
I'VE GOT HIM.
"LATER WE **MUTUALLY** DECIDED, FABLETOWN REGULATIONS BE DAMNED, ONE OF YOUR ARABIAN ALLIES HAD TO LEARN HOW TO USE A **MODERN** WEAPON."
IT'S A BREACH LOADER, WHICH MEANS THE BULLETS GO IN HERE.
HMMM.

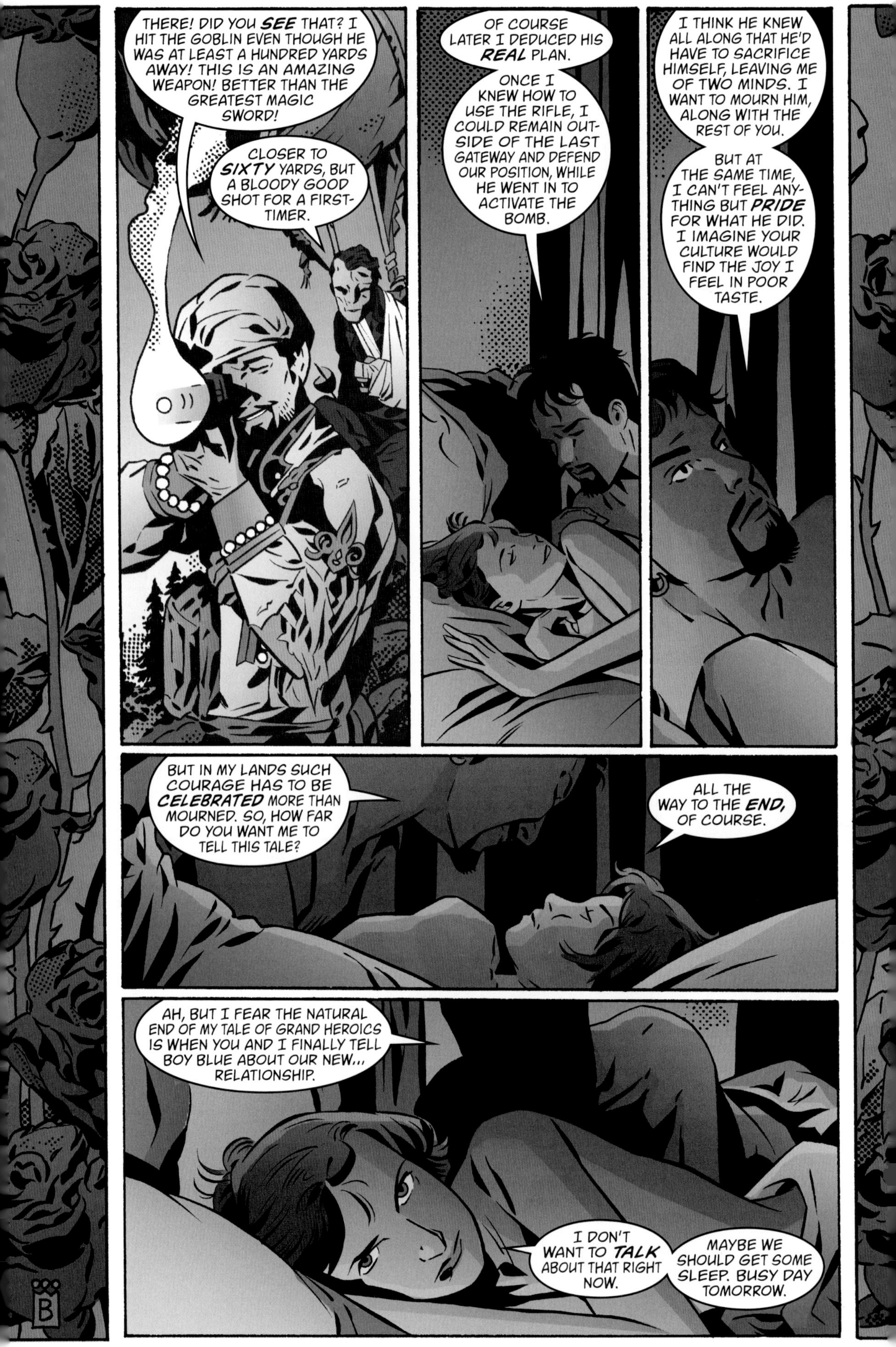
THERE! DID YOU SEE THAT? I HIT THE GOBLIN EVEN THOUGH HE WAS AT LEAST A HUNDRED YARDS AWAY! THIS IS AN AMAZING WEAPON! BETTER THAN THE GREATEST MAGIC SWORD!
CLOSER TO SIXTY YARDS, BUT A BLOODY GOOD SHOT FOR A FIRST-TIMER.
OF COURSE LATER I DEDUCED HIS REAL PLAN.
ONCE I KNEW HOW TO USE THE RIFLE, I COULD REMAIN OUT-SIDE OF THE LAST GATEWAY AND DEFEND OUR POSITION, WHILE HE WENT IN TO ACTIVATE THE BOMB.
I THINK HE KNEW ALL ALONG THAT HE'D HAVE TO SACRIFICE HIMSELF, LEAVING ME OF TWO MINDS. I WANT TO MOURN HIM, ALONG WITH THE REST OF YOU.
BUT AT THE SAME TIME, I CAN'T FEEL ANY-THING BUT PRIDE FOR WHAT HE DID. I IMAGINE YOUR CULTURE WOULD FIND THE JOY I FEEL IN POOR TASTE.
BUT IN MY LANDS SUCH COURAGE HAS TO BE CELEBRATED MORE THAN MOURNED. SO, HOW FAR DO YOU WANT ME TO TELL THIS TALE?
ALL THE WAY TO THE END, OF COURSE.
AH, BUT I FEAR THE NATURAL END OF MY TALE OF GRAND HEROICS IS WHEN YOU AND I FINALLY TELL BOY BLUE ABOUT OUR NEW... RELATIONSHIP.
I DON'T WANT TO TALK ABOUT THAT RIGHT NOW.
MAYBE WE SHOULD GET SOME SLEEP. BUSY DAY TOMORROW.

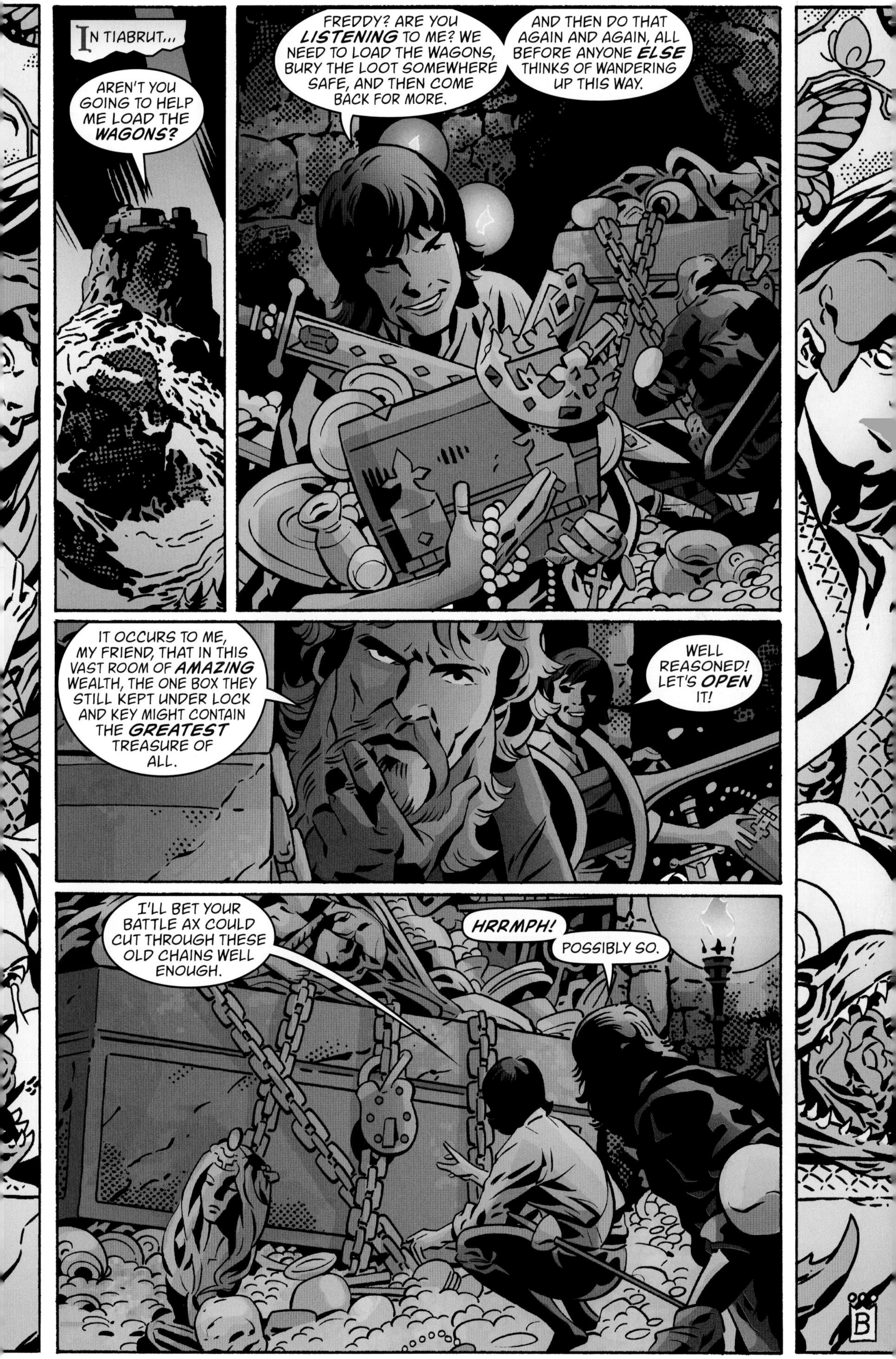

IN TIABRUT...
AREN'T YOU GOING TO HELP ME LOAD THE **WAGONS?**
FREDDY? ARE YOU **LISTENING** TO ME? WE NEED TO LOAD THE WAGONS, BURY THE LOOT SOMEWHERE SAFE, AND THEN COME BACK FOR MORE.
AND THEN DO THAT AGAIN AND AGAIN, ALL BEFORE ANYONE **ELSE** THINKS OF WANDERING UP THIS WAY.
IT OCCURS TO ME, MY FRIEND, THAT IN THIS VAST ROOM OF **AMAZING** WEALTH, THE ONE BOX THEY STILL KEPT UNDER LOCK AND KEY MIGHT CONTAIN THE **GREATEST** TREASURE OF ALL.
WELL REASONED! LET'S **OPEN** IT!
I'LL BET YOUR BATTLE AX COULD CUT THROUGH THESE OLD CHAINS WELL ENOUGH.
HRRMPH!
POSSIBLY SO.

STILL, IT WOULD LIKELY RUIN MY AX'S *BLADE,* THOUGH.

SO WHAT? COMPARED TO WHAT MIGHT BE *INSIDE* THE STONE BOX, WHAT'S ONE MEASLY *AX?*

TRUE.

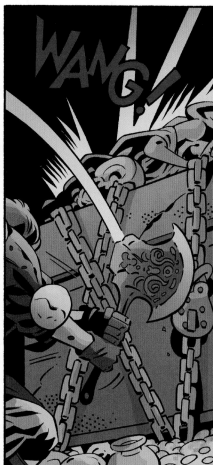

WANG!

BUY YOUR- SELF A THOUSAND MORE WHEN WE'RE *DONE* HERE!

HIT IT! GIVE IT A GREAT *WHACK!*

HMMM. TOUGH CHAIN.

TRY IT AGAIN! REALLY GIVE IT A *GOOD ONE* THIS TIME!

WANG!

YOU *DID* IT! QUICK! LET'S OPEN THE BOX AND SEE THE GREATEST TREASURE OF ALL!

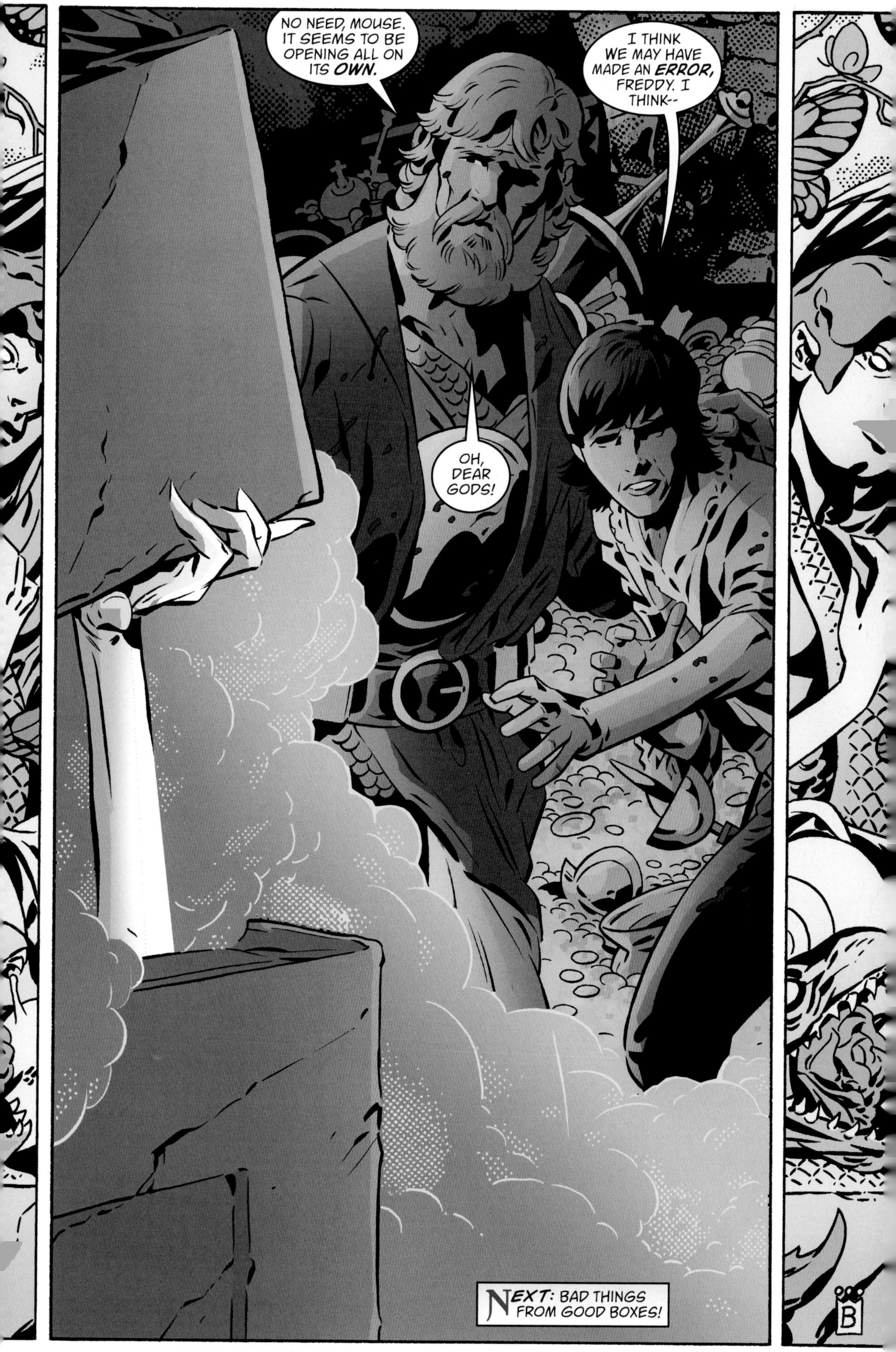
NO NEED, MOUSE. IT SEEMS TO BE OPENING ALL ON ITS OWN.
I THINK WE MAY HAVE MADE AN ERROR, FREDDY. I THINK--
OH, DEAR GODS!
NEXT: BAD THINGS FROM GOOD BOXES!

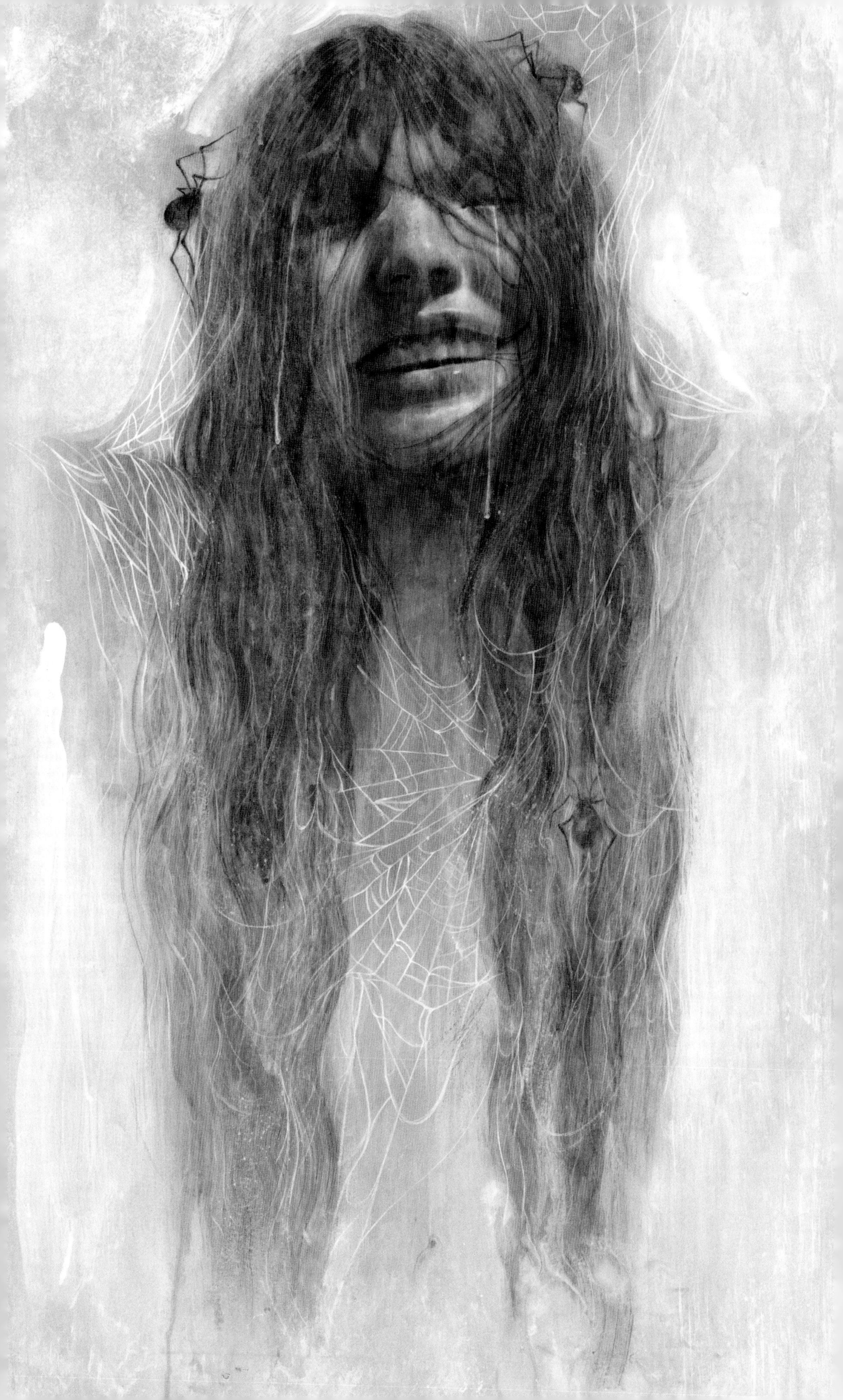

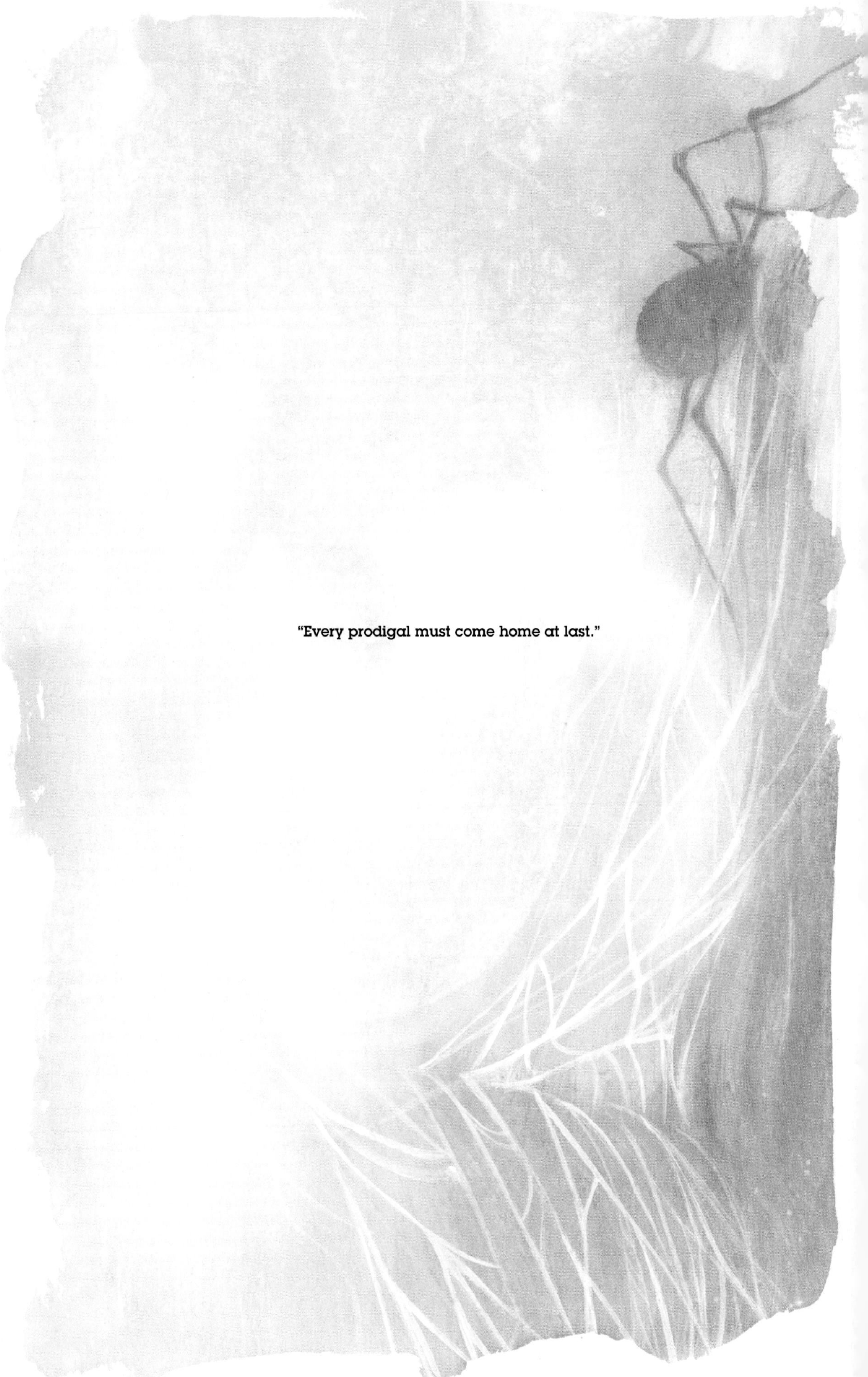

"Every prodigal must come home at last."

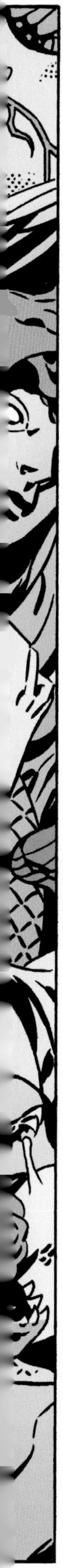

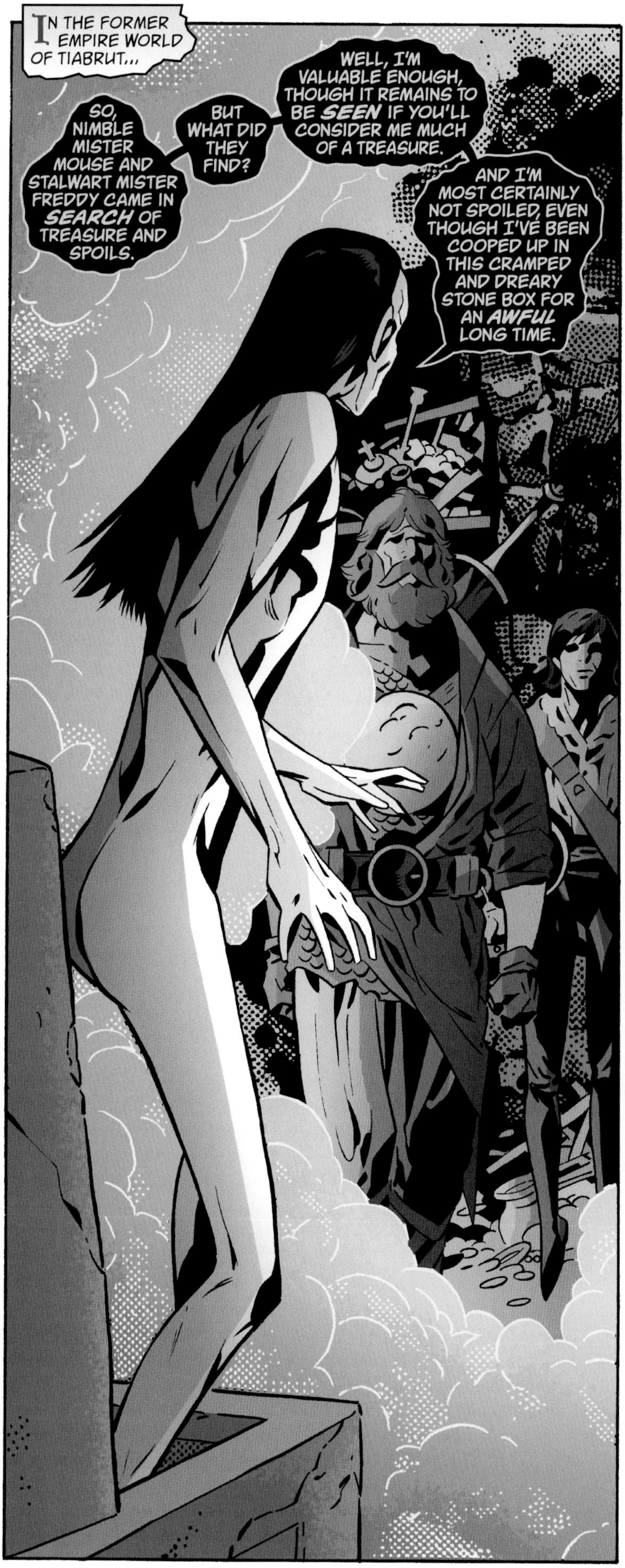
In the former Empire world of Tiabrut...
So, nimble Mister Mouse and stalwart Mister Freddy came in *search* of treasure and spoils.
But what did they find?
Well, I'm valuable enough, though it remains to be *seen* if you'll consider me much of a treasure.
And I'm most certainly not spoiled, even though I've been cooped up in this cramped and dreary stone box for an *awful* long time.

BOXES

Chapter Two of THE DARK AGES

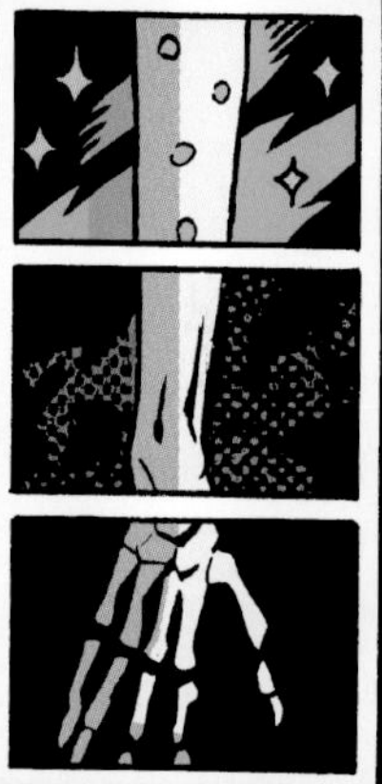

Bill Willingham writer/creator

Mark Buckingham penciller

Andrew Pepoy inker

Lee Loughridge colors

Todd Klein letters

James Jean cover

Angela Rufino associate editor

Shelly Bond editor

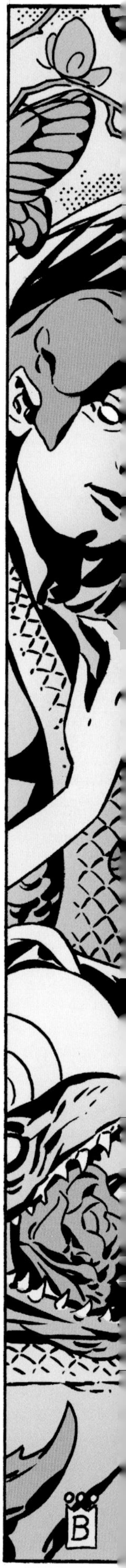

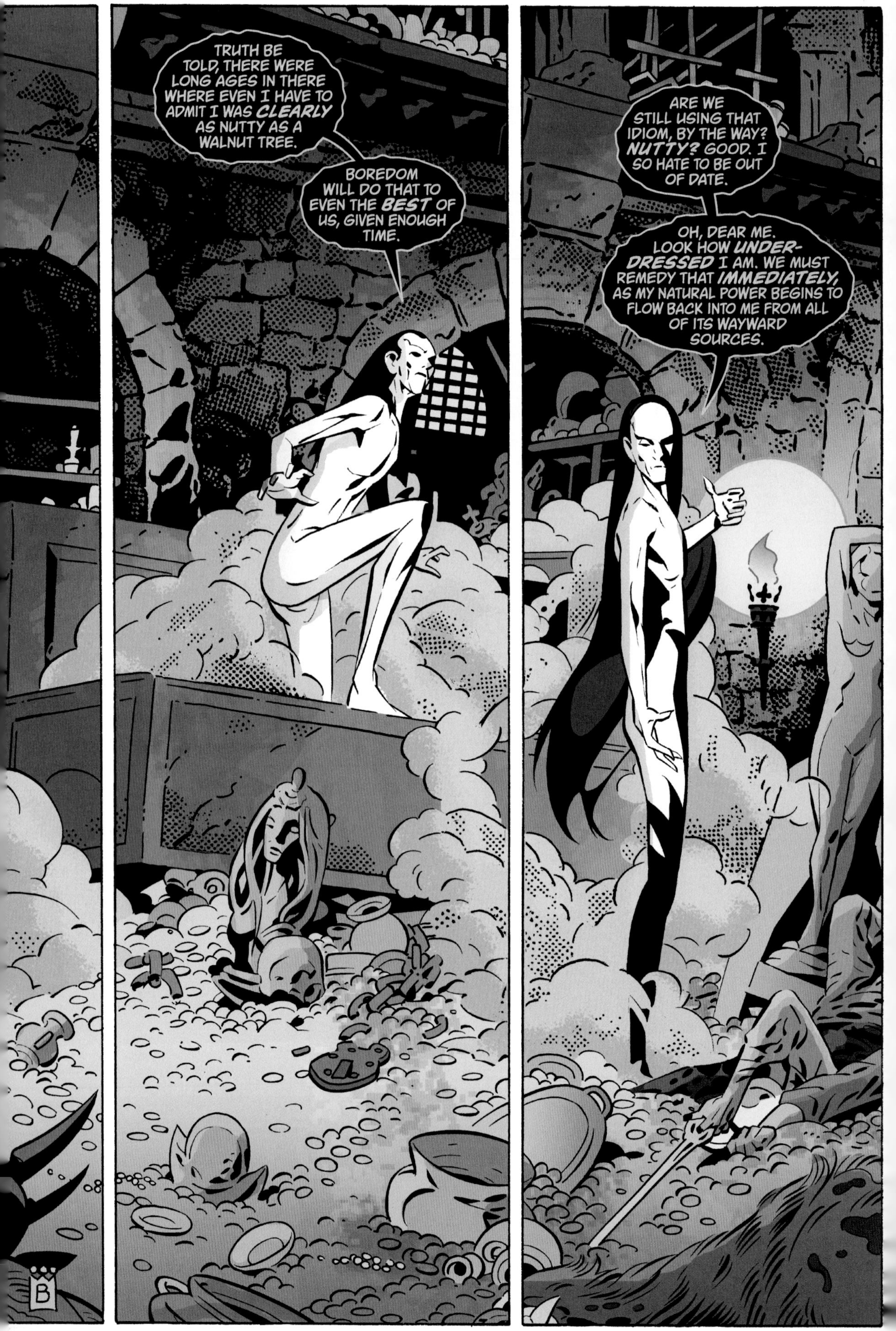
TRUTH BE TOLD, THERE WERE LONG AGES IN THERE WHERE EVEN I HAVE TO ADMIT I WAS CLEARLY AS NUTTY AS A WALNUT TREE.
BOREDOM WILL DO THAT TO EVEN THE BEST OF US, GIVEN ENOUGH TIME.
ARE WE STILL USING THAT IDIOM, BY THE WAY? NUTTY? GOOD. I SO HATE TO BE OUT OF DATE.
OH, DEAR ME. LOOK HOW UNDER-DRESSED I AM. WE MUST REMEDY THAT IMMEDIATELY, AS MY NATURAL POWER BEGINS TO FLOW BACK INTO ME FROM ALL OF ITS WAYWARD SOURCES.

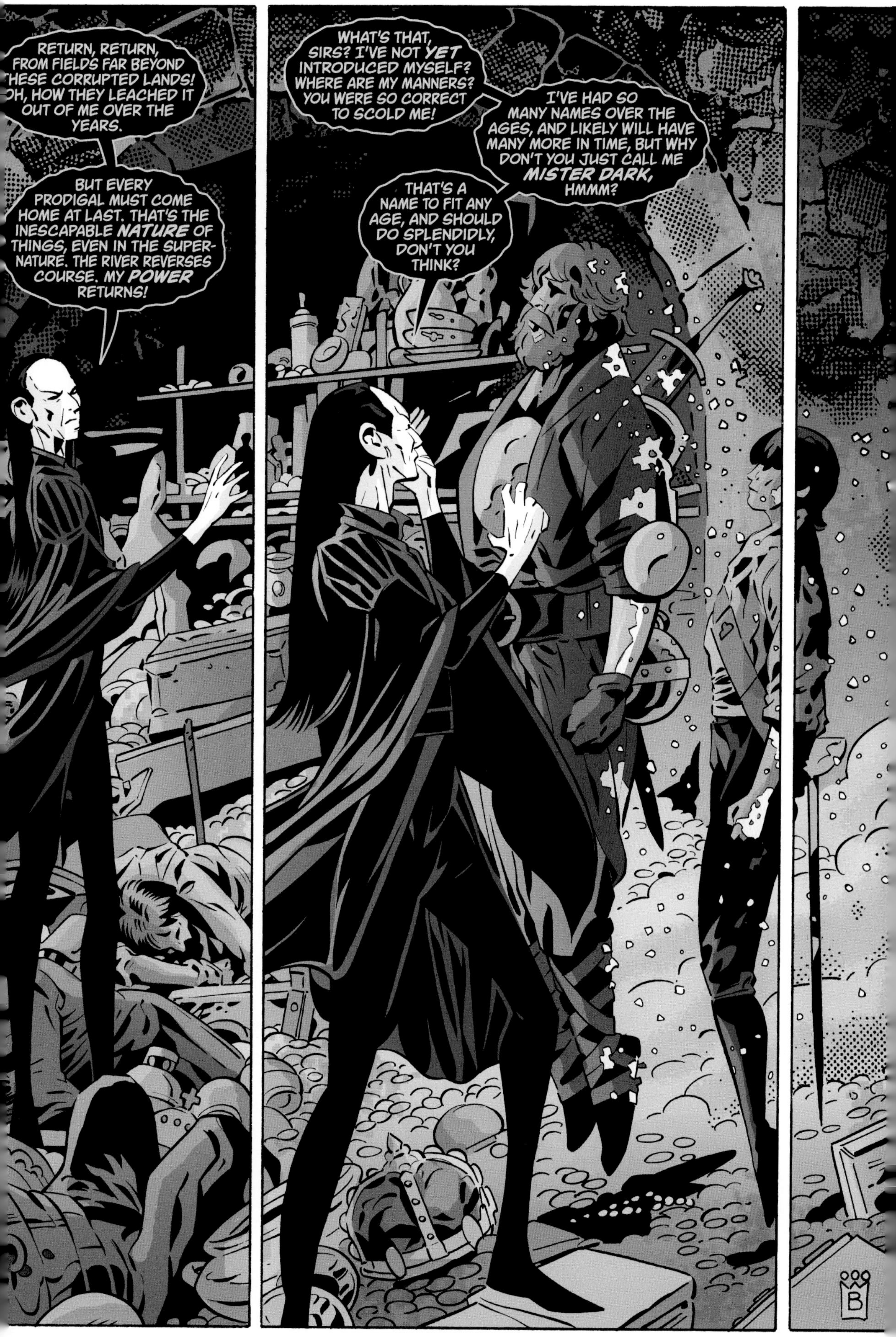
RETURN, RETURN, FROM FIELDS FAR BEYOND THESE CORRUPTED LANDS! OH, HOW THEY LEACHED IT OUT OF ME OVER THE YEARS.
BUT EVERY PRODIGAL MUST COME HOME AT LAST. THAT'S THE INESCAPABLE NATURE OF THINGS, EVEN IN THE SUPER-NATURE. THE RIVER REVERSES COURSE. MY POWER RETURNS!
WHAT'S THAT, SIRS? I'VE NOT YET INTRODUCED MYSELF? WHERE ARE MY MANNERS? YOU WERE SO CORRECT TO SCOLD ME!
I'VE HAD SO MANY NAMES OVER THE AGES, AND LIKELY WILL HAVE MANY MORE IN TIME, BUT WHY DON'T YOU JUST CALL ME MISTER DARK, HMMM?
THAT'S A NAME TO FIT ANY AGE, AND SHOULD DO SPLENDIDLY, DON'T YOU THINK?

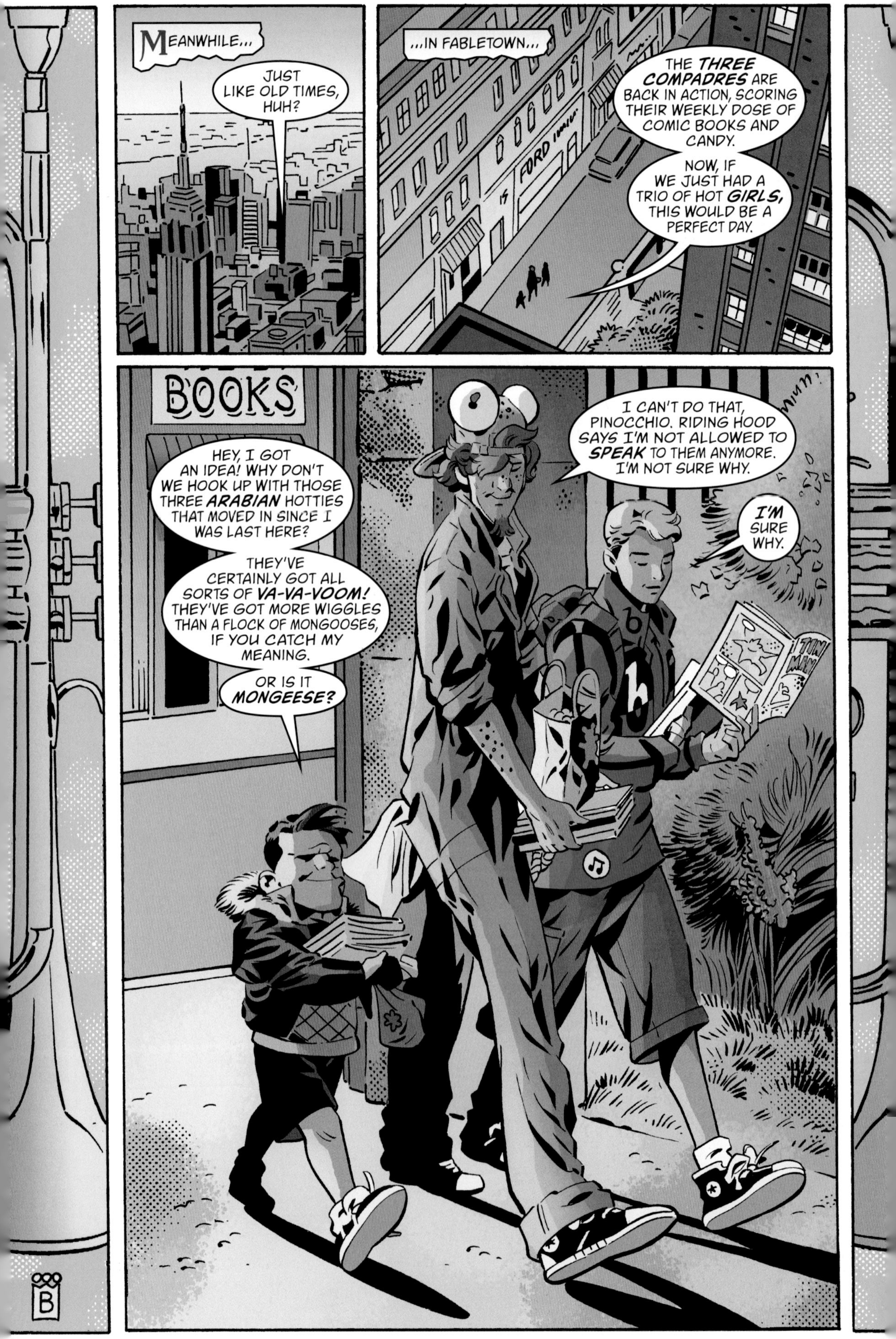
MEANWHILE...
JUST LIKE OLD TIMES, HUH?
...IN FABLETOWN...
THE THREE COMPADRES ARE BACK IN ACTION, SCORING THEIR WEEKLY DOSE OF COMIC BOOKS AND CANDY.
NOW, IF WE JUST HAD A TRIO OF HOT GIRLS, THIS WOULD BE A PERFECT DAY.
BOOKS
HEY, I GOT AN IDEA! WHY DON'T WE HOOK UP WITH THOSE THREE ARABIAN HOTTIES THAT MOVED IN SINCE I WAS LAST HERE?
THEY'VE CERTAINLY GOT ALL SORTS OF VA-VA-VOOM! THEY'VE GOT MORE WIGGLES THAN A FLOCK OF MONGOOSES, IF YOU CATCH MY MEANING.
OR IS IT MONGEESE?
I CAN'T DO THAT, PINOCCHIO. RIDING HOOD SAYS I'M NOT ALLOWED TO SPEAK TO THEM ANYMORE. I'M NOT SURE WHY.
I'M SURE WHY.

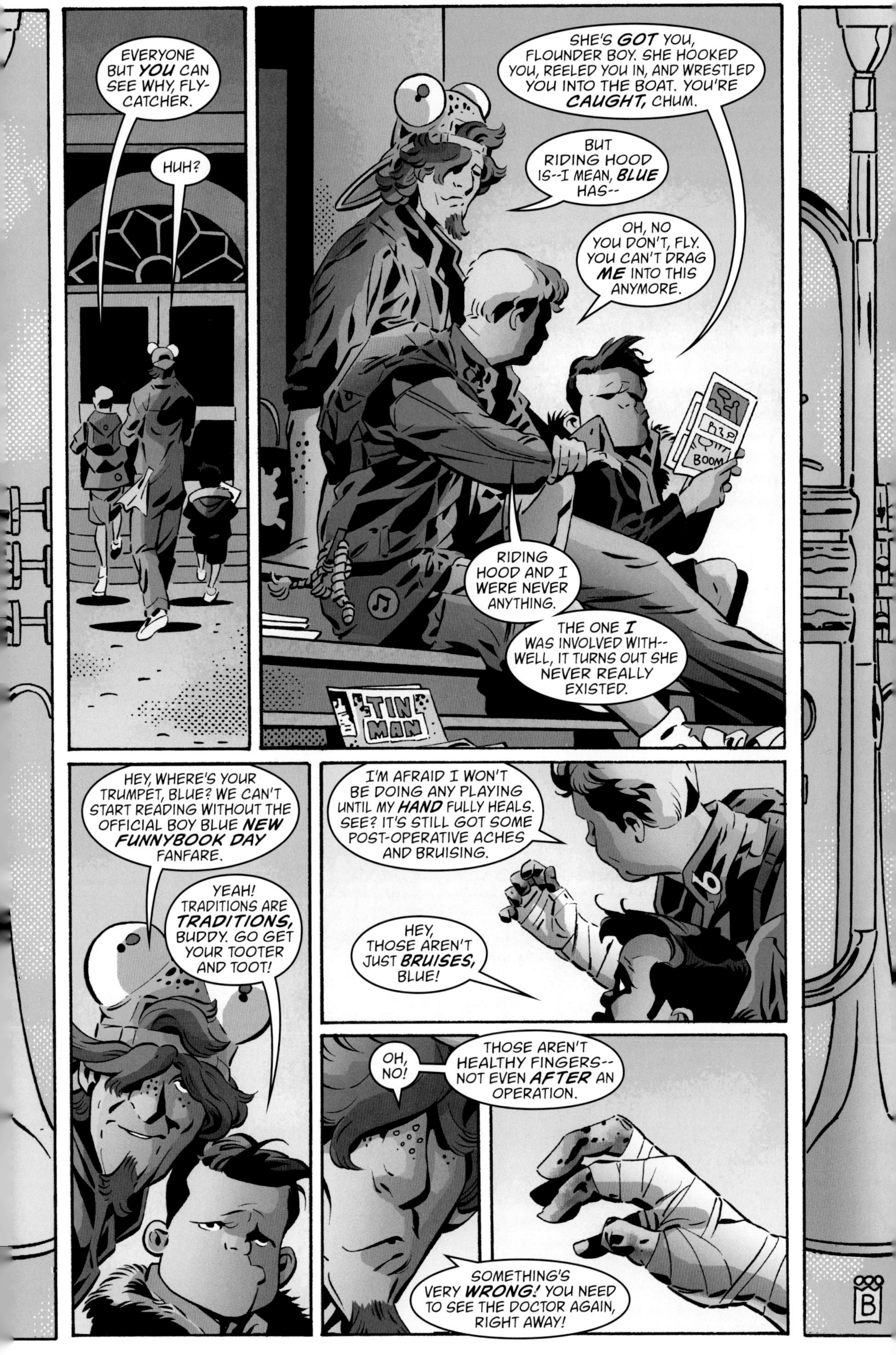
EVERYONE BUT *YOU* CAN SEE WHY, FLY-CATCHER.
HUH?
SHE'S *GOT* YOU, FLOUNDER BOY. SHE HOOKED YOU, REELED YOU IN, AND WRESTLED YOU INTO THE BOAT. YOU'RE *CAUGHT,* CHUM.
BUT RIDING HOOD IS--I MEAN, *BLUE* HAS--
OH, NO YOU DON'T, FLY. YOU CAN'T DRAG *ME* INTO THIS ANYMORE.
BOOM
RIDING HOOD AND I WERE NEVER ANYTHING.
THE ONE *I* WAS INVOLVED WITH-- WELL, IT TURNS OUT SHE NEVER REALLY EXISTED.
TIN MAN
HEY, WHERE'S YOUR TRUMPET, BLUE? WE CAN'T START READING WITHOUT THE OFFICIAL BOY BLUE *NEW FUNNYBOOK DAY* FANFARE.
YEAH! TRADITIONS ARE *TRADITIONS,* BUDDY. GO GET YOUR TOOTER AND TOOT!
I'M AFRAID I WON'T BE DOING ANY PLAYING UNTIL MY *HAND* FULLY HEALS. SEE? IT'S STILL GOT SOME POST-OPERATIVE ACHES AND BRUISING.
HEY, THOSE AREN'T JUST *BRUISES,* BLUE!
OH, NO!
THOSE AREN'T HEALTHY FINGERS-- NOT EVEN *AFTER* AN OPERATION.
SOMETHING'S VERY *WRONG!* YOU NEED TO SEE THE DOCTOR AGAIN, RIGHT AWAY!

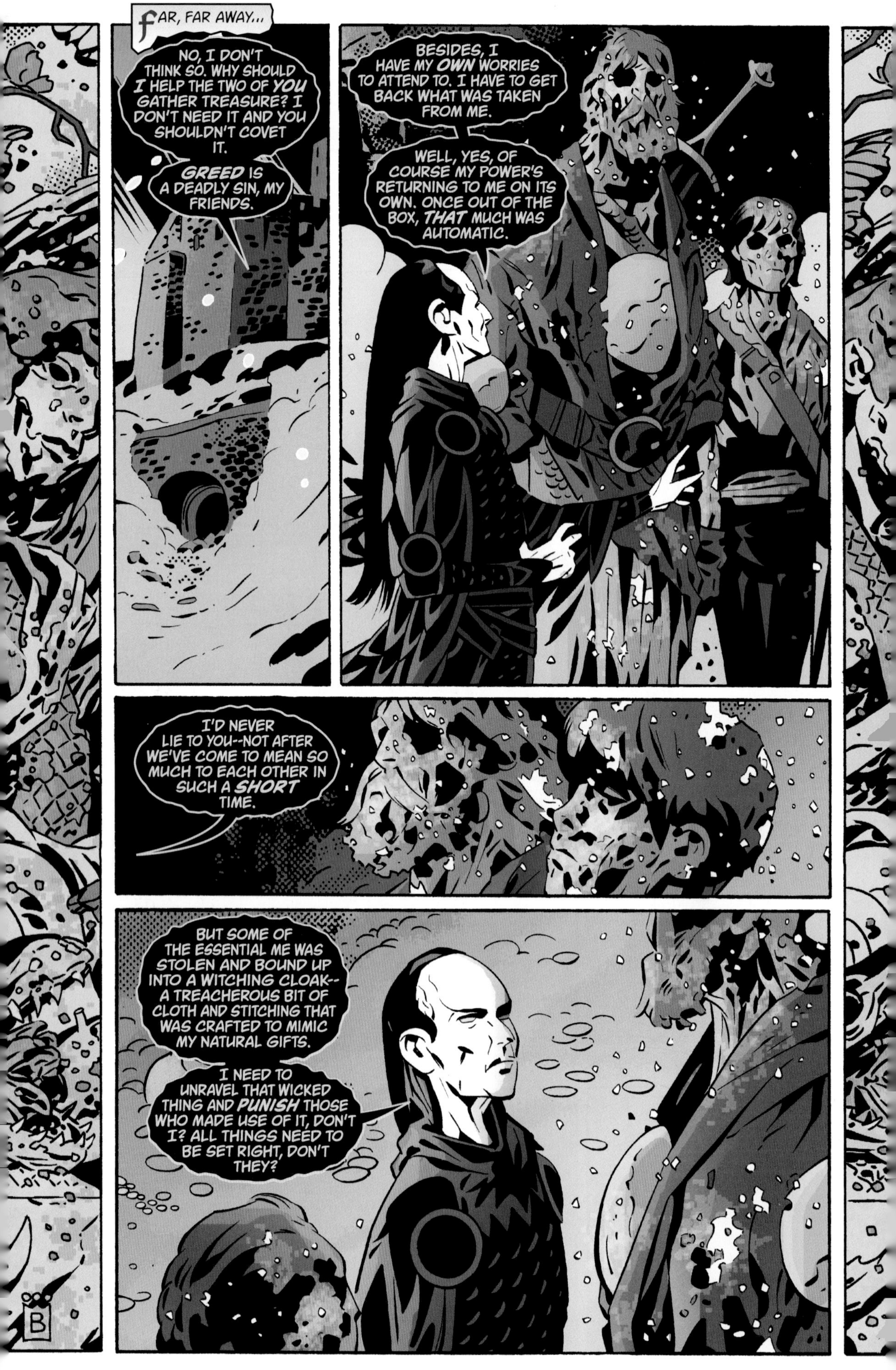
FAR, FAR AWAY...
NO, I DON'T THINK SO. WHY SHOULD I HELP THE TWO OF YOU GATHER TREASURE? I DON'T NEED IT AND YOU SHOULDN'T COVET IT.
GREED IS A DEADLY SIN, MY FRIENDS.
BESIDES, I HAVE MY OWN WORRIES TO ATTEND TO. I HAVE TO GET BACK WHAT WAS TAKEN FROM ME.
WELL, YES, OF COURSE MY POWER'S RETURNING TO ME ON ITS OWN. ONCE OUT OF THE BOX, THAT MUCH WAS AUTOMATIC.
I'D NEVER LIE TO YOU--NOT AFTER WE'VE COME TO MEAN SO MUCH TO EACH OTHER IN SUCH A SHORT TIME.
BUT SOME OF THE ESSENTIAL ME WAS STOLEN AND BOUND UP INTO A WITCHING CLOAK-- A TREACHEROUS BIT OF CLOTH AND STITCHING THAT WAS CRAFTED TO MIMIC MY NATURAL GIFTS.
I NEED TO UNRAVEL THAT WICKED THING AND PUNISH THOSE WHO MADE USE OF IT, DON'T I? ALL THINGS NEED TO BE SET RIGHT, DON'T THEY?

EVEN THOUGH YOU'VE CUT OFF MY ABILITY TO CONJURE, I STILL HAVE **CONNECTIONS** IN PLACE TO MY OLD EMPIRE.

I CAN SENSE WHEN CERTAIN THINGS HAVE BEEN DISRUPTED, AND THEY HAVE. ONE OF THE **BROADCAST BOXES** HAS BEEN OPENED.

AND WHAT MIGHT THEY BE?

AH, SO YOU DON'T KNOW **EVERY-THING,** DO YOU?

THE BOXES WERE USED TO POWER MY **SORCERERS CORPS** BY BROADCASTING WHATEVER MAGICAL SOURCE WAS CON-TAINED WITHIN.

ONE OR MORE PER WORLD WOULD BE ENOUGH TO SUPPLY--

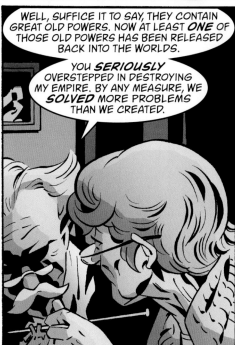

WELL, SUFFICE IT TO SAY, THEY CONTAIN GREAT OLD POWERS. NOW AT LEAST **ONE** OF THOSE OLD POWERS HAS BEEN RELEASED BACK INTO THE WORLDS.

YOU **SERIOUSLY** OVERSTEPPED IN DESTROYING MY EMPIRE. BY ANY MEASURE, WE **SOLVED** MORE PROBLEMS THAN WE CREATED.

SOMETHING THAT TOOK CENTURIES AND ENTIRE ARMIES TO SAFELY LOCK AWAY IS LOOSE AGAIN AND **YOU** CAUSED IT.

I WONDER HOW LONG WE'LL BE ABLE TO SURVIVE THE RESULTS OF YOUR NOBLE **MEDDLING.**

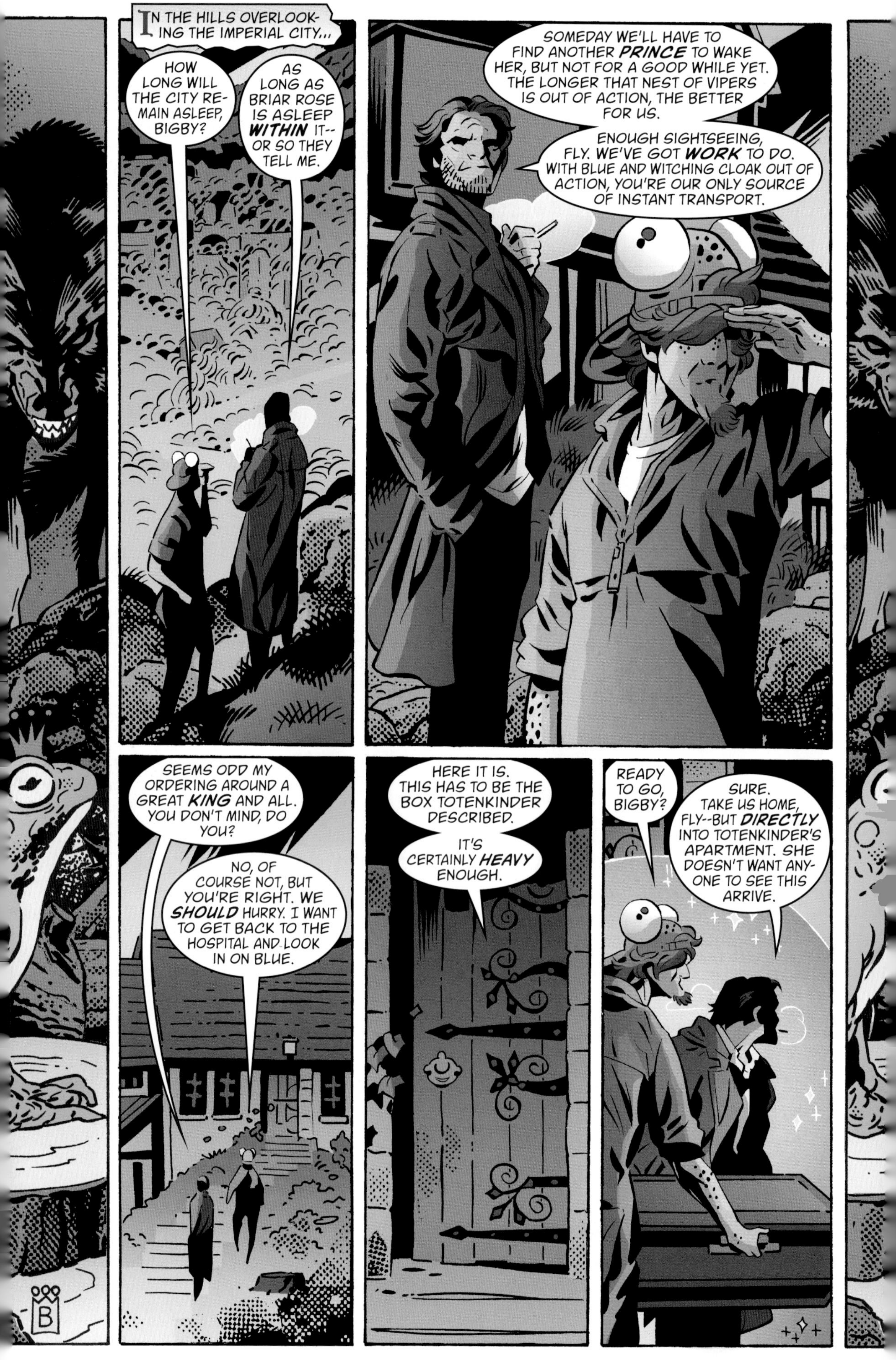
IN THE HILLS OVERLOOKING THE IMPERIAL CITY...
HOW LONG WILL THE CITY REMAIN ASLEEP, BIGBY?
AS LONG AS BRIAR ROSE IS ASLEEP WITHIN IT-- OR SO THEY TELL ME.
SOMEDAY WE'LL HAVE TO FIND ANOTHER PRINCE TO WAKE HER, BUT NOT FOR A GOOD WHILE YET. THE LONGER THAT NEST OF VIPERS IS OUT OF ACTION, THE BETTER FOR US.
ENOUGH SIGHTSEEING, FLY. WE'VE GOT WORK TO DO. WITH BLUE AND WITCHING CLOAK OUT OF ACTION, YOU'RE OUR ONLY SOURCE OF INSTANT TRANSPORT.
SEEMS ODD MY ORDERING AROUND A GREAT KING AND ALL. YOU DON'T MIND, DO YOU?
NO, OF COURSE NOT, BUT YOU'RE RIGHT. WE SHOULD HURRY. I WANT TO GET BACK TO THE HOSPITAL AND LOOK IN ON BLUE.
HERE IT IS. THIS HAS TO BE THE BOX TOTENKINDER DESCRIBED.
IT'S CERTAINLY HEAVY ENOUGH.
READY TO GO, BIGBY?
SURE. TAKE US HOME, FLY--BUT DIRECTLY INTO TOTENKINDER'S APARTMENT. SHE DOESN'T WANT ANYONE TO SEE THIS ARRIVE.

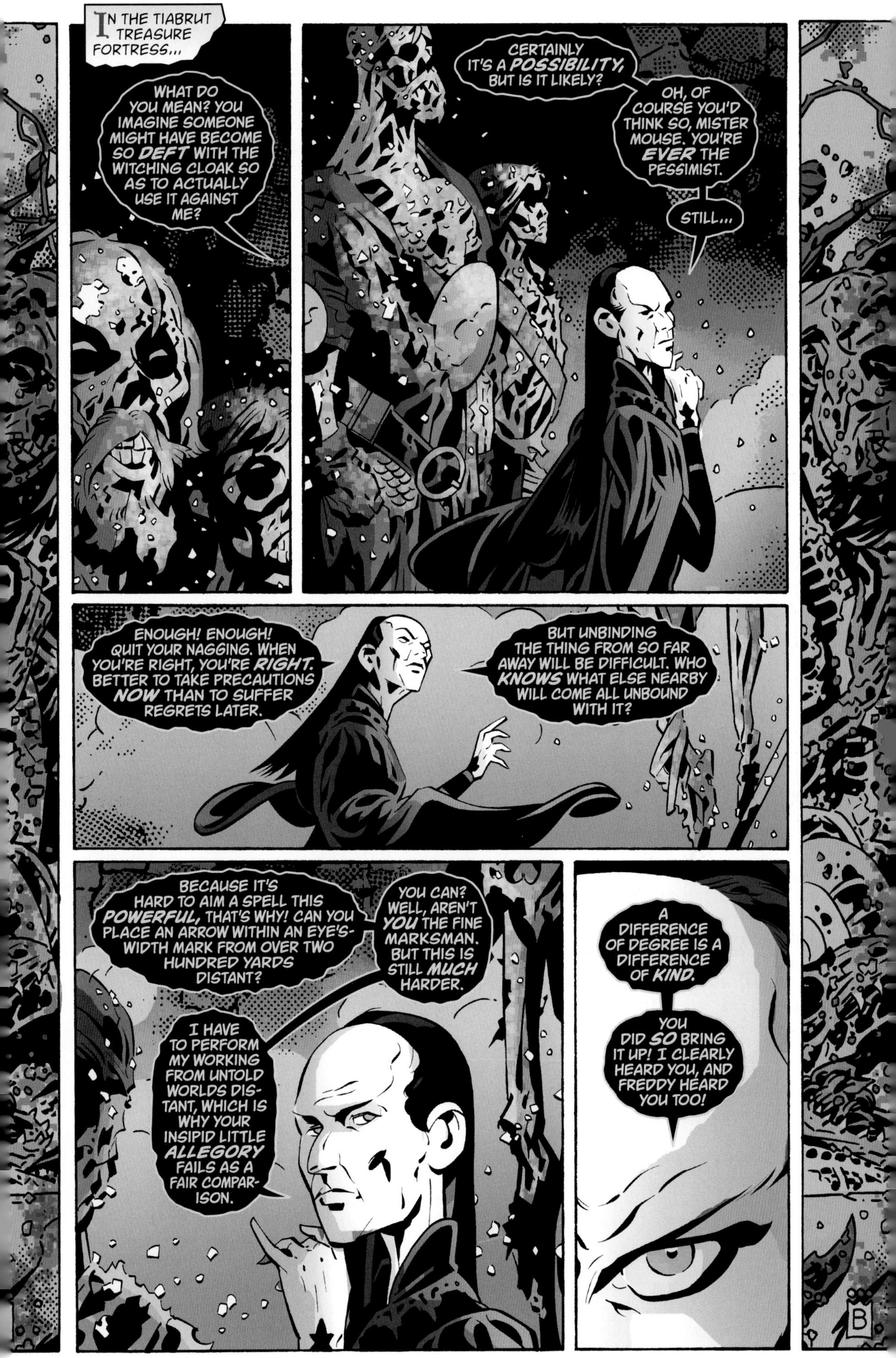
IN THE TIABRUT TREASURE FORTRESS...
WHAT DO YOU MEAN? YOU IMAGINE SOMEONE MIGHT HAVE BECOME SO DEFT WITH THE WITCHING CLOAK SO AS TO ACTUALLY USE IT AGAINST ME?
CERTAINLY IT'S A POSSIBILITY, BUT IS IT LIKELY?
OH, OF COURSE YOU'D THINK SO, MISTER MOUSE. YOU'RE EVER THE PESSIMIST.
STILL...
ENOUGH! ENOUGH! QUIT YOUR NAGGING. WHEN YOU'RE RIGHT, YOU'RE RIGHT. BETTER TO TAKE PRECAUTIONS NOW THAN TO SUFFER REGRETS LATER.
BUT UNBINDING THE THING FROM SO FAR AWAY WILL BE DIFFICULT. WHO KNOWS WHAT ELSE NEARBY WILL COME ALL UNBOUND WITH IT?
BECAUSE IT'S HARD TO AIM A SPELL THIS POWERFUL, THAT'S WHY! CAN YOU PLACE AN ARROW WITHIN AN EYE'S-WIDTH MARK FROM OVER TWO HUNDRED YARDS DISTANT?
YOU CAN? WELL, AREN'T YOU THE FINE MARKSMAN. BUT THIS IS STILL MUCH HARDER.
I HAVE TO PERFORM MY WORKING FROM UNTOLD WORLDS DISTANT, WHICH IS WHY YOUR INSIPID LITTLE ALLEGORY FAILS AS A FAIR COMPARISON.
A DIFFERENCE OF DEGREE IS A DIFFERENCE OF KIND.
YOU DID SO BRING IT UP! I CLEARLY HEARD YOU, AND FREDDY HEARD YOU TOO!

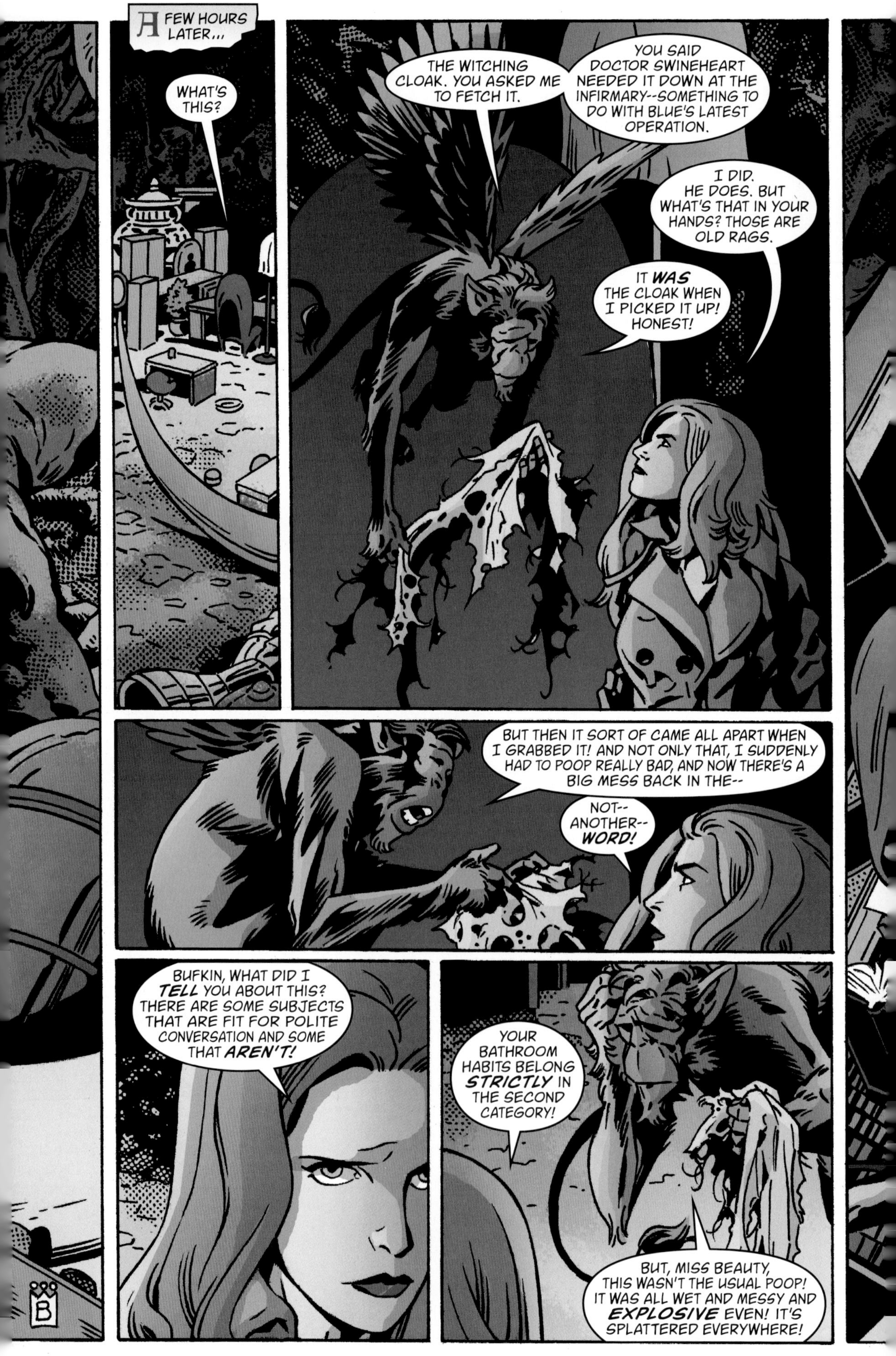
A FEW HOURS LATER...
WHAT'S THIS?
THE WITCHING CLOAK. YOU ASKED ME TO FETCH IT.
YOU SAID DOCTOR SWINEHEART NEEDED IT DOWN AT THE INFIRMARY--SOMETHING TO DO WITH BLUE'S LATEST OPERATION.
I DID. HE DOES. BUT WHAT'S THAT IN YOUR HANDS? THOSE ARE OLD RAGS.
IT WAS THE CLOAK WHEN I PICKED IT UP! HONEST!
BUT THEN IT SORT OF CAME ALL APART WHEN I GRABBED IT! AND NOT ONLY THAT, I SUDDENLY HAD TO POOP REALLY BAD, AND NOW THERE'S A BIG MESS BACK IN THE--
NOT-- ANOTHER-- WORD!
BUFKIN, WHAT DID I TELL YOU ABOUT THIS? THERE ARE SOME SUBJECTS THAT ARE FIT FOR POLITE CONVERSATION AND SOME THAT AREN'T!
YOUR BATHROOM HABITS BELONG STRICTLY IN THE SECOND CATEGORY!
BUT, MISS BEAUTY, THIS WASN'T THE USUAL POOP! IT WAS ALL WET AND MESSY AND EXPLOSIVE EVEN! IT'S SPLATTERED EVERYWHERE!

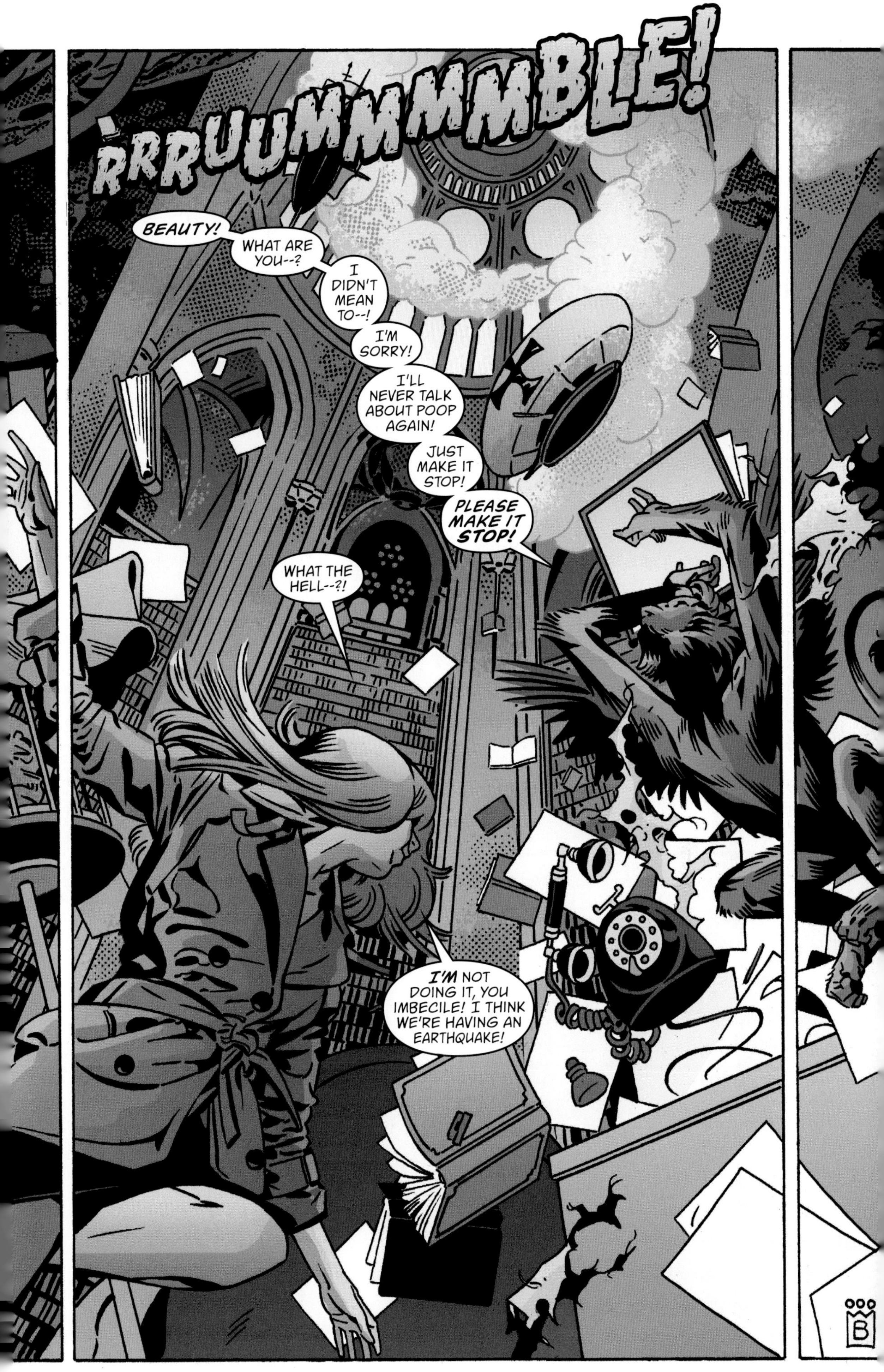

RRRUUMMMMMBLE!
BEAUTY!
WHAT ARE YOU--?
I DIDN'T MEAN TO--!
I'M SORRY!
I'LL NEVER TALK ABOUT POOP AGAIN!
JUST MAKE IT STOP!
PLEASE MAKE IT STOP!
WHAT THE HELL--?!
I'M NOT DOING IT, YOU IMBECILE! I THINK WE'RE HAVING AN EARTHQUAKE!

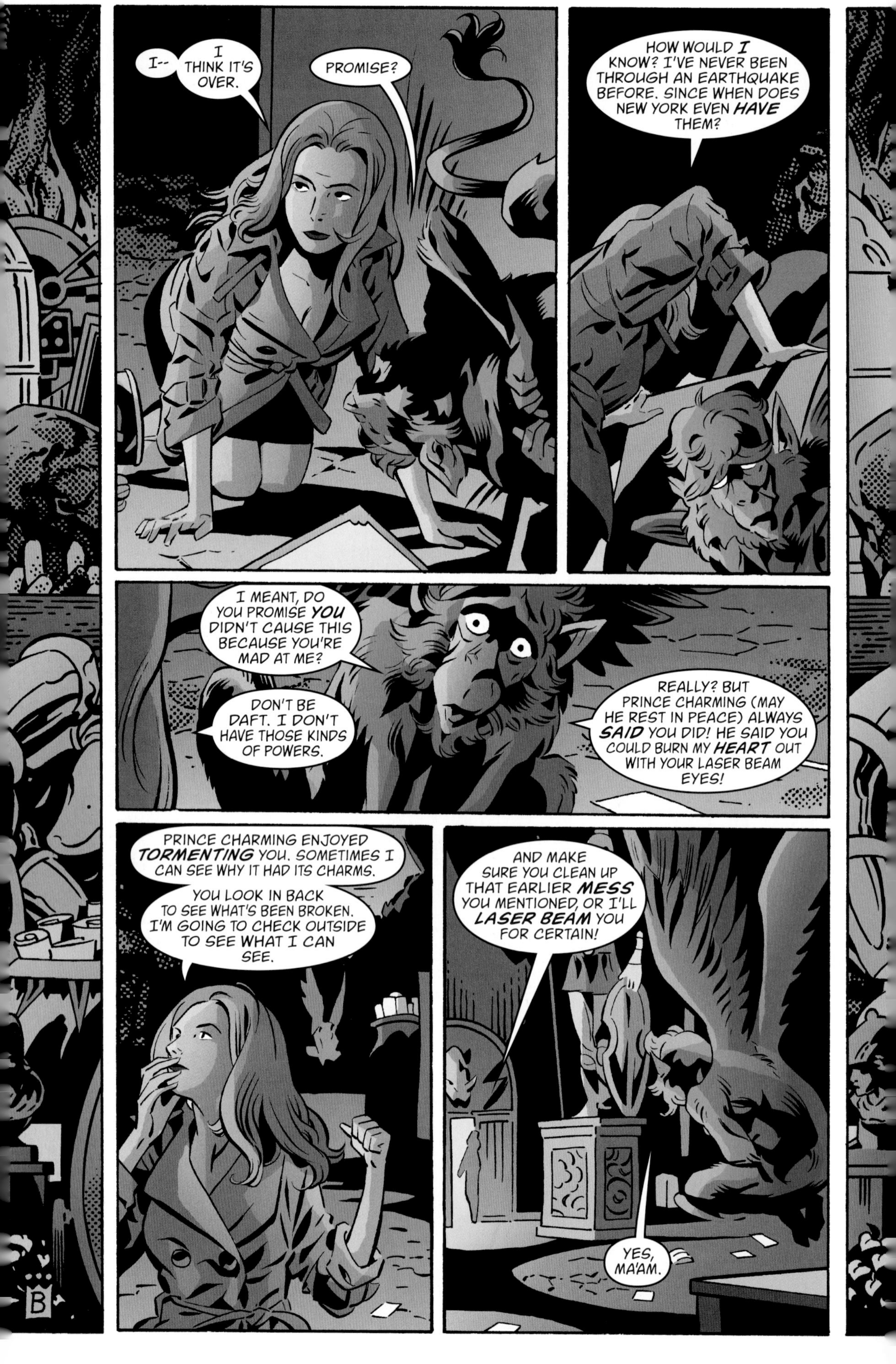
I--
I THINK IT'S OVER.
PROMISE?
HOW WOULD *I* KNOW? I'VE NEVER BEEN THROUGH AN EARTHQUAKE BEFORE. SINCE WHEN DOES NEW YORK EVEN *HAVE* THEM?
I MEANT, DO YOU PROMISE *YOU* DIDN'T CAUSE THIS BECAUSE YOU'RE MAD AT ME?
DON'T BE DAFT. I DON'T HAVE THOSE KINDS OF POWERS.
REALLY? BUT PRINCE CHARMING (MAY HE REST IN PEACE) ALWAYS *SAID* YOU DID! HE SAID YOU COULD BURN MY *HEART* OUT WITH YOUR LASER BEAM EYES!
PRINCE CHARMING ENJOYED *TORMENTING* YOU. SOMETIMES I CAN SEE WHY IT HAD ITS CHARMS.
YOU LOOK IN BACK TO SEE WHAT'S BEEN BROKEN. I'M GOING TO CHECK OUTSIDE TO SEE WHAT I CAN SEE.
AND MAKE SURE YOU CLEAN UP THAT EARLIER *MESS* YOU MENTIONED, OR I'LL *LASER BEAM* YOU FOR CERTAIN!
YES, MA'AM.

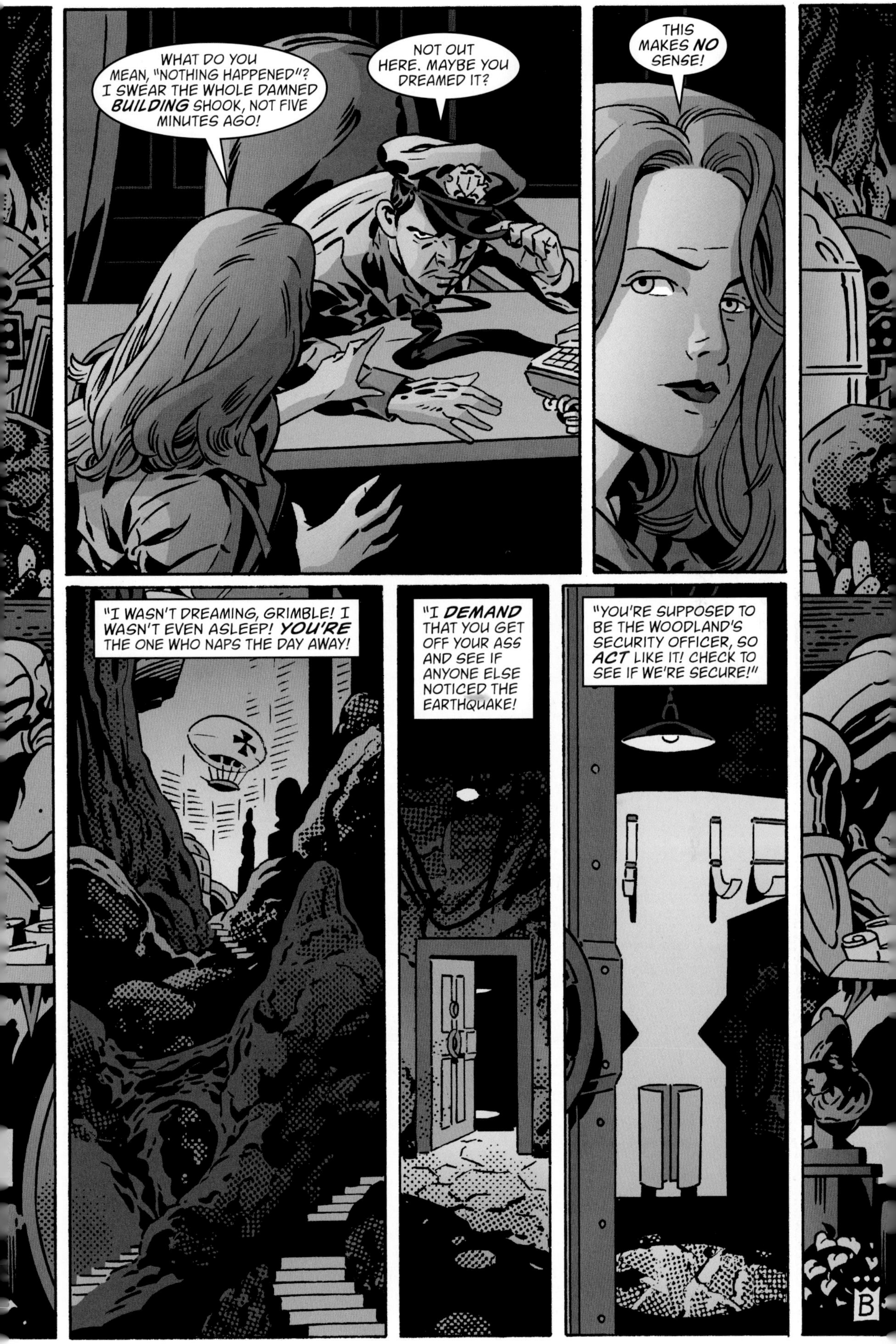
WHAT DO YOU MEAN, "NOTHING HAPPENED"? I SWEAR THE WHOLE DAMNED **BUILDING** SHOOK, NOT FIVE MINUTES AGO!
NOT OUT HERE. MAYBE YOU DREAMED IT?
THIS MAKES **NO** SENSE!
"I WASN'T DREAMING, GRIMBLE! I WASN'T EVEN ASLEEP! ***YOU'RE*** THE ONE WHO NAPS THE DAY AWAY!
"I ***DEMAND*** THAT YOU GET OFF YOUR ASS AND SEE IF ANYONE ELSE NOTICED THE EARTHQUAKE!
"YOU'RE SUPPOSED TO BE THE WOODLAND'S SECURITY OFFICER, SO ***ACT*** LIKE IT! CHECK TO SEE IF WE'RE SECURE!"

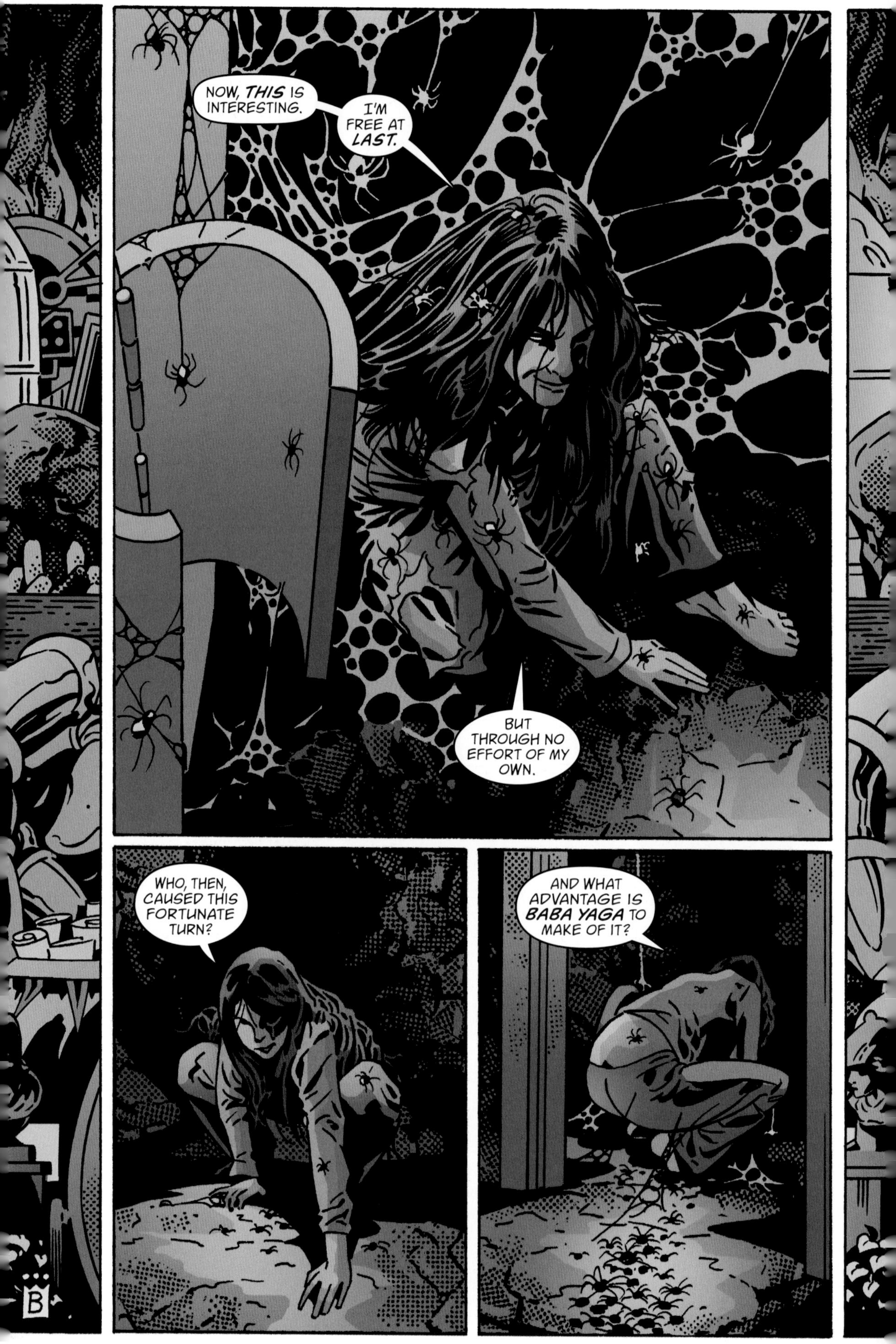
NOW, THIS IS INTERESTING.
I'M FREE AT LAST.
BUT THROUGH NO EFFORT OF MY OWN.
WHO, THEN, CAUSED THIS FORTUNATE TURN?
AND WHAT ADVANTAGE IS BABA YAGA TO MAKE OF IT?

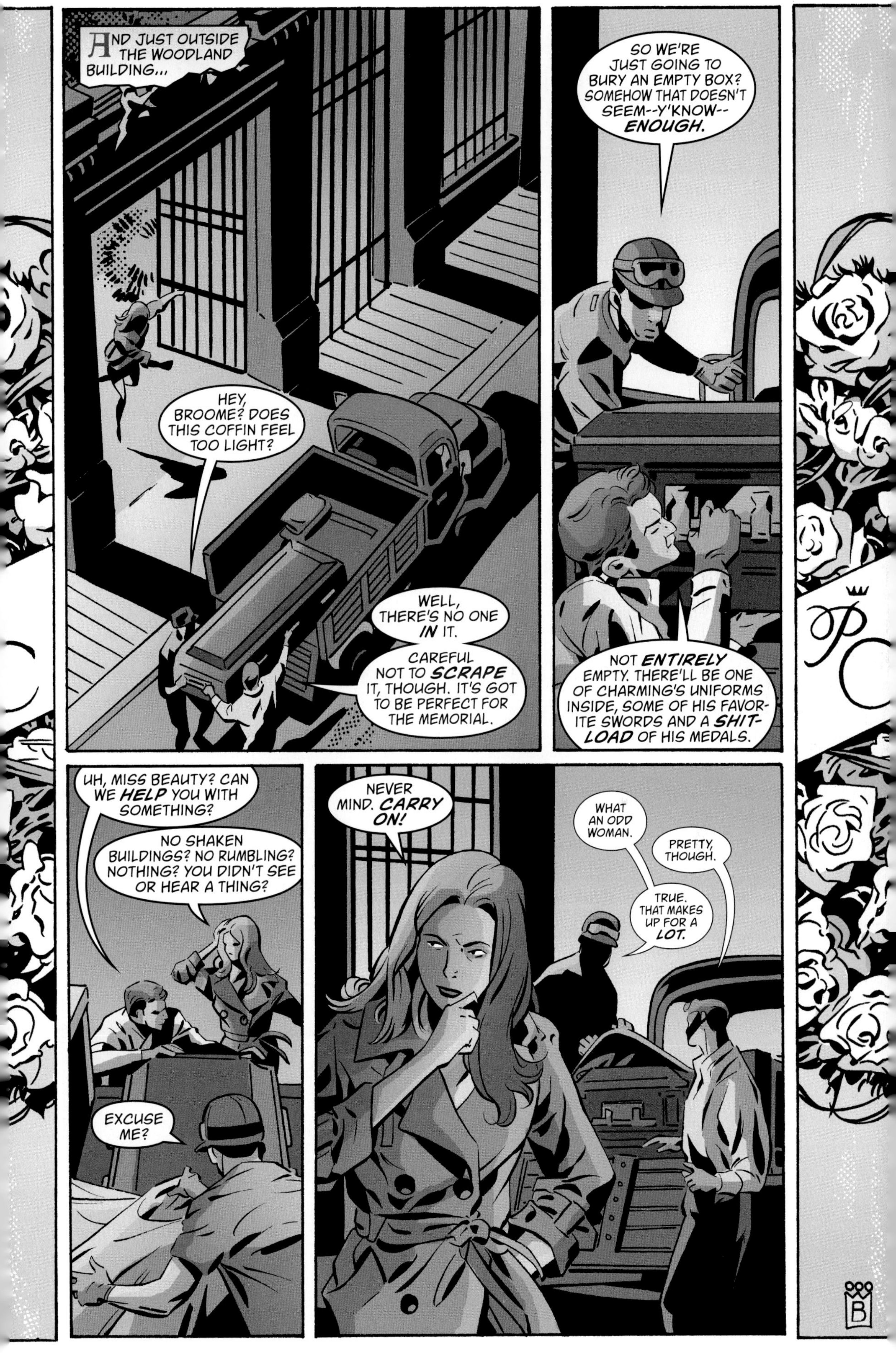
AND JUST OUTSIDE THE WOODLAND BUILDING...
HEY, BROOME? DOES THIS COFFIN FEEL TOO LIGHT?
WELL, THERE'S NO ONE *IN* IT.
CAREFUL NOT TO *SCRAPE* IT, THOUGH. IT'S GOT TO BE PERFECT FOR THE MEMORIAL.
SO WE'RE JUST GOING TO BURY AN EMPTY BOX? SOMEHOW THAT DOESN'T SEEM--Y'KNOW-- *ENOUGH.*
NOT *ENTIRELY* EMPTY. THERE'LL BE ONE OF CHARMING'S UNIFORMS INSIDE, SOME OF HIS FAVORITE SWORDS AND A *SHIT-LOAD* OF HIS MEDALS.
UH, MISS BEAUTY? CAN WE *HELP* YOU WITH SOMETHING?
NO SHAKEN BUILDINGS? NO RUMBLING? NOTHING? YOU DIDN'T SEE OR HEAR A THING?
EXCUSE ME?
NEVER MIND. *CARRY ON!*
WHAT AN ODD WOMAN.
PRETTY, THOUGH.
TRUE. THAT MAKES UP FOR A *LOT.*

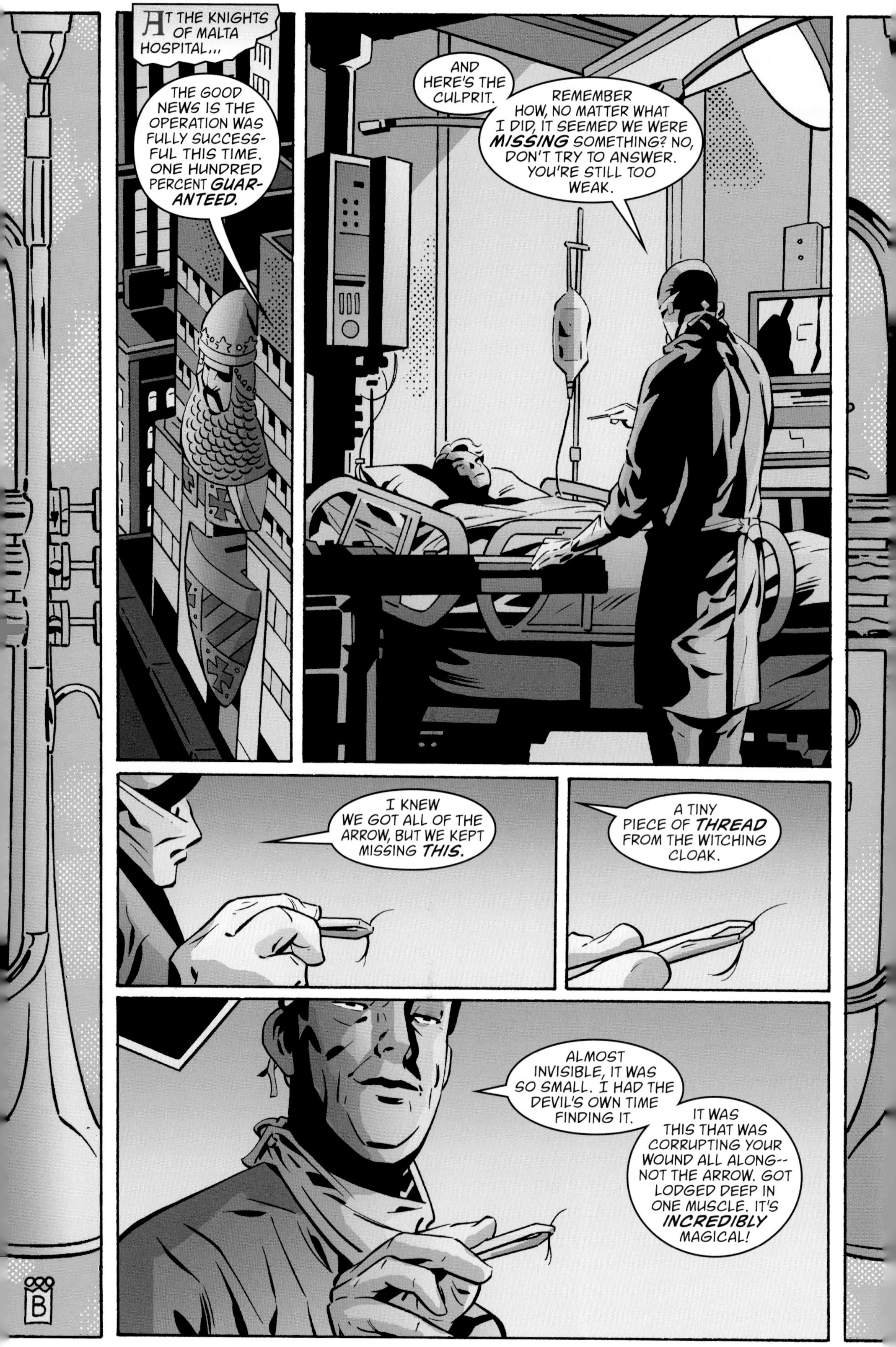
AT THE KNIGHTS OF MALTA HOSPITAL...
THE GOOD NEWS IS THE OPERATION WAS FULLY SUCCESS-FUL THIS TIME. ONE HUNDRED PERCENT GUAR-ANTEED.
AND HERE'S THE CULPRIT.
REMEMBER HOW, NO MATTER WHAT I DID, IT SEEMED WE WERE MISSING SOMETHING? NO, DON'T TRY TO ANSWER. YOU'RE STILL TOO WEAK.
I KNEW WE GOT ALL OF THE ARROW, BUT WE KEPT MISSING THIS.
A TINY PIECE OF THREAD FROM THE WITCHING CLOAK.
ALMOST INVISIBLE, IT WAS SO SMALL. I HAD THE DEVIL'S OWN TIME FINDING IT.
IT WAS THIS THAT WAS CORRUPTING YOUR WOUND ALL ALONG--NOT THE ARROW. GOT LODGED DEEP IN ONE MUSCLE. IT'S INCREDIBLY MAGICAL!

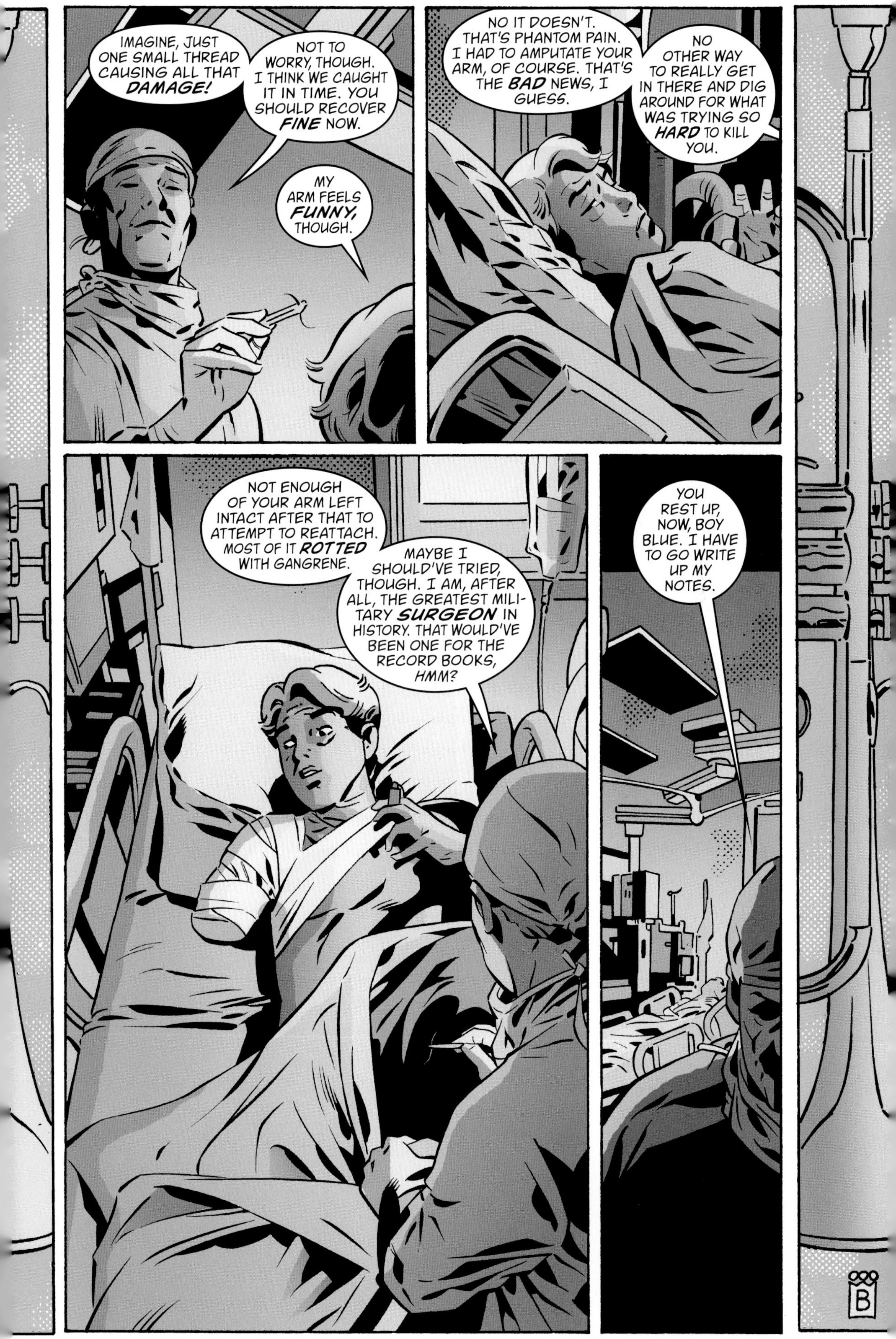
IMAGINE, JUST ONE SMALL THREAD CAUSING ALL THAT DAMAGE!
NOT TO WORRY, THOUGH. I THINK WE CAUGHT IT IN TIME. YOU SHOULD RECOVER FINE NOW.
MY ARM FEELS FUNNY, THOUGH.
NO IT DOESN'T. THAT'S PHANTOM PAIN. I HAD TO AMPUTATE YOUR ARM, OF COURSE. THAT'S THE BAD NEWS, I GUESS.
NO OTHER WAY TO REALLY GET IN THERE AND DIG AROUND FOR WHAT WAS TRYING SO HARD TO KILL YOU.
NOT ENOUGH OF YOUR ARM LEFT INTACT AFTER THAT TO ATTEMPT TO REATTACH. MOST OF IT ROTTED WITH GANGRENE.
MAYBE I SHOULD'VE TRIED, THOUGH. I AM, AFTER ALL, THE GREATEST MILITARY SURGEON IN HISTORY. THAT WOULD'VE BEEN ONE FOR THE RECORD BOOKS, HMM?
YOU REST UP, NOW, BOY BLUE. I HAVE TO GO WRITE UP MY NOTES.

NEXT: THE GREAT UNBINDING

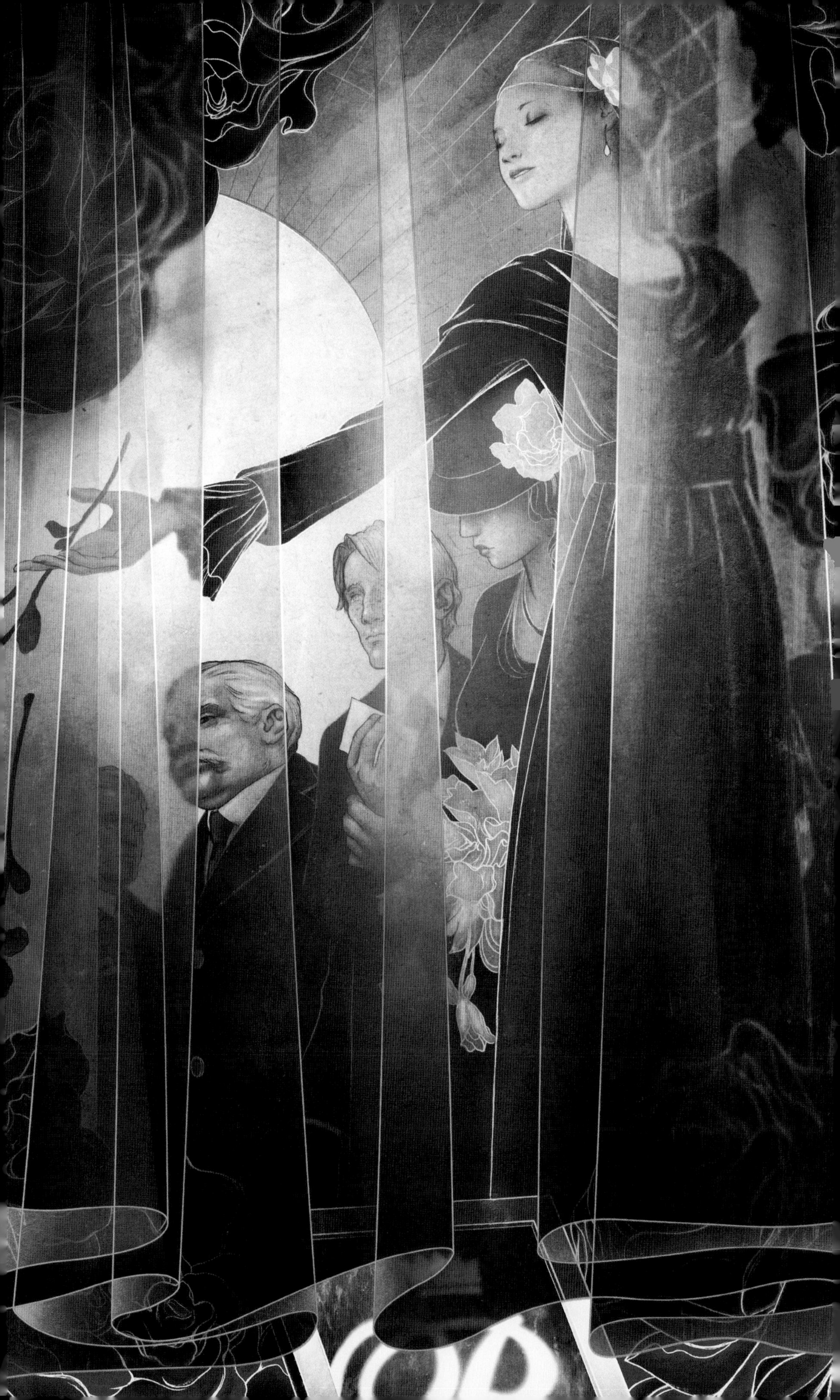

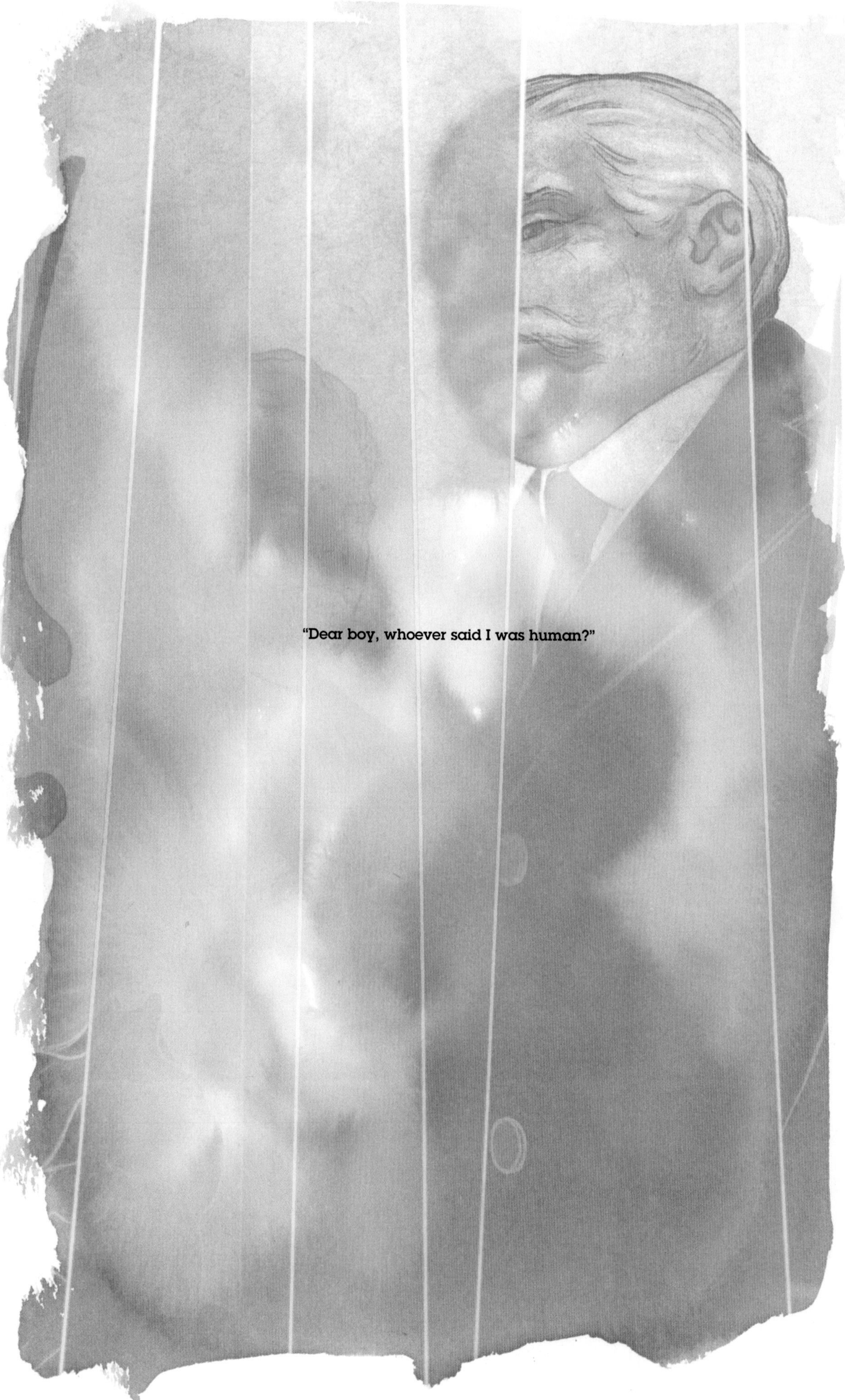

"Dear boy, whoever said I was human?"

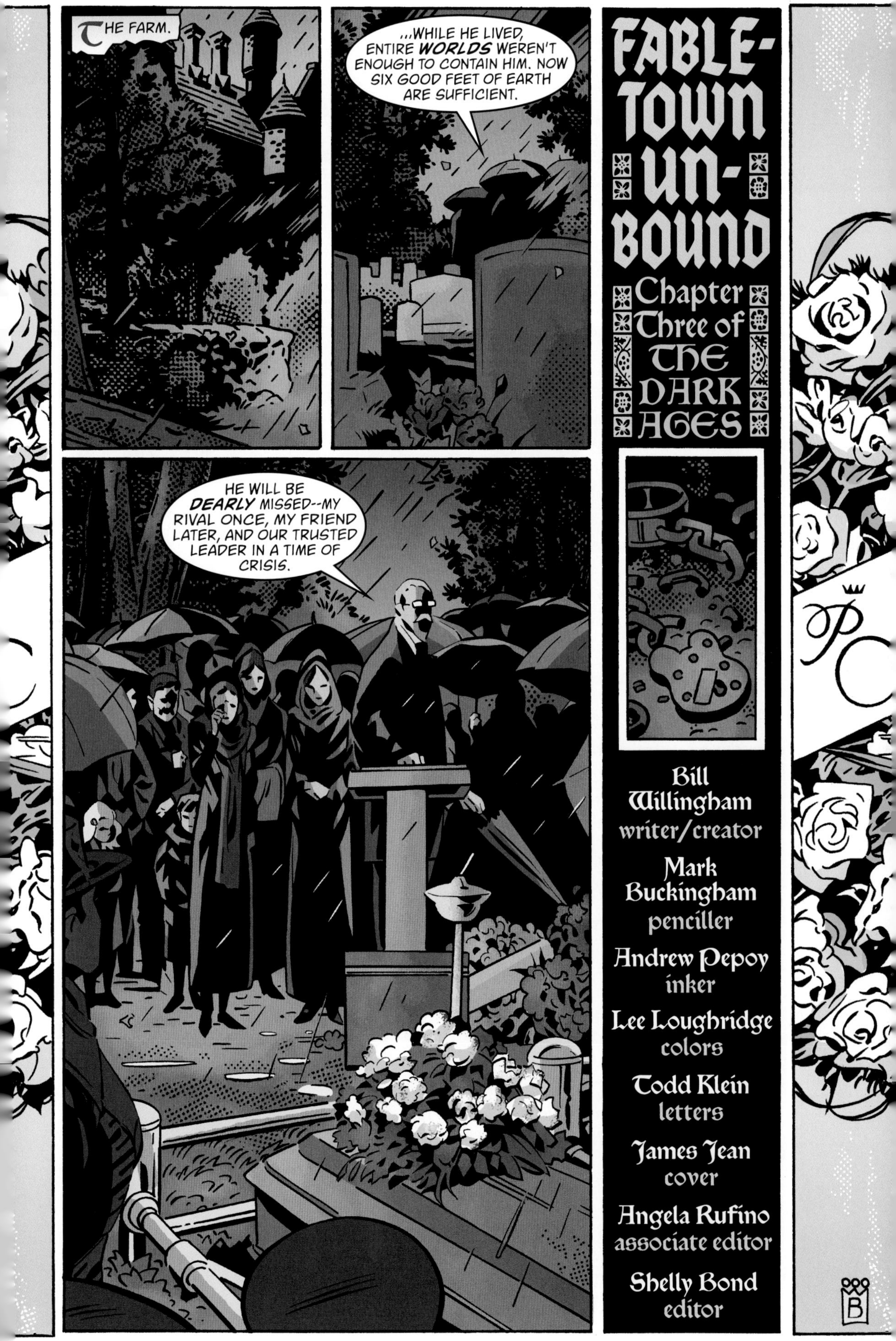
THE FARM.
...WHILE HE LIVED, ENTIRE WORLDS WEREN'T ENOUGH TO CONTAIN HIM. NOW SIX GOOD FEET OF EARTH ARE SUFFICIENT.
HE WILL BE DEARLY MISSED--MY RIVAL ONCE, MY FRIEND LATER, AND OUR TRUSTED LEADER IN A TIME OF CRISIS.
FABLE-TOWN UN-BOUND
Chapter Three of THE DARK AGES
Bill Willingham writer/creator
Mark Buckingham penciller
Andrew Pepoy inker
Lee Loughridge colors
Todd Klein letters
James Jean cover
Angela Rufino associate editor
Shelly Bond editor

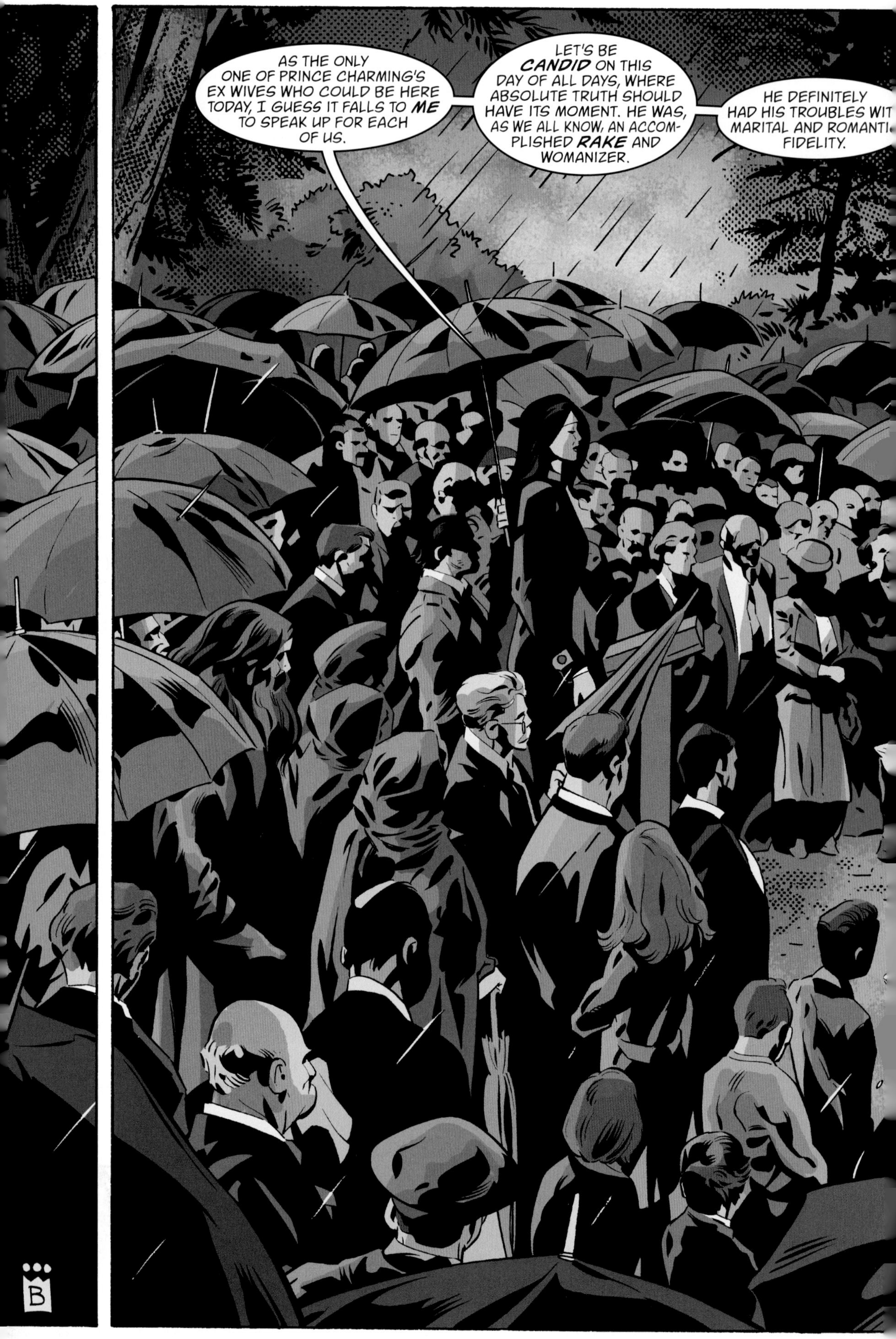
AS THE ONLY ONE OF PRINCE CHARMING'S EX WIVES WHO COULD BE HERE TODAY, I GUESS IT FALLS TO *ME* TO SPEAK UP FOR EACH OF US.
LET'S BE *CANDID* ON THIS DAY OF ALL DAYS, WHERE ABSOLUTE TRUTH SHOULD HAVE ITS MOMENT. HE WAS, AS WE ALL KNOW, AN ACCOMPLISHED *RAKE* AND WOMANIZER.
HE DEFINITELY HAD HIS TROUBLES WIT MARITAL AND ROMANTI FIDELITY.

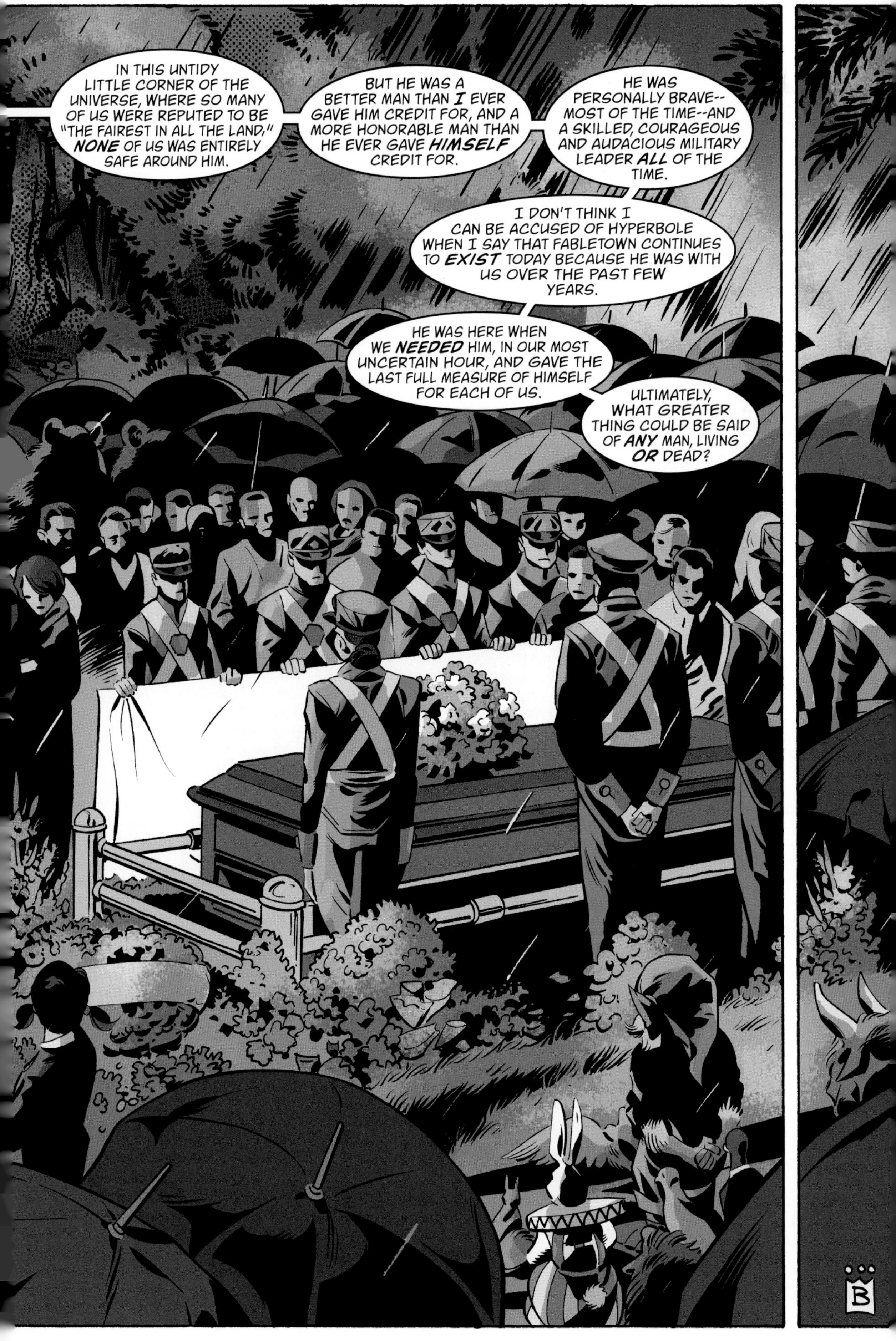
IN THIS UNTIDY LITTLE CORNER OF THE UNIVERSE, WHERE SO MANY OF US WERE REPUTED TO BE "THE FAIREST IN ALL THE LAND," NONE OF US WAS ENTIRELY SAFE AROUND HIM.
BUT HE WAS A BETTER MAN THAN I EVER GAVE HIM CREDIT FOR, AND A MORE HONORABLE MAN THAN HE EVER GAVE HIMSELF CREDIT FOR.
HE WAS PERSONALLY BRAVE--MOST OF THE TIME--AND A SKILLED, COURAGEOUS AND AUDACIOUS MILITARY LEADER ALL OF THE TIME.
I DON'T THINK I CAN BE ACCUSED OF HYPERBOLE WHEN I SAY THAT FABLETOWN CONTINUES TO EXIST TODAY BECAUSE HE WAS WITH US OVER THE PAST FEW YEARS.
HE WAS HERE WHEN WE NEEDED HIM, IN OUR MOST UNCERTAIN HOUR, AND GAVE THE LAST FULL MEASURE OF HIMSELF FOR EACH OF US.
ULTIMATELY, WHAT GREATER THING COULD BE SAID OF ANY MAN, LIVING OR DEAD?

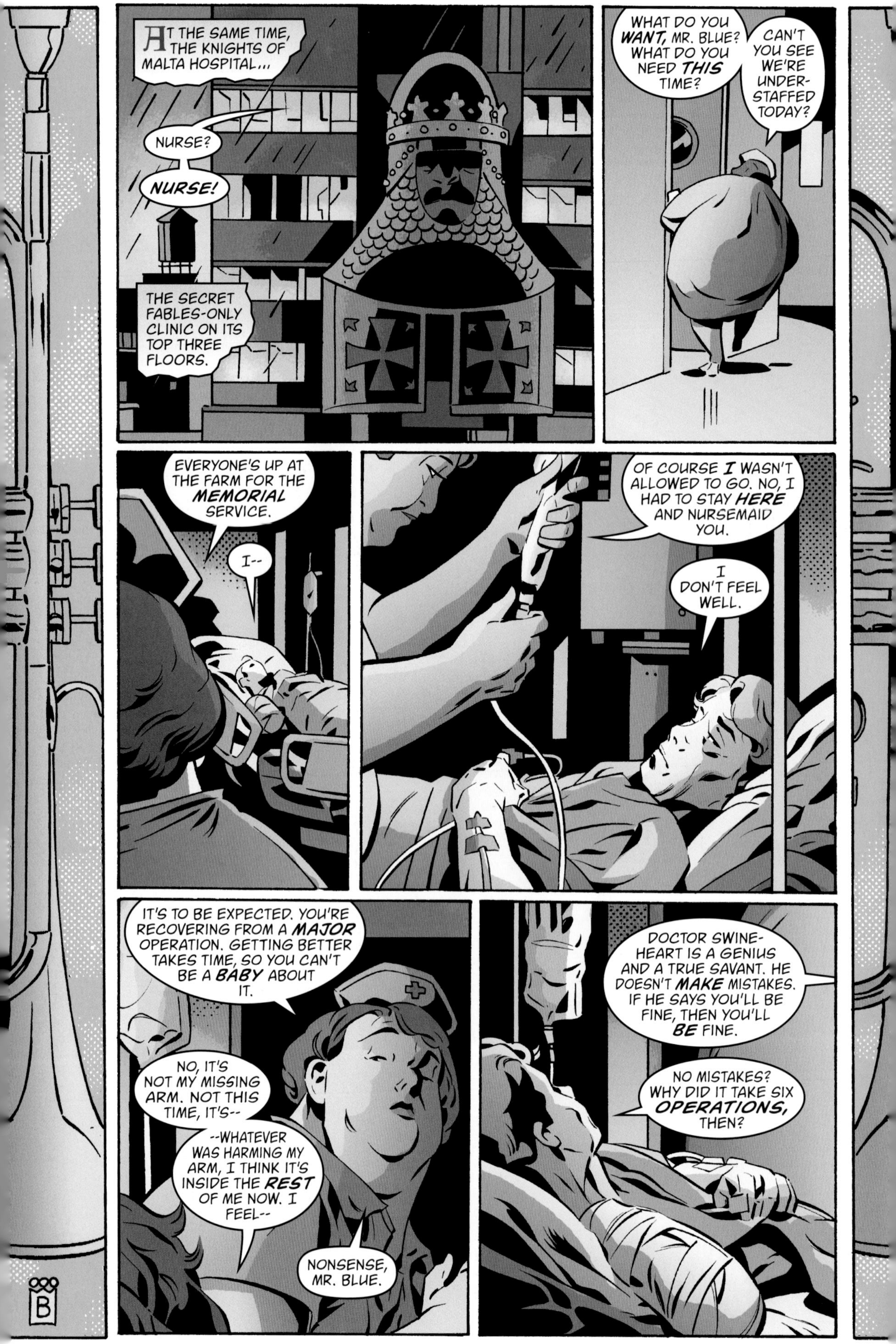
AT THE SAME TIME, THE KNIGHTS OF MALTA HOSPITAL...
NURSE?
NURSE!
THE SECRET FABLES-ONLY CLINIC ON ITS TOP THREE FLOORS.
WHAT DO YOU WANT, MR. BLUE? WHAT DO YOU NEED THIS TIME?
CAN'T YOU SEE WE'RE UNDER-STAFFED TODAY?
EVERYONE'S UP AT THE FARM FOR THE MEMORIAL SERVICE.
I--
OF COURSE I WASN'T ALLOWED TO GO. NO, I HAD TO STAY HERE AND NURSEMAID YOU.
I DON'T FEEL WELL.
IT'S TO BE EXPECTED. YOU'RE RECOVERING FROM A MAJOR OPERATION. GETTING BETTER TAKES TIME, SO YOU CAN'T BE A BABY ABOUT IT.
NO, IT'S NOT MY MISSING ARM. NOT THIS TIME, IT'S--
--WHATEVER WAS HARMING MY ARM, I THINK IT'S INSIDE THE REST OF ME NOW. I FEEL--
NONSENSE, MR. BLUE.
DOCTOR SWINE-HEART IS A GENIUS AND A TRUE SAVANT. HE DOESN'T MAKE MISTAKES. IF HE SAYS YOU'LL BE FINE, THEN YOU'LL BE FINE.
NO MISTAKES? WHY DID IT TAKE SIX OPERATIONS, THEN?

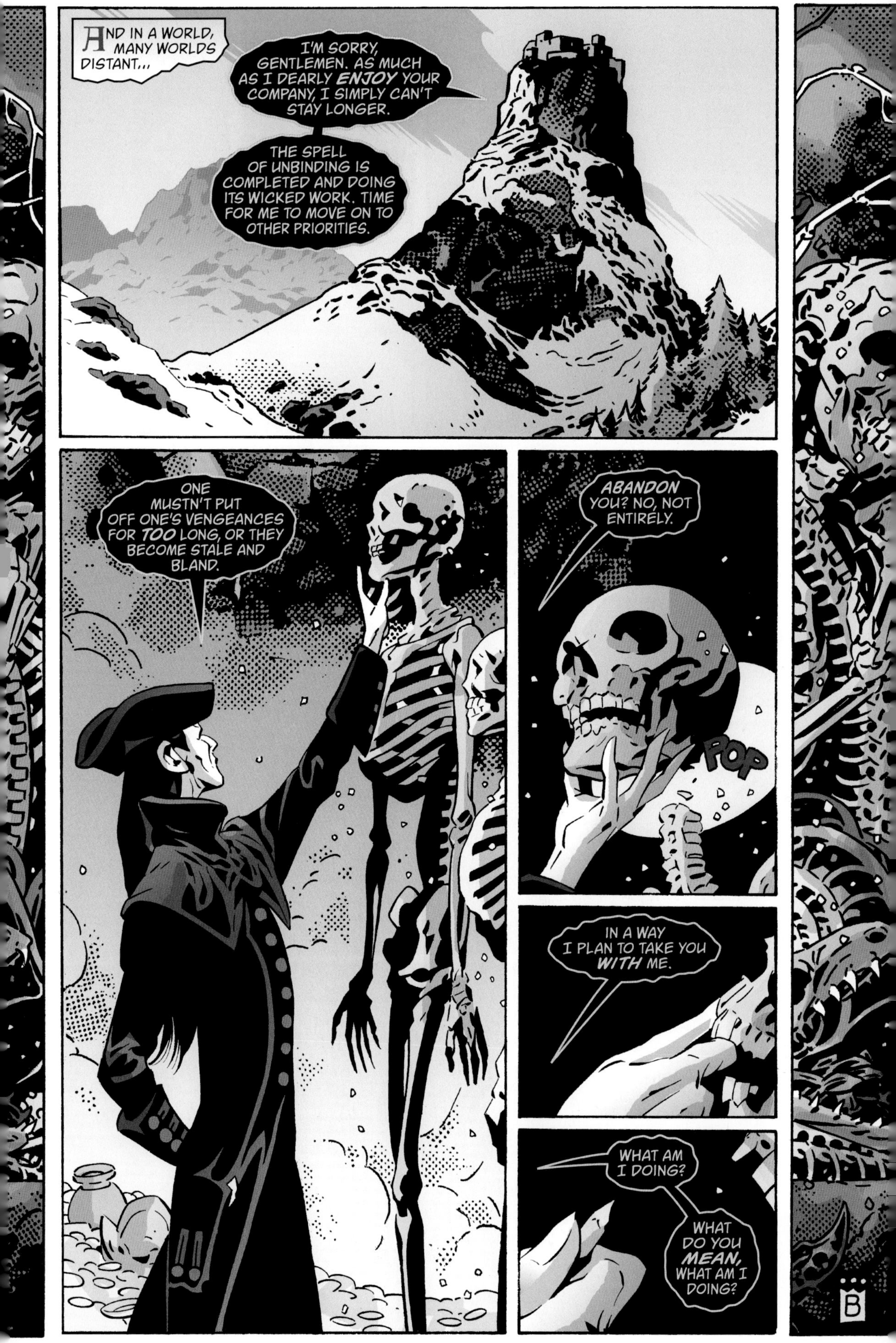
AND IN A WORLD, MANY WORLDS DISTANT...
I'M SORRY, GENTLEMEN. AS MUCH AS I DEARLY ENJOY YOUR COMPANY, I SIMPLY CAN'T STAY LONGER.
THE SPELL OF UNBINDING IS COMPLETED AND DOING ITS WICKED WORK. TIME FOR ME TO MOVE ON TO OTHER PRIORITIES.
ONE MUSTN'T PUT OFF ONE'S VENGEANCES FOR TOO LONG, OR THEY BECOME STALE AND BLAND.
ABANDON YOU? NO, NOT ENTIRELY.
POP
IN A WAY I PLAN TO TAKE YOU WITH ME.
WHAT AM I DOING?
WHAT DO YOU MEAN, WHAT AM I DOING?
B

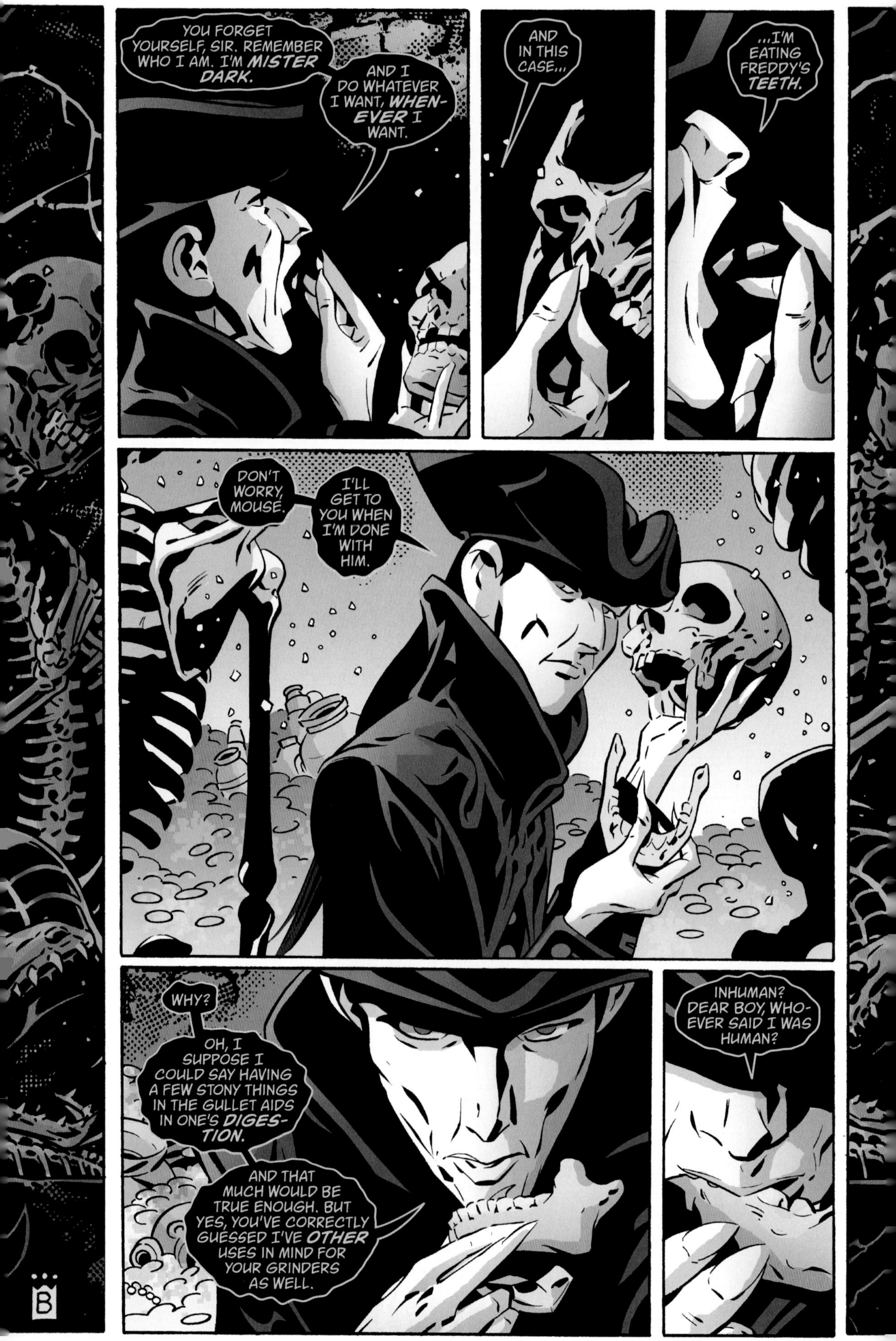
YOU FORGET YOURSELF, SIR. REMEMBER WHO I AM. I'M MISTER DARK.
AND I DO WHATEVER I WANT, WHENEVER I WANT.
AND IN THIS CASE...
...I'M EATING FREDDY'S TEETH.
DON'T WORRY, MOUSE.
I'LL GET TO YOU WHEN I'M DONE WITH HIM.
WHY?
OH, I SUPPOSE I COULD SAY HAVING A FEW STONY THINGS IN THE GULLET AIDS IN ONE'S DIGESTION.
AND THAT MUCH WOULD BE TRUE ENOUGH. BUT YES, YOU'VE CORRECTLY GUESSED I'VE OTHER USES IN MIND FOR YOUR GRINDERS AS WELL.
INHUMAN? DEAR BOY, WHOEVER SAID I WAS HUMAN?

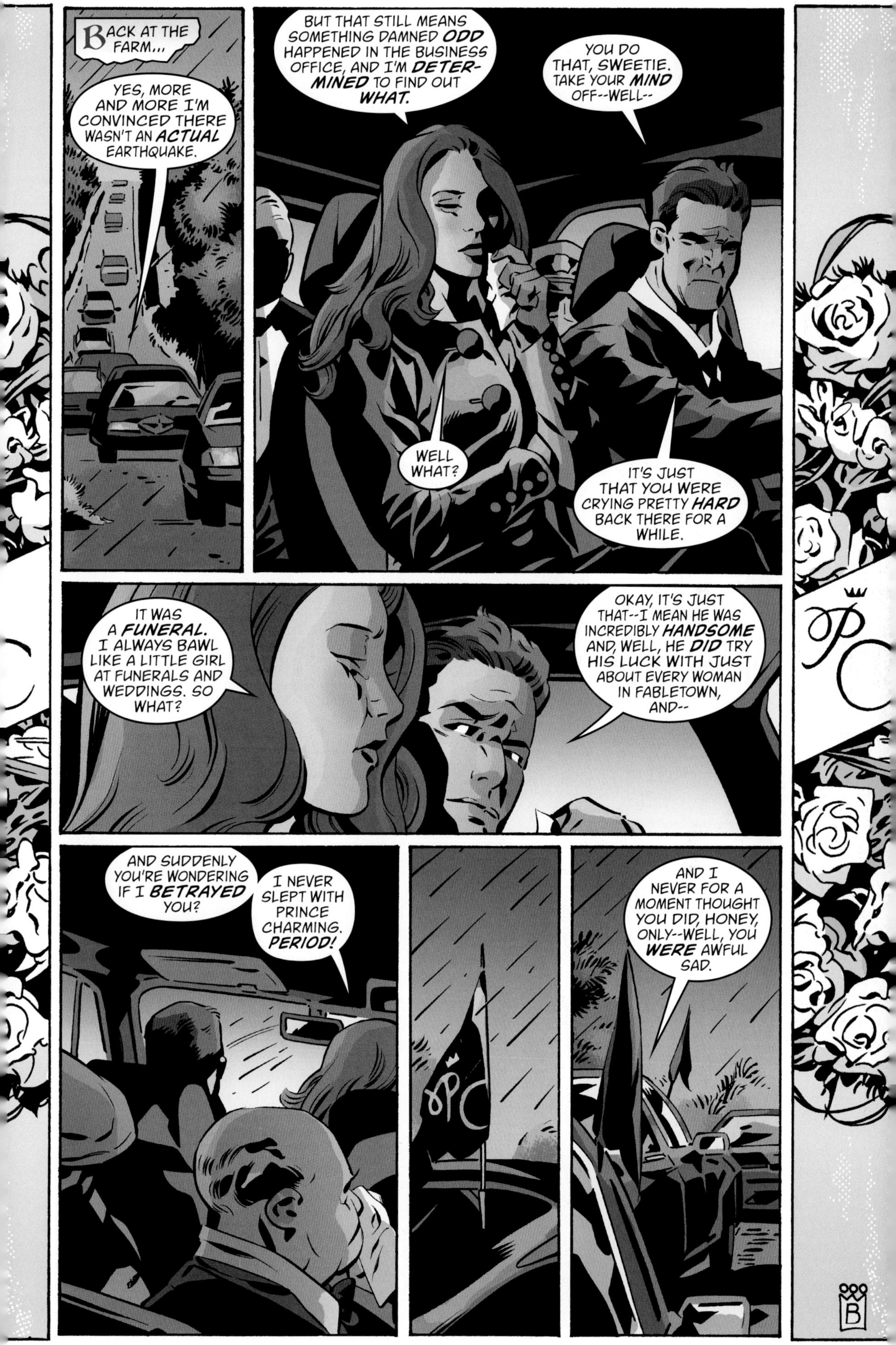
BACK AT THE FARM...
YES, MORE AND MORE I'M CONVINCED THERE WASN'T AN ACTUAL EARTHQUAKE.
BUT THAT STILL MEANS SOMETHING DAMNED ODD HAPPENED IN THE BUSINESS OFFICE, AND I'M DETERMINED TO FIND OUT WHAT.
YOU DO THAT, SWEETIE. TAKE YOUR MIND OFF--WELL--
WELL WHAT?
IT'S JUST THAT YOU WERE CRYING PRETTY HARD BACK THERE FOR A WHILE.
IT WAS A FUNERAL. I ALWAYS BAWL LIKE A LITTLE GIRL AT FUNERALS AND WEDDINGS. SO WHAT?
OKAY, IT'S JUST THAT--I MEAN HE WAS INCREDIBLY HANDSOME AND, WELL, HE DID TRY HIS LUCK WITH JUST ABOUT EVERY WOMAN IN FABLETOWN, AND--
AND SUDDENLY YOU'RE WONDERING IF I BETRAYED YOU?
I NEVER SLEPT WITH PRINCE CHARMING. PERIOD!
AND I NEVER FOR A MOMENT THOUGHT YOU DID, HONEY, ONLY--WELL, YOU WERE AWFUL SAD.

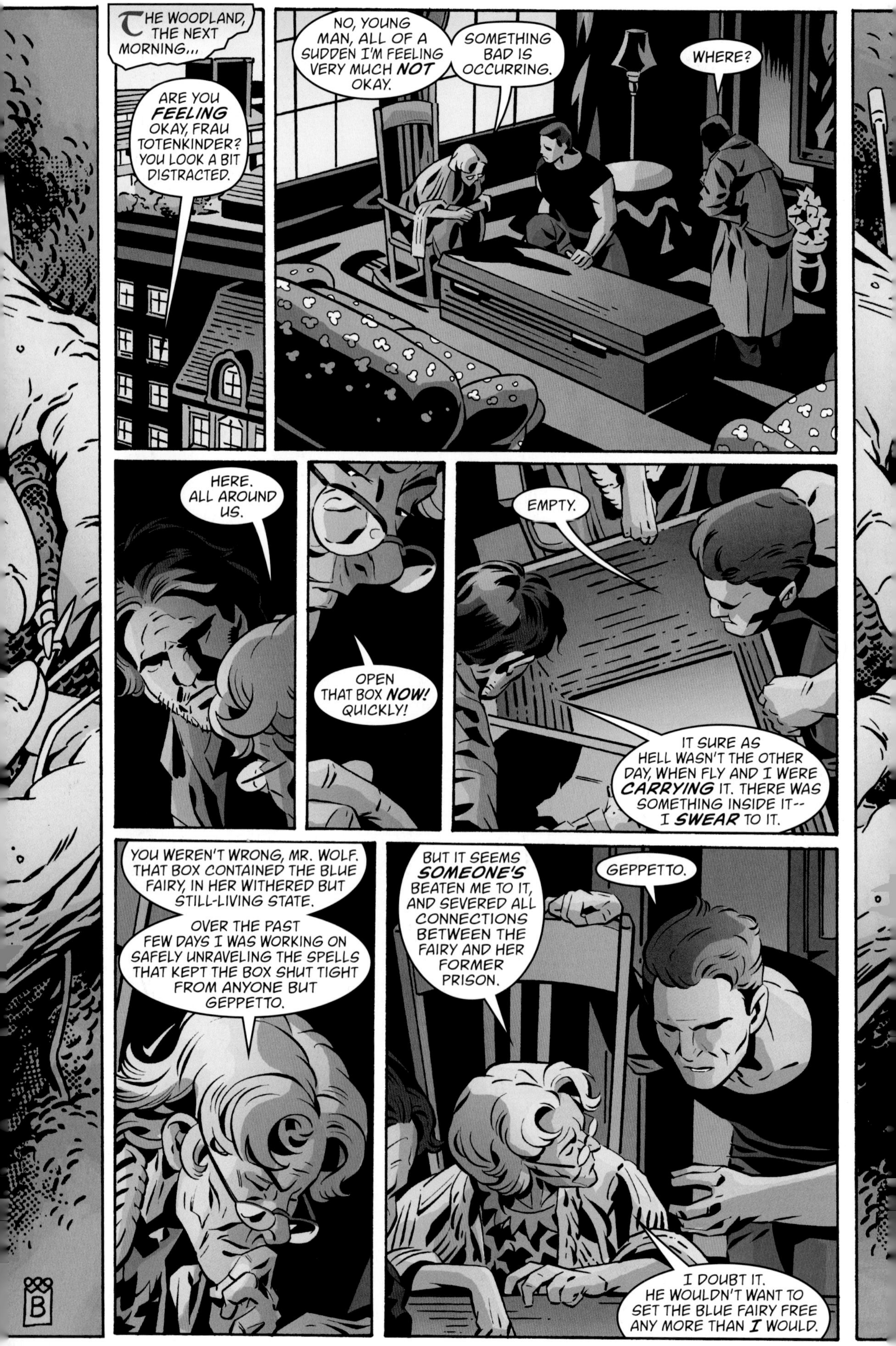
THE WOODLAND, THE NEXT MORNING...
ARE YOU FEELING OKAY, FRAU TOTENKINDER? YOU LOOK A BIT DISTRACTED.
NO, YOUNG MAN, ALL OF A SUDDEN I'M FEELING VERY MUCH NOT OKAY.
SOMETHING BAD IS OCCURRING.
WHERE?
HERE. ALL AROUND US.
OPEN THAT BOX NOW! QUICKLY!
EMPTY.
IT SURE AS HELL WASN'T THE OTHER DAY, WHEN FLY AND I WERE CARRYING IT. THERE WAS SOMETHING INSIDE IT-- I SWEAR TO IT.
YOU WEREN'T WRONG, MR. WOLF. THAT BOX CONTAINED THE BLUE FAIRY, IN HER WITHERED BUT STILL-LIVING STATE.
OVER THE PAST FEW DAYS I WAS WORKING ON SAFELY UNRAVELING THE SPELLS THAT KEPT THE BOX SHUT TIGHT FROM ANYONE BUT GEPPETTO.
BUT IT SEEMS SOMEONE'S BEATEN ME TO IT, AND SEVERED ALL CONNECTIONS BETWEEN THE FAIRY AND HER FORMER PRISON.
GEPPETTO.
I DOUBT IT. HE WOULDN'T WANT TO SET THE BLUE FAIRY FREE ANY MORE THAN I WOULD.

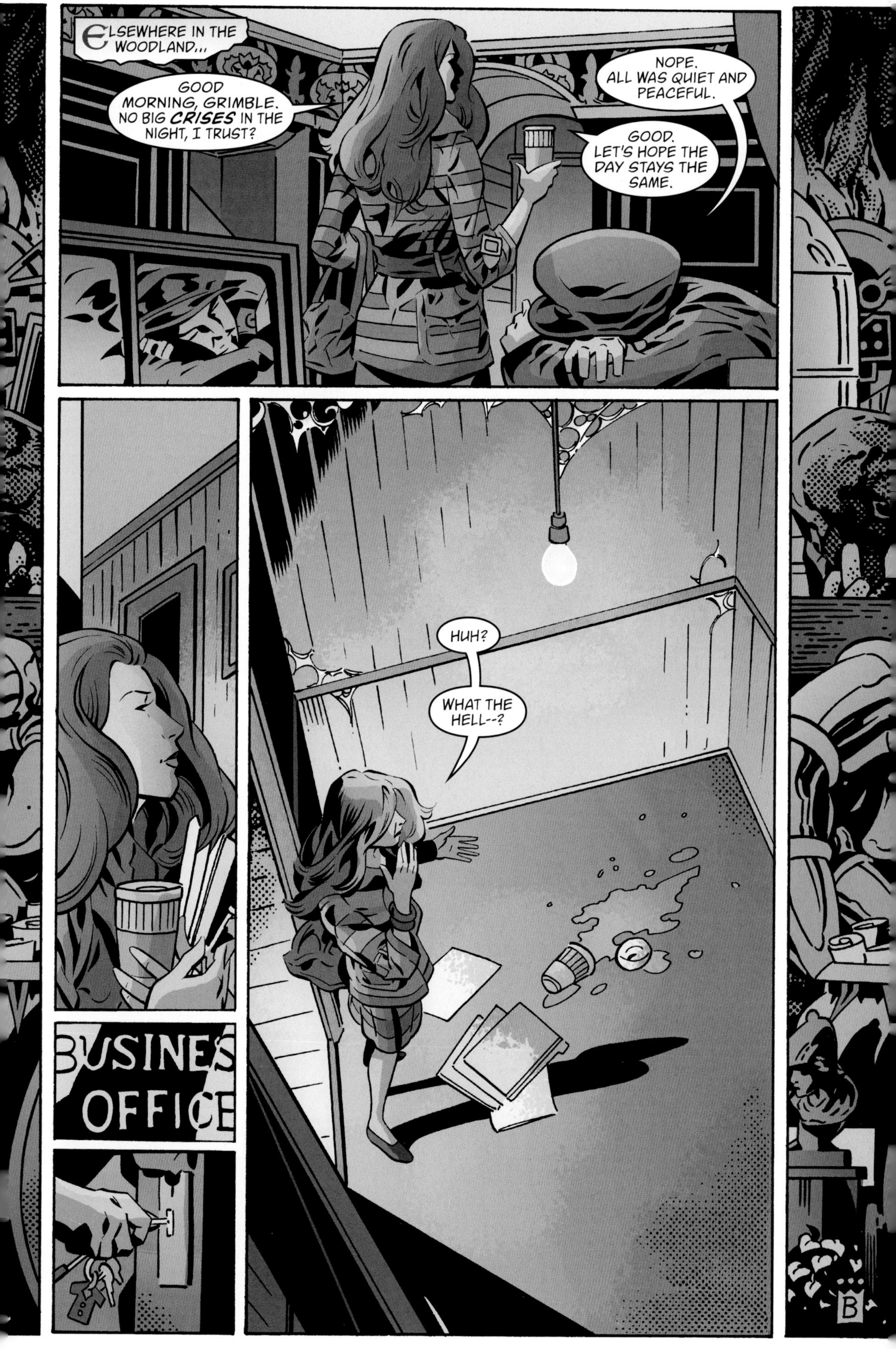
ELSEWHERE IN THE WOODLAND...
GOOD MORNING, GRIMBLE. NO BIG *CRISES* IN THE NIGHT, I TRUST?
NOPE. ALL WAS QUIET AND PEACEFUL.
GOOD. LET'S HOPE THE DAY STAYS THE SAME.
BUSINES OFFICE
HUH?
WHAT THE HELL--?

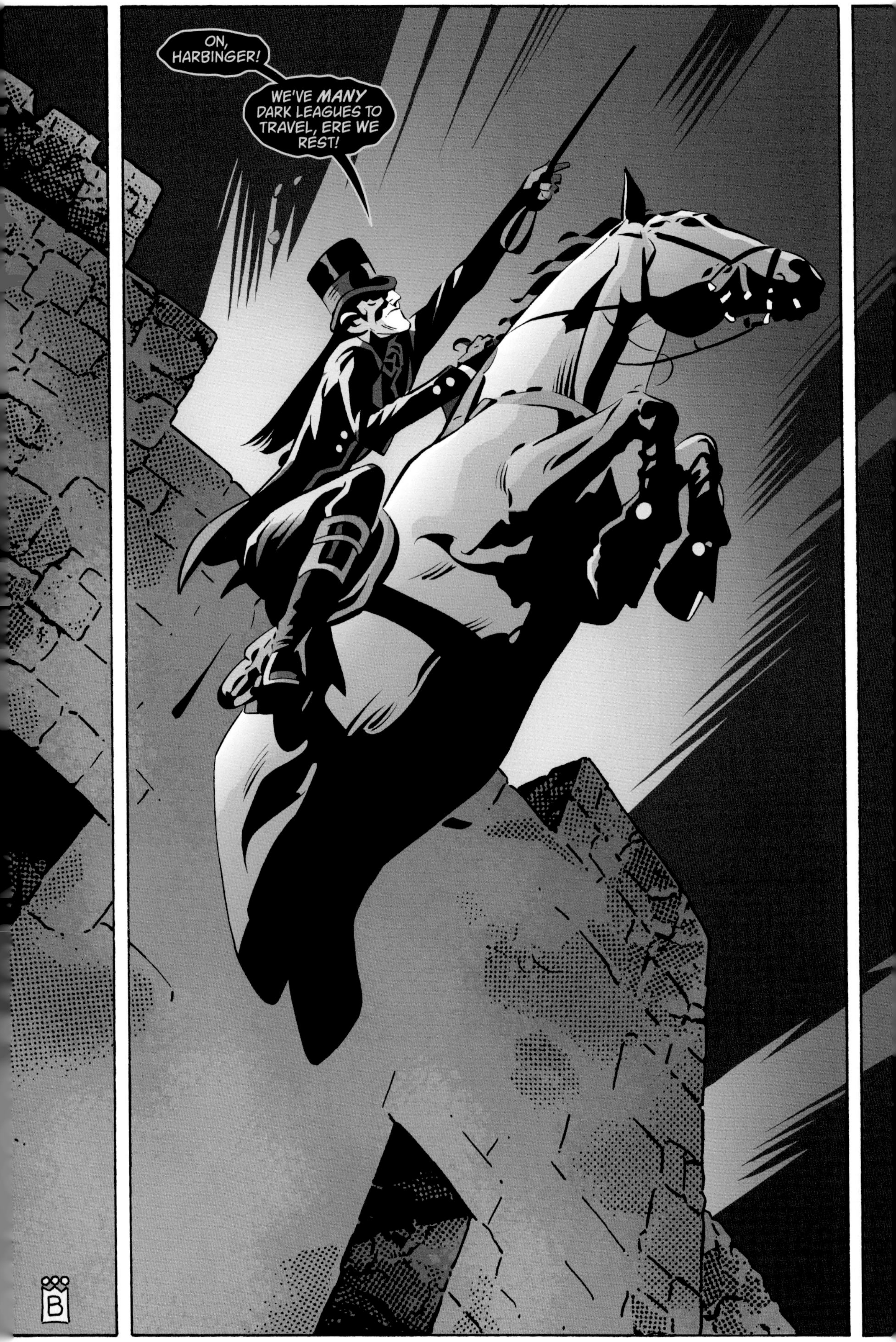
ON, HARBINGER!
WE'VE MANY DARK LEAGUES TO TRAVEL, ERE WE REST!
B

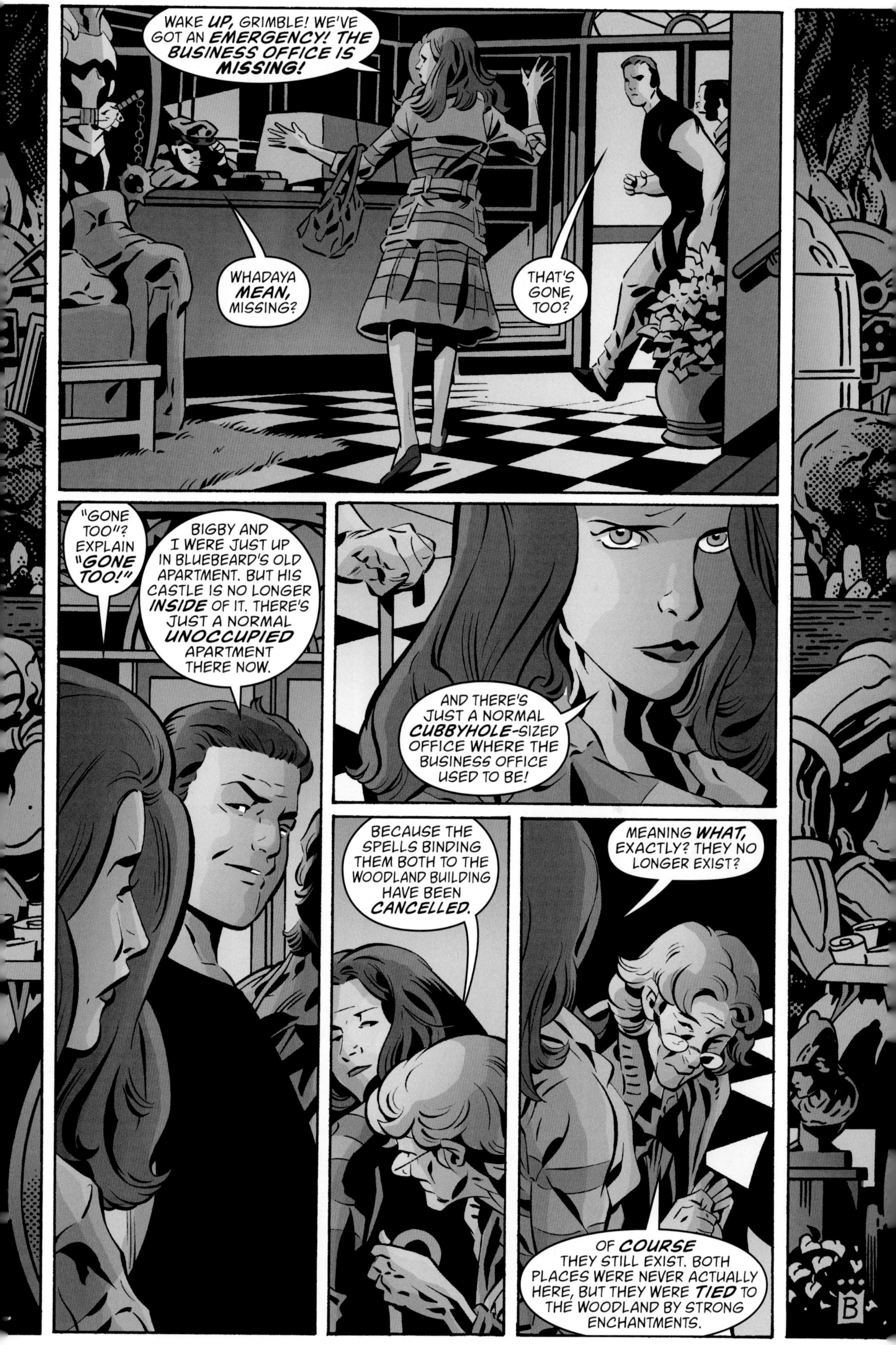

WAKE UP, GRIMBLE! WE'VE GOT AN EMERGENCY! THE BUSINESS OFFICE IS MISSING!
WHADAYA MEAN, MISSING?
THAT'S GONE, TOO?
"GONE TOO"? EXPLAIN "GONE TOO!"
BIGBY AND I WERE JUST UP IN BLUEBEARD'S OLD APARTMENT. BUT HIS CASTLE IS NO LONGER INSIDE OF IT. THERE'S JUST A NORMAL UNOCCUPIED APARTMENT THERE NOW.
AND THERE'S JUST A NORMAL CUBBYHOLE-SIZED OFFICE WHERE THE BUSINESS OFFICE USED TO BE!
BECAUSE THE SPELLS BINDING THEM BOTH TO THE WOODLAND BUILDING HAVE BEEN CANCELLED.
MEANING WHAT, EXACTLY? THEY NO LONGER EXIST?
OF COURSE THEY STILL EXIST. BOTH PLACES WERE NEVER ACTUALLY HERE, BUT THEY WERE TIED TO THE WOODLAND BY STRONG ENCHANTMENTS.

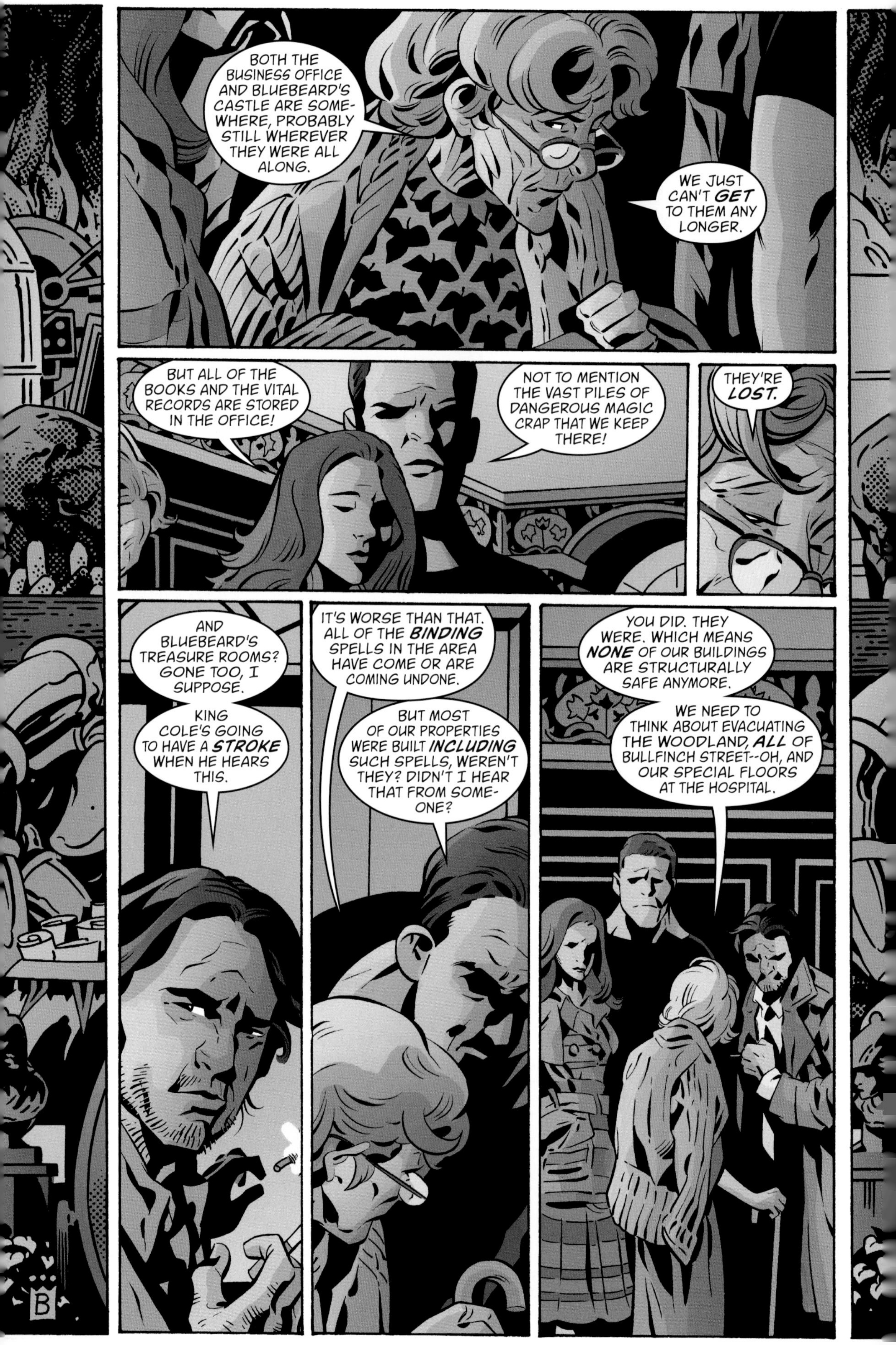
BOTH THE BUSINESS OFFICE AND BLUEBEARD'S CASTLE ARE SOMEWHERE, PROBABLY STILL WHEREVER THEY WERE ALL ALONG.
WE JUST CAN'T *GET* TO THEM ANY LONGER.
BUT ALL OF THE BOOKS AND THE VITAL RECORDS ARE STORED IN THE OFFICE!
NOT TO MENTION THE VAST PILES OF DANGEROUS MAGIC CRAP THAT WE KEEP THERE!
THEY'RE *LOST.*
AND BLUEBEARD'S TREASURE ROOMS? GONE TOO, I SUPPOSE.
KING COLE'S GOING TO HAVE A *STROKE* WHEN HE HEARS THIS.
IT'S WORSE THAN THAT. ALL OF THE *BINDING* SPELLS IN THE AREA HAVE COME OR ARE COMING UNDONE.
BUT MOST OF OUR PROPERTIES WERE BUILT *INCLUDING* SUCH SPELLS, WEREN'T THEY? DIDN'T I HEAR THAT FROM SOMEONE?
YOU DID. THEY WERE. WHICH MEANS *NONE* OF OUR BUILDINGS ARE STRUCTURALLY SAFE ANYMORE.
WE NEED TO THINK ABOUT EVACUATING THE WOODLAND, *ALL* OF BULLFINCH STREET--OH, AND OUR SPECIAL FLOORS AT THE HOSPITAL.

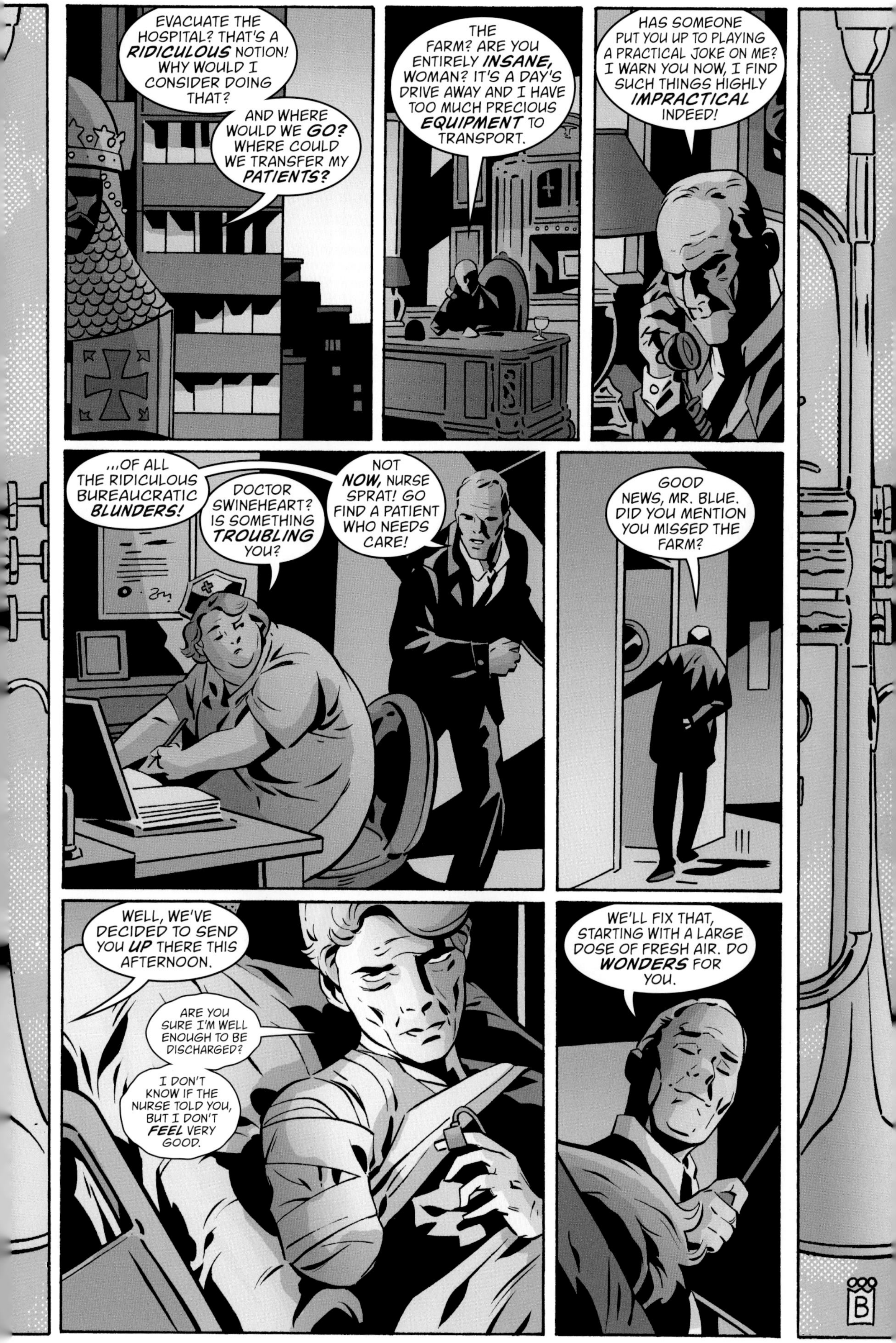
EVACUATE THE HOSPITAL? THAT'S A RIDICULOUS NOTION! WHY WOULD I CONSIDER DOING THAT?
AND WHERE WOULD WE GO? WHERE COULD WE TRANSFER MY PATIENTS?
THE FARM? ARE YOU ENTIRELY INSANE, WOMAN? IT'S A DAY'S DRIVE AWAY AND I HAVE TOO MUCH PRECIOUS EQUIPMENT TO TRANSPORT.
HAS SOMEONE PUT YOU UP TO PLAYING A PRACTICAL JOKE ON ME? I WARN YOU NOW, I FIND SUCH THINGS HIGHLY IMPRACTICAL INDEED!
...OF ALL THE RIDICULOUS BUREAUCRATIC BLUNDERS!
DOCTOR SWINEHEART? IS SOMETHING TROUBLING YOU?
NOT NOW, NURSE SPRAT! GO FIND A PATIENT WHO NEEDS CARE!
GOOD NEWS, MR. BLUE. DID YOU MENTION YOU MISSED THE FARM?
WELL, WE'VE DECIDED TO SEND YOU UP THERE THIS AFTERNOON.
ARE YOU SURE I'M WELL ENOUGH TO BE DISCHARGED?
I DON'T KNOW IF THE NURSE TOLD YOU, BUT I DON'T FEEL VERY GOOD.
WE'LL FIX THAT, STARTING WITH A LARGE DOSE OF FRESH AIR. DO WONDERS FOR YOU.

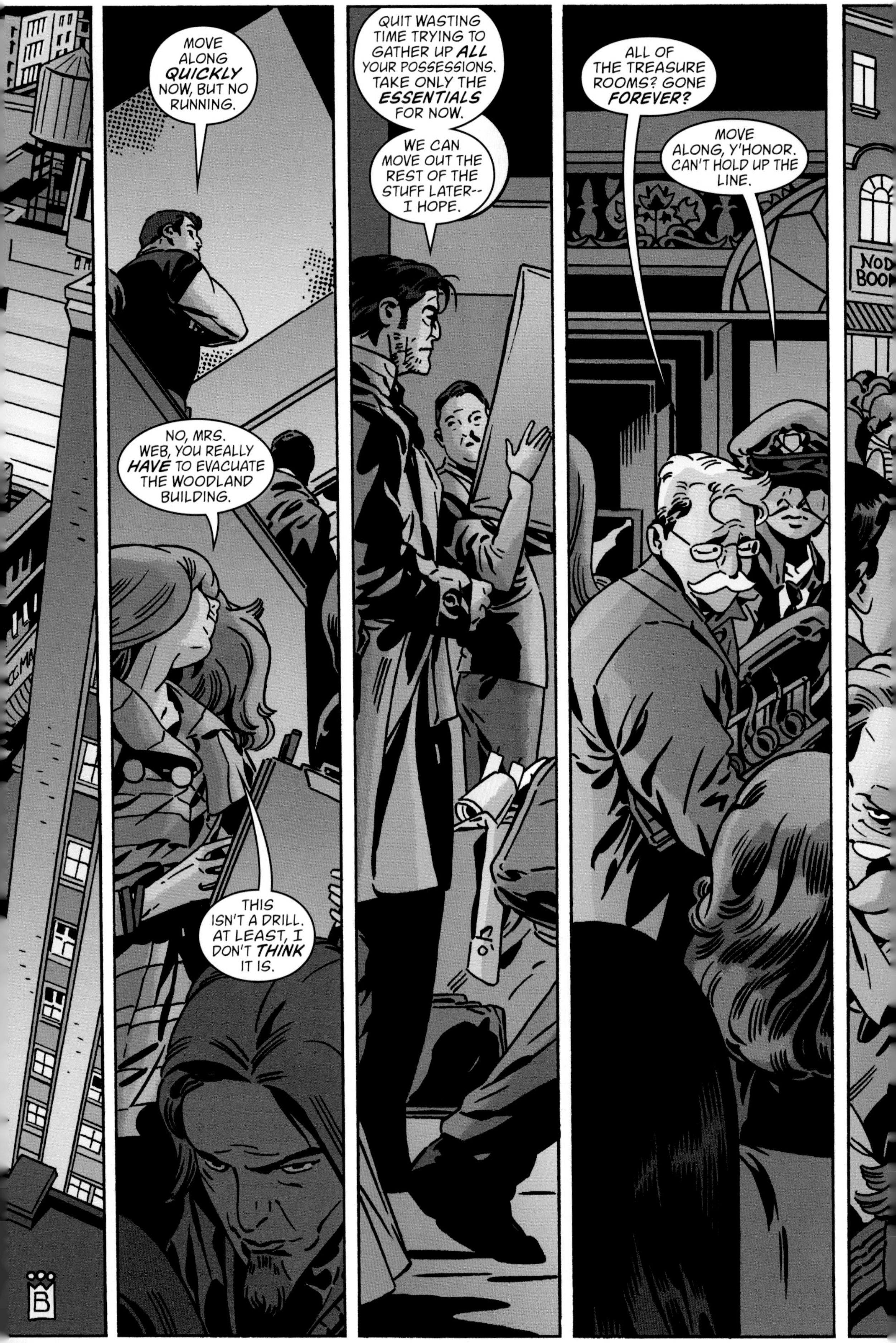
MOVE ALONG QUICKLY NOW, BUT NO RUNNING.
NO, MRS. WEB, YOU REALLY HAVE TO EVACUATE THE WOODLAND BUILDING.
THIS ISN'T A DRILL. AT LEAST, I DON'T THINK IT IS.
QUIT WASTING TIME TRYING TO GATHER UP ALL YOUR POSSESSIONS. TAKE ONLY THE ESSENTIALS FOR NOW.
WE CAN MOVE OUT THE REST OF THE STUFF LATER-- I HOPE.
ALL OF THE TREASURE ROOMS? GONE FOREVER?
MOVE ALONG, Y'HONOR. CAN'T HOLD UP THE LINE.

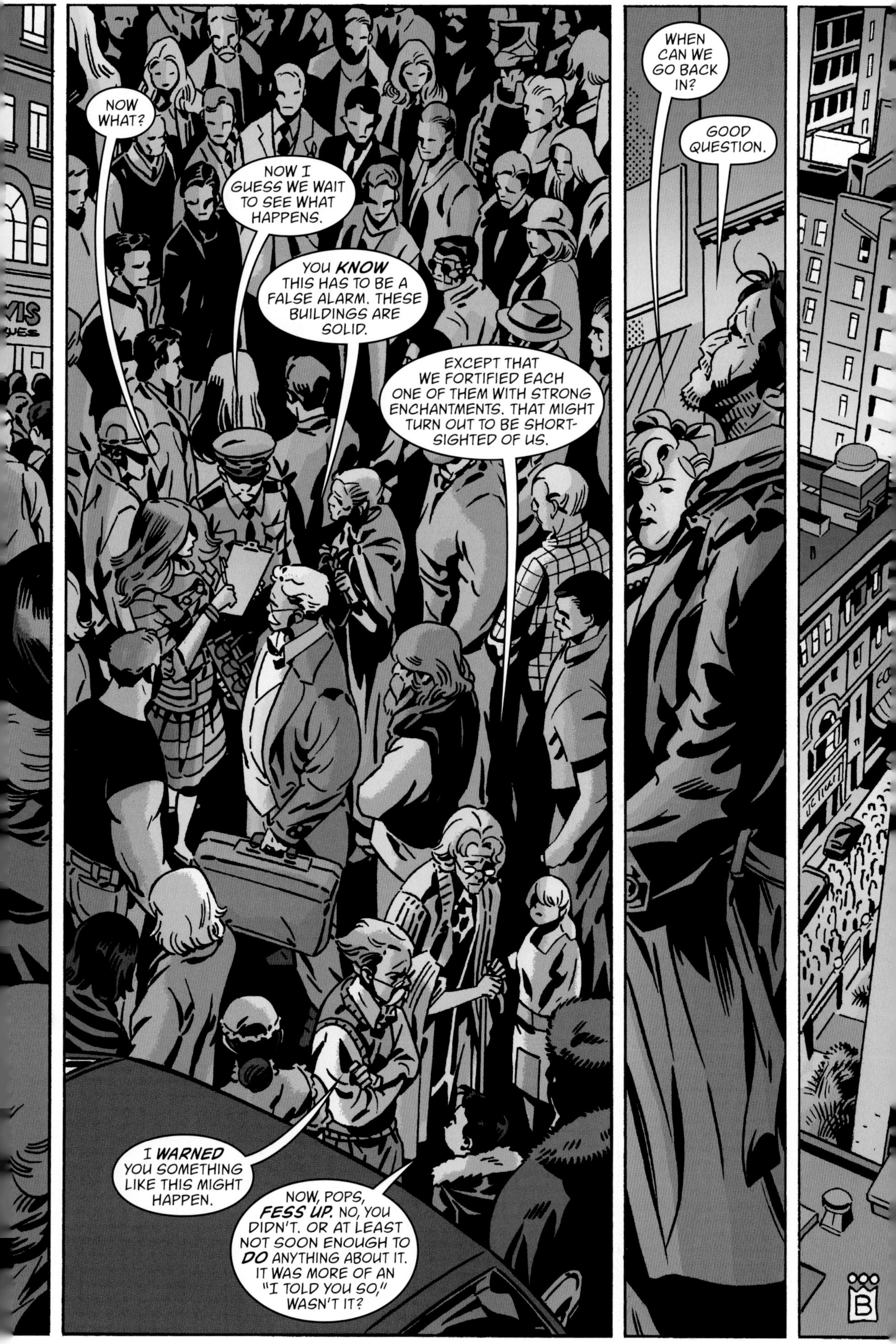
NOW WHAT?
NOW I GUESS WE WAIT TO SEE WHAT HAPPENS.
YOU *KNOW* THIS HAS TO BE A FALSE ALARM. THESE BUILDINGS ARE SOLID.
EXCEPT THAT WE FORTIFIED EACH ONE OF THEM WITH STRONG ENCHANTMENTS. THAT MIGHT TURN OUT TO BE SHORT-SIGHTED OF US.
I *WARNED* YOU SOMETHING LIKE THIS MIGHT HAPPEN.
NOW, POPS, ***FESS UP.*** NO, YOU DIDN'T. OR AT LEAST NOT SOON ENOUGH TO ***DO*** ANYTHING ABOUT IT. IT WAS MORE OF AN "I TOLD YOU SO," WASN'T IT?
WHEN CAN WE GO BACK IN?
GOOD QUESTION.

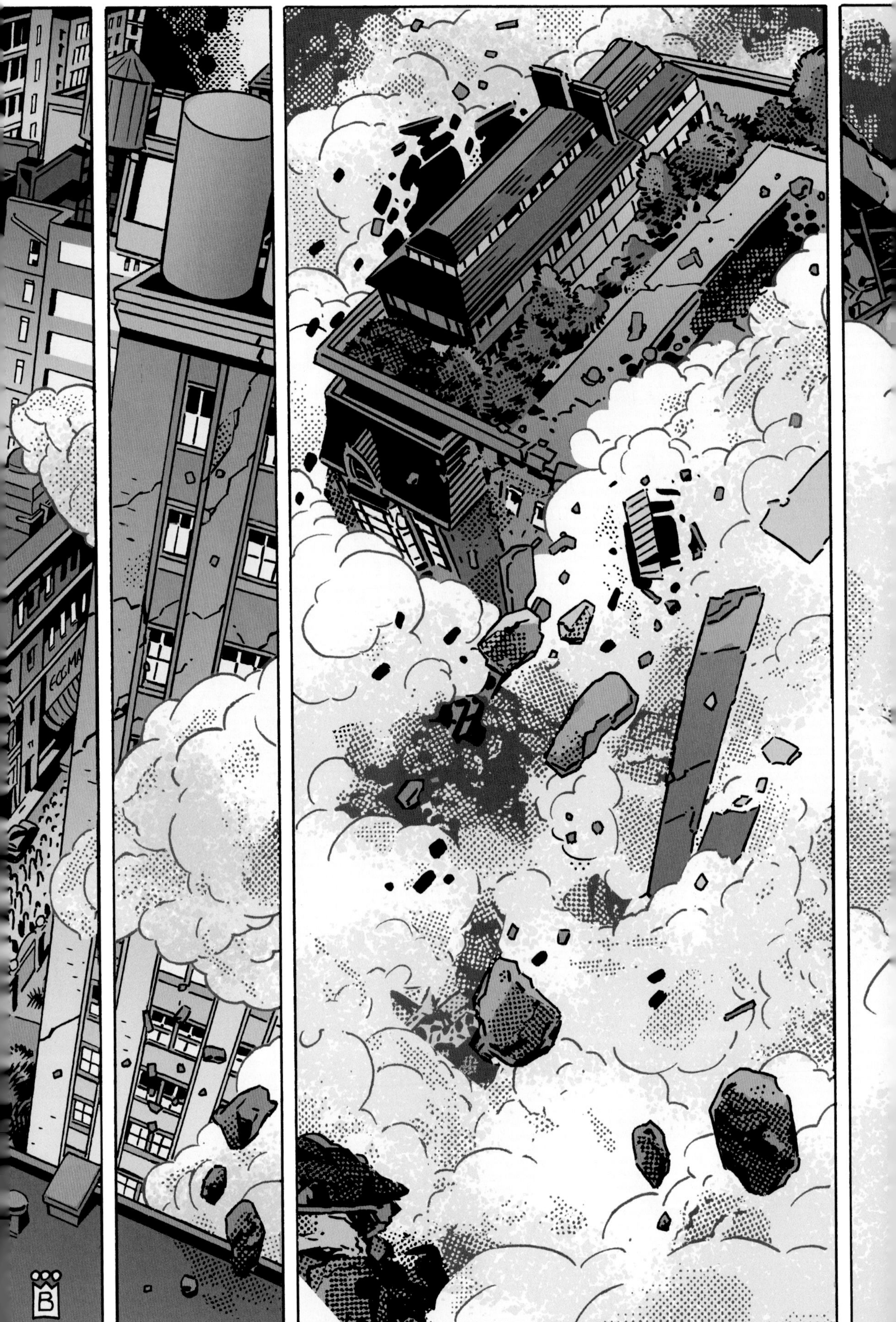

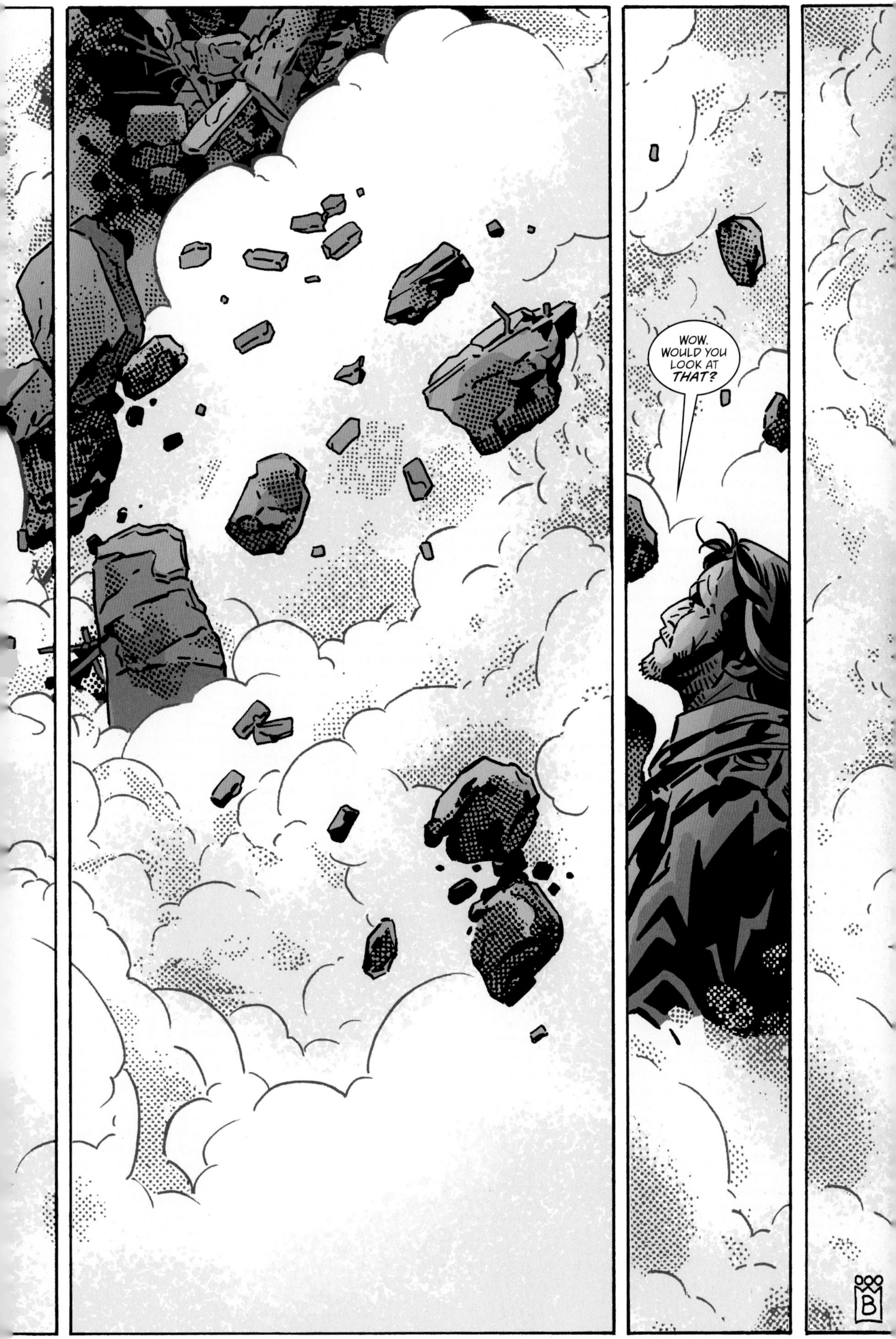
WOW. WOULD YOU LOOK AT THAT?

NEXT: OUR DARKEST HOUR

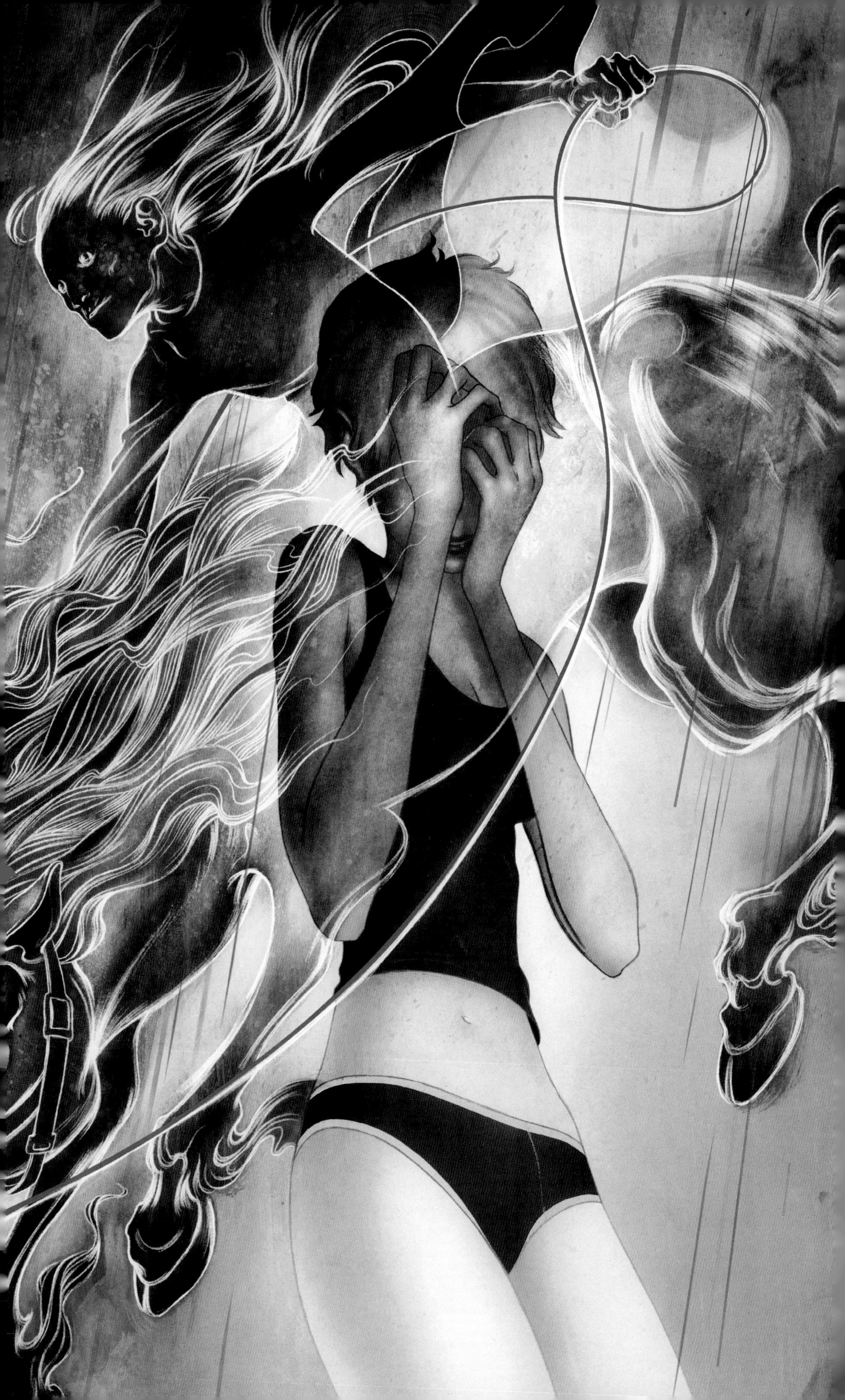

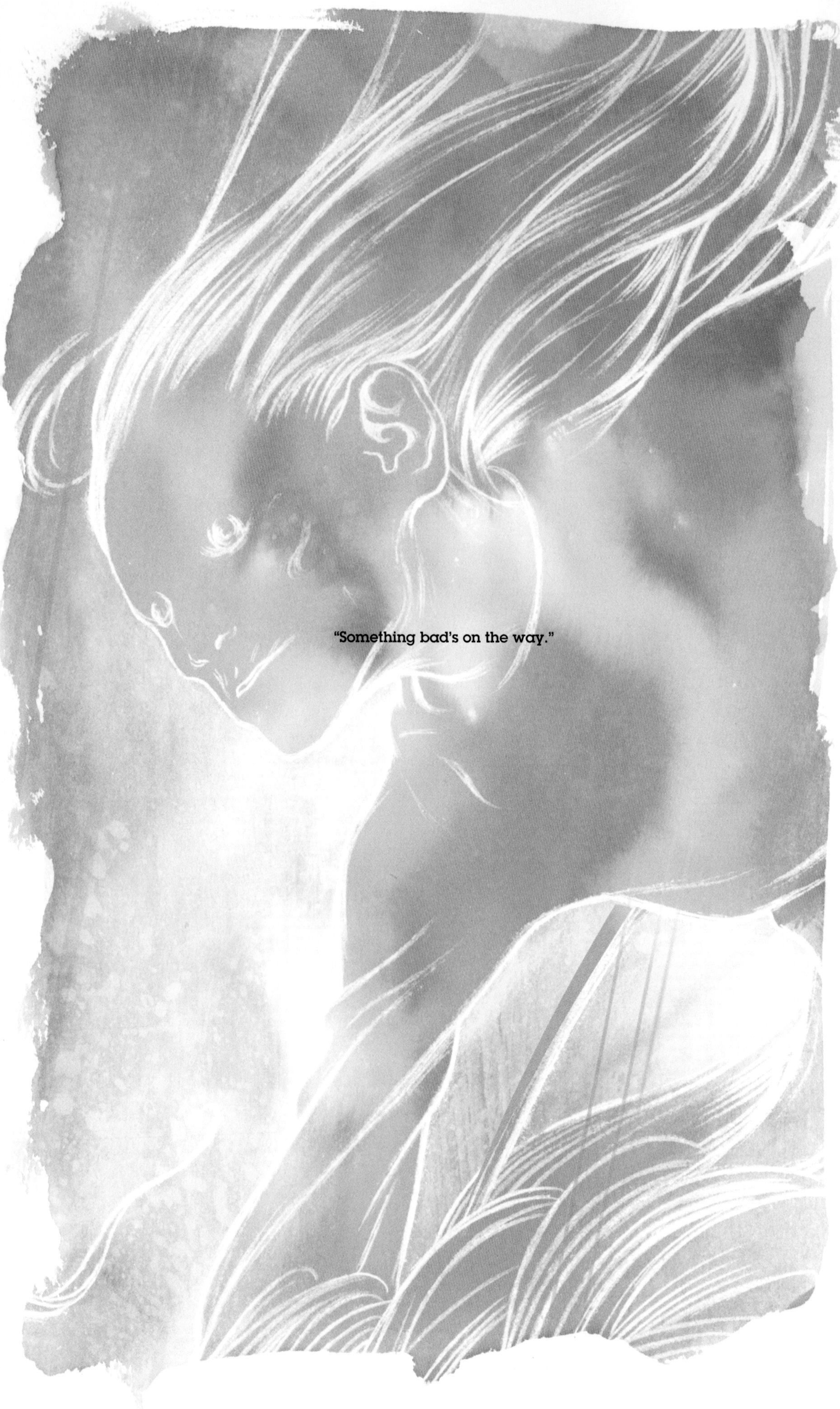
"Something bad's on the way."

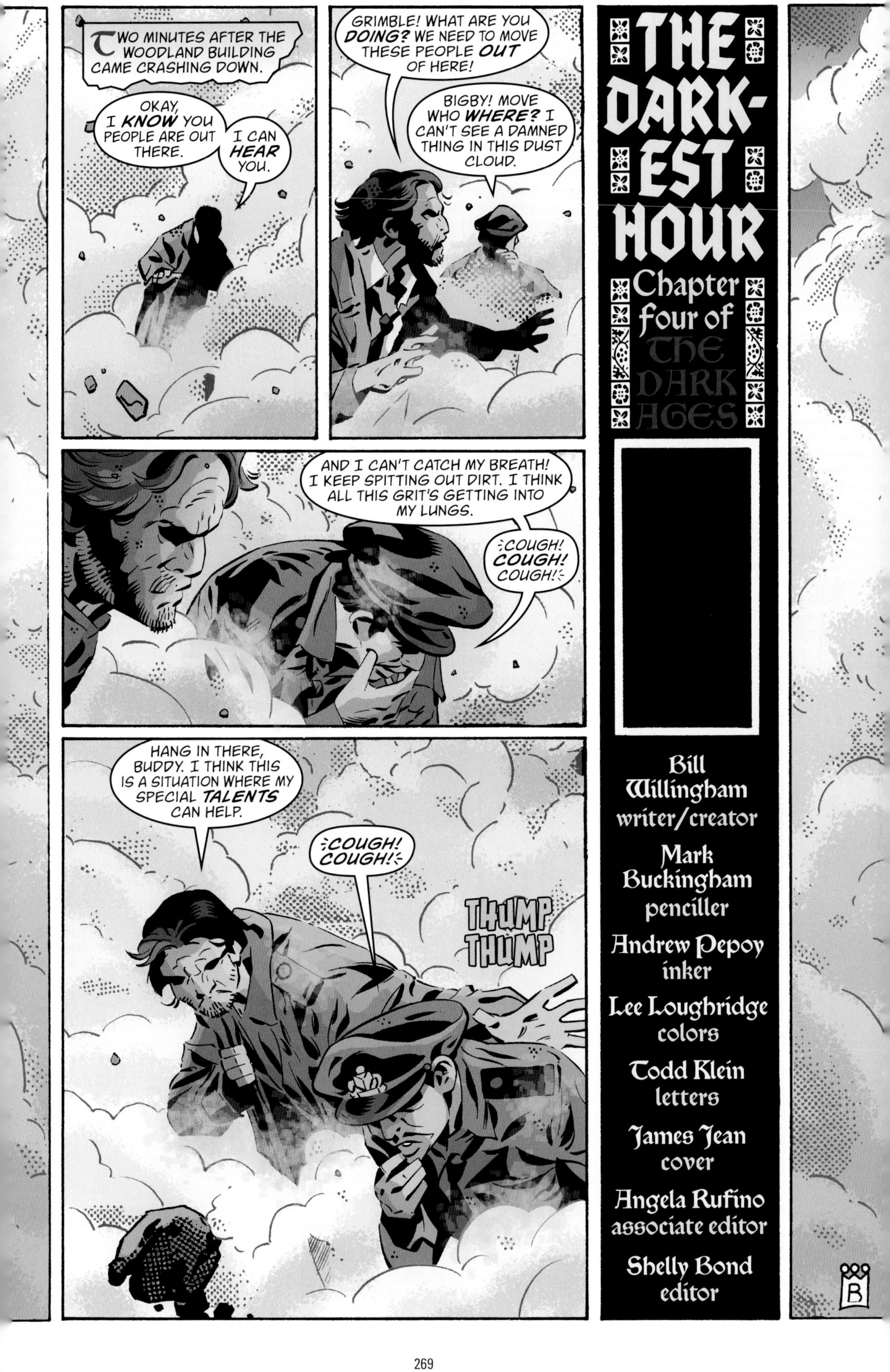
TWO MINUTES AFTER THE WOODLAND BUILDING CAME CRASHING DOWN.
OKAY, I KNOW YOU PEOPLE ARE OUT THERE.
I CAN HEAR YOU.
GRIMBLE! WHAT ARE YOU DOING? WE NEED TO MOVE THESE PEOPLE OUT OF HERE!
BIGBY! MOVE WHO WHERE? I CAN'T SEE A DAMNED THING IN THIS DUST CLOUD.
AND I CAN'T CATCH MY BREATH! I KEEP SPITTING OUT DIRT. I THINK ALL THIS GRIT'S GETTING INTO MY LUNGS.
COUGH! COUGH! COUGH!
HANG IN THERE, BUDDY. I THINK THIS IS A SITUATION WHERE MY SPECIAL TALENTS CAN HELP.
COUGH! COUGH!
THUMP THUMP
THE DARKEST HOUR
Chapter four of THE DARK AGES
Bill Willingham writer/creator
Mark Buckingham penciller
Andrew Pepoy inker
Lee Loughridge colors
Todd Klein letters
James Jean cover
Angela Rufino associate editor
Shelly Bond editor

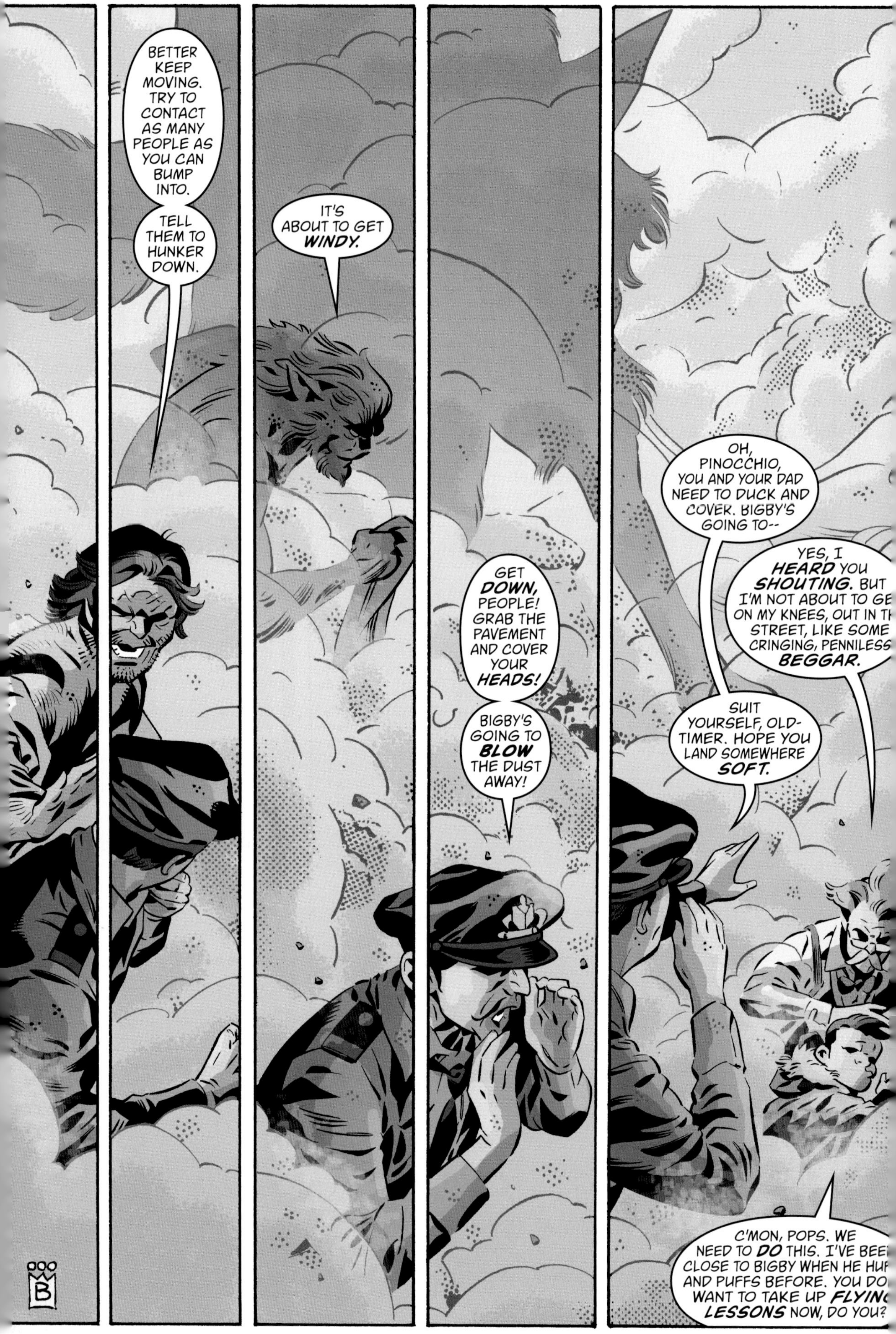
BETTER KEEP MOVING. TRY TO CONTACT AS MANY PEOPLE AS YOU CAN BUMP INTO.
TELL THEM TO HUNKER DOWN.
IT'S ABOUT TO GET **WINDY.**
GET **DOWN,** PEOPLE! GRAB THE PAVEMENT AND COVER YOUR **HEADS!**
BIGBY'S GOING TO **BLOW** THE DUST AWAY!
OH, PINOCCHIO, YOU AND YOUR DAD NEED TO DUCK AND COVER. BIGBY'S GOING TO--
YES, I **HEARD** YOU **SHOUTING.** BUT I'M NOT ABOUT TO GE ON MY KNEES, OUT IN TH STREET, LIKE SOME CRINGING, PENNILESS **BEGGAR.**
SUIT YOURSELF, OLD-TIMER. HOPE YOU LAND SOMEWHERE **SOFT.**
C'MON, POPS. WE NEED TO **DO** THIS. I'VE BEE CLOSE TO BIGBY WHEN HE HUF AND PUFFS BEFORE. YOU DO WANT TO TAKE UP **FLYIN** **LESSONS** NOW, DO YOU?

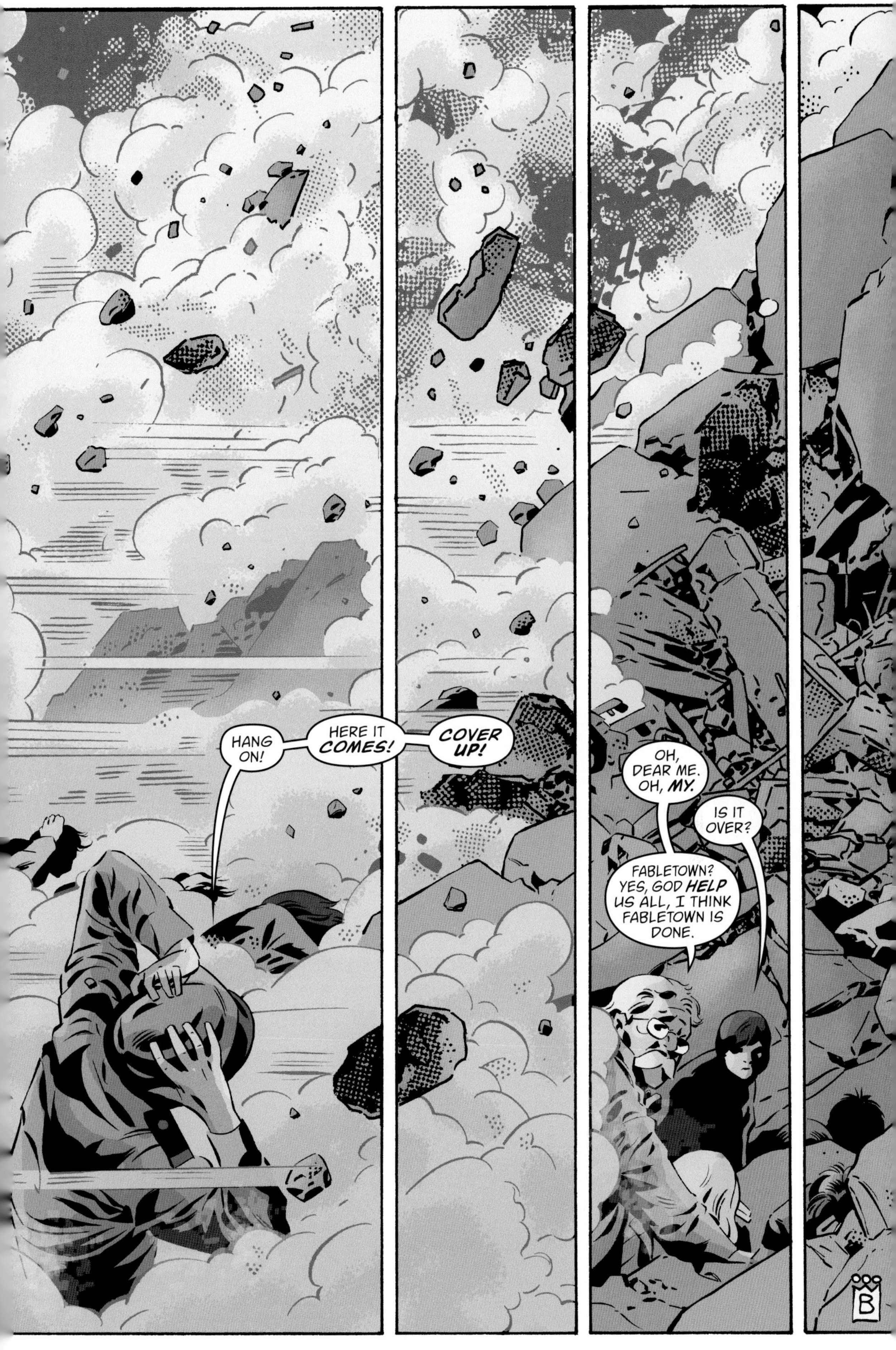
HANG ON!
HERE IT COMES!
COVER UP!
OH, DEAR ME. OH, MY.
IS IT OVER?
FABLETOWN? YES, GOD HELP US ALL, I THINK FABLETOWN IS DONE.

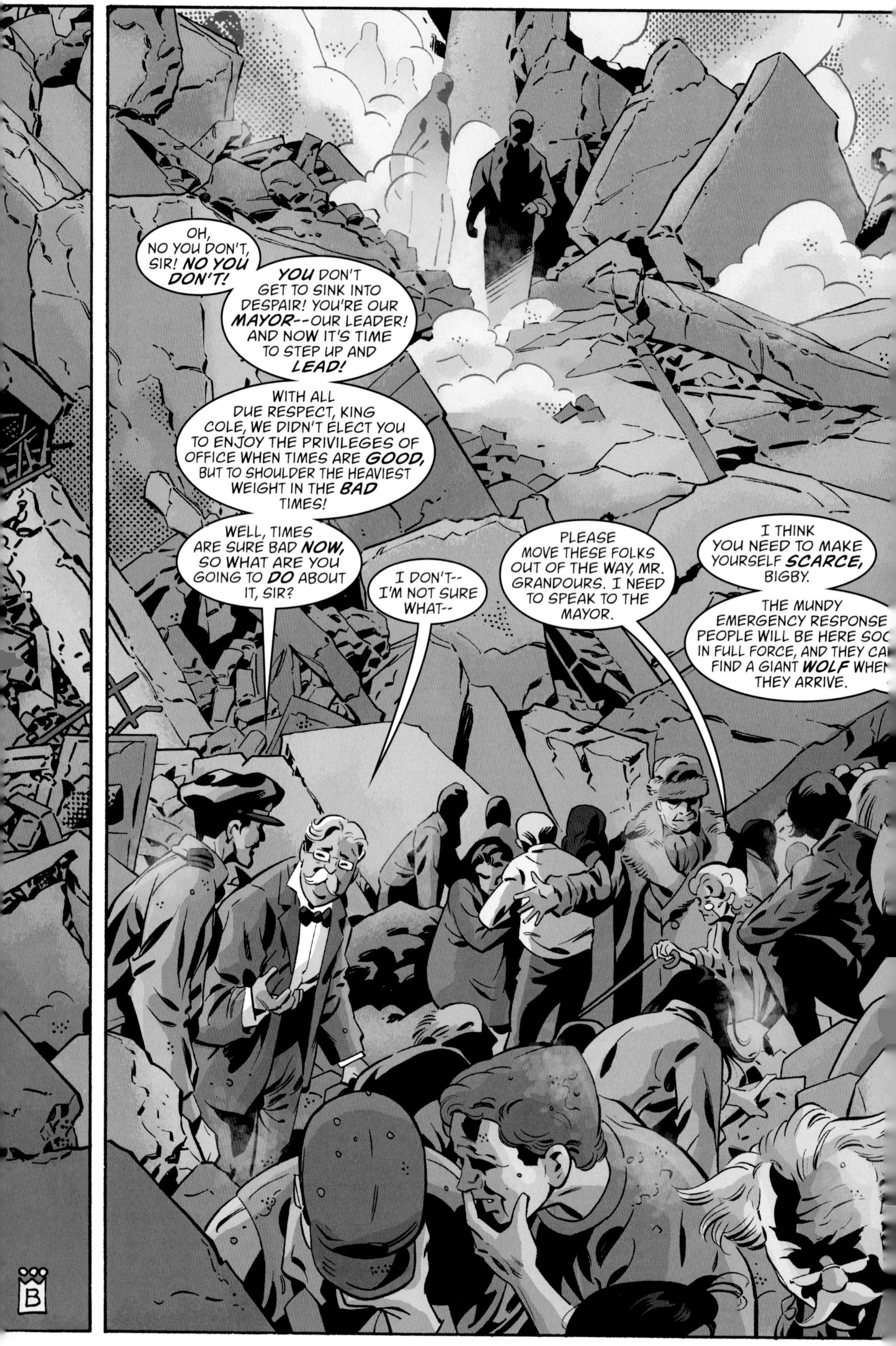
OH, NO YOU DON'T, SIR! NO YOU DON'T!
YOU DON'T GET TO SINK INTO DESPAIR! YOU'RE OUR MAYOR--OUR LEADER! AND NOW IT'S TIME TO STEP UP AND LEAD!
WITH ALL DUE RESPECT, KING COLE, WE DIDN'T ELECT YOU TO ENJOY THE PRIVILEGES OF OFFICE WHEN TIMES ARE GOOD, BUT TO SHOULDER THE HEAVIEST WEIGHT IN THE BAD TIMES!
WELL, TIMES ARE SURE BAD NOW, SO WHAT ARE YOU GOING TO DO ABOUT IT, SIR?
I DON'T--I'M NOT SURE WHAT--
PLEASE MOVE THESE FOLKS OUT OF THE WAY, MR. GRANDOURS. I NEED TO SPEAK TO THE MAYOR.
I THINK YOU NEED TO MAKE YOURSELF SCARCE, BIGBY.
THE MUNDY EMERGENCY RESPONSE PEOPLE WILL BE HERE SOO IN FULL FORCE, AND THEY CA FIND A GIANT WOLF WHE THEY ARRIVE.

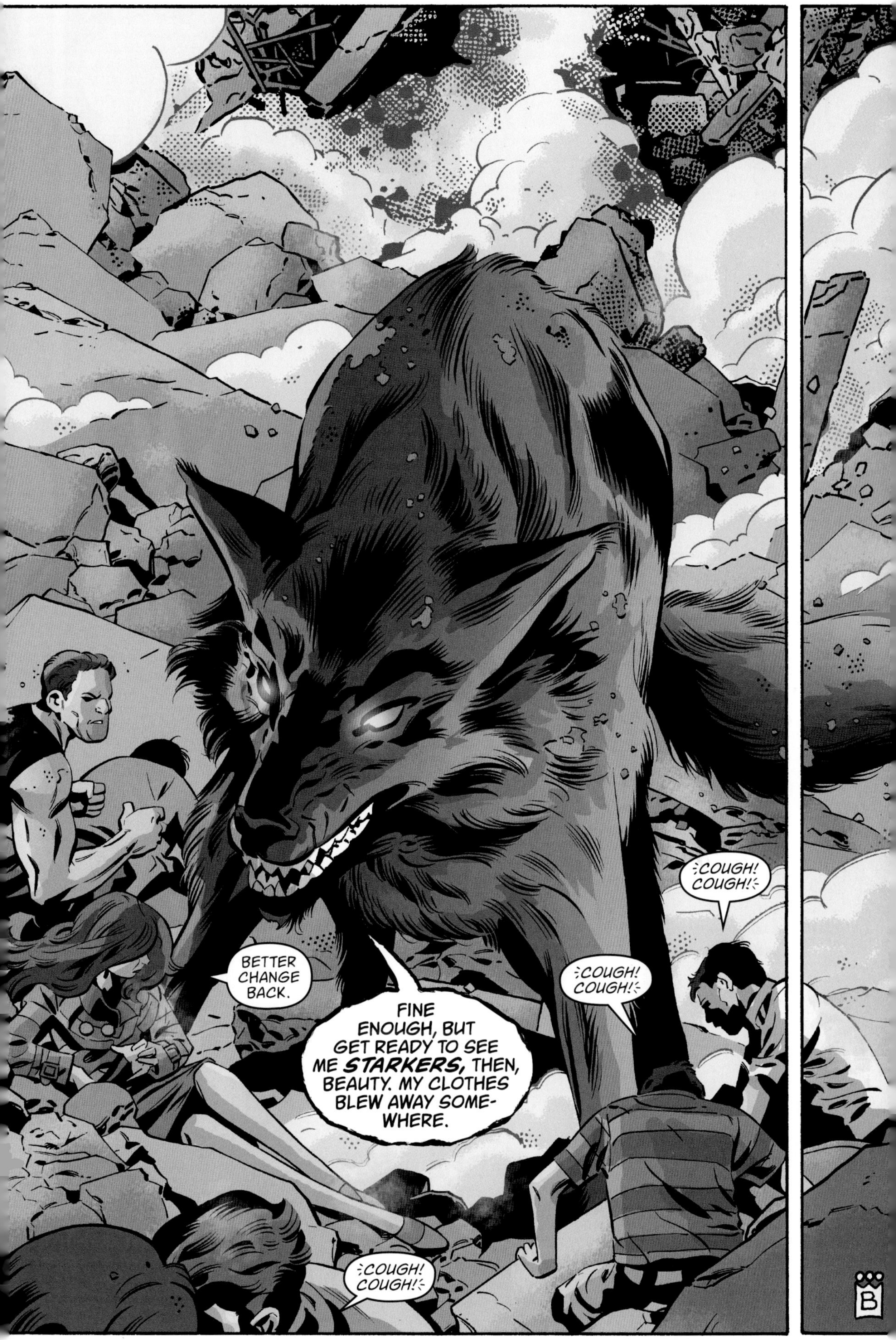
:COUGH! COUGH!:
BETTER CHANGE BACK.
FINE ENOUGH, BUT GET READY TO SEE ME STARKERS, THEN, BEAUTY. MY CLOTHES BLEW AWAY SOME-WHERE.
:COUGH! COUGH!:
:COUGH! COUGH!:

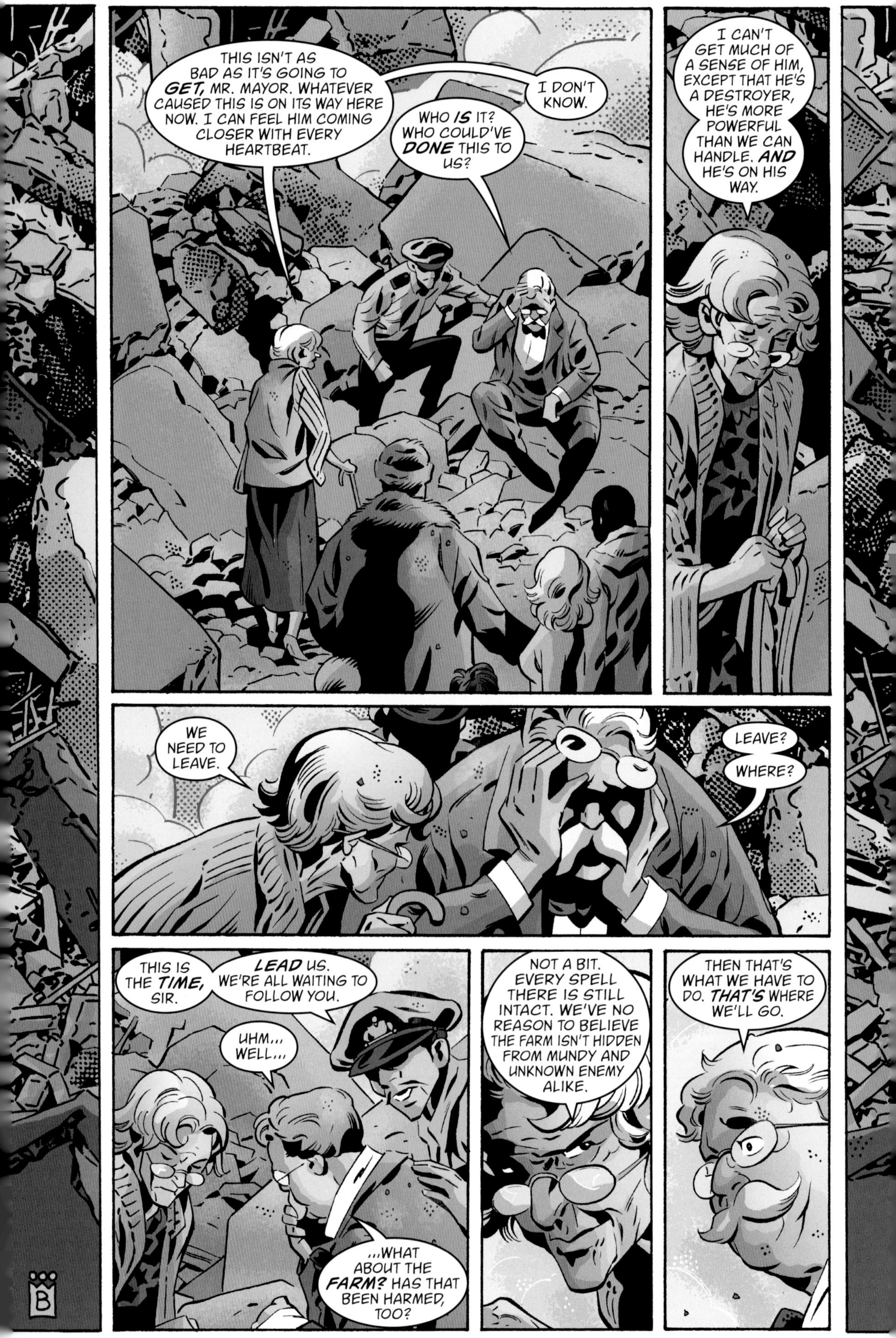
THIS ISN'T AS BAD AS IT'S GOING TO **GET,** MR. MAYOR. WHATEVER CAUSED THIS IS ON ITS WAY HERE NOW. I CAN FEEL HIM COMING CLOSER WITH EVERY HEARTBEAT.
WHO ***IS*** IT? WHO COULD'VE ***DONE*** THIS TO US?
I DON'T KNOW.
I CAN'T GET MUCH OF A SENSE OF HIM, EXCEPT THAT HE'S A DESTROYER, HE'S MORE POWERFUL THAN WE CAN HANDLE. ***AND*** HE'S ON HIS WAY.
WE NEED TO LEAVE.
LEAVE?
WHERE?
THIS IS THE ***TIME,*** SIR.
LEAD US. WE'RE ALL WAITING TO FOLLOW YOU.
UHM... WELL...
...WHAT ABOUT THE ***FARM?*** HAS THAT BEEN HARMED, TOO?
NOT A BIT. EVERY SPELL THERE IS STILL INTACT. WE'VE NO REASON TO BELIEVE THE FARM ISN'T HIDDEN FROM MUNDY AND UNKNOWN ENEMY ALIKE.
THEN THAT'S WHAT WE HAVE TO DO. ***THAT'S*** WHERE WE'LL GO.

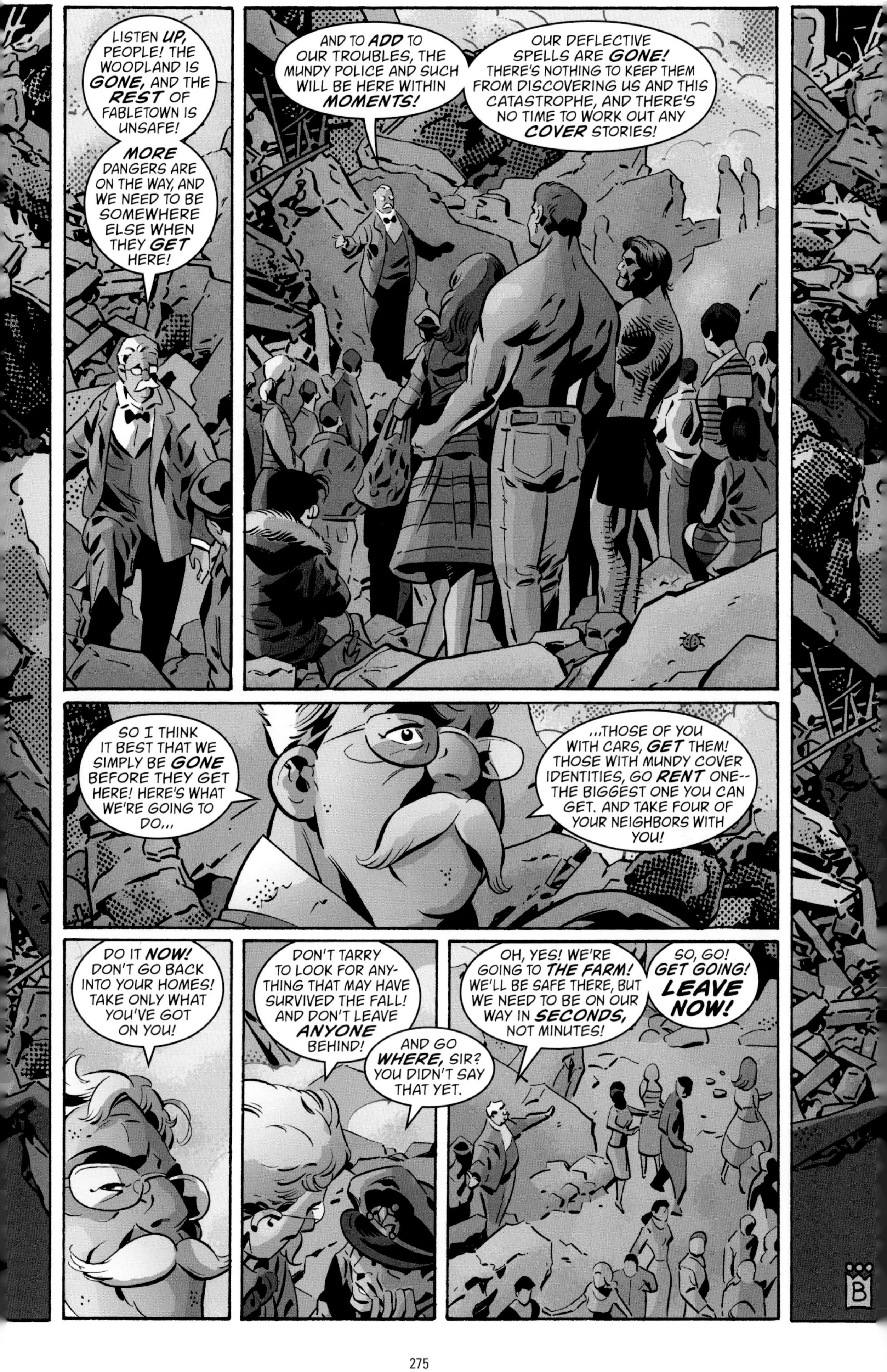

LISTEN UP, PEOPLE! THE WOODLAND IS GONE, AND THE REST OF FABLETOWN IS UNSAFE!
MORE DANGERS ARE ON THE WAY, AND WE NEED TO BE SOMEWHERE ELSE WHEN THEY GET HERE!
AND TO ADD TO OUR TROUBLES, THE MUNDY POLICE AND SUCH WILL BE HERE WITHIN MOMENTS!
OUR DEFLECTIVE SPELLS ARE GONE! THERE'S NOTHING TO KEEP THEM FROM DISCOVERING US AND THIS CATASTROPHE, AND THERE'S NO TIME TO WORK OUT ANY COVER STORIES!
SO I THINK IT BEST THAT WE SIMPLY BE GONE BEFORE THEY GET HERE! HERE'S WHAT WE'RE GOING TO DO...
...THOSE OF YOU WITH CARS, GET THEM! THOSE WITH MUNDY COVER IDENTITIES, GO RENT ONE-- THE BIGGEST ONE YOU CAN GET. AND TAKE FOUR OF YOUR NEIGHBORS WITH YOU!
DO IT NOW! DON'T GO BACK INTO YOUR HOMES! TAKE ONLY WHAT YOU'VE GOT ON YOU!
DON'T TARRY TO LOOK FOR ANY-THING THAT MAY HAVE SURVIVED THE FALL! AND DON'T LEAVE ANYONE BEHIND!
AND GO WHERE, SIR? YOU DIDN'T SAY THAT YET.
OH, YES! WE'RE GOING TO THE FARM! WE'LL BE SAFE THERE, BUT WE NEED TO BE ON OUR WAY IN SECONDS, NOT MINUTES!
SO, GO! GET GOING! LEAVE NOW!

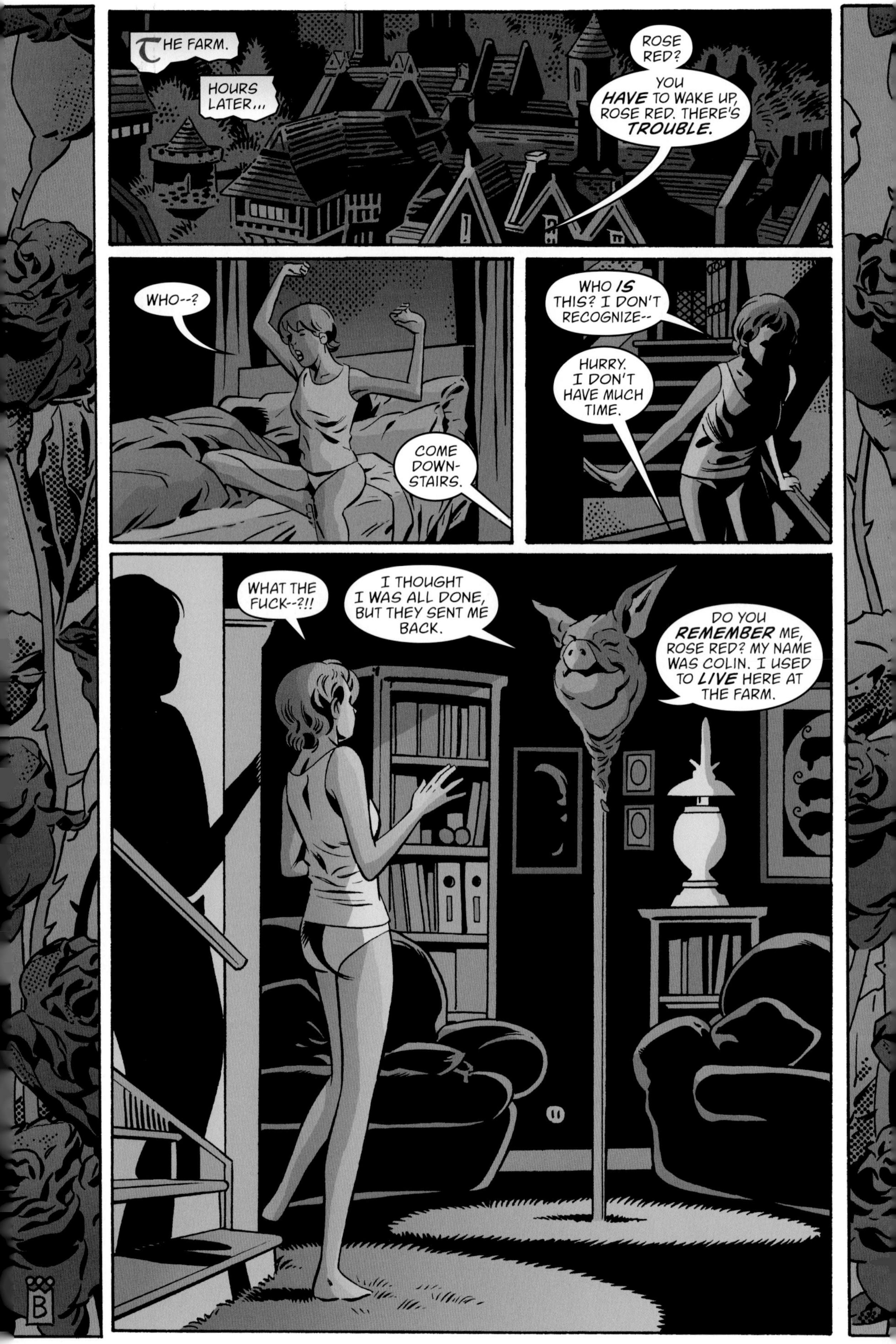
THE FARM.
HOURS LATER...
ROSE RED?
YOU HAVE TO WAKE UP, ROSE RED. THERE'S TROUBLE.
WHO--?
COME DOWN-STAIRS.
WHO IS THIS? I DON'T RECOGNIZE--
HURRY. I DON'T HAVE MUCH TIME.
WHAT THE FUCK--?!!
I THOUGHT I WAS ALL DONE, BUT THEY SENT ME BACK.
DO YOU REMEMBER ME, ROSE RED? MY NAME WAS COLIN. I USED TO LIVE HERE AT THE FARM.

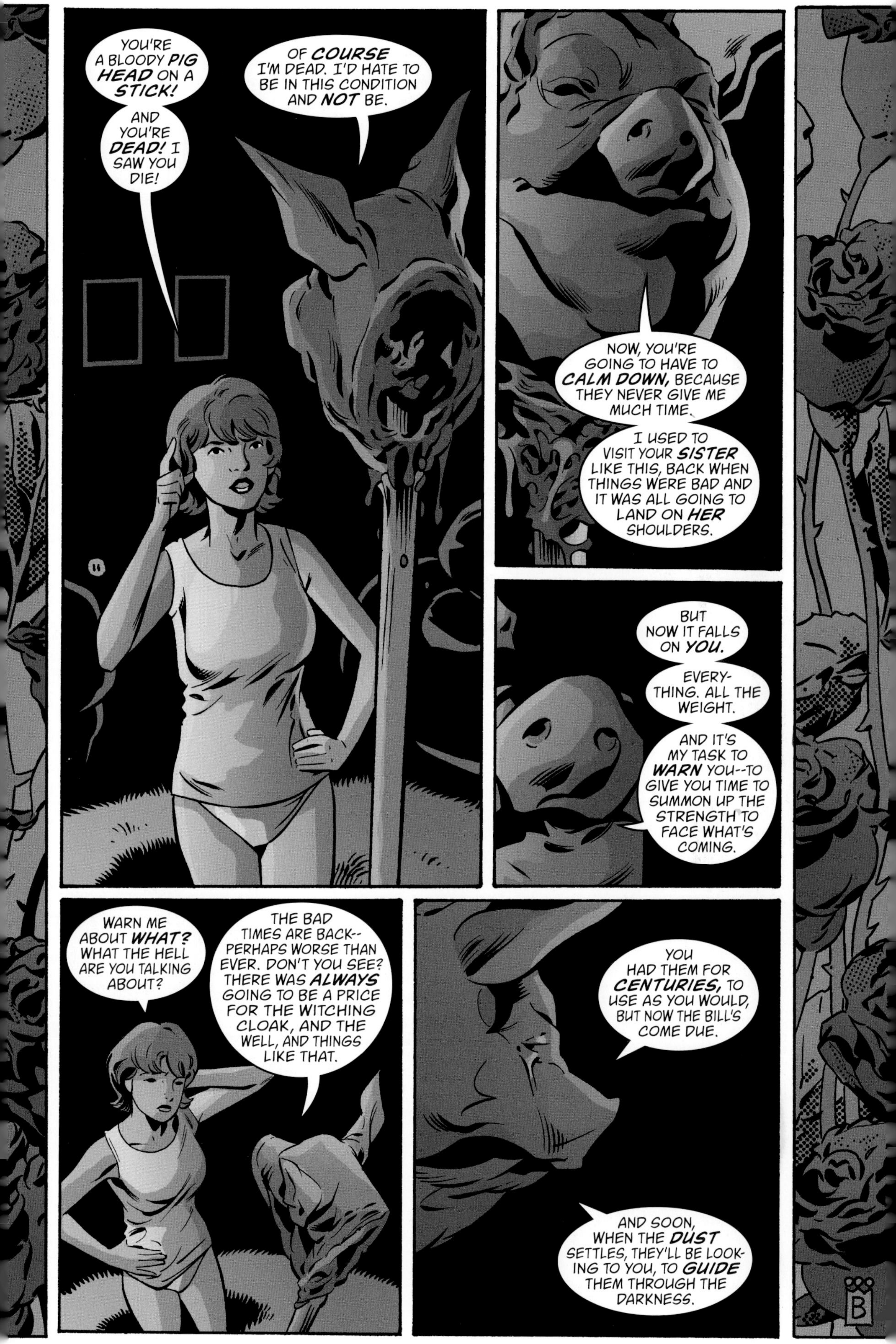
YOU'RE A BLOODY PIG HEAD ON A STICK!
AND YOU'RE DEAD! I SAW YOU DIE!
OF COURSE I'M DEAD. I'D HATE TO BE IN THIS CONDITION AND NOT BE.
NOW, YOU'RE GOING TO HAVE TO CALM DOWN, BECAUSE THEY NEVER GIVE ME MUCH TIME.
I USED TO VISIT YOUR SISTER LIKE THIS, BACK WHEN THINGS WERE BAD AND IT WAS ALL GOING TO LAND ON HER SHOULDERS.
BUT NOW IT FALLS ON YOU.
EVERY-THING. ALL THE WEIGHT.
AND IT'S MY TASK TO WARN YOU--TO GIVE YOU TIME TO SUMMON UP THE STRENGTH TO FACE WHAT'S COMING.
WARN ME ABOUT WHAT? WHAT THE HELL ARE YOU TALKING ABOUT?
THE BAD TIMES ARE BACK--PERHAPS WORSE THAN EVER. DON'T YOU SEE? THERE WAS ALWAYS GOING TO BE A PRICE FOR THE WITCHING CLOAK, AND THE WELL, AND THINGS LIKE THAT.
YOU HAD THEM FOR CENTURIES, TO USE AS YOU WOULD, BUT NOW THE BILL'S COME DUE.
AND SOON, WHEN THE DUST SETTLES, THEY'LL BE LOOK-ING TO YOU, TO GUIDE THEM THROUGH THE DARKNESS.

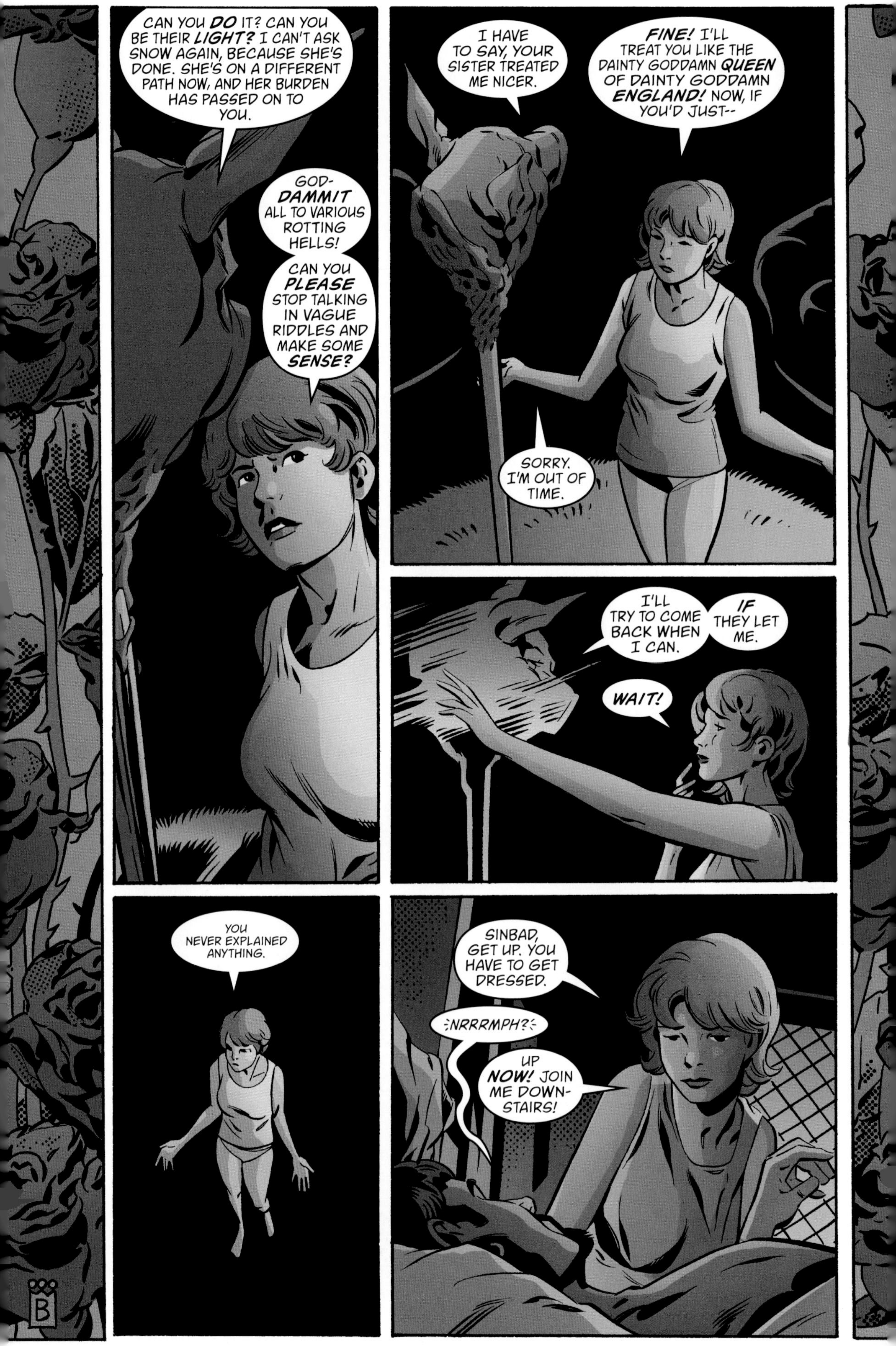
CAN YOU DO IT? CAN YOU BE THEIR LIGHT? I CAN'T ASK SNOW AGAIN, BECAUSE SHE'S DONE. SHE'S ON A DIFFERENT PATH NOW, AND HER BURDEN HAS PASSED ON TO YOU.
GOD-DAMMIT ALL TO VARIOUS ROTTING HELLS!
CAN YOU PLEASE STOP TALKING IN VAGUE RIDDLES AND MAKE SOME SENSE?
I HAVE TO SAY, YOUR SISTER TREATED ME NICER.
FINE! I'LL TREAT YOU LIKE THE DAINTY GODDAMN QUEEN OF DAINTY GODDAMN ENGLAND! NOW, IF YOU'D JUST--
SORRY. I'M OUT OF TIME.
I'LL TRY TO COME BACK WHEN I CAN.
IF THEY LET ME.
WAIT!
YOU NEVER EXPLAINED ANYTHING.
SINBAD, GET UP. YOU HAVE TO GET DRESSED.
NRRRMPH?
UP NOW! JOIN ME DOWN-STAIRS!

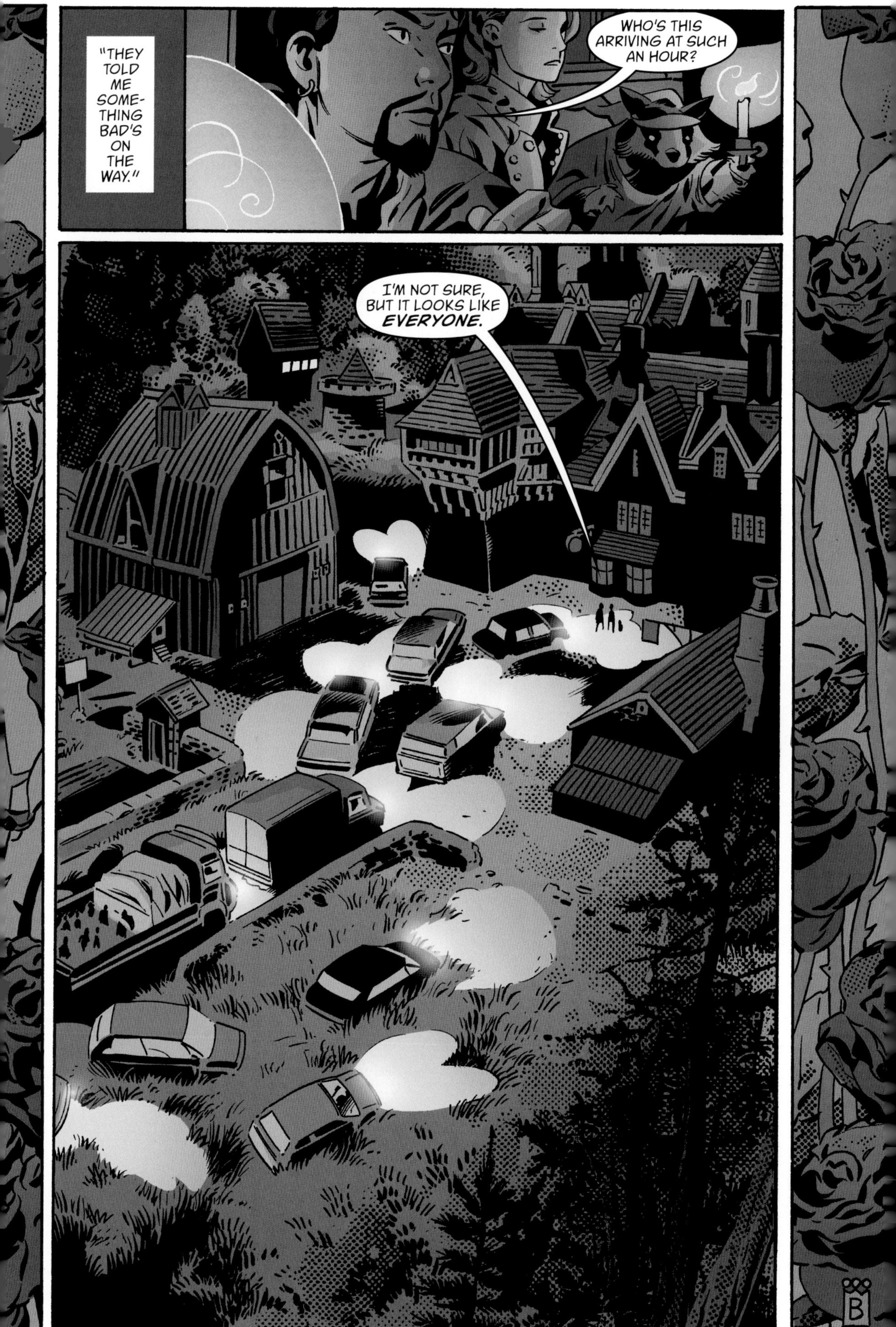
"THEY TOLD ME SOMETHING BAD'S ON THE WAY."
WHO'S THIS ARRIVING AT SUCH AN HOUR?
I'M NOT SURE, BUT IT LOOKS LIKE *EVERYONE*.

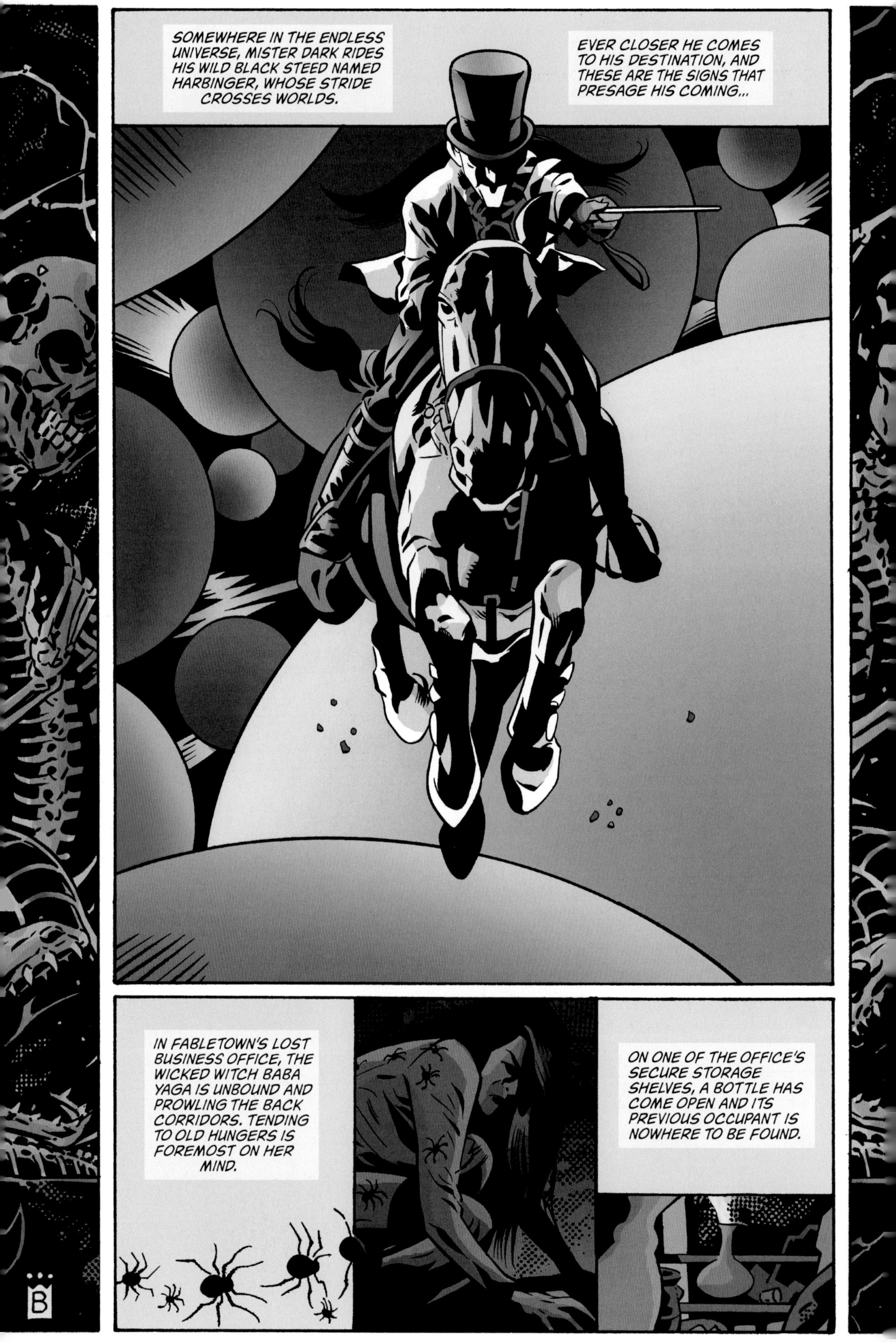
SOMEWHERE IN THE ENDLESS UNIVERSE, MISTER DARK RIDES HIS WILD BLACK STEED NAMED HARBINGER, WHOSE STRIDE CROSSES WORLDS.
EVER CLOSER HE COMES TO HIS DESTINATION, AND THESE ARE THE SIGNS THAT PRESAGE HIS COMING...
IN FABLETOWN'S LOST BUSINESS OFFICE, THE WICKED WITCH BABA YAGA IS UNBOUND AND PROWLING THE BACK CORRIDORS. TENDING TO OLD HUNGERS IS FOREMOST ON HER MIND.
ON ONE OF THE OFFICE'S SECURE STORAGE SHELVES, A BOTTLE HAS COME OPEN AND ITS PREVIOUS OCCUPANT IS NOWHERE TO BE FOUND.

AND AT THE NORTH POLE...

PAPA, WHAT'S WRONG?

I WAS WORKING ON THE NAUGHTY AND NICE LISTS, MAMA, AND **LOOK!**

THE NAUGHTY LIST IS GROWING OUT OF CONTROL. ALL OF THESE CHILDREN SUDDENLY WAKING UP TO THE USUALLY DORMANT KERNELS OF *EVIL* THAT SLEEP INSIDE ALL OF US.

I'VE BEEN WRITING FOR HOURS AND *STILL* THE NAMES ARE COMING TO ME.

MR. BOGEY MAN?

AND IN THEIR SLUMBERS THE WORLD OVER, CHILDREN WAKE IN THE NIGHT, KNOWING THAT SOMETHING IS ABOUT TO COME CRAWLING OUT FROM UNDER THE BED.

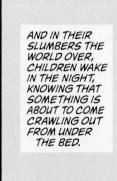

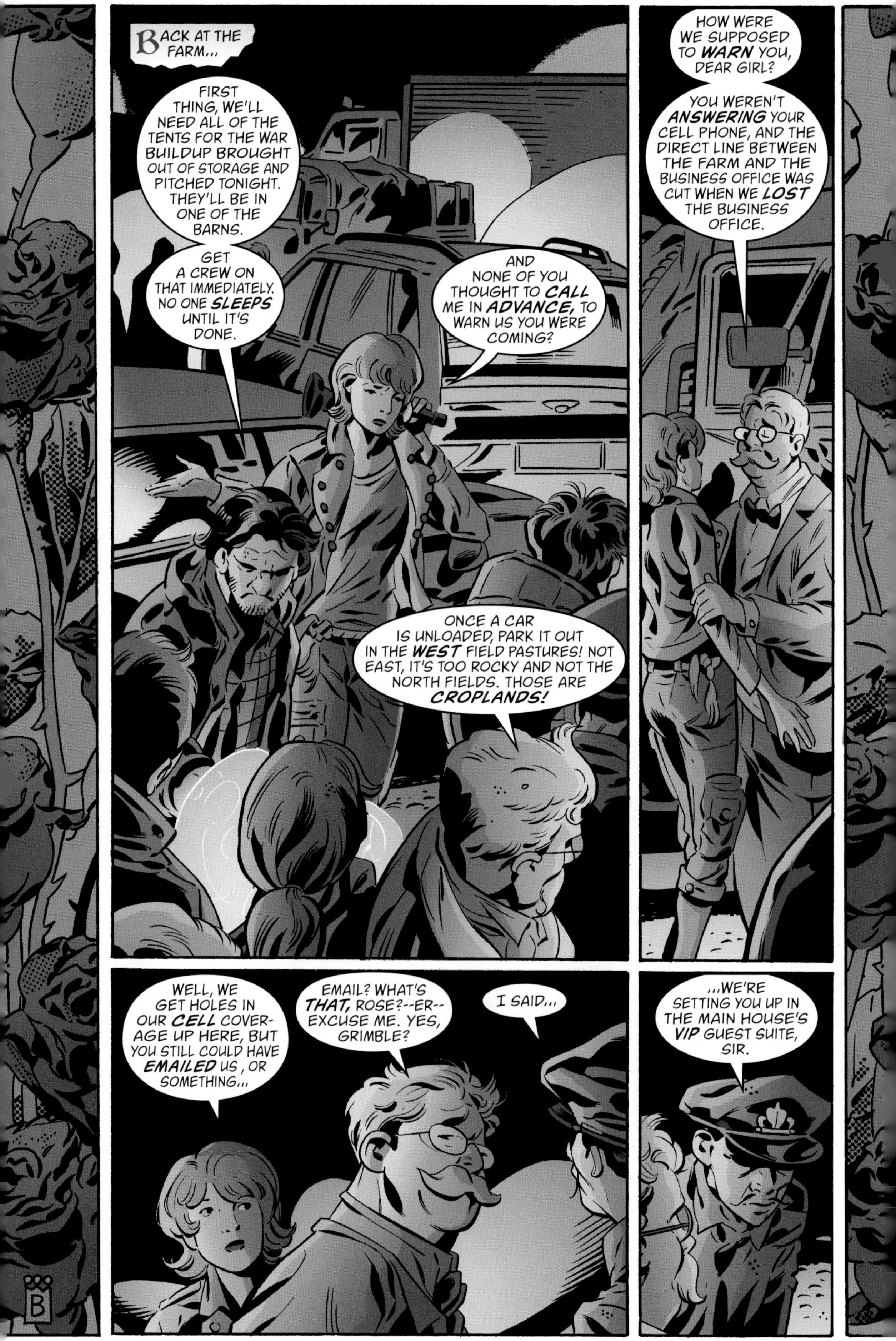

BACK AT THE FARM...
FIRST THING, WE'LL NEED ALL OF THE TENTS FOR THE WAR BUILDUP BROUGHT OUT OF STORAGE AND PITCHED TONIGHT. THEY'LL BE IN ONE OF THE BARNS.
GET A CREW ON THAT IMMEDIATELY. NO ONE SLEEPS UNTIL IT'S DONE.
AND NONE OF YOU THOUGHT TO CALL ME IN ADVANCE, TO WARN US YOU WERE COMING?
ONCE A CAR IS UNLOADED, PARK IT OUT IN THE WEST FIELD PASTURES! NOT EAST, IT'S TOO ROCKY AND NOT THE NORTH FIELDS. THOSE ARE CROPLANDS!
HOW WERE WE SUPPOSED TO WARN YOU, DEAR GIRL?
YOU WEREN'T ANSWERING YOUR CELL PHONE, AND THE DIRECT LINE BETWEEN THE FARM AND THE BUSINESS OFFICE WAS CUT WHEN WE LOST THE BUSINESS OFFICE.
WELL, WE GET HOLES IN OUR CELL COVERAGE UP HERE, BUT YOU STILL COULD HAVE EMAILED US, OR SOMETHING...
EMAIL? WHAT'S THAT, ROSE?--ER--EXCUSE ME. YES, GRIMBLE?
I SAID...
...WE'RE SETTING YOU UP IN THE MAIN HOUSE'S VIP GUEST SUITE, SIR.
B

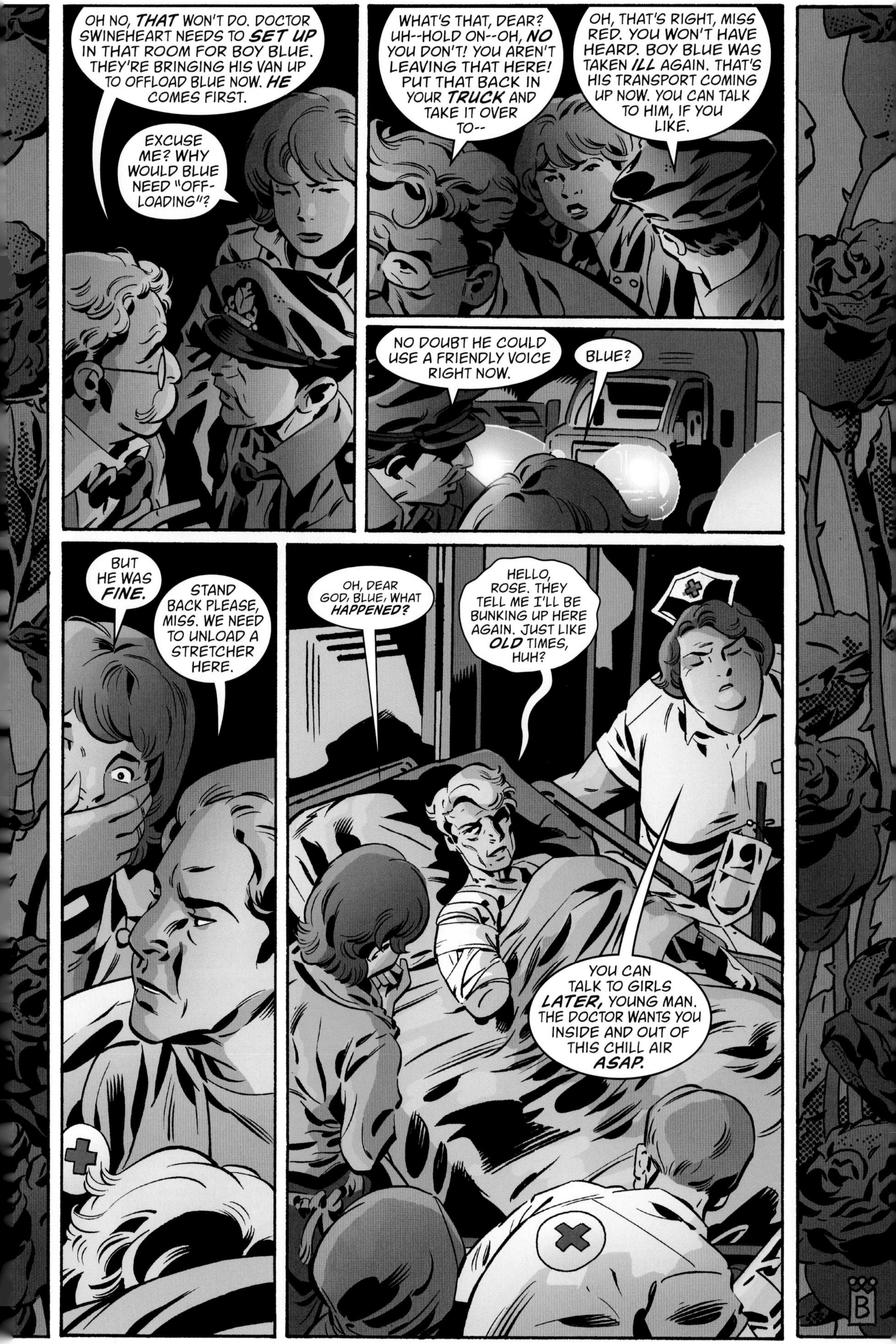

OH NO, THAT WON'T DO. DOCTOR SWINEHEART NEEDS TO SET UP IN THAT ROOM FOR BOY BLUE. THEY'RE BRINGING HIS VAN UP TO OFFLOAD BLUE NOW. HE COMES FIRST.
EXCUSE ME? WHY WOULD BLUE NEED "OFF-LOADING"?
WHAT'S THAT, DEAR? UH--HOLD ON--OH, NO YOU DON'T! YOU AREN'T LEAVING THAT HERE! PUT THAT BACK IN YOUR TRUCK AND TAKE IT OVER TO--
OH, THAT'S RIGHT, MISS RED. YOU WON'T HAVE HEARD. BOY BLUE WAS TAKEN ILL AGAIN. THAT'S HIS TRANSPORT COMING UP NOW. YOU CAN TALK TO HIM, IF YOU LIKE.
NO DOUBT HE COULD USE A FRIENDLY VOICE RIGHT NOW.
BLUE?
BUT HE WAS FINE.
STAND BACK PLEASE, MISS. WE NEED TO UNLOAD A STRETCHER HERE.
OH, DEAR GOD, BLUE, WHAT HAPPENED?
HELLO, ROSE. THEY TELL ME I'LL BE BUNKING UP HERE AGAIN. JUST LIKE OLD TIMES, HUH?
YOU CAN TALK TO GIRLS LATER, YOUNG MAN. THE DOCTOR WANTS YOU INSIDE AND OUT OF THIS CHILL AIR ASAP.

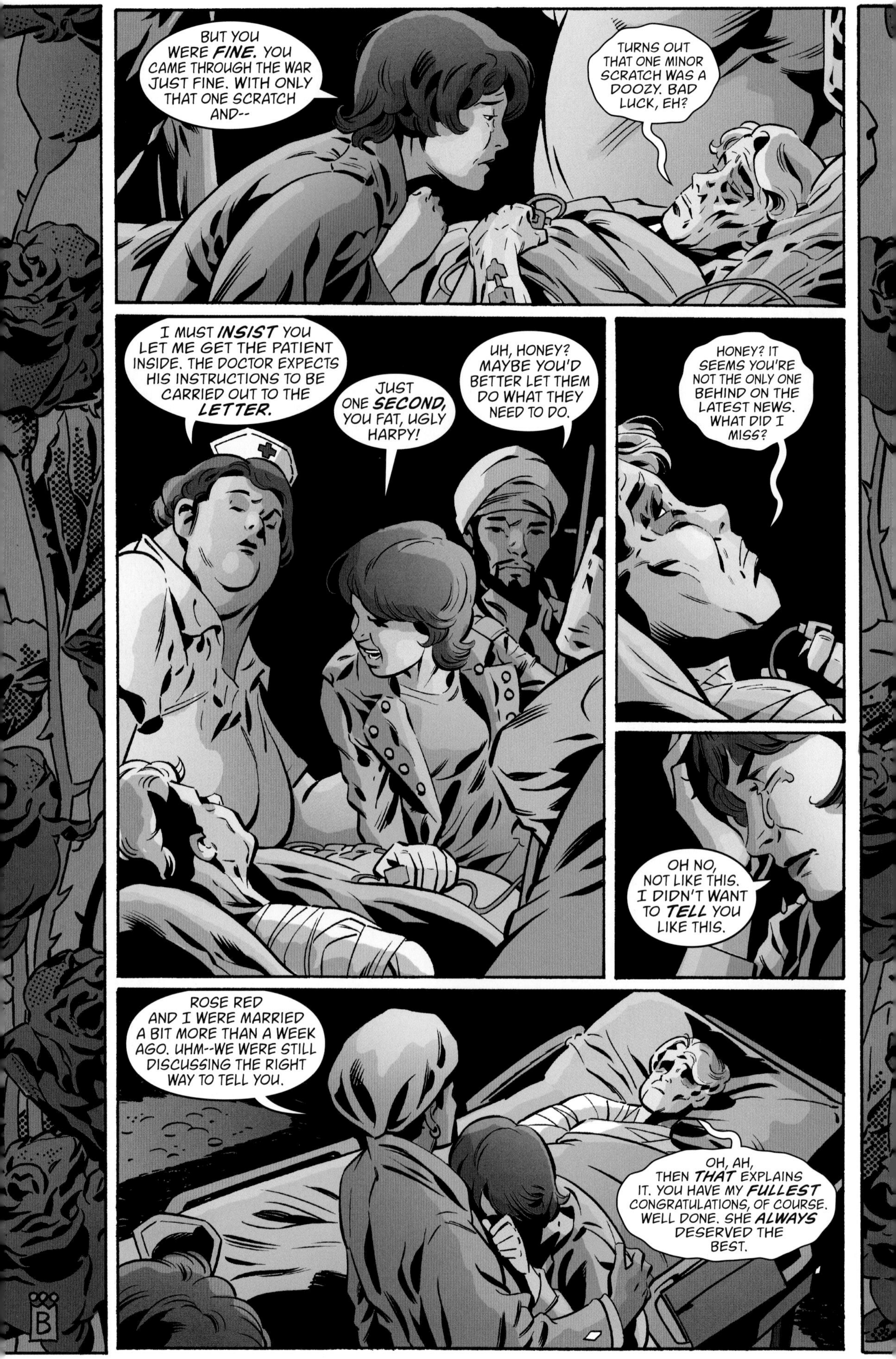
BUT YOU WERE ***FINE.*** YOU CAME THROUGH THE WAR JUST FINE. WITH ONLY THAT ONE SCRATCH AND--
TURNS OUT THAT ONE MINOR SCRATCH WAS A DOOZY. BAD LUCK, EH?
I MUST ***INSIST*** YOU LET ME GET THE PATIENT INSIDE. THE DOCTOR EXPECTS HIS INSTRUCTIONS TO BE CARRIED OUT TO THE ***LETTER.***
JUST ONE ***SECOND,*** YOU FAT, UGLY HARPY!
UH, HONEY? MAYBE YOU'D BETTER LET THEM DO WHAT THEY NEED TO DO.
HONEY? IT SEEMS YOU'RE NOT THE ONLY ONE BEHIND ON THE LATEST NEWS. WHAT DID I MISS?
OH NO, NOT LIKE THIS. I DIDN'T WANT TO ***TELL*** YOU LIKE THIS.
ROSE RED AND I WERE MARRIED A BIT MORE THAN A WEEK AGO. UHM--WE WERE STILL DISCUSSING THE RIGHT WAY TO TELL YOU.
OH, AH, THEN ***THAT*** EXPLAINS IT. YOU HAVE MY ***FULLEST*** CONGRATULATIONS, OF COURSE. WELL DONE. SHE ***ALWAYS*** DESERVED THE BEST.

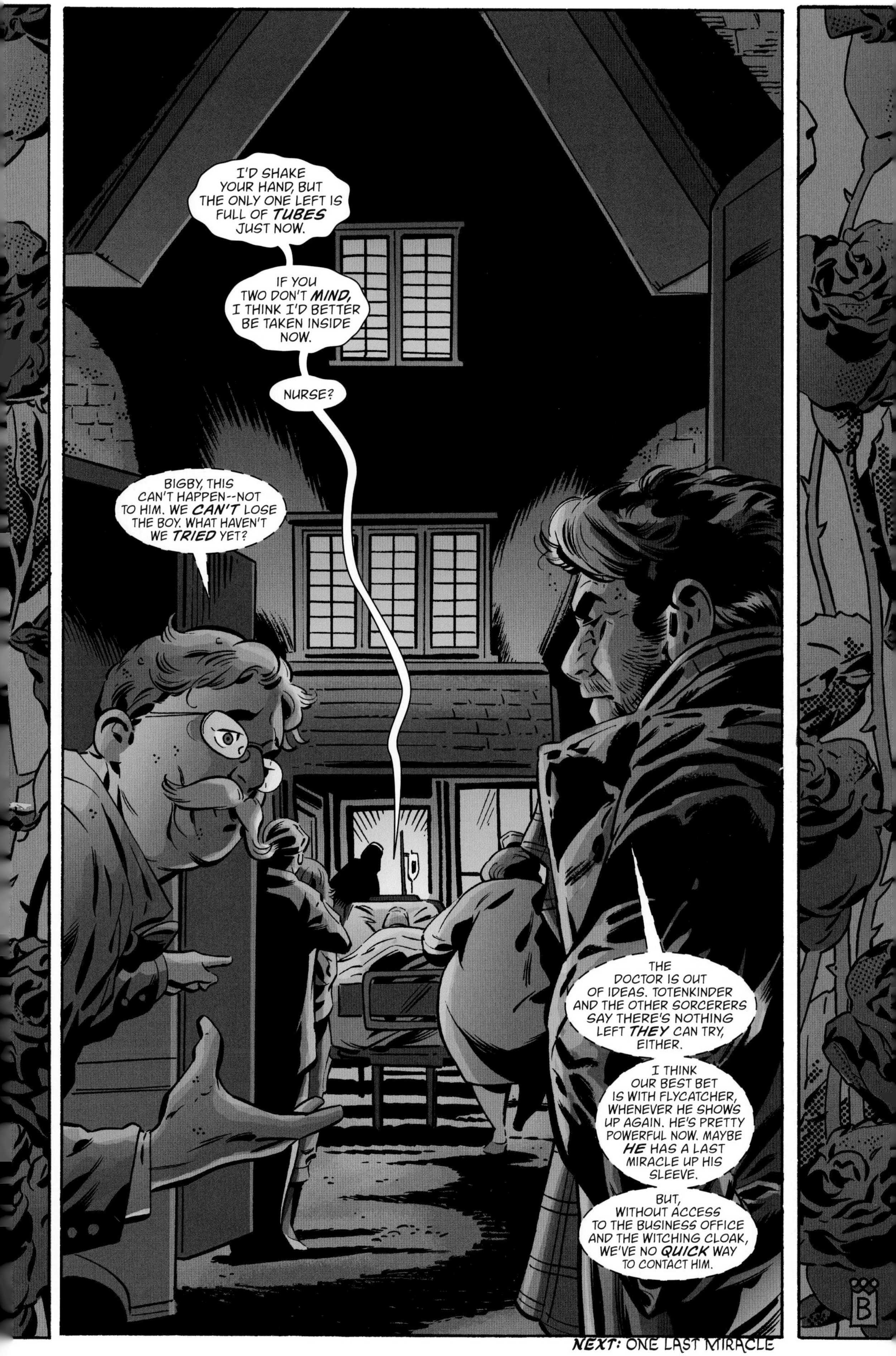
I'D SHAKE YOUR HAND, BUT THE ONLY ONE LEFT IS FULL OF TUBES JUST NOW.
IF YOU TWO DON'T MIND, I THINK I'D BETTER BE TAKEN INSIDE NOW.
NURSE?
BIGBY, THIS CAN'T HAPPEN--NOT TO HIM. WE CAN'T LOSE THE BOY. WHAT HAVEN'T WE TRIED YET?
THE DOCTOR IS OUT OF IDEAS. TOTENKINDER AND THE OTHER SORCERERS SAY THERE'S NOTHING LEFT THEY CAN TRY, EITHER.
I THINK OUR BEST BET IS WITH FLYCATCHER, WHENEVER HE SHOWS UP AGAIN. HE'S PRETTY POWERFUL NOW. MAYBE HE HAS A LAST MIRACLE UP HIS SLEEVE.
BUT, WITHOUT ACCESS TO THE BUSINESS OFFICE AND THE WITCHING CLOAK, WE'VE NO QUICK WAY TO CONTACT HIM.

NEXT: ONE LAST MIRACLE

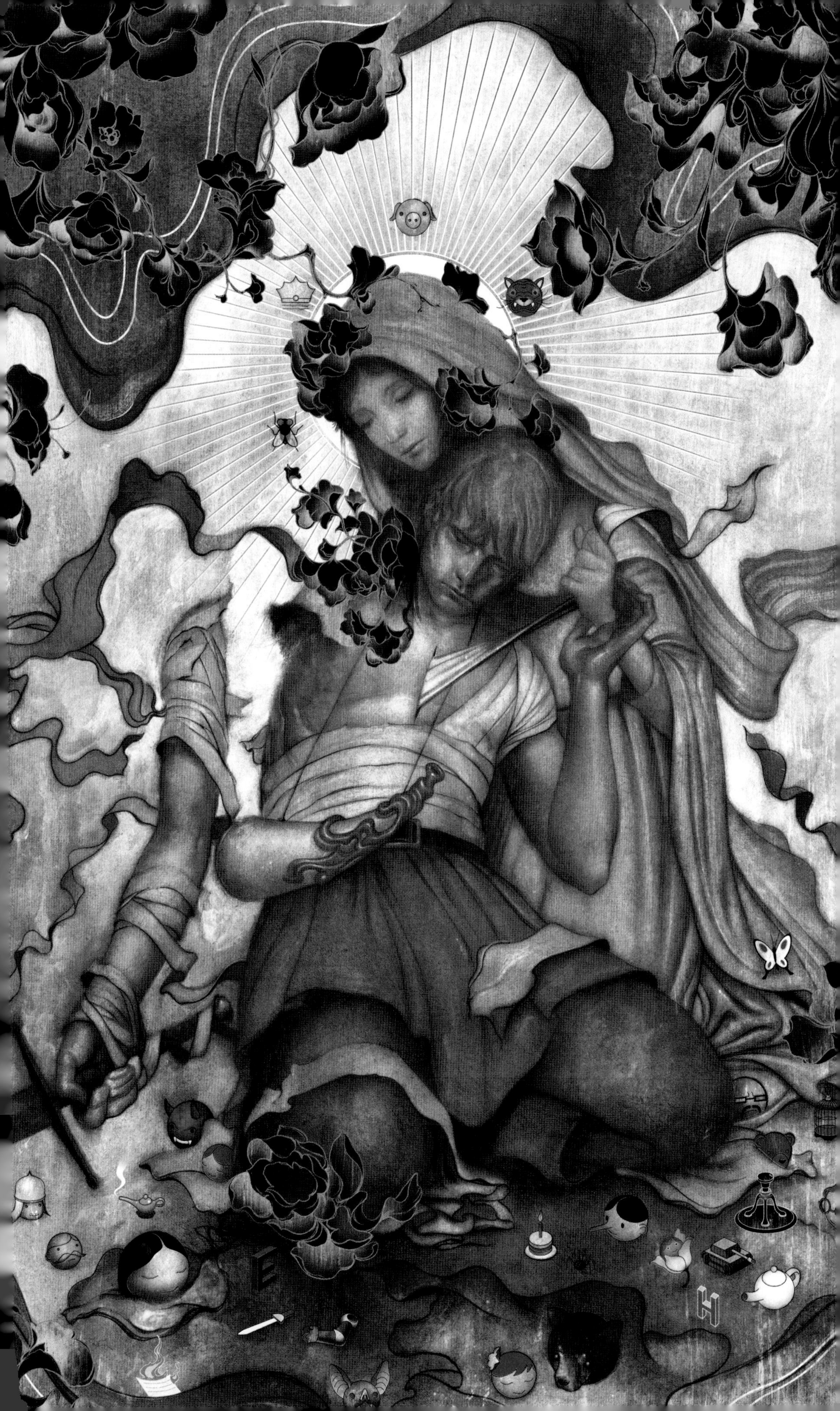

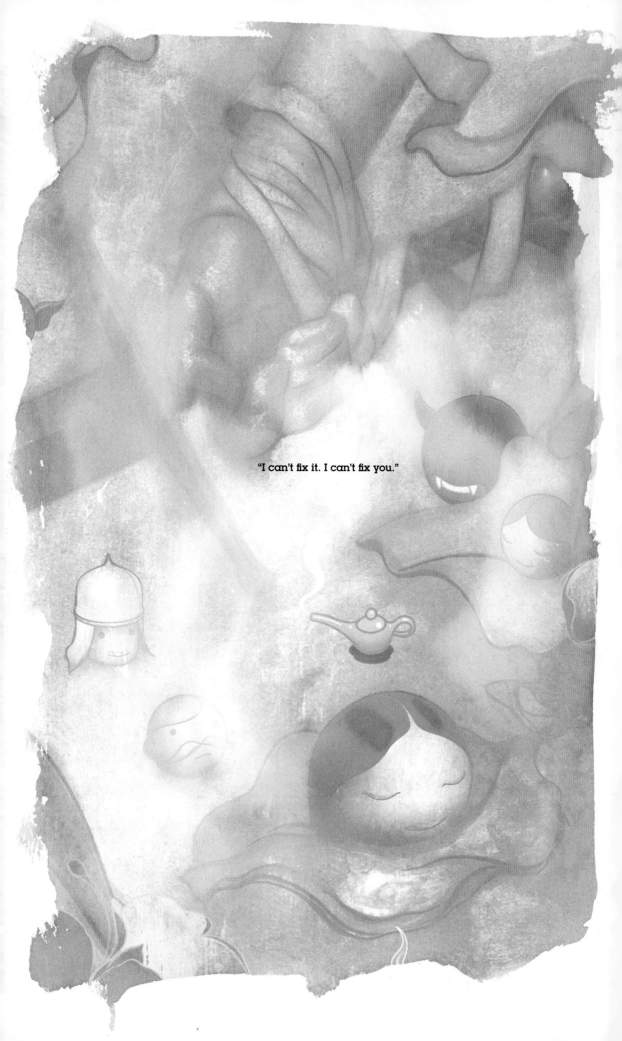

"I can't fix it. I can't fix you."

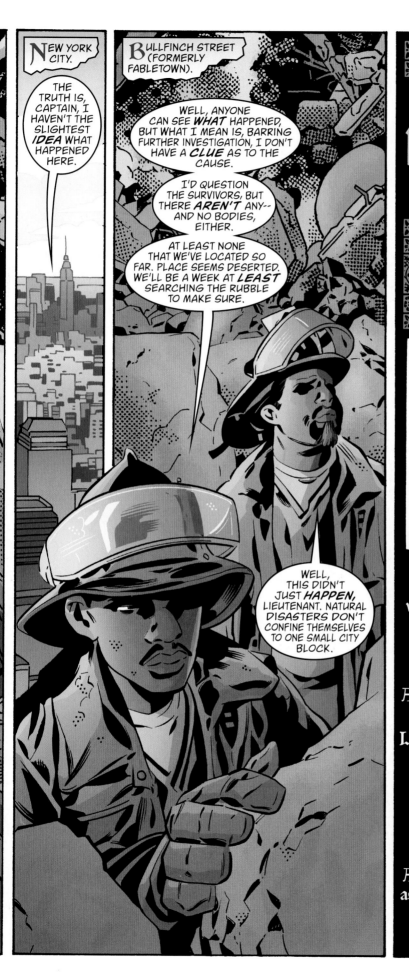

NEW YORK CITY.

THE TRUTH IS, CAPTAIN, I HAVEN'T THE SLIGHTEST *IDEA* WHAT HAPPENED HERE.

BULLFINCH STREET (FORMERLY FABLETOWN).

WELL, ANYONE CAN SEE *WHAT* HAPPENED, BUT WHAT I MEAN IS, BARRING FURTHER INVESTIGATION, I DON'T HAVE A *CLUE* AS TO THE CAUSE.

I'D QUESTION THE SURVIVORS, BUT THERE *AREN'T* ANY-- AND NO BODIES, EITHER.

AT LEAST NONE THAT WE'VE LOCATED SO FAR. PLACE SEEMS DESERTED. WE'LL BE A WEEK AT *LEAST* SEARCHING THE RUBBLE TO MAKE SURE.

WELL, THIS DIDN'T JUST *HAPPEN*, LIEUTENANT. NATURAL DISASTERS DON'T CONFINE THEMSELVES TO ONE SMALL CITY BLOCK.

THE BLUE HORI-ZON

Chapter five of THE DARK AGES

Bill Willingham
writer/creator

Mark Buckingham
penciller

Andrew Pepoy
inker

Lee Loughridge
colors

Todd Klein
letters

James Jean
cover

Angela Rufino
associate editor

Shelly Bond
editor

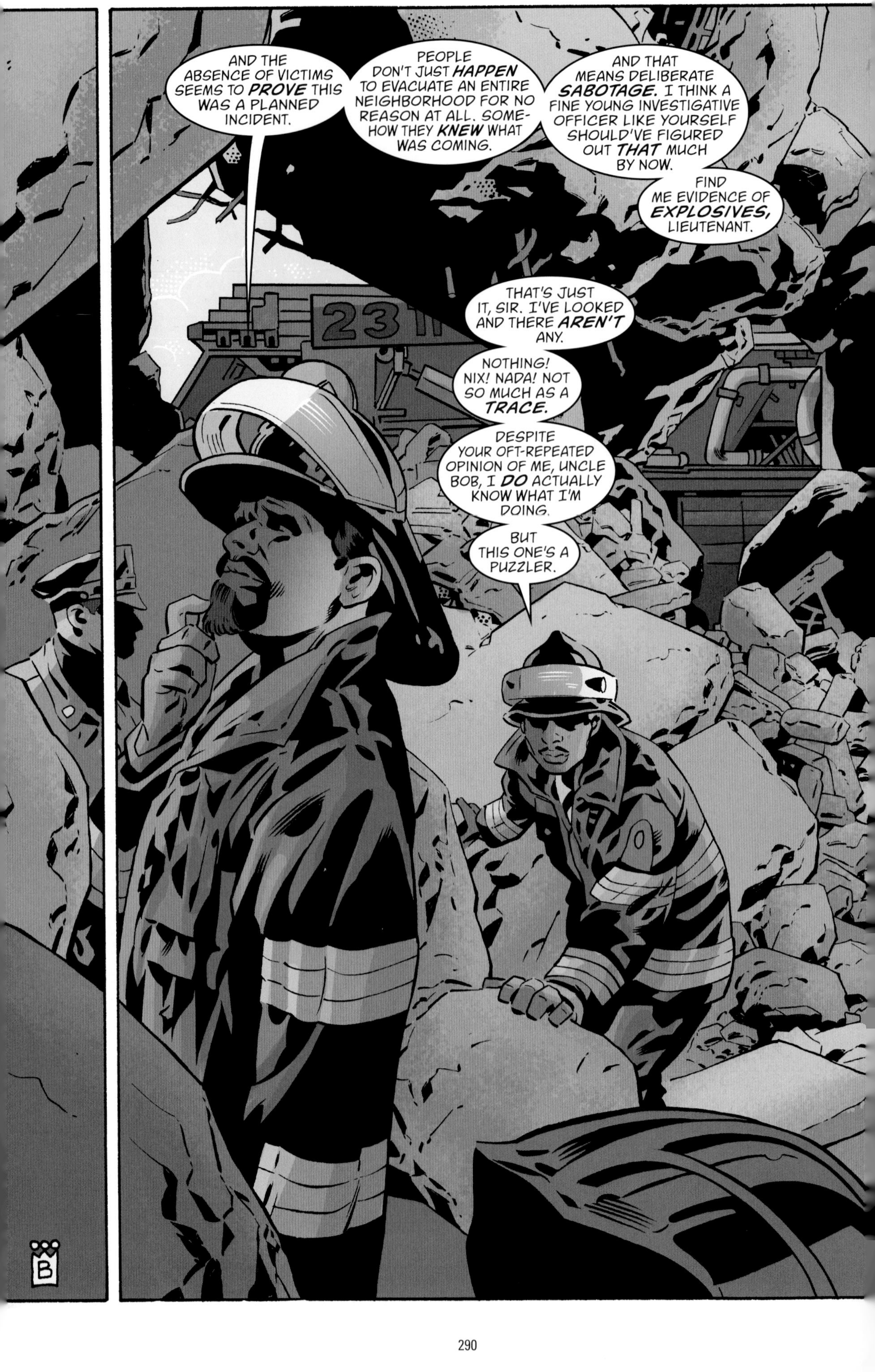
AND THE ABSENCE OF VICTIMS SEEMS TO **PROVE** THIS WAS A PLANNED INCIDENT.
PEOPLE DON'T JUST **HAPPEN** TO EVACUATE AN ENTIRE NEIGHBORHOOD FOR NO REASON AT ALL. SOME-HOW THEY **KNEW** WHAT WAS COMING.
AND THAT MEANS DELIBERATE **SABOTAGE.** I THINK A FINE YOUNG INVESTIGATIVE OFFICER LIKE YOURSELF SHOULD'VE FIGURED OUT **THAT** MUCH BY NOW.
FIND ME EVIDENCE OF **EXPLOSIVES,** LIEUTENANT.
23
THAT'S JUST IT, SIR. I'VE LOOKED AND THERE **AREN'T** ANY.
NOTHING! NIX! NADA! NOT SO MUCH AS A **TRACE.**
DESPITE YOUR OFT-REPEATED OPINION OF ME, UNCLE BOB, I **DO** ACTUALLY KNOW WHAT I'M DOING.
BUT THIS ONE'S A PUZZLER.

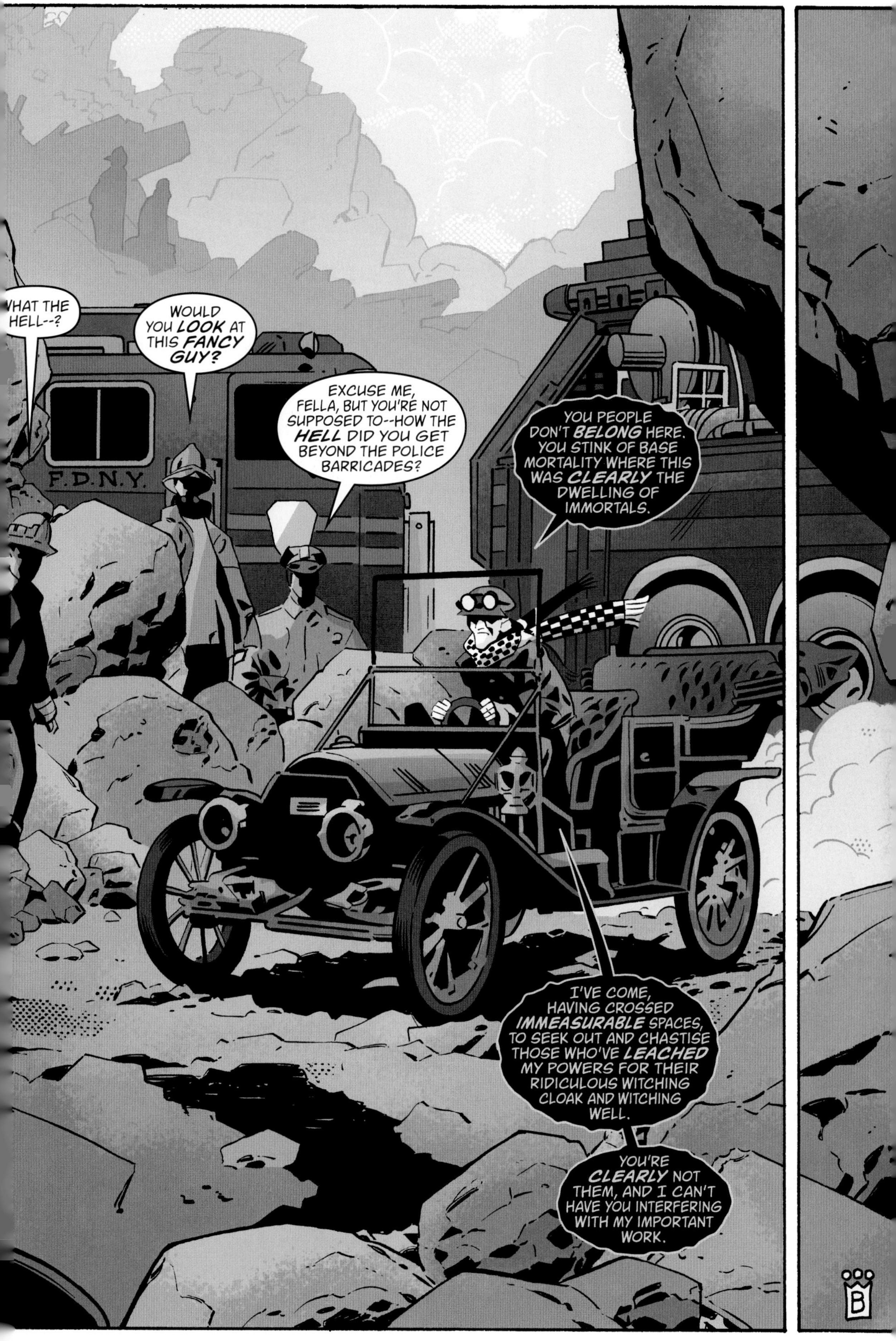
WHAT THE HELL--?
WOULD YOU LOOK AT THIS FANCY GUY?
EXCUSE ME, FELLA, BUT YOU'RE NOT SUPPOSED TO--HOW THE HELL DID YOU GET BEYOND THE POLICE BARRICADES?
F.D.N.Y.
YOU PEOPLE DON'T BELONG HERE. YOU STINK OF BASE MORTALITY WHERE THIS WAS CLEARLY THE DWELLING OF IMMORTALS.
I'VE COME, HAVING CROSSED IMMEASURABLE SPACES, TO SEEK OUT AND CHASTISE THOSE WHO'VE LEACHED MY POWERS FOR THEIR RIDICULOUS WITCHING CLOAK AND WITCHING WELL.
YOU'RE CLEARLY NOT THEM, AND I CAN'T HAVE YOU INTERFERING WITH MY IMPORTANT WORK.

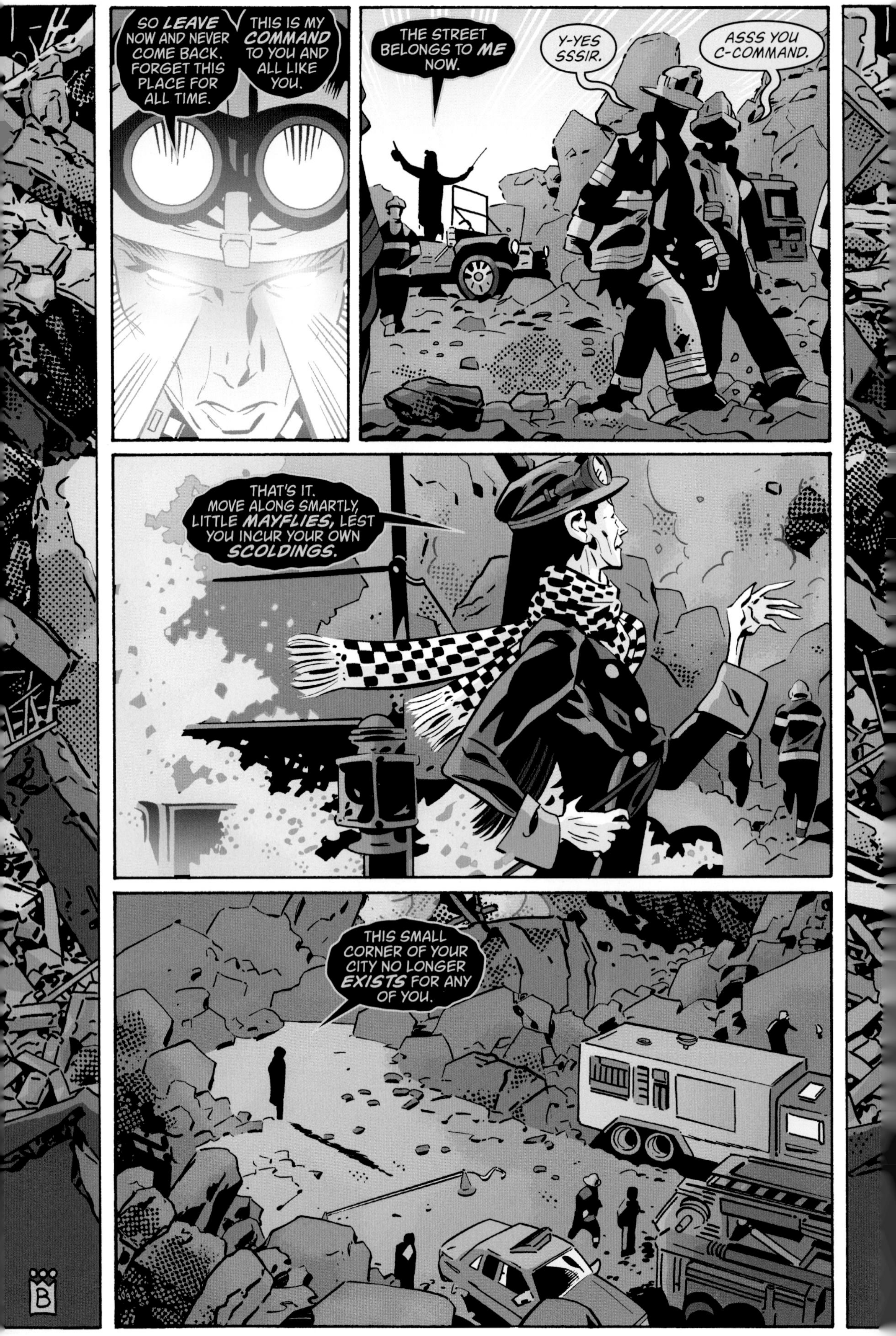
SO LEAVE NOW AND NEVER COME BACK. FORGET THIS PLACE FOR ALL TIME.
THIS IS MY COMMAND TO YOU AND ALL LIKE YOU.
THE STREET BELONGS TO ME NOW.
Y-YES SSSIR.
ASSS YOU C-COMMAND.
THAT'S IT. MOVE ALONG SMARTLY, LITTLE MAYFLIES, LEST YOU INCUR YOUR OWN SCOLDINGS.
THIS SMALL CORNER OF YOUR CITY NO LONGER EXISTS FOR ANY OF YOU.

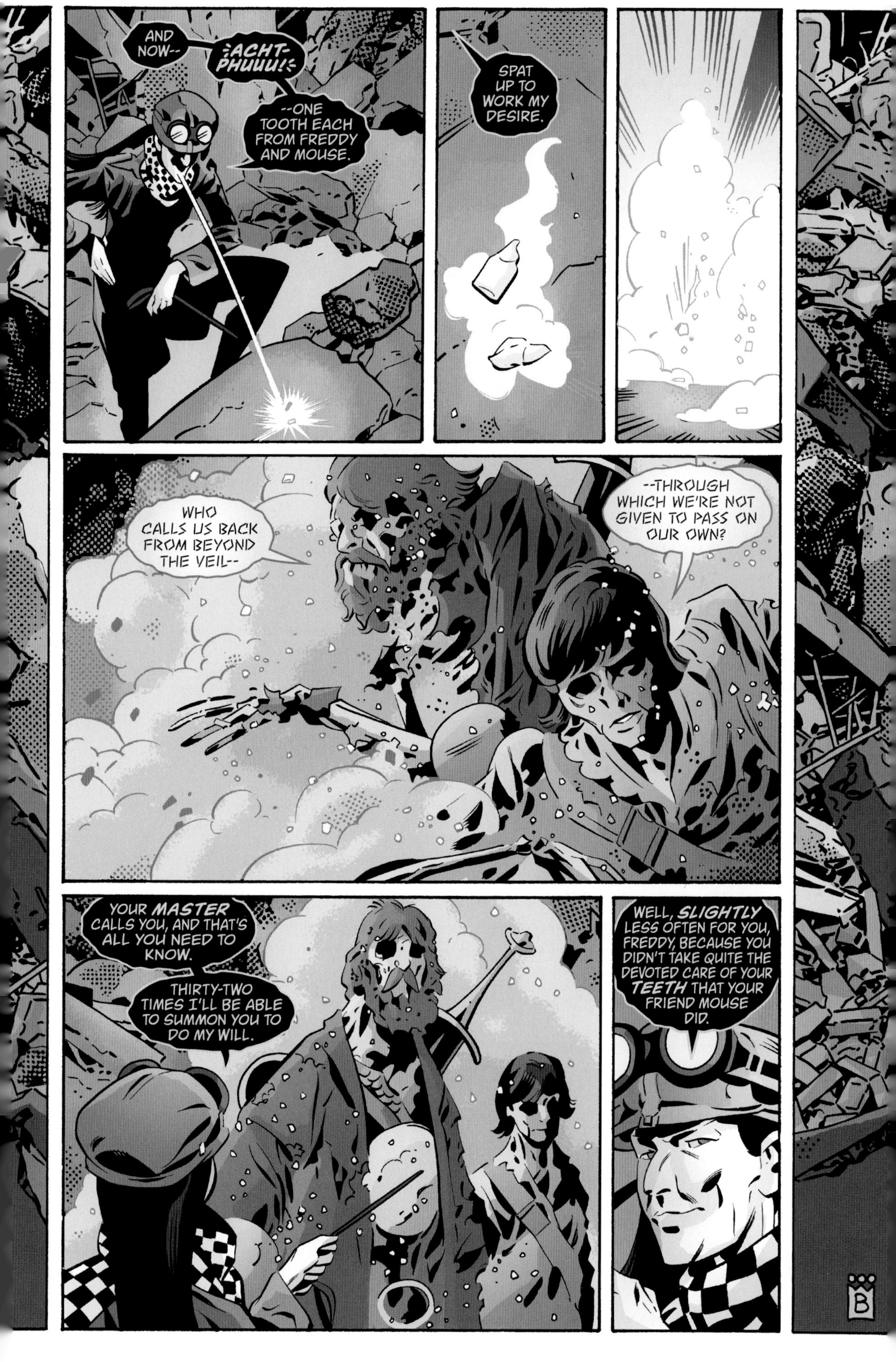
AND NOW--
ACHT-PHUUU!
--ONE TOOTH EACH FROM FREDDY AND MOUSE.
SPAT UP TO WORK MY DESIRE.
WHO CALLS US BACK FROM BEYOND THE VEIL--
--THROUGH WHICH WE'RE NOT GIVEN TO PASS ON OUR OWN?
YOUR MASTER CALLS YOU, AND THAT'S ALL YOU NEED TO KNOW.
THIRTY-TWO TIMES I'LL BE ABLE TO SUMMON YOU TO DO MY WILL.
WELL, SLIGHTLY LESS OFTEN FOR YOU, FREDDY, BECAUSE YOU DIDN'T TAKE QUITE THE DEVOTED CARE OF YOUR TEETH THAT YOUR FRIEND MOUSE DID.

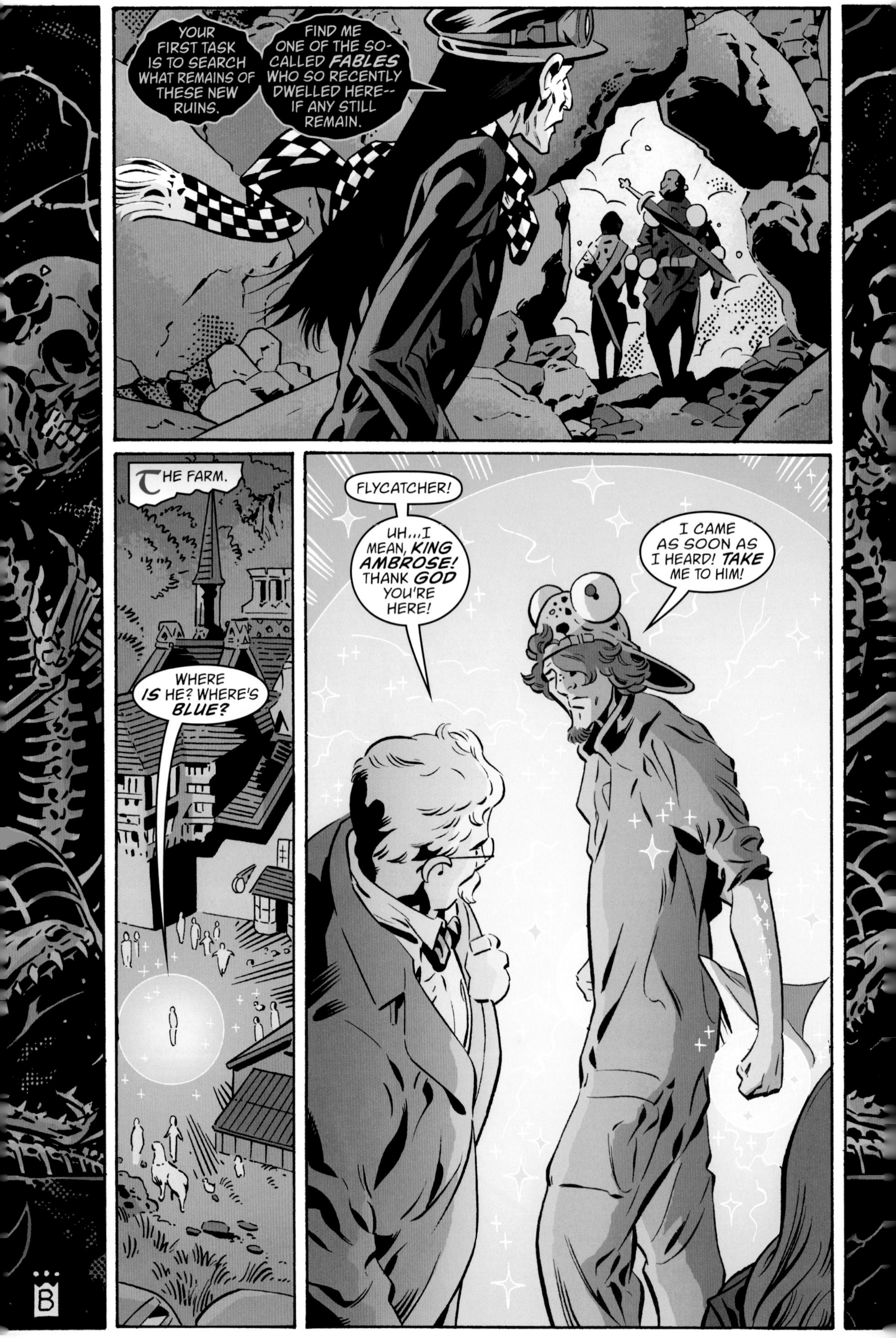
YOUR FIRST TASK IS TO SEARCH WHAT REMAINS OF THESE NEW RUINS.
FIND ME ONE OF THE SO-CALLED FABLES WHO SO RECENTLY DWELLED HERE-- IF ANY STILL REMAIN.
THE FARM.
WHERE IS HE? WHERE'S BLUE?
FLYCATCHER!
UH...I MEAN, KING AMBROSE! THANK GOD YOU'RE HERE!
I CAME AS SOON AS I HEARD! TAKE ME TO HIM!

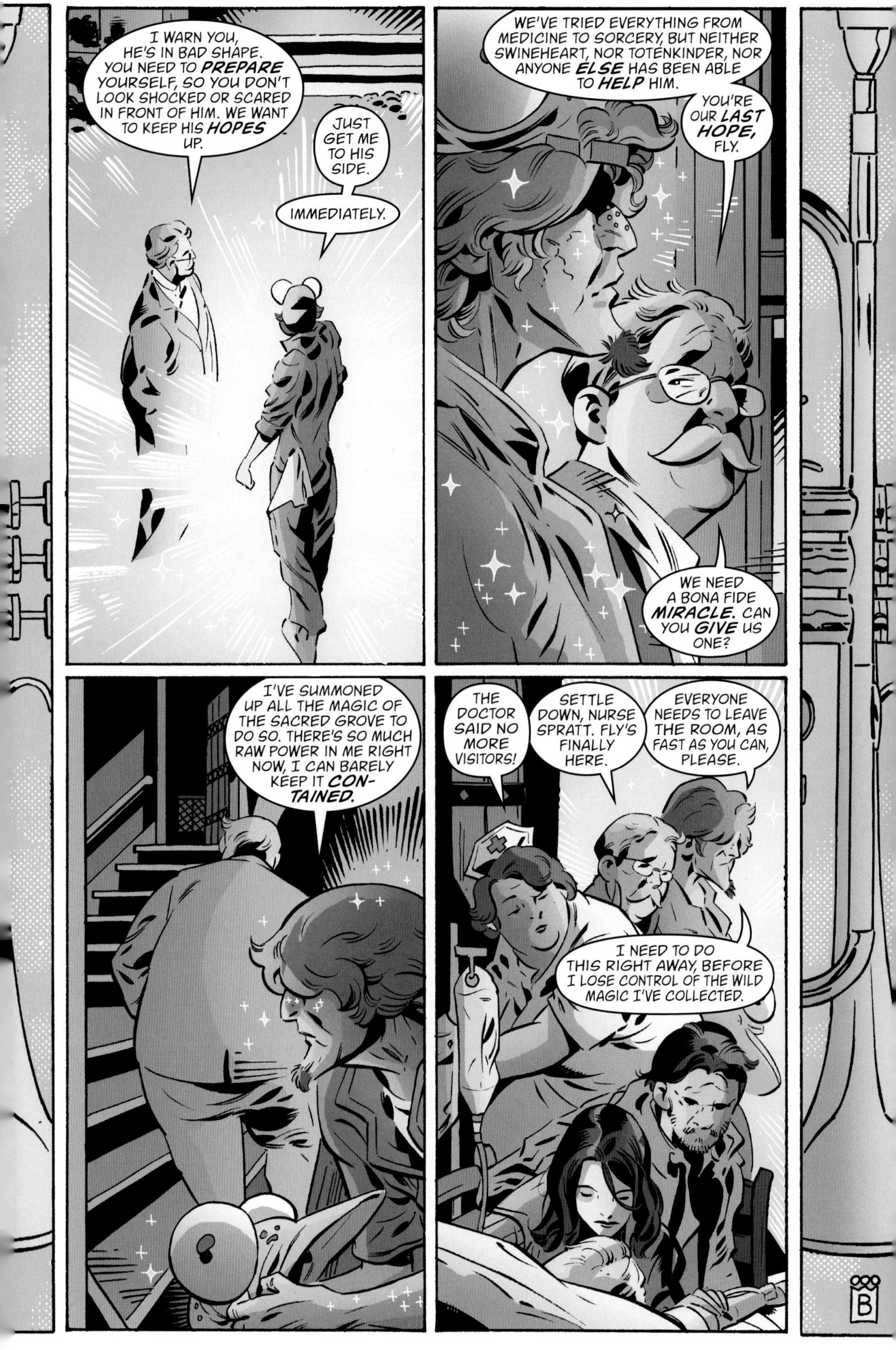

I WARN YOU, HE'S IN BAD SHAPE. YOU NEED TO PREPARE YOURSELF, SO YOU DON'T LOOK SHOCKED OR SCARED IN FRONT OF HIM. WE WANT TO KEEP HIS HOPES UP.
JUST GET ME TO HIS SIDE.
IMMEDIATELY.
WE'VE TRIED EVERYTHING FROM MEDICINE TO SORCERY, BUT NEITHER SWINEHEART, NOR TOTENKINDER, NOR ANYONE ELSE HAS BEEN ABLE TO HELP HIM.
YOU'RE OUR LAST HOPE, FLY.
WE NEED A BONA FIDE MIRACLE. CAN YOU GIVE US ONE?
I'VE SUMMONED UP ALL THE MAGIC OF THE SACRED GROVE TO DO SO. THERE'S SO MUCH RAW POWER IN ME RIGHT NOW, I CAN BARELY KEEP IT CON-TAINED.
THE DOCTOR SAID NO MORE VISITORS!
SETTLE DOWN, NURSE SPRATT. FLY'S FINALLY HERE.
EVERYONE NEEDS TO LEAVE THE ROOM, AS FAST AS YOU CAN, PLEASE.
I NEED TO DO THIS RIGHT AWAY, BEFORE I LOSE CONTROL OF THE WILD MAGIC I'VE COLLECTED.

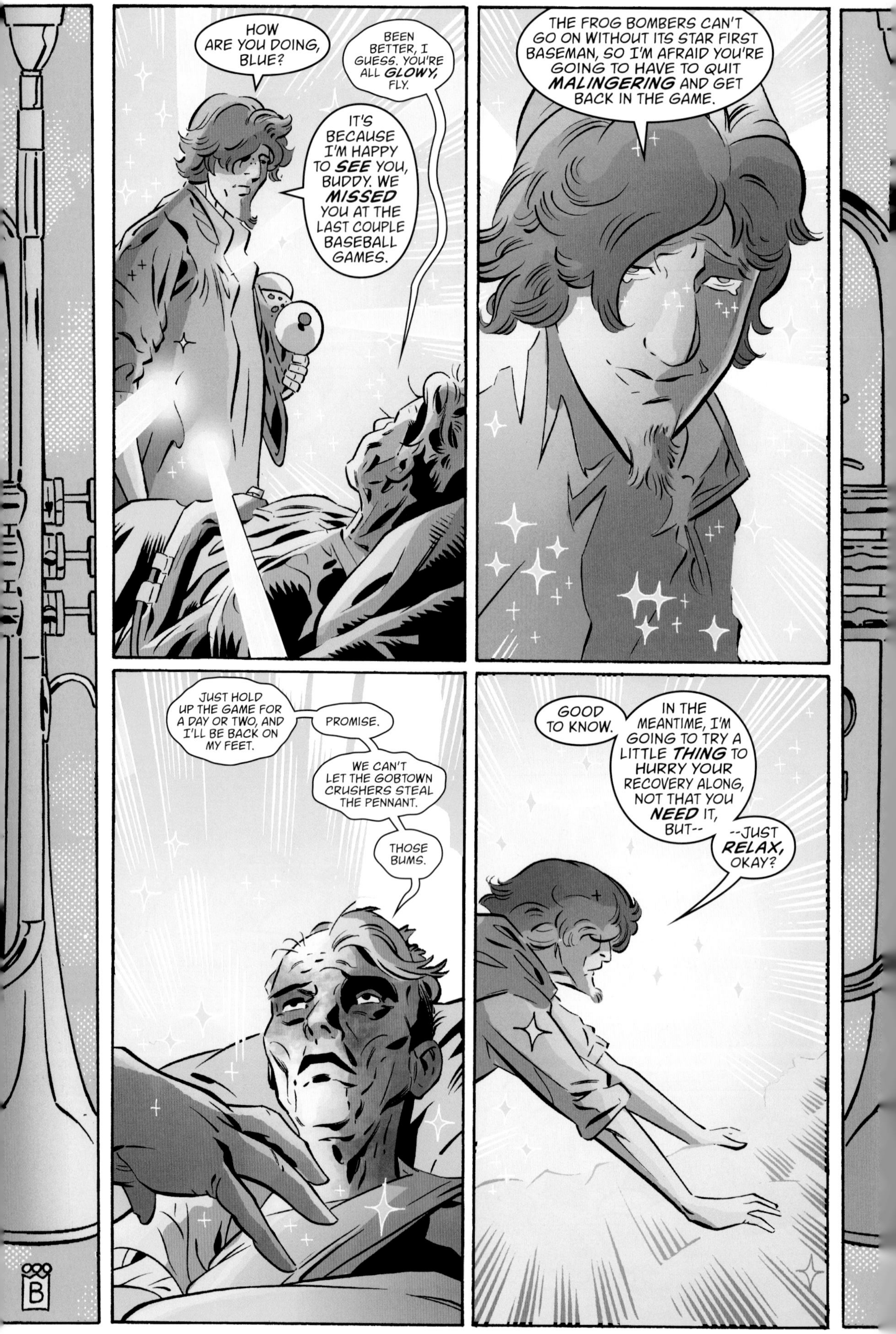
HOW ARE YOU DOING, BLUE?
BEEN BETTER, I GUESS. YOU'RE ALL GLOWY, FLY.
IT'S BECAUSE I'M HAPPY TO SEE YOU, BUDDY. WE MISSED YOU AT THE LAST COUPLE BASEBALL GAMES.
THE FROG BOMBERS CAN'T GO ON WITHOUT ITS STAR FIRST BASEMAN, SO I'M AFRAID YOU'RE GOING TO HAVE TO QUIT MALINGERING AND GET BACK IN THE GAME.
JUST HOLD UP THE GAME FOR A DAY OR TWO, AND I'LL BE BACK ON MY FEET.
PROMISE.
WE CAN'T LET THE GOBTOWN CRUSHERS STEAL THE PENNANT.
THOSE BUMS.
GOOD TO KNOW.
IN THE MEANTIME, I'M GOING TO TRY A LITTLE THING TO HURRY YOUR RECOVERY ALONG, NOT THAT YOU NEED IT, BUT--
--JUST RELAX, OKAY?

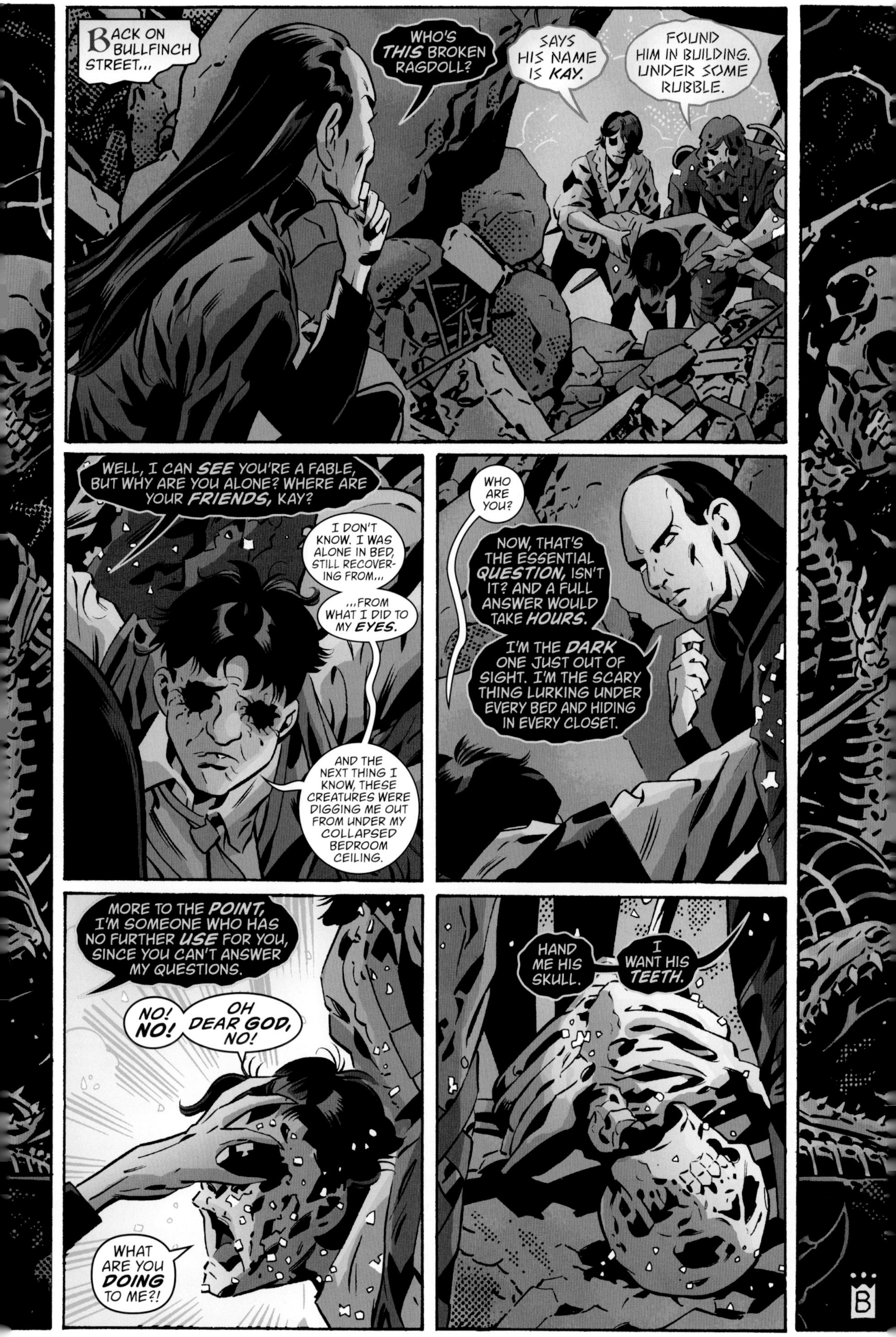

BACK ON BULLFINCH STREET...
WHO'S THIS BROKEN RAGDOLL?
SAYS HIS NAME IS KAY.
FOUND HIM IN BUILDING. UNDER SOME RUBBLE.
WELL, I CAN SEE YOU'RE A FABLE, BUT WHY ARE YOU ALONE? WHERE ARE YOUR FRIENDS, KAY?
I DON'T KNOW. I WAS ALONE IN BED, STILL RECOVERING FROM...
...FROM WHAT I DID TO MY EYES.
AND THE NEXT THING I KNOW, THESE CREATURES WERE DIGGING ME OUT FROM UNDER MY COLLAPSED BEDROOM CEILING.
WHO ARE YOU?
NOW, THAT'S THE ESSENTIAL QUESTION, ISN'T IT? AND A FULL ANSWER WOULD TAKE HOURS.
I'M THE DARK ONE JUST OUT OF SIGHT. I'M THE SCARY THING LURKING UNDER EVERY BED AND HIDING IN EVERY CLOSET.
MORE TO THE POINT, I'M SOMEONE WHO HAS NO FURTHER USE FOR YOU, SINCE YOU CAN'T ANSWER MY QUESTIONS.
NO! NO!
OH DEAR GOD, NO!
WHAT ARE YOU DOING TO ME?!
HAND ME HIS SKULL.
I WANT HIS TEETH.

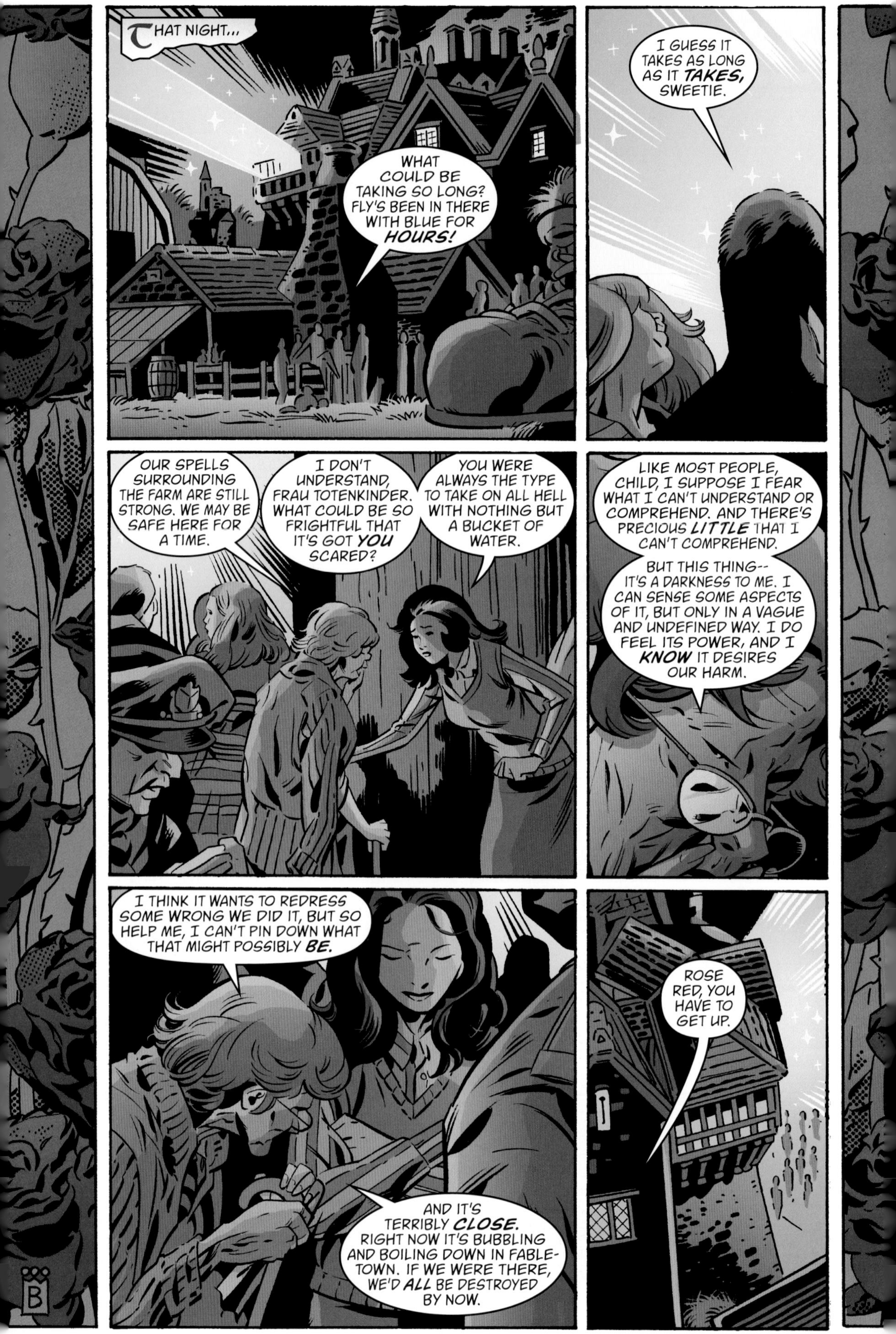
THAT NIGHT...
WHAT COULD BE TAKING SO LONG? FLY'S BEEN IN THERE WITH BLUE FOR HOURS!
I GUESS IT TAKES AS LONG AS IT TAKES, SWEETIE.
OUR SPELLS SURROUNDING THE FARM ARE STILL STRONG. WE MAY BE SAFE HERE FOR A TIME.
I DON'T UNDERSTAND, FRAU TOTENKINDER. WHAT COULD BE SO FRIGHTFUL THAT IT'S GOT YOU SCARED?
YOU WERE ALWAYS THE TYPE TO TAKE ON ALL HELL WITH NOTHING BUT A BUCKET OF WATER.
LIKE MOST PEOPLE, CHILD, I SUPPOSE I FEAR WHAT I CAN'T UNDERSTAND OR COMPREHEND. AND THERE'S PRECIOUS LITTLE THAT I CAN'T COMPREHEND.
BUT THIS THING-- IT'S A DARKNESS TO ME. I CAN SENSE SOME ASPECTS OF IT, BUT ONLY IN A VAGUE AND UNDEFINED WAY. I DO FEEL ITS POWER, AND I KNOW IT DESIRES OUR HARM.
I THINK IT WANTS TO REDRESS SOME WRONG WE DID IT, BUT SO HELP ME, I CAN'T PIN DOWN WHAT THAT MIGHT POSSIBLY BE.
AND IT'S TERRIBLY CLOSE. RIGHT NOW IT'S BUBBLING AND BOILING DOWN IN FABLE-TOWN. IF WE WERE THERE, WE'D ALL BE DESTROYED BY NOW.
ROSE RED, YOU HAVE TO GET UP.

LEAVE ME ALONE. I'M TIRED.

NO, DARLING, YOU'RE DEPRESSED, AND ALTHOUGH I UNDERSTAND, I CAN'T ALLOW YOU TO INDULGE IT RIGHT NOW. NO MATTER *HOW* MISERABLE YOU FEEL, YOU NEED TO GET UP.

YOU'RE THE FARM'S LEADER. YOU NEED TO BE DOWNSTAIRS WITH THE OTHERS, PARTICIPATING IN BLUE'S VIGIL. SORRY, BUT YOU SIMPLY CAN'T HIDE AWAY UP HERE.

THEY NEED YOU. *WE* NEED YOU.

THAT'S WHERE YOU'RE *WRONG*, SINBAD, DARLING. NO ONE NEEDS ME FOR NOTHING. DON'T YOU GET IT? I'M THE *BAD* SISTER. I'M THE PERENNIAL FUCKUP.

YOU MARRIED THE WRONG SISTER. *SNOW'S* THE LEADER. SHE'LL TAKE OVER DOWN THERE. JUST WATCH AND WAIT.

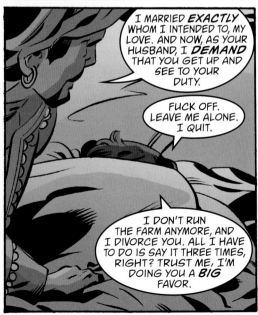

I MARRIED *EXACTLY* WHOM I INTENDED TO, MY LOVE. AND NOW, AS YOUR HUSBAND, I *DEMAND* THAT YOU GET UP AND SEE TO YOUR DUTY.

FUCK OFF. LEAVE ME ALONE. I QUIT.

I DON'T RUN THE FARM ANYMORE, AND I DIVORCE YOU. ALL I HAVE TO DO IS SAY IT THREE TIMES, RIGHT? TRUST ME, I'M DOING YOU A *BIG* FAVOR.

I DIVORCE YOU.

I DIVORCE YOU.

I DIVORCE YOU.

HAPPY? NOW, GET OUT AND LET ME *SLEEP*.

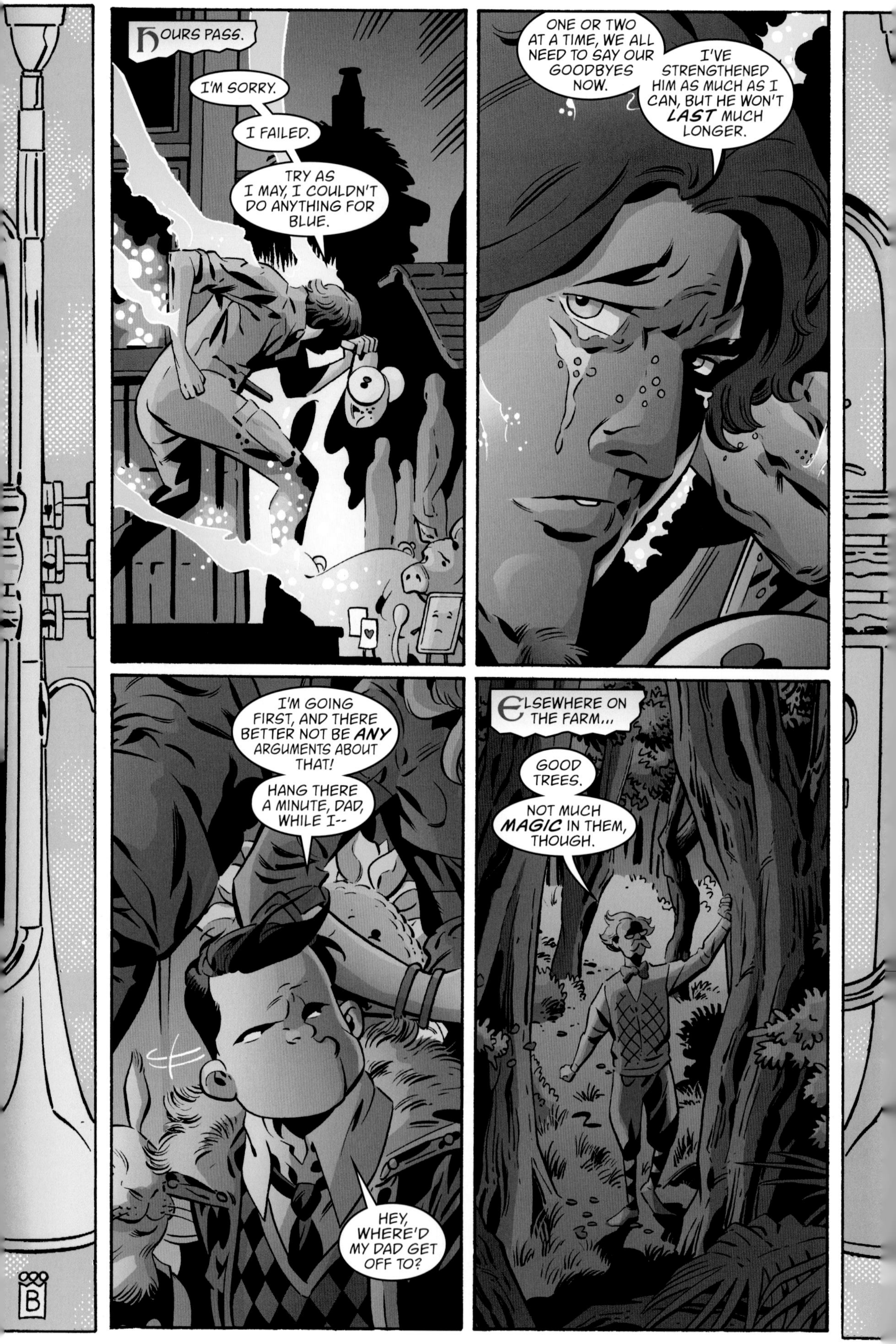
HOURS PASS.
I'M SORRY.
I FAILED.
TRY AS I MAY, I COULDN'T DO ANYTHING FOR BLUE.
ONE OR TWO AT A TIME, WE ALL NEED TO SAY OUR GOODBYES NOW.
I'VE STRENGTHENED HIM AS MUCH AS I CAN, BUT HE WON'T LAST MUCH LONGER.
I'M GOING FIRST, AND THERE BETTER NOT BE ANY ARGUMENTS ABOUT THAT!
HANG THERE A MINUTE, DAD, WHILE I--
HEY, WHERE'D MY DAD GET OFF TO?
ELSEWHERE ON THE FARM...
GOOD TREES.
NOT MUCH MAGIC IN THEM, THOUGH.

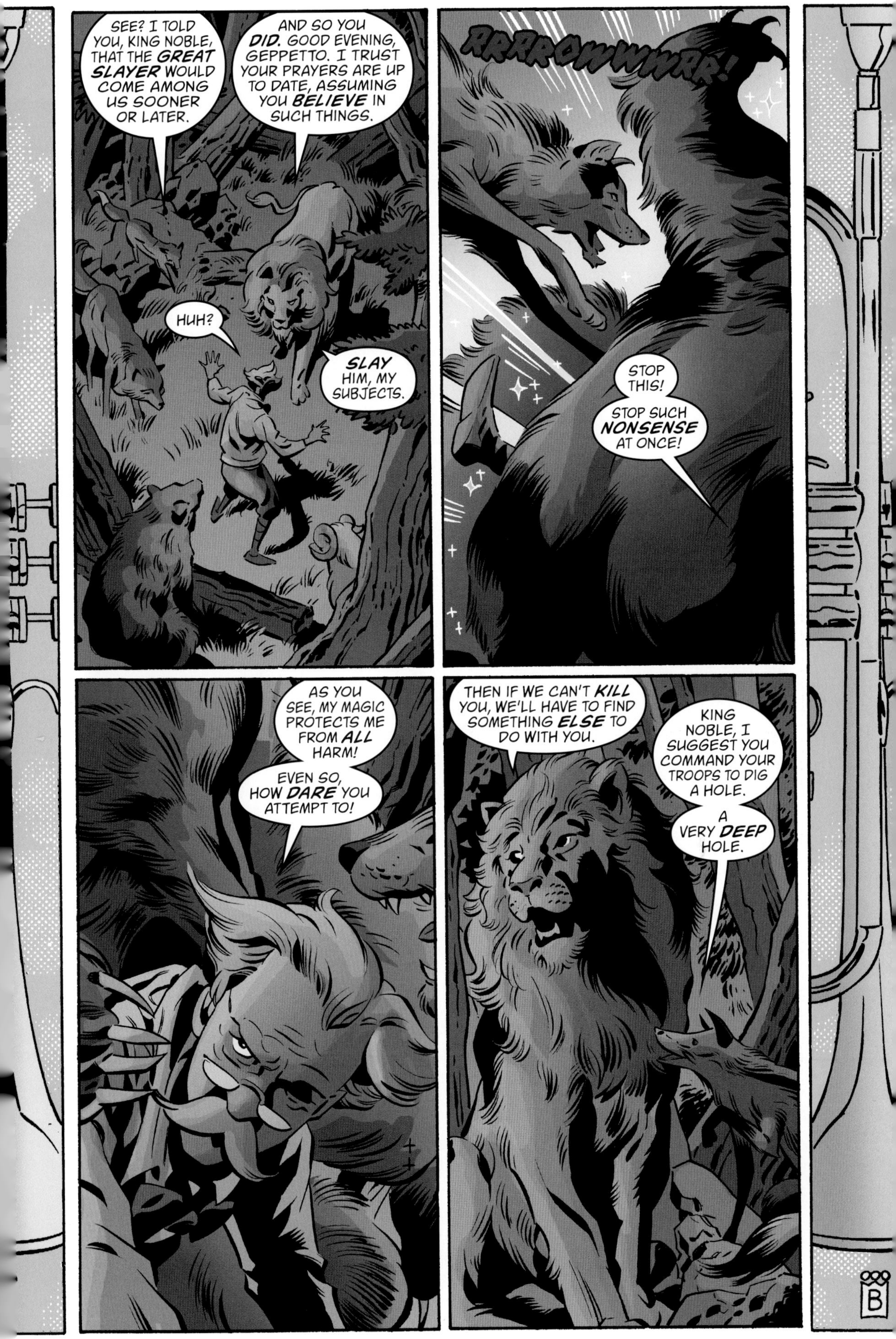
SEE? I TOLD YOU, KING NOBLE, THAT THE GREAT SLAYER WOULD COME AMONG US SOONER OR LATER.
AND SO YOU DID. GOOD EVENING, GEPPETTO. I TRUST YOUR PRAYERS ARE UP TO DATE, ASSUMING YOU BELIEVE IN SUCH THINGS.
HUH?
SLAY HIM, MY SUBJECTS.
RRRROWWWRR!
STOP THIS!
STOP SUCH NONSENSE AT ONCE!
AS YOU SEE, MY MAGIC PROTECTS ME FROM ALL HARM!
EVEN SO, HOW DARE YOU ATTEMPT TO!
THEN IF WE CAN'T KILL YOU, WE'LL HAVE TO FIND SOMETHING ELSE TO DO WITH YOU.
KING NOBLE, I SUGGEST YOU COMMAND YOUR TROOPS TO DIG A HOLE.
A VERY DEEP HOLE.

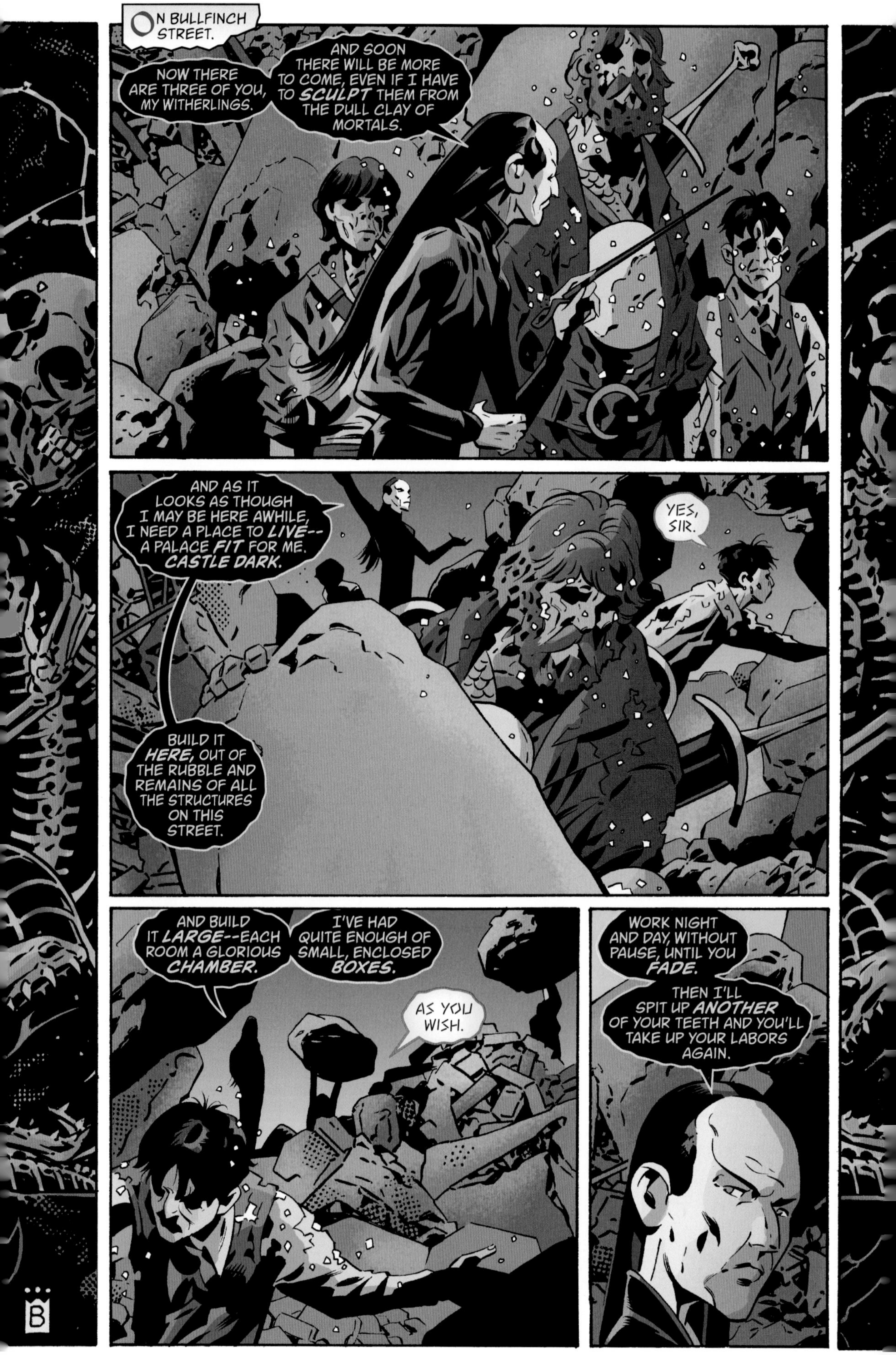
ON BULLFINCH STREET.
NOW THERE ARE THREE OF YOU, MY WITHERLINGS.
AND SOON THERE WILL BE MORE TO COME, EVEN IF I HAVE TO SCULPT THEM FROM THE DULL CLAY OF MORTALS.
AND AS IT LOOKS AS THOUGH I MAY BE HERE AWHILE, I NEED A PLACE TO LIVE-- A PALACE FIT FOR ME. CASTLE DARK.
BUILD IT HERE, OUT OF THE RUBBLE AND REMAINS OF ALL THE STRUCTURES ON THIS STREET.
YES, SIR.
AND BUILD IT LARGE--EACH ROOM A GLORIOUS CHAMBER.
I'VE HAD QUITE ENOUGH OF SMALL, ENCLOSED BOXES.
AS YOU WISH.
WORK NIGHT AND DAY, WITHOUT PAUSE, UNTIL YOU FADE.
THEN I'LL SPIT UP ANOTHER OF YOUR TEETH AND YOU'LL TAKE UP YOUR LABORS AGAIN.

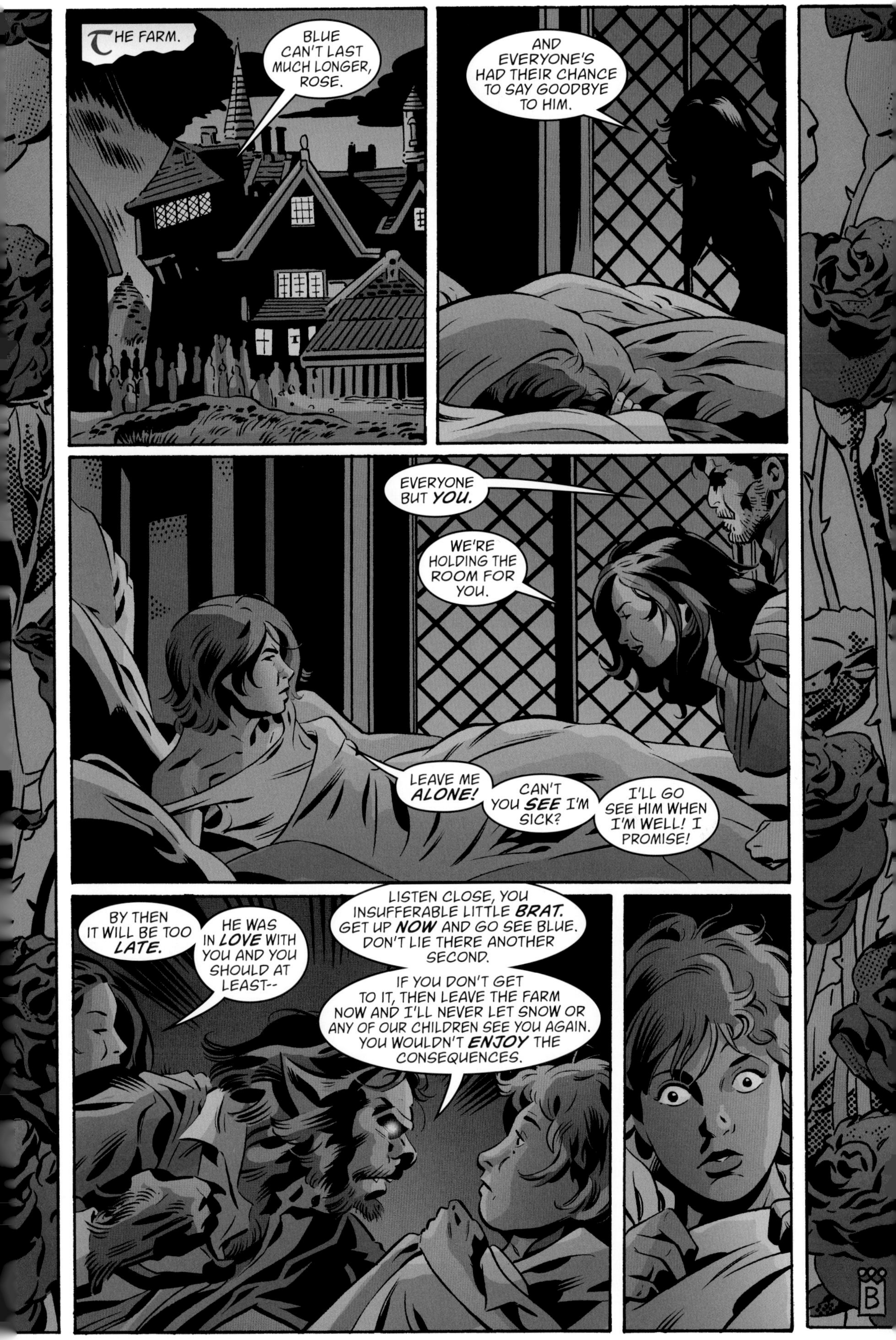
THE FARM.
BLUE CAN'T LAST MUCH LONGER, ROSE.
AND EVERYONE'S HAD THEIR CHANCE TO SAY GOODBYE TO HIM.
EVERYONE BUT YOU.
WE'RE HOLDING THE ROOM FOR YOU.
LEAVE ME ALONE!
CAN'T YOU SEE I'M SICK?
I'LL GO SEE HIM WHEN I'M WELL! I PROMISE!
BY THEN IT WILL BE TOO LATE.
HE WAS IN LOVE WITH YOU AND YOU SHOULD AT LEAST--
LISTEN CLOSE, YOU INSUFFERABLE LITTLE BRAT. GET UP NOW AND GO SEE BLUE. DON'T LIE THERE ANOTHER SECOND.
IF YOU DON'T GET TO IT, THEN LEAVE THE FARM NOW AND I'LL NEVER LET SNOW OR ANY OF OUR CHILDREN SEE YOU AGAIN. YOU WOULDN'T ENJOY THE CONSEQUENCES.

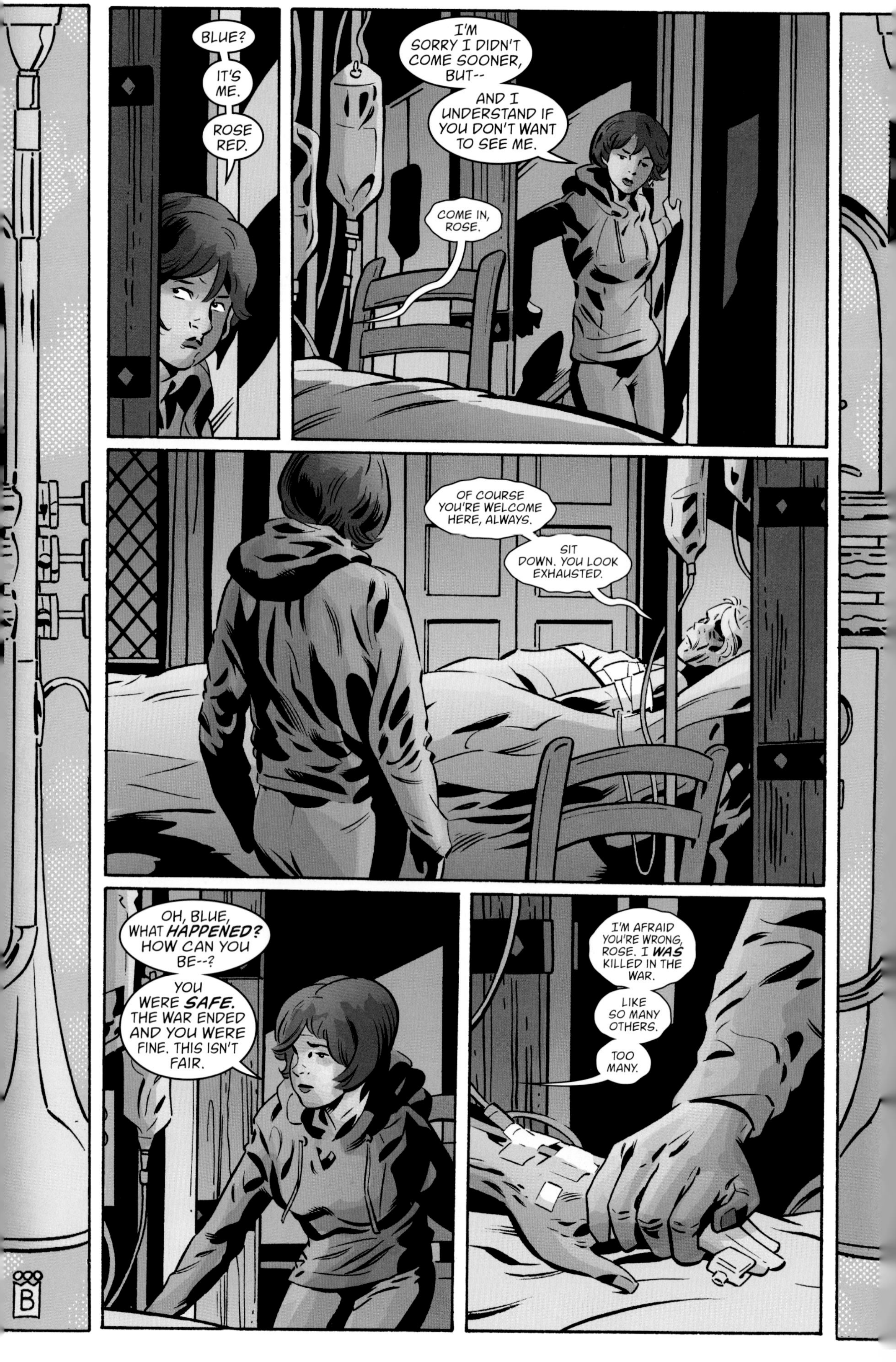
BLUE?
IT'S ME.
ROSE RED.
I'M SORRY I DIDN'T COME SOONER, BUT--
AND I UNDERSTAND IF YOU DON'T WANT TO SEE ME.
COME IN, ROSE.
OF COURSE YOU'RE WELCOME HERE, ALWAYS.
SIT DOWN. YOU LOOK EXHAUSTED.
OH, BLUE, WHAT *HAPPENED?* HOW CAN YOU BE--?
YOU WERE *SAFE.* THE WAR ENDED AND YOU WERE FINE. THIS ISN'T FAIR.
I'M AFRAID YOU'RE WRONG, ROSE. I *WAS* KILLED IN THE WAR.
LIKE SO MANY OTHERS.
TOO MANY.

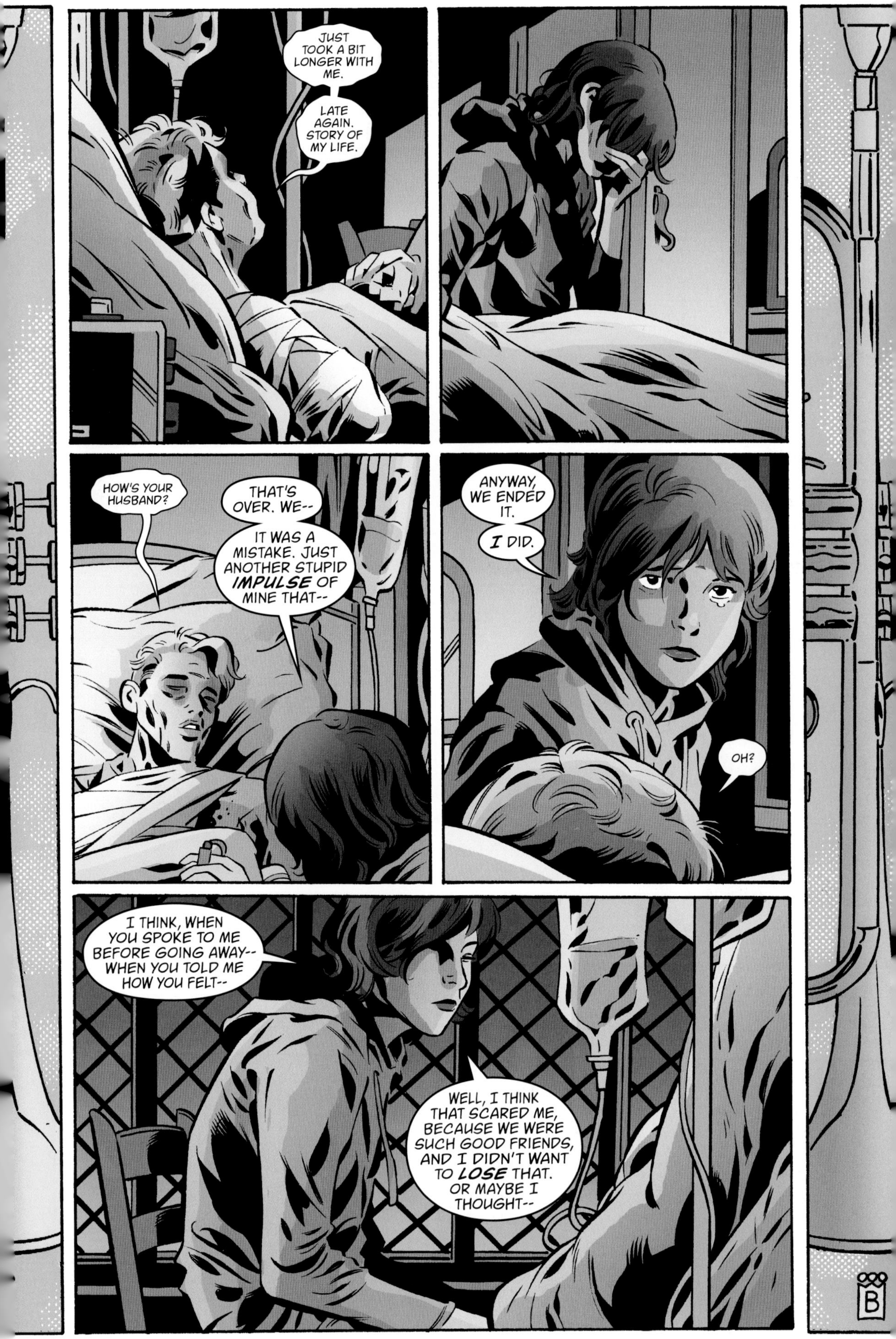

JUST TOOK A BIT LONGER WITH ME.
LATE AGAIN. STORY OF MY LIFE.
HOW'S YOUR HUSBAND?
THAT'S OVER. WE--
IT WAS A MISTAKE. JUST ANOTHER STUPID *IMPULSE* OF MINE THAT--
ANYWAY, WE ENDED IT.
I DID.
OH?
I THINK, WHEN YOU SPOKE TO ME BEFORE GOING AWAY-- WHEN YOU TOLD ME HOW YOU FELT--
WELL, I THINK THAT SCARED ME, BECAUSE WE WERE SUCH GOOD FRIENDS, AND I DIDN'T WANT TO *LOSE* THAT. OR MAYBE I THOUGHT--

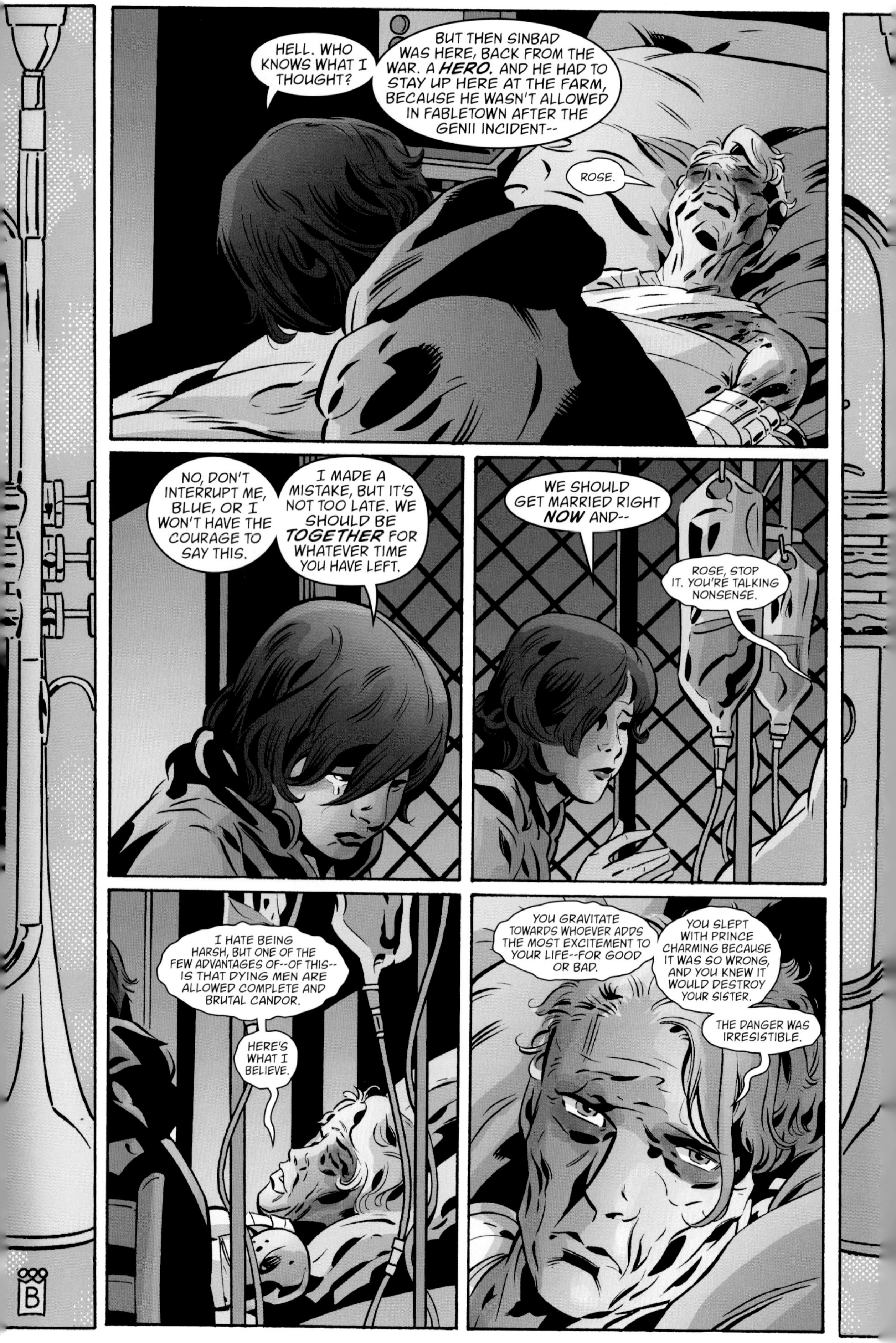
HELL. WHO KNOWS WHAT I THOUGHT?
BUT THEN SINBAD WAS HERE, BACK FROM THE WAR. A **HERO.** AND HE HAD TO STAY UP HERE AT THE FARM, BECAUSE HE WASN'T ALLOWED IN FABLETOWN AFTER THE GENII INCIDENT--
ROSE.
NO, DON'T INTERRUPT ME, BLUE, OR I WON'T HAVE THE COURAGE TO SAY THIS.
I MADE A MISTAKE, BUT IT'S NOT TOO LATE. WE SHOULD BE ***TOGETHER*** FOR WHATEVER TIME YOU HAVE LEFT.
WE SHOULD GET MARRIED RIGHT ***NOW*** AND--
ROSE, STOP IT. YOU'RE TALKING NONSENSE.
I HATE BEING HARSH, BUT ONE OF THE FEW ADVANTAGES OF--OF THIS--IS THAT DYING MEN ARE ALLOWED COMPLETE AND BRUTAL CANDOR.
HERE'S WHAT I BELIEVE.
YOU GRAVITATE TOWARDS WHOEVER ADDS THE MOST EXCITEMENT TO YOUR LIFE--FOR GOOD OR BAD.
YOU SLEPT WITH PRINCE CHARMING BECAUSE IT WAS SO WRONG, AND YOU KNEW IT WOULD DESTROY YOUR SISTER.
THE DANGER WAS IRRESISTIBLE.

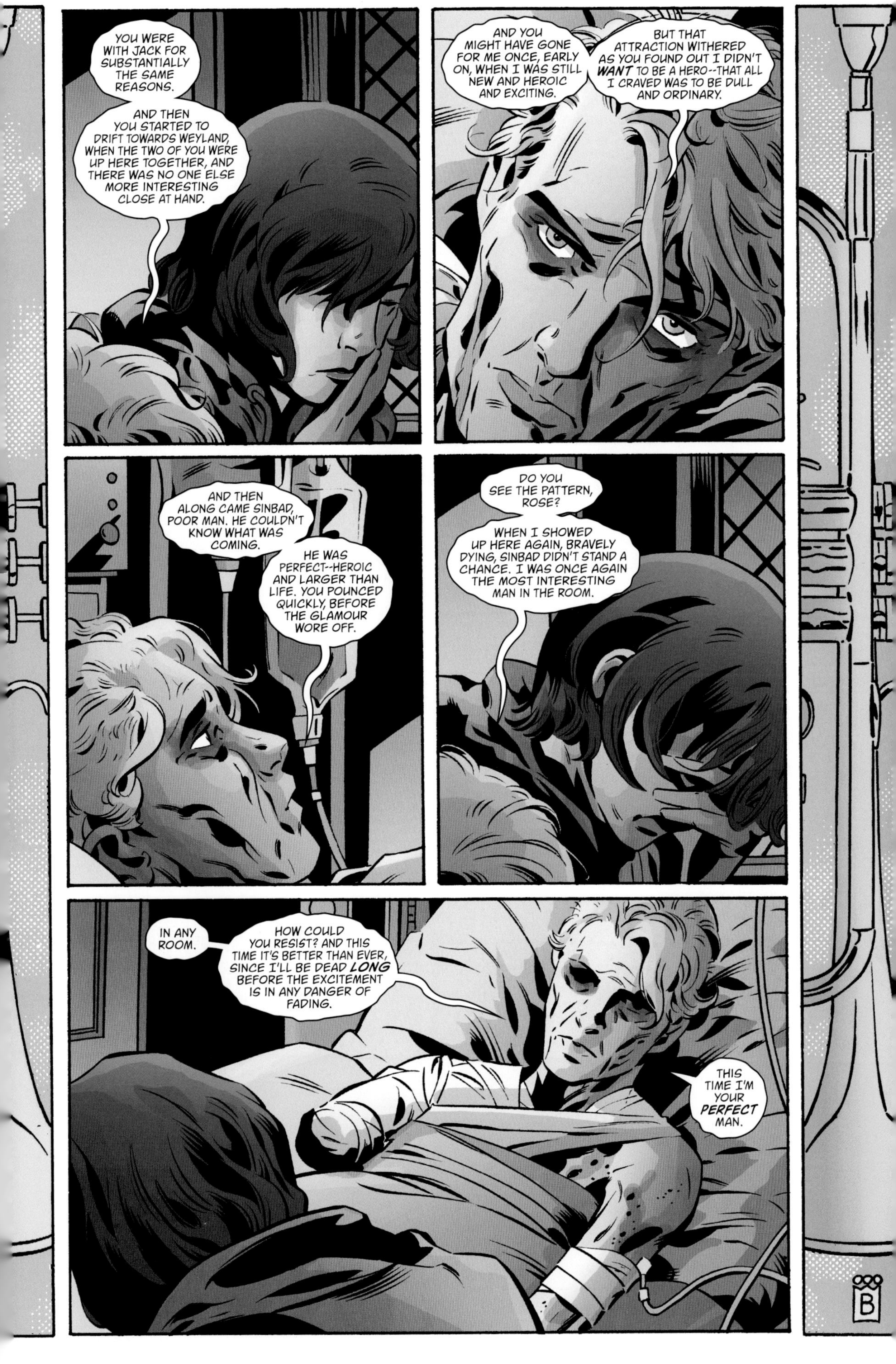
YOU WERE WITH JACK FOR SUBSTANTIALLY THE SAME REASONS.
AND THEN YOU STARTED TO DRIFT TOWARDS WEYLAND, WHEN THE TWO OF YOU WERE UP HERE TOGETHER, AND THERE WAS NO ONE ELSE MORE INTERESTING CLOSE AT HAND.
AND YOU MIGHT HAVE GONE FOR ME ONCE, EARLY ON, WHEN I WAS STILL NEW AND HEROIC AND EXCITING.
BUT THAT ATTRACTION WITHERED AS YOU FOUND OUT I DIDN'T *WANT* TO BE A HERO--THAT ALL I CRAVED WAS TO BE DULL AND ORDINARY.
AND THEN ALONG CAME SINBAD, POOR MAN. HE COULDN'T KNOW WHAT WAS COMING.
HE WAS PERFECT--HEROIC AND LARGER THAN LIFE. YOU POUNCED QUICKLY, BEFORE THE GLAMOUR WORE OFF.
DO YOU SEE THE PATTERN, ROSE?
WHEN I SHOWED UP HERE AGAIN, BRAVELY DYING, SINBAD DIDN'T STAND A CHANCE. I WAS ONCE AGAIN THE MOST INTERESTING MAN IN THE ROOM.
IN ANY ROOM.
HOW COULD YOU RESIST? AND THIS TIME IT'S BETTER THAN EVER, SINCE I'LL BE DEAD *LONG* BEFORE THE EXCITEMENT IS IN ANY DANGER OF FADING.
THIS TIME I'M YOUR *PERFECT* MAN.

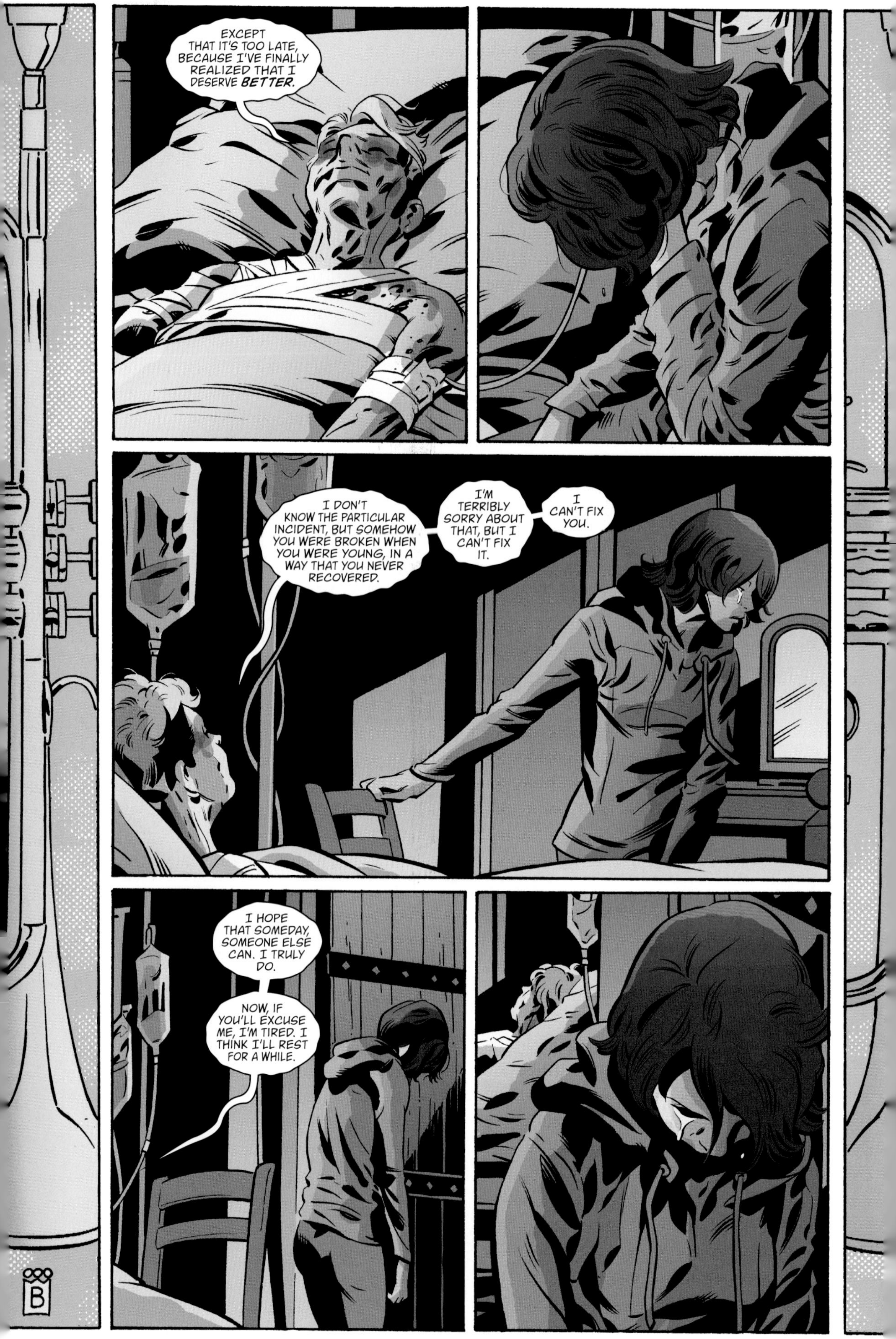
EXCEPT THAT IT'S TOO LATE, BECAUSE I'VE FINALLY REALIZED THAT I DESERVE **BETTER**.
I DON'T KNOW THE PARTICULAR INCIDENT, BUT SOMEHOW YOU WERE BROKEN WHEN YOU WERE YOUNG, IN A WAY THAT YOU NEVER RECOVERED.
I'M TERRIBLY SORRY ABOUT THAT, BUT I CAN'T FIX IT.
I CAN'T FIX YOU.
I HOPE THAT SOMEDAY, SOMEONE ELSE CAN. I TRULY DO.
NOW, IF YOU'LL EXCUSE ME, I'M TIRED. I THINK I'LL REST FOR A WHILE.

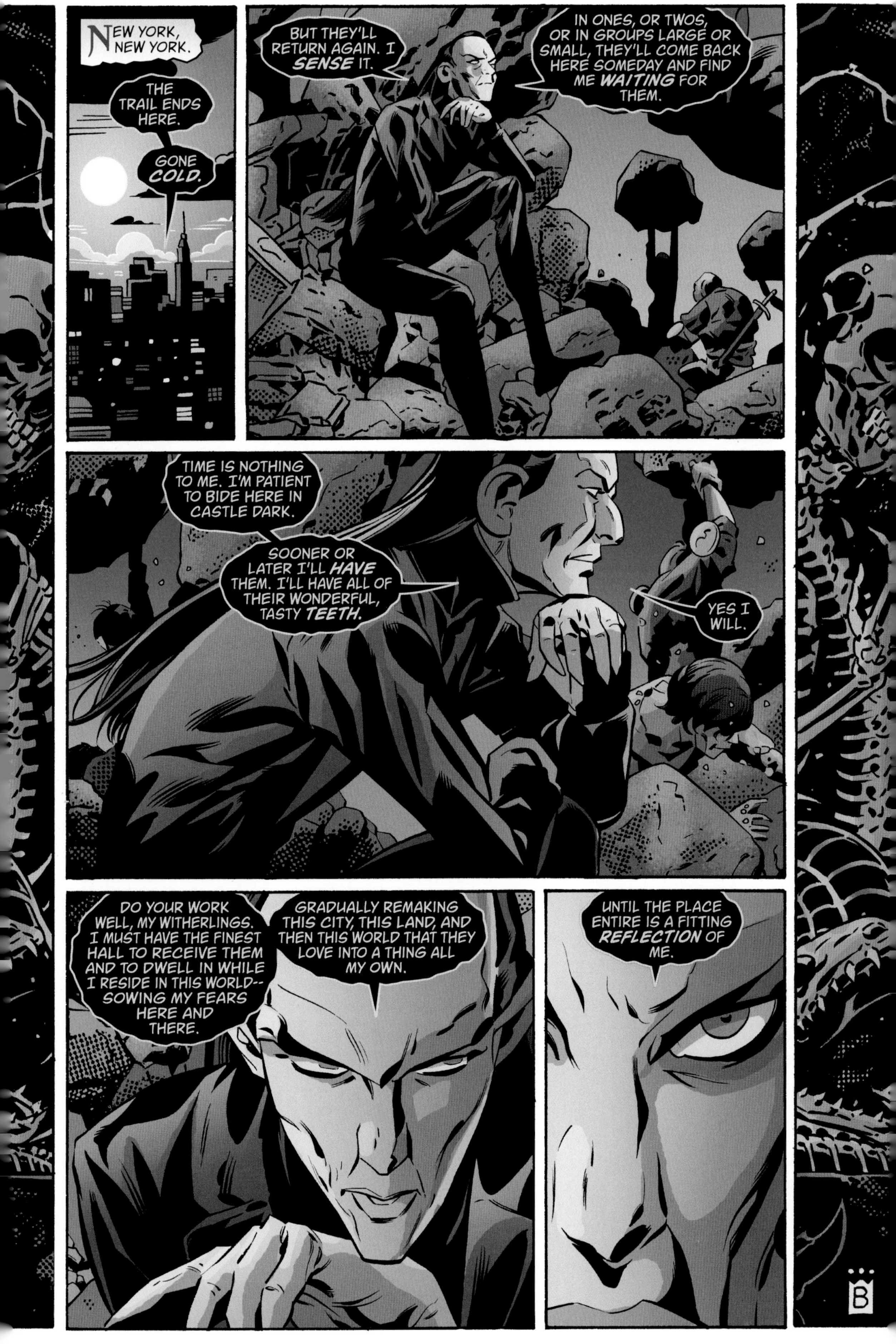
NEW YORK, NEW YORK.
THE TRAIL ENDS HERE.
GONE COLD.
BUT THEY'LL RETURN AGAIN. I SENSE IT.
IN ONES, OR TWOS, OR IN GROUPS LARGE OR SMALL, THEY'LL COME BACK HERE SOMEDAY AND FIND ME WAITING FOR THEM.
TIME IS NOTHING TO ME. I'M PATIENT TO BIDE HERE IN CASTLE DARK.
SOONER OR LATER I'LL HAVE THEM. I'LL HAVE ALL OF THEIR WONDERFUL, TASTY TEETH.
YES I WILL.
DO YOUR WORK WELL, MY WITHERLINGS. I MUST HAVE THE FINEST HALL TO RECEIVE THEM AND TO DWELL IN WHILE I RESIDE IN THIS WORLD-- SOWING MY FEARS HERE AND THERE.
GRADUALLY REMAKING THIS CITY, THIS LAND, AND THEN THIS WORLD THAT THEY LOVE INTO A THING ALL MY OWN.
UNTIL THE PLACE ENTIRE IS A FITTING REFLECTION OF ME.

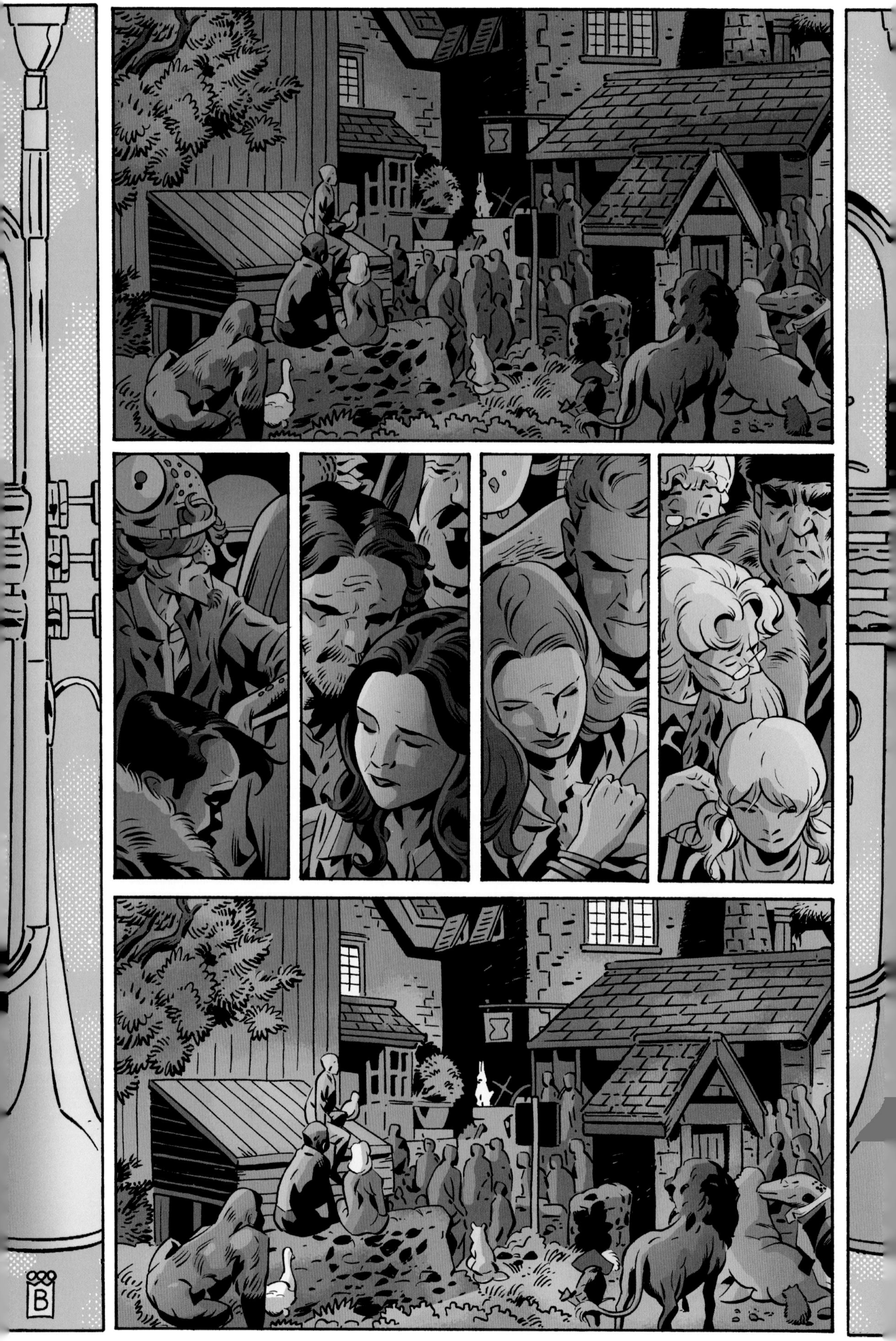

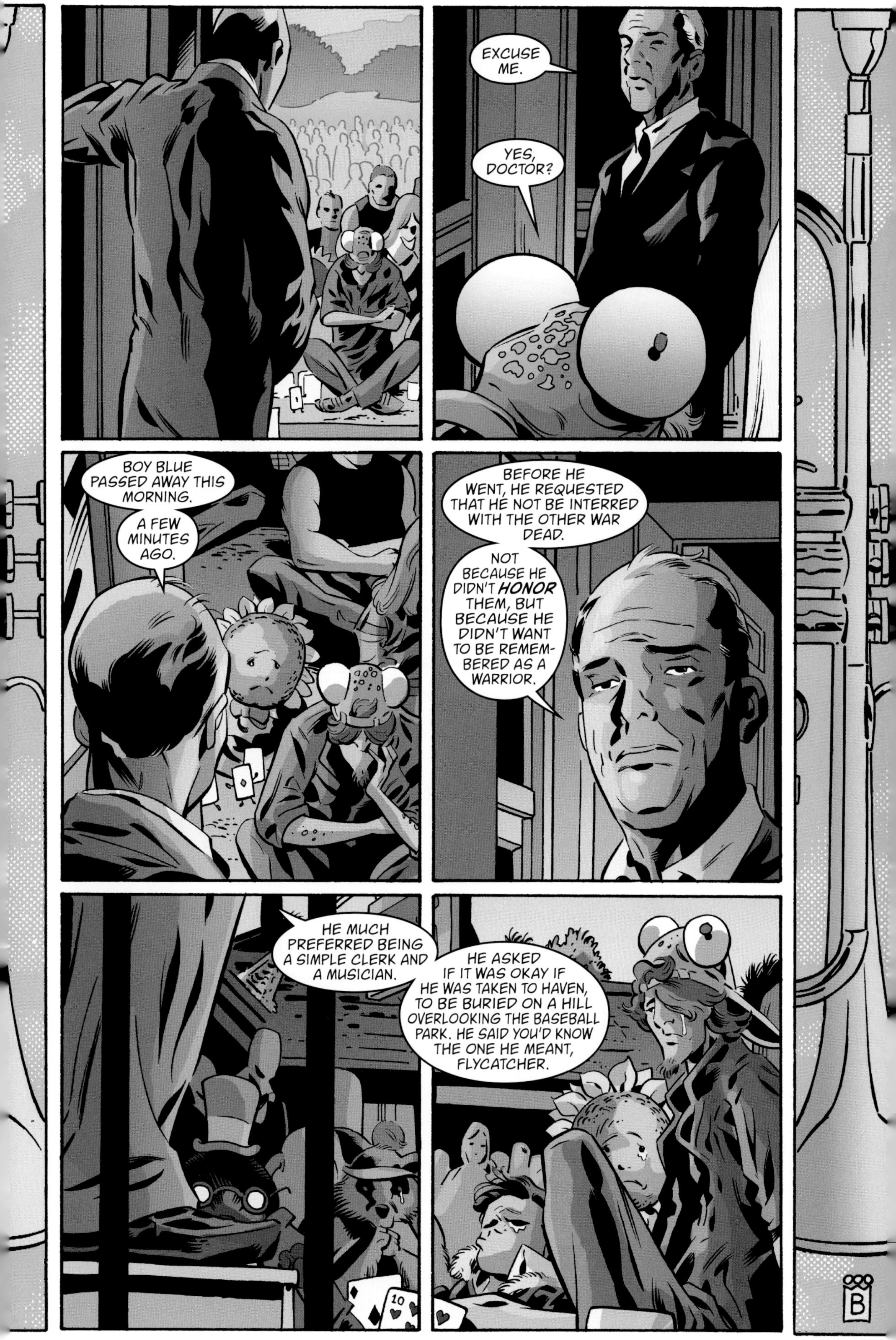
EXCUSE ME.
YES, DOCTOR?
BOY BLUE PASSED AWAY THIS MORNING.
A FEW MINUTES AGO.
BEFORE HE WENT, HE REQUESTED THAT HE NOT BE INTERRED WITH THE OTHER WAR DEAD.
NOT BECAUSE HE DIDN'T ***HONOR*** THEM, BUT BECAUSE HE DIDN'T WANT TO BE REMEMBERED AS A WARRIOR.
HE MUCH PREFERRED BEING A SIMPLE CLERK AND A MUSICIAN.
HE ASKED IF IT WAS OKAY IF HE WAS TAKEN TO HAVEN, TO BE BURIED ON A HILL OVERLOOKING THE BASEBALL PARK. HE SAID YOU'D KNOW THE ONE HE MEANT, FLYCATCHER.

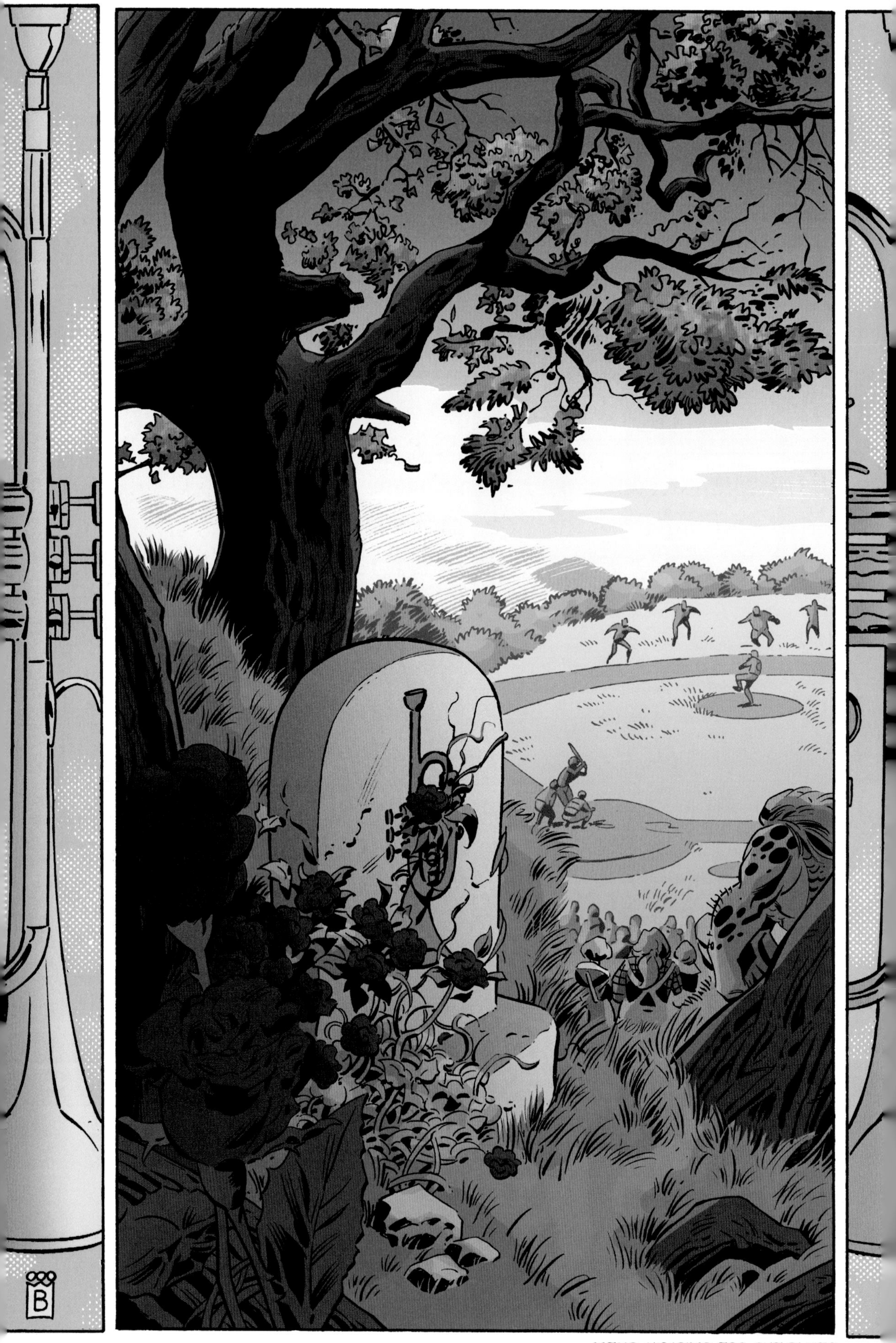

NEXT: WAITING FOR THE BLUES

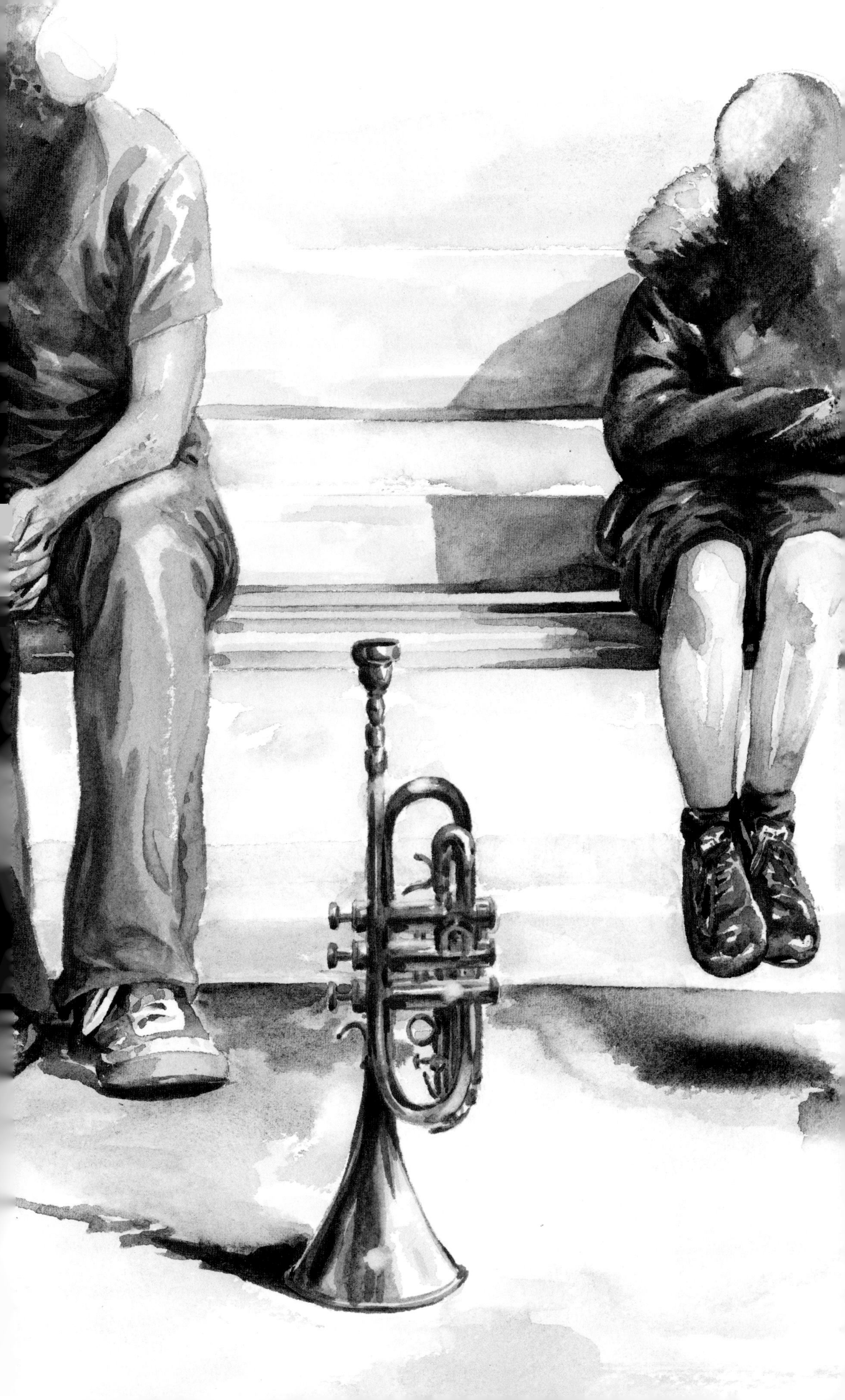

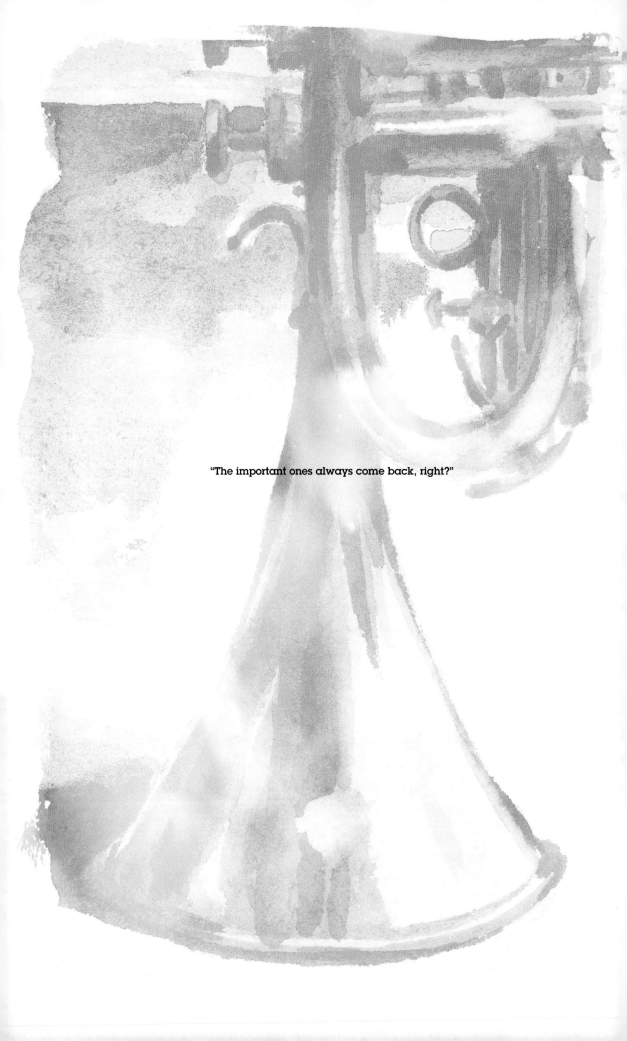

"The important ones always come back, right?"

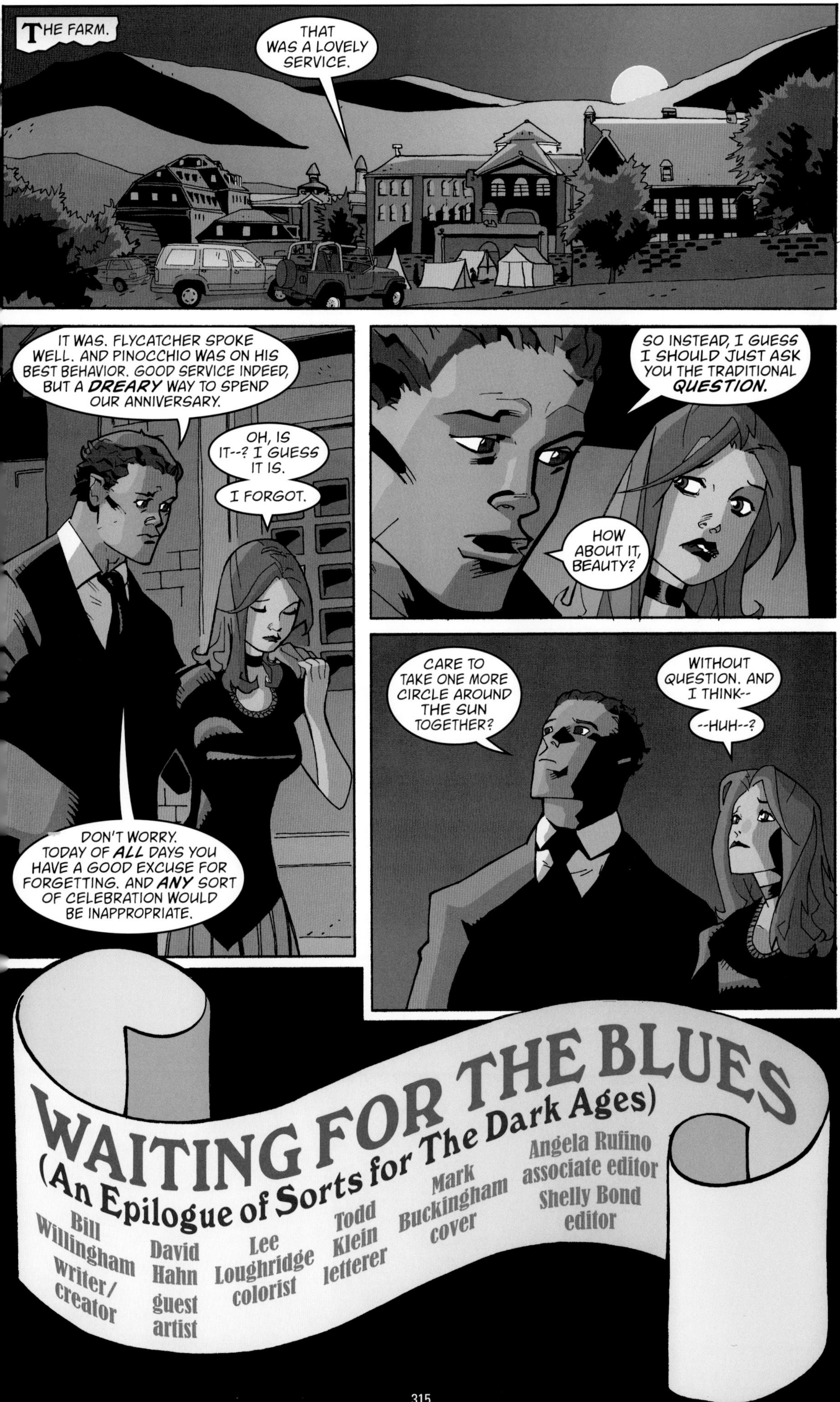
THE FARM.
THAT WAS A LOVELY SERVICE.
IT WAS. FLYCATCHER SPOKE WELL. AND PINOCCHIO WAS ON HIS BEST BEHAVIOR. GOOD SERVICE INDEED, BUT A DREARY WAY TO SPEND OUR ANNIVERSARY.
OH, IS IT--? I GUESS IT IS.
I FORGOT.
DON'T WORRY. TODAY OF ALL DAYS YOU HAVE A GOOD EXCUSE FOR FORGETTING. AND ANY SORT OF CELEBRATION WOULD BE INAPPROPRIATE.
SO INSTEAD, I GUESS I SHOULD JUST ASK YOU THE TRADITIONAL QUESTION.
HOW ABOUT IT, BEAUTY?
CARE TO TAKE ONE MORE CIRCLE AROUND THE SUN TOGETHER?
WITHOUT QUESTION. AND I THINK--
--HUH--?
WAITING FOR THE BLUES
(An Epilogue of Sorts for The Dark Ages)
Bill Willingham writer/creator
David Hahn guest artist
Lee Loughridge colorist
Todd Klein letterer
Mark Buckingham cover
Angela Rufino associate editor
Shelly Bond editor

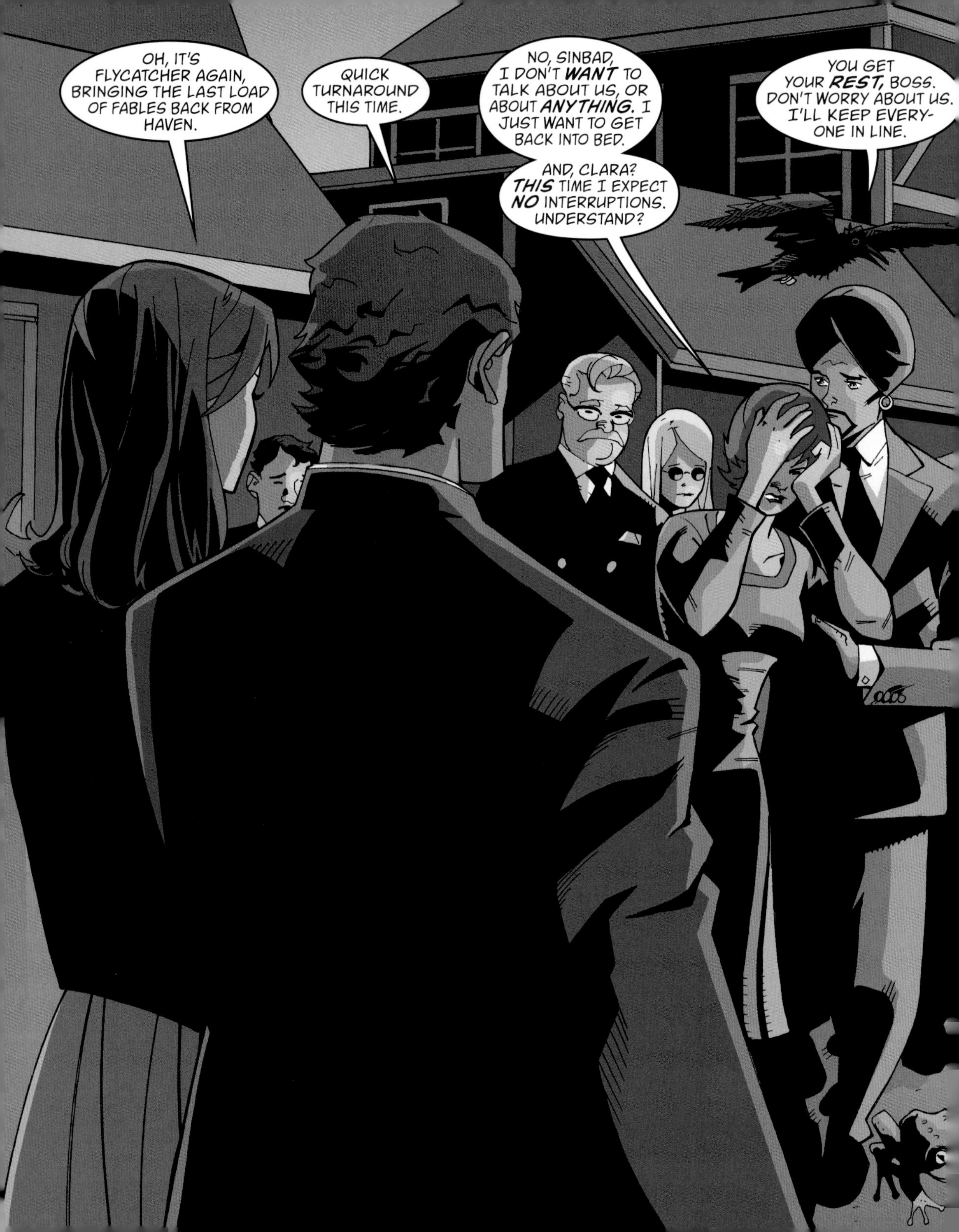
OH, IT'S FLYCATCHER AGAIN, BRINGING THE LAST LOAD OF FABLES BACK FROM HAVEN.
QUICK TURNAROUND THIS TIME.
NO, SINBAD, I DON'T **WANT** TO TALK ABOUT US, OR ABOUT **ANYTHING.** I JUST WANT TO GET BACK INTO BED.
AND, CLARA? **THIS** TIME I EXPECT **NO** INTERRUPTIONS. UNDERSTAND?
YOU GET YOUR **REST,** BOSS. DON'T WORRY ABOUT US. I'LL KEEP EVERY-ONE IN LINE.

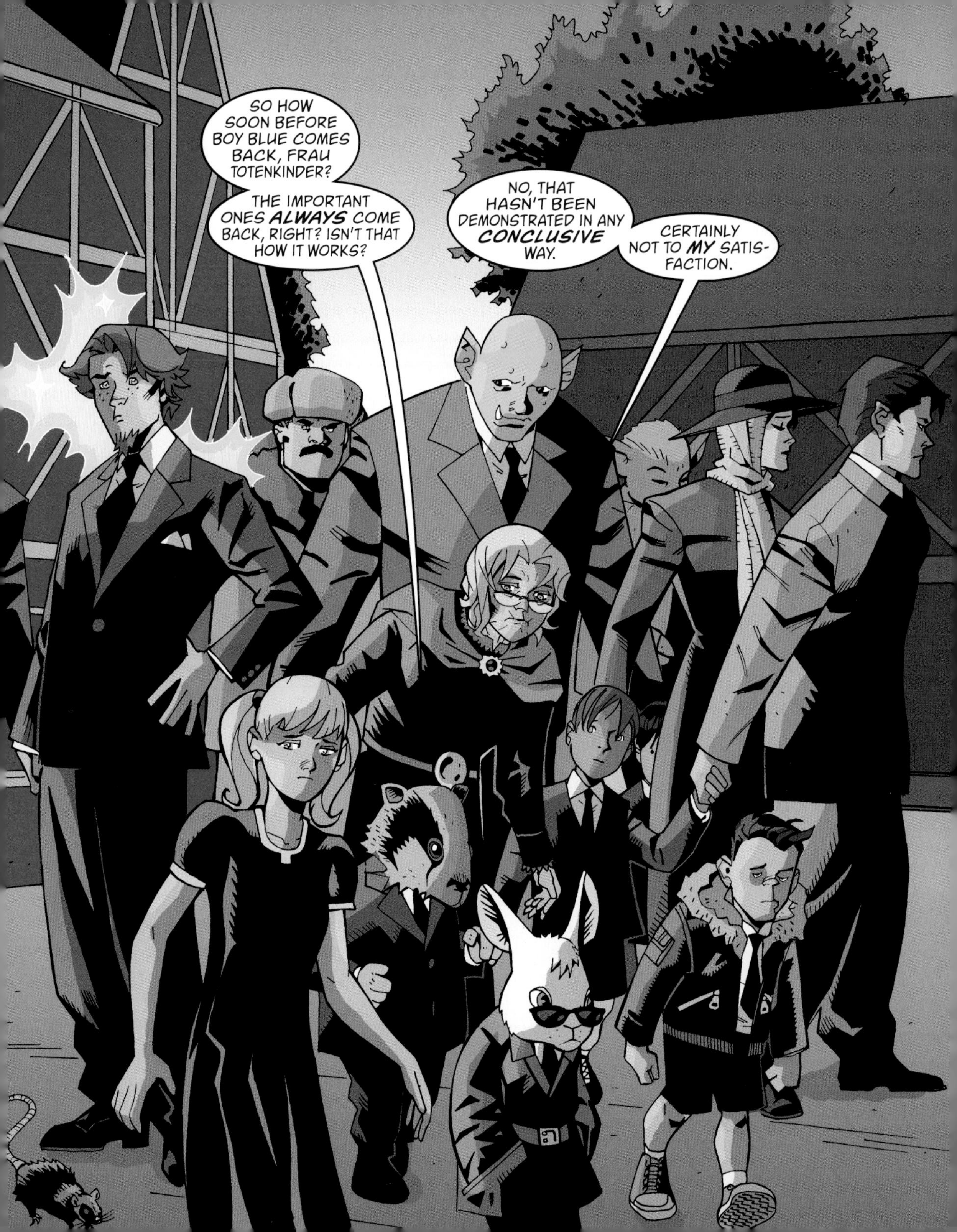
SO HOW SOON BEFORE BOY BLUE COMES BACK, FRAU TOTENKINDER?
THE IMPORTANT ONES ALWAYS COME BACK, RIGHT? ISN'T THAT HOW IT WORKS?
NO, THAT HASN'T BEEN DEMONSTRATED IN ANY CONCLUSIVE WAY.
CERTAINLY NOT TO MY SATIS-FACTION.

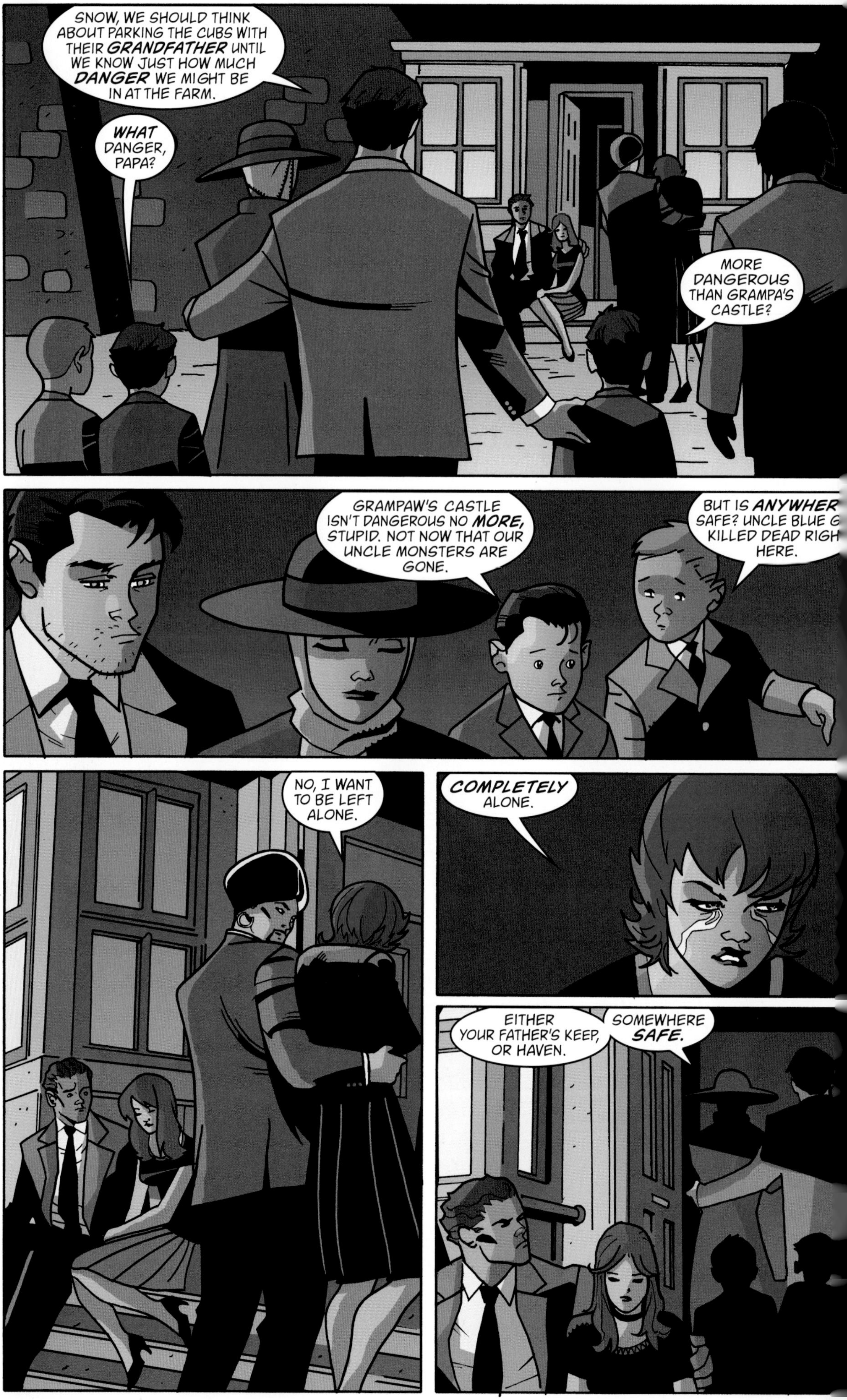
SNOW, WE SHOULD THINK ABOUT PARKING THE CUBS WITH THEIR GRANDFATHER UNTIL WE KNOW JUST HOW MUCH DANGER WE MIGHT BE IN AT THE FARM.
WHAT DANGER, PAPA?
MORE DANGEROUS THAN GRAMPA'S CASTLE?
GRAMPAW'S CASTLE ISN'T DANGEROUS NO MORE, STUPID. NOT NOW THAT OUR UNCLE MONSTERS ARE GONE.
BUT IS ANYWHER SAFE? UNCLE BLUE G KILLED DEAD RIGH HERE.
NO, I WANT TO BE LEFT ALONE.
COMPLETELY ALONE.
EITHER YOUR FATHER'S KEEP, OR HAVEN.
SOMEWHERE SAFE.

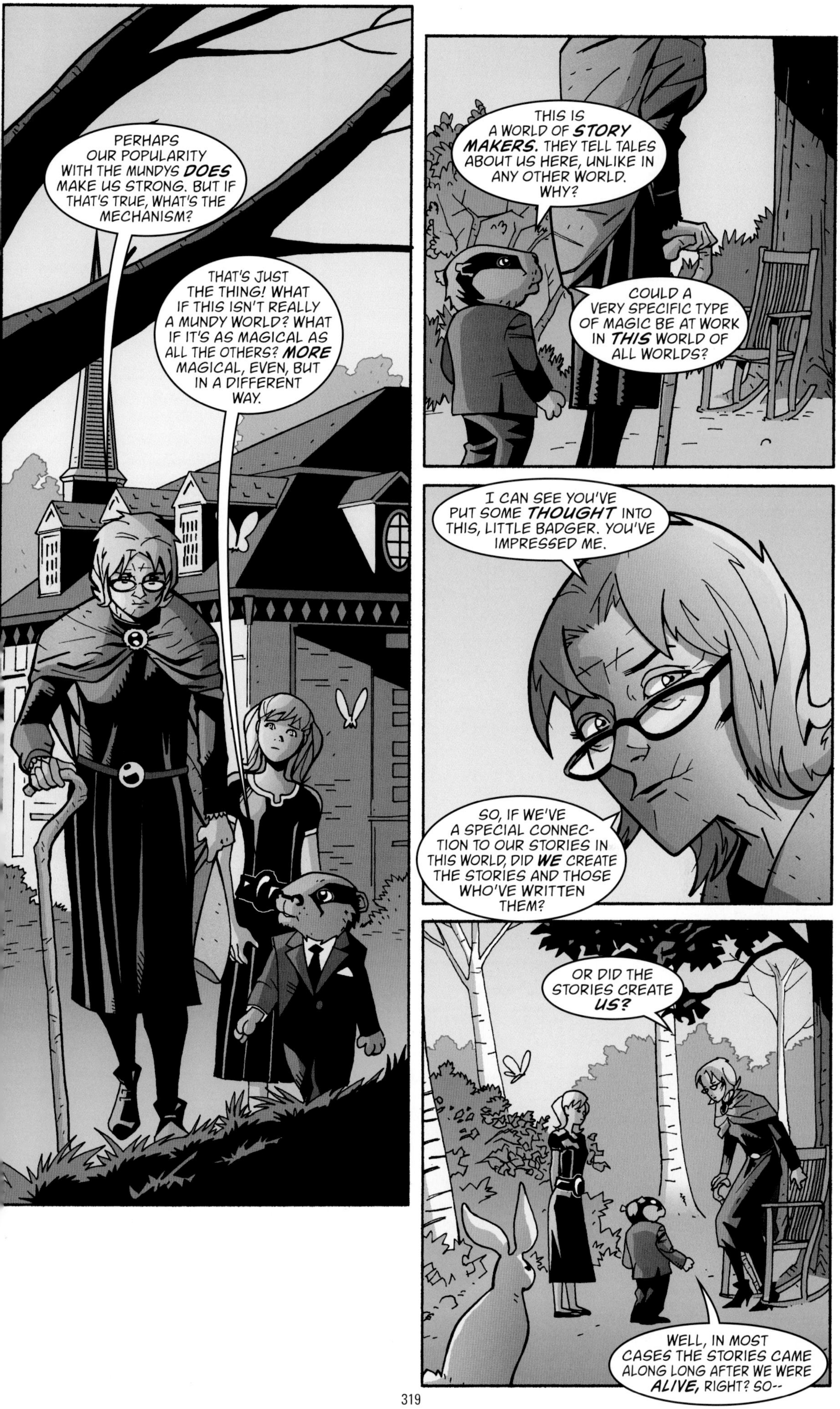
PERHAPS OUR POPULARITY WITH THE MUNDYS **DOES** MAKE US STRONG. BUT IF THAT'S TRUE, WHAT'S THE MECHANISM?
THAT'S JUST THE THING! WHAT IF THIS ISN'T REALLY A MUNDY WORLD? WHAT IF IT'S AS MAGICAL AS ALL THE OTHERS? **MORE** MAGICAL, EVEN, BUT IN A DIFFERENT WAY.
THIS IS A WORLD OF **STORY MAKERS.** THEY TELL TALES ABOUT US HERE, UNLIKE IN ANY OTHER WORLD. WHY?
COULD A VERY SPECIFIC TYPE OF MAGIC BE AT WORK IN **THIS** WORLD OF ALL WORLDS?
I CAN SEE YOU'VE PUT SOME **THOUGHT** INTO THIS, LITTLE BADGER. YOU'VE IMPRESSED ME.
SO, IF WE'VE A SPECIAL CONNECTION TO OUR STORIES IN THIS WORLD, DID **WE** CREATE THE STORIES AND THOSE WHO'VE WRITTEN THEM?
OR DID THE STORIES CREATE **US?**
WELL, IN MOST CASES THE STORIES CAME ALONG LONG AFTER WE WERE **ALIVE,** RIGHT? SO--

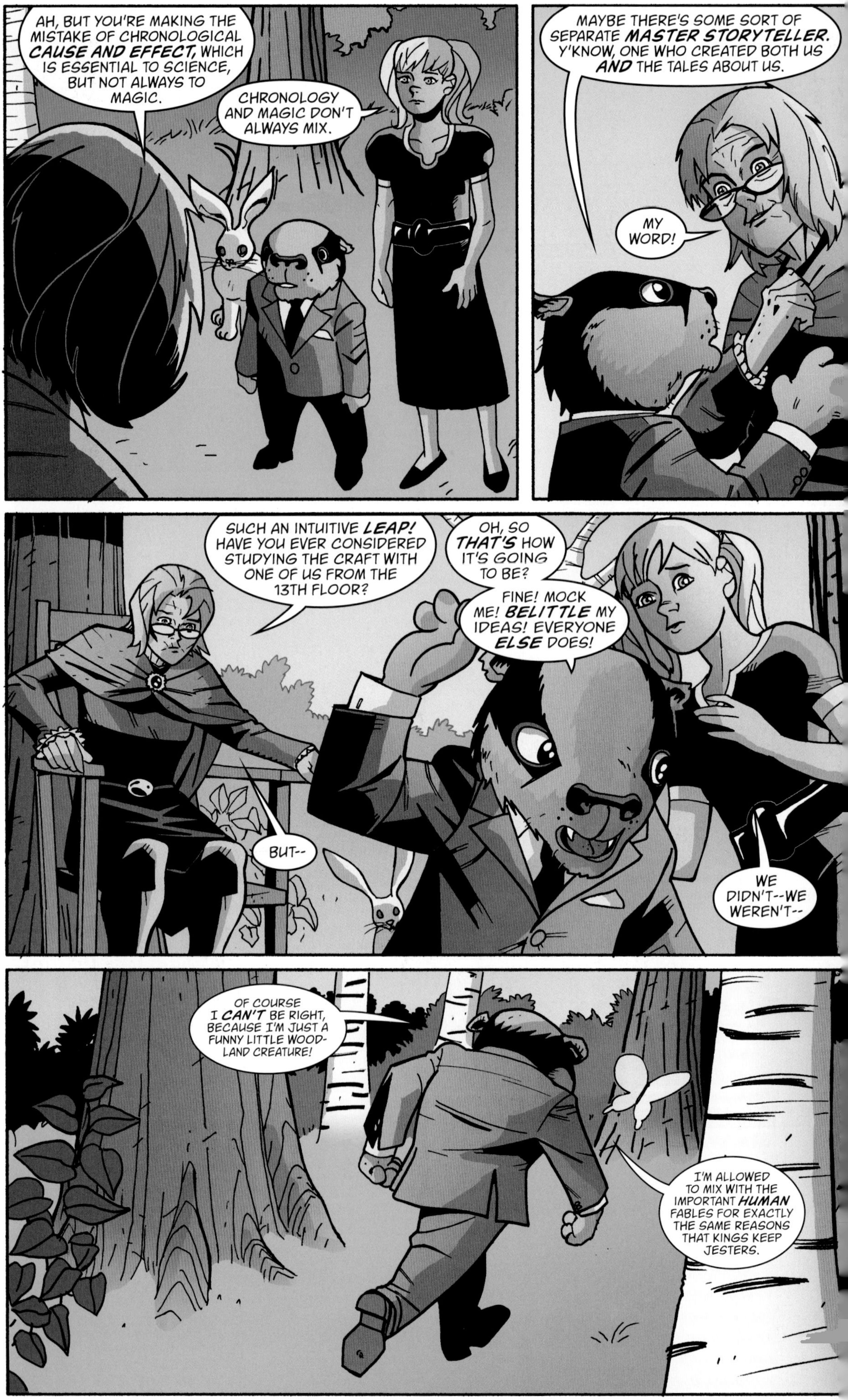
AH, BUT YOU'RE MAKING THE MISTAKE OF CHRONOLOGICAL CAUSE AND EFFECT, WHICH IS ESSENTIAL TO SCIENCE, BUT NOT ALWAYS TO MAGIC.
CHRONOLOGY AND MAGIC DON'T ALWAYS MIX.
MAYBE THERE'S SOME SORT OF SEPARATE MASTER STORYTELLER. Y'KNOW, ONE WHO CREATED BOTH US AND THE TALES ABOUT US.
MY WORD!
SUCH AN INTUITIVE LEAP! HAVE YOU EVER CONSIDERED STUDYING THE CRAFT WITH ONE OF US FROM THE 13TH FLOOR?
OH, SO THAT'S HOW IT'S GOING TO BE?
FINE! MOCK ME! BELITTLE MY IDEAS! EVERYONE ELSE DOES!
BUT--
WE DIDN'T--WE WEREN'T--
OF COURSE I CAN'T BE RIGHT, BECAUSE I'M JUST A FUNNY LITTLE WOODLAND CREATURE!
I'M ALLOWED TO MIX WITH THE IMPORTANT HUMAN FABLES FOR EXACTLY THE SAME REASONS THAT KINGS KEEP JESTERS.

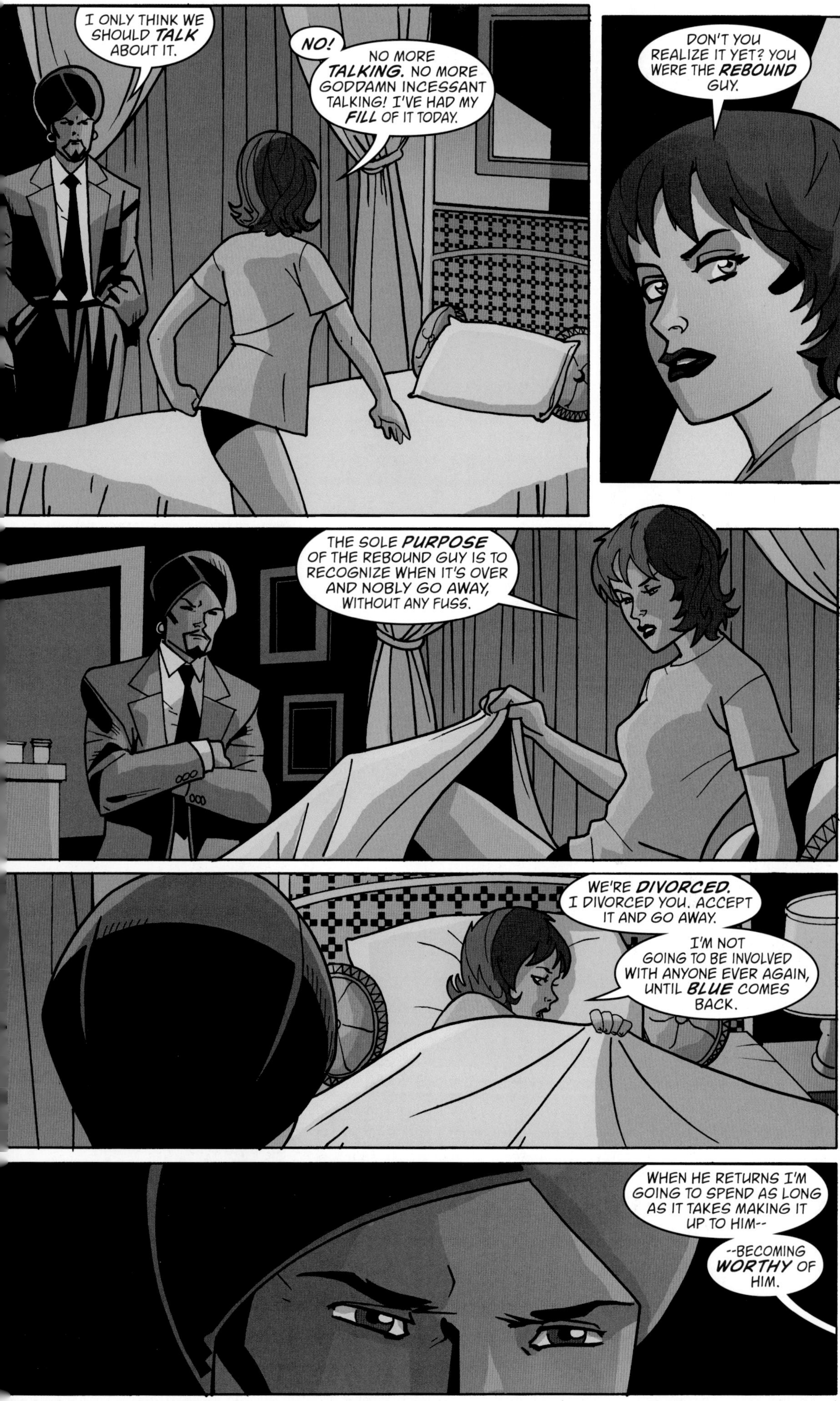

I ONLY THINK WE SHOULD TALK ABOUT IT.
NO!
NO MORE TALKING. NO MORE GODDAMN INCESSANT TALKING! I'VE HAD MY FILL OF IT TODAY.
DON'T YOU REALIZE IT YET? YOU WERE THE REBOUND GUY.
THE SOLE PURPOSE OF THE REBOUND GUY IS TO RECOGNIZE WHEN IT'S OVER AND NOBLY GO AWAY, WITHOUT ANY FUSS.
WE'RE DIVORCED. I DIVORCED YOU. ACCEPT IT AND GO AWAY.
I'M NOT GOING TO BE INVOLVED WITH ANYONE EVER AGAIN, UNTIL BLUE COMES BACK.
WHEN HE RETURNS I'M GOING TO SPEND AS LONG AS IT TAKES MAKING IT UP TO HIM--
--BECOMING WORTHY OF HIM.

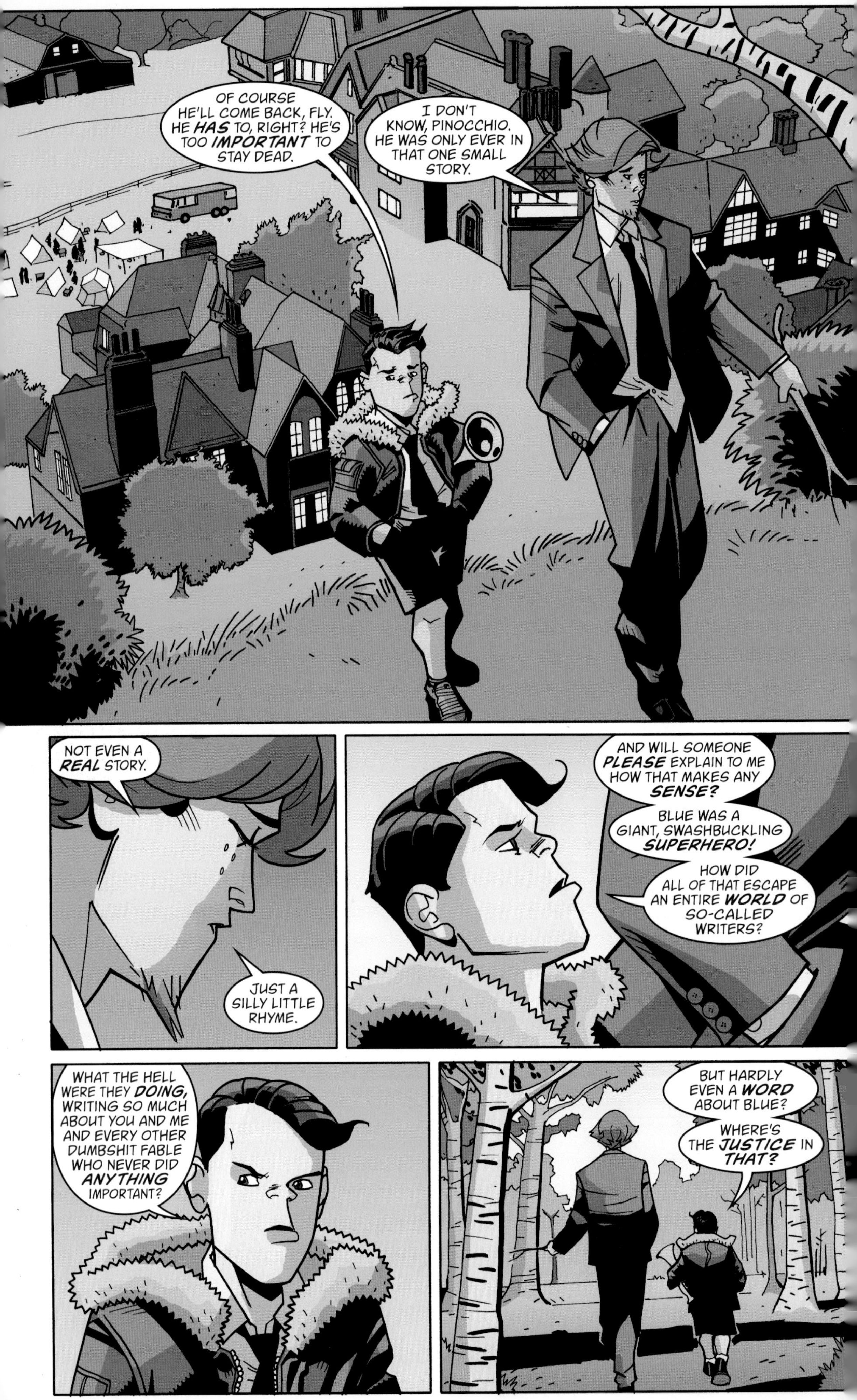
OF COURSE HE'LL COME BACK, FLY. HE HAS TO, RIGHT? HE'S TOO IMPORTANT TO STAY DEAD.
I DON'T KNOW, PINOCCHIO. HE WAS ONLY EVER IN THAT ONE SMALL STORY.
NOT EVEN A REAL STORY.
JUST A SILLY LITTLE RHYME.
AND WILL SOMEONE PLEASE EXPLAIN TO ME HOW THAT MAKES ANY SENSE?
BLUE WAS A GIANT, SWASHBUCKLING SUPERHERO!
HOW DID ALL OF THAT ESCAPE AN ENTIRE WORLD OF SO-CALLED WRITERS?
WHAT THE HELL WERE THEY DOING, WRITING SO MUCH ABOUT YOU AND ME AND EVERY OTHER DUMBSHIT FABLE WHO NEVER DID ANYTHING IMPORTANT?
BUT HARDLY EVEN A WORD ABOUT BLUE?
WHERE'S THE JUSTICE IN THAT?

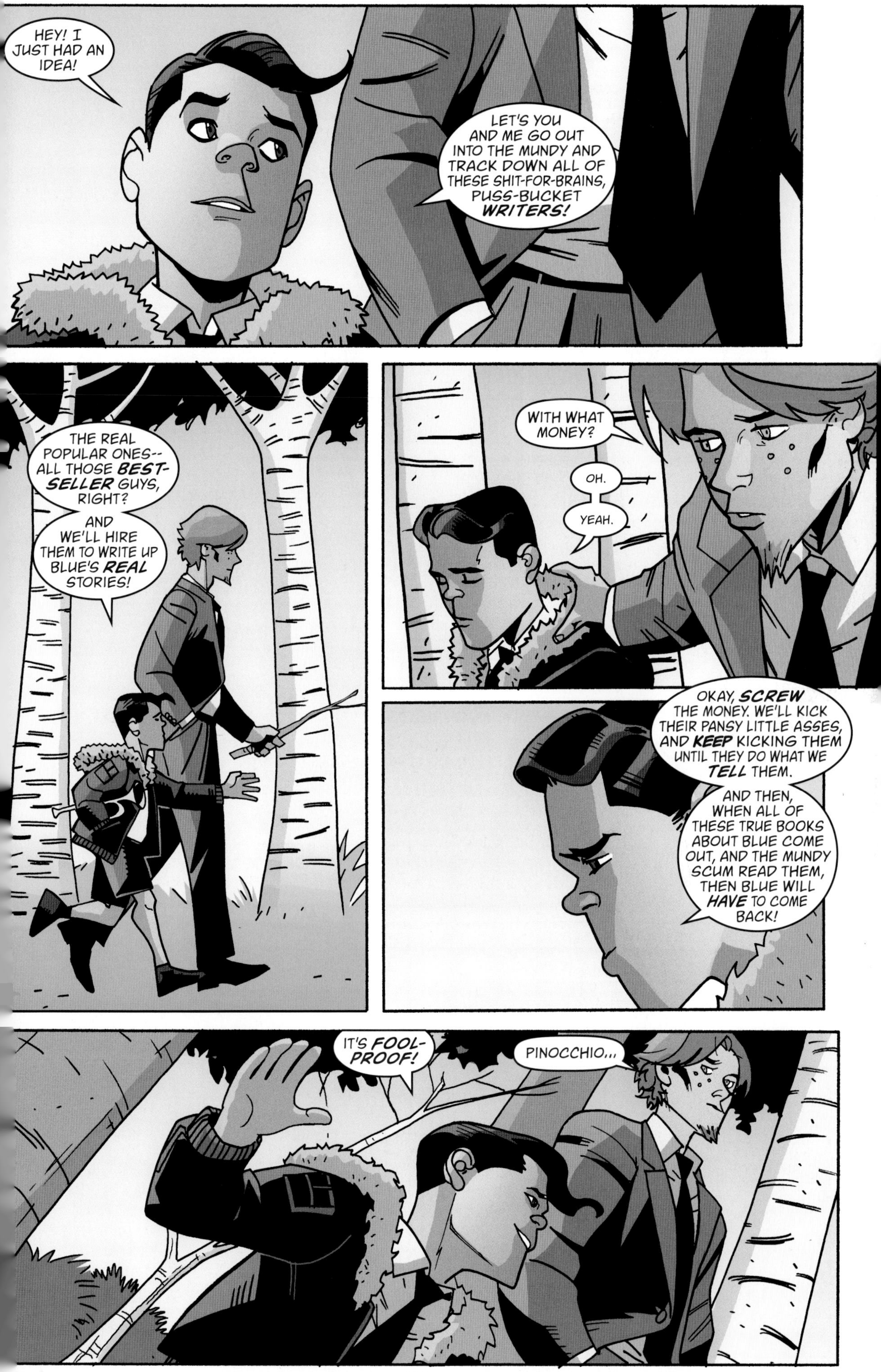
HEY! I JUST HAD AN IDEA!
LET'S YOU AND ME GO OUT INTO THE MUNDY AND TRACK DOWN ALL OF THESE SHIT-FOR-BRAINS, PUSS-BUCKET **WRITERS!**
THE REAL POPULAR ONES--ALL THOSE **BEST-SELLER** GUYS, RIGHT?
AND WE'LL HIRE THEM TO WRITE UP BLUE'S **REAL** STORIES!
WITH WHAT MONEY?
OH.
YEAH.
OKAY, **SCREW** THE MONEY. WE'LL KICK THEIR PANSY LITTLE ASSES, AND **KEEP** KICKING THEM UNTIL THEY DO WHAT WE **TELL** THEM.
AND THEN, WHEN ALL OF THESE TRUE BOOKS ABOUT BLUE COME OUT, AND THE MUNDY SCUM READ THEM, THEN BLUE WILL **HAVE** TO COME BACK!
IT'S **FOOL-PROOF!**
PINOCCHIO...

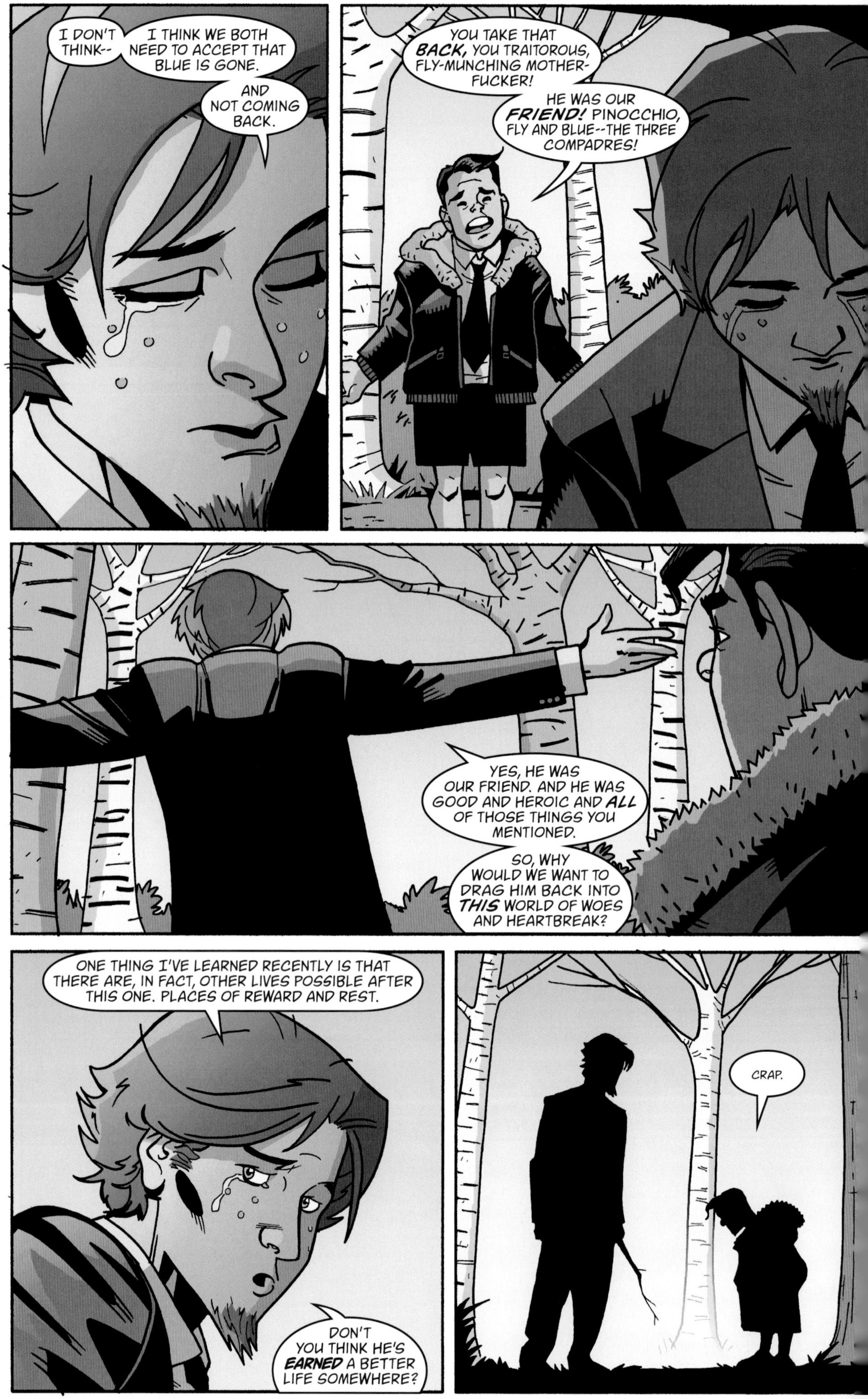
I DON'T THINK--
I THINK WE BOTH NEED TO ACCEPT THAT BLUE IS GONE.
AND NOT COMING BACK.
YOU TAKE THAT BACK, YOU TRAITOROUS, FLY-MUNCHING MOTHER-FUCKER!
HE WAS OUR FRIEND! PINOCCHIO, FLY AND BLUE--THE THREE COMPADRES!
YES, HE WAS OUR FRIEND. AND HE WAS GOOD AND HEROIC AND ALL OF THOSE THINGS YOU MENTIONED.
SO, WHY WOULD WE WANT TO DRAG HIM BACK INTO THIS WORLD OF WOES AND HEARTBREAK?
ONE THING I'VE LEARNED RECENTLY IS THAT THERE ARE, IN FACT, OTHER LIVES POSSIBLE AFTER THIS ONE. PLACES OF REWARD AND REST.
DON'T YOU THINK HE'S EARNED A BETTER LIFE SOMEWHERE?
CRAP.

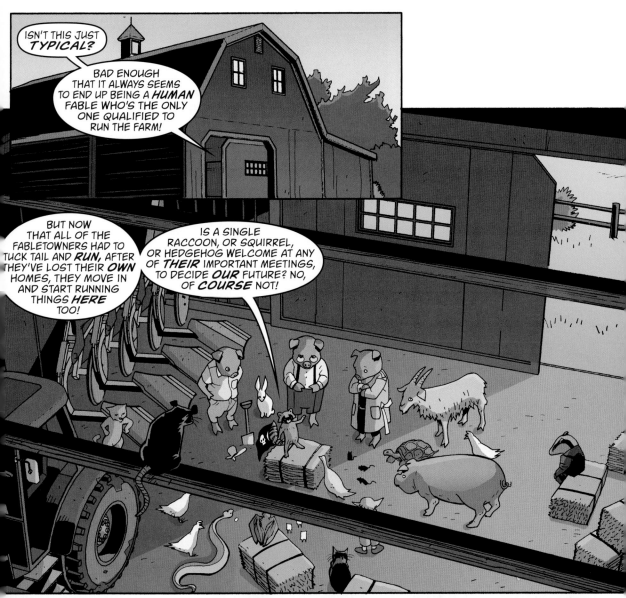

ISN'T THIS JUST *TYPICAL?*

BAD ENOUGH THAT IT ALWAYS SEEMS TO END UP BEING A *HUMAN* FABLE WHO'S THE ONLY ONE QUALIFIED TO RUN THE FARM!

BUT NOW THAT ALL OF THE FABLETOWNERS HAD TO TUCK TAIL AND *RUN,* AFTER THEY'VE LOST THEIR *OWN* HOMES, THEY MOVE IN AND START RUNNING THINGS *HERE* TOO!

IS A SINGLE RACCOON, OR SQUIRREL, OR HEDGEHOG WELCOME AT ANY OF *THEIR* IMPORTANT MEETINGS, TO DECIDE *OUR* FUTURE? NO, OF *COURSE* NOT!

SINCE WE'RE SMALL AND FURRY-- OR FEATHERED--THEY TREAT US LIKE NEWBORN *BABIES* WHO NEED TO BE LOOKED AFTER--

--AND *TOLD* WHAT TO DO!

STOP THIS TALK RIGHT *NOW!*

YOW!

:GULP!:

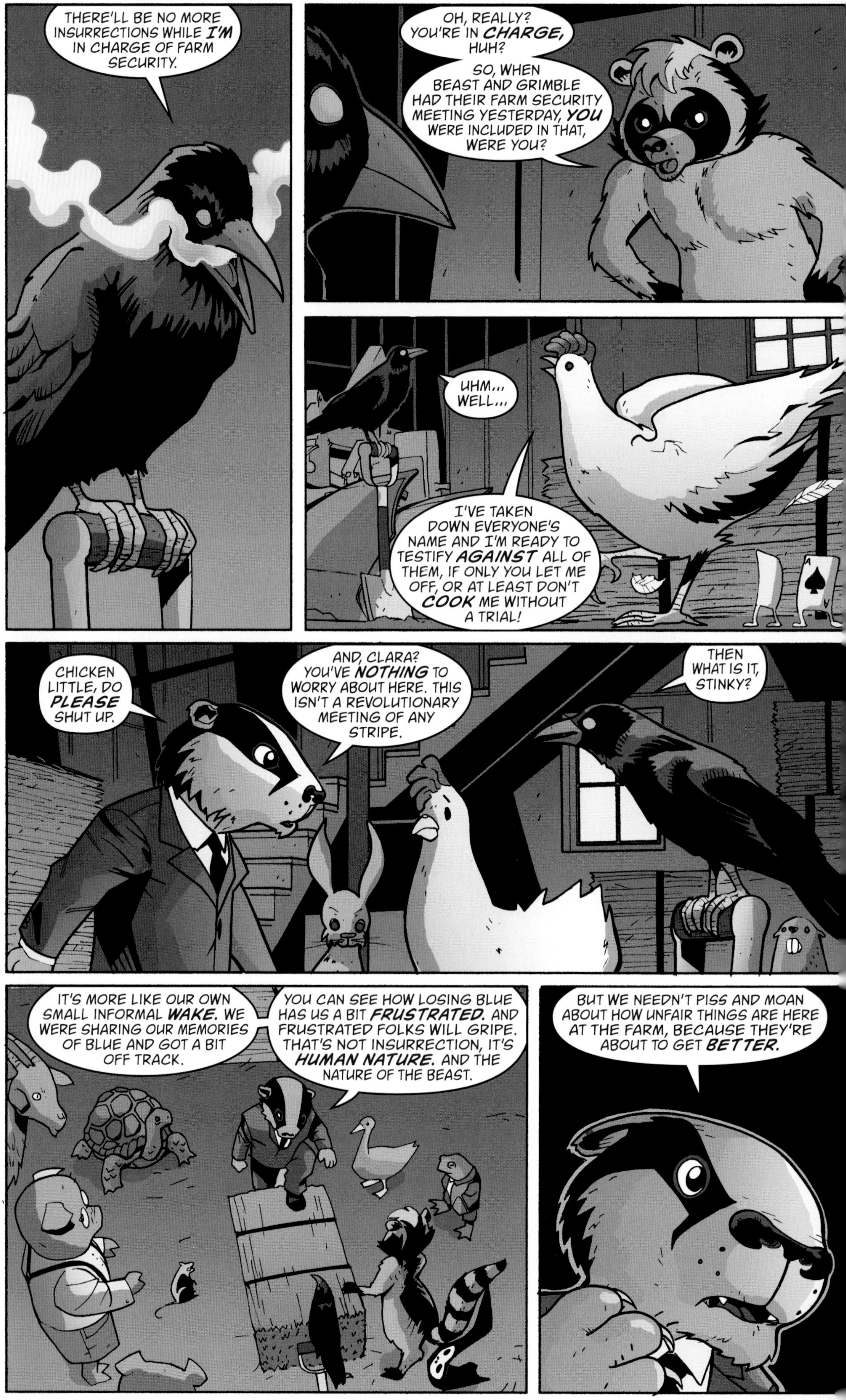
THERE'LL BE NO MORE INSURRECTIONS WHILE *I'M* IN CHARGE OF FARM SECURITY.
OH, REALLY? YOU'RE IN *CHARGE,* HUH?
SO, WHEN BEAST AND GRIMBLE HAD THEIR FARM SECURITY MEETING YESTERDAY, *YOU* WERE INCLUDED IN THAT, WERE YOU?
UHM... WELL...
I'VE TAKEN DOWN EVERYONE'S NAME AND I'M READY TO TESTIFY *AGAINST* ALL OF THEM, IF ONLY YOU LET ME OFF, OR AT LEAST DON'T *COOK* ME WITHOUT A TRIAL!
CHICKEN LITTLE, DO *PLEASE* SHUT UP.
AND, CLARA? YOU'VE *NOTHING* TO WORRY ABOUT HERE. THIS ISN'T A REVOLUTIONARY MEETING OF ANY STRIPE.
THEN WHAT IS IT, STINKY?
IT'S MORE LIKE OUR OWN SMALL INFORMAL *WAKE.* WE WERE SHARING OUR MEMORIES OF BLUE AND GOT A BIT OFF TRACK.
YOU CAN SEE HOW LOSING BLUE HAS US A BIT *FRUSTRATED.* AND FRUSTRATED FOLKS WILL GRIPE. THAT'S NOT INSURRECTION, IT'S *HUMAN NATURE.* AND THE NATURE OF THE BEAST.
BUT WE NEEDN'T PISS AND MOAN ABOUT HOW UNFAIR THINGS ARE HERE AT THE FARM, BECAUSE THEY'RE ABOUT TO GET *BETTER.*

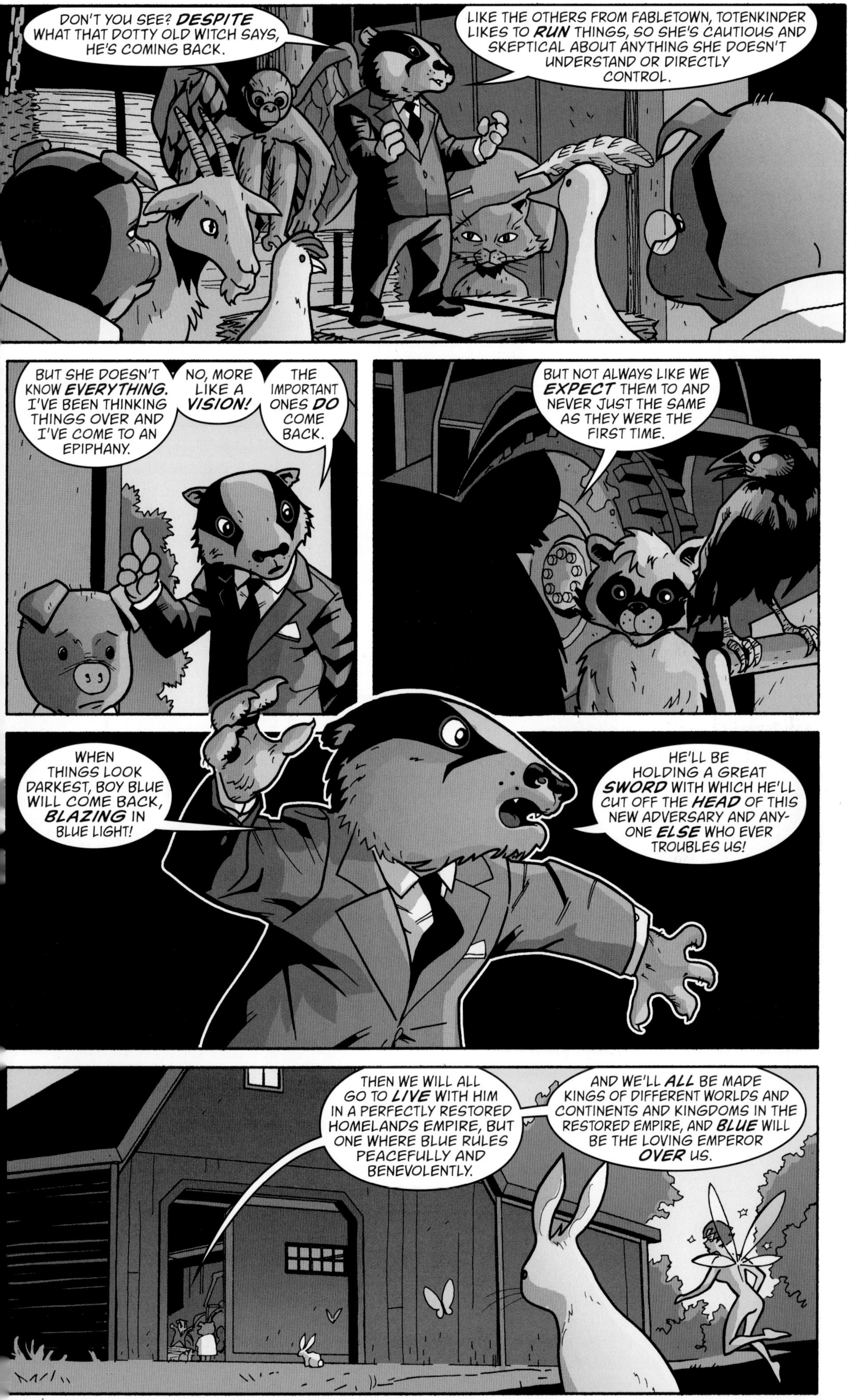
DON'T YOU SEE? DESPITE WHAT THAT DOTTY OLD WITCH SAYS, HE'S COMING BACK.
LIKE THE OTHERS FROM FABLETOWN, TOTENKINDER LIKES TO RUN THINGS, SO SHE'S CAUTIOUS AND SKEPTICAL ABOUT ANYTHING SHE DOESN'T UNDERSTAND OR DIRECTLY CONTROL.
BUT SHE DOESN'T KNOW EVERYTHING. I'VE BEEN THINKING THINGS OVER AND I'VE COME TO AN EPIPHANY.
NO, MORE LIKE A VISION!
THE IMPORTANT ONES DO COME BACK.
BUT NOT ALWAYS LIKE WE EXPECT THEM TO AND NEVER JUST THE SAME AS THEY WERE THE FIRST TIME.
WHEN THINGS LOOK DARKEST, BOY BLUE WILL COME BACK, BLAZING IN BLUE LIGHT!
HE'LL BE HOLDING A GREAT SWORD WITH WHICH HE'LL CUT OFF THE HEAD OF THIS NEW ADVERSARY AND ANYONE ELSE WHO EVER TROUBLES US!
THEN WE WILL ALL GO TO LIVE WITH HIM IN A PERFECTLY RESTORED HOMELANDS EMPIRE, BUT ONE WHERE BLUE RULES PEACEFULLY AND BENEVOLENTLY.
AND WE'LL ALL BE MADE KINGS OF DIFFERENT WORLDS AND CONTINENTS AND KINGDOMS IN THE RESTORED EMPIRE, AND BLUE WILL BE THE LOVING EMPEROR OVER US.

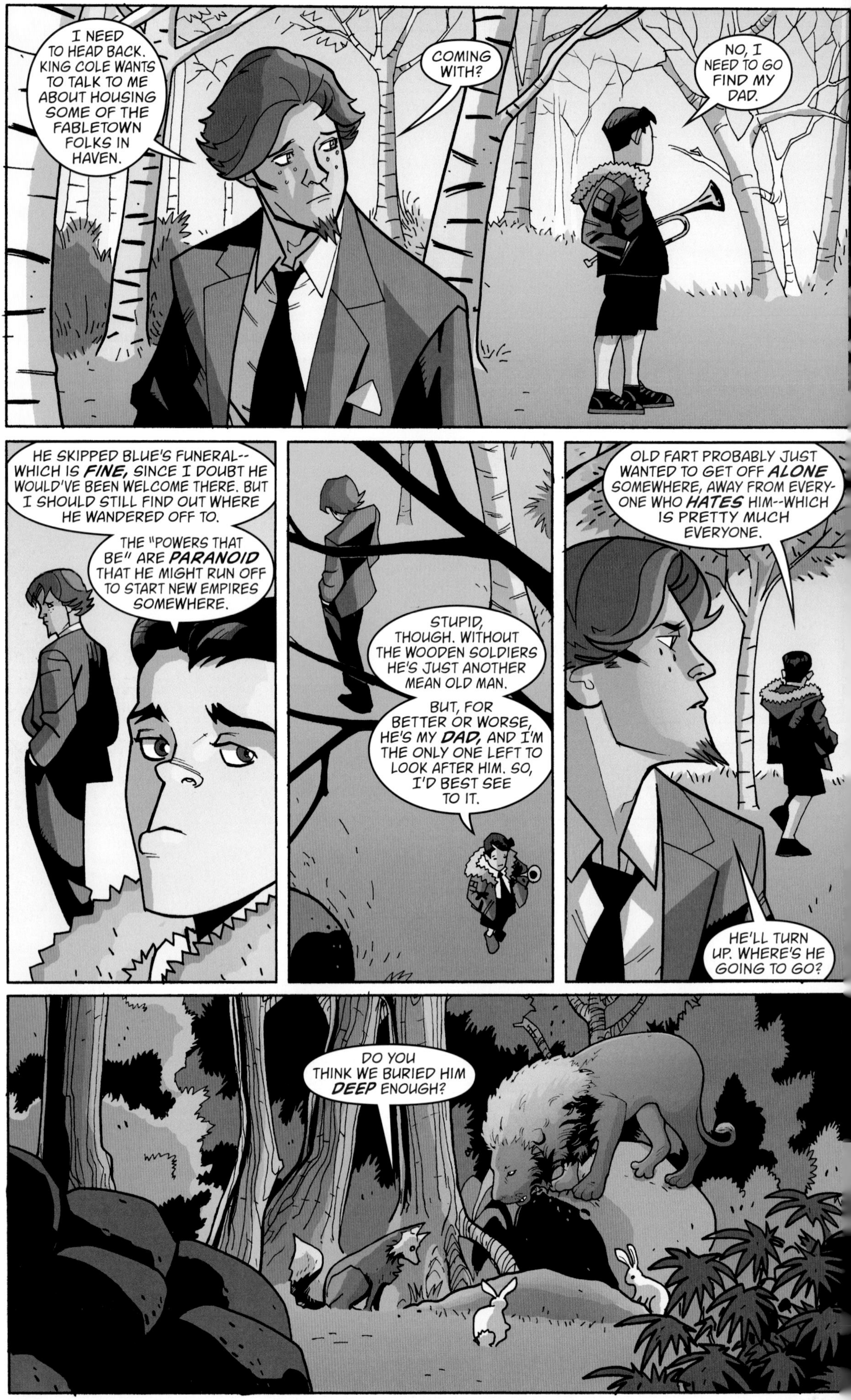
I NEED TO HEAD BACK. KING COLE WANTS TO TALK TO ME ABOUT HOUSING SOME OF THE FABLETOWN FOLKS IN HAVEN.
COMING WITH?
NO, I NEED TO GO FIND MY DAD.
HE SKIPPED BLUE'S FUNERAL--WHICH IS *FINE,* SINCE I DOUBT HE WOULD'VE BEEN WELCOME THERE. BUT I SHOULD STILL FIND OUT WHERE HE WANDERED OFF TO.
THE "POWERS THAT BE" ARE *PARANOID* THAT HE MIGHT RUN OFF TO START NEW EMPIRES SOMEWHERE.
STUPID, THOUGH. WITHOUT THE WOODEN SOLDIERS HE'S JUST ANOTHER MEAN OLD MAN.
BUT, FOR BETTER OR WORSE, HE'S MY *DAD,* AND I'M THE ONLY ONE LEFT TO LOOK AFTER HIM. SO, I'D BEST SEE TO IT.
OLD FART PROBABLY JUST WANTED TO GET OFF *ALONE* SOMEWHERE, AWAY FROM EVERYONE WHO *HATES* HIM--WHICH IS PRETTY MUCH EVERYONE.
HE'LL TURN UP. WHERE'S HE GOING TO GO?
DO YOU THINK WE BURIED HIM *DEEP* ENOUGH?

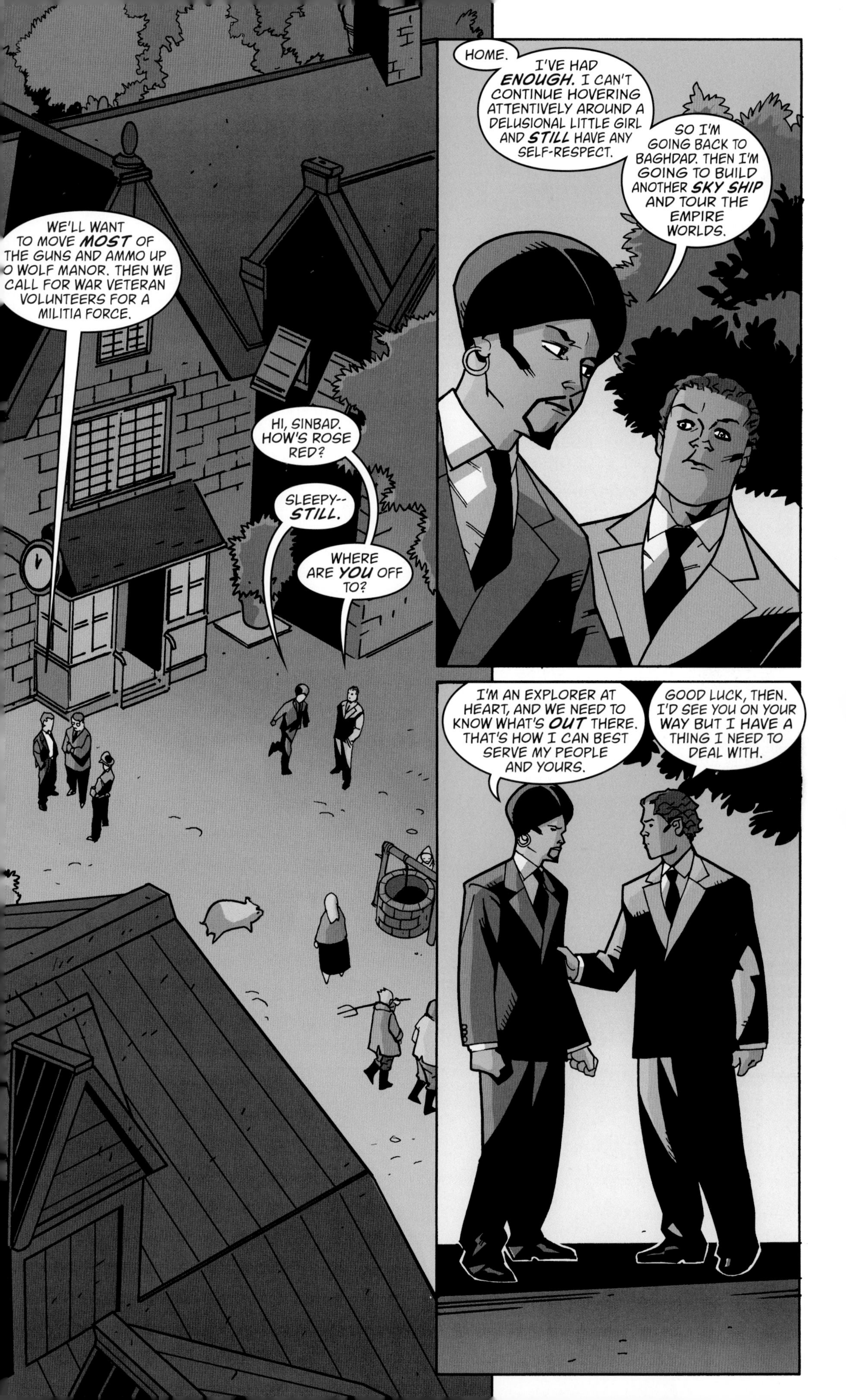
WE'LL WANT TO MOVE **MOST** OF THE GUNS AND AMMO UP O WOLF MANOR. THEN WE CALL FOR WAR VETERAN VOLUNTEERS FOR A MILITIA FORCE.
HI, SINBAD. HOW'S ROSE RED?
SLEEPY-- **STILL.**
WHERE ARE **YOU** OFF TO?
HOME.
I'VE HAD **ENOUGH.** I CAN'T CONTINUE HOVERING ATTENTIVELY AROUND A DELUSIONAL LITTLE GIRL AND **STILL** HAVE ANY SELF-RESPECT.
SO I'M GOING BACK TO BAGHDAD. THEN I'M GOING TO BUILD ANOTHER **SKY SHIP** AND TOUR THE EMPIRE WORLDS.
I'M AN EXPLORER AT HEART, AND WE NEED TO KNOW WHAT'S **OUT** THERE. THAT'S HOW I CAN BEST SERVE MY PEOPLE AND YOURS.
GOOD LUCK, THEN. I'D SEE YOU ON YOUR WAY BUT I HAVE A THING I NEED TO DEAL WITH.

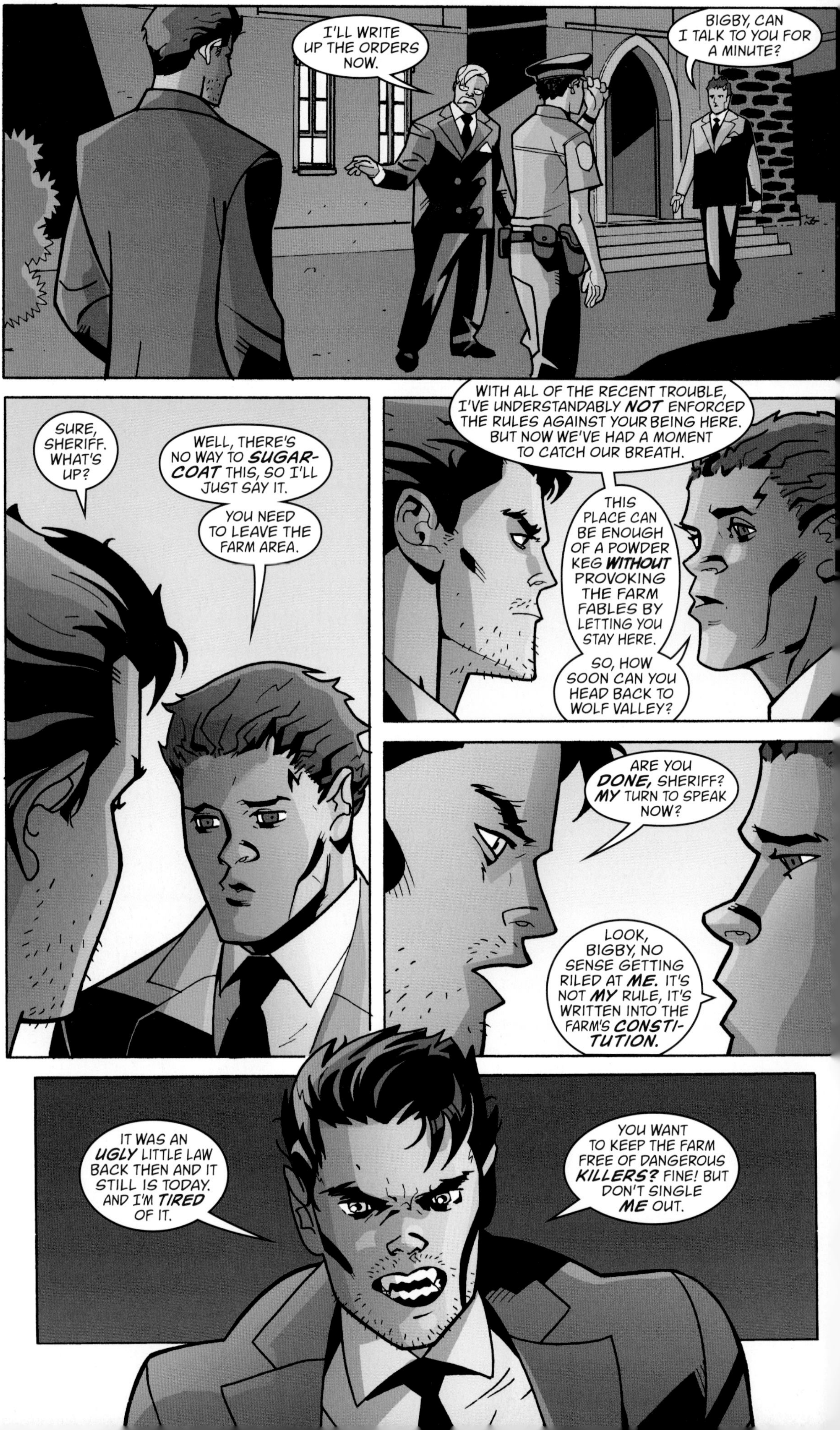
I'LL WRITE UP THE ORDERS NOW.
BIGBY, CAN I TALK TO YOU FOR A MINUTE?
SURE, SHERIFF. WHAT'S UP?
WELL, THERE'S NO WAY TO SUGAR-COAT THIS, SO I'LL JUST SAY IT.
YOU NEED TO LEAVE THE FARM AREA.
WITH ALL OF THE RECENT TROUBLE, I'VE UNDERSTANDABLY NOT ENFORCED THE RULES AGAINST YOUR BEING HERE. BUT NOW WE'VE HAD A MOMENT TO CATCH OUR BREATH.
THIS PLACE CAN BE ENOUGH OF A POWDER KEG WITHOUT PROVOKING THE FARM FABLES BY LETTING YOU STAY HERE.
SO, HOW SOON CAN YOU HEAD BACK TO WOLF VALLEY?
ARE YOU DONE, SHERIFF? MY TURN TO SPEAK NOW?
LOOK, BIGBY, NO SENSE GETTING RILED AT ME. IT'S NOT MY RULE, IT'S WRITTEN INTO THE FARM'S CONSTI-TUTION.
IT WAS AN UGLY LITTLE LAW BACK THEN AND IT STILL IS TODAY. AND I'M TIRED OF IT.
YOU WANT TO KEEP THE FARM FREE OF DANGEROUS KILLERS? FINE! BUT DON'T SINGLE ME OUT.

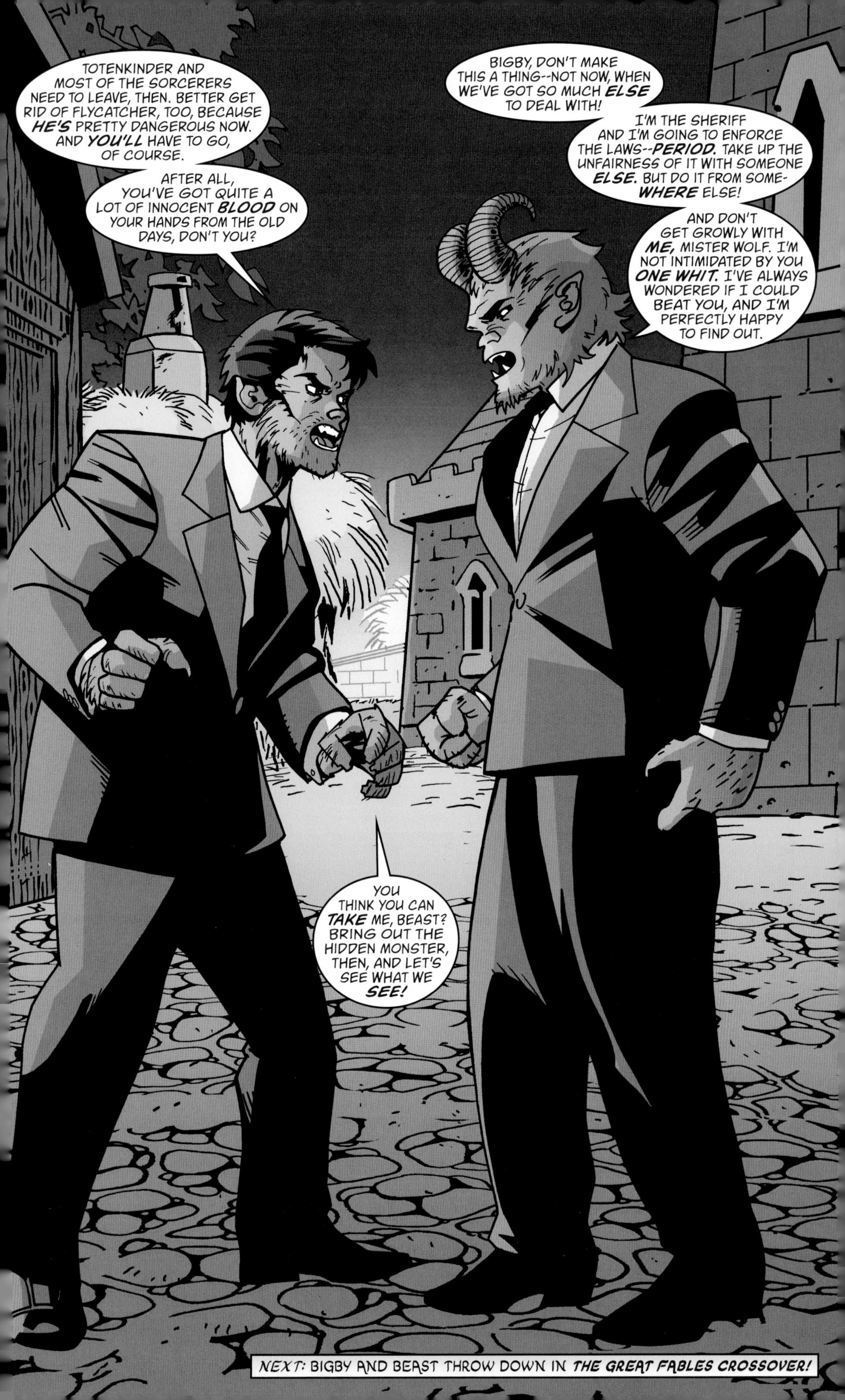
TOTENKINDER AND MOST OF THE SORCERERS NEED TO LEAVE, THEN. BETTER GET RID OF FLYCATCHER, TOO, BECAUSE *HE'S* PRETTY DANGEROUS NOW. AND *YOU'LL* HAVE TO GO, OF COURSE.
AFTER ALL, YOU'VE GOT QUITE A LOT OF INNOCENT *BLOOD* ON YOUR HANDS FROM THE OLD DAYS, DON'T YOU?
BIGBY, DON'T MAKE THIS A THING--NOT NOW, WHEN WE'VE GOT SO MUCH *ELSE* TO DEAL WITH!
I'M THE SHERIFF AND I'M GOING TO ENFORCE THE LAWS--*PERIOD.* TAKE UP THE UNFAIRNESS OF IT WITH SOMEONE *ELSE.* BUT DO IT FROM SOME-*WHERE* ELSE!
AND DON'T GET GROWLY WITH *ME,* MISTER WOLF. I'M NOT INTIMIDATED BY YOU *ONE WHIT.* I'VE ALWAYS WONDERED IF I COULD BEAT YOU, AND I'M PERFECTLY HAPPY TO FIND OUT.
YOU THINK YOU CAN *TAKE* ME, BEAST? BRING OUT THE HIDDEN MONSTER, THEN, AND LET'S SEE WHAT WE *SEE!*
NEXT: BIGBY AND BEAST THROW DOWN IN *THE GREAT FABLES CROSSOVER!*

HOMELAND RECOVERY PART ONE OF FIVE

Bill Willingham writer/creator | Peter Gross artist | Lee Loughridge colors | Todd Klein letters | Angela Rufino assoc. editor | Shelly Bond editor

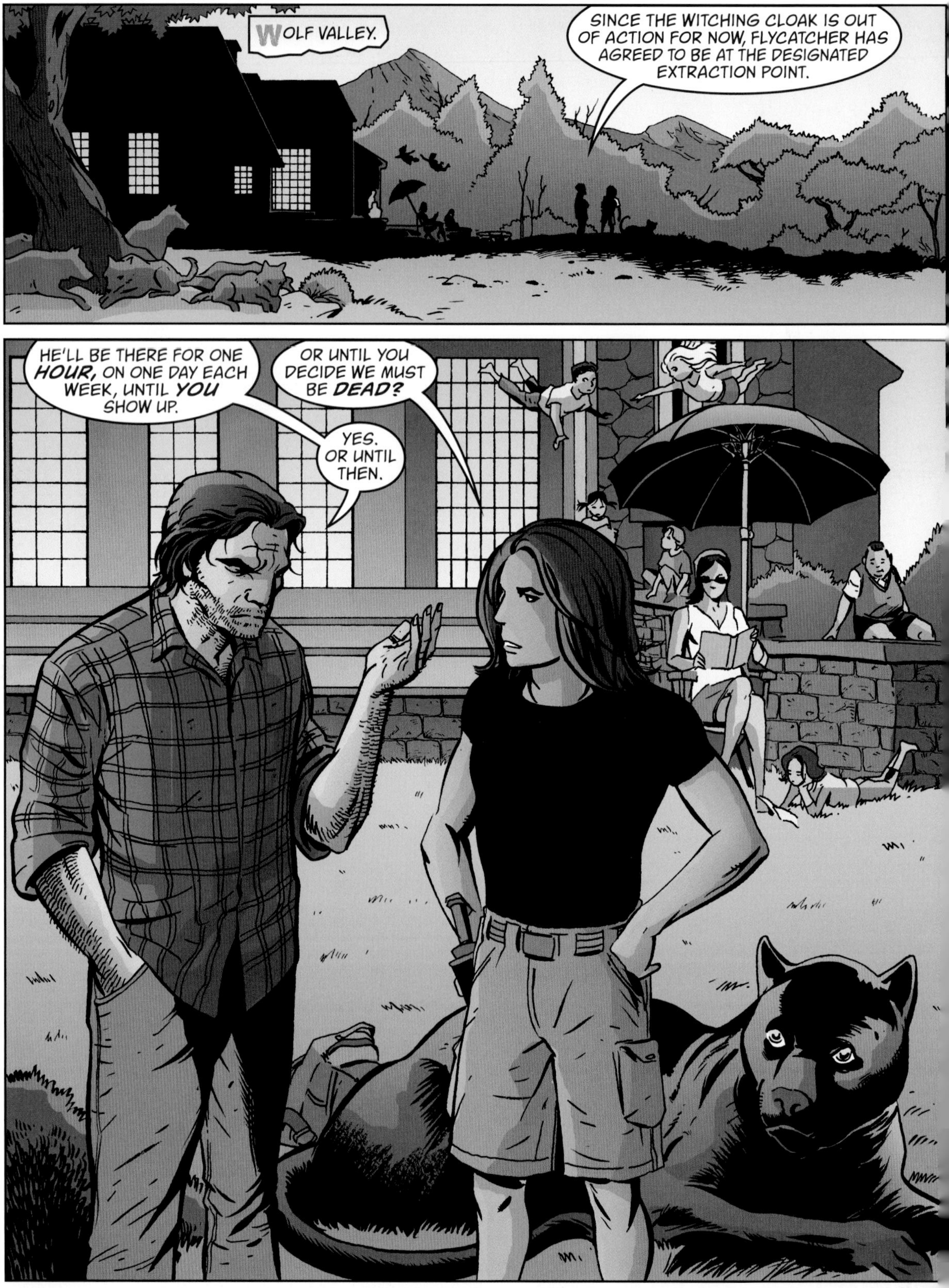
WOLF VALLEY.
SINCE THE WITCHING CLOAK IS OUT OF ACTION FOR NOW, FLYCATCHER HAS AGREED TO BE AT THE DESIGNATED EXTRACTION POINT.
HE'LL BE THERE FOR ONE HOUR, ON ONE DAY EACH WEEK, UNTIL YOU SHOW UP.
OR UNTIL YOU DECIDE WE MUST BE DEAD?
YES. OR UNTIL THEN.

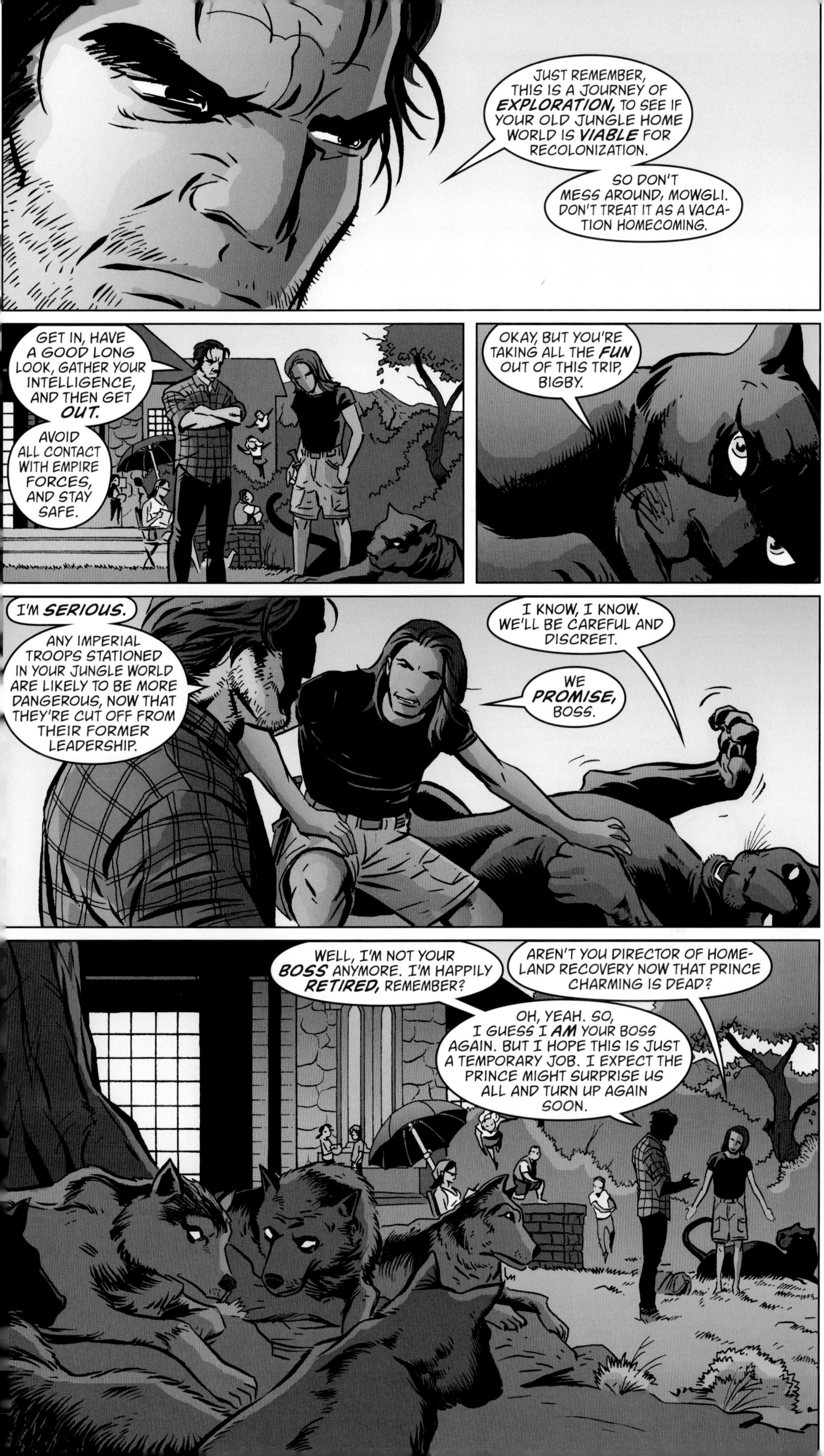
JUST REMEMBER, THIS IS A JOURNEY OF ***EXPLORATION,*** TO SEE IF YOUR OLD JUNGLE HOME WORLD IS ***VIABLE*** FOR RECOLONIZATION.
SO DON'T MESS AROUND, MOWGLI. DON'T TREAT IT AS A VACA-TION HOMECOMING.
GET IN, HAVE A GOOD LONG LOOK, GATHER YOUR INTELLIGENCE, AND THEN GET ***OUT.***
AVOID ALL CONTACT WITH EMPIRE FORCES, AND STAY SAFE.
OKAY, BUT YOU'RE TAKING ALL THE ***FUN*** OUT OF THIS TRIP, BIGBY.
I'M ***SERIOUS.***
ANY IMPERIAL TROOPS STATIONED IN YOUR JUNGLE WORLD ARE LIKELY TO BE MORE DANGEROUS, NOW THAT THEY'RE CUT OFF FROM THEIR FORMER LEADERSHIP.
I KNOW, I KNOW. WE'LL BE CAREFUL AND DISCREET.
WE ***PROMISE,*** BOSS.
WELL, I'M NOT YOUR ***BOSS*** ANYMORE. I'M HAPPILY ***RETIRED,*** REMEMBER?
AREN'T YOU DIRECTOR OF HOME-LAND RECOVERY NOW THAT PRINCE CHARMING IS DEAD?
OH, YEAH. SO, I GUESS I ***AM*** YOUR BOSS AGAIN. BUT I HOPE THIS IS JUST A TEMPORARY JOB. I EXPECT THE PRINCE MIGHT SURPRISE US ALL AND TURN UP AGAIN SOON.

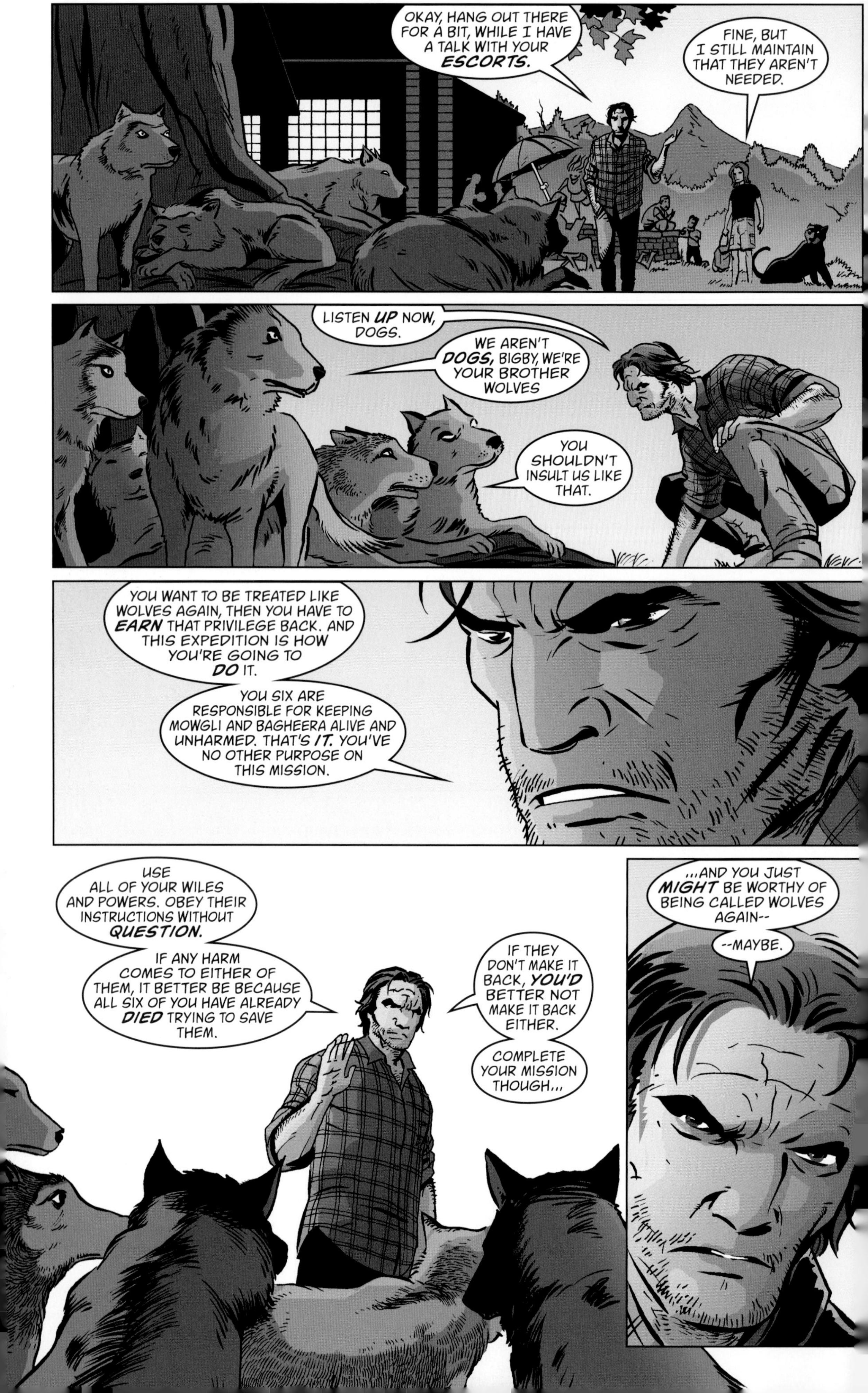
OKAY, HANG OUT THERE FOR A BIT, WHILE I HAVE A TALK WITH YOUR ESCORTS.
FINE, BUT I STILL MAINTAIN THAT THEY AREN'T NEEDED.
LISTEN UP NOW, DOGS.
WE AREN'T DOGS, BIGBY, WE'RE YOUR BROTHER WOLVES
YOU SHOULDN'T INSULT US LIKE THAT.
YOU WANT TO BE TREATED LIKE WOLVES AGAIN, THEN YOU HAVE TO EARN THAT PRIVILEGE BACK. AND THIS EXPEDITION IS HOW YOU'RE GOING TO DO IT.
YOU SIX ARE RESPONSIBLE FOR KEEPING MOWGLI AND BAGHEERA ALIVE AND UNHARMED. THAT'S IT. YOU'VE NO OTHER PURPOSE ON THIS MISSION.
USE ALL OF YOUR WILES AND POWERS. OBEY THEIR INSTRUCTIONS WITHOUT QUESTION.
IF ANY HARM COMES TO EITHER OF THEM, IT BETTER BE BECAUSE ALL SIX OF YOU HAVE ALREADY DIED TRYING TO SAVE THEM.
IF THEY DON'T MAKE IT BACK, YOU'D BETTER NOT MAKE IT BACK EITHER.
COMPLETE YOUR MISSION THOUGH...
...AND YOU JUST MIGHT BE WORTHY OF BEING CALLED WOLVES AGAIN--
--MAYBE.

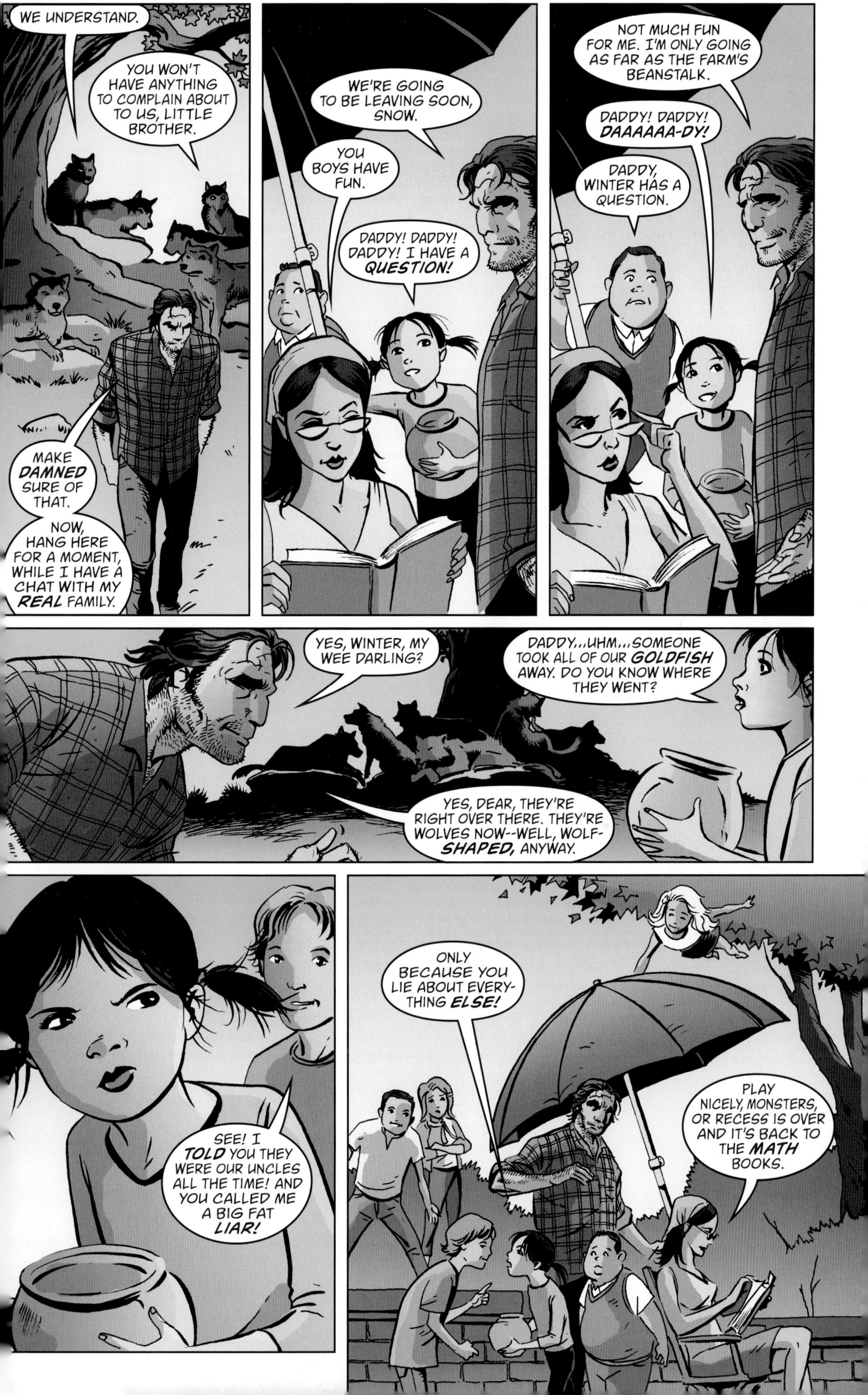
WE UNDERSTAND.
YOU WON'T HAVE ANYTHING TO COMPLAIN ABOUT TO US, LITTLE BROTHER.
MAKE DAMNED SURE OF THAT.
NOW, HANG HERE FOR A MOMENT, WHILE I HAVE A CHAT WITH MY REAL FAMILY.
WE'RE GOING TO BE LEAVING SOON, SNOW.
YOU BOYS HAVE FUN.
DADDY! DADDY! DADDY! I HAVE A QUESTION!
NOT MUCH FUN FOR ME. I'M ONLY GOING AS FAR AS THE FARM'S BEANSTALK.
DADDY! DADDY! DAAAAAA-DY!
DADDY, WINTER HAS A QUESTION.
YES, WINTER, MY WEE DARLING?
DADDY...UHM...SOMEONE TOOK ALL OF OUR GOLDFISH AWAY. DO YOU KNOW WHERE THEY WENT?
YES, DEAR, THEY'RE RIGHT OVER THERE. THEY'RE WOLVES NOW--WELL, WOLF-SHAPED, ANYWAY.
SEE! I TOLD YOU THEY WERE OUR UNCLES ALL THE TIME! AND YOU CALLED ME A BIG FAT LIAR!
ONLY BECAUSE YOU LIE ABOUT EVERY-THING ELSE!
PLAY NICELY, MONSTERS, OR RECESS IS OVER AND IT'S BACK TO THE MATH BOOKS.

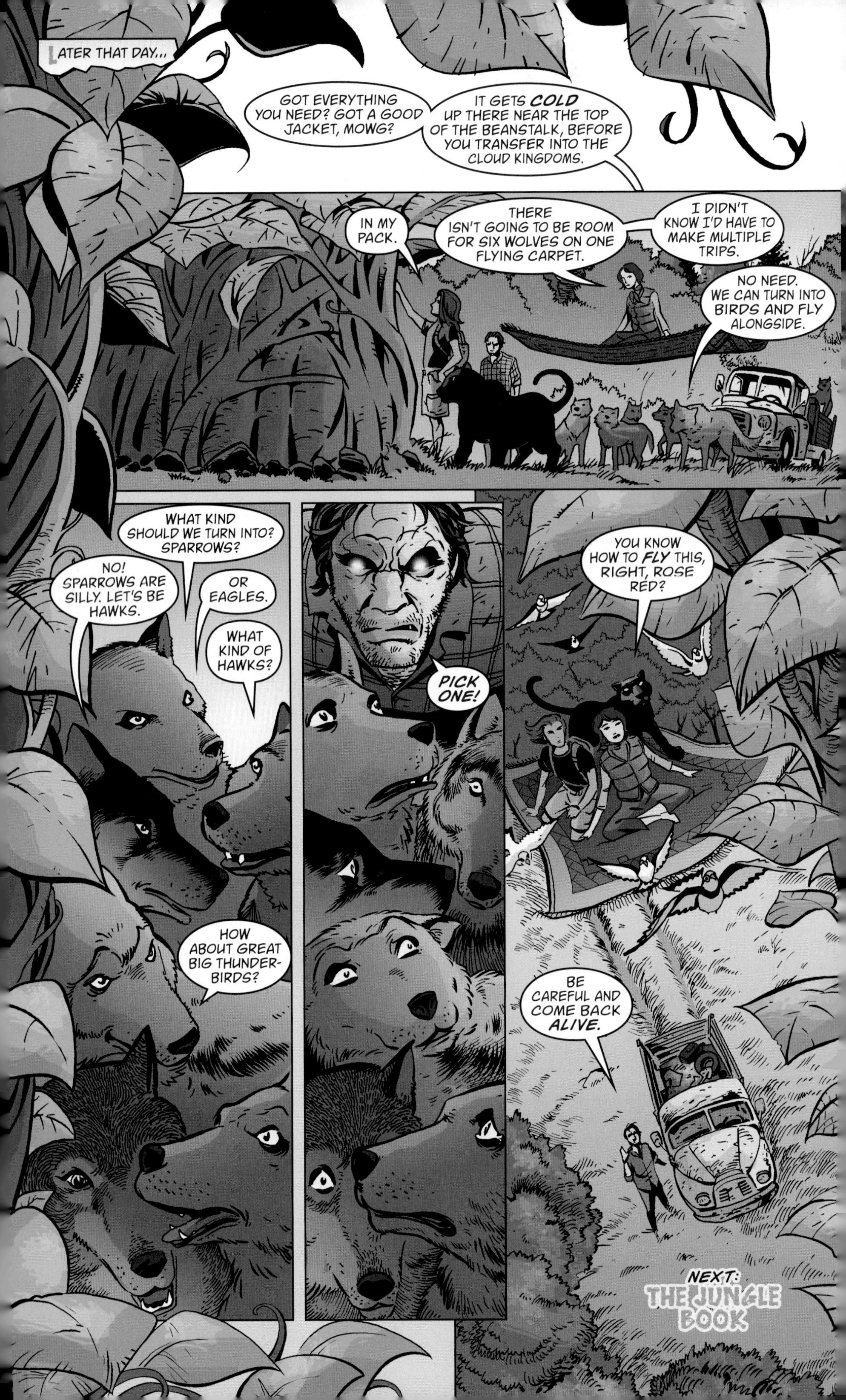
LATER THAT DAY...
GOT EVERYTHING YOU NEED? GOT A GOOD JACKET, MOWG?
IT GETS COLD UP THERE NEAR THE TOP OF THE BEANSTALK, BEFORE YOU TRANSFER INTO THE CLOUD KINGDOMS.
IN MY PACK.
THERE ISN'T GOING TO BE ROOM FOR SIX WOLVES ON ONE FLYING CARPET.
I DIDN'T KNOW I'D HAVE TO MAKE MULTIPLE TRIPS.
NO NEED. WE CAN TURN INTO BIRDS AND FLY ALONGSIDE.
WHAT KIND SHOULD WE TURN INTO? SPARROWS?
NO! SPARROWS ARE SILLY. LET'S BE HAWKS.
OR EAGLES.
WHAT KIND OF HAWKS?
HOW ABOUT GREAT BIG THUNDER-BIRDS?
PICK ONE!
YOU KNOW HOW TO FLY THIS, RIGHT, ROSE RED?
BE CAREFUL AND COME BACK ALIVE.
NEXT: THE JUNGLE BOOK

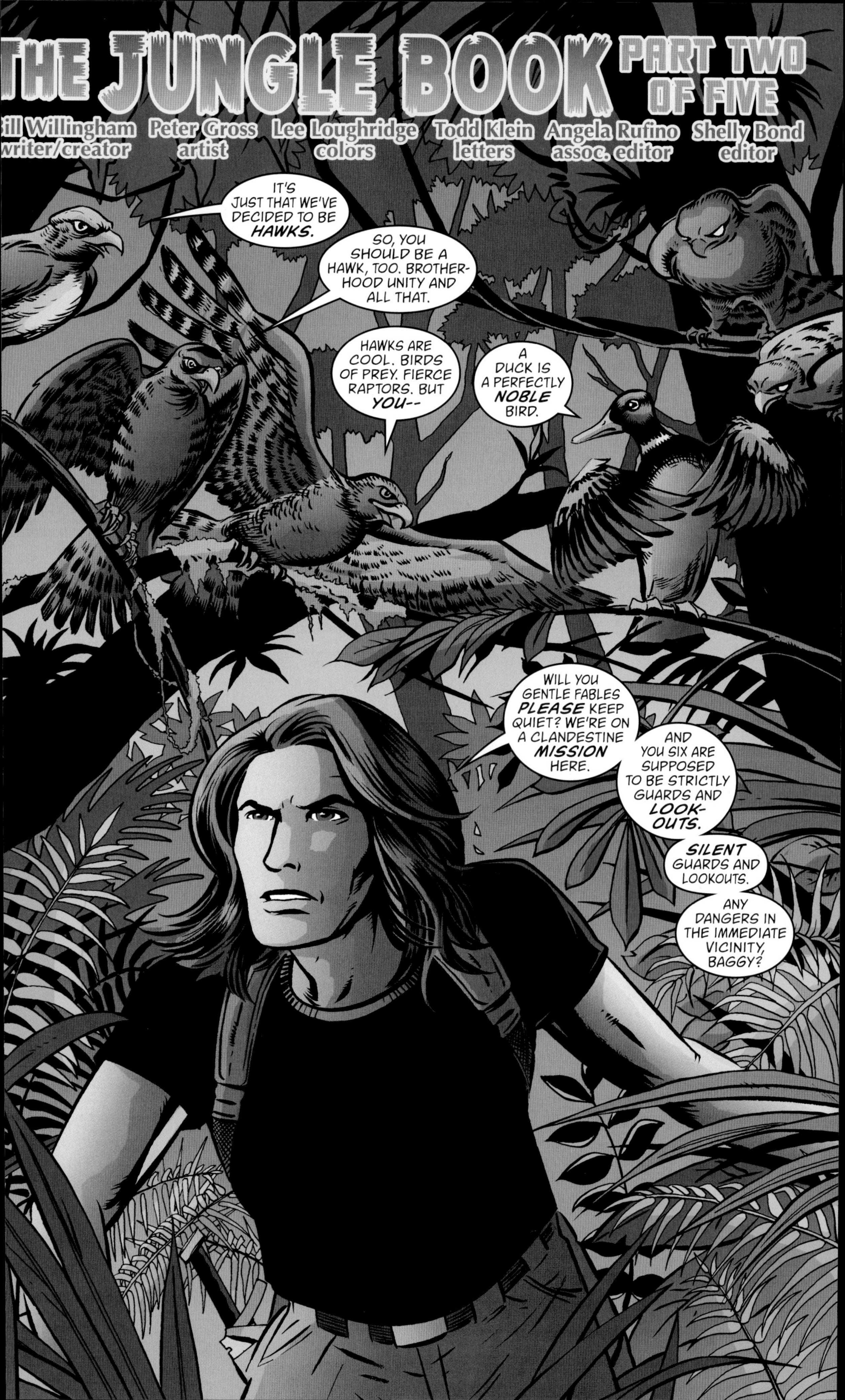
THE JUNGLE BOOK PART TWO OF FIVE
Bill Willingham writer/creator
Peter Gross artist
Lee Loughridge colors
Todd Klein letters
Angela Rufino assoc. editor
Shelly Bond editor
IT'S JUST THAT WE'VE DECIDED TO BE HAWKS.
SO, YOU SHOULD BE A HAWK, TOO. BROTHERHOOD UNITY AND ALL THAT.
HAWKS ARE COOL. BIRDS OF PREY. FIERCE RAPTORS. BUT YOU--
A DUCK IS A PERFECTLY NOBLE BIRD.
WILL YOU GENTLE FABLES PLEASE KEEP QUIET? WE'RE ON A CLANDESTINE MISSION HERE.
AND YOU SIX ARE SUPPOSED TO BE STRICTLY GUARDS AND LOOKOUTS.
SILENT GUARDS AND LOOKOUTS.
ANY DANGERS IN THE IMMEDIATE VICINITY, BAGGY?

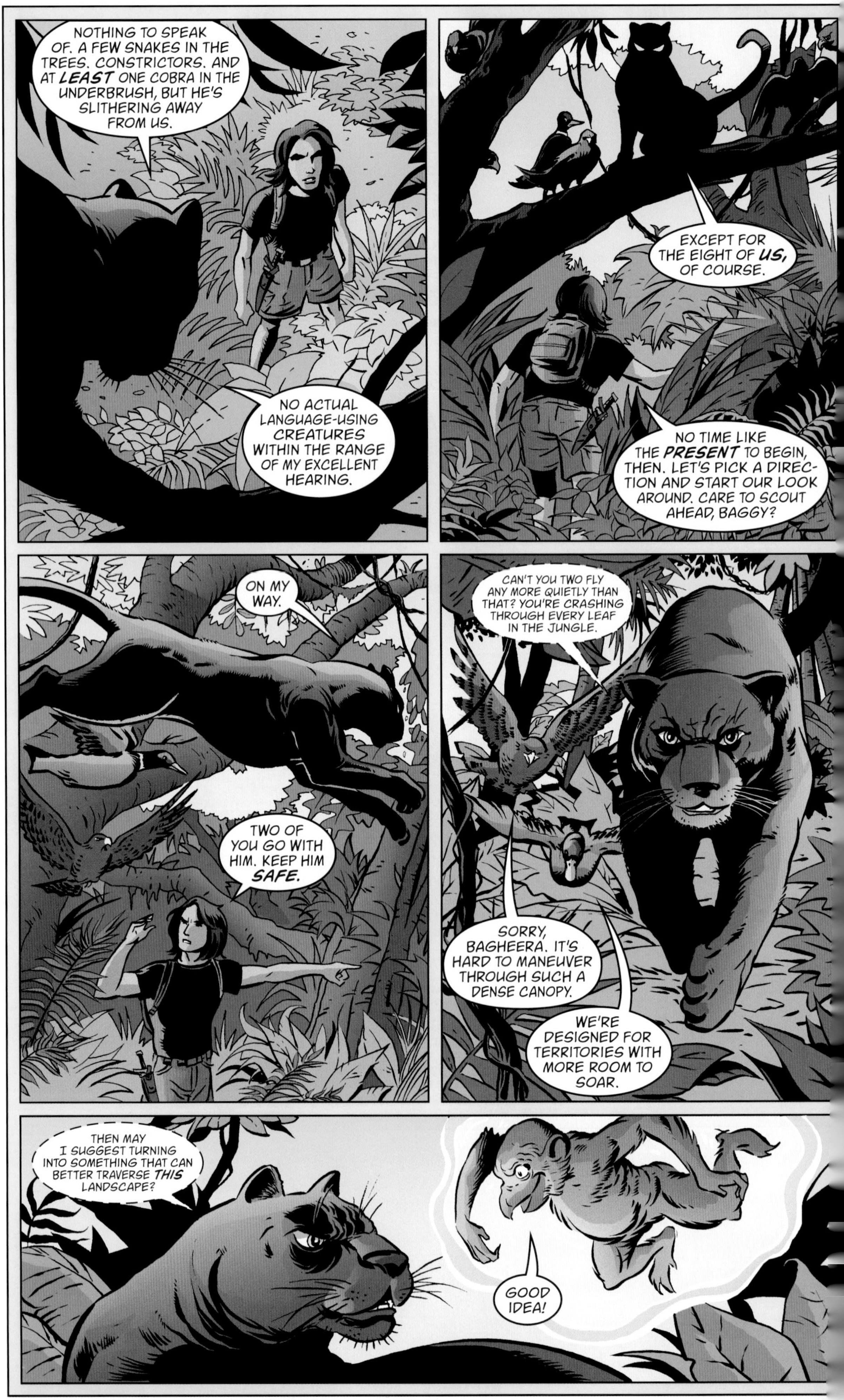
NOTHING TO SPEAK OF. A FEW SNAKES IN THE TREES. CONSTRICTORS. AND AT *LEAST* ONE COBRA IN THE UNDERBRUSH, BUT HE'S SLITHERING AWAY FROM US.
NO ACTUAL LANGUAGE-USING CREATURES WITHIN THE RANGE OF MY EXCELLENT HEARING.
EXCEPT FOR THE EIGHT OF *US*, OF COURSE.
NO TIME LIKE THE *PRESENT* TO BEGIN, THEN. LET'S PICK A DIRECTION AND START OUR LOOK AROUND. CARE TO SCOUT AHEAD, BAGGY?
ON MY WAY.
TWO OF YOU GO WITH HIM. KEEP HIM *SAFE*.
CAN'T YOU TWO FLY ANY MORE QUIETLY THAN THAT? YOU'RE CRASHING THROUGH EVERY LEAF IN THE JUNGLE.
SORRY, BAGHEERA. IT'S HARD TO MANEUVER THROUGH SUCH A DENSE CANOPY.
WE'RE DESIGNED FOR TERRITORIES WITH MORE ROOM TO SOAR.
THEN MAY I SUGGEST TURNING INTO SOMETHING THAT CAN BETTER TRAVERSE *THIS* LANDSCAPE?
GOOD IDEA!

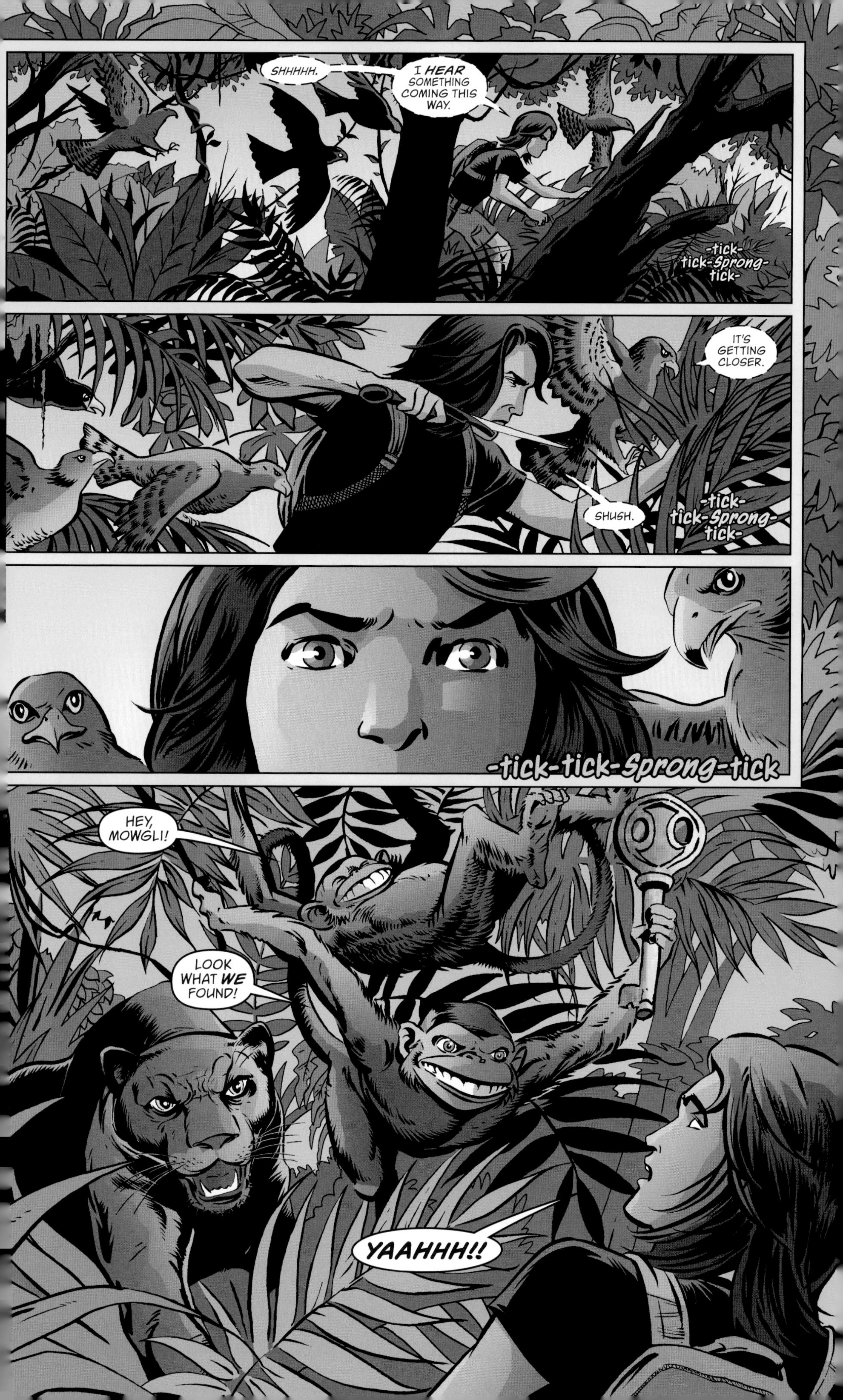
SHHHHH.
I *HEAR* SOMETHING COMING THIS WAY.
-tick-tick-Sprong-tick-
IT'S GETTING CLOSER.
SHUSH.
-tick-tick-Sprong-tick-
-tick-tick-Sprong-tick
HEY, MOWGLI!
LOOK WHAT *WE* FOUND!
YAAHHH!!

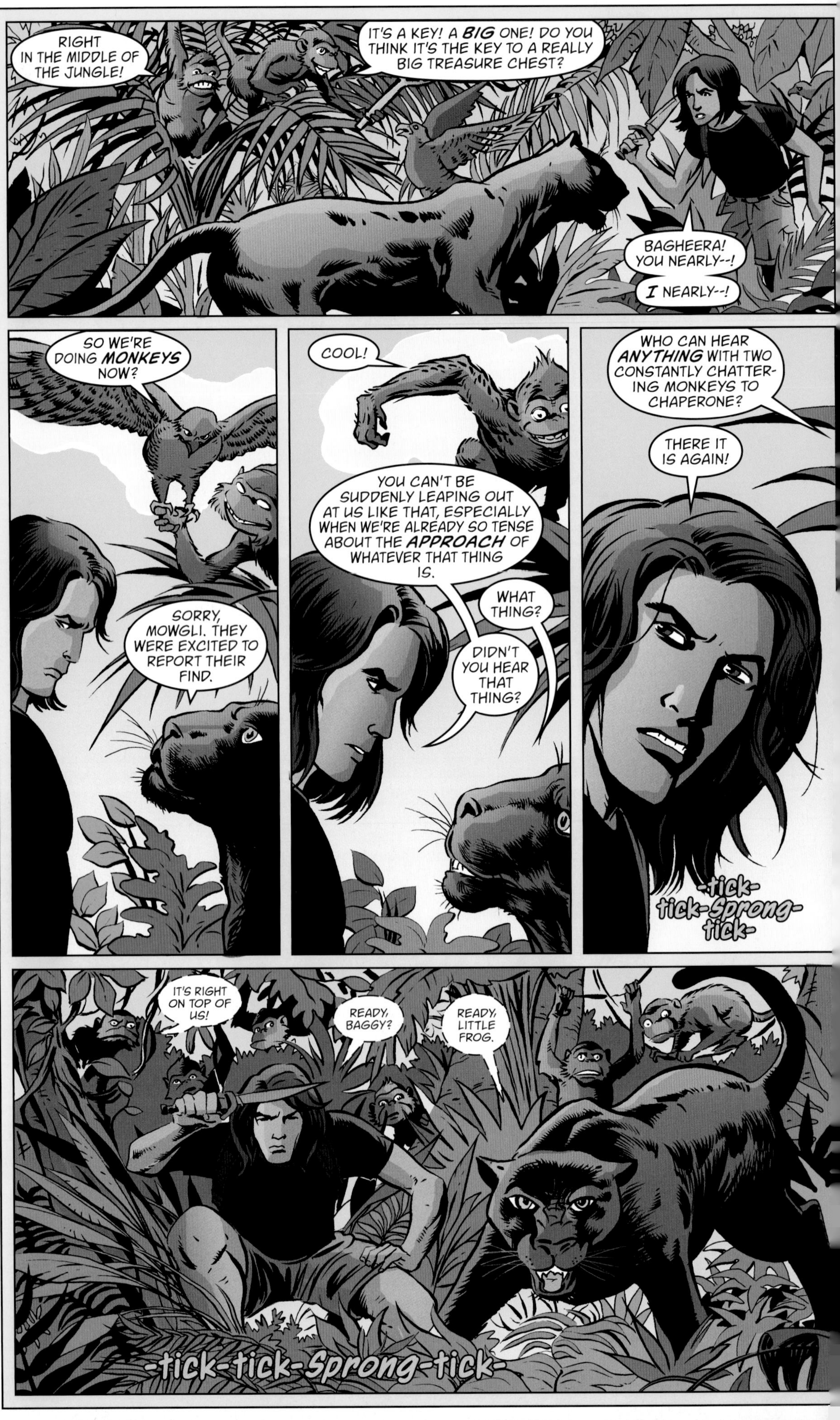
RIGHT IN THE MIDDLE OF THE JUNGLE!
IT'S A KEY! A BIG ONE! DO YOU THINK IT'S THE KEY TO A REALLY BIG TREASURE CHEST?
BAGHEERA! YOU NEARLY--!
I NEARLY--!
SO WE'RE DOING MONKEYS NOW?
SORRY, MOWGLI. THEY WERE EXCITED TO REPORT THEIR FIND.
COOL!
YOU CAN'T BE SUDDENLY LEAPING OUT AT US LIKE THAT, ESPECIALLY WHEN WE'RE ALREADY SO TENSE ABOUT THE APPROACH OF WHATEVER THAT THING IS.
WHAT THING?
DIDN'T YOU HEAR THAT THING?
WHO CAN HEAR ANYTHING WITH TWO CONSTANTLY CHATTERING MONKEYS TO CHAPERONE?
THERE IT IS AGAIN!
-tick-tick-Sprong-tick-
IT'S RIGHT ON TOP OF US!
READY, BAGGY?
READY, LITTLE FROG.
-tick-tick-Sprong-tick-

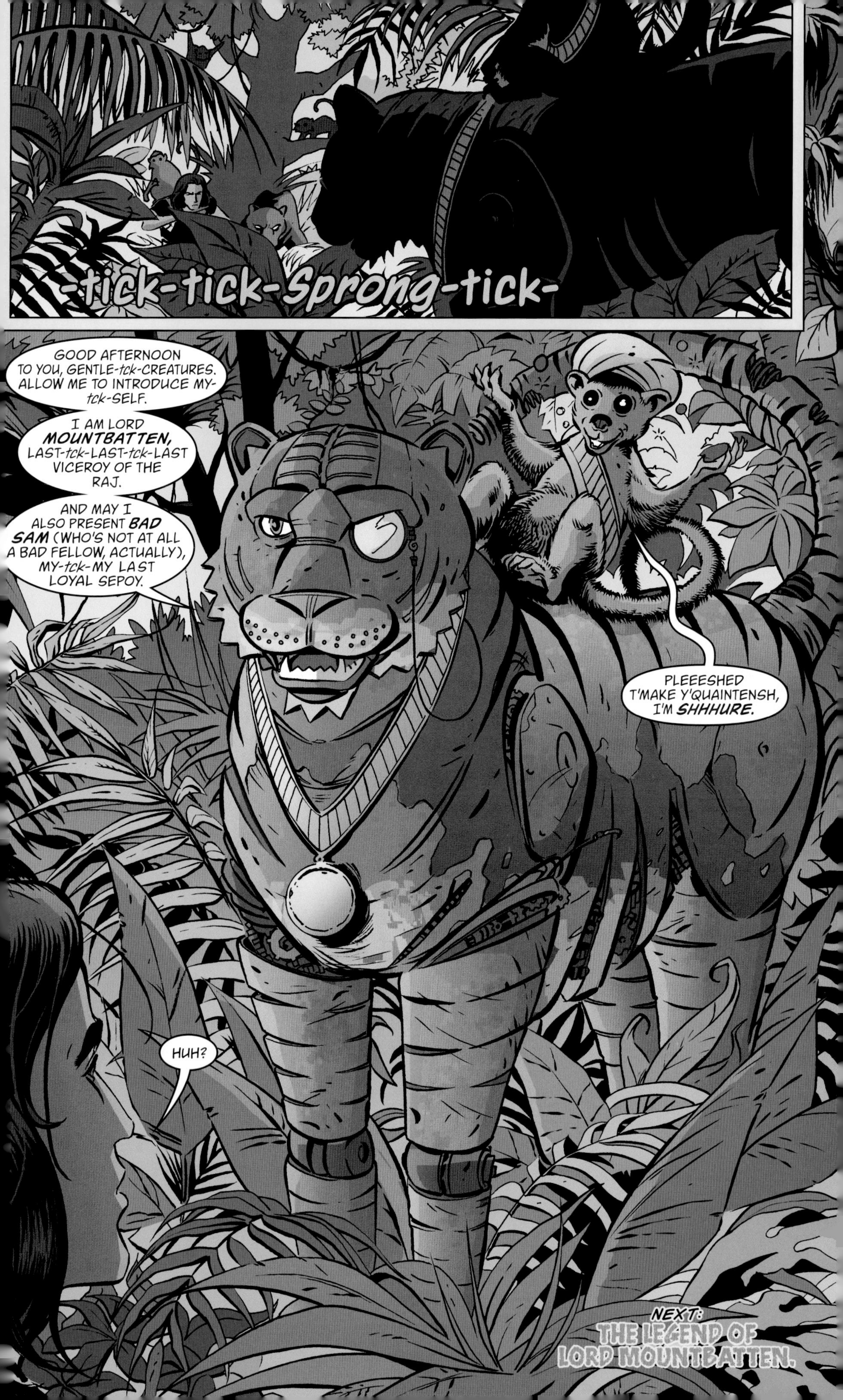
-tick-tick-Sprong-tick-
GOOD AFTERNOON TO YOU, GENTLE-*tck*-CREATURES. ALLOW ME TO INTRODUCE MY-*tck*-SELF.
I AM LORD **MOUNTBATTEN,** LAST-*tck*-LAST-*tck*-LAST VICEROY OF THE RAJ.
AND MAY I ALSO PRESENT **BAD SAM** (WHO'S NOT AT ALL A BAD FELLOW, ACTUALLY), MY-*tck*-MY LAST LOYAL SEPOY.
PLEEESHED T'MAKE Y'QUAINTENSH, I'M **SHHHURE.**
HUH?
NEXT: THE LEGEND OF LORD MOUNTBATTEN.

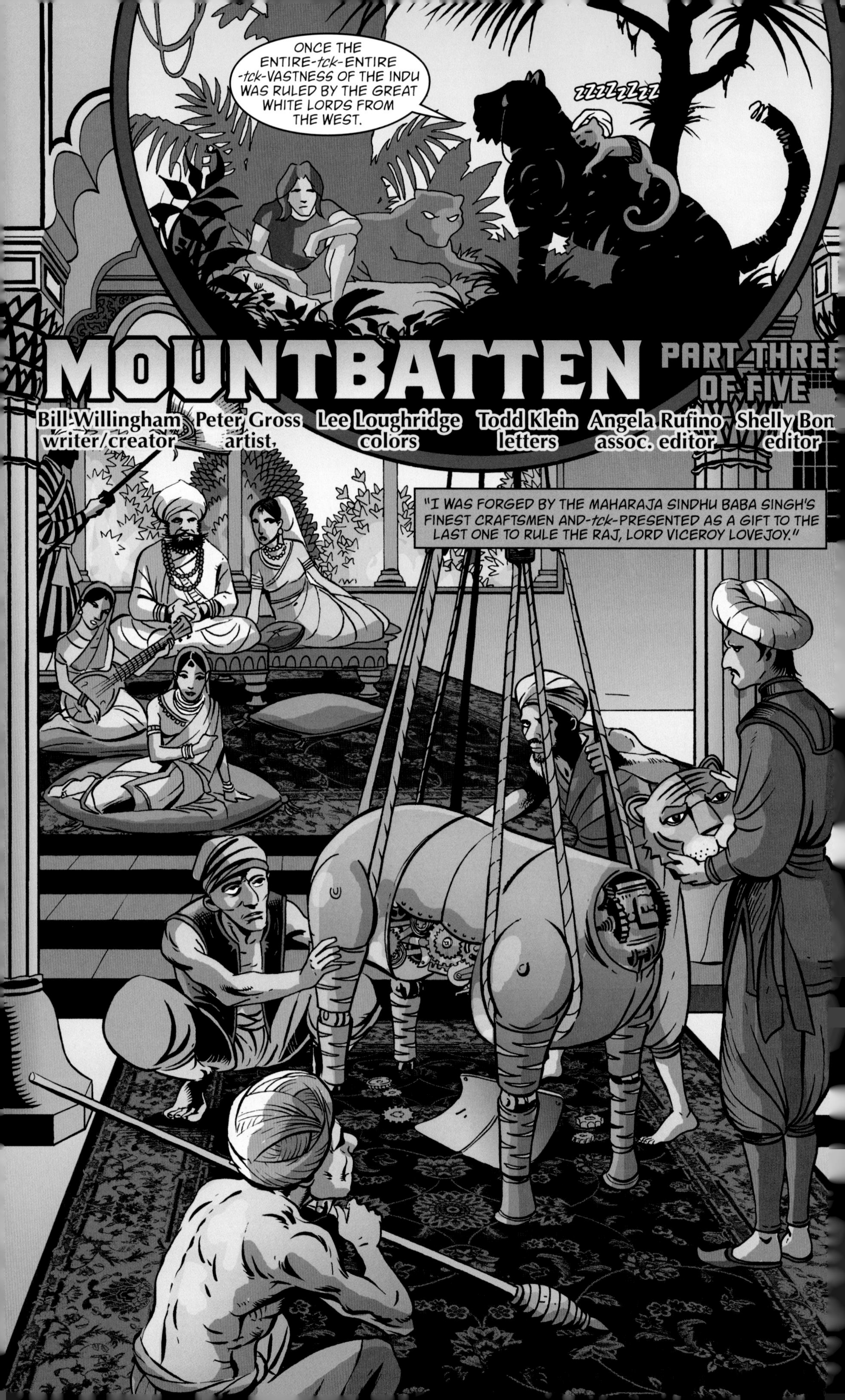
ONCE THE ENTIRE-*tck*-ENTIRE -*tck*-VASTNESS OF THE INDU WAS RULED BY THE GREAT WHITE LORDS FROM THE WEST.
ZZZZZZZZ
MOUNTBATTEN
PART THREE OF FIVE
Bill Willingham writer/creator
Peter Gross artist
Lee Loughridge colors
Todd Klein letters
Angela Rufino assoc. editor
Shelly Bon editor
"I WAS FORGED BY THE MAHARAJA SINDHU BABA SINGH'S FINEST CRAFTSMEN AND-*tck*-PRESENTED AS A GIFT TO THE LAST ONE TO RULE THE RAJ, LORD VICEROY LOVEJOY."

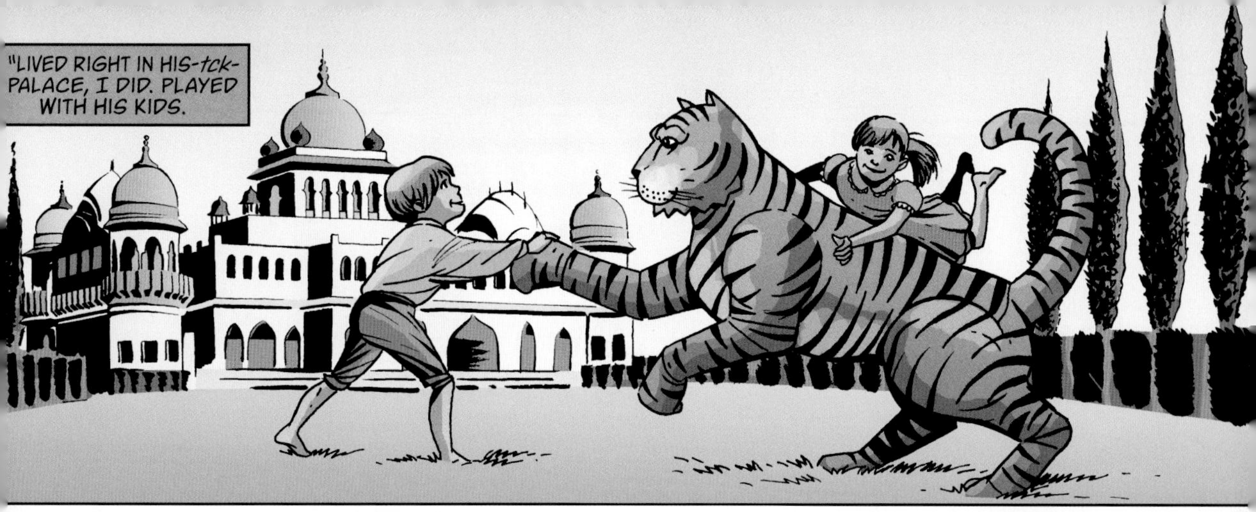
"LIVED RIGHT IN HIS-*tck*-PALACE, I DID. PLAYED WITH HIS KIDS.

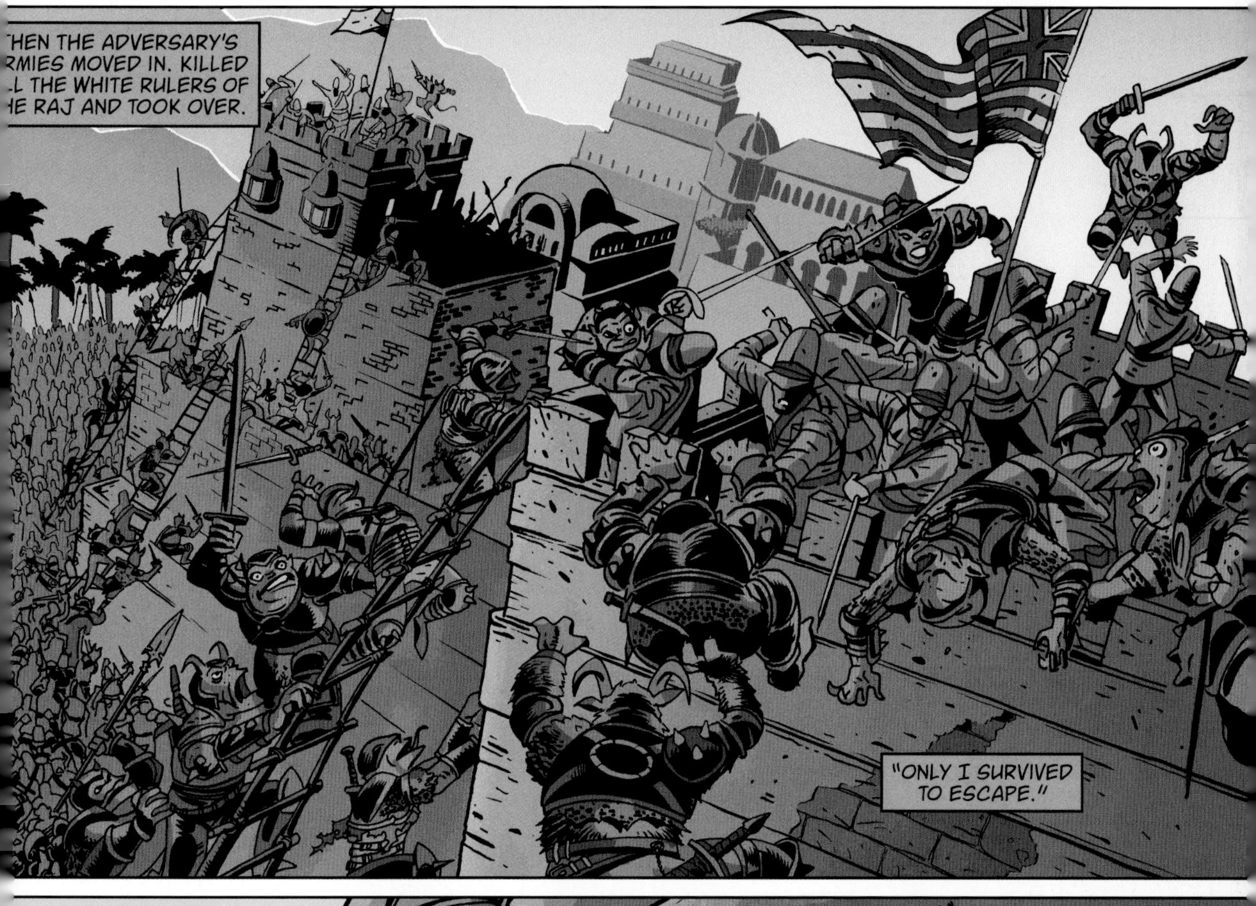
THEN THE ADVERSARY'S RMIES MOVED IN. KILLED L THE WHITE RULERS OF E RAJ AND TOOK OVER.
"ONLY I SURVIVED TO ESCAPE."

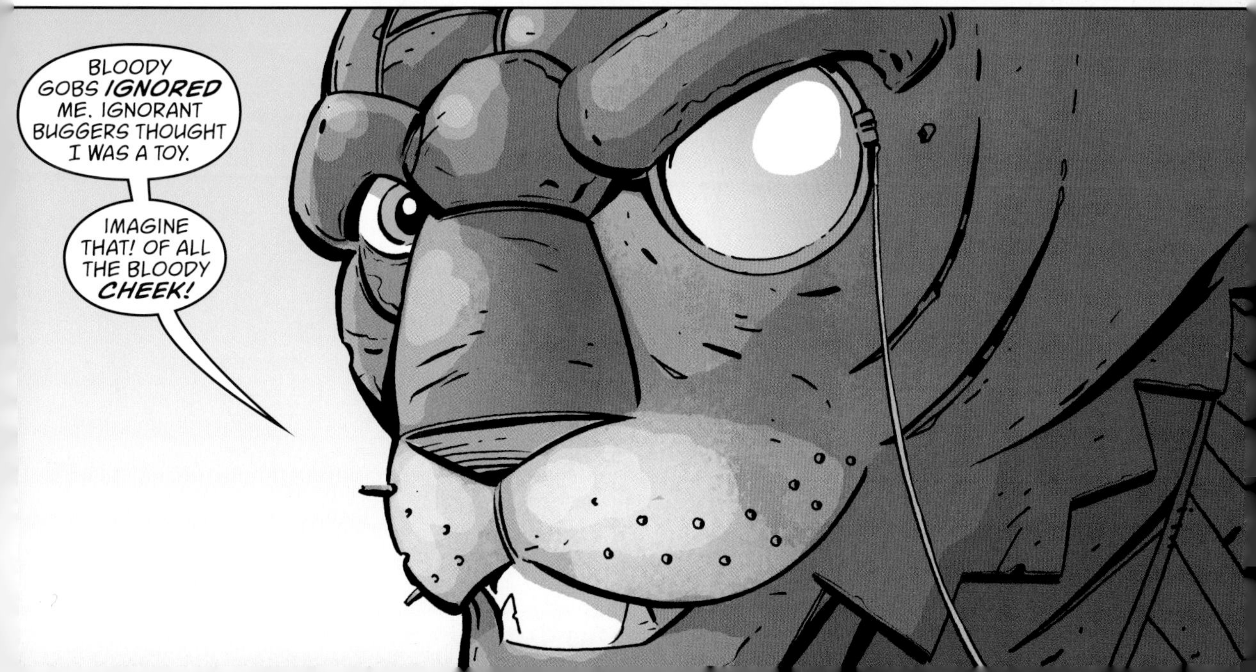
BLOODY GOBS ***IGNORED*** ME. IGNORANT BUGGERS THOUGHT I WAS A TOY.
IMAGINE THAT! OF ALL THE BLOODY ***CHEEK!***

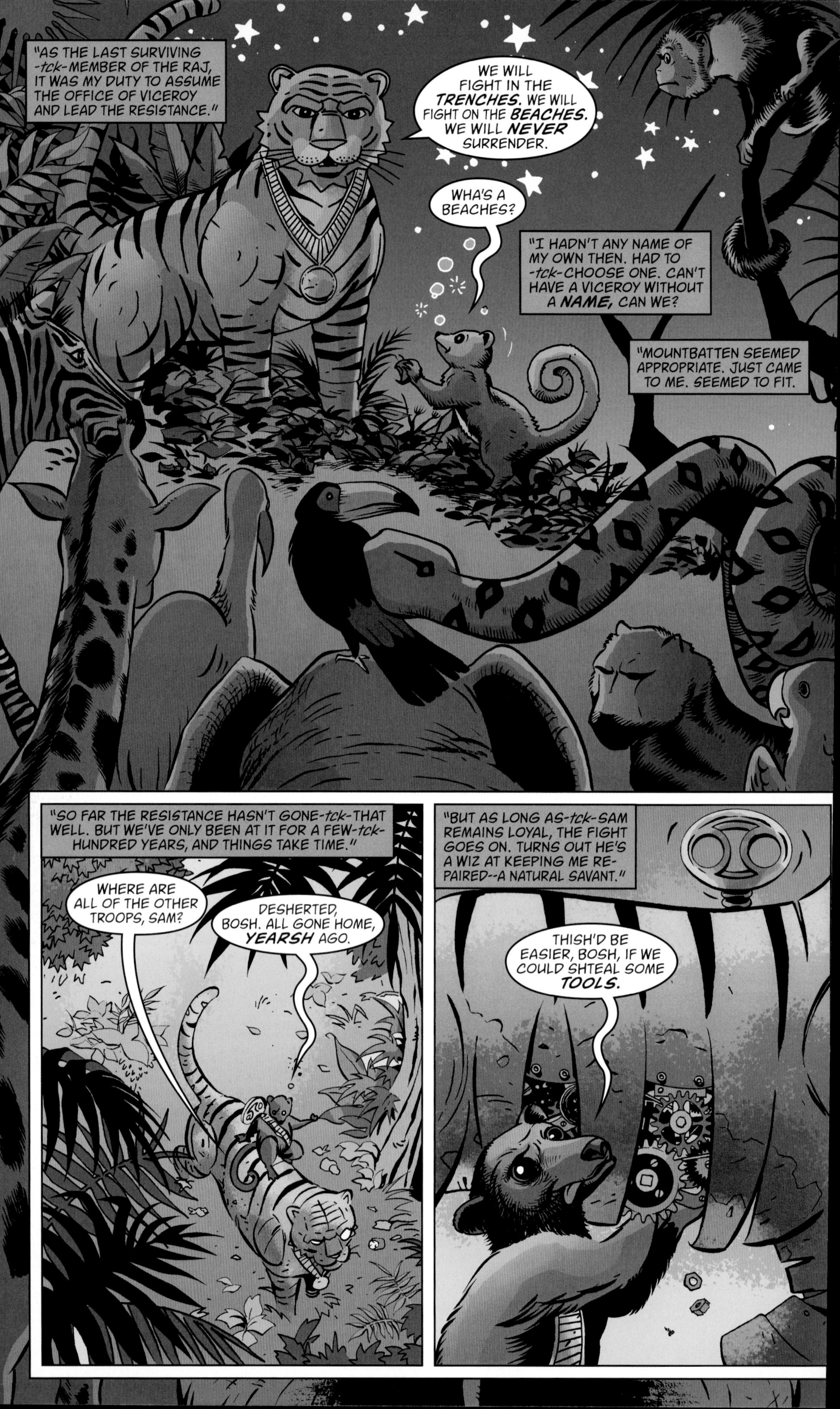
"AS THE LAST SURVIVING -*tck*- MEMBER OF THE RAJ, IT WAS MY DUTY TO ASSUME THE OFFICE OF VICEROY AND LEAD THE RESISTANCE."
WE WILL FIGHT IN THE **TRENCHES.** WE WILL FIGHT ON THE **BEACHES.** WE WILL **NEVER** SURRENDER.
WHA'S A BEACHES?
"I HADN'T ANY NAME OF MY OWN THEN. HAD TO -*tck*- CHOOSE ONE. CAN'T HAVE A VICEROY WITHOUT A **NAME,** CAN WE?
"MOUNTBATTEN SEEMED APPROPRIATE. JUST CAME TO ME. SEEMED TO FIT.
"SO FAR THE RESISTANCE HASN'T GONE -*tck*- THAT WELL. BUT WE'VE ONLY BEEN AT IT FOR A FEW -*tck*- HUNDRED YEARS, AND THINGS TAKE TIME."
WHERE ARE ALL OF THE OTHER TROOPS, SAM?
DESHERTED, BOSH. ALL GONE HOME, **YEARSH** AGO.
"BUT AS LONG AS -*tck*- SAM REMAINS LOYAL, THE FIGHT GOES ON. TURNS OUT HE'S A WIZ AT KEEPING ME RE-PAIRED--A NATURAL SAVANT."
THISH'D BE EASIER, BOSH, IF WE COULD SHTEAL SOME **TOOLS.**

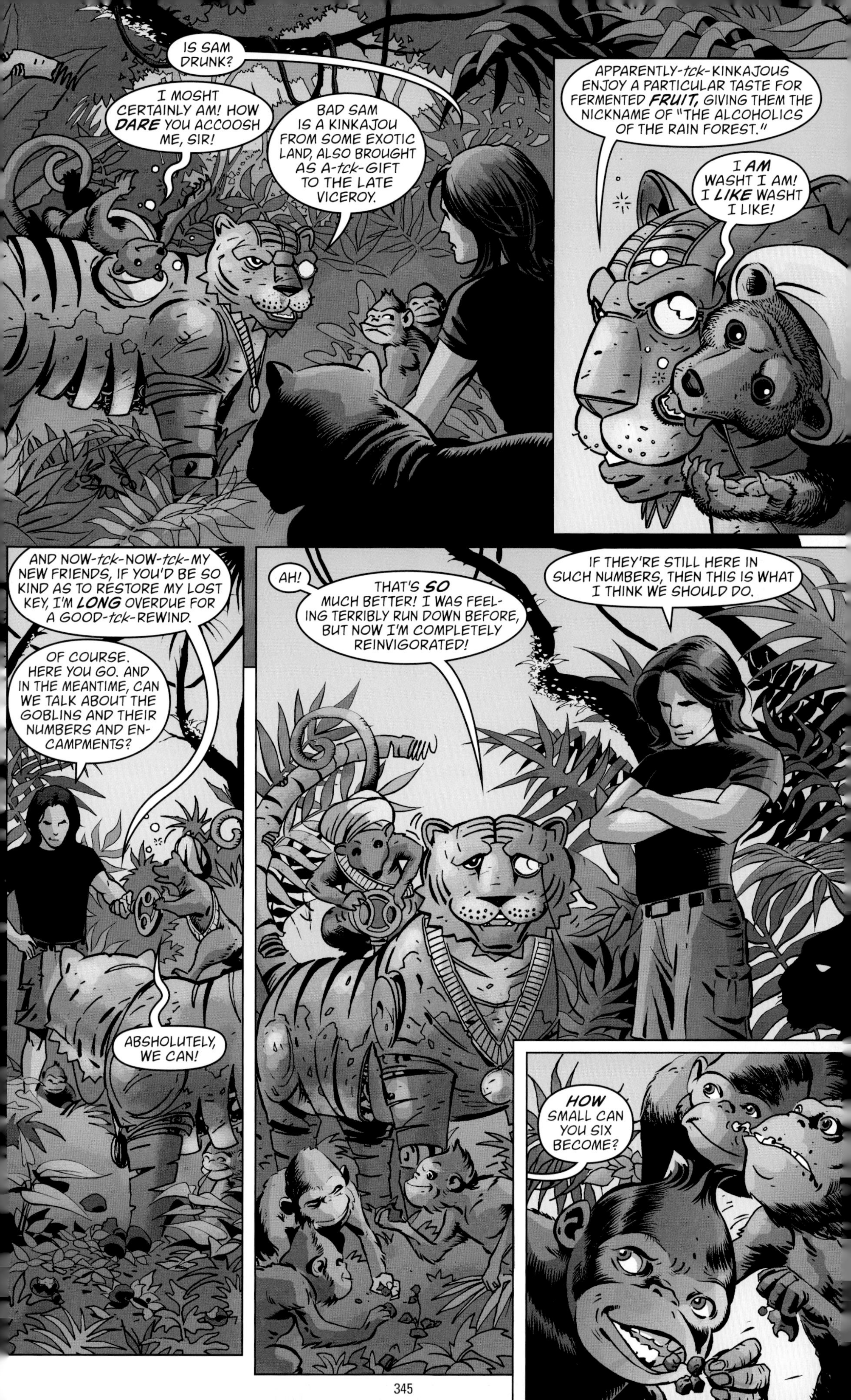
IS SAM DRUNK?
I MOSHT CERTAINLY AM! HOW **DARE** YOU ACCOOSH ME, SIR!
BAD SAM IS A KINKAJOU FROM SOME EXOTIC LAND, ALSO BROUGHT AS A-*tck*-GIFT TO THE LATE VICEROY.
APPARENTLY-*tck*-KINKAJOUS ENJOY A PARTICULAR TASTE FOR FERMENTED ***FRUIT,*** GIVING THEM THE NICKNAME OF "THE ALCOHOLICS OF THE RAIN FOREST."
I ***AM*** WASHT I AM! I ***LIKE*** WASHT I LIKE!
AND NOW-*tck*-NOW-*tck*-MY NEW FRIENDS, IF YOU'D BE SO KIND AS TO RESTORE MY LOST KEY, I'M ***LONG*** OVERDUE FOR A GOOD-*tck*-REWIND.
OF COURSE. HERE YOU GO. AND IN THE MEANTIME, CAN WE TALK ABOUT THE GOBLINS AND THEIR NUMBERS AND ENCAMPMENTS?
ABSHOLUTELY, WE CAN!
AH!
THAT'S ***SO*** MUCH BETTER! I WAS FEELING TERRIBLY RUN DOWN BEFORE, BUT NOW I'M COMPLETELY REINVIGORATED!
IF THEY'RE STILL HERE IN SUCH NUMBERS, THEN THIS IS WHAT I THINK WE SHOULD DO.
HOW SMALL CAN YOU SIX BECOME?

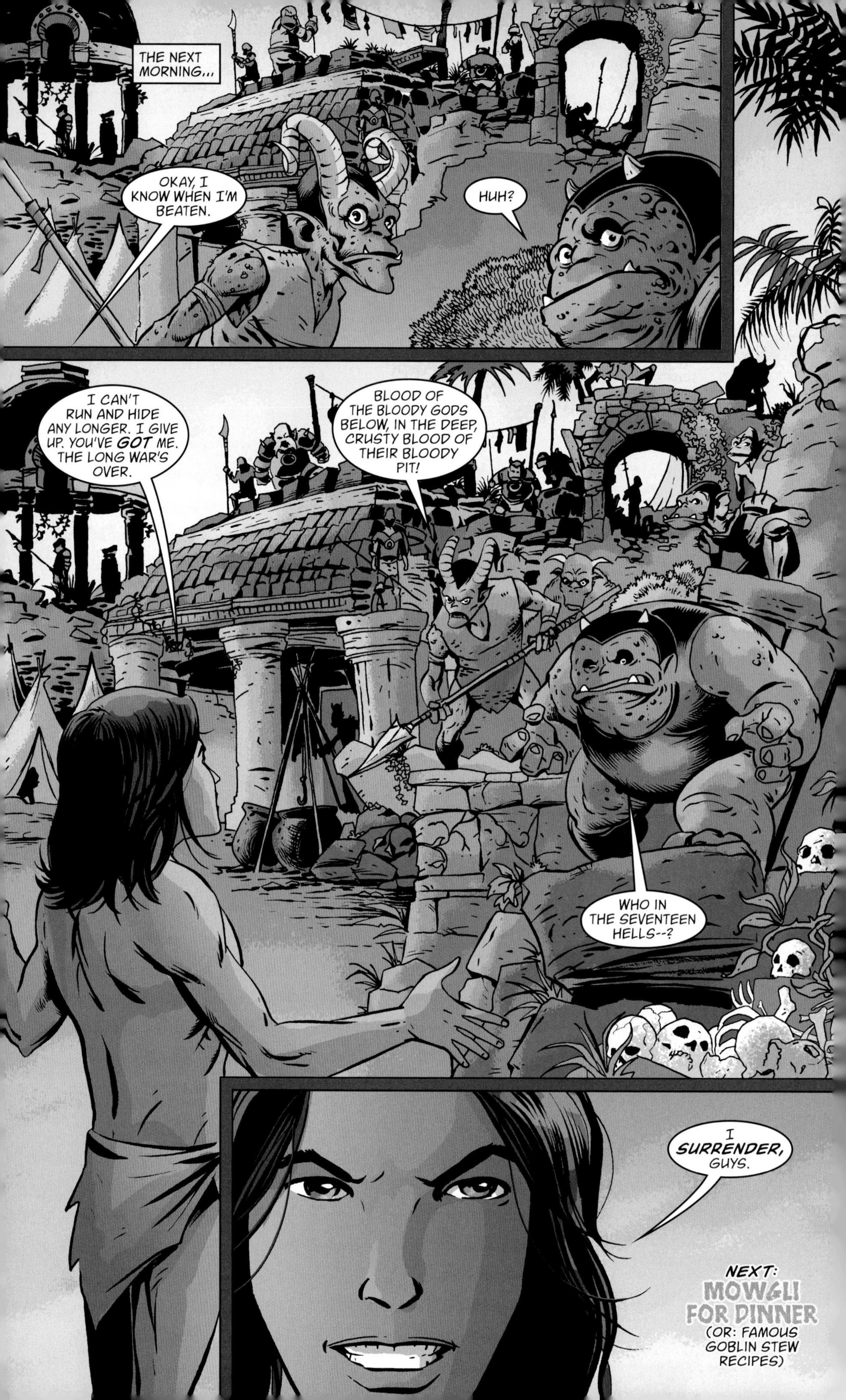
THE NEXT MORNING...
OKAY, I KNOW WHEN I'M BEATEN.
HUH?
I CAN'T RUN AND HIDE ANY LONGER. I GIVE UP. YOU'VE **GOT** ME. THE LONG WAR'S OVER.
BLOOD OF THE BLOODY GODS BELOW, IN THE DEEP, CRUSTY BLOOD OF THEIR BLOODY PIT!
WHO IN THE SEVENTEEN HELLS--?
I **SURRENDER,** GUYS.
NEXT: MOWGLI FOR DINNER (OR: FAMOUS GOBLIN STEW RECIPES)

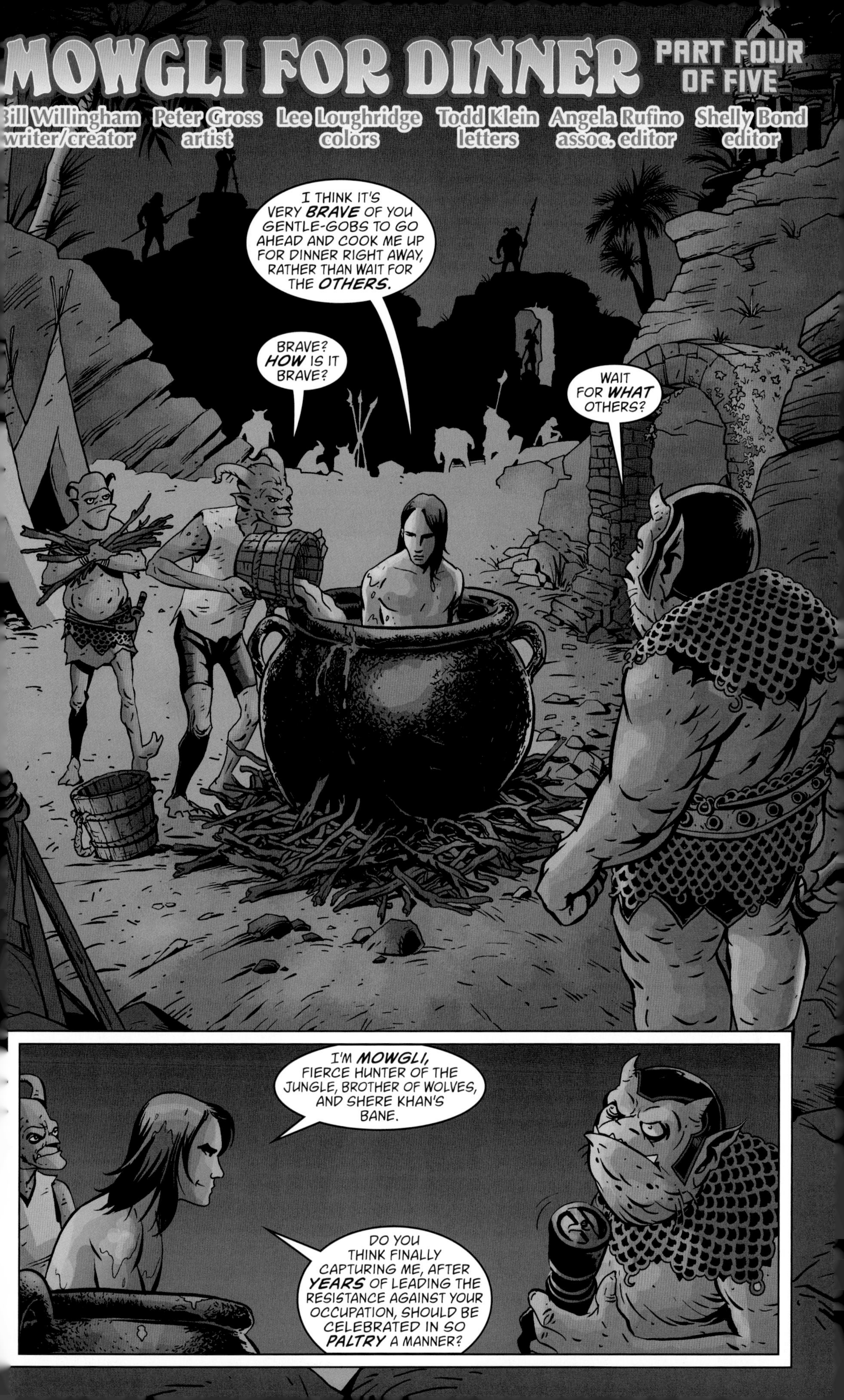
MOWGLI FOR DINNER PART FOUR OF FIVE
Bill Willingham writer/creator
Peter Gross artist
Lee Loughridge colors
Todd Klein letters
Angela Rufino assoc. editor
Shelly Bond editor
I THINK IT'S VERY BRAVE OF YOU GENTLE-GOBS TO GO AHEAD AND COOK ME UP FOR DINNER RIGHT AWAY, RATHER THAN WAIT FOR THE OTHERS.
BRAVE? HOW IS IT BRAVE?
WAIT FOR WHAT OTHERS?
I'M MOWGLI, FIERCE HUNTER OF THE JUNGLE, BROTHER OF WOLVES, AND SHERE KHAN'S BANE.
DO YOU THINK FINALLY CAPTURING ME, AFTER YEARS OF LEADING THE RESISTANCE AGAINST YOUR OCCUPATION, SHOULD BE CELEBRATED IN SO PALTRY A MANNER?

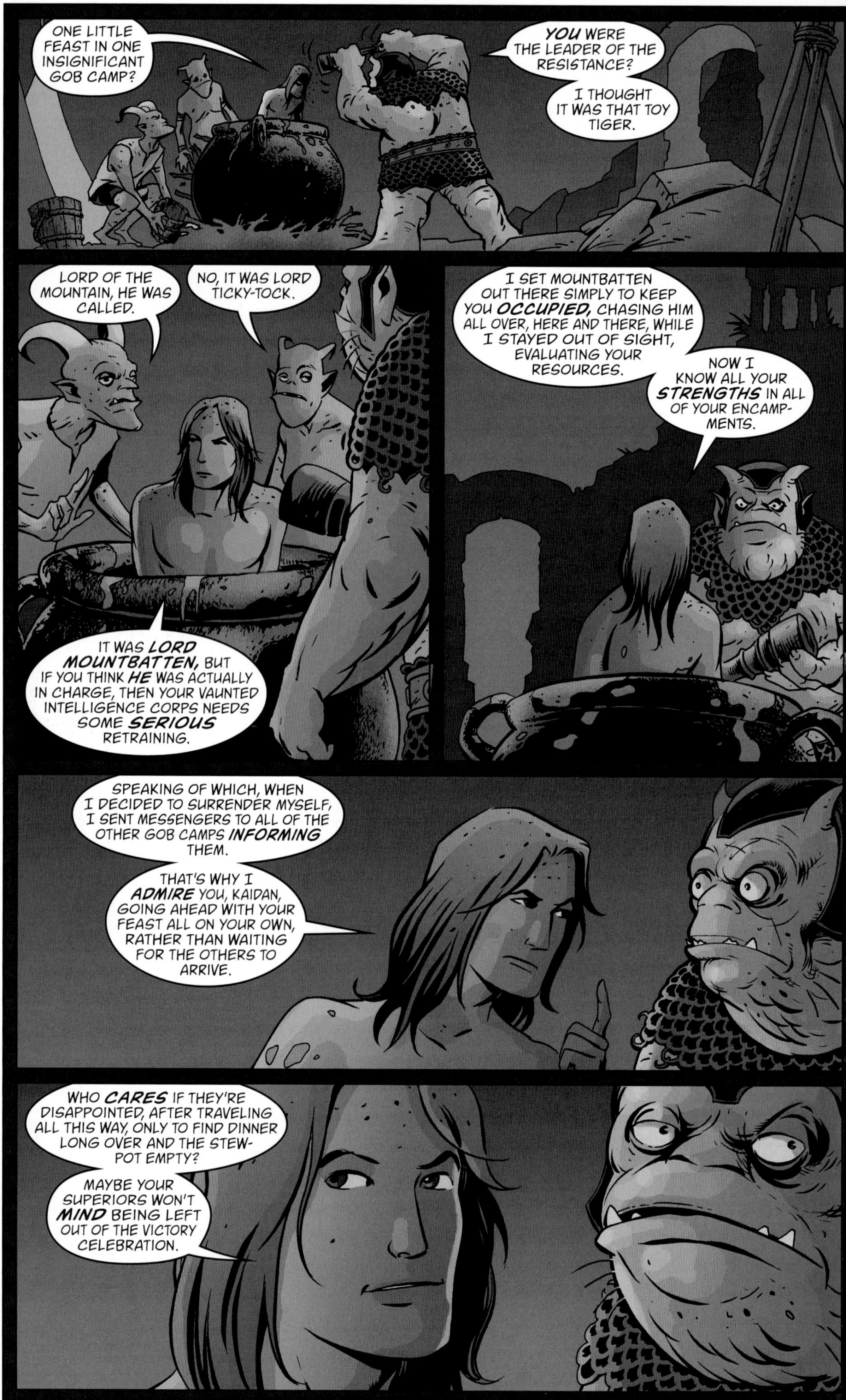
ONE LITTLE FEAST IN ONE INSIGNIFICANT GOB CAMP?
YOU WERE THE LEADER OF THE RESISTANCE?
I THOUGHT IT WAS THAT TOY TIGER.
LORD OF THE MOUNTAIN, HE WAS CALLED.
NO, IT WAS LORD TICKY-TOCK.
IT WAS LORD MOUNTBATTEN, BUT IF YOU THINK HE WAS ACTUALLY IN CHARGE, THEN YOUR VAUNTED INTELLIGENCE CORPS NEEDS SOME SERIOUS RETRAINING.
I SET MOUNTBATTEN OUT THERE SIMPLY TO KEEP YOU OCCUPIED, CHASING HIM ALL OVER, HERE AND THERE, WHILE I STAYED OUT OF SIGHT, EVALUATING YOUR RESOURCES.
NOW I KNOW ALL YOUR STRENGTHS IN ALL OF YOUR ENCAMP-MENTS.
SPEAKING OF WHICH, WHEN I DECIDED TO SURRENDER MYSELF, I SENT MESSENGERS TO ALL OF THE OTHER GOB CAMPS INFORMING THEM.
THAT'S WHY I ADMIRE YOU, KAIDAN, GOING AHEAD WITH YOUR FEAST ALL ON YOUR OWN, RATHER THAN WAITING FOR THE OTHERS TO ARRIVE.
WHO CARES IF THEY'RE DISAPPOINTED, AFTER TRAVELING ALL THIS WAY, ONLY TO FIND DINNER LONG OVER AND THE STEW-POT EMPTY?
MAYBE YOUR SUPERIORS WON'T MIND BEING LEFT OUT OF THE VICTORY CELEBRATION.

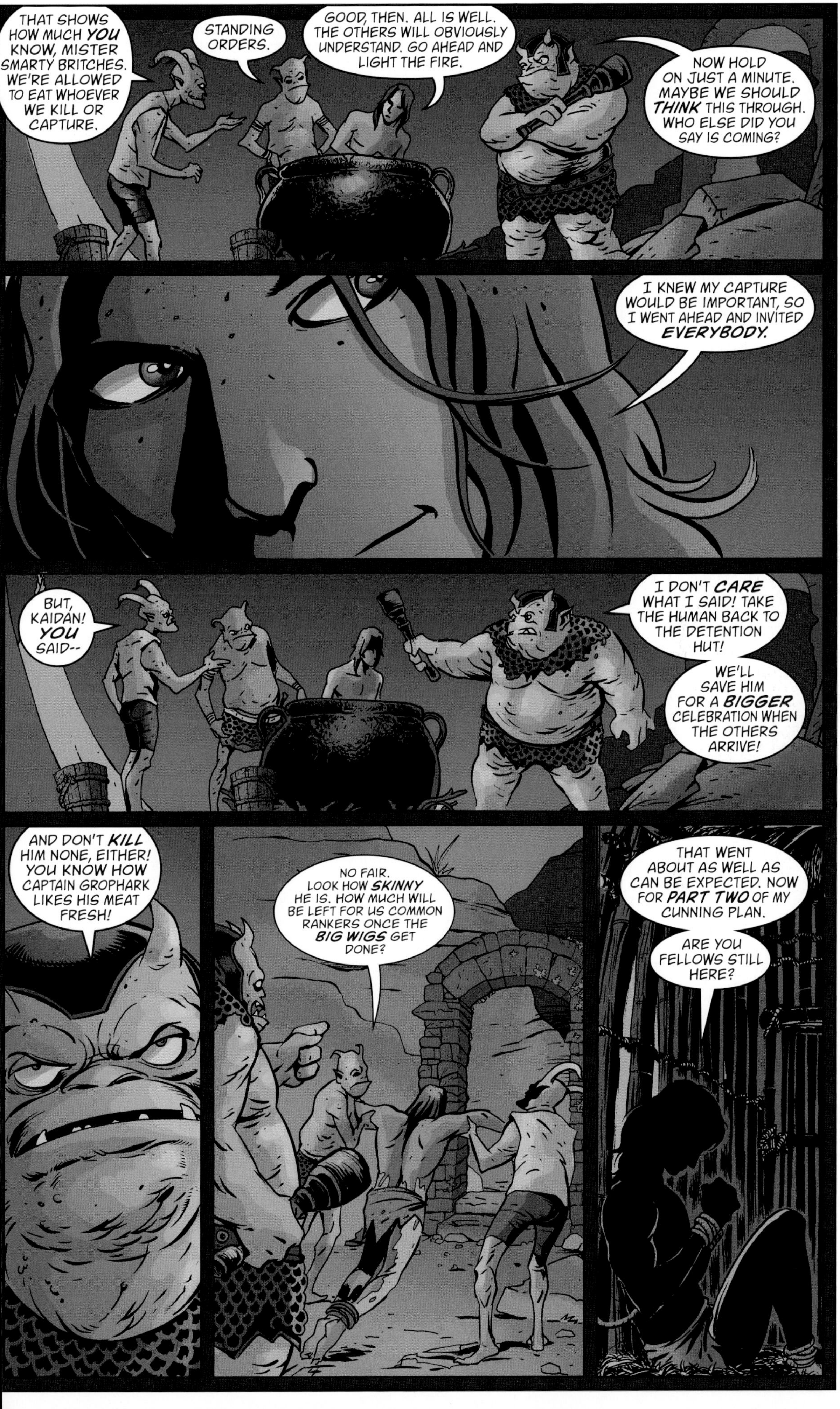
THAT SHOWS HOW MUCH YOU KNOW, MISTER SMARTY BRITCHES. WE'RE ALLOWED TO EAT WHOEVER WE KILL OR CAPTURE.
STANDING ORDERS.
GOOD, THEN. ALL IS WELL. THE OTHERS WILL OBVIOUSLY UNDERSTAND. GO AHEAD AND LIGHT THE FIRE.
NOW HOLD ON JUST A MINUTE. MAYBE WE SHOULD THINK THIS THROUGH. WHO ELSE DID YOU SAY IS COMING?
I KNEW MY CAPTURE WOULD BE IMPORTANT, SO I WENT AHEAD AND INVITED EVERYBODY.
BUT, KAIDAN! YOU SAID--
I DON'T CARE WHAT I SAID! TAKE THE HUMAN BACK TO THE DETENTION HUT!
WE'LL SAVE HIM FOR A BIGGER CELEBRATION WHEN THE OTHERS ARRIVE!
AND DON'T KILL HIM NONE, EITHER! YOU KNOW HOW CAPTAIN GROPHARK LIKES HIS MEAT FRESH!
NO FAIR. LOOK HOW SKINNY HE IS. HOW MUCH WILL BE LEFT FOR US COMMON RANKERS ONCE THE BIG WIGS GET DONE?
THAT WENT ABOUT AS WELL AS CAN BE EXPECTED. NOW FOR PART TWO OF MY CUNNING PLAN.
ARE YOU FELLOWS STILL HERE?

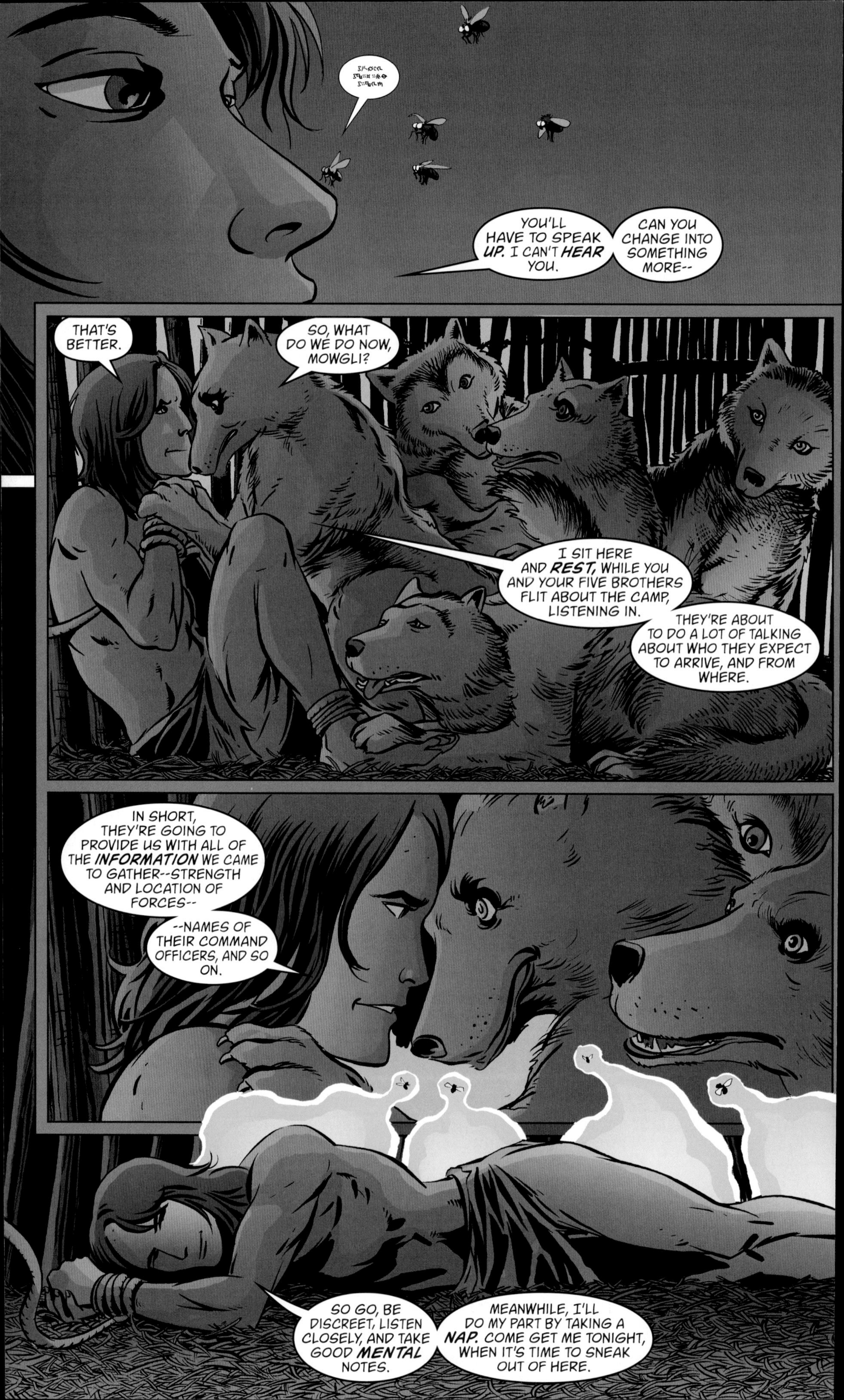
YOU'LL HAVE TO SPEAK UP. I CAN'T HEAR YOU.
CAN YOU CHANGE INTO SOMETHING MORE--
THAT'S BETTER.
SO, WHAT DO WE DO NOW, MOWGLI?
I SIT HERE AND REST, WHILE YOU AND YOUR FIVE BROTHERS FLIT ABOUT THE CAMP, LISTENING IN.
THEY'RE ABOUT TO DO A LOT OF TALKING ABOUT WHO THEY EXPECT TO ARRIVE, AND FROM WHERE.
IN SHORT, THEY'RE GOING TO PROVIDE US WITH ALL OF THE INFORMATION WE CAME TO GATHER--STRENGTH AND LOCATION OF FORCES--
--NAMES OF THEIR COMMAND OFFICERS, AND SO ON.
SO GO, BE DISCREET, LISTEN CLOSELY, AND TAKE GOOD MENTAL NOTES.
MEANWHILE, I'LL DO MY PART BY TAKING A NAP. COME GET ME TONIGHT, WHEN IT'S TIME TO SNEAK OUT OF HERE.

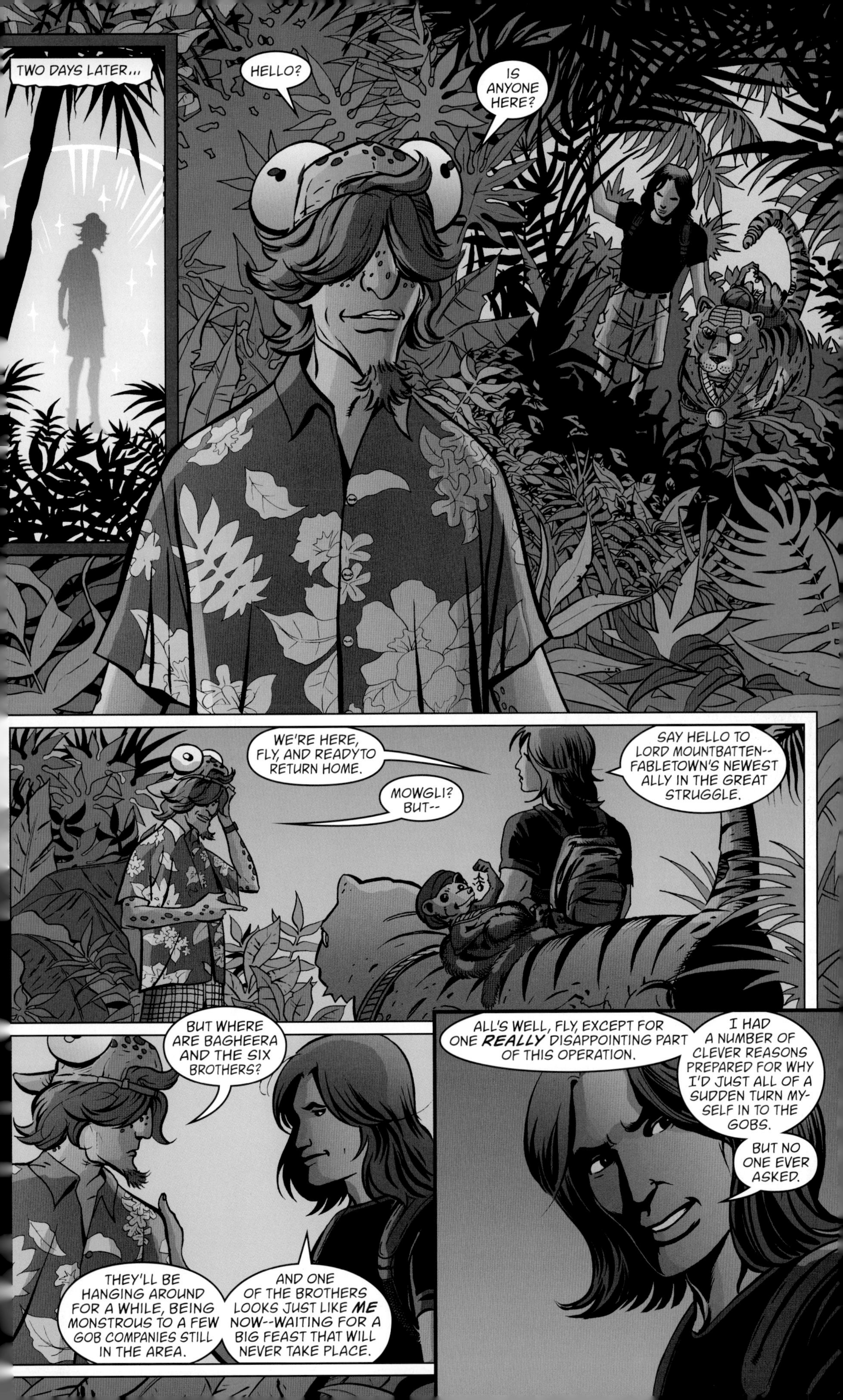
TWO DAYS LATER...
HELLO?
IS ANYONE HERE?
WE'RE HERE, FLY, AND READY TO RETURN HOME.
MOWGLI? BUT--
SAY HELLO TO LORD MOUNTBATTEN--FABLETOWN'S NEWEST ALLY IN THE GREAT STRUGGLE.
BUT WHERE ARE BAGHEERA AND THE SIX BROTHERS?
THEY'LL BE HANGING AROUND FOR A WHILE, BEING MONSTROUS TO A FEW GOB COMPANIES STILL IN THE AREA.
AND ONE OF THE BROTHERS LOOKS JUST LIKE ME NOW--WAITING FOR A BIG FEAST THAT WILL NEVER TAKE PLACE.
ALL'S WELL, FLY, EXCEPT FOR ONE REALLY DISAPPOINTING PART OF THIS OPERATION.
I HAD A NUMBER OF CLEVER REASONS PREPARED FOR WHY I'D JUST ALL OF A SUDDEN TURN MY-SELF IN TO THE GOBS.
BUT NO ONE EVER ASKED.

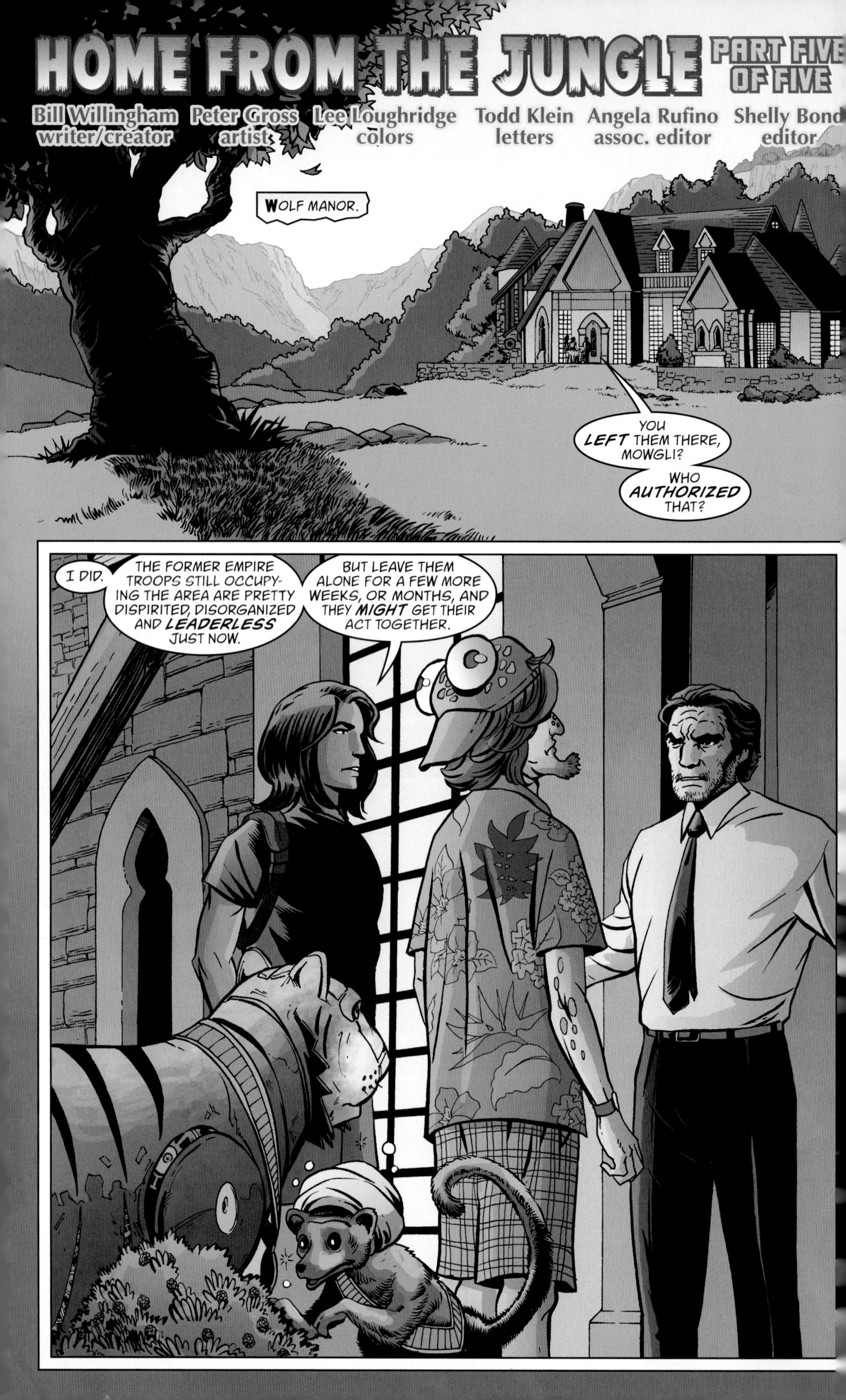
HOME FROM THE JUNGLE PART FIVE OF FIVE
Bill Willingham writer/creator
Peter Gross artist
Lee Loughridge colors
Todd Klein letters
Angela Rufino assoc. editor
Shelly Bond editor
WOLF MANOR.
YOU LEFT THEM THERE, MOWGLI?
WHO AUTHORIZED THAT?
I DID.
THE FORMER EMPIRE TROOPS STILL OCCUPYING THE AREA ARE PRETTY DISPIRITED, DISORGANIZED AND LEADERLESS JUST NOW.
BUT LEAVE THEM ALONE FOR A FEW MORE WEEKS, OR MONTHS, AND THEY MIGHT GET THEIR ACT TOGETHER.

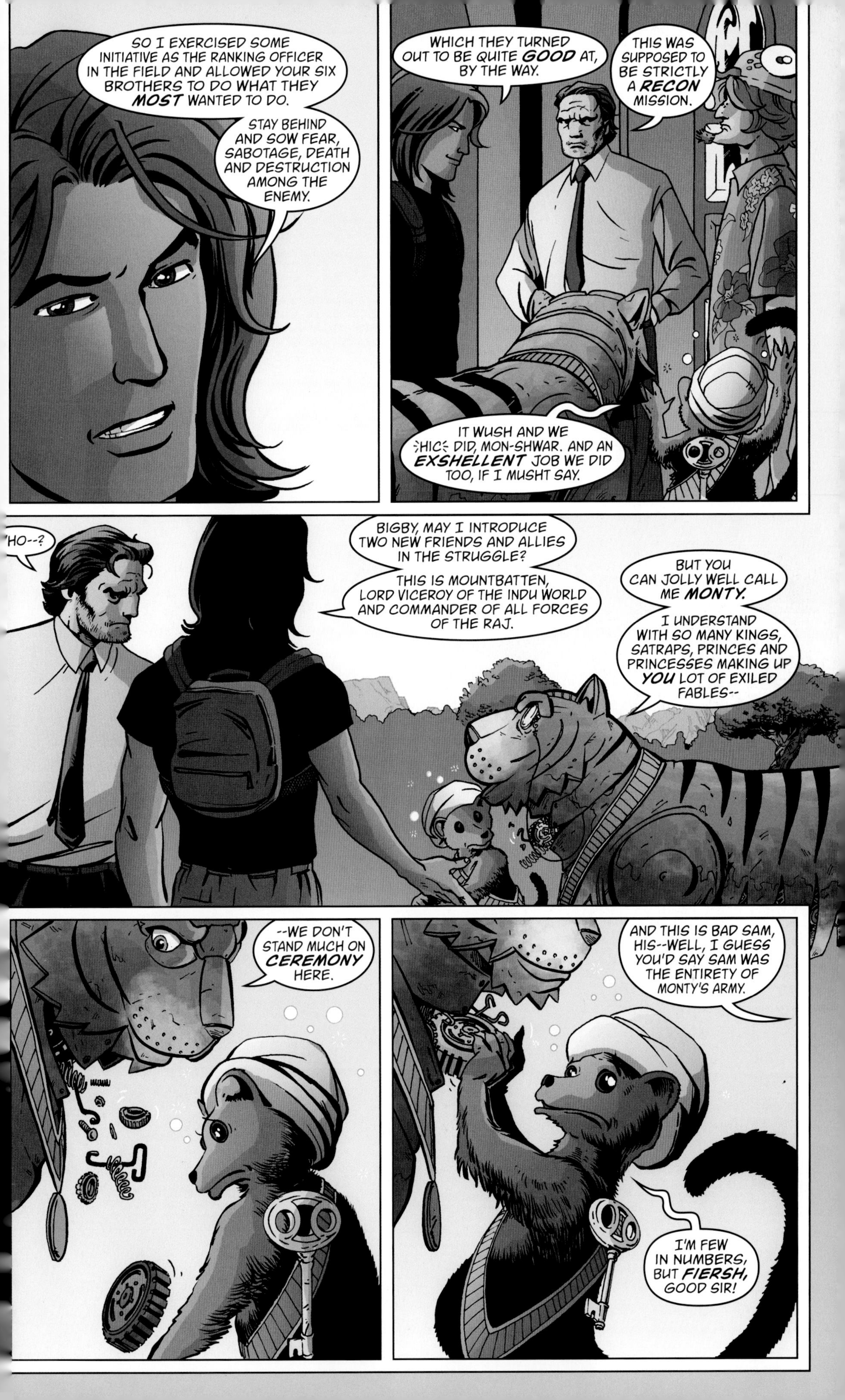
SO I EXERCISED SOME INITIATIVE AS THE RANKING OFFICER IN THE FIELD AND ALLOWED YOUR SIX BROTHERS TO DO WHAT THEY MOST WANTED TO DO.
STAY BEHIND AND SOW FEAR, SABOTAGE, DEATH AND DESTRUCTION AMONG THE ENEMY.
WHICH THEY TURNED OUT TO BE QUITE GOOD AT, BY THE WAY.
THIS WAS SUPPOSED TO BE STRICTLY A RECON MISSION.
IT WUSH AND WE *HIC* DID, MON-SHWAR. AND AN EXSHELLENT JOB WE DID TOO, IF I MUSHT SAY.
HO--?
BIGBY, MAY I INTRODUCE TWO NEW FRIENDS AND ALLIES IN THE STRUGGLE?
THIS IS MOUNTBATTEN, LORD VICEROY OF THE INDU WORLD AND COMMANDER OF ALL FORCES OF THE RAJ.
BUT YOU CAN JOLLY WELL CALL ME MONTY.
I UNDERSTAND WITH SO MANY KINGS, SATRAPS, PRINCES AND PRINCESSES MAKING UP YOU LOT OF EXILED FABLES--
--WE DON'T STAND MUCH ON CEREMONY HERE.
AND THIS IS BAD SAM, HIS--WELL, I GUESS YOU'D SAY SAM WAS THE ENTIRETY OF MONTY'S ARMY.
I'M FEW IN NUMBERS, BUT FIERSH, GOOD SIR!

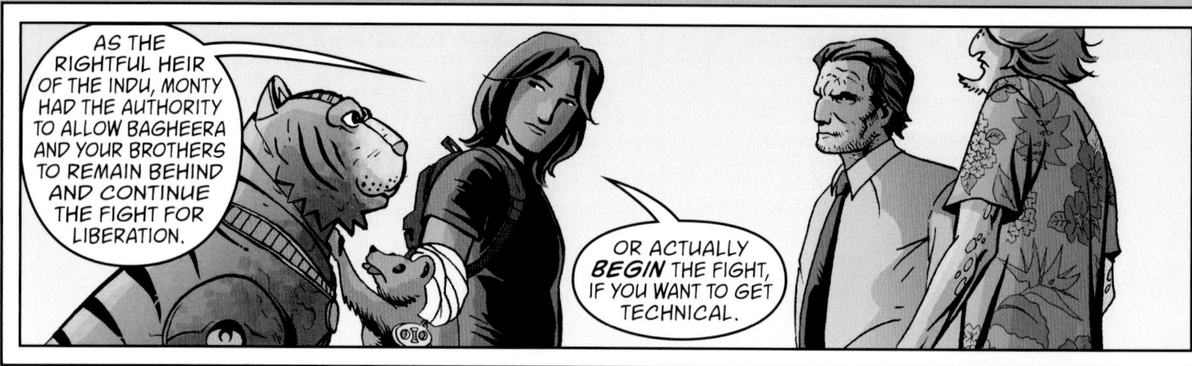
AS THE RIGHTFUL HEIR OF THE INDU, MONTY HAD THE AUTHORITY TO ALLOW BAGHEERA AND YOUR BROTHERS TO REMAIN BEHIND AND CONTINUE THE FIGHT FOR LIBERATION.
OR ACTUALLY BEGIN THE FIGHT, IF YOU WANT TO GET TECHNICAL.
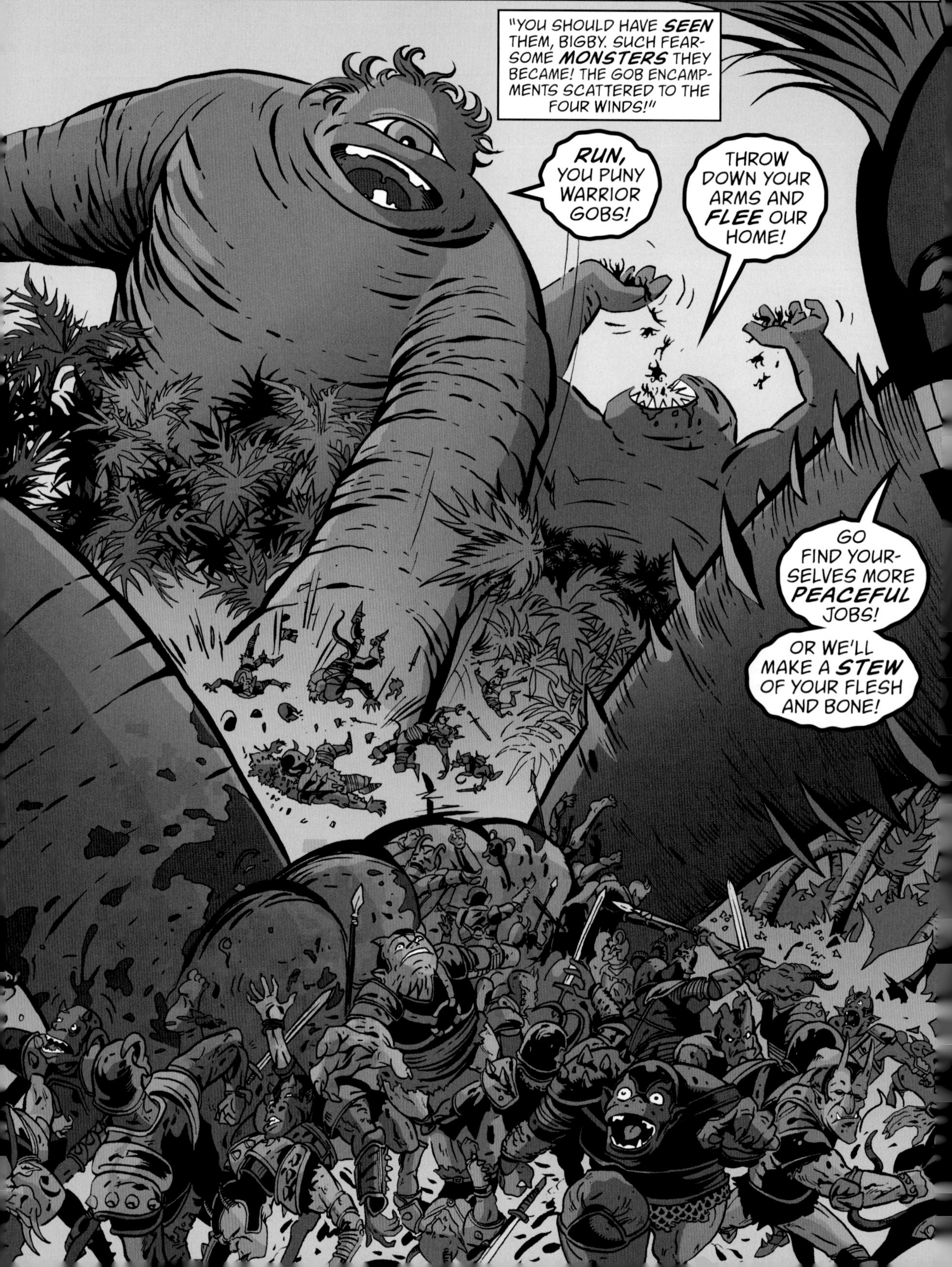
"YOU SHOULD HAVE SEEN THEM, BIGBY. SUCH FEARSOME MONSTERS THEY BECAME! THE GOB ENCAMPMENTS SCATTERED TO THE FOUR WINDS!"
RUN, YOU PUNY WARRIOR GOBS!
THROW DOWN YOUR ARMS AND FLEE OUR HOME!
GO FIND YOURSELVES MORE PEACEFUL JOBS!
OR WE'LL MAKE A STEW OF YOUR FLESH AND BONE!

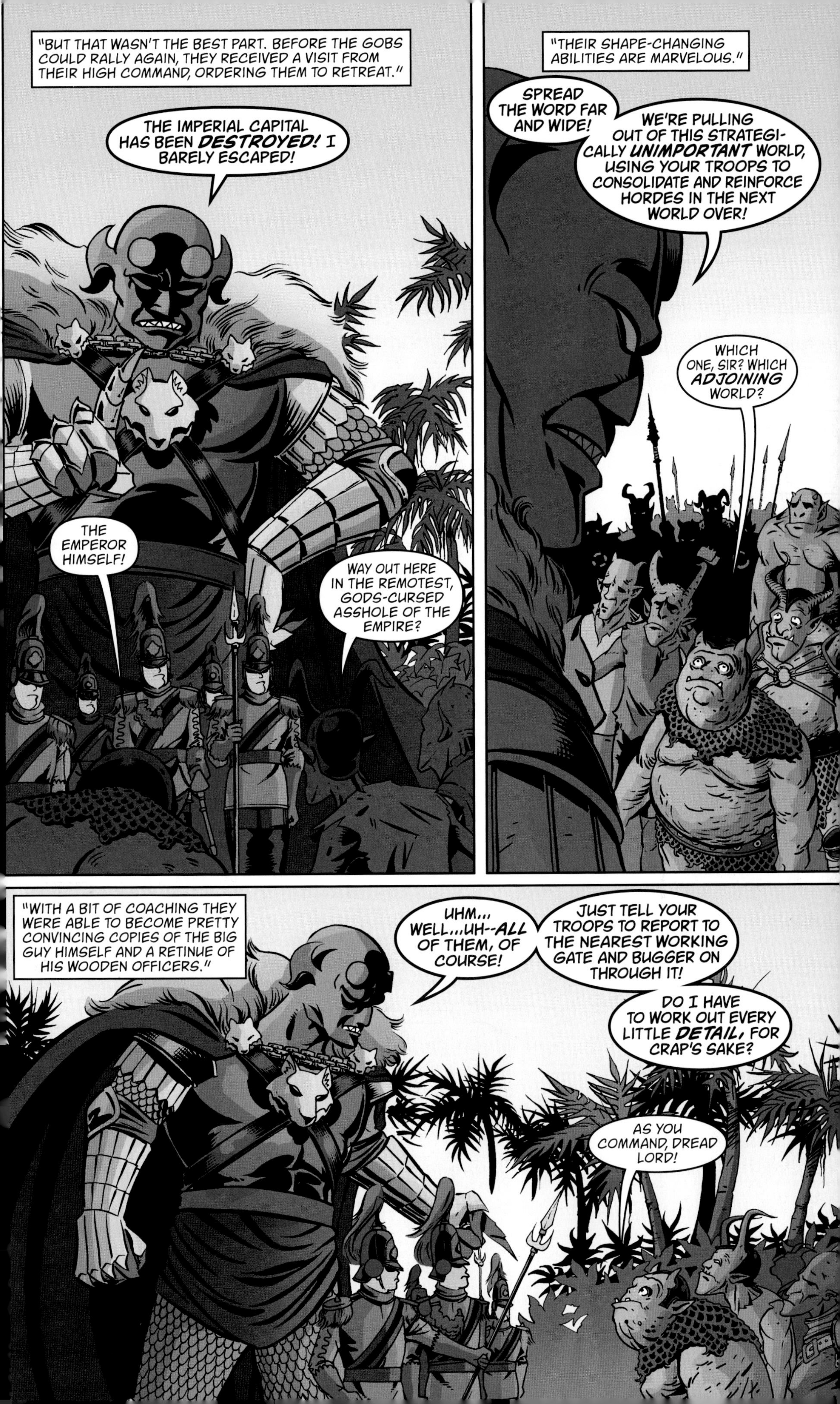
"BUT THAT WASN'T THE BEST PART. BEFORE THE GOBS COULD RALLY AGAIN, THEY RECEIVED A VISIT FROM THEIR HIGH COMMAND, ORDERING THEM TO RETREAT."
THE IMPERIAL CAPITAL HAS BEEN ***DESTROYED!*** I BARELY ESCAPED!
THE EMPEROR HIMSELF!
WAY OUT HERE IN THE REMOTEST, GODS-CURSED ASSHOLE OF THE EMPIRE?
"THEIR SHAPE-CHANGING ABILITIES ARE MARVELOUS."
SPREAD THE WORD FAR AND WIDE!
WE'RE PULLING OUT OF THIS STRATEGICALLY ***UNIMPORTANT*** WORLD, USING YOUR TROOPS TO CONSOLIDATE AND REINFORCE HORDES IN THE NEXT WORLD OVER!
WHICH ONE, SIR? WHICH ***ADJOINING*** WORLD?
"WITH A BIT OF COACHING THEY WERE ABLE TO BECOME PRETTY CONVINCING COPIES OF THE BIG GUY HIMSELF AND A RETINUE OF HIS WOODEN OFFICERS."
UHM... WELL...UH--***ALL*** OF THEM, OF COURSE!
JUST TELL YOUR TROOPS TO REPORT TO THE NEAREST WORKING GATE AND BUGGER ON THROUGH IT!
DO I HAVE TO WORK OUT EVERY LITTLE ***DETAIL,*** FOR CRAP'S SAKE?
AS YOU COMMAND, DREAD LORD!

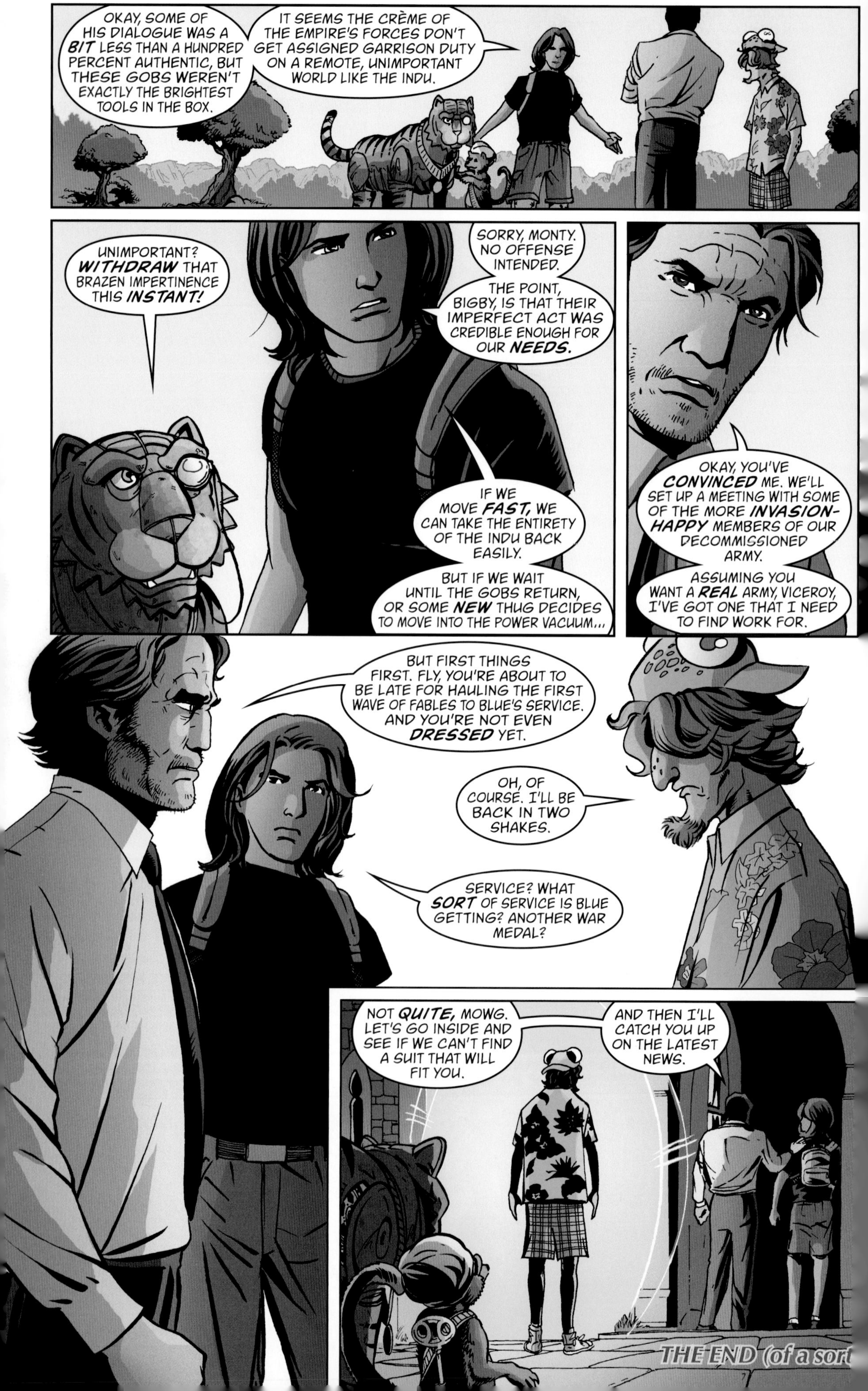
OKAY, SOME OF HIS DIALOGUE WAS A BIT LESS THAN A HUNDRED PERCENT AUTHENTIC, BUT THESE GOBS WEREN'T EXACTLY THE BRIGHTEST TOOLS IN THE BOX.
IT SEEMS THE CRÈME OF THE EMPIRE'S FORCES DON'T GET ASSIGNED GARRISON DUTY ON A REMOTE, UNIMPORTANT WORLD LIKE THE INDU.
UNIMPORTANT? WITHDRAW THAT BRAZEN IMPERTINENCE THIS INSTANT!
SORRY, MONTY. NO OFFENSE INTENDED.
THE POINT, BIGBY, IS THAT THEIR IMPERFECT ACT WAS CREDIBLE ENOUGH FOR OUR NEEDS.
IF WE MOVE FAST, WE CAN TAKE THE ENTIRETY OF THE INDU BACK EASILY.
BUT IF WE WAIT UNTIL THE GOBS RETURN, OR SOME NEW THUG DECIDES TO MOVE INTO THE POWER VACUUM...
OKAY, YOU'VE CONVINCED ME. WE'LL SET UP A MEETING WITH SOME OF THE MORE INVASION-HAPPY MEMBERS OF OUR DECOMMISSIONED ARMY.
ASSUMING YOU WANT A REAL ARMY, VICEROY, I'VE GOT ONE THAT I NEED TO FIND WORK FOR.
BUT FIRST THINGS FIRST. FLY, YOU'RE ABOUT TO BE LATE FOR HAULING THE FIRST WAVE OF FABLES TO BLUE'S SERVICE. AND YOU'RE NOT EVEN DRESSED YET.
OH, OF COURSE. I'LL BE BACK IN TWO SHAKES.
SERVICE? WHAT SORT OF SERVICE IS BLUE GETTING? ANOTHER WAR MEDAL?
NOT QUITE, MOWG. LET'S GO INSIDE AND SEE IF WE CAN'T FIND A SUIT THAT WILL FIT YOU.
AND THEN I'LL CATCH YOU UP ON THE LATEST NEWS.
THE END (of a sort

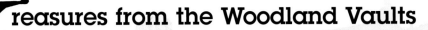

Treasures from the Woodland Vaults

Designs and sketches by Mark Buckingham

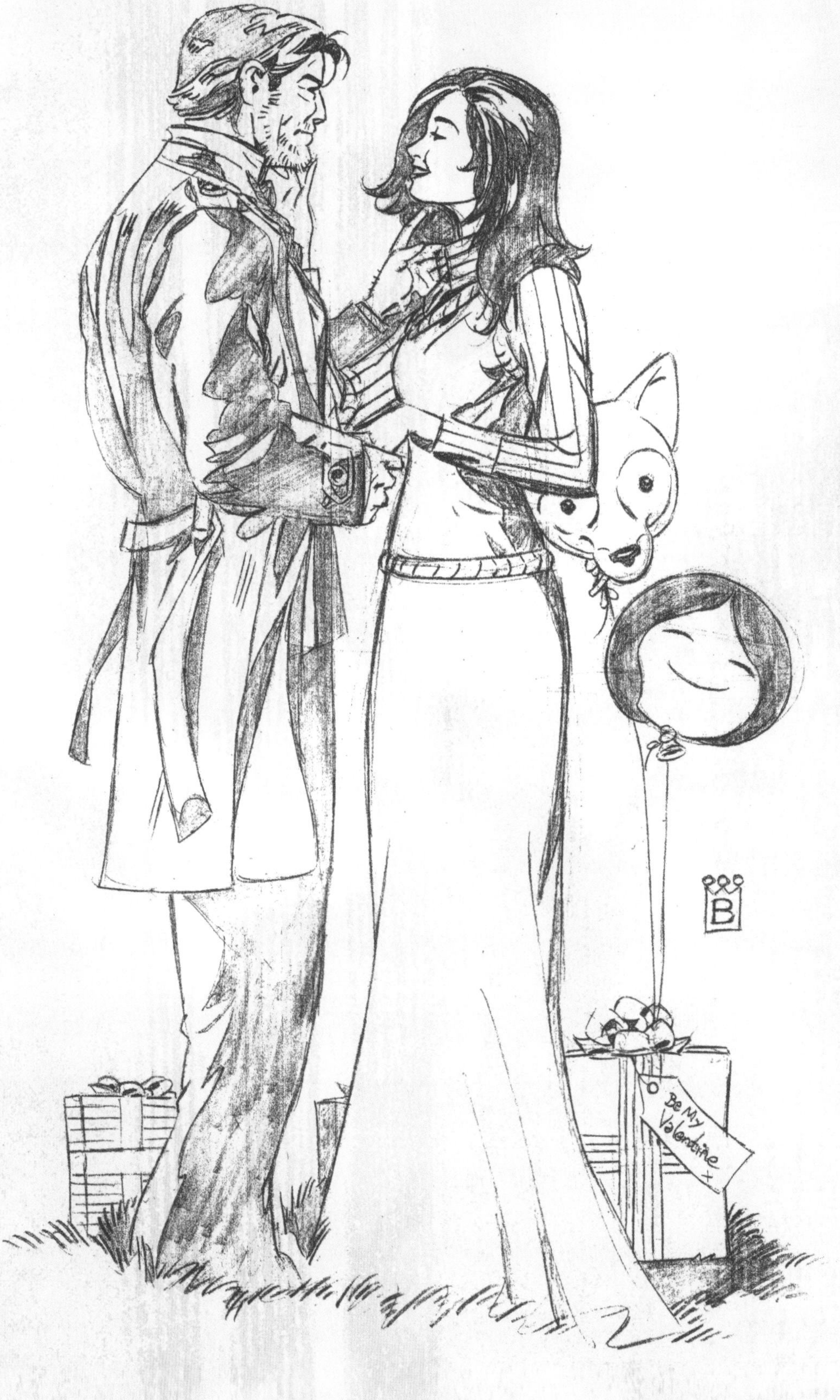
Be My Valentine x

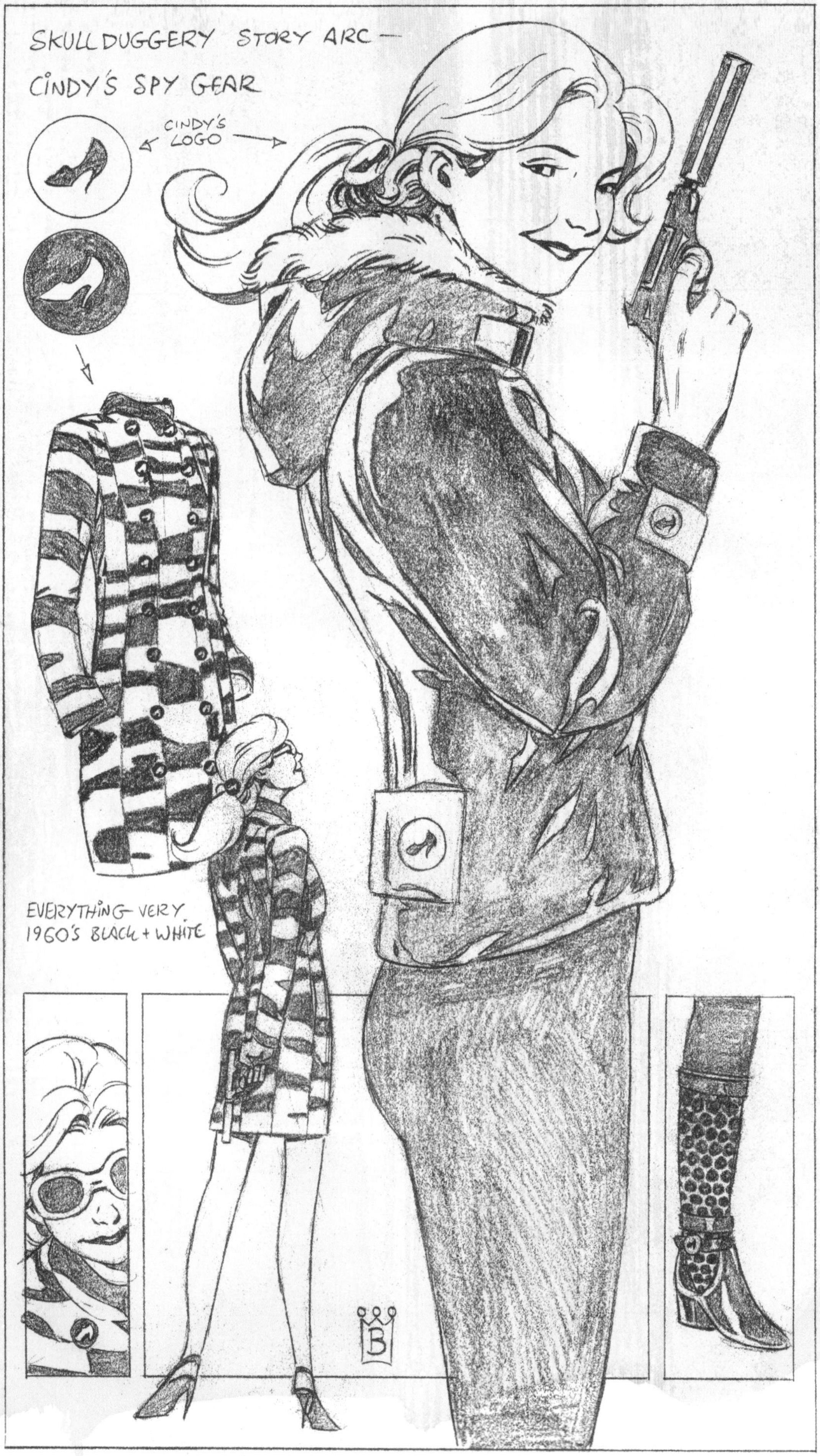
SKULLDUGGERY STORY ARC —
CINDY'S SPY GEAR
CINDY'S LOGO
EVERYTHING VERY 1960'S BLACK + WHITE

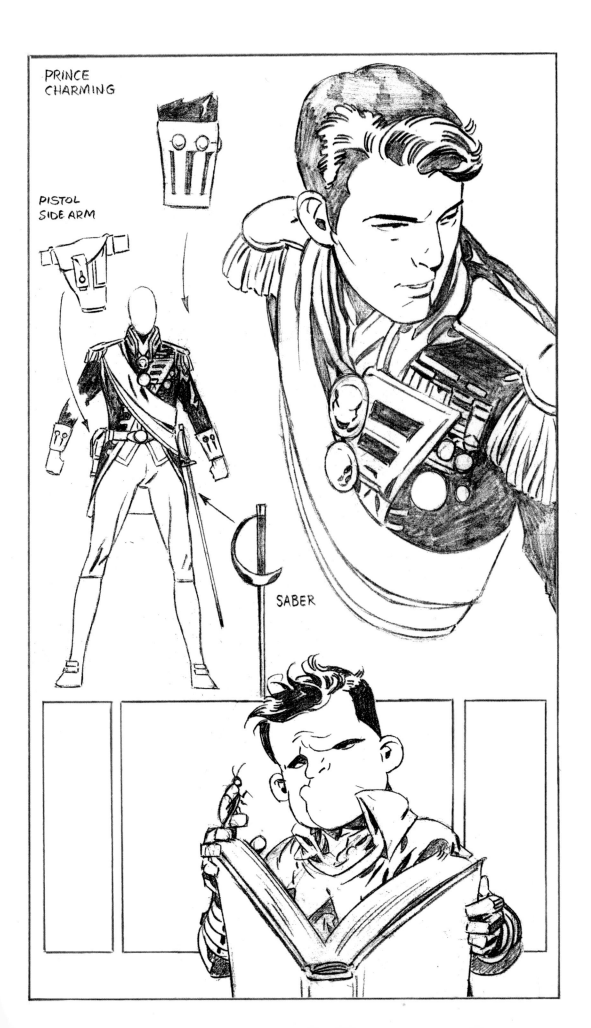

PRINCE
CHARMING

PISTOL
SIDE ARM

SABER

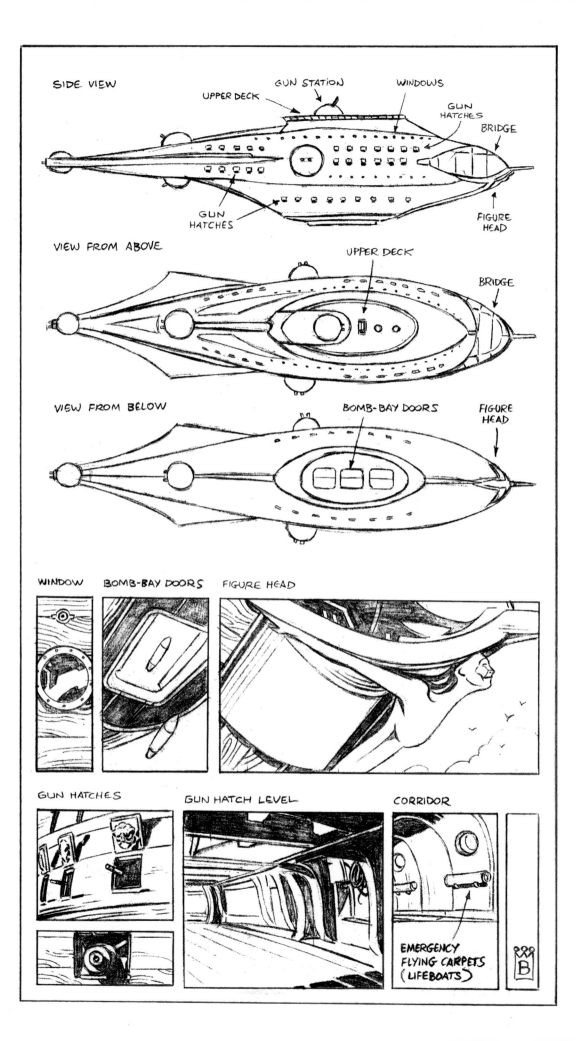

SIDE VIEW

UPPER DECK
GUN STATION
WINDOWS
GUN HATCHES
BRIDGE
GUN HATCHES
FIGURE HEAD

VIEW FROM ABOVE

UPPER DECK
BRIDGE

VIEW FROM BELOW

BOMB-BAY DOORS
FIGURE HEAD

WINDOW   BOMB-BAY DOORS   FIGURE HEAD

GUN HATCHES   GUN HATCH LEVEL   CORRIDOR

EMERGENCY FLYING CARPETS (LIFEBOATS)

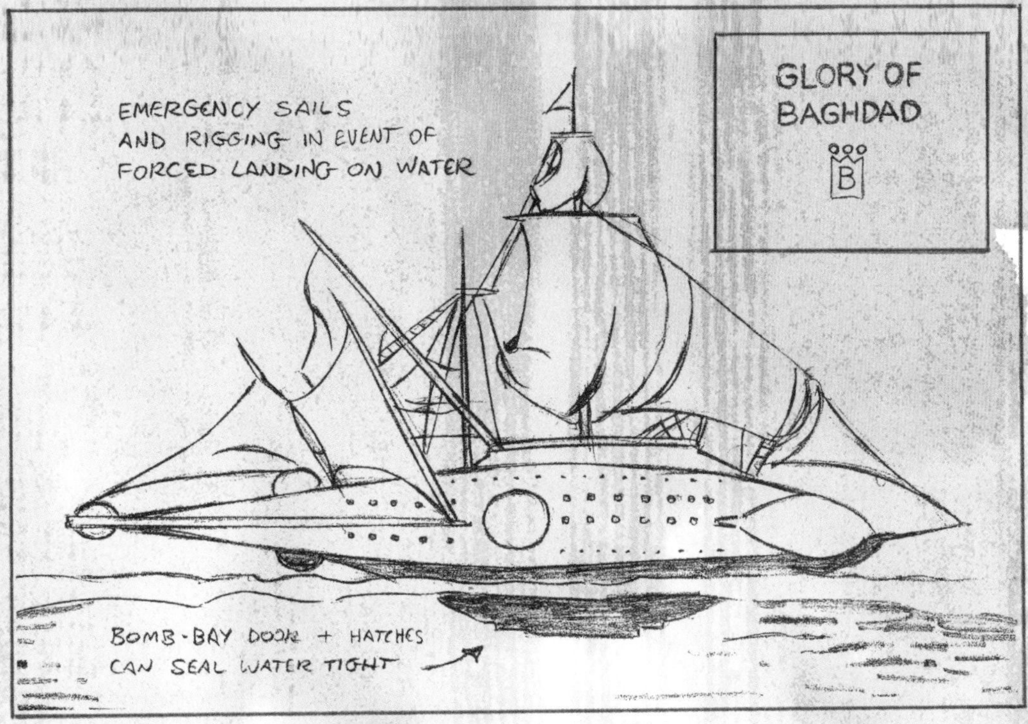
GLORY OF
BAGHDAD
B
EMERGENCY SAILS
AND RIGGING IN EVENT OF
FORCED LANDING ON WATER
BOMB-BAY DOOR + HATCHES
CAN SEAL WATER TIGHT

SKY SHIP
IN FLIGHT

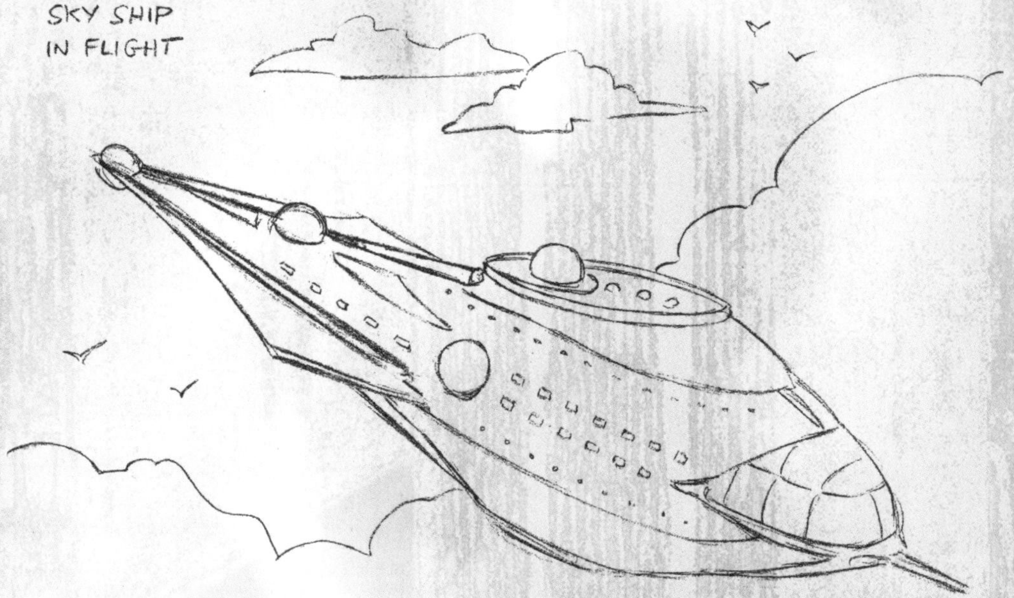

UPPER DECK

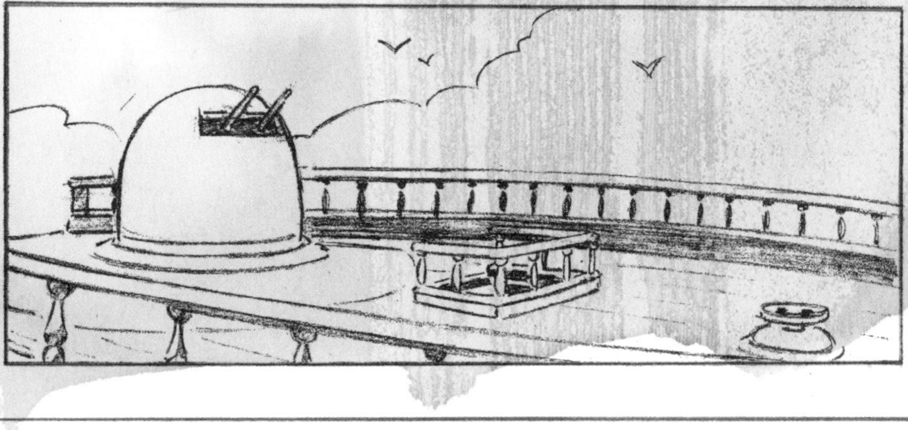

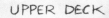

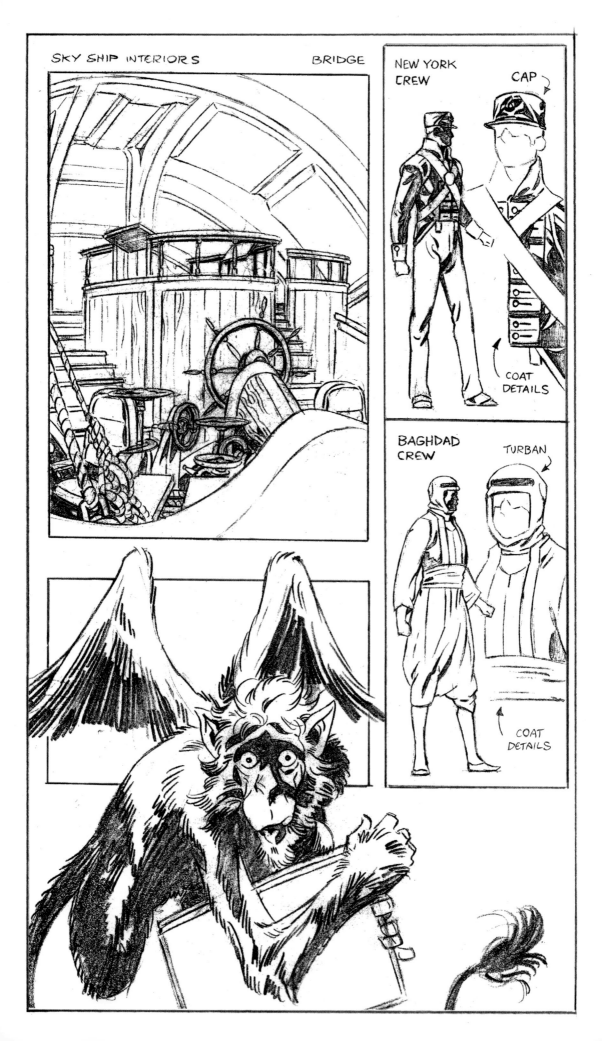

SKY SHIP INTERIORS   BRIDGE

NEW YORK CREW

CAP

COAT DETAILS

BAGHDAD CREW

TURBAN

COAT DETAILS

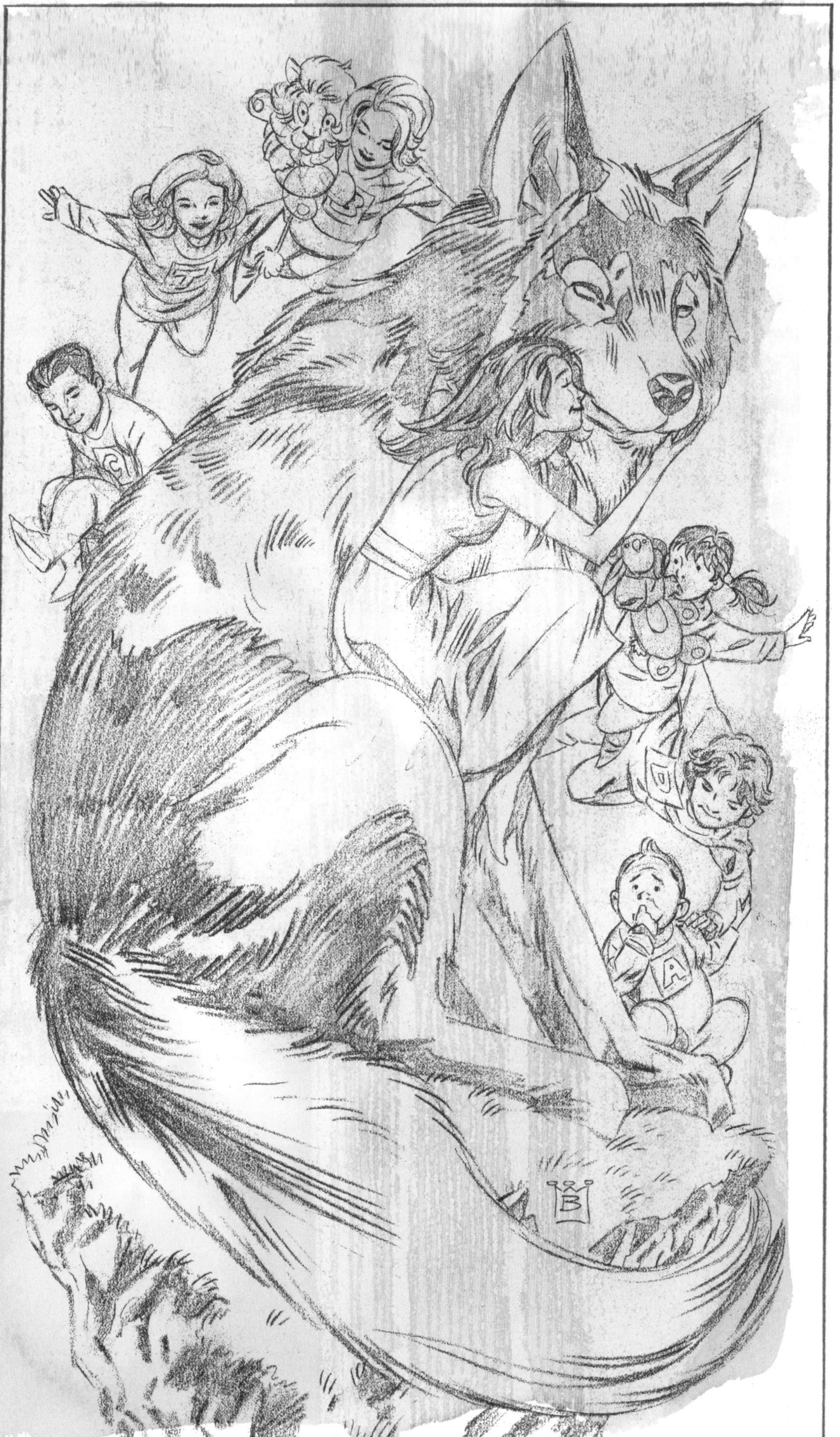

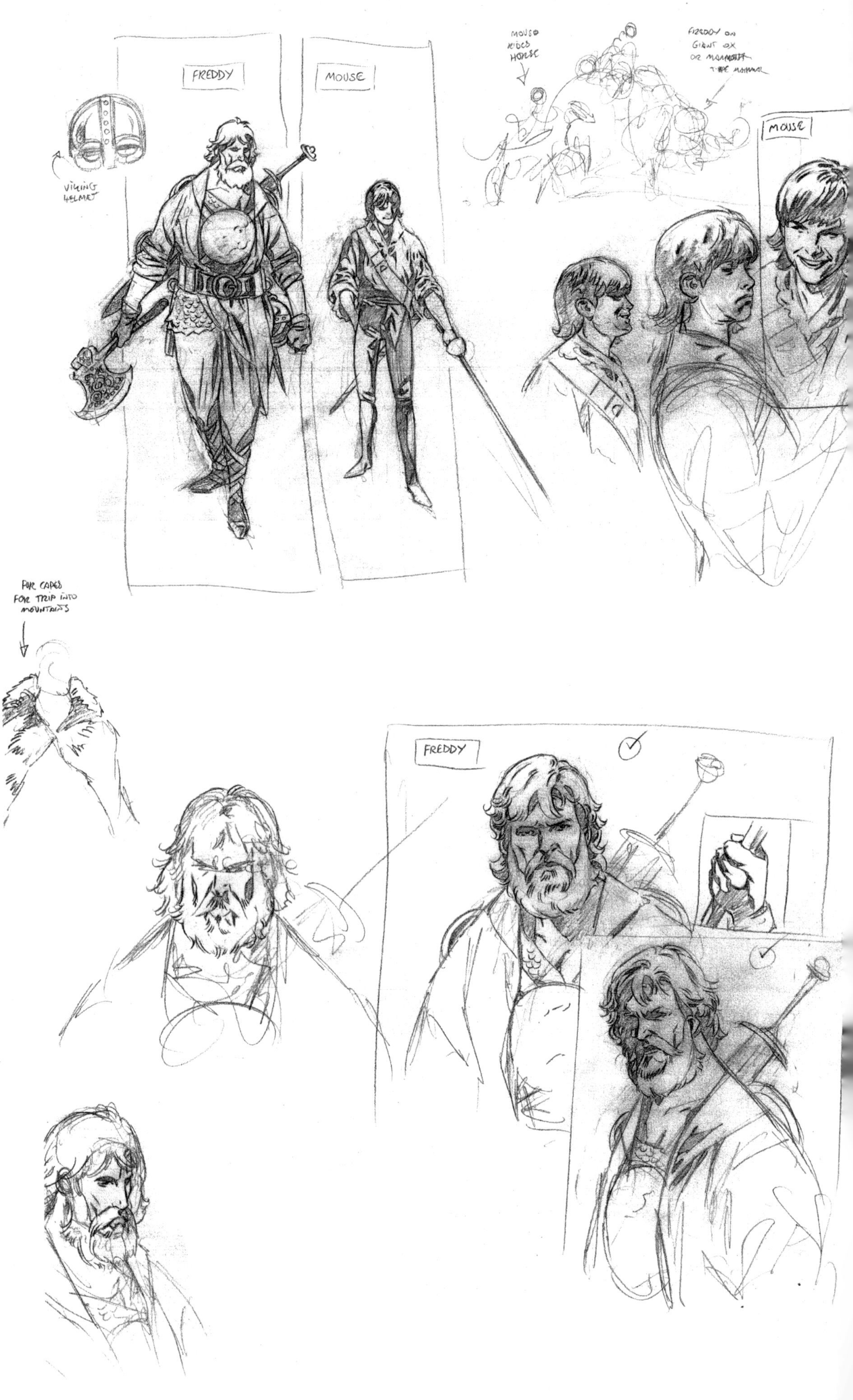
FREDDY
MOUSE
VIKING HELMET
MOUSE RIDES HORSE
FREDDY ON GIANT OX OR
TYPE MAMMAL
MOUSE
FOR CAPES FOR TRIP INTO MOUNTAINS
FREDDY

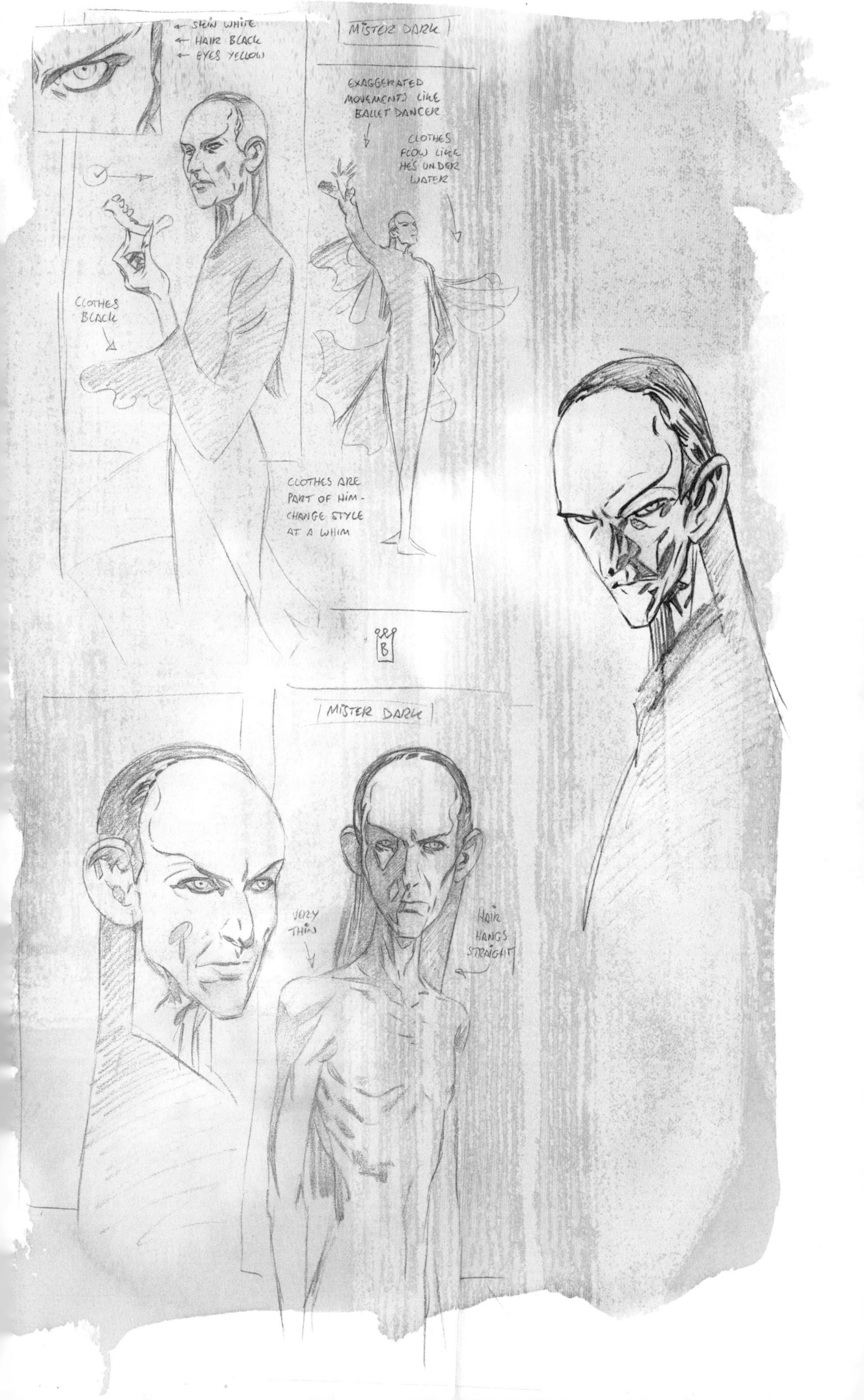
← SKIN WHITE
← HAIR BLACK
← EYES YELLOW
MISTER DARK
EXAGGERATED MOVEMENTS LIKE BALLET DANCER
CLOTHES FLOW LIKE HES UNDER WATER
CLOTHES BLACK
CLOTHES ARE PART OF HIM - CHANGE STYLE AT A WHIM
B
MISTER DARK
VERY THIN
HAIR HANGS STRAIGHT

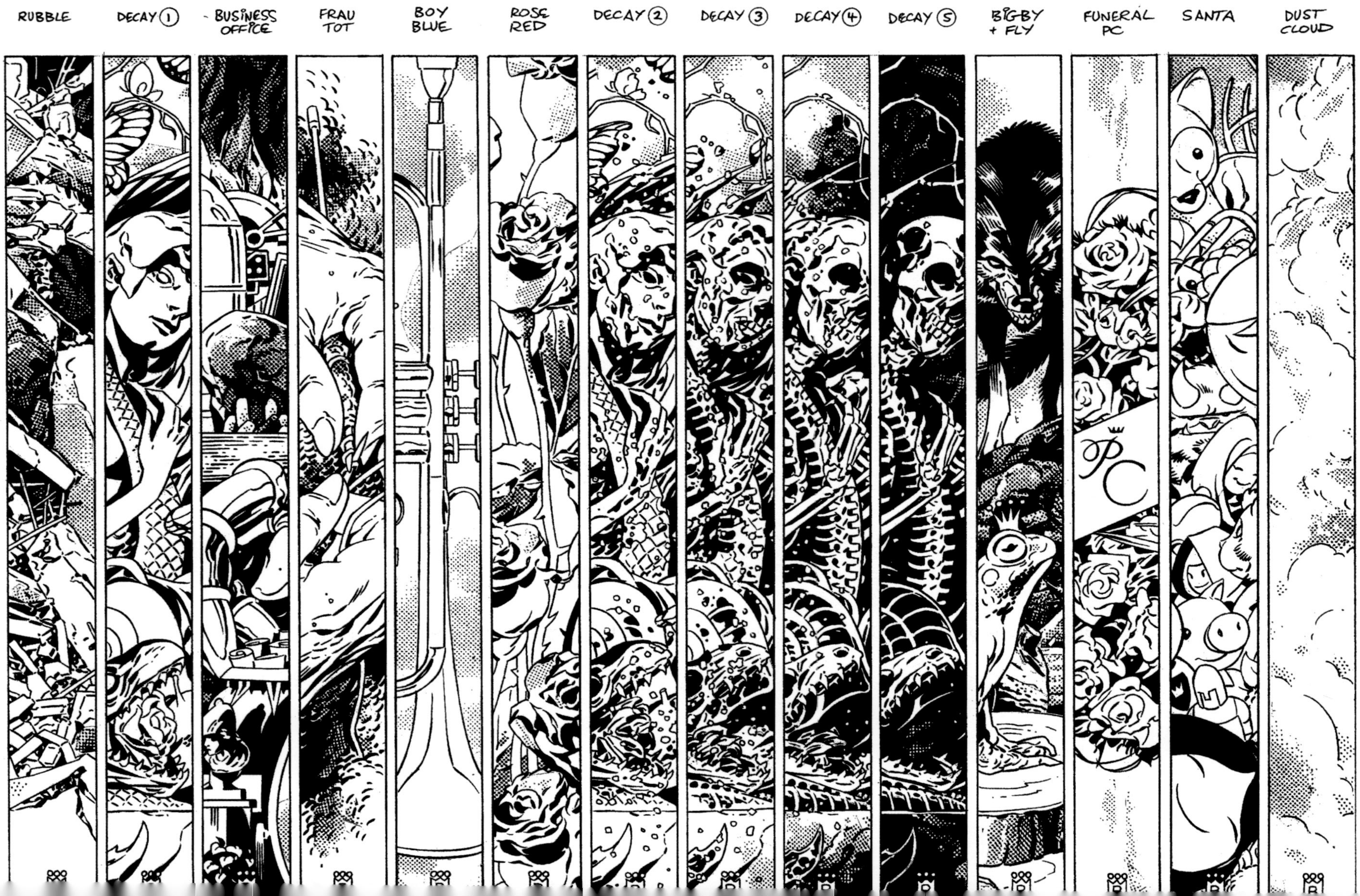
RUBBLE
DECAY 1
BUSINESS OFFICE
FRAU TOT
BOY BLUE
ROSE RED
DECAY 2
DECAY 3
DECAY 4
DECAY 5
BIGBY + FLY
FUNERAL PC
SANTA
DUST CLOUD

Bill Willingham has been writing and sometimes drawing comics for more than twenty years. During that time he's had work published by nearly every publisher in the business and he's created many critically acclaimed comic book series, including *The Elementals*, *Coventry*, PROPOSITION PLAYER and FABLES. His other credits are vast and impressive but far too many to mention here. Currently, he lives in his own personal corner of the American Midwest and can be visited at clockworkstorybook.net.

Born in 1966 in the English seaside town of Clevedon, **Mark Buckingham** has worked in comics professionally since 1988. In addition to illustrating all of Neil Gaiman's run on the post-Alan Moore *Miracleman* in the early 1990s, Buckingham contributed inks to THE SANDMAN and its related miniseries DEATH: THE HIGH COST OF LIVING and DEATH: THE TIME OF YOUR LIFE as well as working on various other titles for Vertigo, DC and Marvel through the end of the decade. Since 2002 he has been the regular penciller for Bill Willingham's FABLES, which has gone on to become one of the most popular and critically acclaimed Vertigo titles of the new millennium.

A thirty-year veteran of the industry, **Steve Leialoha** has worked for nearly every major comics publisher in the course of his distinguished career. Titles featuring his artwork include DC's BATMAN, SUPERMAN and JUSTICE LEAGUE INTERNATIONAL, Vertigo's THE DREAMING, THE SANDMAN PRESENTS: PETREFAX and THE SANDMAN PRESENTS: THE DEAD BOY DETECTIVES, Marvel's *The Uncanny X-Men*, *Spider-Woman* and *Dr. Strange*, Epic's *Coyote*, Harris's *Vampirella* and many of Paradox Press's BIG BOOK volumes. Since 2002 he has inked Bill Willingham's hit Vertigo series FABLES, for which he and penciller Mark Buckingham won the 2007 Eisner Award for Best Penciller/Inker Team. Leialoha also provided pen-and-ink illustrations for Willingham's 2009 FABLES novel, *Peter & Max*.

French-Canadian artist **Niko Henrichon** began his comics career in 2001 with a short story for Bill Willingham's elaborately titled one-shot THE SANDMAN PRESENTS: EVERYTHING YOU ALWAYS WANTED TO KNOW ABOUT DREAMS... BUT WERE AFRAID TO ASK. Between 2003 and 2006 he illustrated the Vertigo graphic novels BARNUM! (written by Howard Chaykin and David Tischman) and PRIDE OF BAGHDAD (written by Brian K. Vaughan). Henrichon's most recent work is a comics adaptation of director Darren Aronofsky's film *Noah*, published first in Europe and then released in North America by Image Comics in 2014. He currently lives in southern France.

Arguably the most handsome man working in the comic book industry today, **Michael "Doc" Allred** is also the most lovable and modest by far. In addition to his dashing good looks and winning personality, "Doc" (as his closest friends call him) is famous for his subpar and borderline talents as an artist and writer. He is probably best known for his cultish creation *Madman*, as well as his history of rock and roll told via the perspective of an alien clone known as *Red Rocket 7*. Allred has also enjoyed passable success creating Marvel mutants with Peter Milligan on the *X-Force* and *X-Statix* series. Out of pity, he was allowed to work on an issue of THE SANDMAN and the stellar series FABLES. Two of Allred's other favorite projects are his issue of DC SOLO (widely regarded as the low point of the series) and his inspired attempt to adapt The Book of Mormon in *The Golden Plates* (a futile effort to earn his way into Heaven). Living on a lake on the Oregon coast, he is blissfully married to his sometime colorist, Laura Allred, and adores his children and grandchildren above all earthly possessions.

Peter Gross is the co-creator (with writer Mike Carey) of the multi-Eisner Award-nominated Vertigo series THE UNWRITTEN and the co-creator (with writer Mark Millar) of *American Jesus* from Image. He is also the illustrator of two of Vertigo's longest-running series, LUCIFER and THE BOOKS OF MAGIC, and he suspects that he might be the only artist/writer who has had work published for Vertigo in every year of the imprint's existence. He lives in Minneapolis, Minnesota, with his wife Jeanne McGee, their daughter Alice, and a cat who looks suspiciously like Tommy Taylor's cat, Mingus.

Wielding a decidedly contemporary style and an eye for crisp detail, **David Hahn** has illustrated issues of *Spider-Man Loves Mary Jane* and *Marvel Adventures: Fantastic Four* for Marvel and BITE CLUB, FABLES, LUCIFER and FRINGE for DC, as well as the licensed title *The Batman Handbook* for Quirk Books. He was nominated for both an Eisner Award and an Ignatz Award for his creator-owned series *Private Beach*, published by Slave Labor Graphics, and he has written and drawn a second creator-owned miniseries, *All Nighter*, for Image Comics. He currently resides in Portland, Oregon, and is a founding member of Portland's Periscope Studio.

An Eisner Award winner and nominee for the Hugo and Inkwell Awards, **Andrew Pepoy** has worked for U.S., British, and French publishers and has inked thousands of pages for dozens of comics titles, including FABLES, *The Simpsons*, *The X-Men*, *Archie* and *Lanfeust*. He is also the creator, writer and artist of his own Harvey Award-nominated series, *The Adventures of Simone & Ajax*, and he has brought his knack for retro glamor with a modern twist to writing and drawing Archie Comics' *Katy Keene* and drawing the *Little Orphan Annie* newspaper strip.

James Jean was born in Taiwan in 1979. Raised in New Jersey, he graduated from New York City's School of Visual Arts in 2001. Along with his award-winning cover art for DC Comics, Jean has produced illustrations for *Time Magazine*, *The New York Times*, *Wired*, *Rolling Stone*, *Spin*, *Playboy*, ESPN, Atlantic Records, Target, Nike, and Prada, among many others. He currently lives and works in Santa Monica.